W9-CGK-531

THE Java™
Programming
Language

Fourth Edition

The Java™ Series

THE Java™
Programming
Language

Fourth Edition

Ken Arnold
James Gosling
David Holmes

✦ Addison-Wesley

Upper Saddle River, NJ • Boston • Indianapolis • San Francisco
New York • Toronto • Montreal • London • Munich • Paris • Madrid
Capetown • Sydney • Tokyo • Singapore • Mexico City

© 2006 Sun Microsystems, Inc.

4150 Network Circle, Santa Clara, California 95054 U.S.A.

All rights reserved.

Use, duplication, or disclosure by the United States Government is subject to the restrictions set forth in DFARS 252.227-7013 (c)(1)(ii) and FAR 52.227-19.

The release described in this book may be protected by one or more U.S. patents, foreign patents, or pending applications.

Sun Microsystems, Inc. (SUN) hereby grants to you a fully-paid, nonexclusive, nontransferable, perpetual, worldwide limited license (without the right to sublicense) under SUN's intellectual property rights that are essential to practice this specification. This license allows and is limited to the creation and distribution of clean room implementations of this specification that: (i) include a complete implementation of the current version of this specification without subsetting or supersetting; (ii) implement all the interfaces and functionality of the standard java.* packages as defined by SUN, without subsetting or supersetting; (iii) do not add any additional packages, classes or methods to the java.* packages; (iv) pass all test suites relating to the most recent published version of this specification that are available from SUN six (6) months prior to any beta release of the clean room implementation or upgrade thereto; (v) do not derive from SUN source code or binary materials; and (vi) do not include any SUN binary materials without an appropriate and separate license from SUN.

Sun, Sun Microsystems, Sun Microsystems Computer Corporation, the Sun logo, the Sun Microsystems Computer Corporation logo, Java, JavaSoft, JavaScript JDBC, JDBC Compliant, JavaOS, JavaBeans and HotJava are trademarks or registered trademarks of Sun Microsystems, Inc. UNIX® is a registered trademark in the United States and other countries, exclusively licensed through X/Open Company, Ltd. Apple and Dylan are trademarks of Apple Computer, Inc. All other product names mentioned herein are the trademarks of their respective owners.

THIS PUBLICATION IS PROVIDED "AS IS" WITHOUT WARRANTY OF ANY KIND, EITHER EXPRESS OR IMPLIED, INCLUDING, BUT NOT LIMITED TO, THE IMPLIED WARRANTIES OF MERCHANTABILITY, FITNESS FOR A PARTICULAR PURPOSE, OR NON-INFRINGEMENT.

THIS PUBLICATION COULD INCLUDE TECHNICAL INACCURACIES OR TYPOGRAPHICAL ERRORS. CHANGES ARE PERIODICALLY ADDED TO THE INFORMATION HEREIN; THESE CHANGES WILL BE INCORPORATED IN NEW EDITIONS OF THE PUBLICATION. SUN MICROSYSTEMS, INC. MAY MAKE IMPROVEMENTS AND/OR CHANGES IN THE PRODUCT(S) AND/OR THE PROGRAM(S) DESCRIBED IN THIS PUBLICATION AT ANY TIME.

Many of the designations used by manufacturers and sellers to distinguish their products are claimed as trademarks. Where those designations appear in this book, and the publisher was aware of a trademark claim, the designations have been printed with initial capital letters or in all capitals.

The authors and publisher have taken care in the preparation of this book, but make no expressed or implied warranty of any kind and assume no responsibility for errors or omissions. No liability is assumed for incidental or consequential damages in connection with or arising out of the use of the information or programs contained herein.

The publisher offers excellent discounts on this book when ordered in quantity for bulk purchases or special sales, which may include electronic versions and/or custom covers and content particular to your business, training goals, marketing focus, and branding interests. For more information, please contact: U. S. Corporate and Government Sales, (800) 382-3419, corpsales@pearsontechgroup.com

For sales outside the U. S., please contact: International Sales, international@pearsoned.com

Visit us on the Web: www.awprofessional.com

Library of Congress Cataloging-in-Publication Data
Arnold, Ken, 1958-
   The Java programming language / Ken Arnold, James Gosling, David Holmes.
        p. cm.
   Includes bibliographical references and index.
   ISBN 0-321-34980-6 (pbk. : alk. paper)
   1. Java (Computer program language) I. Gosling, James. II. Holmes, David (David Colin) III. Title.
   QA76.73.J38A76 2005
   005.13'3--dc22   2005017029

All rights reserved. Printed in the United States of America. This publication is protected by copyright, and permission must be obtained from the publisher prior to any prohibited reproduction, storage in a retrieval system, or transmission in any form or by any means, electronic, mechanical, photocopying, recording, or likewise. For information regarding permissions, write to: Pearson Education, Inc., Rights and Contracts Department, One Lake Street, Upper Saddle River, NJ 07458

ISBN 0321349806

Text printed in the United States on recyled paper at Courier Stoughton in Stoughton, Massachusetts.

3rd Printing   June 2006

This book is dedicated to the Java team
From whose hard work and vision
A mighty oak has grown

To Jareth and Cory—*K.A.*

To Judy and Kate—*J.A.G.*

To Lee, Taylor, and Caitlin —*D.H.*

Contents

Preface

Beautiful buildings are more than scientific. They are true organisms,
spiritually conceived; works of art, using the best technology by inspiration
rather than the idiosyncrasies of mere taste or any averaging by the committee mind.
—Frank Lloyd Wright

THE Java™ programming language has been warmly received by the world community of software developers and Internet content providers. Users of the Internet and World Wide Web benefit from access to secure, platform-independent applications that can come from anywhere on the Internet. Software developers who create applications in the Java programming language benefit by developing code only once, with no need to "port" their applications to every software and hardware platform.

For many, the language was known first as a tool to create applets for the World Wide Web. An *applet* is a mini-application that runs inside a Web page. An applet can perform tasks and interact with users on their browser pages without using resources from the Web server after being downloaded. Some applets may, of course, talk with the server to do their job, but that's their business.

The Java programming language is indeed valuable for distributed network environments like the Web. However, it goes well beyond this domain to provide a powerful general-purpose programming language suitable for building a variety of applications that either do not depend on network features or want them for different reasons. The ability to execute downloaded code on remote hosts in a secure manner is a critical requirement for many organizations.

Other groups use it as a general-purpose programming language for projects in which machine independence is less important. Ease of programming and safety features help you quickly produce working code. Some common programming errors never occur because of features like garbage collection and type-safe references. Support for multithreading caters to modern network-based and graphical user interface–based applications that must attend to multiple tasks simultaneously, and the mechanisms of exception handling ease the task of dealing with error conditions. While the built-in tools are powerful, it is a simple language in which programmers can quickly become proficient.

The Java programming language is designed for maximum portability with as few implementation dependencies as possible. An `int`, for example, is a 32-bit signed two's-complement integer in all implementations, irrespective of the CPU architecture on which the program executes. Defining everything possible about the language and its runtime environment enables users to run compiled code anywhere and share code with anyone who has a Java runtime environment.

ABOUT THIS BOOK

This book teaches the Java programming language to people who are familiar with basic programming concepts. It explains the language without being arduously formal or complete. This book is not an introduction to object-oriented programming, although some issues are covered to establish a common terminology. Other books in this series and much online documentation focus on applets, graphical interfaces, Web sites, databases, components, and other specific kinds of programming tasks. For other references, see "Further Reading" on page 755.

This fourth edition provides integrated coverage of the Java programming language as provided by the Java™ 2 Platform Standard Edition 5.0 and specified by the *Java*™ *Language Specification, Third Edition.* It also covers most of the classes in the main packages (`java.lang`, `java.util`, `java.io`) as implemented in the J2SE™ Development Kit 5.0 (more commonly known as JDK 5.0, or in the older nomenclature JDK 1.5.0).

If you have already read the third edition of this book, you will find some major changes, both in the language and the book, since the 1.3 release that the third edition covered. There are new chapters on generics, enums, and annotations—the major new language features introduced in the 5.0 release—and major new sections on assertions and regular expressions. Some existing material has been restructured to accommodate other changes and to improve the general flow of the text—such as introducing the new boxing and unboxing conversions. But every single chapter has been updated in some way, whether it is a new language feature like variable argument methods; the new enhanced `for` loop construct; a new class such as `Formatter` for formatting text output; or changes to classes and methods caused by the addition of generics (such as the collections utilities and the reflection classes)—change permeates this entire fourth edition.

The Java programming language shares many features common to most programming languages in use today. The language should look familiar to C and C++ programmers because it was designed with C and C++ constructs where the languages are similar. That said, this book is neither a comparative analysis nor a "bridge" tutorial—no knowledge of C or C++ is assumed. C++ programmers, especially, may be as hindered by what they must unlearn as they are helped by their knowledge.

Chapter 1—*A Quick Tour*—gives a quick overview of the language. Programmers who are unfamiliar with object-oriented programming notions should read the quick tour, while programmers who are already familiar with object-oriented programming paradigms will find the quick tour a useful introduction to the object-oriented features of the language. The quick tour introduces some of the basic language features on which examples through the rest of the book are built.

Chapters 2 through 6 cover the object-oriented core features of the language, namely, class declarations that define components of a program, and objects manufactured according to class definitions. Chapter 2—*Classes and Objects*—describes the basis of the language: classes. Chapter 3—*Extending Classes*—describes how an existing class can be *extended,* or *subclassed,* to create a new class with additional data and behavior. Chapter 4—*Interfaces*—describes how to declare interface types that are abstract descriptions of behavior that provide maximum flexibility for class designers and implementors. Chapter 5—*Nested Classes and Interfaces*—describes how classes and interfaces can be declared inside other classes and interfaces, and the benefits that provides. Finally, Chapter 6—*Enumeration Types*—covers the definition and use of type-safe enumeration constants.

Chapters 7 through 10 cover standard constructs common to most languages. Chapter 7—*Tokens, Values, and Variables*—describes the tokens of the language from which statements are constructed, the types defined by the language and their allowed values, and the variables that store data in objects, arrays, or locally within methods. Chapter 8—*Primitives as Types*—explores the relationship between the primitive types and objects of their corresponding wrapper classes, and how boxing and unboxing can transparently convert between them. Chapter 9—*Operators and Expressions*—describes the basic operators of the language, how these operators are used to build expressions, and how expressions are evaluated. Chapter 10—*Control Flow*—describes how control statements direct the order of statement execution.

Chapter 11—*Generic Types*—describes generic types: how they are written and used, their power, and their limitations.

Chapter 12—*Exceptions and Assertions*—describes the language's powerful error-handling capabilities, and the use of assertions to validate the expected behavior of code.

Chapter 13—*Strings and Regular Expressions*—describes the built-in language and runtime support for `String` objects, the underlying character set support, and the powerful utilities for regular expression matching.

Chapter 14—*Threads*—explains the language's view of multithreading. Many applications, such as graphical interface–based software, must attend to multiple tasks simultaneously. These tasks must cooperate to behave correctly, and threads meet the needs of cooperative multitasking.

Chapter 15—*Annotations*—describes the annotation types used to document some of the extra-linguistic properties of classes and method.

Chapter 16—*Reflection*—describes the runtime type introspection mechanism and how you can construct and manipulate objects of unknown type dynamically at runtime.

Chapter 17—*Garbage Collection and Memory*—talks about garbage collection, finalization, and lower-strength reference objects.

Chapter 18—*Packages*—describes how you can group collections of classes and interfaces into separate packages.

Chapter 19—*Documentation Comments*—shows how to write reference documentation in comments.

Chapters 20 through 24 cover the main packages. Chapter 20—*The I/O Package*—describes the input/output system, which is based on *streams*. Chapter 21—*Collections*—covers the *collection* or *container classes* such as sets and lists. Chapter 22—*Miscellaneous Utilities*—covers the rest of the *utility classes* such as bit sets, formatted output, text scanning, and random number generation. Chapter 23—*System Programming*—leads you through the *system classes* that provide access to features of the underlying platform. Chapter 24—*Internationalization and Localization*—covers some of the tools used to create programs that can run in many linguistic and cultural environments.

Chapter 25—*Standard Packages*—briefly explores the packages that are part of the standard platform, giving overviews of those packages not covered in more detail in this book.

Appendix A—*Application Evolution*—looks at some of the issues involved in dealing with the evolution of applications and the Java platform, and the impact this has on some of the new language features.

Appendix B—*Useful Tables*—has tables of information that you may find useful for quick reference.

Finally, *Further Reading* lists works that may be interesting for further reading on complete details, object orientation, programming with threads, software design, and other topics.

EXAMPLES AND DOCUMENTATION

All the code examples in the text have been compiled and run on the latest version of the language available at the time the book was written, which was the JDK 1.5.0_02 product version. Only supported features are covered—deprecated types, methods, and fields are ignored except when unavoidable or when knowledge of the past is necessary to understand the present. We have also covered issues beyond writing programs that simply compile. Part of learning a language is to learn to use it well. For this reason, we have tried to show principles of good programming style and design.

In a few places we refer to online documentation. Development environments provide a way to automatically generate documentation (usually HTML documents) for a compiled class from its documentation comments. This documentation is normally viewed with a Web browser.

ACKNOWLEDGMENTS (FOURTH EDITION)

Once again we are indebted to a group of people who took time out from their hectic schedules (and even their own books!) to give us the benefit of their experiences in making this the best edition yet. Of course, some of those people were also responsible for the huge volume of work required for us to catch up with all the new language and library features, but we won't hold that against them. Much.

On the reviewing side our thanks go first to Yoshiki Shibata. Yoshiki produced the Japanese translation of the third edition and in the process single-handedly discovered at least 85% of the errata. To get the fourth edition as errata free as possible we knew we needed Yoshiki onboard as a reviewer very early on. Yoshiki became our front-line reviewer and nothing went out for general review without his nod of approval. Not only did he provide valuable corrections and feedback on the new material, he also pointed out several areas where there had been language changes that we hadn't been aware of!

Brian Goetz also rates special thanks not only for reviewing the entire edition, but also for re-reviewing various sections that took several iterations to get right. The turnaround times for these re-reviews were very tight and we much appreciate Brian's time at that critical stage.

The remainder of the core reviewing team consisted of Beth Stearns and Kevin Davis, who were able to stay for the long haul, while Bob Withers, Herb Jellinek, Ken Louden, Rich Wardwell, and Kevin Hammond provided valuable feedback on the earlier portions of the text. Thank you all very much.

We'd also like to thank Tim Peierls for supplying the chess example used in the enum chapter; and Keith Lea and Martin Buchholz for valuable reviews of the generics material—thanks!

It will come as no surprise to most that writing the generics chapter (and the related part of the appendix) was the hardest part of this edition. Armed initially only with a draft of the third edition of the *Java Language Specification,* it was never going to be easy to fathom the depths of the new type system, so we brought in the big guns: Neal Gafter, Josh Bloch, Gilad Bracha, and Peter von der Ahé were all instrumental in educating us about generics, and for that we thank them. Peter's in-depth review of the generics chapter was especially valuable and warrants an additional thank you. Of course, the teachers cannot be blamed for the shortcomings of the student, so any errors or omissions in the description of generics are the sole responsibility of the authors. (We'd like to thank Phil Wadler for catching two such omissions in the generics coverage just prior to publication.)

We'd also like to thank the following technical experts for their assistance in specific areas: Doug Lea for reviewing the Java memory model material and providing assistance with concurrent collections; Brian Goetz for checking the overview of the concurrent collections (in addition to everything else); Mike "MadBot" McCloskey for the review of, and assistance with, the use of the Scanner class and the associated regular expression usage; and Jeremy Manson for trying to explain the unfathomable relationship between finalization and the memory model.

Rosemary Simpson seems to always manage to be around when we need her. It's starting to get difficult to find a creative way to say how much we appreciate her indexing, but I'm sure we'll have one by the fifth edition.

On the production side, the path to the fourth edition was a somewhat changeable one. Mike Hendrickson held the reins when the fourth edition was conceived, then handed the reins to Ann Sellers. Ann, with assistance from Ebony Haight, saw the fourth edition through its early gestation, then handed the reins to Greg Doench. Greg, with assistance from Noreen Regina, Stephane Nakib, Tyrrell Albaugh, Elizabeth Ryan, and Mary Lou Nohr saw us through to the ultimate delivery. Thank you all, and to all those behind the scenes.

And thanks as well to Kathy Kerby, Ben Littauer, and Ariana Littauer for being a valuable source of borrowed computrons. It's always nice to have neighbors from whom you can borrow a cup of cycles.

Last, but by no means least, thank you to our families for putting up with the trials and tribulations of authorship once again.

ACKNOWLEDGMENTS (THIRD EDITION)

The third edition required yet more reviews and work, and the helper list is equally critical. Lisa Friendly continued her attempts to keep the project in line; someday we will cooperate better. The set of reviewers included new faces and old friends, all helpful: Joshua Bloch, Joseph Bowbeer, Gilad Bracha, Keith Edwards, Joshua Engel, Rich Gillam, Peter Haggar, Cay Horstmann, Alexander Kuzmin, Doug Lea, Keith Lea, Tim Lindholm, David Mendenhall, Andrew M. Morgan, Ray Ortigas, Brian Preston, Mark Schuldenfrei, Peter Sparago, Guy Steele, Antoine Trux, and our Russian compatriots Leonid Arbouzov, Valery Shakurov, Viatcheslav Rybalov, Eugene Latkin, Dmitri Khukhro, Konstantin Anisimov, Alexei Kaigorodov, Oleg Oleinik, and Maxim Sokolnikov. Several people let us bend their ears to figure out how to approach things better: Peter Jones, Robert W.

Scheifler, Susan Snyder, Guy Steele, Jimmy Torres, and Ann Wollrath. Helen Leary made the logistics work smoothly, as always.

Material support is always provided by the Addison-Wesley team: Julie DiNicola, Mike Hendrickson, and Tracy Russ.

And since the last edition, Peet's Coffee and Tea has opened up on the East Coast, so the eastern part of this writing team can enjoy it regularly. The world continues to improve apace.

ACKNOWLEDGMENTS (SECOND EDITION)

The cast of characters for this second edition is much like the first.

Series Editor Lisa Friendly continued to be doggedly supportive and attentive. The set of reviewers was smaller, overlapping, and certainly as helpful and thorough. Overall reviews by Steve Byrne, Tom Cargill, Mary Dageforde, Tim Lindholm, and Rob Murray were critical to clarity. Brian Beck, Peter Jones, Doug Lea, Bryan O'Sullivan, Sue Palmer, Rosanna Lee, Lori Park, Mark Reinhold, Roger Riggs, Ann Wollrath, and Ken Zadek contributed focused reviews of important parts. Guy Steele's support was ongoing and warm. Rosemary Simpson's extensive and intensive efforts to make a useful index are deeply appreciated. Carla Carlson and Helen Leary gave logistic support that kept all the wheels on the tracks instead of in the ditch. Gerry Wiener provided the Tibetan word on page 550, and we also had help on this from Craig Preston and Takao Miyatani. All who submitted errata and suggestions from the first edition were helpful.

For some inexplicable reason we left the friendly folks of Addison-Wesley off the original acknowledgments—luckily, most of them were present again for this edition. A merged list for both editions includes Kate Duffy, Rosa Gonzales, Mike Hendrickson, Marina Lang, Shannon Patti, Marty Rabinowitz, Sarah Weaver, and Pamela Yee. Others did much that we are blissfully unaware of, but for which we are nonetheless abidingly grateful.

The revision was additionally aided by Josh Bloch, Joe Fialli, Jimmy Torres, Benjamin Renaud, Mark Reinhold, Jen Volpe, and Ann Wollrath.

And Peet's Coffee and Tea continued its supporting role as purveyor to the caffeine-consuming connoisseur.

ACKNOWLEDGMENTS (FIRST EDITION)

No technical book-writing endeavor is an island unto itself, and ours was more like a continent. Many people contributed technical help, excellent reviews, useful information, and book-writing advice.

Contributing editor Henry McGilton of Trilithon Software played the role of "chief editorial firefighter" to help make this book possible. Series editor Lisa Friendly contributed dogged perseverance and support.

A veritable multitude of reviewers took time out of their otherwise busy lives to read, edit, advise, revise, and delete material, all in the name of making this a better book. Kevin Coyle performed one of the most detailed editorial reviews at all levels. Karen Bennet, Mike Burati, Patricia Giencke, Steve Gilliard, Bill Joy, Rosanna Lee, Jon Madison, Brian O'Neill, Sue Palmer, Stephen Perelgut, R. Anders Schneiderman, Susan Sim, Bob Sproull, Guy Steele, Arthur van Hoff, Jim Waldo, Greg Wilson, and Ann Wollrath provided in-depth review. Geoff Arnold, Tom Cargill, Chris Darke, Pat Finnegan, Mick Jordan, Doug Lea, Randall Murray, Roger Riggs, Jimmy Torres, Arthur van Hoff, and Frank Yellin contributed useful comments and technical information at critical junctures.

Alka Deshpande, Sharon Flank, Nassim Fotouhi, Betsy Halstead, Kee Hinckley, Dr. K. Kalyanasundaram, Patrick Martin, Paul Romagna, Susan Snyder, and Nicole Yankelovich collaborated to make possible the five words of non-ISO-Latin-1 text on pages 164 and 550. Jim Arnold provided research help on the proper spelling, usage, and etymology of "smoog" and "moorge." Ed Mooney helped with the document preparation. Herb and Joy Kaiser were our Croatian language consultants. Cookie Callahan, Robert E. Pierce, and Rita Tavilla provided the support necessary to keep this project going at many moments when it would otherwise have stalled with a sputtering whimper.

Thanks to Kim Polese for supplying us the capsule summary of why the Java programming language is important to computer users as well as programmers.

Support and advice were provided at critical moments by Susan Jones, Bob Sproull, Jim Waldo, and Ann Wollrath. And we thank our families, who, besides their loving support, would at times drag us out to play when we should have been working, for which we are deeply grateful.

And thanks to the folks at Peet's Coffee and Tea, who kept us buzzed on the best Java on the planet.

Any errors or shortcomings that remain in this book—despite the combined efforts of these myriads—are completely the responsibility of the authors.

> *Results! Why, man, I have gotten a lot of results.*
> *I know several thousand things that won't work.*
> —Thomas Edison

Calvin and Hobbes quote (page 39) reprinted by permission of Universal Press Syndicate.

"Mail Myself to You," (page 183) words and music by Woody Guthrie. TRO 1962 (renewed), 1963 (renewed) by Ludlow Music, Inc. New York, NY. Used by permission.

CHAPTER 1

A Quick Tour

See Europe! Ten Countries in Seventeen Days!
—Sign in a travel agent's window

THIS chapter is a whirlwind tour of the Java™ programming language that gets you started writing code quickly. We briefly cover the main points of the language, without slowing you down with full-blown detail. Subsequent chapters contain detailed discussions of specific features.

1.1 Getting Started

In the Java programming language, programs are built from *classes.* From a class definition, you can create any number of *objects* that are known as *instances* of that class. Think of a class as a factory with blueprints and instructions to build gadgets—objects are the gadgets the factory makes.

A class contains *members,* the primary kinds being *fields* and *methods.* Fields are data variables belonging either to the class itself or to objects of the class; they make up the *state* of the object or class. Methods are collections of *statements* that operate on the fields to manipulate the state. Statements define the behavior of the classes: they can assign values to fields and other variables, evaluate arithmetic expressions, invoke methods, and control the flow of execution.

Long tradition holds that the first sample program for any language should print "Hello, world":

```
class HelloWorld {
    public static void main(String[] args) {
        System.out.println("Hello, world");
    }
}
```

Use your favorite text editor to type this program source code into a file. Then run the compiler to compile the source of this program into *bytecodes,* the "machine language" for the Java virtual machine (more on this later in this chapter). Details of editing and compiling source vary from system to system—consult your system manuals for specific information. On the system we use most often—the Java™ 2 Platform, Standard Edition (J2SE™) Development Kit (JDK) provided free of charge by Sun Microsystems—you put the source for `HelloWorld` into a file named `HelloWorld.java`. To compile it you type the command

```
javac HelloWorld.java
```

To run the program you type the command

```
java HelloWorld
```

This executes the `main` method of `HelloWorld`. When you run the program, it displays

```
Hello, world
```

Now you have a small program that does something, but what does it mean?

The program declares a class called `HelloWorld` with a single member: a method called `main`. Class members appear between curly braces { and } following the class name.

The `main` method is a special method: the `main` method of a class, if declared exactly as shown, is executed when you run the class as an application. When run, a `main` method can create objects, evaluate expressions, invoke other methods, and do anything else needed to define an application's behavior.

The `main` method is declared `public`—so that anyone can invoke it (in this case the Java virtual machine)—and `static`, meaning that the method belongs to the class and is not associated with a particular instance of the class.

Preceding the method name is the return type of the method. The `main` method is declared `void` because it doesn't return a value and so has no return type.

Following the method name is the *parameter* list for the method—a sequence of zero or more pairs of types and names, separated by commas and enclosed in parentheses (and). The `main` method's only parameter is an array of `String` objects, referred to by the name `args`. Arrays of objects are denoted by the square brackets [] that follow the type name. In this case `args` will contain the program's arguments from the command line with which it was invoked. Arrays and strings are covered later in this chapter. The meaning of `args` for the `main` method is described in Chapter 2 on page 73.

The name of a method together with its parameter list constitute the *signature* of the method. The signature and any modifiers (such as `public` and `static`), the return type, and exception throws list (covered later in this chapter) form the method *header*. A method *declaration* consists of the method header followed by the method *body*—a block of statements appearing between curly braces.

In this example, the body of `main` contains a single statement that invokes the `println` method—the semicolon ends the statement. A method is invoked by supplying an object reference (in this case `System.out`—the `out` field of the `System` class) and a method name (`println`) separated by a dot (`.`).

`HelloWorld` uses the `out` object's `println` method to print a newline-termi- nated string on the standard output stream. The string printed is the *string literal* `"Hello, world"`, which is passed as an argument to `println`. A string literal is a sequence of characters contained within double-quotes `"` and `"`.

Exercise 1.1: Enter, compile, and run `HelloWorld` on your system.

Exercise 1.2: Try changing parts of `HelloWorld` and see what errors you might get.

1.2 Variables

The next example prints a part of the *Fibonacci sequence,* an infinite sequence whose first few terms are

```
1
1
2
3
5
8
13
21
34
```

The Fibonacci sequence starts with the terms 1 and 1, and each successive term is the sum of the previous two terms. A Fibonacci printing program is simple, and it demonstrates how to declare *variables,* write a simple loop, and perform basic arithmetic. Here is the Fibonacci program:

```
class Fibonacci {
    /** Print out the Fibonacci sequence for values < 50 */
    public static void main(String[] args) {
        int lo = 1;
```

```
        int hi = 1;

        System.out.println(lo);
        while (hi < 50) {
            System.out.println(hi);
            hi = lo + hi;          // new hi
            lo = hi - lo;          /* new lo is (sum - old lo)
                                      that is, the old hi */
        }
    }
}
```

This example declares a `Fibonacci` class that, like `HelloWorld`, has a `main` method. The first two lines of `main` are statements declaring two *local* variables: `lo` and `hi`. In this program `hi` is the current term in the series and `lo` is the previous term. Local variables are declared within a block of code, such as a method body, in contrast to fields that are declared as members of a class. Every variable must have a *type* that precedes its name when the variable is declared. The variables `lo` and `hi` are of type `int`, 32-bit signed integers with values in the range -2^{31} through $2^{31}-1$.

The Java programming language has built-in "primitive" data types to support integer, floating-point, boolean, and character values. These primitive types hold numeric data that is understood directly, as opposed to object types defined by programmers. The type of every variable must be defined explicitly. The primitive data types are:

`boolean`	either `true` or `false`
`char`	16-bit Unicode UTF-16 character (unsigned)
`byte`	8-bit integer (signed)
`short`	16-bit integer (signed)
`int`	32-bit integer (signed)
`long`	64-bit integer (signed)
`float`	32-bit floating-point (IEEE 754)
`double`	64-bit floating-point (IEEE 754)

For each primitive type there is also a corresponding object type, generally termed a "wrapper" class. For example, the class `Integer` is the wrapper class for `int`. In most contexts, the language automatically converts between primitive types and objects of the wrapper class if one type is used where the other is expected.

In the Fibonacci program, we declared `hi` and `lo` with initial values of 1. The initial values are set by initialization expressions, using the = operator, when the variables are declared. The = operator (also called the *assignment* operator), sets the variable named on the left-hand side to the value of the expression on the right-hand side.

Local variables are *undefined* prior to initialization. You don't have to initialize them at the point at which you declare them, but if you try to use local variables before assigning a value, the compiler will refuse to compile your program until you fix the problem.

As both `lo` and `hi` are of the same type, we could have used a short-hand form for declaring them. We can declare more than one variable of a given type by separating the variable names (with their initialization expressions) by commas. We could replace the first two lines of main with the single equivalent line

```
int lo = 1, hi = 1;
```

or the much more readable

```
int lo = 1,
    hi = 1;
```

Notice that the presence of line breaks makes no difference to the meaning of the statement—line breaks, spaces, tabs, and other *whitespace* are purely for the programmer's convenience.

The `while` statement in the example demonstrates one way of looping. The expression inside the `while` is evaluated—if the expression is true, the loop's body is executed and the expression is tested again. The `while` is repeated until the expression becomes false. If it never becomes false, the loop will run forever unless something intervenes to break out of the loop, such as a `break` statement or an exception.

The body of the `while` consists of a single statement. That could be a simple statement (such as a method invocation), another control-flow statement, or a *block*—zero or more individual statements enclosed in curly braces.

The expression that `while` tests is a *boolean* expression that has the value `true` or `false`. Boolean expressions can be formed with the *comparison* operators (<, <=, >, >=) to compare the relative magnitudes of two values or with the == operator or != operator to test for equality or inequality, respectively. The boolean expression `hi < 50` in the example tests whether the current high value of the sequence is less than 50. If the high value is less than 50, its value is printed and the next value is calculated. If the high value equals or exceeds 50, control passes to the first line of code following the body of the `while` loop. That is the end of the `main` method in this example, so the program is finished.

To calculate the next value in the sequence we perform some simple arithmetic and again use the = operator to assign the value of the arithmetic expression on the right to the variable on the left. As you would expect, the + operator calculates the sum of its operands, and the - operator calculates the difference. The language defines a number of arithmetic operators for the primitive integer and floating-point types including addition (+), subtraction (-), multiplication (*), and division (/), as well as some other operators we talk about later.

Notice that the `println` method accepts an integer argument in the `Fibonacci` example, whereas it accepted a string argument in the `HelloWorld` example. The `println` method is one of many methods that are *overloaded* so that they can accept arguments of different types. The runtime system decides which method to actually invoke based on the number and types of arguments you pass to it. This is a very powerful tool.

Exercise 1.3: Add a title to the printed list of the `Fibonacci` program.

Exercise 1.4: Write a program that generates a different sequence, such as a table of squares.

1.3   Comments in Code

The English text scattered through the code is in *comments*. There are three styles of comments, all illustrated in the `Fibonacci` example. Comments enable you to write descriptive text alongside your code, annotating it for programmers who may read your code in the future. That programmer may well be *you* months or years later. You save yourself effort by commenting your own code. Also, you often find bugs when you write comments, because explaining what the code is supposed to do forces you to think about it.

Text that occurs between /* and */ is ignored by the compiler. This style of comment can be used on part of a line, a whole line, or more commonly (as in the example) to define a multiline comment. For single line and part line comments you can use // which tells the compiler to ignore everything after it on that line.

The third kind of comment appears at the very top, between /** and */. A comment starting with two asterisks is a *documentation comment* ("doc comment" for short). Documentation comments are intended to describe declarations that follow them. The comment in the previous example is for the `main` method. These comments can be extracted by a tool that uses them to generate reference documentation for your classes. By convention, lines within a documentation comment or a /*...*/ comment have a leading asterisk (which is ignored by documentation tools), which gives a visual clue to readers of the extent of the comment.

1.4 Named Constants

Constants are values like 12, 17.9, and "Strings Like This". Constants, or literals as they are also known, are the way you specify values that are not computed and recomputed but remain, well, constant for the life of a program.

The Fibonacci example printed all Fibonacci numbers with a value less than 50. The constant 50 was used within the expression of the while loop and within the documentation comment describing main. Suppose that you now want to modify the example to print the Fibonacci numbers with values less than 100. You have to go through the source code and locate and modify all occurrences of the constant 50. Though this is trivial in our example, in general it is a tedious and error-prone process. Further, if people reading the code see an expression like hi < 50 they may have no idea what the constant 50 actually represents. Such "magic numbers" hinder program understandability and maintainability.

A *named constant* is a constant value that is referred to by a name. For example, we may choose the name MAX to refer to the constant 50 in the Fibonacci example. You define named constants by declaring fields of the appropriate type, initialized to the appropriate value. That itself does not define a constant, but a field whose value could be changed by an assignment statement. To make the value a constant we declare the field as final. A final field or variable is one that once initialized can never have its value changed—it is *immutable*. Further, because we don't want the named constant field to be associated with instances of the class, we also declare it as static.

We would rewrite the Fibonacci example as follows:

```
class Fibonacci2 {
    static final int MAX = 50;
    /** Print the Fibonacci sequence for values < MAX */
    public static void main(String[] args) {
        int lo = 1;
        int hi = 1;
        System.out.println(lo);
        while (hi < MAX) {
            System.out.println(hi);
            hi = lo + hi;
            lo = hi - lo;
        }
    }
}
```

Modifying the maximum value now requires only one change, in one part of the program, and it is clearer what the loop condition is actually testing.

You can group related constants within a class. For example, a card game might use these constants:

```
class Suit {
    final static int CLUBS    = 1;
    final static int DIAMONDS = 2;
    final static int HEARTS   = 3;
    final static int SPADES   = 4;
}
```

To refer to a `static` member of a class we use the name of the class followed by dot and the name of the member. With the above declaration, suits in a program would be accessed as `Suit.HEARTS`, `Suit.SPADES`, and so on, thus grouping all the suit names within the single name `Suit`. Notice that the order of the modifiers `final` and `static` makes no difference—though you should use a consistent order. We have already accessed static fields in all of the preceding examples, as you may have realized—`out` is a `static` field of class `System`.

Groups of named constants, like the suits, can often be better represented as the members of an *enumeration type,* or *enum* for short. An enum is a special class with predefined instances for each of the named constants the enum represents. For example, we can rewrite our suit example using an enum:

```
enum Suit { CLUBS, DIAMONDS, HEARTS, SPADES }
```

Each enum constant is a static field that refers to the object for that value—such as `Suit.HEARTS`. By representing each named constant as an object rather than just an integer value, you improve the type-safety and so the robustness, of your program. Enums are covered in detail in Chapter 6.

Exercise 1.5: Change the `HelloWorld` application to use a named string constant as the string to print. (A string constant can be initialized with a string literal.)

Exercise 1.6: Change your program from Exercise 1.3 to use a named string constant for the title.

1.5   Unicode Characters

Suppose we were defining a class that dealt with circles and we wanted a named constant that represented the value π. In most programming languages we would name the constant "pi" because in most languages identifiers (the technical term for names) are limited to the letters and digits available in the ASCII character set. In the Java programming language, however, we can do this:

```
class Circle {
    static final double π = 3.14159265358979323846;
    // ...
}
```

The Java programming language moves you toward the world of internationalized software: you write code in *Unicode,* an international character set standard. Unicode basic[1] characters are 16 bits, and together with the supplemental characters (21 bits) provide a character range large enough to write the major languages used in the world. That is why we can use π for the name of the constant in the example. π is a valid letter from the Greek section of Unicode and is therefore valid in source. Most existing code is typed in ASCII, a 7-bit character standard, or ISO Latin-1, an 8-bit character standard commonly called Latin-1. But these characters are translated into Unicode before processing, so the character set is always Unicode.

1.6 Flow of Control

"Flow of control" is the term for deciding which statements in a program are executed and in what order. The `while` loop in the `Fibonacci` program is one control flow statement, as are blocks, which define a sequential execution of the statements they group. Other control flow statements include `for`, `if–else`, `switch`, and `do–while`. We change the Fibonacci sequence program by numbering the elements of the sequence and marking even numbers with an asterisk:

```
class ImprovedFibonacci {

    static final int MAX_INDEX = 9;

    /**
     * Print out the first few Fibonacci numbers,
     * marking evens with a '*'
     */
    public static void main(String[] args) {
        int lo = 1;
        int hi = 1;
```

---

[1] Basic Multilingual Plane, or BMP, in Unicode terminology.

```
        String mark;

        System.out.println("1: " + lo);
        for (int i = 2; i <= MAX_INDEX; i++) {
            if (hi % 2 == 0)
                mark = " *";
            else
                mark = "";
            System.out.println(i + ": " + hi + mark);
            hi = lo + hi;
            lo = hi - lo;
        }
    }
}
```

Here is the new output:

```
1: 1
2: 1
3: 2 *
4: 3
5: 5
6: 8 *
7: 13
8: 21
9: 34 *
```

To number the elements of the sequence, we used a for loop instead of a while loop. A for loop is shorthand for a while loop, with an initialization and increment section added. The for loop in ImprovedFibonacci is equivalent to this while loop:

```
int i = 2;    // define and initialize loop index
while (i <= MAX_INDEX) {
    // ...generate the next Fibonacci number and print it...
    i++;    // increment loop index
}
```

The use of the for loop introduces a new variable declaration mechanism: the declaration of the loop variable in the initialization section. This is a convenient way of defining loop variables that need exist only while the loop is executing, but it applies only to for loops—none of the other control-flow statements allow variables to be declared within the statement itself. The loop variable i is available only within the body of the `for` statement. A loop variable declared in this manner disappears when the loop terminates, which means you can reuse that variable name in subsequent `for` statements.

The ++ operator in this code fragment may be unfamiliar if you're new to C-derived programming languages. The ++ operator increments by one the value of any variable it abuts—the contents of variable `i` in this case. The ++ operator is a *prefix* operator when it comes before its operand, and *postfix* when it comes after. The two forms have slightly different semantics but we defer that discussion until Chapter 9. Similarly, minus-minus (--) decrements by one the value of any variable it abuts and can also be prefix or postfix. In the context of the previous example, a statement like

```
i++;
```

is equivalent to

```
i = i + 1;
```

Expressions where the value assigned to a variable is calculated from the original value of the variable are common enough that there is a short-hand for writing them. For example, another way to write `i = i + 1` is to write

```
i += 1;
```

which adds the value on the right-hand side of the += operator (namely 1) to the variable on the left-hand side (namely `i`). Most of the binary operators (operators that take two operands) can be joined with = in a similar way (such as +=, -=, *=, and /=).

Inside the `for` loop body we use an `if`–`else` statement to see whether the current `hi` value is even. The `if` statement tests the boolean expression between the parentheses. If the expression is `true`, the statement (which can be a block) in the body of the `if` is executed. If the expression is `false`, the statement in the body of the `else` clause is executed. The `else` part is optional. If the `else` is not present, nothing is done when the expression is `false`. After figuring out which (if any) clause to execute, and then actually executing it, control passes to the code following the body of the `if` statement.

The example tests whether `hi` is even using the %, or *remainder,* operator (also known as the *modulus* operator). It produces the remainder after dividing the value on the left side by the value on the right. In this example, if the left-side value is even, the remainder is zero and the ensuing statement assigns a string containing the even-number indicator to `mark`. The `else` clause is executed for odd numbers, setting `mark` to an empty string.

The `println` invocations appear more complex in this example because the arguments to `println` are themselves expressions that must be evaluated before println is invoked. In the first case we have the expression "1: " + lo, which concatenates a string representation of lo (initially 1) to the string literal "1: "— giving a string with the value "1: 1". The + operator is a concatenation operator when at least one of its operands is a string; otherwise, it's an addition operator. Having the concatenation operation appear within the method argument list is a common short-hand for the more verbose and tedious:

```
String temp = "1: " + lo;
System.out.println(temp);
```

The println invocation within the for loop body constructs a string containing a string representation of the current loop count i, a separator string, a string representing the current value of hi and the marker string.

Exercise 1.7: Change the loop in ImprovedFibonacci so that i counts backward instead of forward.

1.7   Classes and Objects

The Java programming language, like many object-oriented programming languages, provides a tool to solve programming problems using the notions of classes and objects. Every object has a class that defines its data and behavior. Each class has three kinds of members:

- ◆ Fields are data variables associated with a class and its objects. Fields store results of computations performed by the class.

- ◆ Methods contain the executable code of a class. Methods are built from statements. The way in which methods are invoked, and the statements contained within those methods, are what ultimately directs program execution.

- ◆ Classes and interfaces can be members of other classes or interfaces (you will learn about interfaces soon).

Here is the declaration of a simple class that might represent a point on a two-dimensional plane:

```
class Point {
    public double x, y;
}
```

This Point class has two fields representing the *x* and *y* coordinates of a point and has (as yet) no methods. A class declaration like this one is, conceptually, a plan that defines what objects manufactured from that class look like, plus sets of instructions that define the behavior of those objects.

Members of a class can have various levels of *visibility* or *accessibility.* The `public` declaration of x and y in the `Point` class means that any code with access to a `Point` object can read and modify those fields. Other levels of accessibility limit member access to code in the class itself or to other related classes.

1.7.1 Creating Objects

Objects are created by expressions containing the `new` keyword. Creating an object from a class definition is also known as *instantiation;* thus, objects are often called *instances.*

Newly created objects are allocated within an area of system memory known as the *heap.* All objects are accessed via *object references*—any variable that may appear to hold an object actually contains a reference to that object. The types of such variables are known as *reference types,* in contrast to the primitive types whose variables hold values of that type. Object references are `null` when they do not reference any object.

Most of the time, you can be imprecise in the distinction between actual objects and references to objects. You can say, "Pass the object to the method" when you really mean "Pass an object reference to the method." We are careful about this distinction only when it makes a difference. Most of the time, you can use "object" and "object reference" interchangeably.

In the `Point` class, suppose you are building a graphics application in which you need to track lots of points. You represent each point by its own concrete `Point` object. Here is how you might create and initialize `Point` objects:

```
Point lowerLeft = new Point();
Point upperRight = new Point();
Point middlePoint = new Point();

lowerLeft.x = 0.0;
lowerLeft.y = 0.0;

upperRight.x = 1280.0;
upperRight.y = 1024.0;

middlePoint.x = 640.0;
middlePoint.y = 512.0;
```

Each `Point` object is unique and has its own copy of the x and y fields. Changing x in the object `lowerLeft`, for example, does not affect the value of x in the object upperRight. The fields in objects are known as *instance variables,* because there is a unique copy of the field in each object (instance) of the class.

When you use new to create an object, a special piece of code, known as a *constructor,* is invoked to perform any initialization the object might need. A constructor has the same name as the class that it constructs and is similar to a method, including being able to accept arguments. If you don't declare a constructor in your class, the compiler creates one for you that takes no arguments and does nothing. When we say "new Point()" we're asking that a Point object be allocated and because we passed in no arguments, the no-argument constructor be invoked to initialize it.

1.7.2   Static or Class Fields

Per-object fields are usually what you need. You usually want a field in one object to be distinct from the field of the same name in every other object instantiated from that class.

Sometimes, though, you want fields that are shared among all objects of that class. These shared variables are known as *class variables*—variables specific to the class as opposed to objects of the class.

Why would you want to use class variables? Consider, for example, the Sony Walkman factory. Each Walkman has a unique serial number. In object terms, each Walkman object has its own unique serial number field. However, the factory needs to keep a record of the next serial number to be assigned. You don't want to keep that number with every Walkman object. You'd keep only one copy of that number in the factory, or, in object terms, as a class variable.

You obtain class-specific fields by declaring them static, and they are therefore commonly called *static fields.* For example, a Point object to represent the origin might be common enough that you should provide it as a static field in the Point class:

```
public static Point origin = new Point();
```

If this declaration appears inside the declaration of the Point class, there will be exactly one piece of data called Point.origin that always refers to an object at (0.0, 0.0). This static field is there no matter how many Point objects are created, even if none are created. The values of x and y are zero because that is the default for numeric fields that are not explicitly initialized to a different value.

You can probably see now why named constants are declared static.

When you see the word "field" in this book, it generally means a per-object field, although the term *non-static field* is sometimes used for clarity.

1.7.3 The Garbage Collector

After creating an object with new, how do you get rid of the object when you no longer want it? The answer is simple—stop referring to it. Unreferenced objects are automatically reclaimed by a *garbage collector,* which runs in the background and tracks object references. When an object is no longer referenced, the garbage collector can remove it from the storage allocation heap, although it may defer actually doing so until a propitious time.

1.8 Methods and Parameters

Objects of the previously defined Point class are exposed to manipulation by any code that has a reference to a Point object, because its fields are declared public. The Point class is an example of the simplest kind of class. Indeed, some classes *are* this simple. They are designed to fit purely internal needs for a package (a group of cooperating classes) or to provide simple data containers when those are all you need.

The real benefits of object orientation, however, come from hiding the implementation of a class behind operations performed on its data. Operations of a class are declared via its *methods*—instructions that operate on an object's data to obtain results. Methods access internal implementation details that are otherwise hidden from other objects. Hiding data behind methods so that it is inaccessible to other objects is the fundamental basis of *data encapsulation.*

If we enhance the Point class with a simple clear method (to clear, or reset the coordinates to zero), it might look like this:

```
public void clear() {
    x = 0.0;
    y = 0.0;
}
```

The clear method has no parameters, hence the empty ( ) pair after its name; clear is declared void because it does not return any value. Inside a method, fields and other methods of the class can be named directly—we can simply say x and y without an explicit object reference.

1.8.1 Invoking a Method

Objects in general do not operate directly on the data of other objects, although, as you saw in the Point class, a class can make its fields publicly accessible. Well-designed classes usually hide their data so that it can be changed only by methods of that class.

To *invoke* a method, you provide an object reference to the *target* object and the method name, separated by a dot. *Arguments* are passed to the method as a comma-separated list of values enclosed in parentheses. Methods that take no arguments still require the parentheses, with nothing between them.

A method can return only a single value as a result. To return more than one value from a method, you must create an object whose purpose is to hold return values in a single unit and then return that object.

When a method is invoked, the flow of execution leaves the current method and starts executing the body of the invoked method. When the invoked method has completed, the current method continues execution with the code after the method invocation. When we start executing the body of the method, the object that was the target of the method invocation is now the *current* or *receiver* object, from the perspective of that method. The arguments passed to the method are accessed via the parameters the method declared.

Here is a method called `distance` that's part of the `Point` class shown in previous examples. The `distance` method accepts another `Point` object as a parameter, computes the Euclidean distance between itself and the other point, and returns a double-precision floating-point result:

```
public double distance(Point that) {
    double xdiff = x - that.x;
    double ydiff = y - that.y;
    return Math.sqrt(xdiff * xdiff + ydiff * ydiff);
}
```

The `return` statement causes a method to stop executing its body and return execution to the invoking method. If an expression is part of the `return` statement then the value of that expression is returned as the value of the method invocation. The type of the expression must be compatible with the return type defined for the method. In the example we use the `sqrt` method of the `Math` library class to calculate the square root of the sum of the squares of the differences between the two *x* and *y* coordinates.

Based on the `lowerLeft` and `upperRight` objects created previously, you could invoke `distance` this way:

```
double d = lowerLeft.distance(upperRight);
```

Here `upperRight` is passed as an argument to `distance`, which sees it as the parameter `that`. After this statement executes, the variable d contains the Euclidean distance between `lowerLeft` and `upperRight`.

1.8.2 The this Reference

Occasionally, the receiving object needs to know its own reference. For example, the receiving object might want to add itself to a list of objects somewhere. An implicit reference named this is available to methods, and this is a reference to the current (receiving) object. The following definition of clear is equivalent to the one just presented:

```
public void clear() {
    this.x = 0.0;
    this.y = 0.0;
}
```

You usually use this as an argument to other methods that need an object reference. The this reference can also be used to explicitly name the members of the current object. Here's another method of Point named move, which sets the x and y fields to specified values:

```
public void move(double x, double y) {
    this.x = x;
    this.y = y;
}
```

The move method uses this to clarify which x and y are being referred to. Naming the parameters x and y is reasonable, because you pass *x* and *y* coordinates to the method. But then those parameters have the same names as the fields, and therefore the parameter names *hide* the field names. If we simply wrote x = x we would assign the value of the x parameter to itself, not to the x field as required. The expression this.x refers to the object's x field, not the x parameter of move.

Exercise 1.8: Add a method to the Point class that sets the current object's coordinates to those of a passed in Point object.

1.8.3 Static or Class Methods

Just as you can have per-class static fields, you can also have per-class static methods, often known as *class methods*. Class methods are usually intended to do operations specific to the class itself, usually on static fields and not on specific instances of that class. Class methods are declared using the static keyword and are therefore also known as *static methods*.

As with the term "field", the word "method" generally means a per-object method, although the term *non-static method* is sometimes used for clarity.

Why would you need static methods? Consider the Sony Walkman factory again. The record of the next serial number to be assigned is held in the factory, not in every Walkman. A method that returned the factory's copy of the next available serial number would be a static method, not a method to operate on specific Walkman objects.

The implementation of `distance` in the previous example uses the static method `Math.sqrt` to calculate a square root. The `Math` class supports many methods that are useful for general mathematical manipulation. These methods are declared as static methods because they do not act on any particular instance of the `Math` class; instead, they group a related set of functionality in the class itself.

A static method cannot directly access non-static members. When a static method is invoked, there's no specific object for the method to operate on, and so no `this` reference. You could work around this by passing an explicit object reference as an argument to the static method. In general, however, static methods perform class-related tasks and non-static methods perform object-related tasks. Asking a static method to work on object fields is like asking the Walkman factory to change the serial number of a Walkman hanging on the belt of a jogger in Golden Gate Park.

1.9   Arrays

Simple variables that hold one value are useful but are not sufficient for many applications. A program that plays a game of cards would want a number of `Card` objects it could manipulate as a whole. To meet this need, you use *arrays*.

An array is a collection of variables all of the same type. The components of an array are accessed by simple integer indexes. In a card game, a `Deck` object might look like this:

```
public class Deck {
    public static final int DECK_SIZE = 52;

    private Card[] cards = new Card[DECK_SIZE];

    public void print() {
        for (int i = 0; i < cards.length; i++)
            System.out.println(cards[i]);
    }
    // ...
}
```

First we declare a constant called DECK_SIZE to define the number of cards in a deck. This constant is public so that anyone can find out how many cards are in a deck. Next we declare a cards field for referring to all the cards. This field is declared private, which means that only the methods in the current class can access it—this prevents anyone from manipulating our cards directly. The modifiers public and private are *access modifiers* because they control who can access a class, interface, field, or method.

We declare the cards field as an array of type Card by following the type name in the declaration with square brackets [and]. We initialize cards to a new array with DECK_SIZE variables of type Card. Each Card element in the array is implicitly initialized to null. An array's length is fixed when it is created and can never change.

The println method invocation shows how array components are accessed. It encloses the index of the desired element within square brackets following the array name.

You can probably tell from reading the code that array objects have a length field that says how many elements the array contains. The *bounds* of an array are integers between 0 and length-1, inclusive. It is a common programming error, especially when looping through array elements, to try to access elements that are outside the bounds of the array. To catch this sort of error, all array accesses are *bounds checked,* to ensure that the index is in bounds. If you try to use an index that is out of bounds, the runtime system reports this by throwing an exception in your program—an ArrayIndexOutOfBoundsException. You'll learn about exceptions a bit later in this chapter.

An array with length zero is an *empty array*. Methods that take arrays as arguments may require that the array they receive is non-empty and so will need to check the length. However, before you can check the length of an array you need to ensure that the array reference is not null. If either of these checks fail, the method may report the problem by throwing an IllegalArgumentException. For example, here is a method that averages the values in an integer array:

```
static double average(int[] values) {
    if (values == null)
        throw new IllegalArgumentException();
    else
        if (values.length == 0)
            throw new IllegalArgumentException();
        else {
            double sum = 0.0;
            for (int i = 0; i < values.length; i++)
                sum += values[i];
```

```
            return sum / values.length;
        }
    }
```

This code works but the logic of the method is almost completely lost in the nested if–else statements ensuring the array is non-empty. To avoid the need for two if statements, we could try to test whether the argument is null *or* whether it has a zero length, by using the boolean inclusive-OR operator (|):

```
    if (values == null | values.length == 0)
        throw new IllegalArgumentException();
```

Unfortunately, this code is not correct. Even if values is null, this code will still attempt to access its length field because the normal boolean operators always evaluate both operands. This situation is so common when performing logical operations that special operators are defined to solve it. The conditional boolean operators evaluate their right-hand operand only if the value of the expression has not already been determined by the left-hand operand. We can correct the example code by using the conditional-OR (||) operator:

```
    if (values == null || values.length == 0)
        throw new IllegalArgumentException();
```

Now if values is null the value of the conditional-OR expression is known to be true and so no attempt is made to access the length field.

The binary boolean operators—AND (&), inclusive-OR (|), and exclusive-OR (^)—are logical operators when their operands are boolean values and bitwise operators when their operands are integer values. The conditional-OR (||) and conditional-AND (&&) operators are logical operators and can only be used with boolean operands.

Exercise 1.9: Modify the Fibonacci application to store the sequence into an array and print the list of values at the end.

Exercise 1.10: Modify the ImprovedFibonacci application to store its sequence in an array. Do this by creating a new class to hold both the value and a boolean value that says whether the value is even, and then having an array of object references to objects of that class.

1.10 String Objects

A `String` class type deals specifically with sequences of character data and provides language-level support for initializing them. The `String` class provides a variety of methods to operate on `String` objects.

You've already seen string literals in examples like the `HelloWorld` program. When you write a statement such as

```
System.out.println("Hello, world");
```

the compiler actually creates a `String` object initialized to the value of the specified string literal and passes that `String` object as the argument to the `println` method.

You don't need to specify the length of a `String` object when you create it. You can create a new `String` object and initialize it all in one statement, as shown in this example:

```
class StringsDemo {
    public static void main(String[] args) {
        String myName = "Petronius";

        myName = myName + " Arbiter";
        System.out.println("Name = " + myName);
    }
}
```

Here we declare a `String` variable called `myName` and initialize it with an object reference to a string literal. Following initialization, we use the `String` concatenation operator (+) to make a new `String` object with new contents and store a reference to this new string object into the variable. Finally, we print the value of `myName` on the standard output stream. The output when you run this program is

```
Name = Petronius Arbiter
```

The concatenation operator can also be used in the short-hand += form, to assign the concatenation of the original string and the given string, back to the original string reference. Here's an upgraded program:

```
class BetterStringsDemo {
    public static void main(String[] args) {
        String myName = "Petronius";
        String occupation = "Reorganization Specialist";

        myName += " Arbiter";
```

```
        myName += " ";
        myName += "(" + occupation + ")";
        System.out.println("Name = " + myName);
    }
}
```

Now when you run the program, you get this output:

```
Name = Petronius Arbiter (Reorganization Specialist)
```

String objects have a `length` method that returns the number of characters in the string. Characters are indexed from 0 through `length()-1`, and can be accessed with the `charAt` method, which takes an integer index and returns the character at that index. In this regard a string is similar to an array of characters, but `String` objects are not arrays of characters and you cannot assign an array of characters to a `String` reference. You can, however, construct a new `String` object from an array of characters by passing the array as an argument to a `String` constructor. You can also obtain an array of characters with the same contents as a string using the `toCharArray` method.

String objects are *read-only,* or *immutable:* The contents of a `String` never change. When you see statements like

```
str = "redwood";
// ... do something with str ..
str = "oak";
```

the second assignment gives a new value to the variable `str`, which is an object reference to a different string object with the contents `"oak"`. Every time you perform operations that seem to modify a `String` object, such as the += operation in `BetterStringsDemo`, you actually get a new read-only `String` object, while the original `String` object remains unchanged. The classes `StringBuilder` and `StringBuffer` provide for mutable strings and are described in Chapter 13, where `String` is also described in detail.

The `equals` method is the simplest way to compare two `String` objects to see whether they have the same contents:

```
if (oneStr.equals(twoStr))
    foundDuplicate(oneStr, twoStr);
```

Other methods for comparing subparts of strings or ignoring case differences are also covered in Chapter 13. If you use == to compare the string objects, you are actually comparing `oneStr` and `twoStr` to see if they refer to the same object, not testing if the strings have the same contents.

Exercise 1.11: Modify the `StringsDemo` application to use different strings.

Exercise 1.12: Modify `ImprovedFibonacci` to store the `String` objects it creates into an array instead of invoking `println` with them directly.

1.10.1 String Conversion and Formatting

The concatenation operator converts primitive values to strings using the `toString` method of the corresponding wrapper class. This conversion doesn't give you any control over the format of the resulting string. Formatted conversion can be done with the `java.util.Formatter` class. A `Formatter` can write its output to a string, a file, or some other output device. For convenience the `System.out.printf` method (for "print formatted") uses a formatter to write to `System.out`. Formatted output uses a *format string* together with a set of values to format. The format string contains normal text together with *format specifiers* that tell the formatter how you want the subsequent values to be formatted. For example, you can print the value of `Math.PI` to three decimal places using

```
System.out.printf("The value of Math.PI is %.3f %n", Math.PI);
```

which prints

```
The value of Math.PI is 3.142
```

whereas using `println` and string concatenation you'd get:

```
The value of Math.PI is 3.141592653589793
```

A format specifier consists of at least two parts: it starts with a % character, and it ends with a conversion indicator. The conversion identifies both the type of the value to format, and the basic form. For example, %f says to format a floating-point value in the usual decimal form, as used for `Math.PI` above, whereas %e says to format a floating point value in scientific notation—for example, 3.142e+00. Integer values can be formatted by %d for normal decimal, or %x for hexadecimal form. A string can be formatted by %s.

The %n conversion causes insertion of the correct line-separator character, something that `println` does automatically for you. The line-separator depends on the current platform and may not be a simple \n (newline) character. If you are familiar with `printf` from the C programming language you need to get used to using %n instead of \n.

A format specifier can provide additional formatting information. You can provide a *width* that indicates the minimum number of characters to print—useful for aligning columns of data. If the formatted value has fewer characters than the width, it is padded with spaces to fit the minimum size. This lets you align values easily. Some conversions also allow a *precision* value to be given, which is written as . followed by a non-negative number. For floating-point values using %f the precision indicates how many decimal places to round to—in the example above the value of Math.PI is rounded to 3 decimal places because of the .3 in the format specifier. If both a width and precision are given they are written in the form *width.precision*. Additional flags in the format specifier can, among other things, request zero padding (instead of spaces) or left-justification (the default is right justification).

Formatted output is covered in detail in Chapter 22.

Exercise 1.13: Rewrite the ImprovedFibonacci program using printf instead of println.

1.11 Extending a Class

One of the major benefits of object orientation is the ability to *extend,* or *subclass,* the behavior of an existing class and continue to use code written for the original class when acting on an instance of the subclass. The original class is known as the *superclass.* When you extend a class to create a new class, the new extended class *inherits* fields and methods of the superclass.

If the subclass does not specifically *override* the behavior of the superclass, the subclass inherits all the behavior of its superclass because it inherits the fields and methods of its superclass. In addition, the subclass can add new fields and methods and so add new behavior.

Consider the Walkman example. The original model had a single jack for one person to listen to the tape. Later models incorporated two jacks so two people could listen to the same tape. In the object-oriented world, the two-jack model extends, or is a subclass of, the basic one-jack model. The two-jack model inherits the characteristics and behavior of the basic model and adds new behavior of its own.

Customers told Sony they wanted to talk to each other while sharing a tape in the two-jack model. Sony enhanced the two-jack model to include two-way communications so people could chat while listening to music. The two-way communications model is a subclass of the two-jack model, inherits all its behavior, and again adds new behavior.

Sony created many other Walkman models. Later models extend the capabilities of the basic model—they subclass the basic model and inherit features and behavior from it.

Let's look at an example of extending a class. Here we extend our former `Point` class to represent a pixel that might be shown on a screen. The new `Pixel` class requires a color in addition to *x* and *y* coordinates:

```
class Pixel extends Point {
    Color color;

    public void clear() {
        super.clear();
        color = null;
    }
}
```

`Pixel` extends both the *data* and *behavior* of its `Point` superclass. `Pixel` extends the data by adding a field named `color`. `Pixel` also extends the behavior of `Point` by overriding `Point`'s `clear` method.

`Pixel` objects can be used by any code designed to work with `Point` objects. If a method expects a parameter of type `Point`, you can hand it a `Pixel` object and it just works. All the `Point` code can be used by anyone with a `Pixel` in hand. This feature is known as *polymorphism*—a single object like `Pixel` can have many (*poly-*) forms (*-morph*) and can be used as both a `Pixel` object and a `Point` object.

`Pixel`'s behavior extends `Point`'s behavior. Extended behavior can be entirely new (adding color in this example) or can be a restriction on old behavior that follows all the original requirements. An example of restricted behavior might be `Pixel` objects that live inside some kind of `Screen` object, restricting x and y to the dimensions of the screen. If the original `Point` class did not forbid restrictions for coordinates, a class with restricted range would not violate the original class's behavior.

An extended class often *overrides* the behavior of its superclass by providing new implementations of one or more of the inherited methods. To do this the extended class defines a method with the same signature and return type as a method in the superclass. In the `Pixel` example, we override `clear` to obtain the proper behavior that `Pixel` requires. The `clear` that `Pixel` inherited from `Point` knows only about `Point`'s fields but obviously can't know about the new `color` field declared in the `Pixel` subclass.

1.11.1 Invoking Methods of the Superclass

To make `Pixel` do the correct "clear" behavior, we provide a new implementation of `clear` that first invokes its superclass's `clear` using the `super` reference. The `super` reference is a lot like the `this` reference described previously except that `super` references things from the superclass, whereas `this` references things from the current object.

The invocation `super.clear()` looks to the superclass to execute `clear` as it would for an object of the superclass—namely, `Point`. After invoking `super.clear()` to clear out the `Point` part of the object, we add new functionality to set `color` to a reasonable empty value. We choose `null`, a reference to no object.

What would happen had we not invoked `super.clear()` in the previous example? `Pixel`'s `clear` method would set `color` to its `null` value, but the `x` and `y` variables that `Pixel` inherited from `Point` would not be set to any "cleared" values. Not clearing all the values of a `Pixel` object, including its `Point` parts, is probably a bug.

When you invoke `super.`*method*`()`, the runtime system looks back up the inheritance hierarchy to the first superclass that contains the required *method*. If `Point` didn't have a `clear` method, for example, the runtime system would look at `Point`'s superclass for such a method and invoke that, and so on.

For all other references, invoking a method uses the actual class of the *object*, not the type of the object *reference*. Here is an example:

```
Point point = new Pixel();
point.clear();   // uses Pixel's clear()
```

In this example, `Pixel`'s version of `clear` is invoked even though the variable that holds the `Pixel` is declared as a `Point` reference. But if we invoke `super.clear()` inside one of `Pixel`'s methods, that invocation will use the `Point` class's implementation of the `clear` method.

1.11.2 The `Object` Class

Classes that do not explicitly extend any other class implicitly extend the `Object` class. All objects are polymorphically of class `Object`, so `Object` is the general-purpose type for references that can refer to objects of any class:

```
Object oref = new Pixel();
oref = "Some String";
```

In this example, `oref` is correctly assigned references to `Pixel` and `String` objects even though those classes have no relationship except that both have `Object` as a superclass. The `Object` class also defines several important methods that you'll learn about in Chapter 3.

1.11.3 Type Casting

The following code fragment seems quite reasonable (if not particularly useful) but results in a compile-time error:

```
String name = "Petronius";
Object obj = name;
name = obj;    // INVALID: won't compile
```

We declare and initialize a `String` reference which we then assign to a general-purpose `Object` reference, and then we try to assign the reference to a `String` back to the `String` reference. Why doesn't this work? The problem is that while a `String` is always an `Object`, an `Object` is not necessarily a `String`, and even though you can see that in this case it really is a `String`, the compiler is not so clever. To help the compiler you have to tell it that the object referred to by `obj` is actually a `String` and so can be assigned to `name`:

```
name = (String) obj;    // That's better!
```

Telling the compiler that the type of an expression is really a different type is known as *type casting* or *type conversion.* You perform a type cast by prefixing the expression with the new type in parentheses. The compiler doesn't automatically trust you when you do this and so it checks that you are telling the truth. A smart compiler may be able to tell at compile time that you are telling the truth; otherwise, it will insert a run time check to verify that the cast really is allowed. If you lie to the compiler and the run time check fails, the runtime system reports this by throwing a `ClassCastException`. As the Java programming language is *strongly typed* there are strict rules concerning assignments between types.

Exercise 1.14: Sketch out a set of classes that reflects the class structure of the Sony Walkman product family we have described. Use methods to hide the data, making all the data `private` and the methods `public`. What methods would belong in the `Walkman` class? Which methods would be added for which extended classes?

1.12 Interfaces

Sometimes you want only to *declare* methods an object must support but not to supply the *implementation* of those methods. As long as their behavior meets specific criteria—called the *contract*—implementation details of the methods are irrelevant. These declarations define a *type,* and any class that implements those methods can be said to have that type, regardless of how the methods are implemented. For example, to ask whether a particular value is contained in a set of values, details of how those values are stored are irrelevant. You want the methods to work equally well with a linked list of values, a hashtable of values, or any other data structure.

To support this, you can define an *interface*. An interface is like a class but has only empty declarations of its methods. The designer of the interface declares the methods that must be supported by classes that *implement* the interface and declares what those methods should do. Here is a Lookup interface for finding a value in a set of values:

```
interface Lookup {
    /** Return the value associated with the name, or
     *  null if there is no such value */
    Object find(String name);
}
```

The Lookup interface declares one method, find, that takes a String and returns the value associated with that name, or null if there is no associated value. In the interface no implementation can be given for the method—a class that implements the interface is responsible for providing a specific implementation—so instead of a method body we simply have a semicolon. Code that uses references of type Lookup (references to objects that implement the Lookup interface) can invoke the find method and get the expected results, no matter what the actual type of the object is:

```
void processValues(String[] names, Lookup table) {
    for (int i = 0; i < names.length; i++) {
        Object value = table.find(names[i]);
        if (value != null)
            processValue(names[i], value);
    }
}
```

A class can implement as many interfaces as you choose. This example implements Lookup using a simple array (methods to set or remove values are left out for simplicity):

```
class SimpleLookup implements Lookup {
    private String[] names;
    private Object[] values;

    public Object find(String name) {
        for (int i = 0; i < names.length; i++) {
```

```
        if (names[i].equals(name))
            return values[i];
    }
    return null;    // not found
}

// ...
}
```

An interface can also declare named constants that are `static` and `final`. Additionally, an interface can declare other *nested* interfaces and even classes. These nested types are discussed in detail in Chapter 5. All the members of an interface are implicitly, or explicitly, `public`—so they can be accessed anywhere the interface itself is accessible.

Interfaces can be extended using the `extends` keyword. An interface can extend one or more other interfaces, adding new constants or new methods that must be implemented by any class that implements the extended interface.

A class's *supertypes* are the class it extends and the interfaces it implements, including all the supertypes of those classes and interfaces. So an object is not only an instance of its particular class but also of any of its supertypes, including interfaces. An object can be used polymorphically with both its superclass and any superinterfaces, including any of their supertypes.

A class's *subtypes* are the classes that extend it, including all of their subtypes. An interface's subtypes are the interfaces that extend it, and the classes that implement it, including all of their subtypes.

Exercise 1.15: Write an interface that extends `Lookup` to declare `add` and `remove` methods. Implement the extended interface in a new class.

1.13 Generic Types

Classes and interfaces can be declared to be *generic types*. A generic class or interface represents a family of related types. For example, in

```
interface List<T> {
    // ... methods of List ...
}
```

`List<T>` (read as "list of T") declares a generic list that can be used for any non-primitive type T. You could use such a declaration to have a list of `Point` objects (`List<Point>`), a list of `String` objects (`List<String>`), a list of `Integer` objects (List<Integer>), and so on. In contrast to a *raw* List, which can hold any kind of Object, a List<String> is known to hold only String objects, and this fact is guaranteed at compile time—if you try to add a plain Object, for example, you'll get a compile-time error.

Consider the Lookup interface from the previous section, it could be declared in a generic form:

```
interface Lookup<T> {
    T find(String name);
}
```

Now, rather than returning Object, the find method returns a T, whatever T may be. We could then declare a class for looking up integers, for example:

```
class IntegerLookup implements Lookup<Integer> {
    private String[] names;
    private Integer[] values;

    public Integer find(String name) {
        for (int i = 0; i < names.length; i++) {
            if (names[i].equals(name))
                return values[i];
        }
        return null;     // not found
    }

    // ...
}
```

Class IntegerLookup is not itself a generic class, rather it implements a generic interface, providing a concrete type—Integer—in place of the abstract type parameter T. Compared to the SimpleLookup class, this class can store items in an array of Integer and find returns an Integer.

How would we modify processValues to work with generic implementations of Lookup? Here's one attempt to do so:

```
void processValues(String[] names, Lookup<Object> table) {
    for (int i = 0; i < names.length; i++) {
        Object value = table.find(names[i]);
        if (value != null)
            processValue(names[i], value);
    }
}
```

This compiles okay, and appears reasonable—`table` is an instance of a class that implements `Lookup` for any kind of `Object`. As `Integer` instances are `Object` instances then we should be able to do this:

```
Lookup<Integer> table = new IntegerLookup();
// ... add entries to table ...
String[] names = { "One", "two" };
processValues(names, table);      // INVALID: won't compile
```

But we find that this code won't compile. The problem is that, as defined, `processValues` will only accept an instance of a class that implements `Lookup<Object>`, and `IntegerLookup` does not do that. Even though `Integer` is a subtype of `Object`, `Lookup<Integer>` is *not* a subtype of `Lookup<Object>` and therefore an instance of the former can not be used where an instance of the latter is required. Is there a way to declare that we want to deal with an instance that implements `Lookup` of anything? Yes—we use what is called a *wildcard* to specify the type parameter:

```
void processValues(String[] names, Lookup<?> table) {
    for (int i = 0; i < names.length; i++) {
        Object value = table.find(names[i]);
        if (value != null)
            processValue(names[i], value);
    }
}
```

The wildcard is written as ? and is read as "of unspecified type", or just as "of some type": `table` is an instance of a class that implements a lookup of some type. We don't know what type, and in this example we don't care. The only thing we know about the type we can lookup is that it must at least be an `Object`, so we can invoke `table.find` and store the return value as an `Object`. Now we can use `IntegerLookup` with `processValues` without a problem.

Suppose in our application we knew that we would always be looking up `Integer` or `Long` or `Double`, etc.—all the subclasses of the `Number` class. We know, from the previous example, that we can't define `processValues` in terms of `Lookup<Number>`, but there is a way to limit the types that the wildcard can represent:

```
void processValues(String[] names,
                   Lookup<? extends Number> table) {
    for (int i = 0; i < names.length; i++) {
        Number value = table.find(names[i]);
        if (value != null)
```

```
            processValue(names[i], value);
        }
    }
```

Where ? on its own is the *unbounded wildcard,* that can represent any type, "? extends X" is a *bounded wildcard:* It can only represent the type X or any type that extends or implements X (depending on whether X is a class or interface). This time in processValues we know that, at worst, table.find will return a Number, so we can store that return value in a variable of type Number.

There is a lot more to generic types and you'll learn about their full power in Chapter 11. Meanwhile, you know enough about them to understand the simple usages that will occur in the early chapters of this book.

1.14 Exceptions

What do you do when an error occurs in a program? In many languages, error conditions are signaled by unusual return values like −1. Programmers often don't check for exceptional values because they may assume that errors "can't happen." On the other hand, adding error detection and recovery to what should be a straightforward flow of logic can complicate that logic to the point where the normal flow is completely obscured. An ostensibly simple task such as reading a file into memory might require about seven lines of code. Error checking and reporting expands this to 40 or more lines. Making normal operation the needle in your code haystack is undesirable.

Checked exceptions manage error handling. Checked exceptions force you to consider what to do with errors where they may occur in the code. If a checked exception is not handled, this is noticed at compile time, not at run time when problems have been compounded because of the unchecked error.

A method that detects an unusual error condition *throws* an exception. Exceptions can be *caught* by code farther back on the calling stack—this invoking code can handle the exception as needed and then continue executing. Uncaught exceptions result in the termination of the thread of execution, but before it terminates the thread's UncaughtExceptionHandler is given the opportunity to respond to the exception as best it can—perhaps doing nothing more than reporting that the exception occurred. Threads and UncaughtExceptionHandlers are discussed in detail in Chapter 14.

An exception is an object, with type, methods, and data. Representing exceptions as objects is useful, because an exception object can include data, methods, or both to report on or recover from specific kinds of exceptions. Exception objects are generally derived from the Exception class, which provides a string

field to describe the error. All exceptions must be subclasses of the class
Throwable, which is the superclass of Exception.

The paradigm for using exceptions is the *try–catch–finally* sequence: you *try*
something; if that something throws an exception, you *catch* the exception; and
finally you clean up from either the normal code path or the exception code path,
whichever actually happened.

Here is a getDataSet method that returns a set of data read from a file. If the
file for the data set cannot be found or if any other I/O exception occurs, this
method throws an exception describing the error. First, we define a new exception
type BadDataSetException to describe such an error. Then we declare that the
method getDataSet throws that exception using a throws clause in the method
header:

```
class BadDataSetException extends Exception { }

class MyUtilities {
    public double[] getDataSet(String setName)
        throws BadDataSetException
    {
        String file = setName + ".dset";
        FileInputStream in = null;
        try {
            in = new FileInputStream(file);
            return readDataSet(in);
        } catch (IOException e) {
            throw new BadDataSetException();
        } finally {
            try {
                if (in != null)
                    in.close();
            } catch (IOException e) {
                ;      // ignore: we either read the data OK
                       // or we're throwing BadDataSetException
            }
        }
    }
    // ... definition of readDataSet ...
}
```

First we turn the data set name into a file name. Then we try to open the file and
read the data using the method readDataSet. If all goes well, readDataSet will
return an array of doubles, which we will return to the invoking code. If opening

or reading the file causes an I/O exception, the catch clause is executed. The catch clause creates a new BadDataSetException object and throws it, in effect translating the I/O exception into an exception specific to getDataSet. Methods that invoke getDataSet can catch the new exception and react to it appropriately. In either case—returning successfully with the data set or catching and then throwing an exception—the code in the finally clause is executed to close the file if it was opened successfully. If an exception occurs during close, we catch it but ignore it—the semicolon by itself forms an *empty statement,* which does nothing. Ignoring exceptions is not a good idea in general, but in this case it occurs either after the data set is successfully read—in which case the method has fulfilled its contract—or the method is already in the process of throwing an exception. If a problem with the file persists, it will be reported as an exception the next time we try to use it and can be more appropriately dealt with at that time.

You will use finally clauses for cleanup code that must always be executed. You can even have a try-finally statement with no catch clauses to ensure that cleanup code will be executed even if uncaught exceptions are thrown.

If a method's execution can result in checked exceptions being thrown, it must declare the types of these exceptions in a throws clause, as shown for the getDataSet method. A method can throw only those checked exceptions it declares—this is why they are called *checked exceptions.* It may throw those exceptions directly with throw or indirectly by invoking a method that throws exceptions. Exceptions of type RuntimeException, Error, or subclasses of these exception types are *unchecked exceptions* and can be thrown anywhere, without being declared.

Checked exceptions represent conditions that, although exceptional, can reasonably be expected to occur, and if they do occur must be dealt with in some way—such as the IOException that may occur reading a file. Declaring the checked exceptions that a method throws allows the compiler to ensure that the method throws only those checked exceptions it declared and no others. This check prevents errors in cases in which your method should handle another method's exceptions but does not. In addition, the method that invokes your method is assured that your method will not result in unexpected checked exceptions.

Unchecked exceptions represent conditions that, generally speaking, reflect errors in your program's logic and cannot be reasonably recovered from at run time. For example, the ArrayIndexOutOfBoundsException thrown when you access outside the bounds of an array tells you that your program calculated an index incorrectly, or failed to verify a value to be used as an index. These are errors that should be corrected in the program code. Given that you can make errors writing any statement it would be totally impractical to have to declare or catch all the exceptions that could arise from those errors—hence they are unchecked.

Exercise 1.16: Add fields to `BadDataSetException` to hold the set name and the I/O exception that signaled the problem so that whoever catches the exception will know details about the error.

1.15 Annotations

Annotations provide information about your program, or the elements of that program (classes, methods, fields, variables, and so forth), in a structured way that is amenable to automated processing by external tools. For example, in many organizations all code that gets written must be reviewed by a programmer other than the author. Keeping track of what code has been reviewed, by whom, and when requires a lot of bookkeeping and is a task most suited to an automated tool—and indeed some code management systems will support this kind of task. Annotations allow you to provide this review information with the code that is being reviewed. For example, here is how you could annotate a class with review information:

```
@Reviewed(reviewer = "Joe Smith", date = 20050331)
public class Point {
    // ...
}
```

An annotation is considered a modifier (like `public` or `static`) and should appear before other modifiers, on a line of its own. It is indicated by an @ character followed by the name of an *annotation type*—in this case `Reviewed`. An annotation type is a special kind of interface, whose members are known as *elements*. Here is the definition of our `Reviewed` annotation type:

```
@interface Reviewed {
    String reviewer();
    int date();
}
```

This is very similar to an interface declaration, except the `interface` keyword is again preceded by the @ character. When you apply an annotation to a program element, you supply values for all of the elements of the annotation type as shown above: The string `"Joe Smith"` is used to set the value of the `reviewer` element, while the `int` value 20050331 is used to set the value of the `date` element. A tool could extract these values from either the source file, or (more often) a compiled class file, and determine, for example, whether a class has been reviewed since it was last modified.

While the language defines the syntax of annotation types, their actual purpose is determined by the tools that recognize them. We won't have anything else to say about annotations until they are discussed in Chapter 15, except to mention where they can be applied.

1.16 Packages

Name conflicts are a major problem when you're developing reusable code. No matter how carefully you pick names for classes, someone else is likely to use that name for a different purpose. If you use simple, descriptive names, the problem gets worse since such names are more likely to be used by someone else who was also trying to use simple, descriptive names. Words like "list," "event," "component," and so on are used often and are almost certain to clash with other people's uses.

The standard solution for name collision in many programming languages is to use a *package prefix* at the front of every class, type, global function, and so on. Prefix conventions create *naming contexts* to ensure that names in one context do not conflict with names in other contexts. These prefixes are usually a few characters long and are usually an abbreviation of the product name, such as Xt for the X-Windows Toolkit.

When code uses only a few packages, the likelihood of prefix conflict is small. However, since prefixes are abbreviations, the probability of a name conflict increases with the number of packages used.

The Java programming language has a formal notion of package that has a set of types and subpackages as members. Packages are named and can be imported. Package names are hierarchical, with components separated by dots. When you use part of a package, either you use its *fully qualified name*—the type name prefixed by the package name, separated by a dot—or you *import* all or part of the package. Importing all, or part, of a package, simply instructs the compiler to look in the package for types that it can't find defined locally. Package names also give you control over name conflicts. If two packages contain classes with the same name, you can use the fully qualified class name for one or both of them.

Here is an example of a method that uses fully qualified names to print the current day and time using the utility class Date (documented in Chapter 22), which, as with all time-based methods, considers time to be in milliseconds since the epoch (00:00:00 GMT, January 1, 1970):

```
class Date1 {
    public static void main(String[] args) {
        java.util.Date now = new java.util.Date();
        System.out.println(now);
    }
}
```

And here is a version that uses `import` to declare the type `Date`:

```
import java.util.Date;

class Date2 {
    public static void main(String[] args) {
        Date now = new Date();
        System.out.println(now);
    }
}
```

When the compiler comes to the declaration of now it determines that the Date type is actually the `java.util.Date` type, because that is the only Date type it knows about. Import statements simply provide information to the compiler; they don't cause files to be "included" into the current file.

The name collision problem is not completely solved by the package mechanism. Two projects can still give their packages the same name. This problem can be solved only by convention. The standard convention is to use the reversed Internet domain name of the organization to prefix the package name. For example, if the Acme Corporation had the Internet domain `acme.com`, it would use package names starting with `com.acme`, as in `com.acme.tools`.

Classes are always part of a package. A package is named by providing a package declaration at the top of the source file:

```
package com.sun.games;

class Card {
    // ...
}
```

If a package is not specified via a `package` declaration, the class is made part of an *unnamed package.* An unnamed package may be adequate for an application (or applet) that is not loaded with any other code. Classes destined for a library should always be written in named packages.

1.17 The Java Platform

The Java programming language is designed to maximize portability. Many details are specifically defined for all implementations. For example, a `double` is a 64-bit IEEE 754 floating-point number. Many languages leave precise definitions to particular implementations, making only general guarantees such as minimum range, or they provide a way to ask the system what the range is on the current platform.

These portable definitions for the Java programming language are specific all the way down to the machine language into which code is translated. Source code is compiled into Java *bytecodes,* which are designed to be run on a Java *virtual machine.* Bytecodes are a machine language for an abstract machine, executed by the virtual machine on each system that supports the Java programming language.[2] Other languages can also be compiled into Java bytecodes.

The virtual machine provides a *runtime* system, which provides access to the virtual machine itself (for example, a way to start the garbage collector) and to the outside world (such as the output stream `System.out`). The runtime system checks security-sensitive operations with a *security manager* or *access controller.* The security manager could, for example, forbid the application to read or write the local disk, or could allow network connections only to particular machines. Exactly what an application is allowed to do, is determined by the *security policy* in force when the application runs.

When classes are loaded into a virtual machine, they will first be checked by a *verifier* that ensures the bytecodes are properly formed and meet security and safety guarantees (for example, that the bytecodes never attempt to use an integer as a reference to gain access to parts of memory).

These features combined give platform independence to provide a security model suitable for executing code downloaded across the network at varying levels of trust. Source code compiled into Java bytecodes can be run on any machine that has a Java virtual machine. The code can be executed with an appropriate level of protection to prevent careless or malicious class writers from harming the system. The level of trust can be adjusted depending on the source of the bytecodes—bytecodes on the local disk or protected network can be trusted more than bytecodes fetched from arbitrary machines elsewhere in the world.

---

[2] A system can, of course, implement the Java virtual machine in silicon—that is, using a special-purpose chip. This does not affect the portability of the bytecodes; it is just another virtual machine implementation.

1.18 Other Topics Briefly Noted

There are several other features that we mention briefly here and cover later in more detail:

- *Threads*—The language has built-in support for creating multithreaded applications. It uses per-object and per-class monitor-style locks to synchronize concurrent access to object and class data. See Chapter 14 for more details.

- *Reflection*—The reflection mechanism (known as runtime type information —RTTI—in some languages) allows browsing of class types and their members, and programmatic manipulation of objects. See Chapter 16 for more information about reflection.

- *I/O*—The `java.io` package provides many different kinds of input and output classes. See Chapter 20 for specifics of the I/O capabilities.

- *Collections*—You will find many useful collection classes, such as `List` and `HashMap` in the `java.util` package. See Chapter 21 for more information about collections.

- *Utility interfaces and classes*—The `java.util` package has many other useful classes, such as `BitSet`, `Scanner`, and `Date`. See Chapter 22 for more information about these utility classes.

- *Internationalization*—If your application is available to people all over the world, you need to be able to adapt the user interface to support interacting with the user in their language, and using their conventions—such as how dates are presented, or how numbers are formatted. There are a number of classes, mainly in the `java.util` and `java.text` packages that aid you in this. Internationalization and localization are discussed in Chapter 24.

> *Careful—we don't want to learn from this!*
> —Calvin and Hobbes

Classes and Objects

First things first, but not necessarily in that order.
—Dr. Who, *Meglos*

THE fundamental programming unit of the Java programming language is the *class*. Classes provide the structure for *objects* and the mechanisms to manufacture objects from a class definition. Classes define *methods:* collections of executable code that are the focus of computation and that manipulate the data stored in objects. Methods provide the behavior of the objects of a class. Although you can compute using only primitive types—integer, floating-point, and so on—almost any interesting program will create and manipulate objects.

Object-oriented programming strictly separates the notion of *what* is to be done from *how* it is done. "What" is described as a set of methods (and sometimes publicly available data) and their associated semantics. This combination—methods, data, and semantics—is often described as a *contract* between the designer of the class and the programmer who uses it because it says what happens when certain methods are invoked on an object. This contract defines a *type* such that all objects that are instances of that type are known to honor that contract.

A common assumption is that the methods declared in a class are its entire contract. The semantics of those operations are also part of the contract, even though they may be described only in documentation. Two methods may have the same name and parameters and throw the same exceptions, but they are not equivalent if they have different semantics. For example, not every method called `print` can be assumed to print a copy of the object. Someone might define a `print` method with the semantics "process interval" or "prioritize nonterminals"—not that we'd recommend this. The contract of the method, both signature and semantics together, defines what it means.

The "how" of an object is defined by its class, which defines the implementation of the methods the object supports. Each object is an *instance* of a class. When a method is invoked on an object, the class is examined to find the code to be run. An object can use other objects to do its job, but we start with simple classes that implement all their own methods directly.

2.1 A Simple Class

Here is a simple class, called Body[1] that could be used to store data about celestial bodies such as comets, asteroids, planets, and stars:

```
class Body {
    public long idNum;
    public String name;
    public Body orbits;

    public static long nextID = 0;
}
```

A class is declared using the keyword class, giving the class a name and listing the class members between curly braces. A class declaration creates a *type name,* so references to objects of that type can be declared with a simple

```
Body mercury;
```

This declaration states that mercury is a variable that can hold a reference to an object of type Body. The declaration does *not* create an object—it declares only a *reference* that is allowed to refer to a Body object. During its existence, the reference mercury may refer to any number of Body objects. These objects must be explicitly created. In this respect, the Java programming language is different from languages in which objects are created when you declare variables.

This first version of Body is poorly designed. This is intentional: We will demonstrate the value of certain language features as we improve the class in this chapter.

2.1.1 Class Members

A class can have three kinds of members:

♦ *Fields* are the data variables associated with a class and its objects and hold the state of the class or object.

---

[1] Good naming is a key part of class design, and Body should really be called CelestialBody or something of that kind. We use Body for brevity, as we refer to it dozens of time throughout the book.

- *Methods* contain the executable code of a class and define the behavior of objects.

- *Nested classes* and *nested interfaces* are declarations of classes or interfaces that occur nested within the declaration of another class or interface.

In this chapter we concentrate on the basic members: fields and methods. Nested members are discussed in Chapter 5.

2.1.2   Class Modifiers

A class declaration can be preceded by class *modifiers* that give the class certain properties:

- *annotations*—Annotations and annotation types are discussed in Chapter 15.

- *public*—A `public` class is publicly accessible: Anyone can declare references to objects of the class or access its public members. Without a modifier a class is only accessible within its own *package.* You'll learn about general access control in Section 2.3 on page 47. Packages and related accessibility issues of classes and members are discussed in Chapter 18.

- *abstract*—An `abstract` class is considered incomplete and no instances of the class may be created. Usually this is because the class contains `abstract` methods that must be implemented by a subclass. You'll learn about this in "Abstract Classes and Methods" on page 97.

- *final*—A `final` class cannot be subclassed. Subclassing is discussed in Chapter 3.

- *strict floating point*—A class declared `strictfp` has all floating-point arithmetic in the class evaluated strictly. See "Strict and Non-Strict Floating-Point Arithmetic" on page 203 for details.

A class cannot be both `final` and `abstract`.

A class declaration can be preceded by several modifiers. Modifiers are allowed in any order, but we recommend that you adopt a consistent order to improve the readability of your code. We always use, and recommend, the order listed.

While we won't be concerned about class modifiers in this chapter you need to know a little about `public` classes. Most Java development tools require that a `public` class be declared in a file with the same name as the class, which means there can only be one `public` class declared per file.

Exercise 2.1: Write a simple `Vehicle` class that has fields for (at least) current speed, current direction in degrees, and owner name.

Exercise 2.2: Write a `LinkedList` class that has a field of type `Object` and a reference to the next `LinkedList` element in the list.

2.2   Fields

A class's variables are called *fields;* the `Body` class's `name` and `orbits` variables are examples. A field declaration consists of a type name followed by the field name and optionally an *initialization clause* to give the field an initial value. Every `Body` object has its own specific instances of three fields: a `long` that uniquely identifies the body from all others, a `String` that is its name, and a reference to another `Body` around which it orbits. Giving each separate object a different instance of the fields means that each object has its own unique state—such fields are known as *instance variables.* Changing the `orbits` field in one `Body` object does not affect the `orbits` field in any other `Body` object.

Field declarations can also be preceded by modifiers that control certain properties of the field:

- ◆ *annotations*—Annotations and annotation types are discussed in Chapter 15.
- ◆ *access modifiers*—These are discussed in Section 2.3 on page 47.
- ◆ *static*—This is discussed below.
- ◆ *final*—This is discussed below.
- ◆ *transient*—This relates to object serialization and is discussed in Section 20.8 on page 549.
- ◆ *volatile*—This relates to synchronization and memory model issues and is discussed in Section 14.10 on page 370.

A field cannot be both `final` and `volatile`.

When multiple modifiers are applied to the same field declaration, we recommend using the order listed above.

2.2.1   Field Initialization

When a field is declared it can be initialized by assigning it a value of the corresponding type. In the `Body` example, the `nextID` field is initialized to the value zero. The initialization expression, or more simply the *initializer,* need not be a constant, however. It could be another field, a method invocation, or an expression involving all of these. The only requirement is that the initializer be of the right type and, if it invokes a method, no checked exceptions may be thrown because there is no surrounding code to catch the exception. For example, the following are all valid initializers:

```
double zero = 0.0;           // constant
double sum = 4.5 + 3.7;      // constant expression
double zeroCopy = zero;      // field
double rootTwo = Math.sqrt(2); // method invocation
double someVal = sum + 2*Math.sqrt(rootTwo); // mixed
```

Although initializers provide a great deal of flexibility in the way fields can be initialized, they are only suitable for simple initialization schemes. For more complex schemes we need additional tools—as we shall soon see.

If a field is not initialized a default initial value is assigned to it depending on its type:

Type	Initial Value
boolean	false
char	'\u0000'
byte, short, int, long	0
float, double	+0.0
object reference	null

2.2.2 Static Fields

Sometimes you want only one instance of a field shared by all objects of a class. You create such fields by declaring them `static`, so they are called *static fields* or *class variables.* When you declare a `static` field in a class only one copy of the field exists, no matter how many instances of the class are created.

In our case, Body has one `static` field, nextID, which contains the next body identifier to use. The nextID field is initialized to zero when the class is initialized after it is loaded (see "Loading Classes" on page 435). You will see that each newly created Body object will be assigned the current value of nextID as its identifier, and the value of nextID will be incremented. Hence, we only want one copy of the nextID field, to be used when creating all Body instances.

Within its own class a `static` field can be referred to directly, but when accessed externally it must usually be accessed using the class name. For example, we could print the value of nextID as follows:

```
System.out.println(Body.nextID);
```

The use of `System.out` itself illustrates accessing a `static` field. When a static member of a class is referenced many times from another class, or when multiple static members of a class are referenced from another class, you can clarify the code, and perhaps save some typing, by using a *static import* statement to name the class of the static member once. This is discussed in detail in Section 2.9 on page 71.

A static member may also be accessed using a reference to an object of that class, such as

```
System.out.println(mercury.nextID);
```

You should avoid this form because it gives the false impression that `nextID` is a member of the object `mercury`, not a member of the class `Body`. It is the type of the reference, not the type of the object it refers to, that determines the class in which to look for the static variable.

In this book when we use the term *field,* we usually mean the non-static kind. When the context makes it ambiguous, we use the term *non-static field* to be clear.

Exercise 2.3: Add a static field to your `Vehicle` class to hold the next vehicle identification number, and a non-static field to the `Vehicle` class to hold each car's ID number.

2.2.3   `final` Fields

A `final` variable is one whose value cannot be changed after it has been initialized—any attempt to assign to such a field will produce a compile-time error. We have seen `final` fields used to define named constants because constants don't change value. In general, a `final` field is used to define an *immutable* property of a class or object—a property that doesn't change for the lifetime of the class or object. Fields that are marked `final` also have special semantics with regard to concurrent access by multiple threads, this is discussed in more detail in Chapter 14.

If a `final` field does not have an initializer it is termed a *blank final.* You would use a blank final when simple initialization is not appropriate for a field. Such fields must be initialized once the class has been initialized (in the case of static `final` fields) or once an object of the class has been fully constructed (for non-static `final` fields). The compiler will ensure that this is done and refuse to compile a class if it determines that a `final` field does not get initialized.

A final field of a primitive type, or of `String` type, that is initialized with a constant expression—that is, an expression whose value can be determined at compile time—is known as a *constant variable.* Constant variables are special because the compiler treats them as values not fields. If your code refers to a constant variable, the compiler does not generate bytecode to load the value of the field from the object, it simply inserts the value directly into the bytecode. This can be a useful optimization, but it means that if the value of your final field needs to be changed, then every piece of code that refers to that field also has to be recompiled.

Whether a property is immutable is determined by the semantics of the application for which the class was designed. When you decide whether a field should be `final`, consider three things:

- Does the field represent an immutable property of the object?
- Is the value of the field always known at the time the object is created?
- Is it always practical and appropriate to set the value of the field when the object is created?

If the property is merely infrequently changed rather than truly immutable then a `final` field is not appropriate. If the value of the field is not known when the object is created then it can't be made `final`, even if it is logically immutable once known. For example, in a simulation of celestial bodies a comet may become trapped by the gravitational pull of a star and commence to orbit that star. Once trapped the comet orbits the star forever or until it is destroyed. In this situation the `orbits` field will hold an immutable value once set, but that value is not known when the comet object is created and so the field cannot be `final`. Finally, if initialization of the field is expensive and the field's value is infrequently needed, then it may be more practical to defer the initialization of the field until its value is needed—this is generally termed *lazy initialization*—which cannot be done to a `final` field.

There are additional considerations concerning `final` fields if your object must be clonable or serializable. These are discussed in "Cloning Objects" on page 101 and "Object Serialization" on page 549, respectively.

Exercise 2.4: Consider your solution to Exercise 2.3. Do you think the identification number field should be `final`?

2.3 Access Control

If every member of every class and object were accessible to every other class and object then understanding, debugging, and maintaining programs would be an almost impossible task. The contracts presented by classes could not be relied on because any piece of code could directly access a field and change it in such a way as to violate the contract. One of the strengths of object-oriented programming is its support for *encapsulation* and *data hiding*. To achieve these we need a way to control who has access to what members of a class or interface, and even to the class or interface itself. This control is specified with *access modifiers* on class, interface, and member declarations.

All members of a class are always available to code in the class itself. To control access from other classes, class members have four possible access modifiers:

◆ *private*—Members declared `private` are accessible only in the class itself.

◆ *package*—Members declared with no access modifier are accessible in classes in the same package, as well as in the class itself. We discuss packages and related accessibility issues in Chapter 18.

◆ *protected*—Members declared `protected` are accessible in subclasses of the class, in classes in the same package, and in the class itself. Extending classes is covered in Chapter 3.

◆ *public*—Members declared `public` are accessible anywhere the class is accessible.

The `private` and `protected` access modifiers apply only to members not to the classes or interfaces themselves (unless nested). For a member to be accessible from a section of code in some class, the member's class must first be accessible from that code.

It is important to realize that access control is performed on a per-class (or interface) level not on a per-object level. This means that members of a class are always accessible from all code written in that class regardless of which instance the code is being applied to. We illustrate this with an example later when we look at how methods can also be used to control access; see Section 2.6.6 on page 65.

You should view public and protected members as contractual, because they can be relied on by code you do not control. Changing them can be impossible after that code relies on public or protected functionality. Package and private access are part of your implementation, hidden from outsiders (classes in the same package should be related).

We declared the Body class's fields `public` because programmers need access to them to do the work the class is designed for. In a later version of the Body class, you will see that such a design is not usually a good idea.

2.4 Creating Objects

In this first version of Body, objects that represent particular celestial bodies are created and initialized like this:

```
Body sun = new Body();
sun.idNum = Body.nextID++;
sun.name = "Sol";
sun.orbits = null; // in solar system, sun is middle

Body earth = new Body();
earth.idNum = Body.nextID++;
earth.name = "Earth";
earth.orbits = sun;
```

First we declare a reference variable (sun) that can refer to objects of type Body. As mentioned before, such a declaration does *not* create an object; it only defines a variable that *references* objects. The object it refers to must be created explicitly.

We create the object sun refers to using new. The new construct is by far the most common way to create objects (we cover the other ways in Chapter 16). When you create an object with new, you specify the type of object you want to create and any arguments for its construction. The runtime system allocates enough space to store the fields of the object and initializes it in ways you will soon see. When initialization is complete, the runtime system returns a reference to the new object.

If the system cannot find enough free space to create the object, it may have to run the garbage collector to try to reclaim space. If the system still cannot find enough free space, new throws an OutOfMemoryError exception.

Having created a new Body object, we initialize its variables. Each Body object needs a unique identifier, which it gets from the static nextID field of Body. The code must increment nextID so that the next Body object created will get a unique identifier.

We then make an earth object in a similar fashion. This example builds a solar system model. In this model, the sun is in the center, and sun's orbits field is null because it doesn't orbit anything. When we create and initialize earth, we set its orbits field to sun. A moon object would have its orbits field set to earth. In a model of the galaxy, the sun would orbit around the black hole presumed to be at the middle of the Milky Way.

You create objects using new, but you never delete them explicitly. The virtual machine manages memory for you using *garbage collection*, which means that objects that you cannot possibly use any longer can have their space automatically reclaimed by the virtual machine without your intervention. If you no longer need an object you should cease referring to it. With local variables in methods this can be as simple as returning from the method—when the method is no longer executing none of its variables can possibly be used. More durable references, such as fields of objects, can be set to `null`. Memory management is discussed in more detail in Chapter 17.

Exercise 2.5: Write a `main` method for your `Vehicle` class that creates a few vehicles and prints their field values.

Exercise 2.6: Write a `main` method for your `LinkedList` class that creates a few objects of type `Vehicle` and places them into successive nodes in the list.

2.5   Construction and Initialization

A newly created object is given an initial state. Fields can be initialized with a value when they are declared, or you can accept their default value, which is sometimes sufficient to ensure a correct initial state. But often you need more than simple initialization to create the initial state. For example, the creating code may need to supply initial data or perform operations that cannot be expressed as simple assignment.

2.5.1   Constructors

For purposes other than simple initialization, classes can have *constructors*. Constructors are blocks of statements that can be used to initialize an object before the reference to the object is returned by new. Constructors have the same name as the class they initialize. Like methods, they take zero or more arguments, but constructors are not methods and thus have no return type. Arguments, if any, are provided between the parentheses that follow the type name when the object is created with new. Constructors are invoked after the instance variables of a newly created object of the class have been assigned their default initial values and after their explicit initializers are executed.

This improved version of the Body class uses both constructors and initializers to set up each new object's initial state:

```
class Body {
    public long idNum;
    public String name = "<unnamed>";
    public Body orbits = null;
```

```
    private static long nextID = 0;

    Body() {
        idNum = nextID++;
    }
}
```

A constructor declaration consists of the class name followed by a (possibly empty) list of parameters within parentheses and a body of statements enclosed in curly braces. Constructors can have any of the same access modifiers as class members, but constructors are *not* members of a class—a distinction you can usually ignore, except when it comes to inheritance. Constructors can also have annotations applied to them; see Chapter 15.

The constructor for Body takes no arguments, but it performs an important function—assigning a proper idNum to the newly created object. In the original code, a simple programmer error—forgetting to assign the idNum or not incrementing nextID after use—could result in different Body objects with the same idNum. That would create bugs in code that relies on the part of the contract that says "All idNum values are different."

By moving responsibility for idNum generation inside the Body class, we have prevented errors of this kind. The Body constructor is now the only entity that assigns idNum and is therefore the only entity that needs access to nextID. We can and should make nextID private so that only the Body class can access it. By doing so, we remove a source of error for programmers using the Body class.

We also are now free to change the way idNum values are assigned to Body objects. A future implementation of this class might, for example, look up the name in a database of known astronomical entities and assign a new idNum only if an idNum had not previously been assigned. This change would not affect any existing code, because existing code is not involved at all in the mechanism for idNum allocation.

The initializers for name and orbits set them to reasonable values. Therefore, when the constructor returns from the following invocations, all data fields in the new Body object have been set to some reasonable initial state. You can then set state in the object to the values you want:

```
Body sun = new Body();   // idNum is 0
sun.name = "Sol";

Body earth = new Body(); // idNum is 1
earth.name = "Earth";
earth.orbits = sun;
```

The Body constructor is invoked when new creates the object but *after* name and orbits have been set to their default initial values.

The case shown here—in which you know the name of the body and what it orbits when you create it—is likely to be fairly common. You can provide another constructor that takes both the name and the orbited body as arguments:

```
Body(String bodyName, Body orbitsAround) {
    this();
    name = bodyName;
    orbits = orbitsAround;
}
```

As shown here, one constructor can invoke another constructor from the same class by using the this() invocation as its first executable statement. This is called an *explicit constructor invocation*. If the constructor you want to invoke has arguments, they can be passed to the constructor invocation—the type and number of arguments used determines which constructor gets invoked. Here we use it to invoke the constructor that has no arguments in order to set up the idNum. This means that we don't have to duplicate the idNum initialization code. Now the allocation code is much simpler:

```
Body sun = new Body("Sol", null);
Body earth = new Body("Earth", sun);
```

The argument list determines which version of the constructor is invoked as part of the new expression.

If provided, an explicit constructor invocation must be the first statement in the constructor. Any expressions that are used as arguments for the explicit constructor invocation must not refer to any fields or methods of the current object—to all intents and purposes there is no current object at this stage of construction.

For completeness, you could also provide a one-argument constructor for constructing a Body object that doesn't orbit anything. This constructor would be used instead of invoking the two-argument Body constructor with a second argument of null:

```
Body(String bodyName) {
    this(bodyName, null);
}
```

and that is exactly what this constructor does, using another explicit constructor invocation.

Some classes always require that the creator supply certain kinds of data. For example, your application might require that all Body objects have a name. To ensure that all statements creating Body objects supply a name, you would define all Body constructors with a name parameter and you wouldn't bother initializing the name field.

Here are some common reasons for providing specialized constructors:

◆ Some classes have no reasonable initial state without parameters.

◆ Providing an initial state is convenient and reasonable when you're constructing some kinds of objects (the two-argument constructor of Body is an example).

◆ Constructing an object can be a potentially expensive operation, so you want objects to have a correct initial state when they're created. For example, if each object of a class had a table, a constructor to specify the initial size would enable the object to create the table with the right size from the beginning instead of creating a table of a default size, which would later be discarded when the method that set the actual size was invoked.

◆ A constructor that isn't `public` restricts who can create objects using it. You could, for example, prevent programmers using your package from creating instances of a class by making all its constructors accessible only inside the package.

Constructors without arguments are so common that there is a term for them: *no-arg* (for "no arguments") constructors. If you don't provide any constructors of any kind in a class, the language provides a default no-arg constructor that does nothing. This constructor—called the *default constructor*—is provided automatically only if no other constructors exist because there are classes for which a no-arg constructor would be incorrect (like the `Attr` class you will see in the next chapter). If you want both a no-arg constructor and one or more constructors with arguments, you must explicitly provide a no-arg constructor. The default constructor has the same accessibility as the class for which it was defined—if the class is `public` then the default constructor is `public`.

Another form of constructor is a *copy constructor*—this constructor takes an argument of the current object type and constructs the new object to be a copy of the passed in object. Usually this is simply a matter of assigning the same values to all fields, but sometimes the semantics of a class dictate more sophisticated actions. Here is a simple copy constructor for Body:

```
Body(Body other) {
    idNum = other.idNum;
    name = other.name;
    orbits = other.orbits;
}
```

Whether this is correct depends on the contract of the class and on what the uniqueness of idNum is supposed to indicate—for this example we won't concern ourselves with that.

This idiom is not used much within the Java class libraries, because the preferred way to make a direct copy of an object is by using the clone method—see "Cloning Objects" on page 101. However, many classes support a more general form of construction that "copies" another object. For example, the StringBuilder and StringBuffer classes (described in Chapter 13) each have a constructor that takes a single CharSequence argument that allows you to copy an existing String, StringBuffer, or StringBuilder object; and the collection classes (described in Chapter 21) each have a constructor that takes another Collection as an argument and so allow one collection to be initialized with the same contents as another (which need not be of exactly the same type). Writing a correct copy constructor requires the same consideration as writing a correct clone method.

Constructors can also be declared to throw checked exceptions. The throws clause comes after the parameter list and before the opening curly brace of the constructor body. If a throws clause exists then any method that invokes this constructor as part of a new expression must either catch the declared exception or itself declare that it throws that exception. Exceptions and throws clauses are discussed in detail in Chapter 12.

Exercise 2.7: Add two constructors to Vehicle: a no-arg constructor and one that takes an initial owner's name. Modify the main program so that it generates the same output it did before.

Exercise 2.8: What constructors should you add to LinkedList?

2.5.2 Initialization Blocks

Another way to perform more complex initialization of fields is to use an *initialization block.* An initialization block is a block of statements that appears within the class declaration, outside of any member, or constructor, declaration and that initializes the fields of the object. It is executed as if it were placed at the beginning of every constructor in the class—with multiple blocks being executed in the order they appear in the class. An initialization block can throw a checked exception only if all of the class's constructors are declared to throw that exception.

For illustration, this variant of the Body class replaces the no-arg constructor with an equivalent initialization block:

```
class Body {
    public long idNum;
    public String name = "<unnamed>";
    public Body orbits = null;

    private static long nextID = 0;

    {
        idNum = nextID++;
    }

    public Body(String bodyName, Body orbitsAround) {
        name = bodyName;
        orbits = orbitsAround;
    }
}
```

Now the two-argument constructor doesn't need to perform the explicit invocation of the no-arg constructor, but we no longer have a no-arg constructor and so everyone is forced to use the two-argument constructor.

This wasn't a particularly interesting use of an initialization block but it did illustrate the syntax. In practice, initialization blocks are most useful when you are writing anonymous inner classes—see Section 5.4 on page 144—that can't have constructors. An initialization block can also be useful to define a common piece of code that all constructors execute. While this could be done by defining a special initialization method, say `init`, the difference is that such a method would not be recognized as construction code and could not, for example, assign values to blank final fields. Initialization is the purpose of having initialization blocks, but in practice you can make it do anything—the compiler won't check what it does. Spreading initialization code all through a class is not a good design, and initialization blocks should be used judiciously, when they express something that cannot easily be done by constructors alone.

2.5.3 Static Initialization

The static fields of a class can have initializers as we have already seen. But in addition we can perform more complex static initialization in a *static initialization block*. A static initialization block is much like a non-static initialization block except it is declared `static`, can only refer to static members of the class, and cannot throw any checked exceptions. For example, creating a static array and initializing its elements sometimes must be done with executable statements. Here is example code to initialize a small array of prime numbers:

```
class Primes {
    static int[] knownPrimes = new int[4];

    static {
        knownPrimes[0] = 2;
        for (int i = 1; i < knownPrimes.length; i++)
            knownPrimes[i] = nextPrime();
    }
    // declaration of nextPrime ...
}
```

The order of initialization within a class is first-to-last—each field initializer or initialization block is executed before the next one, from the beginning of the source to the end. The static initializers are executed after the class is loaded, before it is actually used (see "Preparing a Class for Use" on page 441). With this guarantee, our static block in the example is assured that the knownPrimes array is already created before the initialization code block executes. Similarly, anyone accessing a static field is guaranteed that the field has been initialized.

What if a static initializer in class X invokes a method in Y, but Y's static initializers invoke a method in X to set up *its* static values? This cyclic static initialization cannot be reliably detected during compilation because the code for Y may not be written when X is compiled. If cycles happen, X's static initializers will have been executed only to the point where Y's method was invoked. When Y, in turn, invokes the X method, that method runs with the rest of the static initializers yet to be executed. Any static fields in X that haven't had their initializers executed will still have their default values (false, '\u0000', zero, or null depending on their type).

2.6 Methods

A class's *methods* typically contain the code that understands and manipulates an object's state. Some classes have public or protected fields for programmers to manipulate directly, but in most cases this isn't a very good idea (see "Designing a Class to Be Extended" on page 108). Many objects have tasks that cannot be represented as a simple value to be read or modified but that require computation.

We have already seen a number of examples of methods in Chapter 1—all of our demonstration programs had a main method that was executed by the Java virtual machine. Here is another `main` method that creates a Body object and prints out the values of its fields.

```
class BodyPrint {
    public static void main(String[] args) {
        Body sun = new Body("Sol", null);
        Body earth = new Body("Earth", sun);
        System.out.println("Body " + earth.name +
                        " orbits " + earth.orbits.name +
                        " and has ID " + earth.idNum);
    }
}
```

A method declaration consists of two parts: the *method header* and the *method body*. The *method header* consists of an optional set of modifiers, an optional set of type parameters, the method return type, the signature, and an optional `throws` clause listing the exceptions thrown by the method. The method *signature* consists of the method name and the (possibly empty) parameter type list enclosed in parentheses. All methods must have a return type and signature. Type parameters are used to declare *generic methods* and are discussed in Chapter 11. Exceptions and `throws` clauses are discussed in detail in Chapter 12. The *method body* consists of statements enclosed between curly braces.

The method modifiers consist of the following:

- *annotations*—Annotations and annotation types are discussed in Chapter 15.

- *access modifiers*—These were discussed on page 47.

- *abstract*—An `abstract` method is one whose body has not been defined in this class—the body is specified as a semicolon after the parameter list. A subclass is then responsible for providing a body for this method. This is discussed in Section 3.7 on page 97.

- *static*—This is discussed below.

- *final*—A `final` method cannot be overridden in a subclass. This is discussed in Section 3.6 on page 96.

- *synchronized*—A `synchronized` method has additional semantics related to the control of concurrent threads within a program. This is discussed in Section 14.3 on page 345.

- *native*—This is discussed in Section 2.11 on page 74.

- *strict floating point*—A method declared `strictfp` has all floating-point arithmetic evaluated strictly. If a method is declared within a class declared strictfp, then that method is implicitly declared strictfp. See Section 9.1.3 on page 203 for details.

An abstract method cannot be static, final, synchronized, native, or strict. A native method cannot be strict.

When multiple modifiers are applied to the same method declaration, we recommend using the order listed.

2.6.1   Static Methods

A static method is invoked on behalf of an entire class, not on a specific object instantiated from that class. Such methods are also known as *class methods*. A static method might perform a general task for all objects of the class, such as returning the next available serial number or something of that nature.

A static method can access only static fields and other static methods of the class. This is because non-static members must be accessed through an object reference, and no object reference is available within a static method—there is no this reference.

In this book when we use the term *method*, we usually mean the non-static kind. When the context makes it ambiguous, we use the term *non-static method* to be clear.

Exercise 2.9: Add a static method to Vehicle that returns the highest identification number used thus far.

2.6.2   Method Invocations

Methods are *invoked* as operations on objects via references using the dot (.) operator:

reference.method(arguments)

In the BodyPrint example we invoke the println method on the object referred to by the static reference System.out and passing a single String argument formed by concatenating a number of other strings.

Each method is declared to have a specific number of parameters, each of a specific type. The last parameter of a method can be declared as a sequence of parameters of a given type. This is indicated by an ellipse (...) after the type name. For example, String... is a sequence of zero or more String objects. Sequence parameters allow you to invoke the method by passing in a variable number of arguments, some of which will correspond to that sequence. These variable argument methods are described in the next section.

When a method is invoked the caller must provide an argument of the appropriate type for each of the parameters declared by the method. An argument need not be exactly the same type as its corresponding parameter because some automatic conversions are applied. For example, a `byte` argument can be converted to an `int` parameter, and wrapper objects can be converted to their primitive values (and vice-versa) as needed—see "Boxing Conversions" on page 198.

Methods also have a return type, either a primitive type or a reference type. If a method does not return any value, the place where a return type would go is filled with a `void`.

The `BodyPrint` example illustrates a common situation in which you would like to examine the state of an object. Rather than providing access to all the fields of the object, a class can define a method that returns a string representation of the state of the object. For example, here is a method of the `Body` class to return a `String` that describes the particular `Body` object it is invoked upon:

```java
public String toString() {
    String desc = idNum + " (" + name + ")";
    if (orbits != null)
        desc += " orbits " + orbits.toString();
    return desc;
}
```

This method uses + and += to concatenate `String` objects. It first builds a string that describes the identifier and name. If the body orbits another body, we append the string that describes *that* body by invoking its `toString` method. This recursion builds a string of bodies orbiting other bodies until the chain ends with an object that doesn't orbit anything. The resulting string is then returned to the caller by the `return` statement.

The `toString` method of an object is special—it is invoked to get a `String` when an object is used in a string concatenation expression using the + operator. Consider these expressions:

```java
System.out.println("Body " + sun);
System.out.println("Body " + earth);
```

The `toString` methods of `sun` and `earth` are invoked implicitly and produce the following output:

```
Body 0 (Sol)
Body 1 (Earth) orbits 0 (Sol)
```

All objects have a `toString` method whether their class explicitly defines one or not—this is because all classes extend the class `Object` and it defines the `toString` method. Class extension and the `Object` class are discussed in Chapter 3.

Exercise 2.10: Add a `toString` method to `Vehicle`.

Exercise 2.11: Add a `toString` method to `LinkedList`.

2.6.3   Methods with Variable Numbers of Arguments

The last parameter in a method (or constructor) parameter list can be declared as a sequence of a given type. To indicate that a parameter is a sequence you write an ellipse (. . .) after the parameter type, but before its name. For example, in

```java
public static void print(String... messages) {
    // ...
}
```

the parameter `messages` is declared to be a sequence of `String` objects. Sequence parameters allow a method to be invoked with a variable number of arguments (including zero) that form the sequence. Such methods are known as variable-argument, or more commonly *varargs* methods; methods that don't declare a sequence parameter are known as fixed-argument methods.[2]

The need to process a variable number of arguments can arise in many situations. For example, our Body objects already track which other body they orbit, but it can be useful to know which Body objects they are orbited by. While a given body generally only orbits one other body, it may itself be orbited by many other bodies. To track this we could define an array of Body objects and provide a method to add each orbiting body, one at a time, to that array. That is not an unreasonable solution, but it is much more convenient if we just define a method that can take a sequence of Body objects:

```java
public void setOrbiters(Body... bodies) {
    // ... store the values ...
}
```

You could then use this method in the following way:

```java
Body sun = new Body("Sol", null);
Body earth = new Body("Earth", sun);
Body moon = new Body("Moon", earth);
Body mars = new Body("Mars", sun);
Body phobos = new Body("Phobos", mars);
```

---

[2]   More formally, the number of arguments that can be passed to a method invocation is known as the *arity* of the invocation. Varargs methods are variable-arity methods, while fixed-argument methods are fixed-arity methods.

```
Body deimos = new Body("Deimos", mars);

earth.setOrbiters(moon);
mars.setOrbiters(phobos, deimos);
```

You may be wondering what type the parameter sequence bodies has inside setOrbiters—quite simply it is an array of Body objects. Declaring a parameter as a sequence is nothing more than asking the compiler to construct an array for you and to set its elements to be the arguments actually passed for the sequence. When you invoke a method, the compiler will match each supplied argument to a named parameter. If the compiler finds a sequence parameter then it will bundle all the remaining arguments into an array of the type specified by the sequence parameter—remember a sequence parameter must be the last declared parameter. Of course, those arguments must be of the right type to be stored in the array. If no arguments are left to store in the array then a zero-length array is created and passed as the argument. Knowing this, you could save the compiler the trouble and pass an array yourself:

```
Body[] marsMoons = { phobos, deimos };
mars.setOrbiters(marsMoons);
```

But in most cases it is easier to just let the compiler do its job.

Sometimes the compiler will need some help working out what you intended a particular method invocation to mean. For example, suppose you invoke setOrbiters with the single argument null. Does that mean to pass null as the array (and so have no array) or does it mean to have an array of length one with a null entry? The compiler can't be sure so it will give you a warning. To remove the ambiguity you need to cast null to a suitable type—for a sequence parameter of type T, if you cast to T then you get an array of T of length one with a null entry; if you cast to T[] then you get a null array reference. Other ambiguities can arise in the context of method overloading, but we'll get to those later (see "Overloading Methods" on page 69).

You've already seen an example of another varargs method in use, but may not have realized it. The printf method that was introduced on page 23 is declared to take a String and a sequence of Objects. For each format specifier in the format string, the method expects a corresponding object argument to be passed in.

Exercise 2.12: Considering your Vehicle and LinkedList classes, can you think of a need for any methods that take a variable number of arguments?

2.6.4   Method Execution and Return

When a method is invoked, the flow of control passes from the calling method into
the invoked method and the statements of that method are executed in sequence
according to the semantics of those statements. A method completes execution
and returns to the caller when one of three things happens: a `return` statement is
executed, the end of the method is reached, or an uncaught exception is thrown.

If a method returns any result, it can only return a single result—either a primitive value or a reference to an object. Methods that need to return more than one
result can achieve this effect in several ways: return references to objects that store
the results as fields, take one or more parameters that reference objects in which to
store the results, or return an array that contains the results. Suppose, for instance,
that you want to write a method to return what a particular person can do with a
given bank account. Multiple actions are possible (deposit, withdraw, and so on),
so you must return multiple permissions. You could create a `Permissions` class
whose objects store boolean values to say whether a particular action is allowed:

```
public class Permissions {
    public boolean canDeposit,
                   canWithdraw,
                   canClose;
}
```

Here is a method that fills in the fields to return multiple values:

```
public class BankAccount {
    private long number;       // account number
    private long balance;      // current balance (in cents)

    public Permissions permissionsFor(Person who) {
        Permissions perm = new Permissions();
        perm.canDeposit = canDeposit(who);
        perm.canWithdraw = canWithdraw(who);
        perm.canClose = canClose(who);
        return perm;
    }

    // ... define canDeposit et al ...
}
```

In methods that return a value, every path through the method must either
return a value that is *assignable* to a variable of the declared return type or throw
an exception. The `permissionsFor` method could not return, say, a `String`,

because you cannot assign a String object to a variable of type Permissions. But you could declare the return type of permissionsFor as Object without changing the return statement, because you can assign a Permissions object reference to a variable of type Object, since (as you know) all classes extend Object. The notion of being assignable is discussed in detail in Chapter 3.

2.6.5 Parameter Values

All parameters to methods are passed "by value." In other words, values of parameter variables in a method are copies of the values the invoker specified as arguments. If you pass a double to a method, its parameter is a copy of whatever value was being passed as an argument, and the method can change its parameter's value without affecting values in the code that invoked the method. For example:

```
class PassByValue {
    public static void main(String[] args) {
        double one = 1.0;

        System.out.println("before: one = " + one);
        halveIt(one);
        System.out.println("after:  one = " + one);
    }

    public static void halveIt(double arg) {
        arg /= 2.0;       // divide arg by two
        System.out.println("halved: arg = " + arg);
    }
}
```

The following output illustrates that the value of arg inside halveIt is divided by two without affecting the value of the variable one in main:

```
before: one = 1.0
halved: arg = 0.5
after:  one = 1.0
```

You should note that when the parameter is an object reference, it is the object *reference*—not the object itself—that is passed "by value." Thus, you can change which object a parameter refers to inside the method without affecting the reference that was passed. But if you change any fields of the object or invoke methods

that change the object's state, the object is changed for every part of the program
that holds a reference to it. Here is an example to show this distinction:

```
class PassRef {
    public static void main(String[] args) {
        Body sirius = new Body("Sirius", null);

        System.out.println("before: " + sirius);
        commonName(sirius);
        System.out.println("after:  " + sirius);
    }

    public static void commonName(Body bodyRef) {
        bodyRef.name = "Dog Star";
        bodyRef = null;
    }
}
```

This program produces the following output:

```
before: 0 (Sirius)
after:  0 (Dog Star)
```

Notice that the contents of the object have been modified with a name change,
while the variable sirius still refers to the Body object even though the method
commonName changed the value of its bodyRef parameter variable to null. This
requires some explanation.

The following diagram shows the state of the variables just after main invokes
commonName:

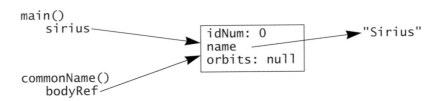

At this point, the two variables sirius (in main) and bodyRef (in commonName)
both refer to the same underlying object. When commonName changes the field
bodyRef.name, the name is changed in the underlying object that the two variables
share. When commonName changes the value of bodyRef to null, only the value of
the bodyRef variable is changed; the value of sirius remains unchanged because

the parameter bodyRef is a pass-by-value copy of sirius. Inside the method commonName, all you are changing is the value in the parameter variable bodyRef, just as all you changed in halveIt was the value in the parameter variable arg. If changing bodyRef affected the value of sirius in main, the "after" line would say "null". However, the variable bodyRef in commonName and the variable sirius in main both refer to the same underlying object, so the change made inside commonName is visible through the reference sirius.

Some people will say incorrectly that objects are passed "by reference." In programming language design, the term *pass by reference* properly means that when an argument is passed to a function, the invoked function gets a reference to the original value, not a copy of its value. If the function modifies its parameter, the value in the calling code will be changed because the argument and parameter use the same slot in memory. If the Java programming language actually had pass-by-reference parameters, there would be a way to declare halveIt so that the above code would modify the value of one, or so that commonName could change the variable sirius to null. This is not possible. The Java programming language does not pass objects by reference; it passes object references by value. Because two copies of the same reference refer to the same actual object, changes made through one reference variable are visible through the other. There is exactly one parameter passing mode—pass by value—and that helps keep things simple.

You can declare method parameters to be final, meaning that the value of the parameter will not change while the method is executing. Had bodyRef been declared final, the compiler would not have allowed you to change its value to null. When you do not intend to change a parameter's value, you can declare it final so the compiler can enforce this expectation. A final declaration can also protect against assigning a value to a parameter when you intended to assign to a field of the same name. The declaration can also help the compiler or virtual machine optimize some expressions using the parameter, because it is known to remain the same. A final modifier on a parameter is an implementation detail that affects only the method's code, not the invoking code, so you can change whether a parameter is final without affecting any invoking code.

2.6.6 Using Methods to Control Access

The Body class with its various constructors is considerably easier to use than its simple data-only form, and we have ensured that the idNum is set both automatically and correctly. But a programmer could still mess up the object by setting its idNum field after construction because the idNum field is public and therefore exposed to change. The idNum should be read-only data. Read-only data in objects is common, but there is no keyword to apply to a field that allows read-only access outside the class while letting the class itself modify the field.

To enforce read-only access, you must either make the field `final`, which makes it read-only for the lifetime of the object, or you must hide it. You hide the field by making the `idNum` field `private` and providing a new method so that code outside the class can read its value using that method:

```
class Body {
    private long idNum;     // now "private"

    public String name = "<unnamed>";
    public Body orbits = null;

    private static long nextID = 0;

    Body() {
        idNum = nextID++;
    }

    public long getID() {
        return idNum;
    }

    //...
}
```

Now programmers who want to use the body's identifier will invoke the `getID` method, which returns the value. There is no longer any way for programmers to modify the identifier—it has effectively become a read-only value outside the class. It can be modified only by the internal methods of the Body class.

Methods that regulate access to internal data are sometimes called *accessor methods.* Their use promotes encapsulation of the class's data.

Even if an application doesn't require fields to be read-only, making fields private and adding methods to set and fetch them enables you to add actions that may be needed in the future. If programmers can access a class's fields directly, you have no control over the values they will use or what happens when values are changed. Additionally, making a field part of the contract of a class locks in the implementation of that class—you can't change the implementation without forcing all clients to be recompiled. For example, a future version of Body may want to look-up the ID number in a database indexed by the body's name and not actually store the ID number in the object at all. Such a change cannot be made if `idNum` is accessible to clients. For these reasons, you will see very few `public` or `protected` fields in subsequent examples in this book.

Methods to get or set a value in an object's state are sometimes said to define a *property* of that object. For example, the `Body` class's `getID` can be said to define an `ID` property for `Body` objects that is retrieved by the `getID` method, and implemented by the `idNum` field. Some automatic systems, including those for the JavaBeans™ component architecture, use these conventions to provide automatic property manipulation systems; see Section 25.3 on page 721. We can and should define the `name` and `orbits` fields to be properties by making them private and providing set and get methods for them:

```java
class Body {
    private long idNum;
    private String name = "<unnamed>";
    private Body orbits = null;

    private static long nextID = 0;

    // constructors omitted ...

    public long getID() { return idNum; }
    public String getName() { return name; }
    public void setName(String newName) {
        name = newName;
    }
    public Body getOrbits() { return orbits; }
    public void setOrbits(Body orbitsAround) {
        orbits = orbitsAround;
    }
}
```

Making a field `final` can be another way to prevent unwanted modifications to a field, but immutability and accessibility should not be confused. If a field is immutable then it should be declared `final` regardless of accessibility. Conversely, if you don't want a field to form part of the contract of a class you should hide it behind a method, regardless of whether the field is read-only or modifiable.

Now that we have made all the fields of `Body` private, we can return to an earlier remark that access control is per-class not per-object. Suppose that a body could be captured by another body and forced to orbit around it, we could define the following method in Body:

```java
public void capture(Body victim) {
    victim.orbits = this;
}
```

If access control were per-object, then the `capture` method when invoked on one object would not be able to access the private `orbits` field of the `victim` body object to modify it. But because access control is per-class, the code of a method in a class has access to all the fields of all objects of that class—it simply needs a reference to the object, such as via a parameter as above. Some object-oriented languages advocate per-object access control, but the Java programming language is not one of them.

Exercise 2.13: Make the fields in your `Vehicle` class `private`, and add accessor methods for the fields. Which fields should have methods to change them, and which should not?

Exercise 2.14: Make the fields in your `LinkedList` class `private`, and add accessor methods for the fields. Which fields should have methods to change them, and which should not?

Exercise 2.15: Add a `changeSpeed` method that changes the current speed of the vehicle to a passed-in value and add a `stop` method that sets the speed to zero.

Exercise 2.16: Add a method to `LinkedList` to return the number of elements in a list.

2.7   `this`

You have already seen (on page 52) how you can use an explicit constructor invocation to invoke another one of your class's constructors at the beginning of a constructor. You can also use the special object reference `this` inside a non-static method, where it refers to the current object on which the method was invoked. There is no `this` reference in a `static` method because there is no specific object being operated on.

The `this` reference is most commonly used as a way to pass a reference to the current object as an argument to other methods. Suppose a method requires adding the current object to a list of objects awaiting some service. It might look something like this:

```
service.add(this);
```

The `capture` method in class `Body` also used `this` to set the value of the victim's `orbits` field to the current object.

An explicit `this` can be added to the beginning of any field access or method invocation in the current object. For example, the assignment to `name` in the Body class two-argument constructor

```
name = bodyName;
```

is equivalent to the following:

```
this.name = bodyName;
```

Conventionally, you use `this` only when it is needed: when the name of the field you need to access is hidden by a local variable or parameter declaration. For example, we could have written the two-argument Body constructor as

```
public Body(String name, Body orbits) {
    this();
    this.name = name;
    this.orbits = orbits;
}
```

The `name` and `orbits` fields are hidden from the constructor by the parameters of the same name. To access, for example, the `name` field instead of the `name` parameter, we prefix it with `this` to specify that the name is for the field belonging to "this" object. Deliberately hiding identifiers in this manner is considered acceptable programming practice only in this idiomatic use in constructors and "set" methods—some coding guidelines and development environments advocate never hiding identifiers, even in these cases. The way in which names are resolved is discussed in "The Meanings of Names" on page 178.

2.8   Overloading Methods

Each method has a *signature,* which is its name and the number and types of its parameters. Two methods can have the same name if they have different numbers or types of parameters and thus different signatures. This feature is called *over-loading* because the simple name of the method has an overloaded (more than one) meaning. When you invoke a method, the compiler uses the number and types of arguments to find the best match from the available overloads. Here are some `orbitsAround` methods for our Body class that return `true` if the current body orbits around the specified body or a body with the specified identifier:

```
public boolean orbitsAround(Body other) {
    return (orbits == other);
}
```

```
public boolean orbitsAround(long id) {
    return (orbits != null && orbits.idNum == id);
}
```

Both methods declare one parameter, but the type of the parameter differs. If the method orbitsAround is invoked with a Body reference as an argument, the version of the method that declares a Body parameter is invoked—that version compares the passed in reference to the body's own orbits reference. If orbitsAround is invoked with a long argument, the version of the method that declares a long parameter is invoked—that version of the method compares the passed in identification number with the idNum field of the object it orbits. If the invocation matches neither of these signatures, the code will not compile.

For varargs methods, a sequence parameter T... is treated as being a parameter of type T[] for overloading purposes. So if two signatures differ only because one declares a sequence and the other an array, then a compile-time error occurs.

The signature does not include the return type or the list of thrown exceptions, and you cannot overload methods based on these factors. A full discussion of how the language chooses which available overloaded method to invoke for a given invocation can be found in "Finding the Right Method" on page 224.

As you may have realized, constructors can also be overloaded in the same way that methods are.

Overloading is typically used when a method or constructor can accept the same information presented in a different form, as in the orbitsAround example, or when it can use a number of parameters, some of which have default values and need not be supplied. For example, the Body class might have two overloaded constructors: one that takes a name and another Body object that it orbits around (as shown on page 55) and a second that takes only a name, indicating that body does not orbit another body.

You should use overloading judiciously and carefully. While overloading based on the number of arguments is usually quite clear, overloading based on the same number but different types of arguments can be confusing. When you add varargs methods to the mix, even overloading based on different numbers of parameters can become confusing when reading or writing invocations of those methods—does that two-argument invocation match two fixed parameters, or one fixed parameter and a sequence with one element, or just a sequence with two elements? For example, the following shows extremely poor use of overloading:

```
public static void print(String title) {
    // ...
}
public static void print(String title, String... messages) {
```

```
        // ...
    }
    public static void print(String... messages) {
        // ...
    }
```

Given the invocation

```
    print("Hello"); // which print ?
```

which `print` method is to be invoked? While not obvious, this example actually has clearly defined behavior: a fixed-argument method will always be selected over a varargs method—again, see "Finding the Right Method" on page 224 for details. So in this case it will invoke the `print` method that takes a single `String` parameter. In contrast, this invocation is ambiguous and results in a compile-time error:

```
    print("Hello", "World");   // INVALID: ambiguous invocation
```

This could be a string and a one-element sequence, or a two-element sequence. The only way to resolve this ambiguity is to pass actual arrays if you intend to match with the sequence parameters:

```
    print("Hello", new String[] {"World"});
    print( new String[] { "Hello", "World" });
```

The first invocation now clearly matches the two-parameter `print` method, and the second clearly matches the single-sequence-parameter `print` method.

You can best avoid such situations by never overloading methods in a way that leads to such ambiguity.

Exercise 2.17: Add two `turn` methods to `Vehicle`: one that takes a number of degrees to turn and one that takes either of the constants `Vehicle.TURN_LEFT` or `Vehicle.TURN_RIGHT`.

2.9   Importing Static Member Names

Static members should generally be referenced using the name of the class to which the static member belongs, as in `System.out` or `Math.sqrt`. This is usually the best practice because it makes clear what your code is referring to. But using the name of the class every time you reference a static field or method can sometimes make your code cluttered and more difficult to understand. For example, suppose you needed to define the mathematical function to calculate the hyperbolic tangent (*tanh*).[3] This can be calculated using the `Math.exp` function:

```
static double tanh(double x) {
    return (Math.exp(x) - Math.exp(-x)) /
           (Math.exp(x) + Math.exp(-x));
}
```

The appearance of `Math` throughout the expression is very distracting and certainly doesn't improve the readability of the code. To alleviate this problem you can tell the compiler that whenever you refer to the method `exp`, you mean the static method `Math.exp`. You do this with a *static import statement:*

```
import static java.lang.Math.exp;
```

A static import statement must appear at the start of a source file, before any class or interface declarations. Given the previous static import statement, anywhere we invoke a method `exp` in our source file it will be taken to mean `Math.exp` (assuming we don't hide it with another declaration of `exp`—see "The Meanings of Names" on page 178). Now we can rewrite our example more clearly as:

```
static double tanh(double x) {
    return (exp(x) - exp(-x)) /
           (exp(x) + exp(-x));
}
```

A static import statement consists of the keyword phrase `import static`, followed by the fully qualified name of the class or interface you are importing the static member from, a dot and then the static member's name. Like all statements it is terminated by a semicolon.

A *static import on demand statement* uses an asterisk (*) instead of a member name. This tells the compiler that if it finds names that it doesn't know about, it should look at the type given by the static import on demand statement to see if it has a static member by that name. If so, the compiler will assume that you intended to refer to the static member. For example, if our hyperbolic tangent function were part of a class that defined many mathematical functions and used many of the static methods and constants of the `Math` class, then we might use a static import on demand statement to import all of those method and constant names:

```
import static java.lang.Math.*;
```

---

[3] This function is part of the math library so there's no need to actually do this.

When names can be imported in this way it is easier for naming conflicts to occur. There are various rules about how static import and static import on demand work with each other and with the other names used in your program. These are explained in more detail in "The Meanings of Names" on page 178.

The use of static imports can help the readability of your code, but if misused they can also make it harder to understand what your code is doing. When the reader sees Math.exp it is quite evident what is being referred to, but a simple exp is not so clear. If you have multiple static import on demand statements, the reader will have to look up each of the types to see if they have a static member named exp. As a general rule you should use static imports to improve the readability and clarity of your code, not to save yourself some typing.

2.10 The main Method

Details of invoking an application vary from system to system, but whatever the details, you must always provide the name of a class that drives the application. When you run a program, the system locates and runs the main method for that class. The main method must be public, static, and void (it returns nothing), and it must accept a single argument of type String[]. Here is an example that prints its arguments:

```java
class Echo {
    public static void main(String[] args) {
        for (int i = 0; i < args.length; i++)
            System.out.print(args[i] + " ");
        System.out.println();
    }
}
```

The String array passed to main contains the *program arguments*. They are usually typed by users when they run the program. For example, on a command-line system such as UNIX or a DOS shell, you might run the Echo application this way:

```
java Echo in here
```

In this command, java is the Java bytecode interpreter, Echo is the name of the class, and the rest of the words are the program arguments. The java command finds the compiled bytecodes for the class Echo, loads them into a Java virtual machine, and invokes Echo.main with the program arguments contained in strings in the String array. The result is the following output:

```
in here
```

The name of the class is not included in the strings passed to `main`. You already know the name because it is the name of the class in which `main` is declared.

An application can have any number of `main` methods because each class in the application can have one. Which class's `main` method is used is specified each time the program is run, as `Echo` was.

Exercise 2.18: Change `Vehicle.main` to create cars with owners whose names are specified on the command line, and then print them.

2.11 Native Methods

If you need to write a program that will use some existing code that isn't written in the Java programming language, or if you need to manipulate some hardware directly, you can write *native methods*. A native method lets you implement a method that can be invoked from the Java programming language but is written in a "native" language, usually C or C++. Native methods are declared using the `native` modifier. Because the method is implemented in another language, the method body is specified as a semicolon. For example, here is a declaration of a native method that queries the operating system for the CPU identifier of the host machine:

```
public native int getCPUID();
```

Other than being implemented in native code, native methods are like all other methods: they can be overloaded, overridden, `final`, `static`, `synchronized`, `public`, `protected`, or `private`. A native method cannot, however, be declared `abstract` or `strictfp`.

If you use a native method, all portability and safety of the code are lost. You cannot, for instance, use a native method in almost any code you expect to download and run from across a network connection (an applet, for example). The downloading system may or may not be of the same architecture, and even if it is, it might not trust your system well enough to run arbitrary native code.

Native methods are implemented using an API provided by the people who wrote the virtual machine on which the code executes. The standard one for C programmers is called JNI—Java Native Interface. Others are being defined for other native languages. A description of these APIs is beyond the scope of this book.

The significant problems we face cannot be solved
by the same level of thinking that created them.
—Albert Einstein

CHAPTER 3

Extending Classes

I am, in point of fact, a particularly haughty and exclusive person,
of pre-Adamite ancestral descent.
You will understand this when I tell you that I can trace
my ancestry back to a protoplasmal primordial atomic globule.
—Gilbert and Sullivan, *The Mikado*

THE quick tour (Chapter 1) described briefly how a class can be *extended,* or *subclassed,* and how an object of an extended class can be used wherever the original class is required. The term for this capability is *polymorphism,* meaning that an object of a given class can have multiple forms, either as its own class or as any class it extends. The new class is a *subclass* or *extended class* of the class it extends; the class that is extended is its *superclass.*

The collection of methods and fields that are accessible from outside a class, together with the description of how those members are expected to behave, is often referred to as the class's *contract.* The contract is what the class designer has promised that the class will do. Class extension provides two forms of inheritance:

- inheritance of *contract* or *type,* whereby the subclass acquires the type of the superclass and so can be used polymorphically wherever the superclass could be used; and

- inheritance of *implementation,* whereby the subclass acquires the implementation of the superclass in terms of its accessible fields and methods.

Class extension can be used for a number of purposes. It is most commonly used for *specialization*—where the extended class defines new behavior and so becomes a specialized version of its superclass. Class extension may involve changing only the implementation of an inherited method, perhaps to make it more efficient. Whenever you extend a class, you create a new class with an expanded contract. You do not, however, change the part of the contract you inherit from the class you extended. Changing the way that the superclass's contract is implemented is reasonable, but you should never change the implementation in a way that violates that contract.

The ability to extend classes interacts with the access control mechanisms to expand the notion of contract that a class presents. Each class can present two different contracts—one for users of the class and one for extenders of the class. Both of these contracts must be carefully designed.

With class extension, inheritance of contract and inheritance of implementation always occur together. However, you can define new types independent of implementation by using *interfaces.* You can also reuse existing implementations, without affecting type, by manually using *composition* and *forwarding.* Interfaces and composition are discussed in Chapter 4.

Class extension that involves generic classes has its own special rules concerning redefining members, overriding, and overloading. These rules are discussed in detail in Chapter 11. In this chapter, generic types are not considered.

3.1   An Extended Class

To demonstrate subclassing, we start with a basic attribute class designed to store name–value pairs. Attribute names are human-readable strings, such as "color" or "location." Attribute values are determined by the kind of attribute; for example, a "location" may have a string value representing a street address, or it may be a set of integer values representing latitude and longitude.

```
public class Attr {
    private final String name;
    private Object value = null;

    public Attr(String name) {
        this.name = name;
    }

    public Attr(String name, Object value) {
        this.name = name;
        this.value = value;
    }

    public String getName() {
        return name;
    }
```

```
    public Object getValue() {
        return value;
    }

    public Object setValue(Object newValue) {
        Object oldVal = value;
        value = newValue;
        return oldVal;
    }

    public String toString() {
        return name + "='" + value + "'";
    }
}
```

An attribute must have a name, so each `Attr` constructor requires a name parameter. The name must be immutable (and so is marked `final`) because it may be used, for example, as a key into a hashtable or sorted list. In such a case, if the `name` field were modified, the attribute object would become "lost" because it would be filed under the old name, not the modified one. Attributes can have any type of value, so the value is stored in a variable of type `Object`. The value can be changed at any time. Both `name` and `value` are `private` members so that they can be accessed only via the appropriate methods. This ensures that the contract of `Attr` is always honored and allows the designer of `Attr` the freedom to change implementation details in the future without affecting clients of the class.

Every class you have seen so far is an extended class, whether or not it is declared as such. A class such as `Attr` that does not explicitly extend another class implicitly extends the `Object` class. `Object` is at the root of the class hierarchy. The `Object` class declares methods that are implemented by all objects—such as the `toString` method you saw in Chapter 2. Variables of type `Object` can refer to any object, whether it is a class instance or an array. The `Object` class itself is described in more detail on page 99.

The next class extends the notion of attribute to store color attributes, which might be strings that name or describe colors. Color descriptions might be color names like "red" or "ecru" that must be looked up in a table, or numeric values that can be decoded to produce a standard, more efficient color representation we call `ScreenColor` (assumed to be defined elsewhere). Decoding a description into a `ScreenColor` object is expensive enough that you would like to do it only once. So we extend the `Attr` class to create a `ColorAttr` class to support a method to retrieve a decoded `ScreenColor` object. We implement it so the decoding is done only once:

```
class ColorAttr extends Attr {
    private ScreenColor myColor; // the decoded color

    public ColorAttr(String name, Object value) {
        super(name, value);
        decodeColor();
    }

    public ColorAttr(String name) {
        this(name, "transparent");
    }

    public ColorAttr(String name, ScreenColor value) {
        super(name, value.toString());
        myColor = value;
    }

    public Object setValue(Object newValue) {
        // do the superclass's setValue work first
        Object retval = super.setValue(newValue);
        decodeColor();
        return retval;
    }

    /** Set value to ScreenColor, not description */
    public ScreenColor setValue(ScreenColor newValue) {
        // do the superclass's setValue work first
        super.setValue(newValue.toString());
        ScreenColor oldValue = myColor;
        myColor = newValue;
        return oldValue;
    }

    /** Return decoded ScreenColor object */
    public ScreenColor getColor() {
        return myColor;
    }
```

```
    /** set ScreenColor from description in getValue */
    protected void decodeColor() {
        if (getValue() == null)
            myColor = null;
        else
            myColor = new ScreenColor(getValue());
    }
}
```

We first create a new `ColorAttr` class that extends the `Attr` class. The `ColorAttr` class does everything the `Attr` class does and adds new behavior. Therefore, the `Attr` class is the superclass of `ColorAttr`, and `ColorAttr` is a subclass of `Attr`. The *class hierarchy* for these classes looks like this, going bottom-up from subclass to superclass:

The extended `ColorAttr` class does three primary things:

- ◆ It provides three constructors: two to mirror its superclass and one to directly accept a `ScreenColor` object.
- ◆ It both overrides and overloads the `setValue` method of its superclass so that it can set the color object when the value is changed.
- ◆ It provides a new `getColor` method to return a value that is the color description decoded into a `ScreenColor` object.

We look at the intricacies of the construction process and the effect of inheritance on the different class members over the next few sections.

Note the use of the `protected` access modifier on the `decodeColor` method. By making this method `protected` it can be accessed in the current class or in a subclass but is not externally visible. We look in detail at what `protected` access really means on page 93.

Exercise 3.1: Starting with the `Vehicle` class from the exercises in Chapter 2, create an extended class called `PassengerVehicle` to add a capability for counting the number of seats available in the car and the number currently occupied. Provide a new `main` method in `PassengerVehicle` to create a few of these objects and print them out.

3.2   Constructors in Extended Classes

An object of an extended class contains state variables (fields) that are inherited from the superclass as well as state variables defined locally within the class. To construct an object of the extended class, you must correctly initialize both sets of state variables. The extended class's constructor can deal with its own state but only the superclass knows how to correctly initialize its state such that its contract is honored. The extended class's constructors must delegate construction of the inherited state by either implicitly or explicitly invoking a superclass constructor.

A constructor in the extended class can directly invoke one of the superclass's constructors using another kind of explicit constructor invocation: the *superclass constructor invocation,* which uses the `super` construct. This is shown in the first constructor of the `ColorAttr` class:

```
public ColorAttr(String name, Object value) {
    super(name, value);
    decodeColor();
}
```

This constructor passes the name and value up to the corresponding two-argument superclass constructor. It then invokes its own `decodeColor` method to make `myColor` hold a reference to the correct `ScreenColor` object.

You can defer the choice of which superclass constructor to use by explicitly invoking one of your class's own constructors using `this` instead of `super`, as shown in the second constructor of `ColorAttr`.

```
public ColorAttr(String name) {
    this(name, "transparent");
}
```

We chose to ensure that every color attribute has a color. If a color value is not supplied we provide a default of `"transparent"`, hence the one-argument constructor invokes the two-argument constructor using a *default argument.*

If you do not invoke a superclass constructor or one of your own constructors as your constructor's first executable statement, the superclass's no-arg constructor is automatically invoked before any statements of the new constructor are executed. That is, your constructor is treated as if

```
super();
```

were its first statement. If the superclass doesn't have a no-arg constructor, you must explicitly invoke another constructor.

The third constructor of `ColorAttr` enables the programmer creating a new `ColorAttr` object to specify the `ScreenColor` object itself.

```
public ColorAttr(String name, ScreenColor value) {
    super(name, value.toString());
    myColor = value;
}
```

The first two constructors must convert their parameters to `ScreenColor` objects using the `decodeColor` method, and that presumably has some overhead. When the programmer already has a `ScreenColor` object to provide as a value, you want to avoid the overhead of that conversion. This is an example of providing a constructor that adds efficiency, not capability.

In this example, `ColorAttr` has constructors with the same signatures as its superclass's constructors. This arrangement is by no means required. Sometimes part of an extended class's benefit is to provide useful parameters to the superclass constructors based on few or no parameters of its own constructor. It is common to have an extended class that has no constructor signatures in common with its superclass.

Constructors are not methods and are not inherited. If the superclass defines a number of constructors and an extended class wishes to have constructors of the same form, then the extended class must explicitly declare each constructor, even if all that constructor does is invoke the superclass constructor of the same form.

3.2.1 Constructor Order Dependencies

When an object is created, memory is allocated for all its fields, including those inherited from superclasses, and those fields are set to default initial values for their respective types (zero for all numeric types, `false` for `boolean`, `'\u0000'` for `char`, and `null` for object references). After this, construction has three phases:

1. Invoke a superclass's constructor.
2. Initialize the fields using their initializers and any initialization blocks.
3. Execute the body of the constructor.

First the implicit or explicit superclass constructor invocation is executed. If an explicit `this` constructor invocation is used then the chain of such invocations is followed until an implicit or explicit superclass constructor invocation is found.

That superclass constructor is then invoked. The superclass constructor is executed in the same three phases; this process is applied recursively, terminating when the constructor for Object is reached because there is no superclass constructor at that point. Any expressions evaluated as part of an explicit constructor invocation are not permitted to refer to any of the members of the current object.

In the second stage all the field initializers and initialization blocks are executed in the order in which they are declared. At this stage references to other fields of the current object are permitted, provided they have already been declared.

Finally, the actual statements of the constructor body are executed. If that constructor was invoked explicitly, then upon completion, control returns to the constructor that invoked it, and executes the rest of its body. This process repeats until the body of the constructor used in the new construct has been executed.

If an exception is thrown during the construction process, the new expression terminates by throwing that exception—no reference to the new object is returned. Because an explicit constructor invocation must be the first statement in a constructor body, it is impossible to catch an exception thrown by another constructor. (If you were allowed to catch such exceptions it would be possible to construct objects with invalid initial states.)

Here is an example you can trace to illustrate the different stages of construction:

```
class X {
    protected int xMask = 0x00ff;
    protected int fullMask;

    public X() {
        fullMask = xMask;
    }

    public int mask(int orig) {
        return (orig & fullMask);
    }
}

class Y extends X {
    protected int yMask = 0xff00;

    public Y() {
```

```
            fullMask |= yMask;
    }
}
```

If you create an object of type Y and follow the construction step by step, here are the values of the fields after each step:

Step	What Happens	xMask	yMask	fullMask
0	Fields set to default values	0	0	0
1	Y constructor invoked	0	0	0
2	X constructor invoked (super)	0	0	0
3	Object constructor invoked	0	0	0
4	X field initialization	0x00ff	0	0
5	X constructor executed	0x00ff	0	0x00ff
6	Y field initialization	0x00ff	0xff00	0x00ff
7	Y constructor executed	0x00ff	0xff00	0xffff

Understanding this ordering is important when you invoke methods during construction. When you invoke a method, you always get the implementation of that method for the actual type of the object. If the method uses fields of the actual type, they may not have been initialized yet. During step 5, if the constructor X invoked mask, it would use a fullMask value of 0x00ff, not 0xffff. This is true even though a later invocation of mask—after the object was completely constructed—would use 0xffff.

Also, imagine that class Y overrides mask with an implementation that explicitly uses the yMask field in its calculations. If the constructor for X used the mask method, it would actually invoke Y's mask method, and at that point yMask would be 0 instead of the expected 0xff00.

Methods you invoke during the construction phase of an object must be designed with these factors in mind. Your constructors should avoid invoking overridable methods—methods that are not private, static, or final. If you do invoke such methods, clearly list them in your documentation to alert anyone wanting to override these methods of their potential unusual use.

Exercise 3.2: Type in the classes X and Y as shown previously, and add print statements to trace the values of the masks. Add a main method and run it to see the results. (Hint: Use the printf method—shown in Chapter 1—with a format specifier of %x to print integers in hexadecimal format.)

Exercise 3.3: If it were critical to set up these masks using the values from the extended class during construction, how could you work around these problems?

3.3   Inheriting and Redefining Members

When you extend a class you can both add new members to a class and redefine existing members. Exactly what effect redefining an inherited member has depends on the kind of member. You'll learn about field and method members here, but we defer discussion of nested members until Chapter 5.

3.3.1   Overriding

In our new `ColorAttr` class we have both *overridden* and *overloaded* the instance method `setValue`:

◆ *Overloading* a method is what you have already learned: providing more than one method with the same name but with different signatures to distinguish them.

◆ *Overriding* a method means replacing the superclass's implementation of a method with one of your own. The signatures must be identical—but the return type can vary in a particular way, as discussed below.

Overloading an inherited method simply means that you have added a new method, with the same name as, but a different signature from, an inherited method. In `ColorAttr` we have gone from having one `setValue` method to having two overloaded forms of the method.

```
public Object setValue(Object newValue) {
    // ...
}
public ScreenColor setValue(ScreenColor newValue) {
    // ...
}
```

This is no different from having overloaded forms of a method declared in the same class.

Overriding a method means that you have replaced its implementation so that when the method is invoked on an object of the subclass, it is the subclass's version of the method that gets invoked. In the `ColorAttr` class, we overrode the `Attr` class's `setValue(Object)` by providing a new `setValue(Object)` method in the `ColorAttr` class that uses the `super` keyword to invoke the superclass's implementation and then invokes `decodeColor`. The `super` reference can be used in method invocations to access methods from the superclass that are overridden in this class. You'll learn about `super` in detail on page 89.

When you're overriding methods, the signature must be the same as in the superclass—if they differ then it is an overload, not an override. The return type of an overriding method is allowed to vary in a specific way: If the return type is a reference type then the overriding method can declare a return type that is a subtype of that declared by the superclass method. Because a reference to a superclass can always hold a reference to an instance of a subclass, this variation is perfectly safe—it is referred to as being a *covariant* return type. We'll see a good example of this when we look at object cloning on page 101. If the return type is a primitive type, then the return type of the overriding method must be identical to that of the superclass method. It is an error if two methods differ only in return type and the compiler will reject your class.

For overriding in a varargs method, as with overloading (see page 60), a sequence parameter of type `T...` is treated the same as a parameter of type `T[]`. This means that an overriding method can "convert" the last array parameter to a sequence, without changing the signature of the method. This allows clients of the subclass to invoke that method with a variable number of arguments. Defining an overriding method that replaces a sequence with an array is allowed, but is strongly discouraged. This is confusing and not useful, so don't do it.[1]

The overriding methods have their own access specifiers. A subclass can change the access of a superclass's methods, but only to provide more access. A method declared `protected` in the superclass can be redeclared `protected` (the usual thing to do) or declared `public`, but it cannot be declared `private` or have package access. Making a method less accessible than it was in a superclass would violate the contract of the superclass, because an instance of the subclass would not be usable in place of a superclass instance.

The overriding method is also allowed to change other method modifiers. The `synchronized`, `native`, and `strictfp` modifiers can be freely varied because they are implementation concerns, as are any annotations—see Chapter 15. The overriding method can be `final` but obviously the method it is overriding cannot—see "Marking Methods and Classes `final`" on page 96 for the implications of `final` methods. An instance method cannot have the same signature as an inherited static method, and vice versa. The overriding method can, however, be made `abstract`, even though the superclass method was not—see "Abstract Classes and Methods" on page 97.

A subclass can change whether a parameter in an overriding method is `final`; a `final` modifier for a parameter is not part of the method signature—it is an implementation detail. Also, the overriding method's `throws` clause can be differ-

---

[1] In the JDK 5.0 release the `javac` compiler issues a (somewhat misleading) warning in both cases. It is expected that the warning when converting to a sequence will be removed. It is possible that in a future release converting from a sequence to an array will be an error.

ent from that of the superclass method's as long as every exception type listed in the overriding method is the same as or a subtype of the exceptions listed in the superclass's method. That is, each type in the overriding method's `throws` clause must be polymorphically compatible with at least one of the types listed in the `throws` clause of the supertype's method. This means that the `throws` clause of an overriding method can have fewer types listed than the method in the superclass, or more specific types, or both. The overriding method can even have no `throws` clause, which means that it results in no checked exceptions. Exceptions and `throws` clauses are described in detail in Chapter 12.

3.3.2   Hiding Fields

Fields cannot be overridden; they can only be *hidden.* If you declare a field in your class with the same name (regardless of type) as one in your superclass, that other field still exists, but it can no longer be accessed directly by its simple name. You must use `super` or another reference of your superclass's type to access it. We show you an example in the next section.

3.3.3   Accessing Inherited Members

When a method accesses an object's member that has been redefined in a subclass, to which member will the method refer—the superclass member or the subclass member? The answer to that depends on the kind of member, its accessibility, and how you refer to it.

When you invoke a method through an object reference, the *actual class of the object* governs which implementation is used. When you access a field, the *declared type of the reference* is used. The following example will help explain:

```
class SuperShow {
    public String str = "SuperStr";

    public void show() {
        System.out.println("Super.show: " + str);
    }
}

class ExtendShow extends SuperShow {
    public String str = "ExtendStr";

    public void show() {
        System.out.println("Extend.show: " + str);
```

```
        }

    public static void main(String[] args) {
        ExtendShow ext = new ExtendShow();
        SuperShow sup = ext;
        sup.show();
        ext.show();
        System.out.println("sup.str = " + sup.str);
        System.out.println("ext.str = " + ext.str);
    }
}
```

There is only one object, but we have two variables containing references to it: One variable has type SuperShow (the superclass) and the other variable has type ExtendedShow (the actual class). Here is the output of the example when run:

```
Extend.show: ExtendStr
Extend.show: ExtendStr
sup.str = SuperStr
ext.str = ExtendStr
```

For the show method, the behavior is as you expect: The actual class of the object, not the type of the reference, governs which version of the method is called. When you have an ExtendShow object, invoking show always calls ExtendShow's show even if you access it through a reference declared with the type SuperShow. This occurs whether show is invoked externally (as in the example) or internally within another method of either ExtendShow or SuperShow.

For the str field, the type of the *reference,* not the actual class of the *object,* determines which class's field is accessed. In fact, each ExtendShow object has *two* String fields, both called str, one of which is hidden by ExtendShow's own, different field called str:

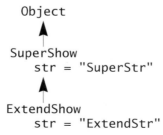

```
            Object

         SuperShow
            str = "SuperStr"

         ExtendShow
            str = "ExtendStr"
```

The field that gets accessed is determined at compile time based on the type of the reference used to access it.

Inside a method, such as `show`, a reference to a field always refers to the field declared in the class in which the method is declared, or else to an inherited field if there is no declaration in that class. So in `SuperShow.show` the reference to `str` is to `SuperShow.str`, whereas in `ExtendShow.show` the reference to `str` is to `ExtendShow.str`.

You've already seen that method overriding enables you to extend existing code by reusing it with objects of expanded, specialized functionality not foreseen by the inventor of the original code. But where fields are concerned, it is hard to think of cases in which hiding them is a useful feature.

If an existing method had a parameter of type `SuperShow` and accessed `str` with that object's reference, it would always get `SuperShow.str` even if the method were actually handed an object of type `ExtendShow`. If the classes were designed to use a method instead of a field to access the string, the overriding method would be invoked in such a case and the `ExtendShow.str` could be returned. This hiding behavior is often another reason to prefer defining classes with private data accessed only by methods, which are overridden, not hidden.

Hiding fields is allowed because implementors of existing superclasses must be free to add new `public` or `protected` fields without breaking subclasses. If the language forbade using the same field name in a superclass and a subclass, adding a new field to an existing superclass could potentially break any subclasses already using those names.

If adding new fields to existing superclasses would break some unknown number of subclasses, you'd be effectively immobilized, unable to add `public` or `protected` fields to a superclass. Purists might well argue that classes should have only `private` data, but you get to decide on your style.

3.3.4   Accessibility and Overriding

A method can be overridden only if it is *accessible*. If the method is not accessible then it is not inherited, and if it is not inherited it can't be overridden. For example, a `private` method is not accessible outside its own class. If a subclass defines a method that coincidentally has the same signature and return type as the superclass's private method, they are completely unrelated—the subclass method does *not* override the superclass's private method.

What does this mean in practice? An external invocation of the subclass method (assuming it is accessible outside its class) results in the subclass implementation being invoked. This is normal behavior. But notice that in the superclass, any invocations of the private method result in the superclass's implementation of the method being invoked, not any like-named method in a subclass. In short, invocations of private methods always invoke the implementation of the method declared in the current class.

When a method is inaccessible because the superclass and subclass are in different packages things are more complicated. We defer a discussion of this until Chapter 18.

3.3.5   Hiding Static Members

Static members within a class—whether fields or methods—cannot be overridden, they are always hidden. The fact that they are hidden has little effect, however—each static field or method should always be accessed via the name of its declaring class, hence the fact that it gets hidden by a declaration in a subclass is of little consequence. If a reference is used to access a static member then, as with instance fields, static members are always accessed based on the declared type of the reference, not the type of the object referred to.

3.3.6   The super Keyword

The super keyword is available in all non-static methods of a class. In field access and method invocation, super acts as a reference to the current object as an instance of its superclass. Using super is the only case in which the type of the reference governs selection of the method implementation to be used. An invocation of super.*method* always uses the implementation of *method* the superclass defines (or inherits). It does not use any overriding implementation of that method further down the class hierarchy. Here is an example that shows super in action:

```
class Base {
    /** return the class name */
    protected String name() {
        return "Base";
    }
}

class More extends Base {
    protected String name() {
        return "More";
    }

    protected void printName() {
        Base sref = (Base) this;
```

```
            System.out.println("this.name()  = " + this.name());
            System.out.println("sref.name()  = " + sref.name());
            System.out.println("super.name() = " + super.name());
        }
    }
```

Although `sref` and `super` both refer to the same object using the type `Base`, only `super` will ignore the real class of the object to use the superclass's implementation of `name`. The reference `sref` will act the same way `this` acts, selecting an implementation of `name` based on the actual class of the object. Here is the output of `printName`:

```
    this.name()  = More
    sref.name()  = More
    super.name() = Base
```

3.4 Type Compatibility and Conversion

The Java programming language is *strongly typed,* which means that it checks for type compatibility at compile time in most cases—preventing incompatible assignments by forbidding anything questionable. Now that you understand the basic type relationship defined by subclasses and superclasses, we can revisit a few details regarding the compatibility of reference types within assignments (implicit or explicit) and conversion between types. The full rules for how and when type conversions are applied, for both reference and primitive types, are discussed in "Type Conversions" on page 216.

3.4.1 Compatibility

When you assign the value of an expression to a variable, either as part of an initializer, assignment statement, or implicitly when an argument value is assigned to a method parameter, the type of the expression must be compatible with the type of the variable. For reference types this means that the type of the expression must be the same type as, or a subtype of, the declared type of the variable—or can be converted to such a type. For example, any method that expects an `Attr` object as a parameter will accept a `ColorAttr` object because `ColorAttr` is a subtype of `Attr`. This is called *assignment compatibility.*[2] But the converse is not true—you

---

[2] There is a slight difference between direct assignment and parameter passing—see the discussion on page 218.

cannot assign an `Attr` object to a variable of type `ColorAttr`, or pass an `Attr` object as an argument when a `ColorAttr` is expected.

The same rule applies for the expression used on a `return` statement within a method. The type of the expression must be assignment compatible with the declared return type of the method.

The `null` object reference is a special case in that it is assignment compatible with all reference types, including array types—a reference variable of any type can be assigned `null`.

The types higher up the type hierarchy are said to be *wider,* or *less specific,* than the types lower down the hierarchy. The lower types are said to be *narrower,* or *more specific,* than their supertypes. When you are expecting a supertype and receive a subtype, a *widening conversion* takes place. Such a conversion causes the subtype object to be treated as an instance of the supertype and can be checked at compile time. No action is needed by the programmer in a widening conversion. Going the other way—taking a reference to a supertype and converting it to a reference to a subtype—is known as a *narrowing conversion.* Narrowing conversions must be explicitly requested using the *cast* operator.

A variable, or an expression, of primitive type can be automatically converted to a reference type using an instance of the wrapper class corresponding to that primitive type—such as an `int` value becoming an `Integer` object. Conversely, a reference to a wrapper object can be converted to the primitive value that is being wrapped. These primitive–to–wrapper conversions (termed *boxing* conversions) are discussed in Chapter 8. The existence of the boxing conversions means that a variable of type `Object` can be assigned the value of any expression that you can form in the Java programming language.

The type compatibility of an expression in a given context (assignment, argument-passing, operand, etc.) is affected by different type conversions that can be applied manually or automatically, depending on that context. Widening and boxing conversions are examples of type conversions that will be automatically applied in some contexts. The different type conversions that exist and the contexts in which they are applied are discussed in "Type Conversions" on page 216. If an expression requires multiple conversions, or if there is no applicable automatic conversion (as in the case of a narrowing conversion), then you must tell the compiler what conversion to apply by using the cast operator.

3.4.2 Explicit Type Casting

A cast is used to tell the compiler that an expression should be treated as having the type specified by the cast—and when applied to primitive types can also affect the value of the expression. A cast consists of a type name within parentheses, applied to an expression. In the previous example we used a widening cast in `printName` to convert the type of `this` to its superclass type:

```
Base sref = (Base) this;
```

This cast was unnecessary but emphasized that we really wanted the current object to be treated as an instance of its superclass. If we then try to assign `sref` back to a reference of the narrower `More` type, an explicit cast is essential:

```
More mref = (More) sref;
```

Even though we know the object referred to is of the right type, the compiler still requires an explicit cast.

A widening conversion is also known as an *upcast* because it casts from one type to another further up the type hierarchy—it is also a *safe cast* because it is always valid. A narrowing conversion is also known as a *downcast* because it casts from one type to another, further down the inheritance hierarchy—it is also an *unsafe cast* because it may not be valid.

When a cast is used to request a conversion, the compiler does not assume that the conversion is correct. If the compiler can tell that is cast is correct, then it can apply the cast. If the compiler can tell that a cast is incorrect then a compile time error can occur. If the compiler cannot ascertain that the cast is correct at compile time, then a run time check will be performed. If the run time check fails because the cast is incorrect, then a `ClassCastException` is thrown.

3.4.3   Testing for Type

You can test the class of an object by using the `instanceof` operator, which evaluates to `true` if the expression on its left is a reference type that is assignment compatible with the type name on its right, and `false` otherwise. Because `null` is not an instance of any type `instanceof` for `null` always returns `false`. Using `instanceof` you can safely downcast a reference, knowing that no exception will be thrown. For example:

```
if (sref instanceof More)
    mref = (More) sref;
```

Note that we still have to apply the cast—that's to convince the compiler that we really meant to use the object as a subclass instance.

Type testing with `instanceof` is particularly useful when a method doesn't require an object of a more extended type but if passed such an object it can make use of the extended functionality. For example, a `sort` method may accept a general `List` type as an argument, but if it actually receives a `SortedList` then it doesn't have to do anything:

```
public static void sort(List list) {
    if (list instanceof SortedList)
        return;
    // else sort the list ...
}
```

3.5   What protected Really Means

We noted briefly that making a class member `protected` means it can be accessed by classes that extend that class, but that is loose language. More precisely, beyond being accessible within the class itself and to code within the same package (see Chapter 18), a protected member can also be accessed from a class through object references that are of at least the same type as the class—that is, references of the class's type or one its subtypes. An example will make this easier to understand.

Consider a linked-list implementation of a queue, class `SingleLinkQueue`, with methods `add` and `remove` for storing an object at the tail of the queue and removing the object from the head of the queue, respectively. The nodes of the queue are made up of `Cell` objects that have a reference to the next cell in the queue and a reference to the object stored in the current cell.

```
class Cell {
    private Cell next;
    private Object element;
    public Cell(Object element) {
        this.element = element;
    }
    public Cell(Object element, Cell next) {
        this.element = element;
        this.next = next;
    }
    public Object getElement() {
        return element;
    }
    public void setElement(Object element) {
        this.element = element;
    }
    public Cell getNext() {
```

```
        return next;
    }
    public void setNext(Cell next) {
        this.next = next;
    }
}
```

A queue then consists of a reference to the head and tail cells and the implementation of add and remove.

```
public class SingleLinkQueue {
    protected Cell head;
    protected Cell tail;

    public void add(Object item) {/* ... */}
    public Object remove() {/* ... */}
}
```

We make the head and tail references protected so that extended classes can manipulate the linked-list cells directly, rather than having to use add and remove—which would involve wrapping and unwrapping the elements each time.

One group decides that it needs a priority queue in which items are stored in a specific order rather than always being inserted at the tail. So it defines a PriorityQueue class in another package that extends SingleLinkQueue and overrides add to insert the object in the right place. The PriorityQueue class's implementation of add can access the head and tail fields inherited from SingleLinkQueue—the code is in a subclass of SingleLinkQueue and the type of the object reference used (this) is the same as that subclass, namely PriorityQueue, so access to the protected members is allowed. This is what you would expect.

The group designing the priority queue needs an additional feature—it wants to be able to merge two priority queues. In a merge operation the target queue ends up with the elements of both queues, while the queue with which it was merged becomes empty. The merge operation starts like this:

```
public void merge(PriorityQueue q) {
    Cell first = q.head;
    // ...
}
```

We are not accessing the protected member of the current object, but the protected member of an object passed as an argument. This is allowed because the class attempting the access is PriorityQueue and the type of the reference q is also `PriorityQueue`. If q were a subclass of `PriorityQueue` this access would also be valid.

Later the group determines that there is a new requirement: It wants to be able to merge a `SingleLinkQueue` with a `PriorityQueue`. So it defines an over-loaded version of `merge` that starts like this:

```
public void merge(SingleLinkQueue q) {
    Cell first = q.head;
    // ...
}
```

But this code won't compile.

The problem is that the class attempting to access the `protected` member is `PriorityQueue` while the type of the reference to the object being accessed is `SingleLinkQueue`. `SingleLinkQueue` is not the same as, nor a subclass of, `PriorityQueue`, so the access is not allowed. Although each `PriorityQueue` is a `SingleLinkQueue`, not every `SingleLinkQueue` is a `PriorityQueue`.

The reasoning behind the restriction is this: Each subclass inherits the contract of the superclass and expands that contract in some way. Suppose that one sub-class, as part of its expanded contract, places constraints on the values of protected members of the superclass. If a different subclass could access the protected mem-bers of objects of the first subclass then it could manipulate them in a way that would break the first subclass's contract—and this should not be permissible.

Protected `static` members can be accessed in any extended class. If `head` were a static field, any method (static or not) in `PriorityQueue` could access it. This is allowed because a subclass can't modify the contract of its static members because it can only hide them, not override them—hence, there is no danger of another class violating that contract.

Members declared `protected` are also available to any code within the pack-age of the class. If these different queue classes were in the same package, they could access one another's `head` and `tail` fields, as could any unrelated type in that package. Classes in the same package are assumed to be fairly trustworthy and not to violate each other's contracts—see Chapter 18. In the list "private, package, protected, public," each access level adds to the kinds of code to which a member is accessible.

3.6   Marking Methods and Classes `final`

Marking a method `final` means that no extended class can override the method to change its behavior. In other words, this is the *final* version of that method. Entire classes can also be marked `final`:

```
final class NoExtending {
    // ...
}
```

A class marked `final` cannot be extended by any other class, and all the methods of a final class are themselves effectively `final`.

Final classes and methods can improve security. If a class is `final`, nobody can declare a class that extends it, and therefore nobody can violate its contract. If a method is `final`, you can rely on its implementation details (unless it invokes non-`final` methods, of course). You could use `final`, for example, on a `validatePassword` method to ensure that it does what it is advertised to do instead of being overridden to always return `true`. Or you can mark as `final` the class that contains the method so that it can never be extended to confuse the implementation of `validatePassword`.

Marking a method or class `final` is a serious restriction on the use of the class. If you make a method `final`, you should really intend that its behavior be completely fixed. You restrict the flexibility of your class for other programmers who might want to use it as a base from which to add functionality to their code. Marking an entire class `final` prevents anyone else from extending your class, limiting its usefulness to others. If you make anything `final`, be sure that you want to create these restrictions.

In many cases, you can achieve the security of marking a whole class `final` by leaving the class extensible and instead marking each method in the class as `final`. In this way, you can rely on the behavior of those methods while still allowing extensions that can add functionality without overriding methods. Of course, fields that the `final` methods rely on should be `final` or `private`, or else an extended class could change behavior by changing those fields.

Another ramification of `final` is that it simplifies optimizations. When a non-`final` method is invoked, the runtime system determines the actual class of the object, binds the method invocation to the correct implementation of the method for that type, and then invokes that implementation. But if, for example, the `getName` method was `final` in the `Attr` class and you had a reference to an object of type `Attr` or any extended type, it can take fewer steps to invoke the method. In the simplest case, such as `getName`, an invocation can be replaced with the actual body of the method. This mechanism is known as *inlining*. An inlined method makes the following two statements perform the same:

```
System.out.println("id = " + rose.name);
System.out.println("id = " + rose.getName());
```

Although the two statements are equally efficient, a `getName` method allows the `name` field to be read-only and gives you the benefits of abstraction, allowing you to change the implementation.

The same optimizations can be applied to private and static methods, because they too cannot be overridden.

Some type checks become faster with `final` classes. In fact, many type checks become compile time checks, and errors can be caught earlier. If the compiler encounters a reference to a `final` class, it knows that the object referred to is exactly that type. The entire class hierarchy for that class is known, so the compiler can check whether any use is valid or invalid. With a non-`final` reference, some checks can happen only at run time.

Exercise 3.4: Which methods (if any) of `Vehicle` and `PassengerVehicle` might reasonably be made `final`?

3.7   Abstract Classes and Methods

An extremely useful feature of object-oriented programming is the concept of the *abstract class*. Using abstract classes, you can declare classes that define only part of an implementation, leaving extended classes to provide specific implementation of some or all of the methods. The opposite of *abstract* is *concrete*—a class that has only concrete methods, including implementations of any abstract methods inherited from superclasses, is a concrete class.

Abstract classes are helpful when some of the behavior is defined for most or all objects of a given type, but other behavior makes sense only for particular classes and not for a general superclass. Such a class is declared `abstract`, and each method not implemented in the class is also marked `abstract`. (If you need to define some methods but you don't need to provide any implementation, you probably want to use interfaces, which are described in Chapter 4.)

For example, suppose you want to create a benchmarking harness to provide an infrastructure for writing benchmarked code. The class implementation could understand how to drive and measure a benchmark, but it couldn't know in advance which benchmark would be run. Most `abstract` classes fit a pattern in which a class's particular area of expertise requires someone else to provide a missing piece—this is commonly known as the "Template Method" pattern. In many cases the expertise methods are good candidates for being `final` so that the expertise cannot be compromised in any way. In this benchmarking example, the missing piece is code that needs to be benchmarked. Here is what such a class might look like:

```
abstract class Benchmark {
    abstract void benchmark();

    public final long repeat(int count) {
        long start = System.nanoTime();
        for (int i = 0; i < count; i++)
            benchmark();
        return (System.nanoTime() - start);
    }
}
```

Any class with any `abstract` methods must be declared `abstract`. This redundancy helps the reader quickly see that the class is `abstract` without scanning to see whether any method in the class is declared `abstract`.

The `repeat` method provides the benchmarking expertise. It can time a run of `count` repetitions of the benchmark. The method `System.nanoTime` returns a timestamp in nanoseconds—see page 665. By subtracting the starting time from the finishing time you get an approximation of the time spent executing the benchmark. If the timing needs become more complex (perhaps measuring the time of each run and computing statistics about the variations), this method can be enhanced without affecting any extended class's implementation of its specialized benchmark code.

The `abstract` method `benchmark` must be implemented by each subclass that is not `abstract` itself. This is why it has no implementation in this class, just a declaration. Here is an example of a simple `Benchmark` extension:

```
class MethodBenchmark extends Benchmark {
    /** Do nothing, just return. */
    void benchmark() {
    }

    public static void main(String[] args) {
        int count = Integer.parseInt(args[0]);
        long time = new MethodBenchmark().repeat(count);
        System.out.println(count + " methods in " +
                              time + " nanoseconds");
    }
}
```

This class times how long it takes to invoke an empty method benchmark, plus the loop overhead. You can now time method invocations by running the application `MethodBenchmark` with the number of times to repeat the test. The count is taken from the program arguments and decoded using the `Integer` class's `parseInt` method on the argument string, as described in "String Conversions" on page 316.

Any class can override methods from its superclass to declare them `abstract`, turning a concrete method into an `abstract` one at that point in the type tree. This technique is useful, for example, when a class's default implementation is invalid for a part of the class hierarchy.

You cannot create an object of an `abstract` class because there would be no valid implementation for some methods that might well be invoked.

Exercise 3.5: Write a new extended class that benchmarks something else, such as how long it takes to run a loop from zero to some passed-in parameter.

Exercise 3.6: Change `Vehicle` so that it has an `EnergySource` object reference, which is associated with the `Vehicle` in its constructor. `EnergySource` must be an `abstract` class, because a `GasTank` object's measure of fullness will differ from that of a `Battery` object. Put an `abstract` empty method in `EnergySource` and implement it in `GasTank` and `Battery` classes. Add a `start` method to `Vehicle` that ensures that the energy source isn't `empty`.

3.8   The `Object` Class

The `Object` class is the root of the class hierarchy. Every class directly or indirectly extends `Object` and so a variable of type `Object` can refer to any object, whether a class instance or an array. For example, the `Attr` class can hold an attribute of any type, so its `value` field was declared to be of type `Object`. Such a class cannot hold primitive types directly, but can hold references to the associated wrapper class—see Chapter 8.

The `Object` class defines a number of methods that are inherited by all objects. These methods fall into two categories: general utility methods and methods that support threads. Thread support is covered in Chapter 14. This section describes the utility methods and how they affect classes. The utility methods are:

public boolean **equals(Object obj)**

> Compares the receiving object and the object referenced by `obj` for equality, returning `true` if they have the same value and `false` if they don't. If you want to determine whether two references refer to the same object, you can compare them using `==` and `!=`. The `equals` method is concerned with value

equality. The default implementation of `equals` in `Object` assumes that an object is equal only to itself, by testing if `this == obj`.

`public int` **hashCode()**

Returns a hash code for this object. Each object has a hash code for use in hashtables. The default implementation returns a value that is usually different for different objects. It is used when storing objects in hashed collections, as described in Chapter 21.

`protected Object` **clone()** `throws CloneNotSupportedException`

Returns a clone of this object. A *clone* is a new object that is a copy of the object on which `clone` is invoked. Cloning is discussed in the next section.

`public final Class<?>` **getClass()**

Returns the *type token* that represents the class of this object. For each class T there is a type token `Class<T>` (read as "class of T") that is an instance of the generic class `Class` described in "The `Class` Class" on page 399. When invoked on an instance of `Object` this method will return an instance of `Class<Object>`; when invoked on an instance of `Attr` it will return an instance of `Class<Attr>`, and so forth.

`protected void` **finalize()** `throws Throwable`

Finalizes the object during garbage collection. This method is discussed in detail in "Finalization" on page 449.

`public String` **toString()**

Returns a string representation of the object. The `toString` method is implicitly invoked whenever an object reference is used within a string concatenation expression as an operand of the + operator. The `Object` version of `toString` constructs a string containing the class name of the object, an @ character, and a hexadecimal representation of the instance's hash code.

Both the `hashCode` and `equals` methods should be overridden if you want to provide a notion of equality different from the default implementation provided in the `Object` class. The default is that any two different objects are not equal and their hash codes are usually distinct.

If your class has a notion of equality in which two different objects can be equal, those two objects must return the same value from `hashCode`. The mechanism used by hashed collections relies on `equals` returning `true` when it finds a key of the same value in the table. For example, the `String` class overrides `equals` to return `true` if the two `String` objects have the same contents. It also overrides `hashCode` to return a hash based on the contents of the `String` so that two strings with the same contents have the same `hashCode`.

The term *identity* is used for reference equality: If two references are identical, then == between the two will be `true`. The term *equivalence* describes value equality—objects that may or may not be identical, but for which `equals` will return `true`. So one can say that the default implementation of `equals` is that equivalence is the same as identity. A class that defines a broader notion of equality can have objects that are not identical be equivalent by overriding `equals` to return `true` based on the states of the objects rather than their identities.

Some hashtables, such as `java.util.IdentityHashMap`, are concerned with identity of objects, not equivalence. If you need to write such a hashtable, you want hash codes corresponding to the identity of objects, not their states. The method `System.identityHashCode` returns the same value that the `Object` class's implementation of `hashCode` would return for an object if it were not overridden. If you simply use `hashCode` on the objects you are storing, you might get a hash code based on equivalence, not on identity, which could be far less efficient.

Exercise 3.7: Override `equals` and `hashCode` for `ColorAttr`.

3.9 Cloning Objects

The `Object.clone` method helps you write *clone* methods for your own classes. A clone method returns a new object whose initial state is a copy of the current state of the object on which `clone` was invoked. Subsequent changes to the new clone object should not affect the state of the original object.

3.9.1 Strategies for Cloning

There are three important factors in writing a `clone` method:

- ◆ The empty `Cloneable` interface, which you must implement to provide a `clone` method that can be used to clone an object.[3]
- ◆ The `clone` method implemented by the `Object` class, which performs a simple clone by copying all fields of the original object to the new object. This method works for many classes but may need to be supplemented by an overriding method.
- ◆ The `CloneNotSupportedException`, which can be used to signal that a class's `clone` method shouldn't have been invoked.

---

[3] `Cloneable` should have been spelled `Clonable`, but the misspelling was realized too late to be fixed.

A given class can have one of four different attitudes toward `clone`:

- ◆ Support `clone`. Such a class implements `Cloneable` and declares its `clone` method to throw no exceptions.
- ◆ Conditionally support `clone`. Such a class might be a collection class that can be cloned in principle but cannot successfully be cloned unless its contents can be cloned. This kind of class will implement `Cloneable`, but will let its `clone` method pass through any `CloneNotSupportedException` it may receive from other objects it tries to clone. Or a class may have the ability to be cloned itself but not require that all subclasses also have the ability to be cloned.
- ◆ Allow subclasses to support `clone` but don't publicly support it. Such a class doesn't implement `Cloneable`, but if the default implementation of `clone` isn't correct, the class provides a protected `clone` implementation that clones its fields correctly.
- ◆ Forbid `clone`. Such a class does not implement `Cloneable` and provides a `clone` method that always throws `CloneNotSupportedException`.

`Object.clone` checks whether the object on which it was invoked implements the `Cloneable` interface and throws `CloneNotSupportedException` if it does not. Otherwise, `Object.clone` creates a new object of exactly the same type as the original object on which `clone` is invoked and initializes the fields of the new, cloned object to have the same values as the fields of the original object. When `Object.clone` is finished, it returns a reference to the new object.

The simplest way to make a class that can be cloned is to declare that it implements the `Cloneable` interface, and override the `clone` method, redeclaring it to be public:

```
public class MyClass extends HerClass implements Cloneable {
    public MyClass clone()
        throws CloneNotSupportedException {
        return (MyClass) super.clone();
    }
    // ...
}
```

Any other code can now make a clone of a `MyClass` object. In this simple case, all fields of `MyClass` will be assigned by `Object.clone` into the new object that is returned. Note that the overriding implementation declares that it returns an instance of `MyClass`, not `Object`, utilizing the ability to specify a covariant return type—this saves the calling code from having to supply a cast, but we have to supply it internally when returning the value from super.clone().

The clone method in Object has a throws CloneNotSupportedException declaration. This means a class can declare that it can be cloned, but a subclass can decide that it can't be cloned. Such a subclass would implement the Cloneable interface because it extends a class that does so, but the subclass could not, in fact, be cloned. The extended class would make this known by overriding clone to always throw CloneNotSupportedException and documenting that it does so. Be careful—this means that you cannot determine whether a class can be cloned by a run time check to see whether the class implements Cloneable. Some classes that can't be cloned will be forced to signal this condition by throwing an exception.

3.9.2   Correct Cloning

Objects of most classes can be cloned in principle. Even if your class does not support the Cloneable interface, you should ensure that its clone method is correct. In many classes, the default implementation of clone will be wrong because it duplicates a reference to an object that shouldn't be shared. In such cases, clone should be overridden to behave correctly. The default implementation assigns each field from the source to the same field in the destination object.

If, for example, an object has a reference to an array, a clone of one of the objects will refer to the same array. If the array holds read-only data, such a shared reference is probably fine. But if it is a list of objects that should be distinct for each of your objects, you probably don't want the clone's manipulation of its own list to affect the list of the original source object, or vice versa.

Here is an example of the problem. Suppose you have a simple integer stack class:

```java
public class IntegerStack implements Cloneable { // dangerous
    private int[] buffer;
    private int top;

    public IntegerStack(int maxContents) {
        buffer = new int[maxContents];
        top = -1;
    }

    public void push(int val) {
        buffer[++top] = val;
    }
```

```java
    public int pop() {
        return buffer[top--];
    }

    public IntegerStack clone() {
        try {
            return (IntegerStack) super.clone();
        } catch (CloneNotSupportedException e) {
            // Cannot happen -- we support clone
            throw new InternalError(e.toString());
        }
    }

    // ...
}
```

Here we override `clone` to make it public, but we use the default implementation from the `Object` class.

Now let's look at some code that creates an `IntegerStack` object, puts some data onto the stack, and then clones it:

```java
IntegerStack first = new IntegerStack(2);
first.push(2);
first.push(9);
IntegerStack second = first.clone();
```

With the default `clone` method, the data in memory will look something like this:

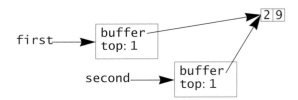

Now consider what happens when future code invokes `first.pop()`, followed by `first.push(17)`. The top element in the stack `first` will change from 9 to 17, which is expected. The programmer will probably be surprised, however, to see that the top element of `second` will *also* change to 17 because there is only one array that is shared by the two stacks.

The solution is to override `clone` to make a copy of the array:

```
public IntegerStack clone() {
    try {
        IntegerStack nObj = (IntegerStack) super.clone();
        nObj.buffer = buffer.clone();
        return nObj;
    } catch (CloneNotSupportedException e) {
        // Cannot happen -- we support
        // clone, and so do arrays
        throw new InternalError(e.toString());
    }
}
```

First the `clone` method invokes `super.clone`. This invocation is very important because the superclass may be working around its own problem of shared objects. If you do not invoke the superclass's method, you solve your own cloning problem but you may create another one. Furthermore, `super.clone` will eventually invoke the method `Object.clone`, which creates an object of the correct type. If the `IntegerStack` implementation of `clone` used new to create an `IntegerStack` object, it would be incorrect for any object that extended `IntegerStack`. The extended class's invocation of `super.clone` would give it an `IntegerStack` object, not an object of the correct, extended type. The return value of `super.clone` is then cast to an `IntegerStack` reference.

`Object.clone` initializes each field in the new clone object by assigning it the value from the same field of the object being cloned. You then need only write special code to deal with fields for which copying the value is incorrect. `IntegerStack.clone` doesn't need to copy the top field, because it is already correct from the "copy values" default. It must, however, make a copy of the `buffer` array, which is done by cloning the array—all arrays can be cloned, with `clone` returning a reference of the same type as the array reference on which `clone` was invoked.

With the specialized `clone` method in place, the example code now creates memory that looks like this:

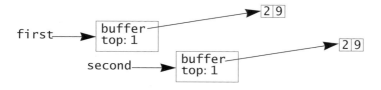

Cloning is an alternative form of construction but is not recognized as construction by the system. This means that you have to be wary of using *blank finals* (see page 46) that can be set only in constructors. If the value of the final field should be a copy of the value in the object being cloned, then there is no problem since `Object.clone` will achieve this. If copying the value is not appropriate for the field then it cannot be declared `final`. In this example, the `buffer` array is immutable for the life of the object, but it can't be declared `final` because its value needs to be explicitly set in `clone`.

If the object that should not be shared between the clone and the original, is not an array, that object should support copying in some way. That may mean that the object itself supports `clone`, or that it has a *copy constructor* that allows a duplicate object to be created. For example, the `String` class does not support `clone` but it does have a copy constructor that creates a new `String` with the same contents as the `String` passed to the constructor. The issues when writing copy constructors are the same as those for writing `clone`—you must decide when a simple field copy is sufficient and when more specific action is required. One advantage the copy constructor has is that it can deal with `final` fields in situations where `clone` cannot.

Sometimes making `clone` work correctly is not worth the trouble, and some classes should not support `clone`. In such cases, you should define a `clone` method that throws `CloneNotSupportedException` so that objects with bad state will never be created by an unsuspecting subclass that uses `clone`.

You can declare that all subclasses of a class must support `clone` properly by overriding your class's `clone` method with one that drops the declaration of `CloneNotSupportedException`. Subclasses implementing the `clone` method cannot throw `CloneNotSupportedException`, because methods in a subclass cannot add an exception to a method. In the same way, if your class makes `clone` public, all extended classes must also have public `clone` methods, because a subclass cannot make a method less visible than it was in its superclass.

3.9.3   Shallow versus Deep Cloning

The default implementation of clone provides what is known as a *shallow* clone or copy—it simply performs a field by field copy. A *deep* clone would clone each object referred to by a field and each entry in an array. This would apply recursively and so deep cloning an object would clone all of the objects reachable from that object. In general, `clone` is overridden to perform a deeper clone whenever a shallow clone is not appropriate—such as in the `IntegerStack` example.

The object serialization mechanism (see page 549) allows you to write entire object graphs to a stream of bytes and, using that generated stream of bytes, create an equivalent copy of the original object graphs. Serialization can provide a way to make deeper copies than those provided by Object.clone.

Exercise 3.8: Make Vehicle and PassengerVehicle into Cloneable types. Which of the four described attitudes should each class take toward cloning? Is the simple copying done by Object.clone correct for the clone methods of these classes?

Exercise 3.9: Write a Garage class whose objects can hold up to some number of Vehicle objects in an array. Make Garage a Cloneable type, and write a proper clone method for it. Write a Garage.main method to test it.

Exercise 3.10: Make your LinkedList class (from the exercises in Chapter 2) Cloneable, with clone returning a new list that refers to the same values as the original list, not clones of the values. In other words, changes to one list should not affect the other list, but changes to the objects referenced by the list would be visible in both lists.

3.10 Extending Classes: How and When

The ability to write extended classes is a large part of the benefits of object-oriented programming. When you extend a class to add new functionality, you create what is commonly termed an *IsA* relationship—the extension creates a new kind of object that "is a" kind of the original class. The IsA relationship is quite different from a *HasA* relationship, in which one object uses another object to store state or do work—it "has a" reference to that other object.

Let's look at an example. Consider a Point class that represents a point in two-dimensional space by an (*x, y*) pair. You might extend Point to create, say, a Pixel class to represent a colored point on a screen. A Pixel IsA Point: anything that is true of a simple Point would also be true of a Pixel. The Pixel class might add mechanisms to represent the color of the pixel or a reference to an object that represents the screen on which the pixel is drawn. As a point in a two-dimensional space (the plane of a display) with an extension to the contract (it has color and a screen), a Pixel IsA Point.

On the other hand, a circle is not a point. Although a circle can be described by a point and a radius, a point has uses that no circle would have. For example, if you had a method to place the center of a rectangle at a particular point, would it really make sense to pass in a circle? A circle HasA center that IsA point, but a circle Is*Not*A point with a radius, and therefore should not be a subclass of Point.

There are times when the correct choice is not obvious and for which different choices will be correct depending on the application. In the end, applications must run and make sense.

Getting IsA versus HasA relationships correct is both subtle and potentially critical. For example, one obvious and common way to design an employee database using object-oriented tools is to use an `Employee` class that has the properties all persons share (such as name and employee number) and extend it to classes for particular kinds of employees, such as `Manager`, `Engineer`, and `FileClerk`.

This design fails in real-world situations, in which one person operates simultaneously in more than one role. For example, an engineer might be an acting manager in a group and must now appear in two guises. As another example, a teaching assistant is often both a student and a staff member at a university.

A more flexible design would create a `Role` class and extend it to create classes for roles such as `Manager`. You would then change the design of the `Employee` class to have a set of `Role` objects. A person could now be associated with an ever-changing set of roles in the organization. We have changed from saying that a manager IsAn employee to saying that manager IsA role, and that an employee can HaveA manager's role as well as other roles.

If the wrong initial choice is made, changing deployed systems will be hard because changes could require major alterations in code. For example, methods in the first employee database design would no doubt rely on the fact that a `Manager` object could be used as an `Employee`. This would no longer be true if we had to change to the role-based design, and all the original code would break.

3.11 Designing a Class to Be Extended

The `Attr` class is an example of a well-designed class—it follows the design principles that you learned in Chapter 2. The fields of the class are `private` and accessible only through accessor methods, thereby protecting them from modifications that violate the class's contract. The `Attr` class presents a clean interface to users of the class and at the same time decouples itself from those classes to allow its own implementation to change in the future.

Given that `ColorAttr` extends `Attr`, should we have designed `Attr` differently to make it more suitable for extension? Should the `name` and `value` fields have been `protected`, instead of `private`, so that a subclass could access them directly? Such decisions require careful thought and consideration of both the benefits and consequences. Making the `Attr` fields protected would not benefit a subclass because all of the actions that can be performed on those fields can be done via the `public` methods that `Attr` provides. On the other hand, making the fields `protected` would prevent any future modifications to the implementation of `Attr` because subclasses could depend on the existence and type of those fields, as well as direct access to them. So in this case, `Attr`'s current design is suited for extension as well as for general use.

In our linked-list queue class, `SingleLinkQueue`, we did make the `head` and `tail` fields `protected`. In that case there was a great performance benefit in allowing the subclass to directly access cells of the linked list—it would be impractical to implement the override of `add` in `PriorityQueue` if the only tools available to use were the original `add` and `remove` methods. The low-level nature of the `SingleLinkQueue` class also means that we are not concerned about locking in implementation details—it is after all a linked-list implementation of a queue and that doesn't really leave much scope for change. If we had written a more general queue class that just happened to be using a linked-list implementation, then it would be a different story.

A non-final class has two interfaces. The *public* interface is for programmers *using* your class. The *protected* interface is for programmers *extending* your class. Do not casually make fields of your classes protected: Both interfaces are real contracts, and both should be designed carefully.

3.11.1 Designing an Extensible Framework

Suppose you want to provide a benchmarking harness for comparing varieties of sorting algorithms. Some things can be said of all sorting algorithm benchmarks: They all have data on which they must operate; that data must support an ordering mechanism; and the number of comparisons and swaps they require to do their work is an important factor in the benchmark.

You can write an `abstract` class that helps you with these features, but you cannot write a general-purpose `sort` method—the actual operations of sorting are determined by each extended class. Here is a `SortDouble` class that sorts arrays of `double` values, tracking the number of swaps, comparisons, and tests required in a `SortMetrics` class we define later:

```
abstract class SortDouble {
    private double[] values;
    private final SortMetrics curMetrics = new SortMetrics();

    /** Invoked to do the full sort */
    public final SortMetrics sort(double[] data) {
        values = data;
        curMetrics.init();
        doSort();
        return getMetrics();
```

```java
        }

        public final SortMetrics getMetrics() {
            return curMetrics.clone();
        }

        /** For extended classes to know the number of elements*/
        protected final int getDataLength() {
            return values.length;
        }

        /** For extended classes to probe elements */
        protected final double probe(int i) {
            curMetrics.probeCnt++;
            return values[i];
        }

        /** For extended classes to compare elements */
        protected final int compare(int i, int j) {
            curMetrics.compareCnt++;
            double d1 = values[i];
            double d2 = values[j];
            if (d1 == d2)
                return 0;
            else
                return (d1 < d2 ? -1 : 1);
        }

        /** For extended classes to swap elements */
        protected final void swap(int i, int j) {
            curMetrics.swapCnt++;
            double tmp = values[i];
            values[i] = values[j];
            values[j] = tmp;
        }

        /** Extended classes implement this -- used by sort */
        protected abstract void doSort();
    }
```

This class defines fields to hold the array being sorted (`values`) and a reference to a metrics object (`curMetrics`) to track the measured operations. To ensure that these counts are correct, `SortDouble` provides routines to be used by extended sorting classes when they need to examine data or perform comparisons and swaps.

When you design a class, you can decide whether to trust its extended classes. The `SortDouble` class is designed not to trust them, and that is generally the best way to design classes for others to extend. A guarded design not only prevents malicious use, it also prevents bugs.

`SortDouble` carefully restricts access to each member to the appropriate level. It uses `final` on all its non-`abstract` methods. These factors are all part of the contract of the `SortDouble` class, which includes protecting the measurement of the sort algorithm from tampering. Making the methods `final` ensures that no extended class overrides these methods to change behavior, and also allows the compiler and runtime system to make them as efficient as possible.

`SortMetrics` objects describe the cost of a particular sorting run. The class has three public fields. Its only task is to communicate data, so there is no need to hide that data behind accessor methods. `SortDouble.getMetrics` returns a copy of the data so that it doesn't give out a reference to its internal data. This prevents both the code that creates `SortDouble` objects and the code in the extended classes from changing the data. Here is the `SortMetrics` class:

```java
final class SortMetrics implements Cloneable {
    public long probeCnt,       // simple data probes
               compareCnt,      // comparing two elements
               swapCnt;         // swapping two elements

    public void init() {
        probeCnt = swapCnt = compareCnt = 0;
    }

    public String toString() {
        return probeCnt + " probes " +
               compareCnt + " compares " +
               swapCnt + " swaps";
    }

    /** This class supports clone */
    public SortMetrics clone() {
        try {
            // default mechanism works
```

```
            return (SortMetrics) super.clone();
        } catch (CloneNotSupportedException e) {
            // can't happen: this and Object both clone
            throw new InternalError(e.toString());
        }
    }
}
```

The following class extends SortDouble. The SimpleSortDouble class implements doSort with a very slow but simple sort algorithm (a "selection sort") whose primary advantage is that it is easy to code and easy to understand:

```
class SimpleSortDouble extends SortDouble {
    protected void doSort() {
        for (int i = 0; i < getDataLength(); i++) {
            for (int j = i + 1; j < getDataLength(); j++) {
                if (compare(i, j) > 0)
                    swap(i, j);
            }
        }
    }
}
```

Now we can write a test harness for sort algorithms that must be changed only slightly to test a new sort algorithm. Here it is shown as a driver for testing the class SimpleSortDouble:

```
public class TestSort {
    static double[] testData = {
                    0.3, 1.3e-2, 7.9, 3.17
                };

    public static void main(String[] args) {
        SortDouble bsort = new SimpleSortDouble();
        SortMetrics metrics = bsort.sort(testData);
        System.out.println("Metrics: " + metrics);
        for (int i = 0; i < testData.length; i++)
            System.out.println("\t" + testData[i]);
    }
}
```

The main method shows how code that drives a test works: It creates an object of a class extended from SortDouble, provides it with the data to be sorted, and invokes `sort`. The `sort` method stores the data, initializes the metrics, and then invokes the abstract method `doSort`. Each extended class implements `doSort` to do its sorting, invoking `getDataLength`, `compare`, and `swap` when it needs to. When `doSort` returns, the counts reflect the number of each operation performed. To test a different algorithm, you can simply change the class name after the `new`. Here is what one run of `TestSort` looks like:

```
Metrics: 0 probes 6 compares 2 swaps
        0.013
        0.3
        3.17
        7.9
```

Now with these classes as examples, let us return to the issue of designing a class to be extended. We carefully designed the protected interface of `SortDouble` to allow extended classes more intimate access to the data in the object but only to things we *want* them to manipulate. The access for each part of the class design has been carefully chosen:

- ◆ *public*—The `public` part of the class is designed for use by the code that tests how expensive the sorting algorithm is. An example of testing code is in `TestSort.main`. This code provides the data to be sorted and gets the results of the test. For the test code, the metrics are read-only. The public `sort` method we provide for the test code ensures that the metrics are initialized before they are used.

  Making the actual `doSort` method `protected` forces the test code to invoke it indirectly by the public `sort` method; thus, we guarantee that the metrics are always initialized and so avoid another possible error.

  To the test code, the only available functionality of the class is to drive a test of a particular sorting algorithm and provide the results. We used methods and access protection to hide the rest of the class, which should not be exposed to the testing code.

- ◆ *protected*—The `protected` part of the class is designed for use by the sorting code to produce a properly metered sort. The `protected` contract lets the sorting algorithm examine and modify the data to produce a sorted list by whatever means the sort desires. It also gives the sorting algorithm a context in which it will be properly driven so that it can be measured. This context is the `doSort` method.

  The extended class is not considered trustworthy, and that is why it can access the data only indirectly, through methods that have access to the data.

For example, to hide a comparison by avoiding `compare`, the sort would have to use `probe` to find out what is in the array. Because calls to `probe` are also metered, this would, in the end, hide nothing.

In addition, `getMetrics` returns a clone of the actual metrics, so a sorting implementation cannot modify the values.

◆ *private*—The class keeps private to itself data that should be hidden from the outside—namely, the data being sorted and the metrics. Outside code cannot access these fields, directly or indirectly.

Recall that to prevent intentional cheating and accidental misuse, `SortDouble` is designed not to trust its extended classes. For example, if `SortDouble.values` (the array being sorted) were `protected` instead of `private`, we could eliminate the `probe` method because sort algorithms normally count only comparisons and swaps. But if we eliminated it, the programmer writing an extended class could avoid using `swap` to swap data. The results would be invalid in ways that might be hard to notice. Counting probes and declaring the array `private` preclude some bugs as well as intentionally devious programming.

If a class is not designed to be extended, it often will be misused by subclasses. If your class will have subclasses, you should design its `protected` parts carefully. The end result may be to have no `protected` members if extended classes need no special access. If you do not design the `protected` part of your class, the class should have no `protected` members, making subclasses rely on its public contract.

Exercise 3.11: Find at least one security hole in `SortDouble` that would let a sorting algorithm cheat on its metrics without getting caught. Fix the security hole. Assume that the sorting algorithm author doesn't get to write `main`.

Exercise 3.12: Write a general-purpose `SortHarness` class that can sort any object type. How would you provide a way to represent ordering for the objects in a general way, given that you cannot use < to compare them?

3.12 Single Inheritance versus Multiple Inheritance

A new class can extend exactly one superclass, a model known as *single inheritance.* Extending a class means that the new class inherits not only its superclass's contract but also its superclass's implementation. Some object-oriented languages employ *multiple inheritance,* in which a new class can have two or more superclasses.

Multiple inheritance is useful when you want a new class to combine multiple contracts and inherit some, or all, of the implementation of those contracts. But when there is more than one superclass, problems arise when a superclass's behavior is inherited in two ways. Assume, for a moment, the following type tree:

This is commonly called *diamond inheritance,* and there is nothing wrong with it. Many legitimate designs show this structure. The problems exist in the inheritance of implementation, when W's implementation stores some state. If class W had, for example, a public field named goggin, and if you had a reference to an object of type Z called zref, what would zref.goggin refer to? It might refer to X's copy of goggin, or it might refer to Y's copy, or X and Y might share a single copy of goggin because Z is really only a W once even though it is both an X and a Y. Resolving such issues is non-trivial and complicates the design and use of class hierarchies. To avoid such issues, the Java programming language uses the single-inheritance model of object-oriented programming.

Single inheritance precludes some useful and correct designs. The problems of multiple inheritance arise from multiple inheritance of implementation, but in many cases multiple inheritance is used to inherit a number of abstract contracts and perhaps one concrete implementation. Providing a means to inherit an abstract contract without inheriting an implementation allows the typing benefits of multiple inheritance without the problems of multiple implementation inheritance. The inheritance of an abstract contract is termed *interface inheritance.* The Java programming language supports interface inheritance by allowing you to declare an interface type—the subject of the next chapter.

> *When we are planning for posterity,*
> *we ought to remember that virtue is not hereditary.*
> —Thomas Paine

CHAPTER 4

Interfaces

*"Conducting" is when you draw "designs" in the nowhere—with your stick,
or with your hands—which are interpreted as "instructional messages"
by guys wearing bow ties who wish they were fishing.*
—Frank Zappa

THE fundamental unit of programming in the Java programming language is the *class,* but the fundamental unit of object-oriented design is the *type.* While classes define types, it is very useful and powerful to be able to define a type without defining a class. *Interfaces* define types in an abstract form as a collection of methods or other types that form the contract for that type. Interfaces contain no implementation and you cannot create instances of an interface. Rather, classes can expand their own types by *implementing* one or more interfaces. An interface is an expression of pure design, whereas a class is a mix of design and implementation.

A class can implement the methods of an interface in any way that the designer of the class chooses. An interface thus has many more possible implementations than a class. Every major class in an application should be an implementation of some interface that captures the contract of that class.

Classes can implement more than one interface. The Java programming language allows multiple inheritance of interface but only single inheritance of implementation—a class can extend only one other class. Classes can use inheritance of interfaces to expand their type and then use, for example, composition to provide an implementation for those interfaces. This design allows the typing flexibility of multiple inheritance while avoiding the pitfalls of multiple implementation inheritance, at the cost of some additional work for the programmer.

In a given class, the classes that are extended and the interfaces that are implemented are collectively called the *supertypes,* and from the viewpoint of the supertypes, the new class is a *subtype.* The new class includes all its supertypes, so a reference to an object of the subtype can be used polymorphically anywhere a reference to an object of any of its supertypes (class or interface) is required. Interface declarations create type names just as class declarations do; you can use the name of an interface as the type name of a variable, and any object whose class implements that interface can be assigned to that variable.

4.1   A Simple Interface Example

Many simple interfaces define a property that is ascribable to a variety of different objects from different classes. These properties are often defined in terms of an object being "able" to do something. For example, in the standard packages there are a number of "ability" interfaces, such as:

- ◆ `Cloneable`—Objects of this type support cloning, as you learned in detail on page 101.
- ◆ `Comparable`—Objects of this type have an ordering that allows them to be compared.
- ◆ `Runnable`—Objects of this type represent a unit of work, that can often execute in an independent thread of control (see Chapter 14).
- ◆ `Serializable`—Objects of this type can be written to an object byte stream for shipping to a new virtual machine, or for storing persistently and then reconstituting into a live object (see "Object Serialization" on page 549).

Let's look at the `Comparable` interface in more detail. This interface can be implemented by any class whose objects can be compared to each other according to the class's "natural ordering." The interface contains a single method:

```
public interface Comparable<T> {
    int compareTo(T obj);
}
```

An interface declaration is similar to a class declaration, except that the keyword `interface` is used instead of `class`. There are also special rules concerning the members of an interface, as you will soon learn.

The `compareTo` method takes a single object argument of type T and compares it to the current object (expected to also be of type T), returning a negative, zero, or positive integer if the current object is less than, equal to, or greater than the argument, respectively.

Consider a variation of the `Point` class we introduced in Chapter 1. The natural ordering for points could be their distance from the origin. We could then make `Point` objects `Comparable`:

```
class Point implements Comparable<Point> {

    /** Origin reference that never changes */
    private static final Point ORIGIN = new Point();

    private int x, y;

    // ... definition of constructors, setters and accessors

    public double distance(Point p) {
        int xdiff = x - p.x;
        int ydiff = y - p.y;
        return Math.sqrt(xdiff * xdiff + ydiff * ydiff);
    }

    public int compareTo(Point p) {
        double pDist = p.distance(ORIGIN);
        double dist  = this.distance(ORIGIN);
        if (dist > pDist)
            return 1;
        else if (dist == pDist)
            return 0;
        else
            return -1;
    }
}
```

First we declare that Point is a Comparable class. A class identifies the interface types that it implements by listing them after the keyword implements, before the class body is defined (and after any extends clause). All such interfaces are the *superinterfaces* of the class. The class must provide an implementation for all of the methods defined in its superinterfaces, or else the class must be declared abstract, thereby requiring that any non-abstract subclass implement them.

The only method we need to implement for the Comparable interface is compareTo, and to actually compare two points we simply compare their distance from the origin.

Interfaces introduce type names just as classes do, so you can declare variables of those types. For example:

```
Comparable<Point> p1;
```

In fact much of the power of interfaces comes from declaring and using only variables of interface type rather than of some specific class type. For example, you can define a general-purpose `sort` routine that can sort any array of `Comparable` objects without regard to what the class of those objects actually is—all the objects in the array should be the same type of course:[1]

```
class Sorter {
    static Comparable<?>[] sort(Comparable<?>[] list) {
        // implementation details ...
        return list;
    }
}
```

References of interface type, however, can be used only to access members of that interface. For example, the following will produce a compile-time error:

```
Comparable<Point> obj = new Point();
double dist = obj.distance(p1); // INVALID: Comparable has
                                // no distance method
```

If you want to treat `obj` as a `Point` object you must explicitly cast it to that type.

You can invoke any of the `Object` methods using a reference of an interface type because no matter what interfaces the object implements, it is always an `Object` and so has those methods. In fact, any interface that does not extend some other interface implicitly has members matching each of the public methods of `Object` (unless the interface explicitly overrides them). Hence, the following is legal:

```
String desc = obj.toString();
```

as is assigning an interface reference to an `Object` reference.

4.2   Interface Declarations

An interface is declared using the keyword `interface`, giving the interface a name and listing the interface members between curly braces.

An interface can declare three kinds of members:

◆ constants (fields)

◆ methods

---

[1]   In Chapter 11 you learn about generic methods, and `sort` should really be defined as such.

♦ nested classes and interfaces

All interface members are implicitly public, but, by convention, the `public` modifier is omitted. Having non-public members in an interface would make little sense; where it does make sense you can use the accessibility of the interface itself to control access to the interface members.

We defer a discussion of nested classes and interfaces until Chapter 5.

4.2.1   Interface Constants

An interface can declare named constants. These constants are defined as fields but are implicitly `public`, `static`, and `final`—again, by convention, the modifiers are omitted from the field declarations. These fields must also have initializers—*blank finals* are not permitted. Annotations can also be applied to the fields—see Chapter 15.

Because interfaces contain no implementation details, they cannot define normal fields—such a definition would be dictating implementation policy to the classes that choose to implement the interface. Interfaces can define named constants because these are useful in the design of types. For example, an interface that had differing levels of verbosity in its contract might have the following:

```
interface Verbose {
    int SILENT  = 0;
    int TERSE   = 1;
    int NORMAL  = 2;
    int VERBOSE = 3;

    void setVerbosity(int level);
    int getVerbosity();
}
```

SILENT, TERSE, NORMAL, and VERBOSE can be passed to the `setVerbosity` method, giving names to constant values that represent specific meanings. In this particular case, the verbosity levels could be more effectively represented as the constants of an enumeration type nested within the `Verbose` interface. Enumeration types are discussed in Chapter 6.

If you need shared, modifiable data in your interface you can achieve this by using a named constant that refers to an object that holds the data. A nested class is good for defining that object, so we defer an example until Chapter 5.

4.2.2   Interface Methods

The methods declared in an interface are implicitly `abstract` because no implementation is, or can be, given for them. For this reason the method body is simply
a semicolon after the method header. By convention, the `abstract` modifier on
the method declaration is omitted.

No other method modifiers are permitted on an interface method declaration,
except for annotations—see Chapter 15. They are implicitly `public` and so can
have no other access modifier. They cannot have modifiers that define implementation characteristics—such as `native`, `synchronized`, or `strictfp`—because
an interface does not dictate implementation, and they cannot be `final` because
they haven't been implemented yet. Of course, the implementation of these methods within a specific class can have any of these modifiers. Interface methods can
never be `static` because `static` methods can't be `abstract`.

4.2.3   Interface Modifiers

An interface declaration can be preceded by interface modifiers:

- *annotations*—Annotations and annotation types are discussed in Chapter 15.
- *public*—A `public` interface is publicly accessible. Without this modifier an
  interface is only accessible within its own package.
- *abstract*—All interfaces are implicitly `abstract` because their methods are
  all abstract—they have no implementation. Again, by convention, the
  `abstract` modifier is always omitted.
- *strict floating point*—An interface declared `strictfp` has all floating-point
  arithmetic, defined within the interface, evaluated strictly. This applies to
  initialization expressions for constants and to all nested types declared in the
  interface. In contrast to classes, this does not imply that each method in the
  interface is implicitly `strictfp` because that is an implementation detail.
  See Section 9.1.3 on page 203 for details.

When multiple modifiers are applied to the same interface declaration, we recommend using the order listed above.

4.3   Extending Interfaces

Interfaces can be extended using the `extends` keyword. Interfaces, unlike classes,
can extend more than one other interface:

```
public interface SerializableRunnable
                    extends java.io.Serializable, Runnable
{
    // ...
}
```

The `SerializableRunnable` interface extends both `java.io.Serializable` and `Runnable`, which means that all methods and constants defined by those interfaces are now part of the `SerializableRunnable` contract, together with any new methods and constants it defines. The interfaces that are extended are the *superinterfaces* of the new interface and the new interface is a *subinterface* of its superinterfaces.

Because interfaces support multiple inheritance, the inheritance graph can contain multiple paths to the same superinterface. This means that constants and methods can be accessed in different ways. However, because interfaces define no implementation of methods, and provide no per-object fields, there are no issues regarding the semantics of this form of multiple inheritance.

4.3.1   Inheriting and Hiding Constants

An extended interface inherits all the constants declared in its superinterfaces. If an interface declares a constant of the same name as an inherited constant, regardless of their types, then the new constant hides the inherited one; this is the same hiding of fields described in "Hiding Fields" on page 86. In the subinterface and in any object implementing the subinterface, any reference to the constant using its simple name will refer to the constant defined in the subinterface. The inherited constant can still be accessed with the qualified name of the constant, that is, the interface name followed by dot and then the constant name—the usual way of referring to static members.

```
interface X {
    int val = 1;
}
interface Y extends X {
    int val = 2;
    int sum = val + X.val;
}
```

Interface Y has two constants: `val` and `sum`. From inside Y, to refer to the hidden `val` in its superinterface you must qualify it as `X.val`. Externally, you can access the constants of Y by using the normal static forms of `Y.val` and `Y.sum`, and of course you can access X's `val` constant by using `X.val`.

These rules are, of course, identical to those concerning the inheritance of static fields in classes.

When a class implements Y you can access the constants in Y as though they were constants declared in the class. For example, given

```
class Z implements Y { }
```

you can do

```
System.out.println("Z.val=" + Z.val + ", Z.sum=" + Z.sum);
```

but there is no way to refer to X.val via Z. However, given an instance of Z you can use an explicit cast to access X.val:

```
Z z = new Z();
System.out.println("z.val=" + z.val +
                   ", ((Y)z).val=" + ((Y)z).val +
                   ", ((X)z).val=" + ((X)z).val);
```

which prints out

```
z.val=2, ((Y)z).val=2, ((X)z).val=1
```

as you would expect. Again these are the same rules that apply to static fields in extended classes—it doesn't matter whether a class inherits a static field from a superclass or a superinterface.

While all these rules are necessary from a language perspective, they have little practical consequence—there are few reasons to hide existing fields, and all accesses to static fields, whether class or interface, should be via the name of the type in which that field is declared.

If an interface inherits two or more constants with the same name, then any simple reference to the constant is ambiguous and results in a compile-time error. For example, given the previous interface declarations and the following:

```
interface C {
    String val = "Interface C";
}
interface D extends X, C { }
```

then the expression D.val is ambiguous—does it mean the integer val or the String reference val? Inside D you would have to explicitly use X.val or C.val.

A class that implements more than one interface, or that extends a class and implements one or more interfaces, can experience the same hiding and ambiguity issues as an interface that extends more than one interface. The class's own static fields can hide the inherited fields of the interfaces it implements or the class it extends, and simple references to multiply-inherited non-hidden fields will be ambiguous.

4.3.2 Inheriting, Overriding, and Overloading Methods

A subinterface inherits all the methods declared in its superinterfaces. If a declared method in a subinterface has the same signature (name and parameter list) as an inherited method and the same, or covariant, return type, then the new declaration *overrides* any and all existing declarations. Overriding in interfaces, unlike overriding in classes, has no semantic effect—the interface effectively contains multiple declarations of the same method, but in any one implementing class there can only be one implementation of that method.

Similarly, if an interface inherits more than one method with the same signature, or if a class implements different interfaces containing a method with the same signature, there is only one such method. The implementation of this method is ultimately defined by the class implementing the interfaces, and there is no ambiguity there. If the methods have the same signature but different return types, then one of the return types must be a subtype of all the others, otherwise a compile-time error occurs. The implementation must define a method that returns that common subtype.

The real issue is whether a single implementation of the method can honor all the contracts implied by that method being part of the different interfaces. This may be an impossible requirement to satisfy in some circumstances. For example:

```
interface CardDealer {
    void draw();           // flip top card
    void deal();           // distribute cards
    void shuffle();
}
interface GraphicalComponent {
    void draw();           // render on default device
    void draw(Device d);   // render on 'd'
    void rotate(int degrees);
    void fill(Color c);
}
interface GraphicalCardDealer
    extends CardDealer, GraphicalComponent { }
```

Here it is difficult to write an implementation of draw() that can satisfy the two different contracts independently. If you try to satisfy them simultaneously, you are unlikely to achieve the desired results: flipping a card each time the screen gets repainted.

As with overriding in class extension, the overriding method is not permitted to throw more checked exceptions than the method it overrides. If two or more method declarations are inherited, without overriding, and differ in the exceptions they throw, then the implementation of that method must satisfy all the `throws` clauses of those declarations. Again the main issue is whether such distinct methods can have a single implementation that honors all contracts. We look further at the issues of overriding and exception throwing in Chapter 12.

If a declared method has the same name but different parameters from an inherited method, then the declared method is an *overloaded* form of the inherited method. The eventual class implementation will provide a method body for each of the overloaded forms.

If a declared method differs only in return type from an inherited method, or if two inherited methods differ only in return type where one type is not a subtype of the other, you will get a compile-time error.

4.4   Working with Interfaces

The previous chapter introduced the `Attr` class and showed how to extend it to make specialized types of attribute objects. Now all you need is the ability to associate attributes with objects.

The first decision to make is whether having attributes is reflected in the type of the object. An object could, if you chose, contain a set of attributes and allow programmers access to that set. Or you could say that being able to store attributes on an object is a part of its type and so should be part of the type hierarchy. Both positions are legitimate. We believe that representing the ability to hold attributes in the type hierarchy is most useful. We will create an `Attributed` type to be used for objects that can be attributed by attaching `Attr` objects to them.

To create an `Attributed` type you could define a class that would form the superclass for all attributed objects. But then programmers must decide whether to inherit from `Attributed` or from some other useful class. Instead we make `Attributed` into an interface:

```
public interface Attributed {
    void add(Attr newAttr);
    Attr find(String attrName);
    Attr remove(String attrName);
    java.util.Iterator<Attr> attrs();
}
```

This interface declares four methods: one for adding a new attribute to an `Attributed` object; one for finding whether an attribute of a given name has been added to that object; one for removing an attribute from an object; and one for accessing all of the attributes currently attached to the object.

When we add an attribute to an object, that object considers itself the owner of that `Attr` instance until it is removed. If the attribute has its value changed or is shared among a number of objects, then the expectation is that the programmer makes such changes and performs such sharing in a manner that makes sense to the application. If the programmer is not to be trusted in this, then methods should specify that they make *defensive copies* of parameters, and/or return values, such that no harmful changes can occur.

The attributes are accessed through an `Iterator` object returned from the `attrs` method. `Iterator` is a generic interface defined in `java.util` for *collection classes* to use to provide access to their contents (see "Iteration" on page 571). In effect, the `Attributed` interface defines a collection type—a set of attributes—so we use the normal mechanism for accessing the contents of a collection, namely, the `Iterator` type. Using `Iterator` has another benefit: It is easy to implement `Attributed` with a standard collection class (such as `HashMap`) that uses `Iterator`, as you'll soon see.

Many classes that provide an `Iterator` declare that they implement the `Iterable` interface, which defines the single method `iterator` to return an `Iterator` instance. Although an `Attributed` object does provide an `Iterator`, it would be wrong to have `Attributed` extend `Iterable` or to rename `attrs` as `iterator`, because that would restrict the ability of the class implementing `Attributed` to control its own iteration behavior. For example, it would mean that an `Attributed` collection class would not be able to provide an iterator for its elements rather than its attributes.

4.4.1 Implementing Interfaces

Interfaces describe contracts in a pure, abstract form, but an interface is interesting only if a class implements it.

Some interfaces are purely abstract—they do not have any useful general implementation but must be implemented afresh for each new class. Most interfaces, however, may have several useful implementations. In the case of our `Attributed` interface, we can imagine several possible implementations that use various strategies to store a set of attributes.

One strategy might be simple and fast when only a few attributes are in a set; another one might be optimized for attribute sets that are queried more often than they are changed; yet another design might be optimized for sets that change frequently. If there were a package of various implementations for the `Attributed` interface, a class might choose to implement the `Attributed` interface through any one of them or through its own implementation.

As an example, here is a simple implementation of `Attributed` that uses the utility `java.util.HashMap` class. The class `AttributedImpl` declares that it `implements` the interface `Attributed`, so the class must implement all the interface's methods. `AttributedImpl` implements the methods using a `HashMap`, described in "HashMap" on page 590. Later, this implementation is used to implement the `Attributed` interface for a specific set of objects to which you would want to add attributes. First, here is the `AttributedImpl` class:

```java
import java.util.*;

class AttributedImpl implements Attributed, Iterable<Attr> {
    protected Map<String, Attr> attrTable =
        new HashMap<String, Attr>();

    public void add(Attr newAttr) {
        attrTable.put(newAttr.getName(), newAttr);
    }

    public Attr find(String name) {
        return attrTable.get(name);
    }

    public Attr remove(String name) {
        return attrTable.remove(name);
    }

    public Iterator<Attr> attrs() {
        return attrTable.values().iterator();
    }

    public Iterator<Attr> iterator() {
        return attrs();
    }
}
```

The initializer for `attrTable` creates a `HashMap` object to hold attributes. This `HashMap` object does most of the actual work. The `HashMap` class uses the key object's `hashCode` method to hash any object it is given as a key. No explicit hash method is needed since `String` already provides a good `hashCode` implementation.

When a new attribute is added, the `Attr` object is stored in the hash map under its name, and then you can easily use the hash map to find and remove attributes by name. The `attrs` method returns the `Iterator` for the hash map's values, giving access to all the attributes of the current object.

We chose to make this implementation of `Attributed` also implement `Iterable<Attr>`, as the attributes are the only things an `AttributedImpl` contains. To do this, we had to define the `iterator` method to return the same value as the `attrs` method.

4.4.2 Using an Implementation

You can use an implementing class like `AttributedImpl` by simply extending the class. This is the simplest tool when it is available because all the methods and their implementations are inherited. But if you need to support more than one interface or extend a different class, you must use a different approach. The most common approach is to create an object of an implementing class and *forward* all the methods of the interface to that object, returning any values—this is often called *composition*.

In composition and forwarding, each method in the class that is inherited from the interface invokes the implementation from another object and returns the result. Here is an implementation of the `Attributed` interface that uses an `AttributedImpl` object to build an attributed version of our previously defined celestial body class `Body`:

```
import java.util.Iterator;

class AttributedBody extends Body
    implements Attributed
{
    private AttributedImpl attrImpl = new AttributedImpl();

    public AttributedBody() {
        super();
    }

    public AttributedBody(String name, Body orbits) {
        super(name, orbits);
    }

    // Forward all Attributed methods to the attrImpl object

    public void add(Attr newAttr)
        { attrImpl.add(newAttr); }
```

```
        public Attr find(String name)
            { return attrImpl.find(name); }
        public Attr remove(String name)
            { return attrImpl.remove(name); }
        public Iterator<Attr> attrs()
            { return attrImpl.attrs(); }
    }
```

The declaration that `AttributedBody` extends `Body` and implements `Attributed` defines the contract of `AttributedBody`. The implementations of all `Body`'s methods are inherited from the `Body` class itself. Each method of `Attributed` is implemented by forwarding the invocation to the `AttributedImpl` object's equivalent method, returning its value (if any). This also means that you must add a field of type `AttributedImpl` to use in the forwarding methods and initialize that field to refer to an `AttributedImpl` object.

Forwarding is both straightforward and much less work than implementing `Attributed` from scratch. Forwarding also enables you to quickly change the implementation you use, should a better implementation of `Attributed` become available at some future date. However, forwarding must be set up manually and that can be tedious and sometimes error prone.

4.5   Marker Interfaces

Some interfaces do not declare any methods but simply mark a class as having some general property. The `Cloneable` interface is such a *marker* interface—it has neither methods nor constants, but marks a class as partaking in the cloning mechanism (see page 101).

Marker interfaces are the degenerate case of a contract because they define no language-level behavior—no methods or values. All their contract is in the documentation that describes the expectations you must satisfy if your class implements that interface. The interfaces `Serializable` and `Externalizable` (described in "Object Serialization" on page 549) are marker interfaces, as are both `java.rmi.Remote` (see "java.rmi—Remote Method Invocation" on page 727) and `java.util.EventListener` (see "java.awt—The Abstract Window Toolkit" on page 717).

Marker interfaces can have a profound impact on the behavior of the classes that implement them—consider `Cloneable`. Do not be fooled into thinking that they are unimportant merely because they have no methods.

4.6   When to Use Interfaces

An interface defines a type with an abstract contract. An abstract class also defines a type with an abstract contract. Which should you use and when?

There are two major differences between interfaces and abstract classes:

♦ Interfaces provide a form of multiple inheritance, because you can implement multiple interfaces. A class can extend only one other class, even if that class has only abstract methods.

♦ An abstract class can have a partial implementation, protected parts, static methods, and so on, whereas interfaces are limited to public constants and public methods with no implementation.

These differences usually direct the choice of which tool is best to use in a particular implementation. If multiple inheritance is important or even useful, interfaces are used. However, an abstract class enables you to provide some or all of the implementation so that it can be inherited easily, rather than by explicit forwarding. Additionally, an abstract class can control the implementation of certain methods by making them `final`—for example, our `SortDouble` class in Chapter 3 ensures that sorting is done correctly. However, if you find yourself writing an abstract class with all abstract methods, you're really writing an interface.

Any major class you expect to be extended, whether abstract or not, should be an implementation of an interface. Although this approach requires a little more work on your part, it enables a whole category of use that is otherwise precluded. For example, suppose we had created an `Attributed` class instead of an `Attributed` interface with an `AttributedImpl` implementation class. In that case, programmers who wanted to create new classes that extended other existing classes could never use `Attributed`, since you can extend only one class—the class `AttributedBody` could never have been created. Because `Attributed` is an interface, programmers have a choice: They can extend `AttributedImpl` directly and avoid the forwarding, or, if they cannot extend, they can at least use composition and forwarding to implement the interface. And if the general implementation provided is incorrect, they can write their own implementation. You can even provide multiple possible implementations of the interface to prospective users. Whatever implementation strategy programmers prefer, the objects they create are `Attributed`.

Exercise 4.1: Rewrite your solution to Exercise 3.6 on page 99 using an interface for `EnergySource` instead of an abstract class.

Exercise 4.2: Rewrite your solution to Exercise 3.12 on page 114 using an interface if you didn't write it that way in the first place.

Exercise 4.3: Should the `LinkedList` class from previous exercises be an interface? Rewrite it that way with an implementation class before you decide.

Exercise 4.4: Design a collection class hierarchy using only interfaces.

Exercise 4.5: Think about whether the following types should be represented as interfaces, abstract classes, or concrete classes: (a) `TreeNode` to represent nodes in an N-ary tree; (b) `TreeWalker` to walk the tree in a particular order (such as depth-first or breadth-first); (c) `Drawable` for objects that can be drawn by a graphics system; (d) `Application` for programs that can be run from a graphical desktop.

Exercise 4.6: What changes in your assumptions about each of the problems in Exercise 4.5 would make you change your answers?

> *There are two ways of constructing a software design:*
> *one way is to make it so simple that there are obviously no deficiencies;*
> *the other is to make it so complicated that there are no obvious deficiencies.*
> *—C.A.R. Hoare*

CHAPTER 5

Nested Classes and Interfaces

Every nonzero finite-dimensional inner product space has an orthonormal basis.
It makes sense when you don't think about it.
—Math Professor, U.C. Berkeley

CLASSES and interfaces can be declared inside other classes and interfaces, either as members or within blocks of code. These *nested classes* and *nested interfaces* can take a number of different forms, each with its own properties.

The ability to define nested types serves two main purposes. First, nested classes and nested interfaces allow types to be structured and scoped into logically related groups. Second, and more important, nested classes can be used to connect logically related objects simply and effectively. This latter capability is used extensively by event frameworks, such as the one used in AWT (see "java.awt— The Abstract Window Toolkit" on page 717) and the JavaBeans™ component architecture (see "java.beans—Components" on page 721).

A nested type is considered a part of its enclosing type and the two share a trust relationship in which each can access all members of the other. Differences between nested types depend on whether the nested type is a class or an interface, and whether the enclosing type is a class or an interface. Nested types are either static or not: The former allows simple structuring of types; the latter defines a special relationship between a nested object and an object of the enclosing class. Static nested types are more basic, so we cover them first.

5.1 Static Nested Types

A nested class or interface that is declared as a static member of its enclosing class or interface acts just like any non-nested, or top-level, class or interface, except that its name and accessibility are defined by its *enclosing type.* The name

133

of a nested type is expressed as *EnclosingName.NestedName*. The nested type is accessible only if the enclosing type is accessible.

Static nested types serve as a structuring and scoping mechanism for logically related types. However, static nested types are members of their enclosing type and as such can access all other members of the enclosing type including private ones—through an appropriate object reference of course. This gives the nested type a special, privileged relationship with the enclosing type.

Because static nested types are members of their enclosing type, the same accessibility rules apply to them as for other members. For classes this means that a static nested class or interface can have private, package, protected, or public access, while for interfaces, nested types are implicitly public.

5.1.1   Static Nested Classes

The static nested class is the simplest form of nested class. You declare one by preceding the class declaration with the `static` modifier. When nested in an interface, a class declaration is always static and the modifier is, by convention, omitted. A static nested class acts just like any top-level class. It can extend any other class (including the class it is a member of),[1] implement any interface and itself be used for further extension by any class to which it is accessible. It can be declared `final` or `abstract`, just as a top-level class can, and it can have annotations applied to it.

Static nested classes serve as a mechanism for defining logically related types within a context in which that type makes sense. For example, on page 62 we showed a `Permissions` class that bears information about a `BankAccount` object. Because the `Permissions` class is related to the contract of the `BankAccount` class—it is how a `BankAccount` object communicates a set of permissions—it is a good candidate to be a nested class:

```
public class BankAccount {
    private long number;     // account number
    private long balance;    // current balance (in cents)

    public static class Permissions {
        public boolean canDeposit,
                       canWithdraw,
                       canClose;
```

---

[1]   This is a very common structuring idiom.

```
        }
        // ...
    }
```

The `Permissions` class is defined inside the `BankAccount` class, making it a member of that class. When `permissionsFor` returns a `Permissions` object, it can refer to the class simply as `Permissions` in the same way it can refer to `balance` without qualification: `Permissions` is a member of the class. The full name of the class is `BankAccount.Permissions`. This full name clearly indicates that the class exists as part of the `BankAccount` class, not as a stand-alone type. Code outside the `BankAccount` class must use the full name, for example:

```
BankAccount.Permissions perm = acct.permissionsFor(owner);
```

If `BankAccount` were in a package named `bank`, the full name of the class would be `bank.BankAccount.Permissions` (packages are discussed in Chapter 18). In your own code, you could import the class `BankAccount.Permissions` and then use the simple name `Permissions`, but you would lose the important information about the subsidiary nature of the class.

Static nested classes are members of their enclosing type. Static nested classes enclosed in an interface are implicitly public; if enclosed by a class, you can declare them to be accessible in any way you like. You can, for example, declare a class that is an implementation detail to be `private`. We declare `Permissions` to be `public` because programmers using `BankAccount` need to use the class.

Since `Permissions` is a member of `BankAccount`, the `Permissions` class can access all other members of `BankAccount`, including all inherited members. For example, if `Permissions` declared a method that took a `BankAccount` object as an argument, that method would be able to directly access both the `number` and `balance` fields of that account. In this sense the nested class is seen as part of the implementation of the enclosing class and so is completely trusted.

There is no restriction on how a static nested class can be extended—it can be extended by any class to which it is accessible. Of course, the extended class does not inherit the privileged access that the nested class has to the enclosing class.

Nested enum classes are always static, although by convention the `static` modifier is omitted from the `enum` declaration. Enum classes are described in Chapter 6.

5.1.2 Nested Interfaces

Nested interfaces are also always static and again, by convention the `static` modifier is omitted from the interface declaration. They serve simply as a structuring mechanism for related types. When we look at non-static nested classes you will see that they are inherently concerned with implementation issues. Since inter-faces do not dictate implementation they cannot be non-static.

Exercise 5.1: Consider the `Attr` class and `Attributed` interface from Chapter 4. Should one of these be a nested type of the other? If so, which way makes the most sense?

5.2   Inner Classes

Non-static nested classes are called *inner classes.* Non-static class members are associated with instances of a class—non-static fields are instance variables and non-static methods operate on an instance. Similarly, an inner class is also (usu-ally) associated with an instance of a class, or more specifically an instance of an inner class is associated with an instance of its enclosing class—the *enclosing instance* or *enclosing object.*

You often need to closely tie a nested class object to a particular object of the enclosing class. Consider, for example, a method for the `BankAccount` class that lets you see the last action performed on the account, such as a deposit or with-drawal:

```
public class BankAccount {
    private long number;    // account number
    private long balance;   // current balance (in cents)
    private Action lastAct; // last action performed

    public class Action {
        private String act;
        private long amount;
        Action(String act, long amount) {
            this.act = act;
            this.amount = amount;
        }
        public String toString() {
            // identify our enclosing account
            return number + ": " + act + " " + amount;
        }
    }

    public void deposit(long amount) {
        balance += amount;
```

```
            lastAct = new Action("deposit", amount);
    }

    public void withdraw(long amount) {
        balance -= amount;
        lastAct = new Action("withdraw", amount);
    }
    // ...
}
```

The class `Action` records a single action on the account. It is not declared `static`, and that means its objects exist relative to an object of the enclosing class.

The relationship between an `Action` object and its `BankAccount` object is established when the `Action` object is created, as shown in the `deposit` and `withdraw` methods. When an inner class object is created, it must be associated with an object of its enclosing class. Usually, inner class objects are created inside instance methods of the enclosing class, as in `deposit` and `withdraw`. When that occurs the current object `this` is associated with the inner object by default. The creation code in `deposit` is the same as the more explicit

```
    lastAct = this.new Action("deposit", amount);
```

Any `BankAccount` object could be substituted for `this`. For example, suppose we add a transfer operation that takes a specified amount from one account and places it in the current account—such an action needs to update the `lastAct` field of both account objects:

```
    public void transfer(BankAccount other, long amount) {
        other.withdraw(amount);
        deposit(amount);
        lastAct = this.new Action("transfer", amount);
        other.lastAct = other.new Action("transfer", amount);
    }
```

In this case we bind the second `Action` object to the `other BankAccount` object and store it as the last action of the other account. Each `BankAccount` object should only refer to `Action` objects for which that `BankAccount` object is the enclosing instance. It would make no sense above, for example, to store the same `Action` object in both the current `lastAct` field and `other.lastAct`.

An inner class declaration is just like a top-level class declaration except for one restriction—inner classes cannot have static members (including static nested types), except for final static fields that are initialized to constants or expressions built up from constants. The rationale for allowing constants to be declared in an inner class is the same as that for allowing them in interfaces—it can be convenient to define constants within the type that uses them.

As with top-level classes, inner classes can extend any other class—including its enclosing class[2]—implement any interface and be extended by any other class. An inner class can be declared `final` or `abstract`, and can have annotations applied to it.

Exercise 5.2: Create a version of `BankAccount` that records the last ten actions on the account. Add a `history` method that returns a `History` object that will return `Action` objects one at a time via a `next` method, returning `null` at the end of the list. Should `History` be a nested class? If so, should it be static or not?

5.2.1   Accessing Enclosing Objects

The `toString` method of `Action` directly uses the `number` field of its enclosing `BankAccount` object. A nested class can access all members of its enclosing class—including private fields and methods—without qualification because it is part of the enclosing class's implementation. An inner class can simply name the members of its enclosing object to use them. The names in the enclosing class are all said to be *in scope.* The enclosing class can also access the private members of the inner class, but only by an explicit reference to an inner class object such as `lastAct`. While an object of the inner class is always associated with an object of the enclosing class, the converse is not true. An object of the enclosing class need not have any inner class objects associated with it, or it could have many.

When `deposit` creates an `Action` object, a reference to the enclosing `BankAccount` object is automatically stored in the new `Action` object. Using this saved reference, the `Action` object can always refer to the enclosing `BankAccount` object's `number` field by the simple name `number`, as shown in `toString`. The name of the reference to the enclosing object is `this` preceded by the enclosing class name—a form known as *qualified-`this`.* For example, `toString` could reference the `number` field of the enclosing `BankAccount` object explicitly:

```
return BankAccount.this.number + ": " + act + " " + amount;
```

The qualified-`this` reference reinforces the idea that the enclosing object and the inner object are tightly bound as part of the same implementation of the enclosing class. This is further reinforced by the *qualified-`super`* reference, which

---

[2]   It is hard to think of a reason why you would want to do this, and easy to get a headache reasoning about what it means.

allows access to members of the enclosing instance's superclass that have been hidden, or overridden, by the enclosing class. For example, given a class T that extends S, within T we can invoke the superclass implementation of a method m, by using `super.m()` in an expression. Similarly, in an inner class of T, we can invoke the same implementation of m using `T.super.m()` in an expression—a qualified-`super` reference—and similarly for fields of S hidden by fields in T.

A nested class can have its own nested classes and interfaces. References to enclosing objects can be obtained for any level of nesting in the same way: the name of the class and `this`. If class X encloses class Y which encloses class Z, code in Z can explicitly access fields of X by using `X.this`.

The language does not prevent you from deeply nesting classes, but good taste should. A doubly nested class such as Z has three name scopes: itself, its immediate enclosing class Y, and outermost class X. Someone reading the code for Z must understand each class thoroughly to know in which context an identifier is bound and which enclosing object was bound to which nested object. We recommend nesting only one level under most circumstances. Nesting more than two levels invites a readability disaster and should probably never be attempted.

5.2.2 Extending Inner Classes

An inner class can be extended just as any static nested class or top-level class can. The only requirement is that objects of the extended class must still be associated with objects of the original enclosing class or a subclass. Usually this is not a problem because the extended inner class is often declared within an extension of the outer class:

```
class Outer {
    class Inner { }
}

class ExtendedOuter extends Outer {
    class ExtendedInner extends Inner { }
    Inner ref = new ExtendedInner();
}
```

The `ref` field is initialized when an `ExtendedOuter` object is created. The creation of the `ExtendedInner` instance uses the default no-arg constructor of `ExtendedInner`, which in turn implicitly invokes the default no-arg constructor of `Inner` by using `super`. The constructor for `Inner` requires an object of `Outer` to bind to, which in this case is implicitly the current object of `ExtendedOuter`.

If the enclosing class of the inner subclass is not a subclass of `Outer`, or if the inner subclass is not itself an inner class, then an explicit reference to an object of

Outer must be supplied when the Inner constructor is invoked via super. For example:

```
class Unrelated extends Outer.Inner {
    Unrelated(Outer ref) {
        ref.super();
    }
}
```

When the construction of an Unrelated object reaches the point where the superclass constructor is invoked, there must be an object of class Outer to which the superclass object can be bound. Since Unrelated is not itself an inner class of Outer, there is no implicit enclosing object. Similarly, because Unrelated is not a subclass of Outer, the current object of Unrelated is not a valid enclosing object. We must provide an explicit reference to an Outer object for the superclass object to bind to. We chose to supply that reference using an argument to the Unrelated constructor, which uses it as an explicit binding reference in the invocation of the superclass constructor.

Note that you cannot use the inner class creation syntax to externally provide an Outer object, as in

```
Outer ref = new Outer();
Unrelated u = ref.new Unrelated(); // INVALID
```

because this syntax supplies an enclosing object for the Unrelated class and Unrelated is *not* an inner class.

An inner class can extend another, unrelated, inner class provided an appropriate enclosing instance is supplied to the superclass, as just described. The resulting inner class then has two enclosing instances—one for the extended class and one for the superclass. Such designs are convoluted, however, and are best avoided.

5.2.3   Inheritance, Scoping, and Hiding

Within an inner class, all names declared within the enclosing class are said to be *in scope*—they can be used as if the inner class code were declared in the outer class. An inner class's own fields and methods (and nested types) can *hide* those of the enclosing object. There are two ways in which this can occur:

- ◆ a field or method is declared in the inner class
- ◆ a field or method is inherited by the inner class

In both cases any use of the simple name refers to the member of the inner class, whether declared or inherited. The enclosing object's field or method must be accessed explicitly using a qualified-`this` expression.

In the second case, the use of the simple name can mislead a reader of the code. Consider the following:

```
class Host {
    int x;

    class Helper extends Unknown {
        void increment() { x++; }    // Not what you think!
    }
}
```

The `increment` method appears to increment the `x` field of the enclosing `Host` instance. In fact, `Unknown` also declares a field `x` and that field is inherited by `Helper`. The inherited `x` field hides the `x` field from the enclosing scope, and so it is the inherited `x` field that is incremented not the field that is seen in the source code! To avoid giving the reader the wrong impression about what the code is doing, you should avoid the use of simple names in this situation. Instead, the reference to `x` should be explicitly qualified as either `this.x` or `Host.this.x`, depending on which field it is meant to refer to.

An inner class method with the same name as an enclosing class method hides all overloaded forms of the enclosing class method, even if the inner class itself does not declare those overloaded forms. For example:

```
class Outer {
    void print() { }
    void print(int val) { }

    class Inner {
        void print() { }
        void show() {
            print();
            Outer.this.print();
            print(1);    // INVALID: no Inner.print(int)
        }
    }
}
```

Here the declaration of `Inner.print` hides all forms of `Outer.print`. When `Inner.show` invokes `print(1)`, the compiler reports that `Inner` has no method `print` that takes an integer argument. The `show` method must explicitly qualify the method invocation with `Outer.this`. There is a good reason to do this. Normally, a set of overloaded methods within a class have the same basic contract—they just operate on different parameter types. If an inner class method happens to have the same name as an enclosing class method, there is no reason to assume that it supports the same contract—consequently, the hiding of the enclosing class's overloaded forms prevents a completely unrelated method from being accidentally invoked. As usual, there are few reasons to hide fields or methods in this way, so the issue is best avoided in the first place. The details of how method invocations are resolved are discussed in "Finding the Right Method" on page 224.

5.3   Local Inner Classes

You can define inner classes in code blocks, such as a method body, constructor, or initialization block. These *local inner classes* are not members of the class of which the code is a part but are local to that block, just as a local variable is. Such classes are completely inaccessible outside the block in which they are defined—there is simply no way to refer to them. But instances of such classes are normal objects that can be passed as arguments and returned from methods, and they exist until they are no longer referenced. Because local inner classes are inaccessible, they can't have access modifiers, nor can they be declared `static` because, well, they are local *inner* classes. All of the other class modifiers, including annotations, can be applied, though only `strictfp` and annotations have practical applications.

A local inner class can access all the variables that are in scope where the class is defined—local variables, method parameters, instance variables (assuming it is a non-static block), and static variables. The only restriction is that a local variable or method parameter can be accessed only if it is declared `final`. The reason for this restriction relates mainly to multithreading issues (see Chapter 14) and ensures that all such variables have well-defined values when accessed from the inner class. Given that the method accessing the local variable or parameter could be invoked after the completion of the method in which the local class was defined—and hence the local variables and parameters no longer exist—the value of those variables must be frozen before the local class object is created. If needed, you can copy a non-final variable into a final one that is subsequently accessed by the local inner class.

Consider the standard interface `Iterator` defined in the `java.util` package. This interface defines a way to iterate through a group of objects. It is commonly used to provide access to the elements in a container object but can be used for any general-purpose iteration:

```
package java.util;

public interface Iterator<E> {
    boolean hasNext();
    E next() throws NoSuchElementException;
    void remove() throws UnsupportedOperationException,
                         IllegalStateException;
}
```

The hasNext method returns true if next has more elements to return. The remove method removes from the collection the last element returned by next. But remove is optional, which means an implementation is allowed to throw UnsupportedOperationException. If remove is invoked before next, or is invoked multiple times after a single call to next, then IllegalStateException is thrown. NoSuchElementException—also part of the java.util package—is thrown if next is invoked when there are no more elements. See "Iteration" on page 571 for more details.

Here is a simple method that returns an Iterator to walk through an array of Object instances:

```
public static Iterator<Object>
    walkThrough(final Object[] objs) {

    class Iter implements Iterator<Object> {
        private int pos = 0;
        public boolean hasNext() {
            return (pos < objs.length);
        }
        public Object next() throws NoSuchElementException {
            if (pos >= objs.length)
                throw new NoSuchElementException();
            return objs[pos++];
        }
        public void remove() {
            throw new UnsupportedOperationException();
        }
    }
```

```
        return new Iter();
    }
```

The `Iter` class is local to the `walkThrough` method; it is not a member of the enclosing class. Because `Iter` is local to the method, it has access to all the final variables of the method—in particular the parameter `objs`. It defines a `pos` field to keep track of where it is in the `objs` array. (This code assumes that `Iterator` and `NoSuchElementException` are imported from `java.util` in the source that contains `walkThrough`.)

Members of local inner classes can hide the local variables and parameters of the block they are declared in, just as they can hide instance fields and methods. The rules discussed on page 140 apply in all cases. The only difference is that once a local variable or parameter has been hidden it is impossible to refer to it.

5.3.1   Inner Classes in Static Contexts

We stated that an inner class is *usually* associated with an instance of the enclosing class. It is possible to declare a local inner class, or an anonymous inner class (see next section), in a *static context:* within a static method, a static initialization block, or as part of a static initializer. In these static contexts there is no corresponding instance of the enclosing class, and so the inner class instance has no enclosing class instance. In these circumstances, any attempt to use a qualified-`this` expression to refer to an enclosing class's instance fields or methods will result in a compile-time error.

5.4   Anonymous Inner Classes

When a local inner class seems too much for your needs, you can declare *anonymous classes* that extend a class or implement an interface. These classes are defined at the same time they are instantiated with `new`. For example, consider the `walkThrough` method. The class `Iter` is fairly lightweight and is not needed outside the method. The name `Iter` doesn't add much value to the code—what is important is that it is an `Iterator` object. The `walkThrough` method could use an anonymous inner class instead:

```
public static Iterator<Object>
    walkThrough(final Object[] objs) {

    return new Iterator<Object>() {
        private int pos = 0;
```

```
                public boolean hasNext() {
                    return (pos < objs.length);
                }
                public Object next() throws NoSuchElementException {
                    if (pos >= objs.length)
                        throw new NoSuchElementException();
                    return objs[pos++];
                }
                public void remove() {
                    throw new UnsupportedOperationException();
                }
            };
    }
```

Anonymous classes are defined in the new expression itself, as part of a statement. The type specified to new is the supertype of the anonymous class. Because `Iterator` is an interface, the anonymous class in `walkThrough` implicitly extends `Object` and implements `Iterator`. An anonymous class cannot have an explicit `extends` or `implements` clause, nor can it have any modifiers, including annotations.

Anonymous inner classes cannot have explicit constructors declared because they have no name to give the constructor. If an anonymous inner class is complex enough that it needs explicit constructors then it should probably be a local inner class. In practice, many anonymous inner classes need little or no initialization. In either case, an anonymous inner class can have initializers and initialization blocks that can access the values that would logically have been passed as a constructor argument. The only construction problem that remains is the need to invoke an explicit superclass constructor. To solve this problem the new expression is written as if a superclass instance were being constructed, and that constructor is invoked as the superclass constructor. For example, the following anonymous subclass of `Attr` (see page 76) invokes the single-argument `Attr` constructor and overrides `setValue` to print out the new value each time it is changed:

```
    Attr name = new Attr("Name") {
        public Object setValue(Object nv) {
            System.out.println("Name set to " + nv);
            return super.setValue(nv);
        }
    };
```

In the `Iterator` example we invoked the no-arg superclass constructor for `Object`—the only constructor that can ever be used when an anonymous inner class has an interface type.

Anonymous classes are simple and direct but can easily become very hard to read. The further they nest, the harder they are to understand. The nesting of the anonymous class code that will execute in the future inside the method code that is executing now adds to the potential for confusion. You should probably avoid anonymous classes that are longer than about six lines, and you should use them in only the simplest of expressions. We stretch this rule in the `walkThrough` example because the sole purpose of the method is to return that object, but when a method does more, anonymous classes must be kept quite small or the code becomes illegible. When anonymous classes are used properly, they are a good tool for keeping simple classes simple. When misused, they create impenetrable inscrutability.

5.5 Inheriting Nested Types

Nested types, whether static classes, interfaces, or inner classes, are inherited the same way that fields are inherited. A declaration of a nested type with the same name as that of an inherited nested type *hides* the definition of the inherited type. The actual type referred to is determined by the type of the reference used. Within a given class, the actual nested type referred to is the one defined in the current class or inherited in the current class.

Consider a framework that models devices that can be connected by different ports. The class `Device` is an abstract class that captures some common behavior of all devices. A port also has some common generic behavior so it is also modeled as an abstract class and, because ports exist only within devices, the `Port` class is made an inner class of `Device`. A concrete device class defines the state for the device and the concrete inner port classes for that device. During construction of a concrete device class, references to the concrete ports of that class are initialized:

```
abstract class Device {
    abstract class Port {
        // ...
    }
    // ...
}
class Printer extends Device {
    class SerialPort extends Port {
```

NESTED CLASSES AND INTERFACES   **147**

```
        // ...
    }
    Port serial = new SerialPort();
}
```

A concrete device can itself be extended, as can the concrete inner port classes, to specialize their behavior.

```
class HighSpeedPrinter extends Printer {
    class SerialPort extends Printer.SerialPort {
        // ...
    }
}
```

The intent is that the class `HighSpeedPrinter.SerialPort` overrides the class `Printer.SerialPort` so that `serial` is set to refer to the correct type of object. But the class `Printer` is not affected by the new subclass of `SerialPort` defined inside `HighSpeedPrinter`, even though the new subclass seems to have the same name.

One solution to this design problem is to abstract construction of the inner class objects into a *factory method* which can then be overridden in a subclass to construct the right kind of inner class. For example:

```
class Printer extends Device {
    class SerialPort extends Port {
        // ...
    }
    Port serial = createSerialPort();
    protected Port createSerialPort() {
        return new SerialPort();
    }
}
```

The `HighSpeedPrinter` class now defines its specialized inner class and overrides the factory method to construct an instance of that class. Now that we realize that nested type definitions hide and don't override, we aren't tempted to use the same name for the inner class, for we know that hiding is usually a bad thing.

```
class HighSpeedPrinter extends Printer {
    class EnhancedSerialPort extends SerialPort {
        // ...
    }
    protected Port createSerialPort() {
```

```
        return new EnhancedSerialPort();
    }
}
```

Now when a HighSpeedPrinter is constructed and the initializers in Printer execute, we invoke the overriding createSerialPort method that returns an instance of EnhancedSerialPort.

This is one example of a situation in which a method of the subclass is invoked before the subclass object has been fully constructed and so care must be taken to ensure that things work correctly. For example, if EnhancedSerialPort initializes a field using a field from the enclosing HighSpeedPrinter instance, then at the time the EnhancedSerialPort object is constructed, the fields of the enclosing object will have the default "zero" values for their type.

An alternative design would have the constructor for HighSpeedPrinter simply reassign serial to refer to an EnhancedSerialPort object. However, that approach causes the unnecessary construction of the original SerialPort object, and that construction may be non-trivial and undesirable—in this example it may involve configuring hardware.

5.6   Nesting in Interfaces

You declare nested classes and interfaces in an interface for the same reason that you declare nested classes and interfaces in a class: nested classes and interfaces allow you to associate types that are strongly related to an interface inside that interface. For example, a class that was used only to return multiple values from an interface's method could be represented as a nested class in that interface:

```
interface Changeable {
    class Record {
        public Object changer;
        public String changeDesc;
    }

    Record getLastChange();
    // ...
}
```

The method getLastChange returns a Changeable.Record object that contains the object that made the change and a string describing the change. This class has meaning relative only to the Changeable interface, so making a top-level class not only is unnecessary but would also separate it from the context of its use. As a nested class it is tightly bound to its origin and context, but it is a normal class in every other regard.

Another use for a nested class within an interface is to define a (partial or complete) default implementation for that interface. A class that implements the interface could then choose to extend the default implementation class or to forward method invocations to an instance of that class.

Any class or interface nested inside an interface is public and static.

5.6.1 Modifiable Variables in Interfaces

We mentioned on page 121 that if you need shared, modifiable data in an interface, then a nested class is a simple way of achieving this. Declare a nested class whose fields hold the shared data, and whose methods provide access to that data, then maintain a reference to an instance of that class. For example:

```
interface SharedData {
    class Data {
        private int x = 0;
        public int getX() { return x; }
        public void setX(int newX) { x = newX; }
    }
    Data data = new Data();
}
```

Now all implementors and users of `SharedData` can share common state via the `data` reference.

5.7 Implementation of Nested Types

How the compiler and runtime system deal with nested types would ideally be transparent to the programmer. Unfortunately, this is not quite the case. Nested types were added as a language extension, and that extension had to maintain compatibility with older Java virtual machines. Consequently, nested types are implemented in terms of a source code transformation that the compiler applies.

As a programmer, the only thing you should need to know about this process is the naming conventions that are used. Consider a static, or non-local, nested type defined as `Outer.Inner`. This is the source name for the class. At the virtual machine level the class is renamed as `Outer$Inner`—in essence, dots in a nested name are converted to dollar signs. For local inner classes, the transformation is less specific because these classes are inaccessible, hence their name is less important—such classes are named `Outer$NInner`, where `Inner` is the name of the local class and N is a sequence of one or more digits. For anonymous inner classes the names have the form `Outer$N`, where N is a sequence of one or more digits.

These issues have to be dealt with in two main cases. First, when bundling the class files for your applications you have to recognize all the strange files with $ in their name. Second, if you use the reflection mechanism discussed in Chapter 16 to create nested class instances, you'll need to know the transformed name. But in most programming the transformed name is something you can blissfully ignore.

> *"A power so great, it can only be used for Good or Evil!"*
> —Firesign Theatre, "The Giant Rat of Summatra"

CHAPTER 6

Enumeration Types

Four be the things I am wiser to know: Idleness, sorrow, a friend, and a foe.
Four be the things I'd been better without: Love, curiosity, freckles, and doubt.
Three be the things I shall never attain: Envy, content, and sufficient champagne.
Three be the things I shall have till I die: Laughter and hope and a sock in the eye.
—Dorothy Parker, "Inventory"

AN *enumeration type*—sometimes known as an *enumerated type,* or more simply as an *enum*—is a type for which all values for the type are known when the type is defined. For example, an enum representing the suits in a deck of cards would have the possible values hearts, diamonds, clubs, and spades; and an enum for the days of the week would have the values Monday, Tuesday, Wednesday, Thursday, Friday, Saturday, and Sunday.

In some programming languages, enums are nothing more than a set of named integer values, but in the Java programming language an enum is a special kind of class, with an instance that represents each value of the enum.

6.1 A Simple Enum Example

An enum for the suits in a deck of cards can be declared as follows:

```
enum Suit { CLUBS, DIAMONDS, HEARTS, SPADES }
```

In this basic form, an enum declaration consists of the keyword `enum`, an identifier that names the enum, and a body that simply names each of the values, or *con-*

stants, of the enum.[1] By convention, enum constants always have uppercase names. The enum constants are static fields of the class:

```
Suit currentSuit = ... ;
if (currentSuit == Suit.DIAMONDS) ... ;
```

Each enum constant actually refers to an instance of the enum class. You cannot construct an instance of an enum by using new—it is as if the enum had no accessible constructors. You may only use those objects created for the enum constants.

While this simple usage appears little different from declaring a set of named integer constants, it has the significant difference of being completely type-safe: It is impossible to assign anything to a reference of type Suit except one of the four defined Suit enum constants or null. As you will see, enums also provide much more sophisticated usage than can be achieved with named integer constants.

Exercise 6.1: Define simple enums for the days of the week and traffic light colors.

Exercise 6.2: Redo your solution to Exercise 2.17 to use an enum to represent the TURN_LEFT and TURN_RIGHT constants. What advantage is there to using the enum?

Exercise 6.3: Redefine the Verbose interface from Section 4.2.1 on page 121 to use an enum for the verbosity level instead of integer constants.

6.2   Enum Declarations

An enum is a special kind of class, but an enum declaration has restrictions on its form and use that are different from those of a normal class. An enum declaration is like a class declaration with two exceptions: The keyword enum is used instead of class, and before declaring any class members (or initialization blocks) an enum must first declare all of its enum constants. If an enum does declare anything other than its enum constants, then the list of enum constants must be terminated by a semicolon. For example, this variation of Suit provides a method to tell you how many suits there are:

---

[1]   The term *enum constant* refers to those values, like CLUBS and DIAMONDS, declared in the enum type. Enum types can also have normal constants, just like other classes, that are static final fields of various types. We always use "enum constant" to refer to the former, and plain "constant" to refer to the latter.

```
enum Suit {
    CLUBS, DIAMONDS, HEARTS, SPADES;

    public static int getSize() { return 4; }
}
```

For convenience, you're allowed to have a comma after the last enum constant (but before the semicolon if present), whether or not any other class declarations follow. This is useful for declaring an enum constant per line:

```
enum Suit {
    CLUBS,
    DIAMONDS,
    HEARTS,
    SPADES,
}
```

Being able to keep the extraneous comma allows you to reorder lines without having to remember to add the comma to the old last line or remove it from the new last line. (Array initialization lists have the same feature—see page 175.)

An enum cannot be declared to `extend` another type because all enums implicitly extend `java.lang.Enum`, which we discuss a little later. Nor can any other type extend an enum (not even another enum), because all enum types act as if they are implicitly `final`. An enum can declare that it implements one or more interfaces—in fact all enums are implicitly `Serializable` (see "Object Serialization" on page 549) and `Comparable`.

The possible members of an enum include all the class members: fields, methods, and nested types, including nested enums—though it should be rare to require such sophistication: The main attraction of enums is their simplicity. The enum constants themselves are implicitly static fields with the same type as the enum.

Every enum type *E* has two static methods that are automatically generated for it by the compiler:

public static *E*[] **values()**
> Returns an array containing each of the enum constants in the order in which they were declared.

public static *E* **valueOf(String name)**
> Returns the enum constant with the given name. If the name does not match an enum constant name exactly then an `IllegalArgumentException` is thrown.

Note that the length of the array returned by `values` tells you how many enum constants there are in the enum, so the `getSize` method we demonstrated is not needed in practice.

An enum type is not allowed to override the `finalize` method from `Object`. Enum instances may never be finalized (see "Finalization" on page 449).

6.2.1   Enum Modifiers

An enum declaration can be preceded by certain modifiers:

◆ *annotations*—Annotations and annotation types are discussed in Chapter 15.

◆ *access modifiers*—Nested enum declarations can have any of the access modifiers, while a top-level enum, as for a top-level class, is either `public` or in the absence of an access modifier, accessible only within its own package.

◆ *static*—All nested enums are implicitly `static` because they contain static members. By convention, the `static` modifier is always omitted.

◆ *strict floating point*—All floating-point arithmetic within an enum declared to be `strictfp` is evaluated strictly. See Section 9.1.3 on page 203 for details.

When multiple modifiers are applied to the same enum declaration, we recommend using the order listed above.

An enum cannot be declared `abstract` because you cannot extend it to provide missing method implementations—however, an enum can declare `abstract` methods. You'll shortly see how this apparent contradiction is resolved.

An enum also cannot be explicitly declared `final`, though it acts as if it were final. You'll shortly see why this is so, too.

6.3   Enum Constant Declarations

The simplest enum constant declaration just gives a name for each enum constant, as you have seen. Such enum constants implicitly define a public, static, and final field with the given name and of the same type as the enum. These implicit fields are initialized by constructing an instance of the enum as described below. An enum constant declaration cannot have modifiers applied to it, except for annotations (see Chapter 15).

6.3.1 Construction

An enum constant declaration that consists of only a name causes an object of the enum type to be created with the (implicit or explicit) no-arg constructor. An enum can declare arbitrary constructors, just like any other class. You select which constructor should be used for a particular enum constant by supplying arguments that match the constructor parameter types:

```
enum Suit {
    CLUBS("CLUBS"),
    DIAMONDS("DIAMONDS"),
    HEARTS("HEARTS"),
    SPADES("SPADES");

    String name;
    Suit(String name) { this.name = name; }

    public String toString() { return name; }
}
```

Here each `Suit` value has a `name` field set by the constructor that takes a `String`, and in each enum constant declaration we provide the desired name argument. This is such a common thing to want with enum constants, however, that this functionality has been built-in so you don't have to write the name strings yourself—invoking the `name` method on an enum constant will return its name as a `String`.

You can get a feel for how an enum is internally defined from the following pseudo-code, which shows a mock class definition for the above `Suit` enum:

```
class Suit extends Enum<Suit>     // pseudo-code only
    implements Comparable<Suit>, Serializable {

    public static final Suit CLUBS = new Suit("CLUBS");
    public static final Suit DIAMONDS = new Suit("DIAMONDS");
    public static final Suit HEARTS = new Suit("HEARTS");
    public static final Suit SPADES = new Suit("SPADES");

    String name;

    Suit(String name) { this.name = name; }
    public String toString() { return name; }

    // ... compiler generated methods ...
}
```

There is a bit more to the detail, but the above gives you the general idea.

The constructor to invoke is determined according to the usual rules for matching argument types with constructor parameter types—see "Finding the Right Method" on page 224.

There are three restrictions on the definition of an enum constructor:

◆ All enum constructors are private. While you can use the `private` access modifier in the constructor declaration, by convention it is omitted. Private constructors ensure that an enum type cannot be instantiated directly.

◆ The constructor cannot explicitly invoke a superclass constructor. The chaining to the super constructor is handled automatically by the compiler.

◆ An enum constructor cannot use a non-constant static field of the enum.

This last restriction requires a little explanation. Because each enum constant is a static field of the enum type, the constructors are executed during static initialization of the enum class. The enum constant declarations must be the first declarations in the type, so the constructors for these values will always be the first code executed during static initialization. Any other static fields will be initialized afterward. So if a constructor were to refer to a static (non-constant) field of the enum, it would see the default uninitialized value. This would nearly always be an error, and so it is simply disallowed.

The work-around is quite straight-forward: Declare a static initialization block that does what the constructor would like to have done. This block can refer to any enum constant or can iterate through all of them because all will have been constructed before the block can execute.

Exercise 6.4: Expand your traffic light color enum from Exercise 6.1 on page 152 so that each enum constant has a suitable `Color` object that can be retrieved with `getColor`.

6.3.2   Constant Specific Behavior

Many enums define simple, passive types whose sole purpose is to provide the named enum constants—an enum like `Suit` is a good example. Occasionally, enum constants will have state associated with them that will be set by a constructor and accessed with a method on the enum. For example, consider an enum that defined the nine planets of our solar system, and that allowed the mass of each planet to be set and queried. In some circumstances, the enum may represent an entity with inherent behavior that varies between the different enum constants—this is known as *constant-specific behavior.*

Suppose you were writing a computer chess program[2] and you wanted to represent the different kinds of chess pieces, you might use a simple enum like this:

```
enum ChessPiece {
    PAWN, ROOK, BISHOP, KNIGHT, KING, QUEEN;
}
```

The rules for manipulating the different chess pieces could be defined in a class ChessRules, which might then have a method that returns the set of reachable positions for a given kind of piece, given its current position:

```
Set<Position> reachable(ChessPiece type, Position current) {
    if (type == ChessPiece.PAWN)
        return pawnReachable(current);
    else if (type == ChessPiece.ROOK)
        return rookReachable(current);
    // ...
    else if (type == ChessPiece.QUEEN)
        return queenReachable(current);
    else
        throw new Error("Unknown type");
}
```

The job of reachable is to dispatch actual calculations to methods that know how to handle specific chess pieces, so it has to consider all the possible values of the chess piece type that was passed to it. Whenever you see a chain of if–else statements, as above, or equivalently a switch statement (which you'll learn about in Chapter 10) that distinguishes different objects or types of object, ask yourself if there is a way to have the object decide what needs to be done—after all, each object knows what it is. In this case, why can't you ask the chess piece for its set of reachable positions? It turns out you can—by adding constant-specific behavior to the enum:

```
enum ChessPiece {
    PAWN {
        Set<Position> reachable(Position current) {
            return ChessRules.pawnReachable(current);
        }
    },
    ROOK {
        Set<Position> reachable(Position current) {
```

---

[2] This example is based on an example given by Tim Peierls.

```
                return ChessRules.rookReachable(current);
            }
        },
        // ...
        QUEEN {
            Set<Position> reachable(Position current) {
                return ChessRules.queenReachable(current);
            }
        };

        // declare the methods defined by this enum
        abstract Set<Position> reachable(Position current);
}
```

This time each named enum constant is followed by a class body that defines the methods for that enum constant—in this case dispatching to the appropriate ChessRules method as before. The advantage of dispatching in the enum constants themselves is that you can't forget to handle the case for a specific value. Looking at the original code for reachable you can see that it would be easy to leave out one of the values, only realizing this at runtime when the error is thrown. Also note that even though we have covered all the possible values in reachable, we still must have that final else clause because the compiler won't check to see if we have covered all possible values and the method must either return a value or throw an exception. By using constant-specific methods we moved the checking for completeness to compile time, which is always a good thing, and we avoided writing code that should never get executed.

The classes that are defined for each enum constant are effectively anonymous inner classes that extend the enclosing enum type—which is why you can't actually declare an enum to be final: Even though it can't be directly extended, it can be implicitly extended by these anonymous inner classes.

As with other anonymous inner classes, the enum constant class body can define arbitrary instance fields, and methods, but it can't declare static members or define constructors. Also note that because enum constants are implicitly static fields, these anonymous inner classes have no enclosing instance.

To be directly accessible, the methods defined for each enum constant must be declared as methods of the enum type itself—either explicitly, as above for reachable, or implicitly by an interface the enum implements. An enum type is allowed to declare an abstract method, only if there is an implementation of that method for each and every enum constant.

Exercise 6.5: Redo Exercise 6.4 making `getColor` an abstract method and defining constant-specific methods for each enum constant to return the correct `Color` object. Would you recommend using constant-specific methods to do this?

6.4 `java.lang.Enum`

All enum types implicitly extend `java.lang.Enum`,[3] but no class is allowed to extend `Enum` directly. Although `Enum` does provide some methods that can be useful for working with enums, its main role is to establish some useful properties for all enum types:

- The `clone` method is overridden to be declared `final` and to throw `CloneNotSupportedException`—making it impossible to ever clone an enum instance.

- The `hashCode` and `equals` methods are overridden and declared `final`— ensuring consistent and efficient hashing for enums, and ensuring that equivalence is the same as identity.

- The `compareTo` method of interface `java.lang.Comparable` is implemented and defined such that enum constants have a natural ordering based on their order of declaration—the first declared enum constant has the lowest position in the ordering.

Enum also provides a `toString` implementation that returns the name of the enum constant, as we have mentioned, but which you can chose to override. It also provides a `final name` method that also returns the name of the enum constant as a `String`. The difference between these two methods is that `name` will return the exact name of the enum constant, while `toString` may be overridden to return a more "user friendly" version of the name—for example, returning `"Diamonds"` instead of `"DIAMONDS"`.

The additional methods of Enum are:

`public final int ordinal()`

> Returns the ordinal value of an enum constant. Enum constants are given ordinal values based on the order they are declared: the first declared constant has an ordinal value of zero, the second has an ordinal value of one, etc.

---

[3] Enum is actually a generic class defined as `Enum<T extends Enum<T>>`. This circular definition is probably the most confounding generic type definition you are likely to encounter. We're assured by the type theorists that this is quite valid and significant, and that we should simply not think about it too much, for which we are grateful.

```
public final Class<E> getDeclaringClass()
```
    Returns the `Class` object representing the enum type of this enum constant. This will be different from the value returned by `Object.getClass` for any enum constant that is set to an anonymous inner class object.

The `Enum` class also provides a static utility method, `valueOf`, that takes a class object for an enum type, and a name, and returns the named enum constant from the given enum. If the enum doesn't have a enum constant by that name then `IllegalArgumentException` is thrown.

In addition to the `Enum` class, there are two highly efficient enum-specific collection classes: `EnumSet` defines a set for use with enum values, and `EnumMap` is a specialized map for which keys are enum values. These specialized collection classes are described further in Chapter 21.

6.5   To Enum or Not

The more sophisticated the type you are considering defining as an enum, the more thought you must give to whether enum is the right way to express that type. For simple uses like card suits, days of the week, and even the simple chess piece enum, all that is necessary is that you have a closed set of well-known instances— the decision to define an enum takes almost no thought.

When an enum declares enum constants with constant-specific behavior, additional considerations need to be made. The more sophisticated the behavior of a type, the more likely an application might need to specialize that behavior. Specialization of behavior is done through subclassing, and you cannot subclass an enum. Even something as innocuous as defining a logging, or profiling version of a given enum type is precluded. The same considerations that go into declaring a class `final` apply to choosing whether to declare a sophisticated enum.

There is little an enum can do that you couldn't do by declaring distinct classes. But the packaging that enum provides is far more convenient to use, though with some restrictions, as you've seen. Additionally, enums are a part of the language and are recognized by other parts of the language. For example, enum constants can be used directly with a `switch` statement (see page 232) whereas normal object references can not. Unless you need specialization through subclassing, it will almost always be better to use an enum type than to define your own classes.

CENSUS TAKER TO HOUSEWIFE: *Did you ever have the measles, and, if so, how many?*

CHAPTER 7

Tokens, Values, and Variables

There's nothing remarkable about it.
All one has to do is hit the right keys at the right time
and the instrument plays itself.
—Johann Sebastian Bach

A program starts as a sequence of characters contained in a file—the source code. Interpreting those characters, according to the rules of a given language, is the job of the compiler, or interpreter. Some characters will represent the names of variables, others will be special keywords used by the language, still others will be operators or "punctuation" characters used to separate the other elements. All of these textual constructs form the *lexical elements* of the program. These lexical elements must be identified as keywords, comments, literals, variables, operators, or whatever else is appropriate for the given language. In this chapter we look at the basic lexical elements of a Java program, the literal values that can be expressed and the different kinds of variables that can hold those values.

7.1 Lexical Elements

One of the first phases of compilation is the *scanning* of the lexical elements into *tokens*. This phase ignores *whitespace* and *comments* that appear in the text—so the language must define what form whitespace and comments take. The remaining sequence of characters must then be parsed into tokens.

7.1.1 Character Set

Most programmers are familiar with source code that is prepared using one of two major families of character representations: ASCII and its variants (including

Latin-1) and EBCDIC. Both character sets contain characters used in English and several other Western European languages.

The Java programming language, on the other hand, is written in a 16-bit encoding of *Unicode.* The Unicode standard originally supported a 16-bit character set, but has expanded to allow for up to 21-bit characters with a maximum value of 0x10ffff. The characters above the value 0x00ffff are termed the *supplementary* characters. Any particular 21-bit value is termed a *code point.* To allow all characters to be represented by 16-bit values, Unicode defines an encoding format called UTF-16, and this is how the Java programming language represents text. In UTF-16 all the values between 0x0000 and 0xffff map directly to Unicode characters. The supplementary characters are encoded by a pair of 16-bit values: The first value in the pair comes from the *high-surrogates* range, and the second comes from the *low-surrogates* range. Methods that want to work with individual code point values can either accept a UTF-16 encoded `char[]` of length two, or a single `int` that holds the code point directly. An individual `char` in a UTF-16 sequence is termed a *code unit.*

The first 256 characters of Unicode are the Latin-1 character set, and most of the first 128 characters of Latin-1 are equivalent to the 7-bit ASCII character set. Current environments read ASCII or Latin-1 files, converting them to Unicode on the fly.[1]

Few existing text editors support Unicode characters, so you can use the *escape sequence* \u*xxxx* to encode Unicode characters, where each *x* is a hexadecimal digit (0–9, and a–f or A–F to represent decimal values 10–15). This sequence can appear anywhere in code—not only in character and string constants but also in identifiers. More than one u may appear at the beginning; thus, the character ⬦ can be written as \u0b87 or \uuu0b87.[2] Also note that if your editor does support Unicode characters (or a subset), you may need to tell your compiler if your source code contains any character that is not part of the default character

---

[1] The Java programming language tracks the Unicode standard. See "Further Reading" on page 755 for reference information. The currently supported Unicode version is listed in the documentation of the `Character` class.

[2] There is a good reason to allow multiple u's. When translating a Unicode file into an ASCII file, you must translate Unicode characters that are outside the ASCII range into an escape sequence. Thus, you would translate ⬦ into \u0b87. When translating back, you make the reverse substitution. But what if the original Unicode source had not contained ⬦ but had used \u0b87 instead? Then the reverse translation would not result in the original source (to the parser, it would be equivalent, but possibly not to the reader of the code). The solution is to have the translator add an extra u when it encounters an existing \u*xxxx,* and have the reverse translator remove a u and, if there aren't any left, replace the escape sequence with its equivalent Unicode character.

encoding for your system—such as through a command-line option that names the source character set.

Exercise 7.1: Just for fun, write a "Hello, World" program entirely using Unicode escape sequences.

7.1.2   Comments

Comments within source code exist for the convenience of human programmers. They play no part in the generation of code and so are ignored during scanning. There are three kinds of comments:

`// comment`	Characters from `//` to the end of the line are ignored.
`/* comment */`	All characters between `/*` and the next `*/` are ignored.
`/** comment */`	All characters between `/**` and the next `*/` are ignored. These documentation comments come immediately before identifier declarations and are included in automatically generated documentation. These comments are described in Chapter 19.

Comments can include any valid Unicode character, such as yin-yang (`\u262f`), asterism (`\u2042`), interrobang (`\u203d`), won (`\u20a9`), scruple (`\u2108`), or a snowman (`\u2603`).[3]

Comments do not nest. This following tempting code does not compile:

```
/* Comment this out for now: not implemented
    /* Do some really neat stuff */
    universe.neatStuff();
*/
```

The first `/*` starts a comment; the very next `*/` ends it, leaving the code that follows to be parsed; and the invalid, stand-alone `*/` is a syntax error. The best way to remove blocks of code from programs is either to put a `//` at the beginning of each line or use `if (false)` like this:

```
if (false) {
    // invoke this method when it works
    dwim();
}
```

---

[3]   These characters are ☯, ⁂, ‽, ₩, ⸮, and ☃, respectively.

This technique requires that the code to be removed is complete enough to compile without error. In this case we assume that the `dwim` method is defined somewhere.

7.1.3   Tokens

The *tokens* of a language are its basic words. A parser breaks source code into tokens and then tries to figure out which statements, identifiers, and so forth make up the code. *Whitespace* (spaces, tabs, newlines, and form feeds) is not significant except to separate tokens or as the contents of character or string literals. You can take any valid code and replace any amount of intertoken whitespace (whitespace outside strings and characters) with a different amount of whitespace (but not none) without changing the meaning of the program.

Whitespace must be used to separate tokens that would otherwise constitute a single token. For example, in the statement

```
return 0;
```

you cannot drop the space between `return` and 0 because that would create

```
return0;
```

consisting of the single identifier `return0`. Use extra whitespace appropriately to make your code human-readable, even though the parser ignores it. Note that the parser treats comments as whitespace.

The tokenizer is a "greedy" tokenizer. It grabs as many characters as it can to build up the next token, not caring if this creates an invalid sequence of tokens. So because ++ is longer than +, the expression

```
j = i+++++i;    // INVALID
```

is interpreted as the invalid expression

```
j = i++ ++ +i;  // INVALID
```

instead of the valid

```
j = i++ + ++i;
```

7.1.4   Identifiers

Identifiers, used for names of declared entities such as variables, constants, and labels, must start with a letter, followed by letters, digits, or both. The terms *letter* and *digit* are broad in Unicode: If something is considered a letter or digit in a human language, you can probably use it in identifiers. "Letters" can come from

Armenian, Korean, Gurmukhi, Georgian, Devanagari, and almost any other script written in the world today. Thus, not only is kitty a valid identifier, but mačka, кошка, پیشی, புனைக்குட்டி, and 猫 are, too.[4] Letters also include any currency symbol (such as $, ¥, and £) and connecting punctuation (such as _).

Any difference in characters within an identifier makes that identifier unique. Case is significant: A, a, á, À, Å, and so on are different identifiers. Characters that look the same, or nearly the same, can be confused. For example, the Latin capital letter n "N" and the Greek capital ν "N" look alike but are different characters (\u004e and \u039d, respectively). The only way to avoid confusion is to write each identifier in one language—and thus in one known set of characters—so that programmers trying to type the identifier will know whether you meant E or E.[5]

Identifiers can be as long as you like, but use some taste. Identifiers that are too long are hard to use correctly and actually obscure your code.

7.1.5 Keywords

Language keywords cannot be used as identifiers because they have special meaning within the language. The following table lists the keywords (keywords marked with a [†] are reserved but currently unused):

abstract	continue	for	new	switch
assert	default	goto[†]	package	synchronized
boolean	do	if	private	this
break	double	implements	protected	throw
byte	else	import	public	throws
case	enum	instanceof	return	transient
catch	extends	int	short	try
char	final	interface	static	void
class	finally	long	strictfp	volatile
const[†]	float	native	super	while

Although they appear to be keywords, null, true, and false are formally literals, just like the number 12, so they do not appear in the above table. However, you cannot use null, true, or false as identifiers, just as you cannot use 12 as an identifier. These words can be used as parts of identifiers, as in annulled, construe, and falsehood.

---

[4] These are the word "cat" or "kitty" in English, Serbo-Croatian, Russian, Persian, Tamil, and Japanese, respectively.

[5] One is a Cyrillic letter, the other is ASCII. Guess which is which and win a prize.

7.2   Types and Literals

Every expression has a type that determines what values the expression can produce. The type of an expression is determined by the types of values and variables used within that expression. Types are divided into the primitive types and the reference types.

The primitive data types are:

boolean	either `true` or `false`
char	16-bit Unicode UTF-16 code unit (unsigned)
byte	8-bit signed two's-complement integer
short	16-bit signed two's-complement integer
int	32-bit signed two's-complement integer
long	64-bit signed two's-complement integer
float	32-bit IEEE 754 floating-point number
double	64-bit IEEE 754 floating-point number

Each primitive data type has a corresponding class type in the `java.lang` package. These *wrapper classes*—`Boolean`, `Character`, `Byte`, `Short`, `Integer`, `Long`, `Float`, and `Double`—also define useful constants and methods. For example, most wrapper classes declare constants `MIN_VALUE` and `MAX_VALUE` that hold the minimum and maximum values for the associated primitive type.

The `Float` and `Double` classes also have `NaN`, `NEGATIVE_INFINITY`, and `POSITIVE_INFINITY` constants. Both also provide an `isNaN` method that tests whether a floating-point value is "Not a Number"—that is, whether it is the result of a floating-point expression that has no valid result, such as dividing zero by zero. The `NaN` value can be used to indicate an invalid floating-point value; this is similar to the use of `null` for object references that do not refer to anything. The wrapper classes are covered in detail in Chapter 8.

There is no unsigned integer type. If you need to work with unsigned values originating outside your program, they must be stored in a larger signed type. For example, unsigned bytes produced by an analog-to-digital converter, can be read into variables of type `short`.

The reference types are class types, interface types, and array types. Variables of these types can refer to objects of the corresponding type.

Each type has *literals*, which are the way that constant values of that type are written. The next few subsections describe how literal (unnamed) constants for each type are specified.

7.2.1 Reference Literals

The only literal object reference is `null`. It can be used anywhere a reference is expected. Conventionally, `null` represents an invalid or uncreated object. It has no class, not even `Object`, but `null` can be assigned to any reference variable.

7.2.2 Boolean Literals

The boolean literals are `true` and `false`.

7.2.3 Character Literals

Character literals appear with single quotes: `'Q'`. Any valid Unicode character can appear between the quotes. You can use `\u`*xxxx* for Unicode characters inside character literals just as you can elsewhere. Certain special characters can be represented by an *escape sequence:*

`\n`	newline (`\u000A`)
`\t`	tab (`\u0009`)
`\b`	backspace (`\u0008`)
`\r`	return (`\u000D`)
`\f`	form feed (`\u000C`)
`\\`	backslash itself (`\u005C`)
`\'`	single quote (`\u0027`)
`\"`	double quote (`\u0022`)
`\`*ddd*	a `char` by octal value, where each *d* is one of 0–7

Octal character constants can have three or fewer digits and cannot exceed `\377` (`\u00ff`)—for example, the character literal `'\12'` is the same as `'\n'`. Supplemental characters can not be represented in a character literal.

7.2.4 Integer Literals

Integer constants are strings of octal, decimal, or hexadecimal digits. The start of a constant declares the number's base: A 0 (zero) starts an octal number (base 8); a `0x` or `0X` starts a hexadecimal number (base 16); and any other digit starts a decimal number (base 10). All the following numbers have the same value:

```
29 035 0x1D 0X1d
```

Integer constants are `long` if they end in L or l, such as `29L`; L is preferred over l because l (lowercase L) can easily be confused with 1 (the digit one). Otherwise, integer constants are assumed to be of type `int`. If an `int` literal is directly assigned to a `short`, and its value is within the valid range for a `short`, the integer literal is treated as if it were a `short` literal. A similar allowance is made for integer literals assigned to `byte` variables. In all other cases you must explicitly cast when assigning `int` to `short` or `byte` (see "Explicit Type Casts" on page 219).

7.2.5   Floating-Point Literals

Floating-point constants are expressed in either decimal or hexadecimal form. The decimal form consists of a string of decimal digits with an optional decimal point, optionally followed by an exponent—the letter *e* or *E,* followed by an optionally signed integer. At least one digit must be present. All these literals denote the same floating-point number:

```
18.   1.8e1   .18E+2   180.0e-1
```

The hexadecimal form consists of 0x (or 0X), a string of hexadecimal digits with an optional hexadecimal point, followed by a mandatory binary exponent—the letter *p* or *P,* followed by an optionally signed integer. The binary exponent represents scaling by two raised to a power. All these literals also denote the same floating-point number (decimal 18.0):

```
0x12p0   0x1.2p4   0x.12P+8   0x120p-4
```

Floating-point constants are of type `double` unless they are specified with a trailing f or F, which makes them `float` constants, such as `18.0f`. A trailing d or D specifies a `double` constant. There are two zeros: positive (`0.0`) and negative (`-0.0`). Positive and negative zero are considered equal when you use == but produce different results when used in some calculations. For example, if dividing by zero, the expression `1d/0d` is +∞, whereas `1d/-0d` is -∞. There are no literals to represent either infinity or NaN, only the symbolic constants defined in the `Float` and `Double` classes—see Chapter 8.

A `double` constant cannot be assigned directly to a `float` variable, even if the value of the `double` is within the valid `float` range. The only constants you may directly assign to `float` variables and fields are `float` constants.

7.2.6   String Literals

String literals appear with double quotes: `"along"`. Any character can be included in string literals, with the exception of newline and " (double quote). Newlines are not allowed in the middle of strings. If you want to embed a newline character in the string, use the escape sequence \n. To embed a double quote use the escape sequence \". A string literal references an object of type `String`. To learn more about strings, see Chapter 13.

Characters in strings can be specified with the octal digit syntax, but all three octal digits should be used to prevent accidents when an octal value is specified next to a valid octal digit in the string. For example, the string "\0116" is equivalent to "\t6", whereas the string "\116" is equivalent to "N".

7.2.7   Class Literals

Every type (primitive or reference) has an associated instance of class `Class` that represents that type. These instances are often referred to as the *class object* for a given type. You can name the class object for a type directly by following the type name with ".class", as in

```
String.class
java.lang.String.class
java.util.Iterator.class
boolean.class
```

The first two of these class literals refer to the same instance of class `Class` because `String` and `java.lang.String` are two different names for the same type. The third class literal is a reference to the `Class` instance for the `Iterator` interface mentioned on page 129. The last is the `Class` instance that represents the primitive type `boolean`.

Since class `Class` is generic, the actual type of the class literal for a reference type T is `Class<T>`, while for primitive types it is `Class<W>` where W is the wrapper class for that primitive type. But note, for example, that `boolean.class` and `Boolean.class` are two different objects of type `Class<Boolean>`. Generic types are discussed in Chapter 11, and the class `Class` is discussed in Chapter 16.

Exercise 7.2: Write a class that declares a field for each of the primitive numeric types, and try to assign values using the different literal forms—for example, try to assign 3.5f to an `int` field. Which literals can be used with which type of field? Try changing the magnitude of the values used to see if that affects things.

7.3   Variables

A *variable* is a storage location[6]—something that can hold a value—to which a

---

[6]   *Type variables* are not storage locations and are excluded from this discussion. They apply only to generic type declarations and are discussed in Chapter 11.

value can be assigned. Variables include fields, local variables in a block of code, and parameters. A variable *declaration* states the identifier (name), type, and other attributes of a variable. The type part of a declaration specifies which kinds of values and behavior are supported by the declared entity. The other attributes of a variable include *annotations* and *modifiers.* Annotations can be applied to any variable declaration and are discussed in Chapter 15.

7.3.1   Field and Local Variable Declarations

Fields and local variables are declared in the same way. A declaration is broken into three parts: *modifiers,* followed by a *type,* followed by a list of *identifiers.* Each identifier can optionally have an *initializer* associated with it to give it an initial value.

There is no difference between variables declared in one declaration or in multiple declarations of the same type. For example:

```
float x, y;
```

is the same as

```
float x;
float y;
```

Any initializer is expressed as an assignment (with the = operator) of an expression of the appropriate type. For example:

```
float x = 3.14f, y = 2.81f;
```

is the same as the more readable

```
float x = 3.14f,
      y = 2.81f;
```

is the same as the preferred

```
float x = 3.14f;
float y = 2.81f;
```

Field variables are members of classes, or interfaces, and are declared within the body of that class or interface. Fields can be initialized with an initializer, within an initialization block, or within a constructor, but need not be initialized at all because they have default initial values, as discussed on page 44. Field initialization and the modifiers that can be applied to fields were discussed in Chapter 2.

Local variables can be declared anywhere within a block of statements, not just at the start of the block, and can be of primitive or reference type. As a special case, a local variable declaration is also permitted within the initialization section of a for loop—see "for" on page 236. A local variable must be assigned a value before it is used.[7] There is no default initialization value for local variables because failure to assign a starting value for one is usually a bug. The compiler will refuse to compile code that doesn't ensure that assignment takes place before a variable is used:

```
int x;      // uninitialized, can't use
int y = 2;
x = y * y; // now x has a value
int z = x; // okay, safe to use x
```

Local variables cease to exist when the flow of control reaches the end of the block in which they were declared—though any referenced object is subject to normal garbage collection rules.

Apart from annotations, the only modifier that can be applied to a local variable is final. This is required when the local variable will be accessed by a local or anonymous inner class—see also the discussion of final variables below.

7.3.2   Parameter Variables

Parameter variables are the parameters declared in methods, constructors, or catch blocks—see "try, catch, and finally" on page 286. A parameter declaration consists of an optional modifier, a type name, and a single identifier.

Parameters cannot have explicit initializers because they are implicitly initialized with the value of the argument passed when the method or constructor is invoked, or with a reference to the exception object caught in the catch block. Parameter variables cease to exist when the block in which they appear completes.

As with local variables, the only modifiers that can be applied to a parameter are annotations, or the final modifier.

7.3.3   final Variables

The final modifier declares that the value of the variable is set exactly once and will thereafter always have the same value—it is *immutable*. Any variable—fields, local variables, or parameters—can be declared final. Variables that are final

---

[7]   In technical terms there is a concept of a variable being *"definitely assigned."* The compiler won't allow the use of a local variable unless it can determine that it has been definitely assigned a value.

must be initialized before they are used. This is typically done directly in the declaration:

```
final int id = nextID++;
```

You can defer the initialization of a final field or local variable. Such a final variable is called a *blank final*. A blank final field must be initialized within an initialization block or constructor (if it's an instance field) while a blank final local variable, like any local variable, must be initialized before it is used.

Blank final fields are useful when the value of the field is determined by a constructor argument:

```
class NamedObj {
    final String name;

    NamedObj(String name) {
        this.name = name;
    }
}
```

or when you must calculate the value in something more sophisticated than an initializer expression:

```
static final int[] numbers = numberList();
static final int maxNumber; // max value in numbers

static {
    int max = numbers[0];
    for (int num : numbers) {
        if (num > max)
            max = num;
    }
    maxNumber = max;
}

static int[] numberList() {
    // ...
}
```

The compiler will verify that all static final fields are initialized by the end of any static initializer blocks, and that non-static final fields are initialized by the end of all construction paths for an object. A compile-time error will occur if the compiler cannot determine that this happens.

Blank final local variables are useful when the value to be assigned to the variable is conditional on the value of other variables. As with all local variables, the compiler will ensure that a final local variable is initialized before it is used.

Local variables and parameters are usually declared final only when they will be accessed by a local, or anonymous inner, class—though some people advocate always making parameters final, both as a matter of style, and to avoid accidentally assigning a value to a parameter, when a field or other variable was intended. Issues regarding when you should, and should not, use `final` on fields were discussed on page 46.

7.4   Array Variables

Arrays provide ordered collections of elements. Components of an array can be primitive types or references to objects, including references to other arrays. Arrays themselves are objects and extend `Object`. The declaration

```
int[] ia = new int[3];
```

declares an array named `ia` that initially refers to an array of three `int` values.

Array dimensions are omitted in the type declaration of an array variable. The number of components in an array is determined when it is *created* using `new`, not when an array variable is declared. An array object's length is fixed at its creation and cannot be changed. Note that it is the length of the array *object* that is fixed. In the example, a new array of a different size could be assigned to the array variable `ia` at any time.

You access array elements by their position in the array. The first element of an array has index 0 (zero), and the last element has index *length*–1. You access an element by using the name of the array and the index enclosed between [and]. In our example, the first element of the array is `ia[0]` and last element of the array is `ia[2]`. Every index use is checked to ensure that it is within the proper range for that array, throwing an `ArrayIndexOutOfBoundsException` if the index is out of bounds.[8] The index expression must be of type `int`—this limits the maximum size of an array.

---

[8]   The range check can often be optimized away when, for example, it can be proved that a loop index variable is always within range, but you are guaranteed that an index will never be used if it is out of range.

The length of an array is available from its `length` field (which is implicitly `public` and `final`). In our example, the following code would loop over the array, printing each value:

```
for (int i = 0; i < ia.length; i++)
    System.out.println(i + ": " + ia[i]);
```

An array with length zero is said to be an *empty* array. There is a big difference between a `null` array reference and a reference to an empty array—an empty array is a real object, it simply has no elements. Empty arrays are useful for returning from methods instead of returning `null`. If a method can return `null`, then users of the method must explicitly check the return value for `null` before using it. On the other hand, if the method returns an array that may be empty, no special checking is needed provided the user always uses the array length to check valid indices.

If you prefer, you can put the array brackets after the variable name instead of after the type:

```
int ia[] = new int[3];
```

This code is equivalent to the original definition of `ia`. However, the first style is preferable because it places the type declaration entirely in one place.

7.4.1   Array Modifiers

The normal modifiers can be applied to array variables, depending on whether the array is a field or local variable. The important thing to remember is that the modifiers apply to the array variable *not* to the elements of the array the variable references. An array variable that is declared `final` means that the array reference cannot be changed after initialization. It does not mean that array elements cannot be changed. There is no way to apply any modifiers (specifically `final` and `volatile`) to the elements of an array.

7.4.2   Arrays of Arrays

You can have arrays of arrays. The code to declare and print a two-dimensional matrix, for example, might look like this:

```
float[][] mat = new float[4][4];
setupMatrix(mat);
for (int y = 0; y < mat.length; y++) {
    for (int x = 0; x < mat[y].length; x++)
```

```
        System.out.print(mat[y][x] + " ");
    System.out.println();
}
```

The first (left-most) dimension of an array must be specified when the array is created. Other dimensions can be left unspecified, to be filled in later. Specifying more than the first dimension is a shorthand for a nested set of new statements. Our new creation could have been written more explicitly as:

```
float[][] mat = new float[4][];
for (int y = 0; y < mat.length; y++)
    mat[y] = new float[4];
```

One advantage of arrays of arrays is that each nested array can have a different size. You can emulate a 4×4 matrix, but you can also create an array of four int arrays, each of which has a different length sufficient to hold its own data.

7.4.3 Array Initialization

When an array is created, each element is set to the default initial value for its type—zero for the numeric types, '\u0000' for char, false for boolean, and null for reference types. When you declare an array of a reference type, you are really declaring an array of variables of that type. Consider the following code:

```
Attr[] attrs = new Attr[12];

for (int i = 0; i < attrs.length; i++)
    attrs[i] = new Attr(names[i], values[i]);
```

After the initial new of the array, attrs has a reference to an array of 12 variables that are initialized to null. The Attr objects themselves are created only when the loop is executed.

You can initialize arrays with comma separated values inside braces following their declaration. The following array declaration creates and initializes an array:

```
String[] dangers = { "Lions", "Tigers", "Bears" };
```

The following code gives the same result:

```
String[] dangers = new String[3];

dangers[0] = "Lions";
dangers[1] = "Tigers";
dangers[2] = "Bears";
```

When you initialize an array within its declaration, you don't have to explicitly create the array using new—it is done implicitly for you by the system. The length of the array to create is determined by the number of initialization values given. You can use new explicitly if you prefer, but in that case you have to omit the array length, because again it is determined from the initializer list.

```
String[] dangers = new String[]{"Lions", "Tigers", "Bears"};
```

This form of array creation expression allows you to create and initialize an array anywhere. For example, you can create and initialize an array when you invoke a method:

```
printStrings(new String[] { "one", "two", "many" });
```

An unnamed array created with new in this way is called an *anonymous array*.

The last value in the initializer list is also allowed to have a comma after it. This is a convenience for multiline initializers so you can reorder, add, or remove values, without having to remember to add a comma to the old last line, or remove it from the new last line.

Arrays of arrays can be initialized by nesting array initializers. Here is a declaration that initializes an array to the top few rows of Pascal's triangle, with each row represented by its own array:

```
int[][] pascalsTriangle = {
        { 1 },
        { 1, 1 },
        { 1, 2, 1 },
        { 1, 3, 3, 1 },
        { 1, 4, 6, 4, 1 },
    };
```

Indices in an array of arrays work from the outermost inward. For example, in the above array, pascalsTriangle[0] refers to the int array that has one element, pascalsTriangle[1] refers to the int array that has two elements, and so forth.

For convenience, the System class provides an arraycopy method that allows you to assign the values from one array into another, instead of looping through each of the array elements—this is described in more detail in "Utility Methods" on page 665.

7.4.4   Arrays and Types

Arrays are implicit extensions of Object. Given a class X, classes Y and Z that extend X, and arrays of each, the class hierarchy looks something like this:

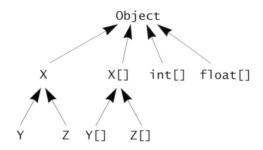

This class relationship allows polymorphism for arrays. You can assign an array to a variable of type Object and cast it back. An array of objects of type Y is usable wherever an array of objects of its supertype X is required. This seems natural but can require a run time check that is sometimes unexpected. An array of X can contain either Y or Z references, but an array of Y cannot contain references to X or Z objects. The following code would generate an ArrayStoreException at run time on either of its final two lines, which violate this rule:

```
Y[] yArray = new Y[3];      // a Y array
X[] xArray = yArray;        // valid: Y is assignable to X
xArray[0] = new Y();
xArray[2] = new X();        // INVALID: can't store X in Y[]
xArray[1] = new Z();        // INVALID: can't store Z in Y[]
```

If xArray were a reference to a real X[] object, it would be valid to store both an X and a Z object into it. But xArray actually refers to a Y[] object so it is not valid to store either an X reference or a Z reference in it. Such assignments are checked at run time if needed to ensure that no improper reference is stored into an array.

Like any other object, arrays are created and are subject to normal garbage collection mechanisms. They inherit all the methods of Object and additionally implement the Cloneable interface (see page 101) and the Serializable interface (see "Object Serialization" on page 549). Since arrays define no methods of their own, but just inherit those of Object, the equals method is always based on identity, not equivalence. The utility methods of the java.util.Arrays class—see "The Arrays Utility Class" on page 607—allow you to compare arrays for equivalence, and to calculate a hash code based on the contents of the array.

The major limitation on the "object-ness" of arrays is that they cannot be extended to add new methods. The following construct is not valid:

```
class ScaleVector extends double[] { // INVALID
    // ...
}
```

In a sense, arrays behave like final classes.

Exercise 7.3: Write a program that calculates Pascal's triangle to a depth of 12, storing each row of the triangle in an array of the appropriate length and putting each of the row arrays into an array of 12 `int` arrays. Design your solution so that the results are printed by a method that prints the array of arrays using the lengths of each array, not a constant 12. Now change the code to use a constant other than 12 without modifying your printing method.

7.5   The Meanings of Names

Identifiers give names to a range of things within our programs—types, variables, fields, methods, and so forth. When you use a particular name in your program, the compiler has to determine what that name refers to, so that it can decide if you are using the name correctly and so that it can generate the appropriate code. The rules for determining the meaning of a name trade off convenience with complexity. At one extreme the language could require that every name in a program be unique—this makes things simple for the compiler but makes life very inconvenient for the programmer. If names are interpreted based on the context in which they are used, the programmer gets the convenience of reusing names (such as always using the name i for a `for` loop counter), but the compiler has to be able to determine what each name means—and so does any human being reading the code.

Name management is achieved with two mechanisms. First, the *namespace* is partitioned to give different namespaces for different kinds of names. Second, scoping is used to control the visibility of names declared in one part of a program to other parts. Different namespaces allow you to give the same name to a method and a field (not that we recommend doing this), and scoping allows you to use the same name for all your `for` loop counters.

There are six different namespaces:

- package names,
- type names,

- ◆ field names,
- ◆ method names,
- ◆ local variable names (including parameters), and
- ◆ labels

When a name is used in a program, its context helps determine what kind of name it is. For example, in the expression x.f = 3, we know that f must be a field—it can't be a package, type, method, or label because we are assigning a value to it, and it can't be a local variable because we are accessing it as a member of x. We know that x must be a typename, or a field, or a local variable that is an object reference—exactly which one is determined by searching the enclosing scope for an appropriate declaration, as you will see.

The use of separate namespaces gives you greater flexibility when writing code (especially when combining code from different sources) but can be abused. Consider this pathological, but perfectly valid, piece of code:

```
package Reuse;
class Reuse {
    Reuse Reuse(Reuse Reuse) {
        Reuse:
        for (;;) {
            if (Reuse.Reuse(Reuse) == Reuse)
                break Reuse;
        }
        return Reuse;
    }
}
```

Every declaration of a name has a scope in which that name can be used. The exact rules differ depending on the kind of name—type name, member name, local variable, and so on. For example, the scope of a parameter in a method is the entire body of that method; the scope of a local variable is the block in which the local variable is declared; the scope of a loop variable declared in the initialization section of a for loop is the rest of that for loop.

A name cannot be used outside its scope—for example, one method in a class cannot refer to the parameter of another method. However, scopes also nest and an inner scope has access to all names declared in the outer scope before the inner scope is entered. For example, the body of a for loop can access the local variables of the method in which it was declared.

When a name that could be a variable is used, the meaning of the name is determined by searching the current and enclosing scopes for declarations of that name in the different namespaces. The search order is:

1. Local variables declared in the code block, for loop, or as parameters to the catch clause of a try statement. Then local variables declared in any enclosing code block. This applies recursively up to the method containing the block, or until there is no enclosing block (as in the case of an initialization block).

2. If the code is in a method or constructor, the parameters to the method or constructor.

3. A field of the class or interface, including any accessible inherited fields.

4. If the type is a nested type, a variable in the enclosing block or field of the enclosing class. If the type is a static nested type, only static fields of an enclosing type are searched. This search rule is applied successively to any enclosing blocks and types further out.

5. A static field of a class, or interface, specifically declared in a static import statement.

6. A static field of a class, or interface, declared in a static import on demand statement.

For method names a similar process as for fields is followed, but starting at step 3, searching for methods in the current class or interface. There are special rules for determining how members of a class are accessed, as you'll see in "Member Access" on page 223.

The order of searching determines which declaration will be found. This implies that names declared in outer scopes can be hidden by names declared in inner scopes. And that means, for example, that local variable names can hide class member names, that nested class members can hide enclosing instance members, and that locally declared class members can hide inherited class members—as you have already seen.[9]

Hiding is generally bad style because a human reading the code must check all levels of the hierarchy to determine which variable is being used. Yet hiding is permitted in order to make local code robust. If hiding outer variables were not allowed, adding a new field to a class or interface could break existing code in

---

[9] Technically, the term *hiding* is reserved for this last case—when an inherited member is hidden by a locally declared member—and the other situations are referred to as *shadowing*. This distinction is not significant for this book so we simply refer to "hiding."

subtypes that used variables of the same name. Scoping is meant as protection for the system as a whole rather than as support for reusing identifier names.

To avoid confusion, hiding is not permitted in nested scopes within a code block. This means that a local variable in a method cannot have the same name as a parameter of that method; that a for loop variable cannot have the same name as a local variable or parameter; and that once there is a local variable called, say, über, you cannot create a new, different variable with the name über in a nested block.

```
{
    int über = 0;
    {
        int über = 2; // INVALID: already defined
        // ...
    }
}
```

However, you can have different (non-nested) for loops in the same block, or different (non-nested) blocks in the same method, that do declare variables with the same name.

If a name appears in a place where a type name is expected, then the different type scopes must be searched for that name. Type scopes are defined by packages. The search order is as follows:

1. The current type including inherited types.
2. A nested type of the current type.
3. Explicitly named imported types.
4. Other types declared in the same package.
5. Implicitly named imported types.

Again, hiding of type names is possible, but a type can always be explicitly referred to by its fully qualified name, which includes package information, such as java.lang.String. Packages and type imports are discussed in Chapter 18.

In order to make an apple pie from scratch, you must first create the universe.
—Carl Sagan, *Cosmos*

CHAPTER 8

Primitives as Types

I'm gonna wrap myself in paper,
I'm gonna dab myself with glue,
Stick some stamps on top of my head!
I'm gonna mail myself to you.
—Woody Guthrie, *Mail Myself to You*

THE separation of primitive types (`byte`, `float`, and so on) and reference types (classes and interfaces) is a trade-off between efficiency and familiarity versus expressiveness and consistency. An object may incur too much overhead where a plain `int` will do, while an `int` may be fast and convenient until you need to store it into a hashtable. To smooth this separation, the Java programming language provides a *wrapper* class corresponding to each of the primitive types. Instances of a given wrapper class contain a value of the corresponding primitive type. The type hierarchy for these classes looks like this:

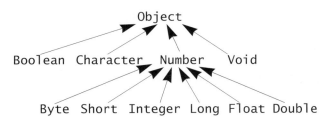

The language provides automatic conversion between primitives and their wrappers in many contexts, specifically when assigning values or passing arguments. For example, you can write:

```
Integer val = 3;
```

And `val` will be assigned a reference to an instance of the `Integer` class that holds the value 3.

Converting a primitive value to a wrapper object is known as a *boxing conversion;* unsurprisingly, extracting a primitive value from a wrapper object is known as an *unboxing conversion.*[1] The details of these conversions are discussed in "Boxing Conversions" on page 198. These automated conversions make it easy to write general purposes classes that are written in terms of `Object` references, but that can handle either reference types or primitive types. The `HashMap` class, for example, stores only references, not primitive types—see "HashMap" on page 590—but an `int` can be passed as a key because it will be converted to an `Integer` instance:

```
int key = ... ;
map.put(key, value);
```

The efficiency and convenience of using an `int` can be maintained, while an object can still be obtained when necessary—the best of both worlds.

A second purpose of the wrapper classes is to provide a home for methods and variables related to the type (such as string conversions and value range constants). Here, for example, is how you might check whether you could use a faster `float` calculation on a particular value or whether the value requires a larger range than a `float` provides and so must be performed as a `double` calculation:

```
double aval = Math.abs(value);
if (Float.MAX_VALUE >= aval && aval >= Float.MIN_VALUE)
    return fasterFloatCalc((float) value);
else
    return slowerDoubleCalc(value);
```

The following sections cover methods and constants specific to each particular wrapper class, but first let's look at some things that are common to most of the wrapper classes.

8.1   Common Fields and Methods

Except where individually noted, the following sections define constructors, constants, and methods that are defined for each of the wrapper classes. The general exception is the `Void` class which supports almost nothing—see page 187.

For the constructors and methods that convert strings into values, each class defines the valid form that the string can take, and these are described in the section for each class. For the numeric types, an invalid string format results in `NumberFormatException` being thrown.

---

[1]   This difference in terminology ("wrap" versus "box") is an historical artifact.

The term *radix,* used in several places in the wrapper classes, is another word for numeric base. For example, decoding a `long` in radix 8 means the same as decoding it in base 8. The allowable range for a radix is 2 through 36.

In the following, *Type* refers to the wrapper class, and *type* is the corresponding primitive type.

8.1.1 Construction

Each wrapper class defines an immutable object for the primitive value that it is wrapping. This means that once a wrapper object has been created, the value represented by that object can never be changed. So, for example, the object created by `new Integer(1)` will always have the value 1, and no methods of class `Integer` allow you to modify this value.

Each wrapper class has the following constructors:

- A constructor that takes a value of the primitive type and creates an object of the corresponding wrapper class. The constructors `Character(char)` and `Integer(int)` are examples.

- A constructor that converts a single `String` parameter into the object's initial value (except `Character`, which has no such constructor)—for example, `new Float("6.02e23")`.

Each wrapper class, *Type,* also has the following methods:

`public static` *Type* **valueOf(*type* t)**
    Returns an object of the specified *Type* with the value t.

`public static` *Type* **valueOf(String str)**
    Returns an object of the specified *Type* with the value parsed from str. `Float.valueOf("6.02e23")` and `Integer.valueOf("16")` are examples. `Character` does not have this method just as it does not have the string-converting constructor.

These methods may return a newly constructed instance or a cached instance. For efficiency, you should always use one of the `valueOf` methods, in preference to direct construction, unless you really need distinct instances that have the same value.

8.1.2 Constants

Each of the wrapper classes, with the exception of `Boolean` define the following three fields:

```
public static final type MIN_VALUE
```
   The minimum value representable by this data type. For example, for Integer this is -2^{31}.

```
public static final type MAX_VALUE
```
   The maximum value representable by this data type. For example, for Integer this is $2^{31}-1$.

```
public static final int SIZE
```
   The number of bits used to represent a value of this type. For example, for Integer this is 32.

All the wrapper classes define the following field:

```
public static final Class<Type> TYPE
```
   A reference to the Class object that represents primitives of this type. These fields are equivalent to the Class objects you can obtain from .class class literal expressions as described in "Class Literals" on page 169. For example, Integer.TYPE is the same Class object you will get from the expression int.class. Note that int.class and Integer.class yield two different Class instances, both of type Class<Integer>.

8.1.3   Common Methods

Each of the wrapper classes implements the Comparable<T> interface and so defines:

```
public int compareTo(Type other)
```
   Returns a value less than, equal to, or greater than zero as the object on which it is invoked is less than, equal to, or greater than the object (of the same type *Type*) passed as a parameter.

For the numeric types, comparison follows the normal arithmetic rules; however, the Float and Double classes have specific ordering properties that differ from float and double—see page 191. For Boolean, the value true is considered greater than false—in contrast to boolean for which the relational operators < and > are not defined. For Character, the comparison is strictly numerical, with no consideration of alphabetic, or locale specific ordering.

   Each class provides a method to extract the wrapped value:

```
public type typeValue()
```
   Returns the primitive value corresponding to the current wrapper object. For example, Integer.valueOf(6).intValue() returns 6.

   And each class overrides the following members of Object:

`public String `**`toString()`**

> Provides a string representation of the wrapper object's value. For the numeric classes base 10 is always used.

`public boolean `**`equals(Object obj)`**

> Returns `true` if the two objects are the same type and wrap the same value. For example, for two `Integer` objects x and y, `x.equals(y)` is true if and only if, `x.intValue() == y.intValue()`. If obj is not of the same type as the current object, or is `null`, `false` is returned.

`public int `**`hashCode()`**

> Returns a value-based hash code for use in hashtables.

The following additional methods convert primitive values to and from strings:

`public static `*`type`*` `**`parse`***`Type`***`(String str)`**

> Converts the string `str` to a value of the specified primitive *type*. For example, `Integer.parseInt("10")` returns the value 10. This is equivalent to invoking the string-converting constructor, and extracting the resulting value with *type*`Value()`, but without constructing an object. `Character` does not have this method just as it does not have the string-converting constructor.

`public static String `**`toString(`***`type`*` `**`val)`**

> Returns a string representation of the given primitive value of type *type*. For example, `Double.toString(0.3e2)` returns the string `"30.0"`.

All wrapper classes have these methods so we do not list them in each class's description. The wrapper class's system property fetch-and-decode methods, described in "System Properties" on page 663, are not discussed in this chapter.

8.2 Void

The `Void` class is the exception to all the preceding rules because it has no values to wrap, provides no methods, and cannot be instantiated. It has only a static TYPE field containing a reference to the `Class` object `void.class`. The language has no `void` type—`void` is a placeholder indicating no return type. The `Void` class represents that lack of an actual return type and is only used in reflection (see "The Method Class" on page 420).

8.3 Boolean

The `Boolean` class represents the `boolean` type as a class. Both the constructor that decodes a string, the `valueOf` method and the `parseBoolean` method understand "true", with any mixture of uppercase and lowercase characters, to be true. Any other string is interpreted as false.

The Boolean class has two static references to objects corresponding to each of the primitive boolean values: Boolean.TRUE and Boolean.FALSE.

8.4   Number

The Number class is an abstract class extended by all wrapper classes that represent primitive numeric types: Byte, Short, Integer, Long, Float, and Double.

The abstract methods of Number return the value of the object converted to any of the numeric types:

```
public byte byteValue()
public short shortValue()
public int intValue()
public long longValue()
public float floatValue()
public double doubleValue()
```

Each extended Number class overrides these methods to convert its own type to any of the others under the same rules used for an explicit cast. For example, given a Float object with the value 32.87, the return value of intValue on the object would be 32, just as "(int) 32.87" would be 32.

8.4.1   The Integer Wrappers

The classes Byte, Short, Integer, and Long extend Number to represent the corresponding integer types as classes. In addition to the standard Number methods, each of the integer wrapper classes supports the following methods:

public static *type* **parse*Type*(String str, int radix)**
> Converts the string str into a numeric value of the specified *type*, using the given radix. For example, Integer.parseInt("1010", 2) returns 10, and Integer.parseInt("-1010", 2) returns –10. The characters in the string must all be valid digits for the given radix, except that the first character may be a minus sign to indicate a negative value. A NumberFormatException is thrown if str contains any other characters (including leading or trailing whitespace), the value is out of range for this type, or radix is out of range.

public static *Type* **valueOf(String str, int radix)**
> Returns a wrapper object of class *Type* with the value obtained by decoding str using the specified radix. Note that there are no equivalent constructors

with this form. This is equivalent to the two-step process of parsing the string and using that value to construct a new wrapper object. For example, `Integer.valueOf("1010", 2)` is equivalent to the more verbose expression new `Integer(Integer.parseInt("1010", 2))`.

public static *Type* **decode(String str)**

Returns a wrapper object of class *Type* with the value obtained by decoding `str`. A leading – character indicates a negative value. The base of the number is encoded in `str`: Hexadecimal numbers start with #, 0x, or 0X, while octal numbers are indicated by a leading 0; otherwise, the number is presumed to be decimal. This is in contrast to the parse*Type* and `valueOf` methods, to which you pass the radix as an argument. For example, `Long.decode("0xABCD")` returns a `Long` with the value 43981, while `Long.decode("ABCD")` throws a `NumberFormatException`. Conversely, `Long.parseLong("0xABCD", 16)` throws a `NumberFormatException`, while `Long.parseLong("ABCD", 16)` returns a `Long` with the value 43981. (The character # is used in many external data formats for hexadecimal numbers, so it is convenient that `decode` understands it.)

For each class, the string-based constructor, parse*Type*(String str) method, and `valueOf` methods work like parse*Type*(String str, int radix), with a radix of 10 if none is specified

In addition, the `Integer` and `Long` classes each have the following methods, where *type* is either `int` or `long`, respectively:

public static String toString(*type* **val, int radix)**

Returns a string representation of the given value in the given radix. If radix is out of range then a radix of 10 is used.

public static String toBinaryString(*type* **val)**

Returns a string representation of the two's complement bit pattern of the given value. For positive values this is the same as `toString(value, 2)`. For negative values the sign of the value is encoded in the bit pattern, not as a leading minus character. For example, `Integer.toBinaryString(-10)` returns `"11111111111111111111111111110110"`. These string representations for negative values cannot be used with corresponding parse*Type* methods because the magnitude represented by the string will always be greater than MAX_VALUE for the given type.

public static String toOctalString(*type* **val)**

Returns a string representation of the given value in an unsigned base 8 format. For example, `Integer.toOctalString(10)` returns `"12"`. Negative values are treated as described in `toBinaryString`. For example, `Integer.toOctalString(-10)` returns `"37777777766"`.

`public static String` **`toHexString(`***`type`* **`val)`**
Returns a string representation of the given value in an unsigned base 16 format. For example, `Integer.toHexString(10)` returns "a". Negative values are treated as described in `toBinaryString`. For example, `Integer.toHexString(-10)` returns "fffffff6".

Note that none of the string formats include information regarding the radix in that format—there is no leading 0 for octal, or 0x for hexadecimal. If radix information is needed then you must construct it yourself.

The `Short`, `Integer`, and `Long` classes have a method `reverseBytes` that returns a value with its constituent bytes in the reverse order to the value passed in. For example, `Integer.reverseBytes(0x0000ABCD)` returns an `int` value with the hexadecimal representation of `0xCDAB0000`. The `Integer` and `Long` classes also provide a family of bit-querying methods:

`public static int` **`bitCount(`***`type`* **`val)`**
Returns the number of one-bits in the two's complement binary representations of `val`.

`public static` *`type`* **`highestOneBit(`***`type`* **`val)`**
Returns a value consisting of all zero-bits, except for a single one-bit, in the same position as the highest-order (left-most) one-bit in `val`.

`public static` *`type`* **`lowestOneBit(`***`type`* **`val)`**
Returns a value consisting of all zero-bits, except for a single one-bit, in the same position as the lowest-order (right-most) one-bit in `val`.

`public static int` **`numberOfLeadingZeros(`***`type`* **`val)`**
Returns the number of zero-bits preceding the highest-order one-bit in `val`.

`public static int` **`numberOfTrailingZeros(`***`type`* **`val)`**
Returns the number of zero-bits following the lowest-order one-bit in `val`.

`public static` *`type`* **`reverse(`***`type`* **`val)`**
Returns the value obtained by reversing the order of the bits in `val`.

`public static` *`type`* **`rotateLeft(`***`type`* **`val,`** **`int distance)`**
Returns the value obtained by rotating the bits in `val` to the left. In a left rotation the high-order bit moved out on the left becomes the lowest-order bit on the right. Rotating to the left by a negative distance is the same as rotating to the right by a positive distance.

`public static` *`type`* **`rotateRight(`***`type`* **`val,`** **`int distance)`**
Returns the value obtained by rotating the bits in `val` to the right. In a right rotation the low-order bit moved out on the right becomes the highest-order bit on the left. Rotating to the right by a negative distance is the same as rotating to the left by a positive distance.

Finally, the `Integer` and `Long` classes also define the mathematical `signum` function. This function takes a value and returns –1, 0, or +1 as the value is negative, zero, or positive, respectively.

8.4.2   The Floating-Point Wrapper Classes

The `Float` and `Double` classes extend `Number` to represent the `float` and `double` types as classes. With only a few exceptions, the names of the methods and constants are the same for both types. In the following list, the types for the `Float` class are shown, but `Float` and `float` can be changed to `Double` and `double`, respectively, to get equivalent fields and methods for the `Double` class. In addition to the standard `Number` methods, `Float` and `Double` have the following constants and methods:

`public final static float` **POSITIVE_INFINITY**
> The value for +∞.

`public final static float` **NEGATIVE_INFINITY**
> The value for –∞.

`public final static float` **NaN**
> Not-a-Number. This constant gives you a way to get a NaN value, not to test one. Surprising as it may be, `NaN == NaN` is always false because a NaN value, not being a number, is equal to no value, not even itself. To test whether a number is NaN, you must use the `isNaN` method.

`public static boolean` **isNaN(float val)**
> Returns `true` if `val` is a Not-a-Number (NaN) value.

`public static boolean` **isInfinite(float val)**
> Returns `true` if `val` is either positive or negative infinity.

`public boolean` **isNaN()**
> Returns `true` if this object's value is a Not-a-Number (NaN) value.

`public boolean` **isInfinite()**
> Returns `true` if this object's value is either positive or negative infinity.

In addition to the usual constructor forms, `Float` has a constructor that takes a `double` argument to use as its initial value after conversion to `float`.

Comparison of `Float` and `Double` objects behaves differently than `float` and `double` values. Each wrapper class defines a sorting order that treats –0 less than +0, NaNs greater than all values (including +∞), and all NaNs equal to each other.

When converting to a string, NaN values return the string `"NaN"`, +∞ returns `"Infinity"` and –∞ returns `"-Infinity"`. The string-taking constructor, and the parse*Type* method are defined in terms of the `valueOf` method, which accepts strings in the following form:

- The values "NaN" or "Infinity" with an optional leading + or – character
- A floating-point literal
- A hexadecimal floating-point literal

In contrast to the integer wrapper classes, the string is first stripped of leading and trailing whitespace. If the literal forms contain a trailing float or double specifier, such as "1.0f", the specifier is ignored and the string is converted directly to a value of the requested type.

To let you manipulate the bits inside a floating-point value's representation, `Float` provides methods to get the bit pattern as an `int`, as well as a way to convert a bit pattern in an `int` to a `float` value (according to the appropriate IEEE 754 floating-point bit layout). The `Double` class provides equivalent methods to turn a `double` value into a `long` bit pattern and vice versa:

public static int **floatToIntBits(float val)**
> Returns the bit representation of the `float` value as an `int`. All NaN values are always represented by the same bit pattern.

public static int **floatToRawIntBits(float val)**
> Equivalent to `floatToIntBits` except that the actual bit pattern for a NaN is returned, rather than all NaNs being mapped to a single value.

public static float **intBitsToFloat(int bits)**
> Returns the `float` corresponding to the given bit pattern.

8.5 Character

The `Character` class represents the `char` type as a class. It provides methods for determining the type of a character (letter, digit, uppercase, and so forth) and for converting between uppercase and lowercase.

Since a `char` is a 16-bit value, and Unicode allows for 21-bit characters, known as *code points,* many of the methods of `Character` are overloaded to take either a `char` or an `int` that represents an arbitrary code point. Such methods are described in combination below and the pseudo-type *codePoint* is used to represent either a `char` or an `int` code point value.

In addition to MIN_VALUE and MAX_VALUE constants, `Character` provides the constants MIN_RADIX and MAX_RADIX, which are the minimum and maximum radices understood by methods that translate between digit characters and integer values or vice versa,. The radix must be in the range 2–36; digits for values greater than 9 are the letters A through Z or their lowercase equivalents. Three methods convert between characters and integer values:

public static int **digit(*codePoint* ch, int radix)**
> Returns the numeric value of ch considered as a digit in the given radix. If the radix is not valid or if ch is not a digit in the radix, –1 is returned. For example, digit('A', 16) returns 10 and digit('9', 10) returns 9, while digit('a', 10) returns –1.

public static int **getNumericValue(*codePoint* ch)**
> Returns the numeric value of the digit ch. For example, the character \u217F is the Roman numeral digit **M**, so getNumericValue('\u217F') returns the value 1000. These numeric values are non-negative. If ch has no numeric value, –1 is returned; if it has a value but is not a non-negative integer, such as the fractional value ¼ ('\u00bc'), getNumericValue returns –2.

public static char **forDigit(int digit, int radix)**
> Returns the character value for the specified digit in the specified radix. If the digit is not valid in the radix, the character '\u0000' is returned. For example, forDigit(10, 16) returns 'a' while forDigit(16, 16) returns '\u0000'.

There are three character cases in Unicode: upper, lower, and title. Uppercase and lowercase are familiar to most people. Titlecase distinguishes characters that are made up of multiple components and are written differently when used in titles, where the first letter in a word is traditionally capitalized. For example, in the string "ljepotica",[2] the first letter is the lowercase letter lj (\u01C9, a letter in the Extended Latin character set that is used in writing Croatian digraphs). If the word appeared in a book title, and you wanted the first letter of each word to be in uppercase, the correct process would be to use toTitleCase on the first letter of each word, giving you "Ljepotica" (using Lj, which is \u01C8). If you incorrectly used toUpperCase, you would get the erroneous string "LJepotica" (using LJ, which is \u01C7).

All case issues are handled as defined in Unicode. For example, in Georgian, uppercase letters are considered archaic, and translation into uppercase is usually avoided. Therefore, toUpperCase will not change lowercase Georgian letters to their uppercase equivalents, although toLowerCase will translate uppercase Georgian letters to lowercase. Because of such complexities, you cannot assume

---

[2] "Ljepotica" is a Croatian diminutive of "beauty," often used as a term of endearment and admiration.

that converting characters to either lower or upper case and then comparing the results will give you a proper case-ignoring comparison. However, the expression

```
Character.toUpperCase(Character.toLowerCase(ch));
```

leaves you with a character that you can compare with another similarly constructed character to test for equality ignoring case distinctions. If the two resulting characters are the same, then the original characters were the same except for possible differences in case. The case conversion methods are:

public static *codePoint* **toLowerCase(***codePoint* **ch)**
>   Returns the lowercase character equivalent of ch. If there is no lowercase equivalent, ch is returned.

public static *codePoint* **toUpperCase(***codePoint* **ch)**
>   Returns the uppercase character equivalent of ch. If there is no uppercase equivalent, ch is returned.

public static *codePoint* **toTitleCase(***codePoint* **ch)**
>   Returns the titlecase character equivalent of ch. If there is no titlecase equivalent, the result of toUpperCase(ch) is returned.

The Character class has many methods to test whether a given character is of a particular type in any Unicode character set (for example, isDigit recognizes digits in Ethiopic and Khmer). The methods are passed a char or int code point and return a boolean that answers a question. These methods are:

Method	Is the Character...
isDefined	a defined Unicode character?
isDigit	a digit?
isIdentifierIgnorable	ignorable in any identifier (such as a direction control directive)?
isISOControl	an ISO control character?
isJavaIdentifierStart	valid to start a source code identifier?
isJavaIdentifierPart	valid after the first character of a source code identifier?
isLetter	a letter?
isLetterOrDigit	a letter or digit?
isLowerCase	a lowercase letter?
isSpaceChar	a space?
isTitleCase	a titlecase letter?
isUnicodeIdentifierStart	valid to start a Unicode identifier?
isUnicodeIdentifierPart	valid after the first character of a Unicode identifier?

Method	Is the Character...
isUpperCase	an uppercase letter?
isWhitespace	a source code whitespace character?

You can also ask whether a char value isLowSurrogate or isHighSurrogate, a specific int code point isSupplementaryCodePoint or isValidCodePoint, or if a pair of char values isSurrogatePair.

Unicode identifiers are defined by the Unicode standard. Unicode identifiers must start with a letter (connecting punctuation such as _ and currency symbols such as ¥ are not letters in Unicode, although they are in the Java programming language) and must contain only letters, connecting punctuation (such as _), digits, numeric letters (such as Roman numerals), combining marks, nonspacing marks, or ignorable control characters (such as text direction markers).

All these types of characters, and several others, are defined by the Unicode standard. The static method getType returns an int that defines a character's Unicode type. The return value is one of the following constants:

COMBINING_SPACING_MARK	MODIFIER_LETTER
CONNECTOR_PUNCTUATION	MODIFIER_SYMBOL
CONTROL	NON_SPACING_MARK
CURRENCY_SYMBOL	OTHER_LETTER
DASH_PUNCTUATION	OTHER_NUMBER
DECIMAL_DIGIT_NUMBER	OTHER_PUNCTUATION
ENCLOSING_MARK	OTHER_SYMBOL
END_PUNCTUATION	PARAGRAPH_SEPARATOR
FINAL_QUOTE_PUNCTUATION	PRIVATE_USE
FORMAT	SPACE_SEPARATOR
INITIAL_QUOTE_PUNCTUATION	START_PUNCTUATION
LETTER_NUMBER	SURROGATE
LINE_SEPARATOR	TITLECASE_LETTER
LOWERCASE_LETTER	UNASSIGNED
MATH_SYMBOL	UPPERCASE_LETTER

Unicode is divided into blocks of related characters. The static nested class Character.Subset is used to define subsets of the Unicode character set. The static nested class Character.UnicodeBlock extends Subset to define a set of standard Unicode character blocks, which are available as static fields of UnicodeBlock. The static method UnicodeBlock.of returns the UnicodeBlock object representing the Unicode character block for a particular character. The UnicodeBlock class also defines constants for all the blocks, such as GREEK,

KATAKANA, TELUGU, and COMBINING_MARKS_FOR_SYMBOLS. The of method will return one of these values, or null if the character is not in any block. For example, the code

```
boolean isShape =
    (Character.UnicodeBlock.of(ch) ==
        Character.UnicodeBlock.GEOMETRIC_SHAPES);
```

tests to see if a character is in the GEOMETRIC_SHAPES block.

Two Subset objects define the same Unicode subset if they are the same object, a semantic enforced in Subset by declaring equals and hashCode to be final, and defining them to have the default Object behavior for these methods. If you define your own subsets for some reason, you should give people a way analogous to of to get a single Subset object for each different kind of Subset you define.

8.5.1 Working with UTF-16

Working with sequences of characters, whether arrays of char, strings, or other types that implement CharSequence (see Chapter 13), is complicated by the fact that supplementary characters need to be encoded as a pair of char values. To assist with this, the Character class defines a range of methods that help with the encoding and decoding of surrogate pairs, and accounting for their existence in a sequence of character values:

public static int **charCount(int codePoint)**
> Returns the number of char values needed to encode the given code point. This returns 2 for supplementary characters, otherwise 1.

public static int **codePointAt(char[] seq, int index)**
> Returns the code point defined at the given index in seq, taking into account that it may be a supplementary character represented by the pair seq[index] and seq[index+1]. There is a variant that takes an additional limit argument that restricts the use of index+1 to be less than a specified value.

public static int **codePointAt(CharSequence seq, int index)**
> Returns the code point defined at the given index in seq, taking into account that it may be a supplementary character represented by the pair seq.charAt(index) and seq.charAt(index+1).

public static int **codePointBefore(char[] seq, int index)**
> Returns the code point defined preceding the given index in seq, taking into account that it may be a supplementary character represented by the pair

`seq[index-2]` and `seq[index-1]`. There is a variant that takes an additional `start` argument, that restricts the use of `index-1` and `index-2` to be greater than or equal to the specified start position.

public static int codePointBefore(CharSequence seq, int index)
Returns the code point defined preceding the given index in `seq`, taking into account that it may be a supplementary character represented by the pair `seq.charAt(index-2)` and `seq.charAt(index-1)`.

public static int
codePointCount(char[] seq, int start, int count)
Returns the number of code points defined in `seq[start]` to `seq[start+length]`, taking into account surrogate pairs. Any unpaired surrogate values count as one code point each.

public static int
codePointCount(CharSequence seq, int start, int end)
Returns the number of code points defined in `seq.charAt(start)` to `seq.charAt(end)`, taking into account surrogate pairs. Any unpaired surrogate values count as one code point each.

public static int offsetByCodePoints(char[] seq, int start,
int count, int index, int numberOfCodePoints)
Returns the index into the array, that is `numberOfCodePoints` away from `index`, considering only the subarray from `seq[start]` to `seq[start+length]`, taking into account surrogate pairs. This allows you to skip a given number of code points, without having to manually loop through the array, keeping track of surrogate pairs. If any unpaired surrogates are found, they count as one code point.

public static int offsetByCodePoints(CharSequence seq, int index,
int numberOfCodePoints)
Returns the index into the CharSequence, that is `numberOfCodePoints` away from `index`, taking into account surrogate pairs.

public static char[] toChars(int codePoint)
Converts a code point to its UTF-16 representation as a one- or two-char array. If `codePoint` is not valid, `IllegalArgumentException` is thrown.

public static int
toChars(int codePoint, char[] dst, int dstBegin)
Converts a code point to its UTF-16 representation, storing it in `dst` starting at `dst[dstBegin]` and returning the number of characters written (either 1 or 2). If `codePoint` is not valid, `IllegalArgumentException` is thrown.

```
public static int toCodePoint(char high, char low)
```
Converts the given surrogate pair of char values to their supplementary code point value. This method does not check that high and low form a valid surrogate pair, so you must check that yourself by using isSurrogatePair.

All of these methods that use indices can throw IndexOutOfBoundsException, if you cause them to try to index outside the given array, or CharSequence, accounting for any imposed limits on the valid range of indices.

8.6   Boxing Conversions

The automatic conversion of a variable of primitive type into an instance of its wrapper class, is termed a *boxing conversion*—the wrapper object acts like a "box" in which the primitive value is held. The opposite conversion, from an instance of a wrapper class to a primitive value, is termed an *unboxing conversion.*

A boxing conversion replaces any primitive value v with a wrapper object of the same value. The wrapper object's type corresponds to the type of v. For example, given

```
Integer val = 3;
```

val will refer to an Integer object because 3 is an int value; val.intValue() will return the value 3.

An unboxing conversion takes a reference to a wrapper object and extracts its primitive value. Building on the previous example,

```
int x = val;
```

is equivalent to the explicit

```
int x = val.intValue();
```

and the value of x is 3. If val was a Short reference, the unboxing of val would invoke val.shortValue(), and so forth. If a wrapper reference is null, an unboxing conversion will throw a NullPointerException.

The boxing and unboxing conversions are applied automatically in many contexts, such as assignment and argument passing, so primitives and reference types can be used almost interchangeably. However, the conversions do not apply everywhere, and in particular you cannot directly dereference a primitive variable, or value, as if it were an object. For example, given the int variable x, as above, the expression x.toString() will not compile. You can, however, apply a cast to the primitive first, such as:

```
((Object) x).toString()
```

The exact contexts in which boxing and unboxing automatically occur are discussed in "Type Conversions" on page 216.

Ideally, you would rely on boxing conversions wherever necessary, without giving it a second thought. In practice, you need to be aware that a boxing conversion may need to allocate an instance of a wrapper class, which consumes memory and which may fail if insufficient memory is available. Given that the wrapper classes are immutable, two objects with the same value can be used interchangeably, and there is no need to actually create two distinct objects. This fact is exploited by requiring that boxing conversions for certain value ranges of certain types always yield the same object. Those types and value ranges are:

Type	Range
boolean	true, false
byte	all values
char	\u0000 to \u00ff
short	-128 to 127
int	-128 to 127

So given the method

```
static boolean sameArgs(Integer a, Integer b) {
    return a == b;
}
```

the following invocation returns `true`:

```
sameArgs(3, 3)
```

while this invocation returns `false`:

```
sameArgs(3, new Integer(3))
```

An implementation of the virtual machine may choose to expand on these types and ranges, and is free to determine when instances of the wrapper classes are first created: They could be created eagerly and all stored in a lookup table, or they could be created as needed.

> *Dare to be naïve.*
> —R. Buckminster Fuller

CHAPTER 9

Operators and Expressions

Work is of two kinds:
first, altering the position of matter at or near the earth's surface relative to other matter;
second, telling other people to do so.
—Bertrand Russell

THIS chapter teaches you about the fundamental computational building blocks of the programming language—namely, operators and expressions. You have already seen a lot of code and have gained familiarity with its components. This chapter describes these basic elements in detail.

Each operator is described in terms of its basic operation, upon operands of the base expected type—such as a numeric primitive type or a reference type. The actual evaluation of an expression in a program may involve type conversions as described in Section 9.4 on page 216.

9.1 Arithmetic Operations

There are several binary arithmetic operators that operate on any of the primitive numerical types:

+	addition
–	subtraction
*	multiplication
/	division
%	remainder

You can also use unary - for negation. The sign of a number can be inverted with code like this:

```
val = -val;
```

For completeness there is also a unary +, as in +2.0.

The exact actions of the binary arithmetic operators depend on the types of operands involved. The following sections look at the different rules for integer and floating-point arithmetic.

9.1.1   Integer Arithmetic

Integer arithmetic is modular two's-complement arithmetic—that is, if a value exceeds the range of its type (int or long), it is reduced modulo the range. So integer arithmetic never overflows or underflows but only wraps.

Integer division truncates toward zero (7/2 is 3, and -7/2 is -3). For integer types, division and remainder obey the rule

```
(x/y)*y + x%y == x
```

So 7%2 is 1, and -7%2 is –1. Dividing by zero or remainder by zero is invalid for integer arithmetic and throws ArithmeticException.

Character arithmetic is integer arithmetic after the char is implicitly converted to int—see "Expression Type" on page 215.

9.1.2   Floating-Point Arithmetic

Floating-point arithmetic can overflow to infinity (become too large for a double or float) or underflow (become too small for a double or float). Underflow results in a loss of precision, possibly enough to yield a zero value.[1] The result of an invalid expression, such as dividing infinity by infinity, is a NaN value—for "Not-a-Number."

Arithmetic with finite operands performs as expected, within the limits of precision of double or float. Signs of floating-point arithmetic results are also as expected. Multiplying two numbers having the same sign results in a positive value; multiplying two numbers having opposite signs results in a negative value.

Adding two infinities results in the same infinity if their signs are the same, and NaN if their signs differ. Subtracting infinities of the same sign produces NaN; subtracting infinities of opposite signs produces an infinity of the same sign as the left operand. For example, $(\infty - (-\infty))$ is ∞. Arithmetic operations involving any value that is NaN have a result that is also NaN. Overflows result in a value that is an infinity of the proper sign. Underflows also result in values of the proper sign. Floating-point arithmetic has a negative zero -0.0, which compares equal to +0.0. Although they compare equal, the two zeros can produce different

---

[1]   Detecting non-zero underflows is a non-trivial task that is beyond the scope of this book.

results. For example, the expression `1f/0f` yields positive infinity and `1f/-0f` yields negative infinity.

If the result of an underflow is `-0.0` and if `-0.0 == 0.0`, how do you test for a negative zero? You must use the zero in an expression where sign matters and then test the result. For example, if `x` has a zero value, the expression `1/x` will yield negative infinity if `x` is negative zero, or positive infinity if `x` is positive zero.

The rules for operations on infinities match normal mathematical expectations. Adding or subtracting any number to or from either infinity results in that infinity. For example, $(-\infty + x)$ is $-\infty$ for any finite number x.

You can get an infinity value from the constants `POSITIVE_INFINITY` and `NEGATIVE_INFINITY` in the wrapper classes `Float` and `Double`. For example, `Double.NEGATIVE_INFINITY` is the `double` value of minus infinity.

Multiplying infinity by zero yields NaN. Multiplying infinity by a non-zero finite number produces an infinity of the appropriate sign.

Floating-point division and remainder can produce infinities or NaN but never throw an exception. This table shows the results of the various combinations:

x	y	x/y	x%y
Finite	± 0.0	$\pm\infty$	NaN
Finite	$\pm\infty$	± 0.0	x
± 0.0	± 0.0	NaN	NaN
$\pm\infty$	Finite	$\pm\infty$	NaN
$\pm\infty$	$\pm\infty$	NaN	NaN

Otherwise, floating-point remainder (%) acts analogously to integer remainder as described earlier. See the `IEEEremainder` method in "`Math` and `StrictMath`" on page 657 for a different remainder calculation.

Exercise 9.1: Write a program that uses the operators +, –, *, and /, on two infinite operands and show the result. Ensure that you try both same signed and opposite-signed infinity values.

9.1.3 Strict and Non-Strict Floating-Point Arithmetic

Floating-point arithmetic can be executed in one of two modes: *FP-strict* or *not FP-strict*. For simplicity, we refer to these as strict and non-strict, respectively. *Strict* floating-point evaluation follows constrained rules about exact floating-point operations: When you execute strict floating-point code you will always get exactly equivalent results on all Java virtual machine implementations. Floating-point arithmetic that is *non-strict* can be executed with somewhat relaxed rules. These rules allow the use of floating-point representations that may avoid some overflows or underflows that would occur if the arithmetic were executed strictly. This means that some applications may run differently on different virtual machines when under non-strict floating point. Non-strict floating point might also execute faster than strict floating point, because the relaxed rules may allow the use of representations that are supported directly by the underlying hardware.

The strictness of floating-point arithmetic is determined by the presence of the modifier `strictfp`, which can be applied to a class, interface, or method. When you declare a method `strictfp`, all the code in the method will be executed according to strict constraints. When you use `strictfp` on a class or interface, all code in the class, including initializers and code in nested types, will be evaluated strictly. To determine if an expression is strict, all methods, classes, and interfaces within which the expression is contained are examined; if any of them is declared `strictfp` then the expression is strict. For example, an inner class declared within a strict outer class, or within a strict method, is also strict. However, strictness is not inherited—the presence of `strictfp` on a class or interface declaration does not cause extended classes or interfaces to be strict.

Constant expressions that require floating point are always evaluated strictly. Otherwise, any code that is not marked as `strictfp` can be executed under rules that do not require repeatable results. If you want to guarantee bit-for-bit exact results across all Java virtual-machine implementations, you should use `strictfp` on relevant methods, classes, and interfaces. You should also note that a virtual machine can satisfy the rules for non-strict floating point by always acting strictly: Non-strict floating point does not *require* the virtual machine to act differently, it offers the virtual machine a degree of freedom to optimize code where repeatable results are not required.

Non-strict floating-point execution allows intermediate results within expressions to take on values with a greater range than allowed by the usual `float` or `double` representations. These extended range representations avoid some underflows and overflows that can happen with the standard representations. Fields, array elements, local variables, parameters, and return values always use the standard representations. When an extended range representation is converted to a standard representation, the closest representable value is used.

If you need a complete understanding of these issues, you should consult *The Java*[TM] *Language Specification, Third Edition*.

9.2   General Operators

In addition to the main arithmetic operators, there are other useful operators for comparing and manipulating values. Member access operators, method invocation and type conversion operators are discussed in following sections.

9.2.1 Increment and Decrement Operators

The ++ and -- operators are the increment and decrement operators, respectively, and can only be applied to numeric variables or numeric array elements. The expression i++ is equivalent to i = i + 1 except that i is evaluated only once. For example, the statement

```
++arr[where()];
```

invokes where only once and uses the result as an index into the array only once. On the other hand, in the statement

```
arr[where()] = arr[where()] + 1;
```

the where method is called twice: once to determine the index on the left-hand side, and a second time to determine the index on the right-hand side. If where returns a different value each time it is invoked, the results will be quite different from those of the ++ expression. To avoid the second invocation of where you would have to store its result in a temporary—hence the increment (and decrement) operator allows a simpler, succinct expression of what you want to do.

The increment and decrement operators can be either *prefix* or *postfix* operators—they can appear either before or after what they operate on. If the operator comes before (prefix), the operation is applied before the value of the expression is returned. If the operator comes after (postfix), the operation is applied after the original value is used. For example:

```
class IncOrder {
    public static void main(String[] args) {
        int i = 16;
        System.out.println(++i + " " + i++ + " " + i);
    }
}
```

The output is

```
17 17 18
```

The expression ++i preincrements the value of i to 17 and evaluates to that value (17); the expression i++ evaluates to the current value of i (17) and postincrements i to have the value 18; finally the expression i is the value of i after the postincrement from the middle term. Modifying a variable more than once in an expression makes code hard to understand, and should be avoided.

The increment and decrement operators ++ and -- can also be applied to char variables to get to the next or previous Unicode character.

9.2.2   Relational and Equality Operators

The language provides a standard set of relational and equality operators, all of which yield `boolean` values:

`>`	greater than
`>=`	greater than or equal to
`<`	less than
`<=`	less than or equal to
`==`	equal to
`!=`	not equal to

Both the relational and equality operators can be applied to the primitive numeric types, with the usual mathematical interpretation applying.

Floating-point values follow normal ordering (–1.0 is less than 0.0 is less than positive infinity) except that NaN is an anomaly. All relational and equality operators that test a number against NaN return `false`, except `!=`, which always returns `true`. This is true even if both values are NaN. For example,

```
Double.NaN == Double.NaN
```

is always `false`. To test whether a value is NaN, use the type-specific NaN testers: the static methods `Float.isNaN(float)` and `Double.isNaN(double)`.[2]

Only the equality operators `==` and `!=` are allowed to operate on boolean values.

These operators can be combined to create a "logical XOR" test. The following code invokes `sameSign` only if both x and y have the same sign (or zero); otherwise, it invokes `differentSign`:

```
if ((x < 0) == (y < 0))
    sameSign();
else
    differentSign();
```

The equality operators can also be applied to reference types. The expression `ref1==ref2` is true if the two references refer to the same object or if both are `null`, even if the two references are of different declared types. Otherwise, it is false.

The equality operators test for reference *identity,* not object *equivalence.* Two references are identical if they refer to the same object; two objects are equivalent

---

[2]   There is one other way to test for NaN: If x has a NaN value, then `x != x` is true. This is interesting but very obscure, so you should use the methods instead.

if they logically have the same value. Equivalence is tested with the `equals` method defined by `Object`, which you should override in classes for which equivalence and identity are different. `Object.equals` assumes an object is equal only to itself. For example, the `String` class overrides `equals` to test whether two `String` objects have the same contents—see Chapter 13.

9.2.3 Logical Operators

The logical operators combine boolean expressions to yield boolean values and provide the common operations of boolean algebra:

`&`	logical AND
`|`	logical inclusive OR
`^`	logical exclusive or (XOR)
`!`	logical negation
`&&`	conditional AND
`||`	conditional OR

A "logical AND" is true if and only if both its operands are true, while a "logical OR" is true if and only if either of its operands are true. The "exclusive OR" operator yields true if either, but not both, of its operands is true—which is the same as testing the equality of the two operands, so we can rewrite our earlier example as:

```
if ((x < 0) ^ (y < 0))
    differentSign();
else
    sameSign();
```

The unary operator `!` negates, or inverts, a boolean, so `!true` is the same as `false` and `!false` is the same as `true`.

Boolean values are normally tested directly—if x and y are booleans, the code

```
if (x || !y) {
    // ...
}
```

is considered cleaner than the equivalent, but more verbose

```
if (x == true || y == false) {
    // ...
}
```

The && ("conditional AND") and || ("conditional OR") operators perform the same logical function as the simple & and | operators, but they avoid evaluating their right operand if the truth of the expression is determined by the left operand—for this reason they are sometimes referred to as "short-circuit operators." For example, consider:

```
if (w && x) {        // outer "if"
    if (y || z) {  // inner "if"
        // ...        inner "if" body
    }
}
```

The inner `if` is executed only if both w and x are `true`. If w is `false` then x will not be evaluated because the expression is already guaranteed to be `false`. The body of the inner `if` is executed if either y or z is `true`. If y is `true`, then z will not be evaluated because the expression is already guaranteed to be `true`.

A lot of code relies on this rule for program correctness or efficiency. For example, the evaluation shortcuts make the following code safe:

```
if (0 <= ix && ix < array.length && array[ix] != 0) {
    // ...
}
```

The range checks are done first. The value `array[ix]` will be accessed only if `ix` is within bounds. There is no "conditional XOR" because the truth of XOR always depends on the value of both operands.

9.2.4   `instanceof`

The `instanceof` operator evaluates whether a reference refers to an object that is an instance of a particular class or interface. The left-hand side is a reference to an object, and the right-hand side is a class or interface name. You learned about `instanceof` on page 92.

9.2.5   Bit Manipulation Operators

The binary bitwise operators are:

&	bitwise AND
|	bitwise inclusive OR
^	bitwise exclusive or (XOR)

The bitwise operators apply only to integer types (including `char`) and perform their operation on each pair of bits in the two operands. The AND of two bits yields a 1 if *both* bits are 1, the OR of two bits yields a 1 if *either* bit is 1, and the XOR of two bits yields a 1 only if the two bits have *different* values. For example:

```
0xf00f & 0x0ff0 yields 0x0000
0xf00f | 0x0ff0 yields 0xffff
0xaaaa ^ 0xffff yields 0x5555
```

There is also a unary bitwise complement operator ~, which toggles each bit in its operand. An `int` with value 0x00003333 has a complemented value of 0xffffcccc.

Although the same characters are used for the bitwise operators and the logical operators, they are quite distinct. The types of the operands determine whether, for example, & is a logical or a bitwise AND. Since logical operators only apply to booleans and bitwise operators only apply to integer types, any expression involving operands of the different types, such as `true & 0xaaaa`, is a compile-time error.

There are other bit manipulation operators to shift bits within an integer value:

`<<`	Shift bits left, filling with zero bits on the right-hand side
`>>`	Shift bits right, filling with the highest (sign) bit on the left-hand side
`>>>`	Shift bits right, filling with zero bits on the left-hand side

The left-hand side of a shift expression is what is shifted, and the right-hand side is how much to shift. For example, `var >>> 2` will shift the bits in `var` two places to the right, dropping the bottom two bits from the end and filling the top two bits with zero.

The two right-shift operators provide for an arithmetic shift (`>>`) and a logical shift (`>>>`). The arithmetic shift preserves the sign of the value by filling in the highest bit positions with the original sign bit (the bit in the highest position). The logical shift inserts zeroes into the high-order bits. It is often used when extracting subsets of bits from a value. For example, in binary coded decimal (BCD) each decimal digit is represented by four bits (0x00 to 0x09—the remaining bit patterns are invalid) and so every byte can encode two decimal digits. To extract the low-order digit you AND the byte with a mask of 0x0f to zero out the high-order digit. To extract the high-order digit you logically right-shift the value by four positions, moving the valid bits down to the least significant positions and filling the new high-order bits with zero:

```
class BCD {
    static int getBCDLowDigit(byte val) {
        return (val & 0x0f);
    }
    static int getBCDHighDigit(byte val) {
        return val >>> 4 ;
    }
}
```

Shift operators have a slightly different type rule from most other binary integer operations. For shift operators, the resulting type is the type of the left-hand operand—that is, the value that is shifted. If the left-hand side of the shift is an int, the result of the shift is an int, even if the shift count is provided as a long.

If the shift count is larger than the number of bits in the word, or if it is negative, the actual count will be different from the provided count. The actual count used in a shift is the count you provide, masked by the size of the type minus one. For a 32-bit int, for example, the mask used is 0x1f (31), so both (n << 35) and (n << -29) are equivalent to (n << 3).

Shift operators can be used only on integer types. In the rare circumstance when you actually need to manipulate the bits in a floating-point value, you can use the conversion methods on the classes Float and Double, as discussed in "The Floating-Point Wrapper Classes" on page 191.

Exercise 9.2: Write a method that determines the number of 1 bits in a passed-in int, by using just the bit manipulation operators (that is, don't use Integer.bitCount). Compare your solution with published algorithms for doing this—see the related reading for "General Programming Techniques" on page 758 for one source.

9.2.6   The Conditional Operator ?:

The *conditional operator* provides a single expression that yields one of two values based on a boolean expression. The statement

```
value = (userSetIt ? usersValue : defaultValue);
```

is equivalent to

```
if (userSetIt)
    value = usersValue;
else
    value = defaultValue;
```

The primary difference between the `if` statement and the `?:` operator is that the latter has a value and so can be used as part of an expression. The conditional operator results in a more compact expression, but programmers disagree about whether it is clearer. We use whichever seems clearer at the time. When to use parentheses around a conditional operator expression is a matter of personal style, and practice varies widely. Parentheses are not required by the language.

The conditional operator expression has a type that is determined by the types of the second and third expressions (`usersValue` and `defaultValue` in the above example). If the types of these expressions are the same then that is the type of the overall expression. Otherwise, the rules get somewhat complicated:

- If one expression is a primitive type and the other can be unboxed to become a compatible primitive type, then the unboxing occurs and the expressions are reconsidered.

- If both expressions are numeric primitive types then the resulting type is also a numeric primitive type, obtained by numeric promotion if needed. For example, in

   ```
   double scale = (halveIt ? 0.5 : 1);
   ```

   the two expressions are of type `double` (`0.5`) and type `int` (`1`). An `int` is assignable to a `double`, so the `1` is promoted to `1.0` and the type of the conditional operator is `double`.

- If one expression is an `int` constant, and the other is `byte`, `short`, or `char`, and the `int` value can fit in the smaller type, then the resulting type is that smaller type.

- If one of the expressions is a primitive type and the other is a reference type that can't be unboxed to get a compatible value, or both expressions are primitive but incompatible, then the primitive type is boxed so that we have two reference types.

- Given two reference types that are different, the type of the expression is the first common parent type. For example, if both expressions were unrelated class types that implemented `Cloneable` then `Cloneable` would be the type of the expression; if one expression was `int` while the other was `String`, then `Object` would be the resulting type.

Note that if either expression has a type of `void` (possible if the expression invokes a method with the `void` return type) then a compile-time error occurs.

This operator is also called the *question/colon operator* because of its form, and the *ternary operator* because it is the only ternary (three-operand) operator in the language.

9.2.7   Assignment Operators

The assignment operator = assigns the value of its right-operand expression to its left operand, which must be a variable (either a variable name or an array element). The type of the expression must be assignment compatible with the type of the variable—an explicit cast may be needed—see Section 9.4 on page 216.

An assignment operation is itself an expression and evaluates to the value being assigned. For example, given an `int z`, the assignment

```
z = 3;
```

has the value 3. This value can be assigned to another variable, which also evaluates to 3 and so that can be assigned to another variable and so forth. Hence, assignments can be chained together to give a set of variables the same value:

```
x = y = z = 3;
```

This also means that assignment can be performed as a side effect of evaluating another expression—though utilizing side effects in expressions is often considered poor style. An acceptable, and common, example of this is to assign and test a value within a loop expression. For example:

```
while ((v = stream.next()) != null)
    processValue(v);
```

Here the next value is read from a stream and stored in the variable v. Provided the value read was not `null`, it is processed and the next value read. Note that as assignment has a lower precedence than the inequality test (see "Operator Precedence and Associativity" on page 221), you have to place the assignment expression within parentheses.

The simple = is the most basic form of assignment operator. There are many other assignment forms. Any binary arithmetic, logical, or bit manipulation operator can be concatenated with = to form another assignment operator—a *compound assignment operator.* For example,

```
arr[where()] += 12;
```

is the same as

```
arr[where()] = arr[where()] + 12;
```

except that the expression on the left-hand side of the assignment is evaluated only once. In the example, `arr[where()]` is evaluated only once in the first expression, but twice in the second expression—as you learned earlier with the ++ operator.

Given the variable `var` of type T, the value `expr`, and the binary operator *op,* the expression

```
var op= expr
```

is equivalent to

```
var = (T) ((var) op (expr))
```

except that `var` is evaluated only once. This means that *op=* is valid only if *op* is valid for the types involved. You cannot, for example, use <<= on a `double` variable because you cannot use << on a `double` value.

Note the parentheses used in the expanded form you just saw. The expression

```
a *= b + 1
```

is analogous to

```
a = a * (b + 1)
```

and not to

```
a = a * b + 1
```

Although a += 1 is the same as ++a and a++, using ++ is considered idiomatic and is preferred.

Exercise 9.3: Review your solution to Exercise 7.3 to see if it can be written more clearly or succinctly with the operators you've learned about in this chapter.

9.2.8   String Concatenation Operator

You can use + to concatenate two strings. Here is an example:

```
String boo = "boo";
String cry = boo + "hoo";
cry += "!";
System.out.println(cry);
```

And here is its output:

```
boohoo!
```

The + operator is interpreted as the string concatenation operator whenever at least one of its operands is a String. If only one of the operands is a String then the other is implicitly converted to a String as discussed in "String Conversions" on page 220.

9.2.9   new

The new operator is a unary prefix operator—it has one operand that follows the operator. Technically, the use of new is known as an *instance creation expression*—because it creates an instance of a class or array. The value of the expression is a reference to the object created. The use of new and the associated issue of constructors was discussed in detail on page 50.

9.3   Expressions

An *expression* consists of operators and their operands, which are evaluated to yield a result. This result may be a variable or a value, or even nothing if the expression was the invocation of a method declared void. An expression may be as simple as a single variable name, or it may be a complex sequence of method invocations, variable accesses, object creations, and the combination of the results of those subexpressions using other operators, further method invocations, and variable accesses.

9.3.1   Order of Evaluation

Regardless of their complexity, the meanings of expressions are always well-defined. Operands to operators will be evaluated left-to-right. For example, given x+y+z, the compiler evaluates x, evaluates y, adds the values together, evaluates z, and adds that to the previous result. The compiler does not evaluate, say, y before x, or z before either y or x. Similarly, argument expressions for method, or constructor, invocations are evaluated from left to right, as are array index expressions for multidimensional arrays.

Order of evaluation matters if x, y, or z has side effects of any kind. If, for instance, x, y, or z are invocations of methods that affect the state of the object or print something, you would notice if they were evaluated in any other order. The language guarantees that this will not happen.

Except for the operators &&, ||, and ?:, every operand of an operator will be evaluated before the operation is performed. This is true even for operations that throw exceptions. For example, an integer division by zero results in an ArithmeticException, but it will do so only after both operands have been fully evaluated. Similarly, all arguments for a method or constructor invocation are evaluated before the invocation occurs.

If evaluation of the left operand of a binary operator causes an exception, no part of the right-hand operand is evaluated. Similarly, if an expression being evaluated for a method, or constructor, argument causes an exception, no argument expressions to the right of it will be evaluated—and likewise for array index expressions. The order of evaluation is very specific and evaluation stops as soon as an exception is encountered.

One further detail concerns object creation with new. If insufficient memory is available for the new object, an OutOfMemoryError exception is thrown. This occurs before evaluation of the constructor arguments occurs—because the value of those arguments is not needed to allocate memory for the object—in which case those arguments won't be evaluated. In contrast, when an array is created, the array dimension expressions must be evaluated first to find out how much memory to allocate—consequently, array creation throws the OutOfMemoryError after the dimension expressions are evaluated.

9.3.2 Expression Type

Every expression has a type. The type of an expression is determined by the types of its component parts and the semantics of operators.

If an arithmetic or bit manipulation operator is applied to integer values, the result of the expression is of type int unless one or both sides are long, in which case the result is long. The exception to this rule is that the type of shift operator expressions are not affected by the type of the right-hand side. All integer operations are performed in either int or long precision, so the smaller byte and short integer types are always promoted to int before evaluation.

If either operand of an arithmetic operator is floating point, the operation is performed in floating-point arithmetic. Such operations are done in float unless at least one operand is a `double`, in which case `double` is used for the calculation and result.

A + operator is a `String` concatenation when either operand to + is of type `String` or if the left-hand side of a += is a `String`.

When used in an expression, a `char` value is converted to an `int` by setting the top 16 bits to zero. For example, the Unicode character `\uffff` would be treated as equivalent to the integer `0x0000ffff`. This treatment is different from the way a `short` with the value `0xffff` would be treated—sign extension makes the `short` equivalent to `-1`, and its `int` equivalent would be `0xffffffff`.

The above are all examples of different type conversions that can occur within an expression, to determine the type of that expression. The complete set of conversions is discussed next.

9.4   Type Conversions

The Java programming language is a *strongly typed* language, which means that it checks for type compatibility at compile time in almost all cases. Incompatible assignments are prevented by forbidding anything questionable. It also provides *cast* operations for times when the compatibility of a type can be determined only at run time, or when you want to explicitly force a type conversion for primitive types that would otherwise lose range, such as assigning a `double` to a `float`. You learned about type compatibility and conversion for reference types on page 90. In this section you will learn about conversions as a whole, for both primitive and reference types, and the contexts in which those conversions are automatically applied.

9.4.1   Implicit Type Conversions

Some kinds of conversions happen automatically, without any work on your part—these are *implicit* conversions.

Any numeric value can be assigned to any numeric variable whose type supports a larger range of values—a *widening primitive* conversion. A `char` can be used wherever an `int` is valid. A floating-point value can be assigned to any floating-point variable of equal or greater precision.

You can also use implicit widening conversion of integer types to floating-point, but not vice versa. There is no loss of range going from integer to floating point, because the range of any floating-point type is larger than the range of any integer.

Preserving magnitude is not the same as preserving the precision of a value. You can lose precision in some implicit conversions. Consider, for example, assigning a `long` to a `float`. The `float` has 32 bits of data and the `long` has 64 bits of data. A `float` stores fewer significant digits than a `long`, even though a `float` stores numbers of a larger range. You can lose data in an assignment of a `long` to a `float`. Consider the following:

```
long orig = 0x7effffff00000000L;
float fval = orig;
long lose = (long) fval;

System.out.println("orig = " + orig);
System.out.println("fval = " + fval);
System.out.println("lose = " + lose);
```

The first two statements create a `long` value and assign it to a `float` value. To show that this loses precision, we explicitly cast `fval` to a `long` and assign it to another variable (explicit casts are covered next). If you examine the output, you can see that the `float` value lost some precision: The `long` variable `orig` that was assigned to the `float` variable `fval` has a different value from the one generated by the explicit cast back into the `long` variable `lose`:

```
orig = 9151314438521880576
fval = 9.1513144E18
lose = 9151314442816847872
```

As a convenience, compile-time constants of integer type can be assigned to smaller integer types, without a cast, provided the value of the constant can actually fit in the smaller type and the integer type is not `long`. For example, the first two assignments are legal while the last is not:

```
short s1 = 27;    // implicit int to short
byte  b1 = 27;    // implicit int to byte
short s3 = 0x1ffff; // INVALID: int value too big for short
```

Such a conversion, from a larger type to a smaller type, is a *narrowing primitive conversion*.

In all, seven different kinds of conversions might apply when an expression is evaluated:

- ◆ Widening or narrowing primitive conversions
- ◆ Widening or narrowing reference conversions
- ◆ Boxing or unboxing conversions
- ◆ String conversions

You have previously seen all of these. There are then five different contexts in which these conversions might be applied, but only some conversions apply in any given context:

◆ *Assignment*—This occurs when assigning the value of an expression to a variable and can involve the following: a widening primitive conversion; a widening reference conversion; a boxing conversion optionally followed by a widening reference conversion; or an unboxing conversion optionally followed by a widening primitive conversion.

If the resulting expression is of type `byte`, `char`, `short`, or `int`, and is a constant expression, then a narrowing primitive conversion can be applied if the variable is of type `byte`, `short`, or `char` and the value will fit in that type—for example, the assignment of the `int` literal 27 to a `short` variable that we saw previously. If the type of the variable is `Byte`, `Short`, or `Character`, then after the narrowing primitive conversion a boxing conversion can be applied:

```
Short s1 = 27;    // implicit int to short to Short
```

◆ *Method invocation*—This occurs when the type of an expression being passed as an argument to a method invocation is checked. Basically, the same conversions apply here as they do for assignment, with the exception that the narrowing primitive conversions are not applied. This means, for example, that a method expecting a `short` parameter will not accept the argument 27 because it is of type `int`—an explicit cast must be used. This restriction makes it easier to determine which method to invoke when overloaded forms of it exist—for example, if you try to pass a `short` to a method that could take an `int` or a `byte`, should the `short` get widened to an `int`, or narrowed to a `byte`?

◆ *Numeric promotion*—Numeric promotion, as discussed in Section 9.3.2 on page 215, ensures that all the operands of an arithmetic expression are of the appropriate type by performing widening primitive conversions, preceded if necessary by unboxing conversions.

◆ *Casts*—Casts potentially allow for any of the conversions, but may fail at runtime—this is discussed in the next section.

◆ *String conversions*—String conversions occur when the string concatenation operation is used (see page 214) and are discussed further in "String Conversions" on page 220.

9.4.2 Explicit Type Casts

When one type cannot be assigned to another type with implicit conversion, often it can be explicitly *cast* to the other type—usually to perform a narrowing conversion. A cast requests a new value of a new type that is the best available representation of the old value in the old type. Some casts are not allowed—for example, a `boolean` cannot be cast to an `int`—but explicit casting can be used to assign a `double` to a `long`, as in this code:

```
double d = 7.99;
long l = (long) d;
```

When a floating-point value is cast to an integer, the fractional part is lost by rounding toward zero; for instance, `(int)-72.3` is `-72`. Methods available in the `Math` and `StrictMath` classes round floating-point values to integers in other ways. See "`Math` and `StrictMath`" on page 657 for details. A floating-point NaN becomes the integer zero when cast. Values that are too large, or too small, to be represented as an integer become `MAX_VALUE` or `MIN_VALUE` for the types `int` and `long`. For casts to `byte`, `short`, or `char`, the floating-point value is first converted to an `int` or `long` (depending on its magnitude), and then to the smaller integer type by chopping off the upper bits as described below.

A `double` can also be explicitly cast to a `float`, or an integer type can be explicitly cast to a smaller integer type. When you cast from a `double` to a `float`, three things can go wrong: you can lose precision, you can get a zero, or you can get an infinity where you originally had a finite value outside the range of a `float`.

Integer types are converted by chopping off the upper bits. If the value in the larger integer fits in the smaller type to which it is cast, no harm is done. But if the larger integer has a value outside the range of the smaller type, dropping the upper bits changes the value, including possibly changing sign. The code

```
short s = -134;
byte b = (byte) s;

System.out.println("s = " + s + ", b = " + b);
```

produces the following output because the upper bits of s are lost when the value is stored in b:

```
s = -134, b = 122
```

A `char` can be cast to any integer type and vice versa. When an integer is cast to a `char`, only the bottom 16 bits of data are used; the rest are discarded. When a `char` is cast to an integer type, any additional upper bits are filled with zeros.

Once those bits are assigned, they are treated as they would be in any other value. Here is some code that casts a large Unicode character to both an `int` (implicitly) and a `short` (explicitly). The `int` is a positive value equal to `0x0000ffff`, because the upper bits of the character were set to zero. But the same bits in the `short` are a negative value, because the top bit of the `short` is the sign bit:

```
class CharCast {
    public static void main(String[] args) {
        int i = '\uffff';
        short s = (short) '\uffff';

        System.out.println("i = " + i);
        System.out.println("s = " + s);
    }
}
```

And here is the program's output:

```
i = 65535
s = -1
```

9.4.3   String Conversions

One special type of implicit conversion involves both the primitive and reference types: string conversion. Whenever a + operator has at least one `String` operand, it is interpreted as the string concatenation operator and the other operand, if not a `String`, is implicitly converted into a `String`. Such conversions are predefined for all primitive types. Objects are converted via the `toString` method, which is either inherited from `Object` or overridden to provide a meaningful string representation. For example, the following method brackets a string with the guillemet characters used for quotation marks in many European languages:

```
public static String guillemete(String quote) {
    return '«' + quote + '»';
}
```

This implicit conversion of primitive types and objects to strings happens only when you're using + or += in expressions involving strings. It does not happen anywhere else. A method, for example, that takes a `String` parameter must be passed a `String`. You cannot pass it an object or primitive type and have it converted implicitly.

When a `null` reference is converted to a `String`, the result is the string `"null"`, hence a `null` reference can be used freely within any string concatenation expression.

9.5   Operator Precedence and Associativity

Operator *precedence* is the "stickiness" of operators relative to each other. Operators have different precedences. For example, relational operators have a higher precedence than boolean logic operators, so you can say

```
if (min <= i && i <= max)
    process(i);
```

without any confusion. Because `*` (multiply) has a higher precedence than `-` (minus), the expression

```
3 - 3 * 5
```

has the value -12, not zero. Precedence can be overridden with parentheses; if zero were the desired value, for example, the following would do the trick:

```
(3 - 3) * 5
```

When two operators with the same precedence appear next to each other, the *associativity* of the operators determines which is evaluated first. Because `+` (add) is left-associative, the expression

```
a + b + c
```

is equivalent to

```
(a + b) + c
```

The following table lists all the operators in order of precedence from highest to lowest. All the operators are binary, except those shown as unary with *expr*, the creation and cast operators (which are also unary), and the conditional operator (which is ternary). Operators with the same precedence appear on the same line of the table:

postfix operators	`[] . (`*params*`) expr++ expr--`
unary operators	`++`*expr* `--`*expr* `+`*expr* `-`*expr* `~ !`
creation or cast	`new (`*type*`)expr`
multiplicative	`* / %`
additive	`+ -`

shift	`<< >> >>>`
relational	`< > >= <= instanceof`
equality	`== !=`
AND	`&`
exclusive OR	`∧`
inclusive OR	`|`
conditional AND	`&&`
conditional OR	`||`
conditional	`?:`
assignment	`= += -= *= /= %= >>= <<= >>>= &= ∧= |=`

All binary operators except assignment operators are left-associative. Assignment is right-associative. In other words, a=b=c is equivalent to a=(b=c), so it is convenient to chain assignments together. The conditional operator ?: is right-associative.

Parentheses are often needed in expressions in which assignment is embedded in a boolean expression, or in which bitwise operations are used. For an example of the former, examine the following code:

```
while ((v = stream.next()) != null)
    processValue(v);
```

Assignment operators have lower precedence than equality operators; without the parentheses, it would be equivalent to

```
while (v = (stream.next() != null)) // INVALID
    processValue(v);
```

and probably not what you want. It is also likely to be invalid code since it would be valid only in the unusual case in which v is boolean.

Many people find the precedence of the bitwise and logical operators &, ∧, and | hard to remember. In complex expressions you should parenthesize these operators for readability and to ensure correct precedence.

Our use of parentheses is sparse—we use them only when code seems otherwise unclear. Operator precedence is part of the language and should be generally understood. Others inject parentheses liberally. Try not to use parentheses everywhere—code becomes illegible, looking like LISP with none of LISP's saving graces.

Exercise 9.4: Using what you've learned in this chapter but without writing code, figure out which of the following expressions are invalid and what the type and values are of the valid expressions:

```
3 << 2L - 1
(3L << 2) - 1
10 < 12 == 6 > 17
10 << 12 == 6 >> 17
13.5e-1 % Float.POSITIVE_INFINITY
Float.POSITIVE_INFINITY + Double.NEGATIVE_INFINITY
Double.POSITIVE_INFINITY - Float.NEGATIVE_INFINITY
0.0 / -0.0 == -0.0 / 0.0
Integer.MAX_VALUE + Integer.MIN_VALUE
Long.MAX_VALUE + 5
(short) 5 * (byte) 10
(i < 15 ? 1.72e3f : 0)
i++ + i++ + --i      // i = 3 at start
```

9.6 Member Access

You use the dot (.) operator—as in ref.method()—to access both instance members or static members of types. Because types can inherit members from their supertypes, there are rules regarding which member is accessed in any given situation. Most of these rules were covered in detail in Chapter 2 and Chapter 3, but we briefly recap them.

You access static members by using either the type name or an object reference. When you use a type name, the member referred to is the member declared in that type (or inherited by it if there was no declaration in that type). When you use an object reference, the declared type of the reference determines which member is accessed, not the type of the object being referred to. Within a class, reference to a static member always refers to the member declared in, or inherited by, that class.

Non-static members are accessed through an object reference—either an explicit reference or implicitly this (or one of the enclosing objects) if the non-static member is a member of the current object (or enclosing object). Fields and nested types are accessed based on the declared type of the object reference. Similarly, within a method, a reference to a field or nested type always refers to the declaration within that class or else the inherited declaration. In contrast, methods are accessed based on the class of the object being referred to. Further, the existence of method overloading means that the system has to determine which method to invoke based on the compile-time type of the arguments used in the invocation; this process is described in detail in the next section. The only operator that can be applied to a method member is the method invocation operator ().

You will get a `NullPointerException` if you use . on a reference with the value `null`, unless you are accessing a static member. In that case the value of the reference is never considered, because only the type of the reference determines the class in which to locate the member.

9.6.1   Finding the Right Method

For an invocation of a method to be correct, you must provide arguments of the proper number and type so that exactly one matching method can be found in the class. If a method is not overloaded, determining the correct method is simple, because only one parameter count is associated with the method name. When overloaded methods are involved choosing the correct method is more complex. The compiler uses a "most specific" algorithm to do the match, the general form of which is as follows:

1. Determine which class or interface to search for the method. Exactly how this is done depends on the form of the method invocation. For example, if the invocation is of a static method using a class name—such as `Math.exp`—then the class to search for `exp` is `Math`. On the other hand, if the method name is not qualified in any way—such as `exp(n)`—then there must be a method by that name in scope at the point where the code invokes the method. That method will be defined in a particular class or interface, and that is the class or interface that will be searched in step 2. You should note that it is only the *name* of the method that is used to determine where to search.

2. Find all the methods in that class or interface that could possibly apply to the invocation—namely, all accessible methods that have the correct name, can take the number of arguments being passed, and whose parameters are of types that can be assigned the values of all the arguments. This matching process occurs in three phases:[3]

   i. The match is attempted without performing any boxing conversions, and without considering the possibility of a variable number of arguments— that is, the compiler looks for a method whose declared number of

---

[3]   These phases were introduced to maintain backwards compatibility with older versions of the Java programming language.

parameters matches the number of arguments, and whose kinds of parameters (either primitive or reference types) match the corresponding arguments provided.

ii. If no matches have been found, the match is attempted again, but this time boxing conversions are considered, so primitives can be passed for objects and vice-versa.

iii. If no matches have been found, the match is attempted again, but this time the possibility of a variable number of arguments is considered, so now the number of arguments might exceed the number of declared parameters.

3. If any method in the set has parameter types that are all assignable to the corresponding parameters of any other method in the set, that other method is removed from the set because it is a less specific method. For example, if the set has a method that takes an `Object` parameter and another that takes a `String` parameter, the `Object` method is removed because a `String` can be assigned to an `Object`, and therefore the method that takes a `String` is more specific. If you pass a `String` argument you want it handled by the method that specializes in strings, not the general one that works with any object.

4. If exactly one method remains, that method is the most specific and will be invoked. If more than one method remains, and they have different signatures, then the invocation is ambiguous and the invoking code invalid because there is no most specific method. If all the remaining methods have the same signature then: if all are abstract then one is chosen arbitrarily; otherwise if only one is not abstract then it is chosen; otherwise the invocation is again ambiguous and is invalid.

The exact details of the algorithm are quite complex, due mainly to the possibility of generic types or methods being involved—see Chapter 11. Interested readers should again consult *The Java*™ *Language Specification, Third Edition,* for those details.

Once a method has been selected, that method determines the expected return type and the possible checked exceptions of that method invocation. If the expected return type is not acceptable in the code (for example, the method returns a `String` but the method call is used as an array subscript) or if the checked exceptions are not dealt with correctly you will get a compile-time error.

For instance, suppose you had the following type hierarchy:

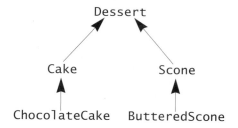

Also suppose you had several overloaded methods that took particular combinations of `Dessert` parameters:

```
void moorge(Dessert d, Scone s)        { /* first form  */ }
void moorge(Cake c, Dessert d)         { /* second form */ }
void moorge(ChocolateCake cc, Scone s) { /* third form  */ }
void moorge(Dessert... desserts)       { /* fourth form */ }
```

Now consider the following invocations of `moorge`:

```
moorge(dessertRef, sconeRef);
moorge(chocolateCakeRef, dessertRef);
moorge(chocolateCakeRef, butteredSconeRef);
moorge(cakeRef, sconeRef);      // INVALID
moorge(sconeRef, cakeRef);
```

All of these invocations might appear to match the fourth form, and indeed without the other overloaded forms they would. But the fourth form, being a method that takes a variable number of arguments, will only be considered by the compiler if it fails to find any candidate methods that explicitly declare two parameters of assignable type.

The first invocation uses the first form of `moorge` because the parameter and argument types match exactly. The second invocation uses the second form because it is the only form for which the provided arguments can be assigned to the parameter types. In both cases, the method to invoke is clear after step 2 in the method-matching algorithm.

The third invocation requires more thought. The list of potential overloads includes all three two-argument forms, because a `ChocolateCake` reference is assignable to any of the first parameter types, a `ButteredScone` reference is assignable to either of the second parameter types, and none of the signatures matches exactly. So after step 2, you have a set of three candidate methods.

Step 3 requires you to eliminate less specific methods from the set. In this case, the first form is removed from the set because the third form is more specific—a `ChocolateCake` reference can be assigned to the first form's `Dessert` parameter and a `Scone` reference can be assigned to the first form's `Scone` parameter, so the first form is less specific. The second form is removed from the set in a similar manner. After this, the set of possible methods has been reduced to one—the third form of `moorge`—and that method form will be invoked.

The fourth invocation is invalid. After step 2, the set of possible matches includes the first and second forms. Because neither form's parameters are assignable to the other, neither form can be removed from the set in step 3. Therefore, you have an ambiguous invocation that cannot be resolved by the compiler, and so it is an invalid invocation of `moorge`. You can resolve the ambiguity by explicitly casting one of the arguments to the `Dessert` type: If you cast `cakeRef`, then the first form is invoked; if you cast `sconeRef`, then the second form is invoked.

The final invocation uses the fourth form. There are no potential candidates after the first phase of step 2, and no boxing conversions to consider, so the compiler now considers the fourth form in phase 3. An invocation with two arguments is compatible with a parameter list that has a single sequence parameter, and the types of the two arguments are assignable to the type of the sequence, so it matches. Because this is the only match after step 2, it is the method chosen.

These rules also apply to the primitive types. An `int`, for example, can be assigned to a `float`, and resolving an overloaded invocation will take that into account just as it considered that a `ButteredScone` reference was assignable to a `Scone` reference. However, implicit integer conversions to smaller types are not applied—if a method takes a `short` argument and you supply an `int` you will have to explicitly cast the `int` to `short`; it won't match the `short` parameter, regardless of its value.

The method resolution process takes place at compile time based on the declared types of the object reference and the argument values. This process determines which form of a method should be invoked, but not which implementation of that method. At run time the actual type of the object on which the method is invoked is used to find an implementation of the method that was determined at compile time.

Methods may not differ only in return type or in the list of exceptions they throw, because there are too many ambiguities to determine which overloaded method is wanted. If, for example, there were two `doppelgänger` methods that differed only in that one returned an `int` and the other returned a `short`, both methods would make equal sense in the following statement:

```
double d = doppelgänger();
```

A similar problem exists with exceptions, because you can catch any, all, or none of the exceptions a method might throw in the code in which you invoke the overloaded method. There would be no way to determine which of two methods to use when they differed only in thrown exceptions.

Such ambiguities are not always detectable at compile time. For example, a superclass may be modified to add a new method that differs only in return type from a method in an extended class. If the extended class is not recompiled, then the error will not be detected. At run time there is no problem because the exact form of the method to be invoked was determined at compile time, so that is the method that will be looked for in the extended class. In a similar way, if a class is modified to add a new overloaded form of a method, but the class invoking that method is not recompiled, then the new method will never be invoked by that class—the form of method to invoke was already determined at compile time and that form is different from that of the new method.

> *Math was always my bad subject.*
> *I couldn't convince my teachers that many of my answers were meant ironically.*
> —Calvin Trillin

CHAPTER **10**

Control Flow

"Would you tell me, please, which way I ought to go from here?"
"That depends a good deal on where you want to get to."
—Lewis Carroll, *Alice in Wonderland*

A program consisting only of a list of consecutive statements is immediately useful because the statements are executed in the order in which they're written. But the ability to control the order in which statements are executed—that is, to test conditions and execute different statements based on the results of the tests—adds enormous value to our programming toolkit. This chapter covers almost all the *control flow statements* that direct the order of execution. Exceptions and assertions are covered separately in Chapter 12.

10.1 Statements and Blocks

The two basic statements are *expression statements* and *declaration statements,* of which you've seen a plethora. Expression statements, such as i++ or method invocations, are expressions that have a semicolon at the end. The semicolon terminates the statement.[1] In fact, a semicolon by itself is a statement that does nothing—the *empty statement.* Not all expressions can become statements, since it would be almost always meaningless to have, for example, an expression such as x <= y stand alone as a statement. Only the following types of expressions can be made into statements by adding a terminating semicolon:

---

[1]   There is a distinction between *terminator* and *separator.* The comma between identifiers in declarations is a separator because it comes between elements in the list. The semicolon is a terminator because it ends each statement. If the semicolon were a statement separator, the last semicolon in a code block would be unnecessary and (depending on the choice of the language designer) possibly invalid.

- ◆ Assignment expressions—those that contain = or one of the *op=* operators
- ◆ Prefix or postfix forms of ++ and --
- ◆ Method calls (whether or not they return a value)
- ◆ Object creation expressions—those that use new to create an object

Declaration statements (formally called *local variable declaration statements*) declare a variable and initialize it to a value, as discussed in Section 7.3.1 on page 170. They can appear anywhere inside a block, not just at the beginning. Local variables exist only as long as the block containing their declaration is executing. Local variables must be initialized before use, either by initialization when declared or by assignment. If any local variable is used before it is initialized, the code will not compile.

Local class declaration statements declare a local inner class that can be used within the block in which it was declared. Local classes were discussed in detail on page 142.

In addition to the expression statements listed, several other kinds of statements, such as if and for statements, affect flow of control through the program. This chapter covers each type of statement in detail.

Curly braces, { and }, group zero or more statements into a *block*. A block can be used where any single statement is allowed because a block *is* a statement, albeit a compound one.

10.2 if–else

The most basic form of conditional control flow is the if statement, which chooses whether to execute statements that follow it. Its syntax is:

```
if (expression)
     statement1
else
     statement2
```

First, the expression—which must be of type boolean or Boolean—is evaluated. If its value is true, then *statement1* is executed; otherwise, if there is an else clause, *statement2* is executed. The else clause is optional.

You can build a series of tests by joining another if to the else clause of a previous if. Here is a method that maps a string—expected to be one of a particular set of words—into an action to be performed with a value:

```java
public void setProperty(String keyword, double value)
    throws UnknownProperty
{
    if (keyword.equals("charm"))
        charm(value);
    else if (keyword.equals("strange"))
        strange(value);
    else
        throw new UnknownProperty(keyword);
}
```

What if there is more than one preceding if without an else? For example:

```java
public double sumPositive(double[] values) {
    double sum = 0.0;

    if (values.length > 1)
        for (int i = 0; i < values.length; i++)
            if (values[i] > 0)
                sum += values[i];
    else    // oops!
        sum = values[0];
    return sum;
}
```

The else clause *looks* as if it is bound to the array length check, but that is a mirage of indentation, and indentation is ignored. Instead, an else clause is bound to the most recent if that does not have one. Thus, the previous block of code is equivalent to

```java
public double sumPositive(double[] values) {
    double sum = 0.0;

    if (values.length > 1)
        for (int i = 0; i < values.length; i++)
            if (values[i] > 0)
                sum += values[i];
            else    // oops!
                sum = values[0];
    return sum;
}
```

This is probably not what was intended. To bind the `else` clause to the first `if`, you can use braces to create blocks:

```
public double sumPositive(double[] values) {
    double sum = 0.0;

    if (values.length > 1) {
        for (int i = 0; i < values.length; i++)
            if (values[i] > 0)
                sum += values[i];
    } else {
        sum = values[0];
    }
    return sum;
}
```

Exercise 10.1: Using `if-else` in a loop, write a method that takes a string parameter and returns a string with all the special characters in the original string replaced by their language equivalents. For example, a string with a " in the middle of it should create a return value with that " replaced by \". (Section 7.2.3 on page 167 lists all special characters).

10.3 `switch`

A `switch` statement allows you to transfer control to a labeled entry point in a block of statements, based on the value of an expression. The general form of a `switch` statement is:

```
switch (expression) {
    case n: statements
    case m: statements

    . . .

    default: statements
}
```

The expression must either be of an integer type (`char`, `byte`, `short`, or `int`, or a corresponding wrapper class) or an enum type. The body of the `switch` statement, known as the *switch block,* contains statements that can be prefixed with `case` labels. A `case` label is an integer or enum constant. If the value of the `switch` expression matches the value of a `case` label then control is transferred to the first statement following that label. If a matching `case` label is not found, control is transferred to the first statement following a `default` label. If there is no `default` label, the entire `switch` statement is skipped.

For example, consider our `Verbose` interface from page 121:

```
interface Verbose {
    int SILENT  = 0;
    int TERSE   = 1;
    int NORMAL  = 2;
    int VERBOSE = 3;

    void setVerbosity(int level);
    int getVerbosity();
}
```

Depending on the verbosity level, the state of the object is dumped, adding new output at greater verbosity levels and then printing the output of the next lower level of verbosity:

```
Verbose v = ... ; // initialized as appropriate
public void dumpState() {
    int verbosity = v.getVerbosity();
    switch (verbosity) {
      case Verbose.SILENT:
        break; // do nothing

      case Verbose.VERBOSE:
        System.out.println(stateDetails);
        // FALLTHROUGH

      case Verbose.NORMAL:
        System.out.println(basicState);
        // FALLTHROUGH

      case Verbose.TERSE:
        System.out.println(summaryState);
        break;

      default:
        throw new IllegalStateException(
                    "verbosity=" + verbosity);
    }
}
```

Once control has transferred to a statement following a case label, the following statements are executed in turn, according to the semantics of those statements, even if those statements have their own different case labels. The FALLTHROUGH comments in the example show where control *falls through* the next case label to the code below. Thus, if the verbosity level is VERBOSE, all three output parts are printed; if NORMAL, two parts are printed; and if TERSE, only one part is printed.

A case or default label does *not* force a break out of the switch. Nor does it imply an end to execution of statements. If you want to stop executing statements in the switch block you must explicitly transfer control out of the switch block. You can do this with a break statement. Within a switch block, a break statement transfers control to the first statement after the switch. This is why we have a break statement after the TERSE output is finished. Without the break, execution would continue through into the code for the default label and throw the exception every time. Similarly, in the SILENT case, all that is executed is the break because there is nothing to print.

Falling through to the next case can be useful in some circumstances. But in most cases a break should come after the code that a case label selects. Good coding style suggests that you always use some form of FALLTHROUGH comment to document an intentional fall-through.

A single statement can have more than one case label, allowing a singular action in multiple cases. For example, here we use a switch statement to decide how to translate a hexadecimal digit into an int:

```
public int hexValue(char ch) throws NonHexDigitException {
    switch (ch) {
      case '0': case '1': case '2': case '3': case '4':
      case '5': case '6': case '7': case '8': case '9':
        return (ch - '0');

      case 'a': case 'b': case 'c':
      case 'd': case 'e': case 'f':
        return (ch - 'a') + 10;

      case 'A': case 'B': case 'C':
      case 'D': case 'E': case 'F':
        return (ch - 'A') + 10;

      default:
        throw new NonHexDigitException(ch);
    }
}
```

There are no `break` statements because the `return` statements exit the switch block (and the whole method) before control can fall through.

You should terminate the last group of statements in a switch with a `break`, `return`, or `throw`, as you would a group of statements in an earlier case. Doing so reduces the likelihood of accidentally falling through the bottom of what *used* to be the last part of the switch when a new `case` is added.

All `case` labels must be enum constants or constant expressions—the expressions must contain only literals or named constants initialized with constant expressions—and must be assignable to the type of the `switch` expression. In any single `switch` statement, each `case` value must be unique, and there can be at most one `default` label.

When you use an enum as a switch expression, you will get no warning if you leave out a case. It is your job to ensure that each case is covered. To safeguard against an enum being redefined to have additional constants, you should always include a `default` case that simply throws an exception.

Only statements directly within the switch block can have `case` labels. This means that you cannot, for example, transfer control to a statement within the switch block that is in the middle of a loop, or a statement within a nested block of code. You can, however, skip the declaration and initialization of a local variable within the switch block (not that we recommend it). The effect of this is that the local variable is still considered to be declared, but the initializer has not been executed. Because local variables must be initialized, any attempt to read the value of that variable will result in a compile-time error—the first use of that variable must be an assignment.

The first statement in a switch block must be labeled, otherwise it is unreachable (all cases will jump over it) and your code will not compile.

Exercise 10.2: Rewrite your method from Exercise 10.1 to use a `switch`.

Exercise 10.3: Using your "days of the week" enum from Exercise 6.1 write a method that takes a day of the week and returns `true` if it is a working day, and `false` otherwise. First use nested `if–else` statements and then a `switch` statement. Which do you think results in clearer code?

10.4 `while` and `do–while`

The `while` loop looks like this:

```
while (expression)
    statement
```

The expression—again either of `boolean` or `Boolean` type—is evaluated and, if it is `true`, the statement (which may be a block) is executed. Once the statement completes, the expression is reevaluated and, if still `true`, the statement is executed again. This repeats until the expression evaluates to `false`, at which point control transfers to after the `while`.

We introduced the `while` loop with our second program in Chapter 1, the `Fibonacci` program:

```
while (hi < MAX) {
    System.out.println(hi);
    hi = lo + hi;
    lo = hi - lo;
}
```

This loops around printing and calculating new Fibonacci values until the highest value computed exceeds the maximum limit.

A `while` loop executes zero or more times since the expression might be `false` the first time it is evaluated. Sometimes you want to execute a loop body at least once, which is why you also have a do–`while` loop:

```
do
    statement
while (expression);
```

Here, the expression is evaluated *after* the statement is executed. While the expression is `true`, the statement is executed repeatedly. The statement in a do–`while` loop is almost always a block.

Exercise 10.4: Select a few previous exercise solutions for which you have used a `for` loop and rewrite it using a `while` loop. Can you also rewrite it using a do–`while` loop? Would you do so? If not, why not?

10.5 for

The `for` statement comes in two forms: a basic and an enhanced form. The basic form is the more general and powerful of the two.

10.5.1 Basic for Statement

You use the basic `for` statement to loop over a range of values from beginning to end. It looks like this:

```
for (initialization-expression;
     loop-expression;
     update-expression)
    statement
```

The *initialization-expression* allows you to declare and/or initialize loop variables, and is executed only once. Then the *loop-expression*—of boolean or Boolean type—is evaluated and if it is true the statement in the body of the loop is executed. After executing the loop body, the *update-expression* is evaluated, usually to update the values of the loop variables, and then the *loop-expression* is reevaluated. This cycle repeats until the *loop-expression* is found to be false. This is roughly equivalent to

```
{
    initialization-expression;
    while (loop-expression) {
        statement
        update-expression;
    }
}
```

except that in a for statement the *update-expression* is always executed if a continue is encountered in the loop body (see "continue" on page 244).

The initialization and update parts of a for loop can be comma-separated lists of expressions. The expressions separated by the commas are, like most operator operands, evaluated from left-to-right. For example, to march two indexes through an array in opposite directions, the following code would be appropriate:

```
for (i = 0, j = arr.length - 1; j >= 0; i++, j--) {
    // ...
}
```

The initialization section of a for loop can also be a local variable declaration statement, as described on page 170. For example, if i and j are not used outside the for loop, you could rewrite the previous example as:

```
for (int i = 0, j = arr.length - 1; j >= 0; i++, j--) {
    // ...
}
```

If you have a local variable declaration, however, each part of the expression after a comma is expected to be a part of that local variable declaration. For example, if you want to print the first MAX members of a linked list you need to both maintain a count and iterate through the list members. You might be tempted to try the following:

```
for (int i = 0, Cell node = head;                    // INVALID
     i < MAX && node != null;
     i++, node = node.next)
{
    System.out.println(node.getElement());
}
```

This will not compile: In a variable declaration the comma separates the different variables being declared, and Cell is a type, not a variable. Declarations of different types of variables are distinct statements terminated by semicolons. If you change the comma to a semicolon, however, you get a for loop with four sections, not three—still an error. If you need to initialize two different types of variables then neither of them can be declared within the for loop:

```
int i;
Cell node;
for (i = 0, node = head;
     i < MAX && node != null;
     i++, node = node.next)
{
    System.out.println(node.getElement());
}
```

Typically, the for loop is used to iterate a variable over a range of values until some logical end to that range is reached. You can define what an iteration range is. A for loop is often used, for example, to iterate through the elements of a linked list or to follow a mathematical sequence of values. This capability makes the for construct more powerful than equivalent constructs in many other languages that restrict for-style constructs to incrementing a variable over a range of values.

Here is an example of such a loop, designed to calculate the smallest value of *exp* such that 10^{exp} is greater than or equal to a value:

```
public static int tenPower(int value) {
    int exp, v;
    for (exp = 0, v = value - 1; v > 0; exp++, v /= 10)
        continue;
    return exp;
}
```

In this case, two variables step through different ranges. As long as the loop variable v is greater than zero, the exponent value is incremented and v is divided by ten. When the loop completes, the value 10^{exp} is the smallest power of ten that is greater than or equal to value. Both the test value and the exponent are updated on each loop iteration. In such cases, a comma-separated list of expressions is a good technique to ensure that the two values are always in lockstep.

The body of this loop is simply a continue statement, which starts the next iteration of the loop. The body of the loop has nothing to do—all the work of the loop is in the test and iteration clauses of the for statement itself. The continue style shown here is one way to show an empty loop body; another way is to put a simple semicolon on a line by itself or to use an empty block with braces. Simply putting a semicolon at the end of the for line is dangerous—if the semicolon is accidentally deleted or forgotten, the statement that follows the for can silently become the body of the for.

All the expressions in the for construct are optional. If *initialization-expression* or *update-expression* is left out, its part in the loop is simply omitted. If *loop-expression* is left out, it is assumed to be true. Thus, one idiomatic way to write an infinite loop is as a "for ever" loop:

```
for (;;)
    statement
```

Presumably, the loop is terminated by some other means, such as a break statement (described later) or by throwing an exception.

Conventionally, the for loop is used only when looping through a range of related values. It is bad style to violate this convention by using initialization or increment expressions that are unrelated to the boolean loop test.

Exercise 10.5: Write a method that takes two char parameters and prints the characters between those two values, including the endpoints.

10.5.2 Enhanced for Statement

The enhanced for statement, often referred to as the *for-each* loop, provides an alternative, more compact form for iterating through a set of values. It looks like this:

```
for (Type loop-variable : set-expression)
    statement
```

The *set-expression* must evaluate to an object that defines the set of values that you want to iterate through, and the *loop-variable* is a local variable of a suitable type for the set's contents. Each time through the loop, *loop-variable* takes on the next value from the set, and *statement* is executed (presumably using the *loop-variable* for something). This continues until no more values remain in the set.

The *set-expression* must either evaluate to an array instance, or an object that implements the interface java.lang.Iterable—which is the case for all of the collection classes you'll see in Chapter 21. Here's an example using an array, where we rewrite the average method we showed on page 19:

```
static double average(int[] values) {
    if (values == null || values.length == 0)
        throw new IllegalArgumentException();

    double sum = 0.0;
    for (int val : values)
        sum += val;

    return sum / values.length;
}
```

The for statement is read "for each val in values" and each time through the loop we add the next value, val, to the sum. This is equivalent to a basic for statement written as follows:

```
for (int j = 0 ; j < values.length; j++) {
    int val = values[j];
    sum += val;
}
```

The advantage of using the for-each loop with arrays is that you don't have to manually maintain the array index and check the array length. The disadvantage is that for-each can only loop forwards through a single array, and only looks at the array elements. If you want to modify an array element you will need to know what index you are working with, and that information is not available in the enhanced for statement.

The main motivation behind the enhanced for statement is to make it more convenient to iterate through collection classes, or more generally anything that implements the Iterable interface. The Iterable interface defines a single method iterator that returns an Iterator for that object (see "Iteration" on page 571). Recalling the AttributedImpl class we defined in Chapter 4, we can define a method to print all the attributes of an AttributedImpl object:

```
static void printAttributes(AttributedImpl obj) {
    for (Attr attr : obj)
        System.out.println(attr);
}
```

Again we read this as "for each `attr` in `obj`" and it is simply a syntactic short-hand for a more verbose basic `for` statement that uses the iterator explicitly:

```
for (Iterator<Attr> iter = obj.iterator();
     iter.hasNext();
     /* no update expression */)
{
    Attr attr = iter.next();
    System.out.println(attr);
}
```

As before the advantage of the enhanced `for` is a simple, syntactic construct for accessing the elements you are iterating through. But you cannot use the iterator's `remove` method to alter the collection, nor can you iterate through multiple collections at the same time. If you need these capabilities you must use the basic `for` statement and an explicit iterator.

10.6 Labels

You can label statements to give them a name by which they can be referred. A label precedes the statement it names; only one label is allowed per statement:

```
label: statement
```

Labels can be referred to only by the `break` and `continue` statements (discussed next).

10.7 break

A `break` statement can be used to exit from any block, not just from a `switch`. There are two forms of `break` statement. The *unlabeled break:*

```
break;
```

and the *labeled break:*

```
break label;
```

An unlabeled break terminates the innermost switch, for, while, or do statement—and so can appear only within one of those statements. A labeled break can terminate any labeled statement.

A break is most often used to break out of a loop. In this example, we are looking for the first empty slot in an array of references to Contained objects:

```
class Container {
    private Contained[] objs;

    // ...

    public void addIn(Contained obj)
        throws NoEmptySlotException
    {
        int i;
        for (i = 0; i < objs.length; i++)
            if (objs[i] == null)
                break;
        if (i >= objs.length)
            throw new NoEmptySlotException();
        objs[i] = obj;      // put it inside me
        obj.inside(this); // let it know it's inside me
    }
}
```

To terminate an outer loop or block, you label the outer statement and use its label name in the break statement:

```
private float[][] matrix;

public boolean workOnFlag(float flag) {
    int y, x;
    boolean found = false;

  search:
    for (y = 0; y < matrix.length; y++) {
        for (x = 0; x < matrix[y].length; x++) {
            if (matrix[y][x] == flag) {
                found = true;
                break search;
            }
        }
    }
```

```
    }
    if (!found)
        return false;

    // do some stuff with flagged value at matrix[y][x]
    return true;
}
```

Here we label the outer for loop and if we find the value we are looking for, we terminate both inner and outer loops by using a labeled break. This simplifies the logic of the loops because we do not need to add a !found clause in the loop expressions.

Note that a labeled break is not a goto. The goto statement would enable indiscriminate jumping around in code, obfuscating the flow of control. A break or continue that references a label, on the other hand, exits from or repeats only that specific labeled block, and the flow of control is obvious by inspection. For example, here is a modified version of workOnFlag that labels a block instead of a loop, allowing us to dispense with the found flag altogether:

```
public boolean workOnFlag(float flag) {
    int y, x;

    search:
    {
        for (y = 0; y < matrix.length; y++) {
            for (x = 0; x < matrix[y].length; x++) {
                if (matrix[y][x] == flag)
                    break search;
            }
        }

        // if we get here we didn't find it
        return false;
    }
    // do some stuff with flagged value at matrix[y][x]
    return true;
}
```

You should use the break statement judiciously, and with thought to the clarity of the resulting code. Arbitrarily jumping out of loops or statements can obscure the flow of control in the code, making it harder to understand and maintain. Some programming styles ban the use of break altogether, but that is an extreme position. Contorting the logic in a loop to avoid the need for a `break` can result in code that is less clear than it would have been with the `break`.

10.8 `continue`

A `continue` statement can be used only within a loop (`for`, `while`, or `do`) and transfers control to the end of the loop's body to continue on with the loop. In the case of `while` and `do` loops, this causes the loop expression to be the next thing evaluated. In a basic `for` loop `continue` causes the update-expression to be evaluated next and then the loop expression. In the enhanced `for` loop execution goes to the next element in the set of values if there is one.

Like the `break` statement, the `continue` statement has an unlabeled form:

```
continue;
```

and a labeled form:

```
continue label;
```

In the unlabeled form, `continue` transfers control to the end of the innermost loop's body. The labeled form transfers control to the end of the loop with that label. The label must belong to a loop statement.

A `continue` is often used to skip over an element of a loop range that can be ignored or treated with trivial code. For example, a token stream that included a simple "skip" token might be handled this way:

```
while (!stream.eof()) {
    token = stream.next();
    if (token.equals("skip"))
        continue;
    // ... process token ...
}
```

A labeled `continue` will break out of any inner loops on its way to the next iteration of the named loop. No label is required on the `continue` in the preceding example since there is only one enclosing loop. Consider, however, nested loops that iterate over the values of a two-dimensional matrix. Suppose that the matrix is symmetric (`matrix[i][j] == matrix[j][i]`). In that case, you need only iterate through half of the matrix. For example, here is a method that doubles each value in a symmetric matrix:

```
static void doubleUp(int[][] matrix) {
    int order = matrix.length;
  column:
    for (int i = 0; i < order; i++) {
        for (int j = 0; j < order; j++) {
            matrix[i][j] = matrix[j][i] = matrix[i][j]*2;
            if (i == j)
                continue column;
        }
    }
}
```

Each time a diagonal element of the matrix is reached, the rest of that row is skipped by continuing with the outer loop that iterates over the columns.

10.9 `return`

A `return` statement terminates execution of a method and returns to the invoker. If the method returns no value, a simple `return` statement will do:

```
return;
```

If the method has a return type, the `return` must include an expression of a type that could be assigned to the return type. For example, if a method returns `double`, a `return` could have an expression that was a `double`, `float`, or integer:

```
protected double nonNegative(double val) {
    if (val < 0)
        return 0;   // an int constant
    else
        return val; // a double
}
```

A `return` can also be used to exit a constructor. Since constructors do not specify a return type, `return` is used without a value. Constructors are invoked as part of the new process that, in the end, returns a reference to a new object, but each constructor plays only a part of that role; no constructor "returns" the final reference.

10.10 What, No goto?

The Java programming language has no `goto` construct that transfers control to an arbitrary statement, although `goto` is common in languages to which the language is related.[2] The primary uses for `goto` in such languages have other solutions:

- Controlling outer loops from within nested loops. Use labeled `break` and `continue` statements to meet this need.
- Skipping the rest of a block of code that is not in a loop when an answer or error is found. Use a labeled `break`.
- Executing cleanup code before a method or block of code exits. Use either a labeled break or, more cleanly, the `finally` construct of the `try` statement covered in Chapter 12.

Labeled `break` and `continue` have the advantage that they transfer control to a strictly limited place. A `finally` block is even stricter as to where it transfers control, and it works in all circumstances, including exceptions. With these constructs you can write clean code without a `goto`.

Furious activity is no substitute for understanding.
—H.H. Williams

---

[2] Although not used `goto` is a reserved keyword, as is `const`. The reason they are reserved is mostly historical: Both of these come from strongly related programming languages, like C and C++, and reserving them helped compilers advise programmers clearly that they were using something that didn't make sense. Occasionally, suggestions are made for how `const` might be used in the Java programming language.

CHAPTER 11

Generic Types

*The problem with people who have no vices
is that generally you can be pretty sure they're going to have some pretty annoying virtues.*
—Elizabeth Taylor

IN the Java programming language, the class `Object` forms the root of the class hierarchy, allowing other classes to deal with arbitrary types of objects by declaring that they work with `Object`. In Chapter 3 you saw a `SingleLinkQueue` class that used `Cell` objects to hold a reference to any `Object` you wanted in the queue. This provides great flexibility, but with some inconvenience: If you know that the elements in question are `String` objects, for example, then you have to cast the result of the `remove` method each time.

This use of `Object` as a generic reference is also potentially unsafe—there is nothing to stop the programmer from mistakenly adding a `Number` instead of a `String`, with the mistake only discovered at runtime when the cast applied to `remove` fails and a `ClassCastException` is thrown. To avoid these problems you could define different queue classes to store particular types of elements, such as `SingleLinkStringQueue` or `SingleLinkNumberQueue`, but this has many drawbacks: It is tedious, inefficient, and error-prone to duplicate code in this way; it is awkward to deal with an arbitrary kind of queue; and you could end up with numerous classes that are identical except for the return and parameter types of a few methods. Ideally, you would like to write a `SingleLinkQueue` that can be specialized to contain any particular kind of object and then, for each queue object, define which type it holds. That is where *generic types* come in.

To start, here's a new version of `Cell` declared as a generic class:

```
class Cell<E> {
    private Cell<E> next;
    private E element;
    public Cell(E element) {
        this.element = element;
```

```
        }
        public Cell(E element, Cell<E> next) {
            this.element = element;
            this.next = next;
        }
        public E getElement() {
            return element;
        }
        public void setElement(E element) {
            this.element = element;
        }
        public Cell<E> getNext() {
            return next;
        }
        public void setNext(Cell<E> next) {
            this.next = next;
        }
    }
```

The class is now declared as Cell<E> (which is read as "Cell of E"). E represents the type of element that a cell object can hold. In this generic version of Cell, everywhere that Object was used in the original Cell class now uses the name E. E is known as a *type variable* for which a concrete type can be substituted. There's nothing special about the name E—it could be ElementType, for example—but E is a nice abbreviation for "element." By convention, type variables have single character names: E for an element type, K for a key type, V for a value type, T for a general type, and so forth.

To create an actual Cell object you have to tell the compiler what specific type you wish to replace E with. For example, a Cell to hold a String could be constructed and referenced as follows:

```
Cell<String> strCell = new Cell<String>("Hello");
```

Note that the concrete type information is required in two places here: in the type declaration of strCell and as part of the constructor invocation.

Of course, our cells aren't used directly like this; rather, they are an internal part of the SingleLinkQueue class, which would look like this:

```
class SingleLinkQueue<E> {
    protected Cell<E> head;
    protected Cell<E> tail;
```

```
    public void add(E item) {
        Cell<E> cell = new Cell<E>(item);
        if (tail == null)
            head = tail = cell;
        else {
            tail.setNext(cell);
            tail = cell;
        }
    }

    public E remove() {
        if (head == null)
            return null;
        Cell<E> cell = head;
        head = head.getNext();
        if (head == null)
            tail = null;  // empty queue
        return cell.getElement();
    }
}
```

A queue with element type E is made up of cells of E. Again, everywhere in the original class that `Object` was used, the type variable E is now used. In addition, each use of `Cell` is replaced with `Cell<E>`.

You can create and use a queue of `String` objects as follows:

```
SingleLinkQueue<String> queue =
    new SingleLinkQueue<String>();
queue.add("Hello");
queue.add("World");
```

Now there is no need for a cast when invoking `remove`:

```
String hello = queue.remove();
```

Nor is it possible to add the wrong kind of element to the queue:

```
queue.add(25);    // INVALID: won't compile
```

Generic types are invaluable in defining these kind of collection classes, as you'll see in Chapter 21, but they have uses in many other situations.

11.1   Generic Type Declarations

The declaration of the class `Cell<E>` is an example of a *generic type declaration.* It declares `Cell` to be a generic class, where the type variable E is known as the *type parameter* of the generic declaration. When you use a type name such as `Cell<String>`, providing a specific *type argument* (`String`) to replace the generic type parameter (E), you thereby introduce a *parameterized type.* This has some similarities to the method invocation process where declared parameters are given the values of specific arguments, so the use of a parameterized type such as `Cell<String>` is also known as a *generic type invocation.*

A generic type declaration can contain multiple type parameters, separated by commas. For example, the `Map` interface (see page 587) defines a generic mapping between keys and values so it is declared as `interface Map<K, V>`, where K is the type parameter for the key type and V is the type parameter for the value type.

When you define a generic class, all invocations of that generic class are simply expressions of that one class. Declaring a variable `strCell` as `Cell<String>` tells the compiler that `strCell` will refer to an object of type `Cell<E>` where E will be `String`. It does not tell the compiler to create a new class `Cell<String>`. `Cell<String>` and `Cell<Number>` are not two separate classes. They are two generic type invocations of the one class—`Cell`—that are applied in two different ways to two different objects. The class `Cell` is known as the *raw type* corresponding to the generic class declaration `Cell<E>`.

The following code shows quite clearly that there is just one class because the value of `same` is `true`:

```
Cell<String> strCell = new Cell<String>("Hello");
Cell<Integer> intCell = new Cell<Integer>(25);
boolean same = (strCell.getClass() == intCell.getClass());
```

This may seem surprising if you thought that `Cell<String>` was a class. But it is only `Cell` that is a class. The use of `<String>` and `<Integer>` in the constructor invocations are not class definitions. They declare information about the type of object being constructed so that the compiler can check that the object is used correctly. At runtime, no generic type information is present in objects. In the example above, the `Cell` object that contains the element `"Hello"` has no knowledge that it was constructed as a `Cell<String>`—that knowledge has been *erased;* a concept we come back to a bit later in the chapter (see page 267).

The fact that there is a single class definition for a generic class, no matter how many different parameterized invocations there may be, has several consequences in regard to what you can and cannot do with generics. We point these out along the way, but they all boil down to this: There is only one class, so you cannot do anything that cannot be done with only one class.

The first consequence of this fact is that a generic class with a type parameter, say E, cannot use E in the type of a static field or anywhere within a static method or static initializer. To do so would require a different field or method for each value of E. Because there is only one class, there is only one actual static field or method, and so the code cannot depend on the value of E. The fact that static members are never dependent on a particular parameterization is reinforced by the rule that you cannot refer to a static member via a parameterized type name. For example, if `SingleLinkQueue` has a static `merge` method, it must be invoked as `SingleLinkQueue.merge`. `SingleLinkQueue<Integer>.merge`, for example, would not compile. To similarly reinforce that there is but a single class object, a class literal such as `SingleLinkQueue.class` can only use the raw class name.

Within a generic class definition, a type parameter can appear in any non-static declaration where you would normally put a concrete type name: in a field declaration, a method return type or parameter type declaration, a local variable declaration, or a nested type declaration. You've seen examples of most of these uses in the `Cell` and `SingleLinkQueue` classes.

Two places where you would usually use a class name but cannot use a type parameter are when creating objects and arrays. For example, here is the wrong way to try to expose the elements of a queue as an array:

```java
class SingleLinkQueue<E> {
    // ...

    public E[] toArray() {
        int size = 0;
        for (Cell<E> c = head; c != null; c = c.getNext())
            size++;

        E[] arr = new E[size];    // INVALID: won't compile

        // ... copy in elements ...
    }
}
```

You cannot instantiate E or create an array of E for the same reason you can't have a static field of type E: There is a single class with a single definition of `toArray`, and the compiler has to know at compile time what code to generate to create any objects or arrays. There is no way for the compiler to generate `new String[size]` or `new Integer[size]` depending on what E happens to be.[1]

---

[1] This is a consequence of there being no parameterized type information within objects at runtime—see Section 11.5 on page 267.

By now you may be wondering how it is that the compiler can do anything with type parameters? The answer to that is deceptively simple: The compiler uses the most general possible type to represent the type parameter (often `Object`) and uses type casting to ensure type correctness. You can think of generics as a (potentially optimized) shorthand for writing all those casts. This is explained in more detail a little later.

So how do you expose the elements of the queue as an array? You could expose the size of the queue and have the caller create, and pass to you, an array of the right size and type—which we show you a little later—or you could have the caller provide the *type token* for E (the `Class` object for the actual type argument) and use reflection to create an array of the right size—see "Genericity and Dynamic Arrays" on page 430.

Exercise 11.1: Revisit the `LinkedList` class that you started back in Exercise 2.2 and rewrite it as a generic class.

Exercise 11.2: Rewrite the `Attr` class from Chapter 3 as a generic class.

Exercise 11.3: Was Exercise 11.2 a good idea? How does `Attr` being generic affect the `Attributed` interface defined in Chapter 4? What does it mean for `Attributed` objects?

11.1.1 Bounded Type Parameters

In the generic class declaration of `Cell<E>`, the type variable E can be replaced by absolutely any reference type. Sometimes it doesn't make sense to allow an arbitrary type argument to be used with a generic type. For example, a sorted collection can hold any type of object as long as that object can be sorted. As you have seen a number of times now, the way to define something that can be sorted is to have it implement the `Comparable` interface. `Comparable` itself is a generic interface, with a single type variable that identifies what type the current type can be compared with. Usually, objects of a given type should only be compared with other objects of that same type, so typically a class `Value` that is comparable will be declared as

```
class Value implements Comparable<Value> {
    // ...
}
```

So a sorted collection would restrict its type parameter to be a type that implements `Comparable`:[2]

```
interface SortedCollection<E extends Comparable<E>> {
    // ... sorted collection methods ...
}
```

Here E is restricted to be a type that "extends" `Comparable<E>` so that you know that no matter what type argument is supplied, it is guaranteed to support the methods of the `Comparable` interface. We say that `Comparable` is the *upper bound* on the type of E, and that E is a *bounded* type parameter. The keyword `extends` is used here in a very general way to mean either "extends" or "implements," depending on whether the type that follows is a class type or an interface type. Any given class can extend only one other class, but multiple interfaces can be implemented by classes or interfaces. A type bound can express such multiple dependencies by declaring that the type parameter extends one class or interface, followed by an ampersand (&) separated list of additional interfaces that must be implemented. For example, a sorted collection of character sequences could be declared as follows:

```
interface SortedCharSeqCollection<E extends Comparable<E>
                                & CharSequence> {
    // ... sorted char sequence collection methods ...
}
```

Such a collection could hold `String` objects, for example.

11.1.2 Nested Generic Types

A nested type can also be declared as a generic type with its own type variables. Because static members cannot refer to type variables of their own class, any type variable in a static nested type is distinct from any type variable in the outer type, even if they have the same name. For example, if `Cell` objects are only intended for use within `SingleLinkQueue` objects, then it would be reasonable for `Cell` to be a static nested class within `SingleLinkQueue`:

```
class SingleLinkQueue<E> {
    static class Cell<E> {
        private Cell<E> next;
        private E element;
```

---

[2] You'll see a little later (page 258) that it's better to actually declare this slightly differently, but for now we keep it simple.

```
        public Cell(E element) {
            this.element = element;
        }
        public Cell(E element, Cell<E> next) {
            this.element = element;
            this.next = next;
        }
        public E getElement() {
            return element;
        }
        /* ... rest of Cell methods as before ... */
    }

    protected Cell<E> head;
    protected Cell<E> tail;

    /* ... rest of SingleLinkQueue methods as before ... */
}
```

The code in Cell and SingleLinkQueue is unchanged except that Cell is declared as a static nested class within SingleLinkQueue. The type variable E is used for both classes because the element type of a cell must always match the element type of the queue it is part of, but they are distinct names. The two different E types are associated in the declarations of head and tail, where the E type parameter of the SingleLinkQueue class defines the parameterized type Cell<E>. As always, you should choose names carefully and avoid confusion. If the type variables should always represent the same type then use the same name; if they can be distinct types, then use different names.

If the nested type is an inner class, then the type variables of the outer class declaration are accessible to it and can be used directly. For example, an alternative design of the queue could use a non-generic inner class to define cell objects:

```
class SingleLinkQueue<E> {
    class Cell {
        private Cell next;
        private E element;
        public Cell(E element) {
            this.element = element;
        }
        public Cell(E element, Cell next) {
            this.element = element;
            this.next = next;
```

```
        }
        public E getElement() {
            return element;
        }
        /* ... rest of Cell methods ... */
    }

    protected Cell head;
    protected Cell tail;

    public void add(E item) {
        Cell cell = new Cell(item);
        if (tail == null)
            head = tail = cell;
        else {
            tail.setNext(cell);
            tail = cell;
        }
    }

    public E remove() {
        if (head == null)
            return null;
        Cell cell = head;
        head = head.getNext();
        if (head == null)
            tail = null;   // empty queue
        return cell.getElement();
    }

    /* ... rest of methods ... */
}
```

This time the element type of the cell is directly tied to the element type of the queue that it is in, and there is no need to declare Cell to be a generic class.

If you do choose to use generic inner classes, a type variable in the inner class hides any type variable with the same name in the outer class and, as always, hiding should be avoided.

Deeply nesting types is even more of a problem when the nested types are generic. Both nested types and generic types add an extra degree of complexity to programs, and their combination can greatly compound that complexity.

11.2 Working with Generic Types

To use a generic type you define a suitable parameterized type that provides the desired type arguments for each type parameter. For example, you previously saw:

```
SingleLinkQueue<String> queue =
        new SingleLinkQueue<String>();
```

The variable queue is of type `SingleLinkQueue<String>`, and the constructor invocation also declares the parameterized type `SingleLinkQueue<String>`. A parameterized type must supply a type argument for each type parameter declared by the generic type.

Working with generic types requires a little more planning than working with non-generic types: When you need to declare a field or local variable, or a method parameter or return type, you need to specify the appropriate parameterized type that you intend to work with. For example, should a field be of type `SingleLinkQueue<String>` or `SingleLinkQueue<Number>`, or should it be able to refer to any queue, perhaps `SingleLinkQueue<Object>`? This seems an easy enough question to answer—indeed it seems we did just answer it: You should specify a type argument that is assignable by all the types you expect. The problem is that the way you specify such a type is not the way we just illustrated because generic types don't form subtypes in the way you might think.

11.2.1 Subtyping and Wildcards

Suppose you want to write a method to sum all of the elements in a `List`—one of the collection interfaces of `java.util` that we describe in Section 21.6 on page 580. Naturally, you can only sum numbers, so you require that the list that gets passed contains only `Number` objects. The following code would seem to do the trick:

```
static double sum(List<Number> list) {
    double sum = 0.0;
    for (Number n : list)
        sum += n.doubleValue();
    return sum;
}
```

The intent is that `sum` can be passed any `List` object that has elements that are compatible with `Number`. But that is not what the parameterized type `List<Number>` means: It means an object compatible with `List` that has elements declared to *be* Number. If you try to invoke sum with a List<Integer>, for example, your code will not compile.

```
List<Integer> list = new ArrayList<Integer>();
list.add(1);
list.add(4);
list.add(9);
double sum = sum(list);    // INVALID: won't compile
```

The problem is that even though Integer is a subtype of Number, List<Integer> is *not* a subtype of List<Number>. Contrast this with arrays, where Integer[] is a subtype of Number[].

We need a way to declare a List of an arbitrary element type that is compatible with Number, and the way to do that is to use the type argument *wildcard* '?':

```
static double sum(List<? extends Number> list) {
    double sum = 0.0;
    for (Number n : list)
        sum += n.doubleValue();
    return sum;
}
```

In this example, the wildcard indicates that we require a List of any type, as long as that type is Number or a subclass of Number. More formally, we've used a *bounded wildcard,* where Number forms the upper bound on the type that is expected: Whatever type we get, it must be at least a Number.

You can also specify that a wildcard type must be the same as, or a supertype of, another. You do this by using the keyword super rather than extends. For example, you could use List<? super Integer> to match a List of Integer or any of its supertypes: List<Integer>, List<Number>, List<Serializable>, List<Comparable<Integer>>, or List<Object>. In this case the type represents the *lower bound* on the wildcard's type.

Note that unlike a bounded type variable, a bounded wildcard can have only a single bound—either an upper bound or a lower bound. For example, if you would like to restrict the type of list to be one containing elements that are at least of class Value and also implement Serializable, you cannot say List<? extends Value & Serializable>.

Of course, you can also have an *unbounded wildcard.* For example, List<?> represents a list of any kind—implicitly the upper bound is Object. But remember that List<?> is not another way of saying List<Object>; rather, it is a way of saying List<? extends Object>.

In contrast to the non-wildcard versions, parameterized types that include a bounded wildcard are related in the way you might have expected. For example,

List<? extends Integer> is a subtype of List<? extends Number>, which is itself a subtype of List<?>. Similarly, List<? super Number> is a subtype of List<? super Integer>. In addition, non-wildcard parameterized types are subtypes of suitably bounded, wildcard parameterized types. For example, List<Number> is a subtype of List<? extends Number>, as is List<Integer>. While this in itself is a good property to have, the difference between the behavior with and without bounded wildcards can be a source of confusion. Perhaps the following diagram will clarify things:

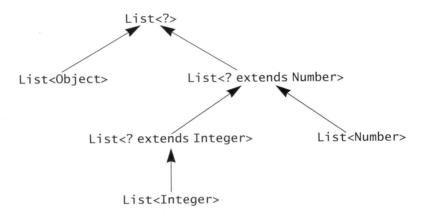

These properties of wildcards make them not only useful but *essential* for effective use of generic types. Whenever a method takes a parameter that is a parameterized type or returns a parameterized type, that parameterized type should almost always be expressed with a wildcard of some form. Typically, parameters use lower-bounded wildcards, while return values use upper bounded wildcards—though if there is a constraint between a parameter type and the return type, it may not be possible to use a wildcard. Even a type bound that is a parameterized type will often be expressed with a wildcard. Recall the example of the SortedCollection<E> interface, in which we constrained the type parameter E such that E extends Comparable<E>. This seemed reasonable: to sort the collection we need the elements to be comparable to each other. In fact, this constraint is overly tight—for two elements of a class T to be comparable to each other, it is not necessary that T extend Comparable<T> but only that T extend Comparable<S> where S is T or any supertype of T. For example, if class Value implements Comparable<Object> then it can still correctly compare two Value objects—it just happens to be able to do more than that. Consequently, SortedCollection should be declared as follows:

```
interface SortedCollection<E extends Comparable<? super E>> {
    // ... sorted collection methods ...
}
```

Wildcards are essential for obtaining the flexibility that we needed in the sum example, but they have a limitation: Because the wildcard represents an unknown type, you can't do anything that requires the type to be known. For example, you can't add an element to a queue referenced through a variable that has an unbounded or upper-bounded wildcard type:[3]

```
SingleLinkQueue<?> strings =
    new SingleLinkQueue<String>();
strings.add("Hello");                   // INVALID: won't compile

SingleLinkQueue<? extends Number> numbers =
    new SingleLinkQueue<Number>();
numbers.add(Integer.valueOf(25));   // INVALID: won't compile
```

This is a reasonable restriction because in general, if passed a queue of an unknown kind, you have no idea what type of object you can store in it. So you can't store a String (or an Object or a Number or ...) in a queue that could require some other kind of element. Nor can you store a Number in a queue in which the elements are known to be Number objects or objects of a subclass of Number—because in the subclass case passing a general Number object would be incorrect. However, given strings above, you could invoke remove and assign the result to an Object reference—because the returned value must be compatible with Object. Similarly, given numbers, you could invoke remove and assign the result to a Number reference—because the returned value must be at least a Number.

In contrast, given a lower-bounded wildcard type, the wildcard is known to be the same as, or a super type of, the bound, so adding an element of the same type as the bound is always correct. For example, this method is perfectly correct:

```
static void addString(SingleLinkQueue<? super String> sq) {
    sq.add("Hello");
}
```

No matter what queue is passed to addString, you're guaranteed that it can hold String objects.

---

[3] Since the reference literal null has no type, the type-system will allow you to invoke add passing null, but this is an uninteresting boundary case with little practical significance.

Wildcards can be used in most declarations: fields, local variables, parameter types, and return types. But you can't use them to name a class or interface in an `extends` or `implements` clause. Any parameterized types that a class (or interface) extends or implements must be concrete types in which the immediate type argument is not a wildcard. For example, you can't define a class that implements `List<?>`. However, the type argument may itself be a parameterized type with a type argument that is a wildcard so implementing `List<List<?>>` is okay.

You'll see more examples of the use of wildcards when we look at the collection classes in detail in Chapter 21.

11.3   Generic Methods and Constructors

Earlier we mentioned how the `SingleLinkQueue` class might want to expose the elements of the queue as an array. We noted then that it was impossible to create an array with the type variable `E` and that instead the caller should pass in an array of the right size and type. Here's a first attempt at defining such a method:

```
public E[] toArray_v1(E[] arr) { // too restrictive!
    int i = 0;
    for (Cell<E> c = head;
        c != null && i < arr.length;
        c = c.getNext())
        arr[i++] = c.getElement();
    return arr;
}
```

This method works. If you invoke `toArray_v1` on an instance of `SingleLinkQueue<String>` and pass a `String[]`, then as many elements from the queue as the array can hold will be copied into it, and then the array will be returned. The problem with this definition, as you may have already surmised from the discussion of wildcards, is that it is too restrictive. It will, in the current example, accept only a `String[]` and not, for example, an `Object[]` even though it is perfectly valid to store `String` objects into an `Object[]`.

Can we use a wildcard to help us out in this situation as well? Unfortunately not. To use a wildcard we'd try writing something like this:

```
public ?[] toArray(?[]) { ... } // INVALID: won't compile
```

But this is simply not legal syntax: A wildcard represents an unknown type in a parameterized type definition and '`?[]`' is not a parameterized type. What you need to do is introduce another type variable, say `T`, and use it to describe the type of the array. And the way you introduce new type variables in a method is to declare the method as a *generic method*.

You declare a generic method by defining type variables between the method modifiers and the method return type, much as you would declare type variables for a generic class or interface. Here is how you would actually define `toArray` as a generic method:

```
public <T> T[] toArray(T[] arr) {
    Object[] tmp = arr;
    int i = 0;
    for (Cell<E> c = head;
         c != null && i < arr.length;
         c = c.getNext())
        tmp[i++] = c.getElement();
    return arr;
}
```

Notice that the type variable T is only used in the method header to constrain the parameter type and the return type to be the same—within the method body we don't really care what type T is. But also note that in the method body we actually work with a local variable of type `Object[]`, which refers to the actual array that is passed in. This is necessary because the array is of type T, but `getElement` returns E, and these are not the same type—T may be `Object` while E is `String`. We could cast E to T for the cast must succeed if T and E are compatible, but such a cast would be an *unchecked cast* and would produce a compiler warning—see "Erasure at Runtime" on page 267—so we bypass the problem by using the `Object[]` variable.

By now you may be asking yourself: "Shouldn't there be some restriction between the types T and E, since they must be compatible?" Logically, there could be such a restriction: T must be E or a supertype of E. Unfortunately, there is no way to express this restriction. Only wildcards can be given a lower type bound, so you cannot write `<T super E>` as a type variable. In any case, such a restriction is not strictly necessary. Suppose you have a `SingleLinkQueue<Object>` that you know you have filled only with `String` instances—why shouldn't you be able to pass `toArray` a `String[]`? Yet `String` is not a supertype of `Object`. So in fact there is no compile-time type checking between T and E to see if they are compatible. We instead rely on the runtime type check that always occurs when a reference is stored into an array.

Generic methods and constructors are typically used when you need to introduce a type variable to constrain the parameterized types of different parameters, or to constrain a parameter and the return type, as with `toArray`. For example, consider a `merge` operation for `SingleLinkQueue` that moves the elements from a source queue into a destination queue. To perform a merge, the elements of the source queue must be the same as, or a subtype of, the elements of the destination queue. You can express this constraint with a generic method by using a wildcard:

```
public static <E> void merge(SingleLinkQueue<E> d,
                             SingleLinkQueue<? extends E> s)
{
    // ... merge s elements into d ...
}
```

We could have introduced a second type variable, say S, to use instead of the wild-card to achieve the same affect. So which is preferable? The general rule is to use wildcards when you can because code with wildcards is generally more readable than code with multiple type parameters. When deciding if you need a type variable, ask yourself if that type variable is used to relate two or more parameters, or to relate a parameter type with the return type. If the answer is no, then a wildcard should suffice. In the above example, S would appear in only one place and so can trivially be replaced by a wildcard.

A generic method need not be declared in a generic type, and if it is then the type variables are distinct. As with inner generic types, if a generic method declares a type variable of the same name as that of a type variable in the method's class or interface, the outer name is hidden. Finally, note that a static method such as merge can be a generic method, though it cannot refer to any type variables of its own generic class.

11.3.1 Generic Invocations and Type Inference

If you invoke a generic method like toArray or merge, the compiler must ensure, as it does for all method invocations, that you pass in arguments of the right type and assign any return value to a variable of the right type. When you create an instance of a generic class, you use a parameterized type to bind a particular type argument to the type variables of the class. Similarly, you can parameterize a method invocation to supply type arguments for the method's type variables. For example, consider this generic method that simply returns its argument:

```
<T> T passThrough(T obj) {
    return obj;
}
```

You can invoke passThrough as a String method:

```
String s1 = "Hello";
String s2 = this.<String>passThrough(s1);
```

This parameterized method invocation tells the compiler that T should be treated as String and that the arguments and return value of passThrough must be verified accordingly.

Fortunately, explicitly parameterizing a method invocation is rarely needed. In the absence of a type argument, the compiler will infer what type to use from the static argument types and the way in which the return type is used. For example, this invocation of passThrough is equivalent to the previous one but relies on type inference to establish the type of T:

```
String s1 = "Hello";
String s2 = passThrough(s1);
```

In this case, the argument type is inferred to be String, which is the static type of the variable s1. This implies that the return type is also String. This is compatible with the assignment to s2 and so the invocation is valid with an inferred type of String.

The following invocations of passThrough are also valid:

```
String s1 = "Hello";
Object o1 = passThrough(s1);            // T => String
Object o2 = passThrough((Object) s1); // T => Object
```

In the first case the argument type is String and the return type is expected to be Object. The inferred type for T is again String, implying that the return type is also String. This is compatible with assignment to the Object variable o1, so the invocation is valid, with an inferred type of String. In the second case the static type of the argument is Object (due to the cast) and so the inferred type is also Object. This makes the return type Object, so again we have a compatible assignment and so a valid invocation. In general, type inference has to find the most specific type in the set of types that satisfy the constraints imposed by the type variables—a non-trivial exercise.

Type inference is based on the static type of the argument expressions that are being passed, not their dynamic types, so the following won't compile:

```
String s1 = "Hello";
s1 = passThrough((Object) s1); // INVALID: won't compile
```

The static argument type of Object requires that T, as the return type of the method, be Object (or a supertype if Object had one) and the String type of s1 requires that T be assignable to String. But there is no such type—you cannot assign an Object to a String reference. Of course, you can inform the compiler that you know the returned object actually is a `String` by inserting an additional cast:

```
s1 = (String) passThrough((Object) s1);
```

The actual type inference process and the rules controlling it are extremely complex, but for the most part you don't need to care what the actual inferred type is as long as the code compiles. For example, if a generic method took two parameters of type T and you invoked it passing a `List<String>` and a `List<Number>`, then the inferred type could be `List<?>`. Inference is also used as part of determining which method to invoke, as you will see shortly.

The inference process may result in simple types like `Object` or `String`, or more complex types for which no single class or interface declaration exists—such as a type that is both `Runnable` and `Cloneable`. These complex types are generally known as *intersection types*. For each constraint on a type variable there will be a set of types that meet that constraint. The intersection of those sets contains the inferred type.

Finally, note that if you do wish to make a parameterized method invocation, you cannot parameterize an invocation that uses just a simple method name:

```
String s1 = "Hello";
String s2 = <String>passThrough(s1); // INVALID: won't compile
```

Instead you must qualify the method name appropriately, such as by using `this` or `super` for instance methods, or the class name for static methods.

11.4 Wildcard Capture

Wildcards represent an unknown type, but whenever a variable that has a wildcard type is used, the compiler must treat it as having some specific type so that it can check for correct usage. This specific (but still unknown) type is referred to as the *capture* of the wildcard. The place you will most commonly come across the capture of a wildcard is in the error messages the compiler produces when you use a parameterized type the wrong way. For example, recall the incorrect attempt to add a `String` object to a queue accessed through an unbounded wildcard reference:

```
SingleLinkQueue<?> strings =
    new SingleLinkQueue<String>();
strings.add("Hello");                  // INVALID: won't compile
```

The error message this produced from the compiler we used was:

```
add(capture of ?) in SingleLinkQueue<capture of ?> cannot be
applied to (java.lang.String)
```

This is telling us that when the wildcard reference `strings` is used, the type of queue is `SingleLinkQueue<capture of ?>`, so the type of the parameter to `add` is also "`capture of ?`". Because `String` is not compatible with "`capture of ?`" the call is not allowed. Even if the wildcard is bounded, as in the earlier example with the queue of numbers ("`? extends Number`"), the type of the parameter to `add` is "`capture of ? extends Number`" which is still not compatible with `Integer`, even though `Integer` is a subtype of `Number`.

If a wildcard is always represented by its capture, it would seem that once you have a wildcard type you can only use it wherever a wildcard type is expected. Indeed this is a basic rule that ensures the integrity of the type system.

However, as it stands this basic rule imposes a rather annoying restriction. A wildcard represents any type. Similarly, the type variable of a generic method represents any type. But under the basic rule a wildcard type can only be used where a wildcard type is expected. This precludes passing wildcard types to generic methods that have a parameter defined by a type variable. Consider the `synchronizedList` utility method from the `Collections` class—part of the `java.util` package discussed in more detail in Chapter 21. Its job is to take an arbitrary list object and return a new list object that is backed by the original, but one for which all the methods are `synchronized` to make access to the list thread-safe (see Chapter 14). The method is declared as follows:

```
static <T> List<T> synchronizedList(List<T> list) { ... }
```

There is no logical reason why we should not be able to pass it a list referenced through a wildcard type:

```
static void processList(List<?> list) {
    List<?> slist = Collections.synchronizedList(list);
    // ... process the list
}
```

To do so is quite safe—and quite convenient!

Although in general you cannot use a `List<?>` where a `List<T>` is expected because the actual type represented by the wildcard is not known to be compatible with T, a special rule bridges the gap that would otherwise exist between wildcard types and the type variables of generic methods. This rule allows (under the right circumstances) the capture of the wildcard to be represented as some unknown generic type X and then to infer in the call that T is X. You don't actually need to know what X is—whatever it is, the resulting use of the list is guaranteed to be type-safe.

This conversion of the capture of the wildcard to the type T is known as *capture conversion* and it complements the other type conversions that we discussed in Section 9.4 on page 216.

For capture conversion to apply, there must be a unique mapping between the capture of the wildcard and the type variable involved. This leads to some general restrictions on when capture conversion can apply.

First, capture conversion won't apply if the type parameter is used with more than one method parameter. Consider a utility method that merges two lists:

```
static <T> List<T> merge(List<T> first, List<T> second) {
    /* ... */
}
```

If you try to pass an argument of type List<?> for first and second it will fail—even if you passed the same reference. The problem is that the process for resolving the method call will essentially replace the type of the first argument with X, the type of the second argument with Y, and then see if T is uniquely determined. But because X is not the same as Y this will not be the case.

Second, you can only apply capture conversion if the type variable is defined at the top-level of the generic type. For example, suppose you had the method

```
static <T> void processListOfLists(List<List<T>> list) {
    /* ... */
}
```

and you tried to invoke it with an argument of type List<List<?>>. The capture of the wildcard would not uniquely determine an element type for the outer List. The method requires a List with elements that are all the same type, but a List with an element type of List<?> could contain a List<String>, a List<Object>, and so forth, so capture conversion does not apply in this case.

Finally, as usual you cannot use a wildcard reference anywhere that the type of the wildcard needs to be known. For example, given the method

```
static <T> void addToList(List<T> list, T t) {
    /* ... */
}
```

you cannot pass a reference of type List<?> because the inferred type of T will be "capture of ?" and there is no type compatible with "capture of ?" that you could possibly pass for the parameter t. Or looking at it the other way, T will be determined by whatever you pass for t, and whatever it is, it cannot be "capture of ?", so the type of T would not be uniquely determined.

11.5   Under the Hood: Erasure and Raw Types

As we have stated a number of times, for each generic type there is only one class, no matter how many different parameterized types are formed from it. This raises the question: What exactly is that type? Given a class like Cell<E>, what type do Cell<String> and Cell<Number> share?

To determine the answer the compiler uses a process called *erasure* (because the compiler essentially erases all generic type information from the compiled class). The erasure of a generic or parameterized type is simply the unadorned type name. This is also known as the *raw type* (see "Raw Types, "Unchecked" Warnings, and Bridge Methods" on page 745). For example, the erasure of Cell<E> is just Cell. The erasure of a type variable is the erasure of its first bound. For example, the erasure of E in <E> is Object—the implicit upper bound. The erasure of E in <E extends Number> is the explicit upper bound of Number, as it is in <E extends Number & Cloneable>, because Number is the first bound. The compiler generates a class definition for the erasure of a generic type by effectively replacing each type variable with its erasure. When a parameterized type is used and the type information from the erasure of the generic type doesn't match what is expected, the compiler inserts a cast. For example, if you invoke remove on an object created as a SingleLinkQueue<String> and assign it to a String reference, the compiler will insert a cast to String because the erasure of the type variable in SingleLinkQueue<E> is just Object.

You need to understand the erasure process because it impacts your programs in two key areas:

+ The runtime actions that can involve generic types
+ Method overloading and overriding

We start with the runtime issues.

11.5.1   Erasure at Runtime

The runtime impact of erasure is simple to state: Nothing that needs to know the value of a type argument at runtime is allowed. This has the following consequences, some of which we have already discussed:

+ You cannot instantiate a type represented only as a type parameter, nor can you create an array of such a type. So for a type variable T you can't do new T() or new T[n].

◆ You cannot create an array whose element type is a parameterized type, with the exception of a parameterized type for which all the type arguments are unbounded wildcards. For example, "new List<String>[1]" is invalid, whereas "new List<?>[1]" is okay.

◆ You cannot use instanceof to see if an object is an instance of a parameterized type, again with the exception of a parameterized type whose type arguments are all unbounded wildcards. The instanceof test is a runtime test, and at runtime the parameterized type has been replaced by its erasure. Since this is unlikely to perform the test you expected, the compiler rejects it. You can replace the parameterized type by its erasure if that is what you really wanted to test.

◆ Casts involving type parameters or parameterized types are replaced with casts to the erasure of that type (see discussion below).

◆ A catch clause cannot declare that it catches an exception represented by a type variable—even if the bound on that type variable is an exception type. The exact type of the exception must be known at compile time. (You can throw an exception so referenced, however, and you can declare the type variable in a method's throws clause.)

◆ A generic class is not allowed to directly or indirectly extend Throwable. Given that you can't catch generic exceptions there is little point in being able to declare them.

◆ You cannot use a parameterized type in a class literal expression (such as SingleLinkQueue<String>.class). This reinforces that there is but one class object.

The restriction on creating arrays of a parameterized type can be limiting but is essential. Consider, for example, an implementation of List that provides a split method that returns the contents of the list split across a number of sublists. It would seem reasonable to return the sublists as an array of lists. So given a class that implements List<T> the split method would return List<T>[]. You could actually declare such a method, but you would have trouble implementing it. You cannot create an array with component type List<T>, and any attempt to return some less specific array type (say List[]) would result in an "unchecked" warning (see below). The reason you cannot create a generic array such as List<T>[] is that correct use of the array cannot be enforced by the type system. This is because array store checks are based on the erasure of the component type not on their actual parameterized type, so you would be allowed to store any kind of List in an array that is supposed to have a component type of List<String>, for example. Not allowing you to create generic arrays avoids this problem. From the programmers perspective, it is better to try to work with a suitable collection of a parameterized type rather than an array. For example, the `split` method could be defined to return `List<List<T>>` instead.

Using unbounded wildcards in array creation and `instanceof` is allowed for parameterized types because such types are effectively equivalent to their raw types. For example, creating a `List<?>[1]` is effectively the same as creating a `List[1]`—an array whose component type is a raw type. However, there is one significant difference between these two forms: The raw type permits unsafe operations but causes the compiler to issue a warning, whereas the wildcard form prohibits unsafe operations, causing a compile-time error.

The absence of generic type information at runtime also means that casts involving type parameters or parameterized types may not have the desired effect: You cannot check whether an object is an instance of a parameterized type, so a cast to that type can not be checked at runtime—except if all type parameters are unbounded wildcards. In an ideal world in which everyone used generics, such casts would simply be disallowed (as is use of `instanceof`). Some degree of interoperability between generic code and non-generic code must be provided, so the casts are allowed but are replaced by casts to the erasure of the type variable or parameterized type, usually causing the compiler to emit an *"unchecked" warning* (see page 745). This warns you that the cast can neither be checked at runtime nor guaranteed to be type-safe at compile time. For example, a method with a `SingleLinkQueue<?>` parameter could cast it to `SingleLinkQueue<String>` and add a `String`. This would cause the compiler to emit an "unchecked" warning. At runtime, the actual cast to `SingleLinkQueue` would succeed even if the queue was actually of type `SingleLinkQueue<Number>`, and the `String` would be added, violating the type integrity of the queue. This violation would only be detected when a `remove` invocation tried to cast the returned instance to `Number`, resulting in a runtime `ClassCastException`. Note, however, that if the cast does not involve a change to the type parameter, then the cast is quite safe and there is no warning. For example, a cast from `Collection<T>` to `List<T>` doesn't require checking anything about T.

Casts involving parameterized types are unavoidable in many circumstances, such as when a method returns a (possibly non-generic) supertype, and the actual object will be of a generic subtype that you need to cast to that subtype. In such circumstances you should use casts that only involve unbounded wildcards, and assign the results to variables that also declare unbounded wildcards. The fact that you need a cast means that you have lost valuable type information and there is no way to restore that information at runtime, so casting to a parameterized type should always involve unbounded wildcards. For example, consider a non-generic version of the `passThrough` method:

```
Object passThrough(Object o) {
    return o;
}
```

and its subsequent use with an instance of List<String>:

```
List<String> l = new ArrayList<String>();
Object o = passThrough(l);

List<String> list1 = (List<String>) o; // unchecked
List<String> list2 = (List) o;         // unchecked; raw type
List<?>      list3 = (List) o;         // OK: but raw type
List<?>      list4 = (List<?>) o;      // OK
```

The attempt to cast to List<String> is effectively a cast to List<?> (or equivalently the raw type List). At runtime we may have a list of some type but we can not be certain it is a List<String>, so the use of the cast gives an "unchecked" warning. The cast to the raw List type is itself okay, but the assignment to list2 raises an "unchecked" warning because again there is no guarantee that the object is a List<String>. You can remove the "unchecked" warning by assigning to a variable of type List<?>, as with list3 above—the cast checks that the object is a list of some kind and that list3 can hold a reference to a list of some kind. You should cast to List<?> instead of simply to List because it clearly expresses that List is a generic type. The raw types exist for integration with legacy code that predates generics; when you are writing code, it's better to consistently stick with the generic expression of the concept instead of the legacy raw type.

The only places where use of a raw type is unavoidable are within a class literal expression and when accessing static members. This reinforces the fact that what you are accessing is independent of any parameterization of the generic type.

In some rare circumstances you may know for certain that a value has a particular parameterized type,[4] even though the type system cannot verify that at runtime, and a cast to that parameterized type (with its ensuing "unchecked" warning) is essential to allow your code to compile. As noted above, the fact that you need the cast means that type information was lost, so your first response to this should be to avoid the loss of type information in the first place. If you cannot do this you should clearly document why the "unchecked" warning is occurring and why you are certain that the lack of a runtime type check is not a problem.

---

[4]   Implementing a `clone` method is one such circumstance—see Section A.3.2 on page 747.

11.5.2 Overloading and Overriding

In Chapter 2 we defined overloaded methods to be methods having the same name but different signatures. Later, in Chapter 3, we defined an overriding method to be a method in a subclass with the same name and the same signature as an accessible method in the supertype. When a method signature involves type variables, these definitions have to be adapted slightly.

First, the definition of "same signature" for two generic methods requires that they have the same number of type variables with the same corresponding bounds. Further, after all the uses of the type variables in the second method are renamed with the names of the type variables from the first method, the formal parameter types must be the same.

Second, rather than requiring the same (or different) signatures we talk about *override-equivalent* signatures: Two methods have override-equivalent signatures if their signatures are the same, or if the erasures of their signatures are the same.

Using the new definitions, two methods are *overloaded* if they have the same name and do not have override-equivalent signatures. Consider this class:

```
class Base<T> {
    void m(int x)      {}
    void m(T t)        {}
    void m(String s) {}
    <N extends Number> void m(N n) {}
    void m(SingleLinkQueue<?> q)      {}
}
```

This defines five different overloads of the method m. Replacing each method's signature by its erasure, we would get the following corresponding set of methods:

```
void m(int x)      {}
void m(Object t) {}
void m(String s) {}
void m(Number n) {}
void m(SingleLinkQueue q) {}
```

It is an error for a class or interface to declare two methods with the same name and the same signature erasure. Consequently, trying to define any of the following versions of m in Base would be an error:

```
void m(Object o) {}
void m(Number n) {}
<G extends String> void m(G g) {}
void m(SingleLinkQueue<Object> q) {}
```

In each case, the erasure of the signature matches the erasure of one of the other signatures.

A method in a subtype *potentially* overrides an accessible method in a super type if the two methods have the same name and have override-equivalent signatures. We say "potentially overrides" because there is an additional requirement to be met: The signature of the subclass method must be the same as that of the superclass method, or it must be the same as the erasure of the signature of the superclass method. This constraint makes overriding a "one-way street": A method without generic types can override a method with generic types, but not the other way around. You are allowed to do this so that you can generify an existing class without breaking previously existing subclasses that overrode methods.

Continuing with the previous example we can extend Base as follows:

```
class Derived<T> extends Base<T> {
    void m(Integer i){}  // new overload
    void m(Object t) {}  // overrides m(T t)
    void m(Number n) {}  // overrides m(N n)
}
```

This introduces one new overloaded form of m and defines two overriding implementations of m.

The simple rule to remember when thinking about overloading and overriding is to always consider the erasure of the method signatures and to remember that you can't add genericity to an inherited method.

11.6 Finding the Right Method—Revisited

In "Finding the Right Method" on page 224, we outlined the basic algorithm used by the compiler to determine which form of a method should be invoked for a given method invocation expression. We can now consider how generic types and generic methods (and constructors) affect that basic algorithm.

The changes to the algorithm can be summarized as follows:

1. If the method invocation includes explicit type arguments, then any potentially applicable generic methods must have the same number of type parameters. Non-generic methods may also be potentially applicable, in which case the actual type arguments are ignored.

2. If there are no explicit type arguments in the invocation, and a generic method might be applicable, then first the type arguments for the generic method are inferred based on the static types of the argument expressions

used in the method invocation. If no types that satisfy all the constraints on the type parameters can be inferred, then the method is not applicable.

3. At each phase, once the set of potentially applicable methods is determined, applicable methods are searched for as previously described. For generic methods, either the explicit (if present) or the inferred type arguments establish whether the argument type is compatible with the formal parameter type.

4. When the most specific method is searched for, type inference is again used when generic methods are being considered. However, this time the type inference is not based on the actual argument expression types; rather, the initial constraint is between the formal parameters of the generic method and the formal parameters of the method against which it is being tested for being most specific. In simple terms, the most specific test considers only the declared parameter types of the methods concerned, not the type of the arguments used in the method invocation. This is clarified in an example below.

5. The search for the maximally specific method is not based on "same or different signature" but rather on whether the signatures are override-equivalent (as previously described) or not.

6. If the maximally specific method is a generic method, then the type of the method invocation expression is the inferred return type of that generic method as determined by the type inference applied as in point 2 above.

For example, consider these two overloads of a method m:

```
void m(String key, Object val) {
    // ...
}

<S, T extends Number> void m(S key, T val) {
    // ...
}
```

Now consider this invocation of m:

```
m("hello", "world");
```

Both forms of m are potentially applicable because they have the right name and the right number of parameters. Both arguments are reference types and neither method has a variable number of parameters, so only phase 1 for finding the applicable methods will occur. First, the type arguments of the generic method must be inferred. Attempting to do so, however, requires that `String` extend `Number`; it does not, so the generic form is not applicable. The non-generic form is applicable because it matches in the first argument type exactly, and in the second a `String` can be assigned to an `Object`. Since there is only one applicable method, it is selected.

Now consider this invocation of `m`:

```
m(new Object(), 29);
```

Again both forms are potentially applicable. The type of the generic method is inferred to be `<Object, Integer>` after applying boxing conversion to the argument 29. The non-generic form fails to match in the first argument because an `Object` is not compatible with a `String`, so it is not applicable. The generic method matches in the first argument exactly, and matches in the second argument after a boxing conversion (phase 2). Consequently, the generic method is the only applicable method.

In contrast, this invocation of `m` is ambiguous:

```
m("hello", Integer.valueOf(29));
```

Both forms are potentially applicable, and again only phase 1 will come into play. The inferred type of the generic method call is `<String, Integer>`. The non-generic form matches exactly in the first argument type and matches in the second argument because an `Integer` is an `Object`. The generic form matches exactly on both argument types. So there are two applicable methods. The next step is to determine which is the most specific method. First, we see if the non-generic method is more specific than the generic method. This is done as follows:

1. Since our second method is generic, type inference is performed, but this time with the initial constraint that `String` is convertible to `S` and that `Object` is convertible to `T`. This infers the types `<String, Object>` for the generic method. Note that the bound on `T` is not considered at this point.

2. A check is made to see if each parameter of the first method is a subtype of the (inferred) type of the corresponding parameter in the second method. In this case the parameter types of the first method and the inferred parameter types of the second method are the same, so the check passes.

3. Since the second method is generic, a second check is then made to see if the types of the parameters of the first method are subtypes of the bounds of the generic type parameters of the second method. Considering the first parameter, the bound of `S` is `Object` and so we are testing whether `String` is a subtype of `Object`—which it is. The bound of `T`, however, is `Number` and the test is if `Object` is a subtype of `Number`—which it is not.

Because the check has failed, the non-generic method is not more specific than the generic method. Now we must see if the generic method is more specific than the non-generic one. This proceeds as follows:

1. The second method is not generic this time, so no type inference occurs.

2. A check is made to see if each parameter of the first method is a subtype of the type of the corresponding parameter in the second method. In this case the check is to see whether S is a subtype of String and T is a subtype of Object. A type variable is a subtype only of its bounds (and their supertypes) so S is a subtype of Object and T is subtype of Number. Because S is a subtype of Object and not String, the check fails.

The check failed, so the generic method is not more specific than the non-generic method. Since neither method is more specific than the other the call is ambiguous and the compiler rejects it as such.

Informally, one method is more specific than another if all calls to the first method could be handled by the second. Looking at the two methods here, the most general signature of the generic method would have parameters of type Object and Number. So if we consider the first parameter, anything we pass to the non-generic method must be a String, and a String is always an Object, so the generic method could accept all first arguments to the first method. So considering just the first parameter, the non-generic method is more specific than the generic method. But conversely, the generic method can accept first arguments that are not String objects, so the generic method is not more specific than the non-generic method. Considering the second parameter, you can pass arbitrary objects to the non-generic method but only Number objects to the generic method. Consequently, the non-generic method is not more specific at the second parameter and so it is not more specific. As neither is more specific, the call is ambiguous.

You can remove the ambiguity in two ways. You can cast the first argument to Object so that the non-generic method is no longer applicable and so the generic version must be called:

```
m((Object) "hello", Integer.valueOf(29));
```

The alternative is to cast the second argument to Object so that the generic method is no longer applicable and so the non-generic version must be called:

```
m("hello", (Object) Integer.valueOf(29));
```

Note that parameterizing the invocation itself does not automatically exclude the non-generic method—its applicability is determined without consideration of the type arguments.

Overloading, even without involving generics, should be used judiciously and only to improve the resulting clarity of the program. With generics added to the mix, it is even easier to create programs in which the intent can only be established by detailed recourse to the language specification. Avoid mixing generic and non-generic overloads of a method unless you have an extremely compelling reason.

11.7   Class Extension and Generic Types

Generic types add an extra dimension to the type system, and force you to think more deeply about how to define classes and interfaces and how to use existing classes and interfaces. You can extend a non-generic type to produce either a generic or a non-generic subtype. You can extend a generic type to produce a generic subtype, or you can extend a specific parameterized type to yield a non-generic subtype, or you can combine both. This degree of flexibility can be overwhelming, but the key thing to focus on is what abstraction your new class or interface represents and what abstraction the class or interface you are inheriting from represents.

For example, the List<E> interface is generic and represents a list of elements of some kind. If you implement that interface then you may be providing a general-purpose implementation that can deal with arbitrary element types, and in that case your class would also be a generic class, such as

```
class GeneralList<E> implements List<E> { /* ... */ }
```

Or you may be providing a specialized implementation that has been hand-crafted to deal with a particular kind of element, say String, and so it won't be generic itself and will implement the parameterized interface List<String>:

```
class StringList implements List<String> { /* ... */ }
```

An existing non-generic class, such as AbstractEventService, may provide base functionality that you have to extend to use a framework within your application. You might define a concrete implementation that has no need of generics:

```
class RemoteEventService extends AbstractEventService {
    /* ... */
}
```

Or you might define a generic service for different kinds of events:

```
class LocalEventService<T extends Event> extends
                    AbstractEventService { /* ... */ }
```

The possibilities really depend on the semantics of the types involved.

When choosing to extend a parameterized type, you need to carefully consider the implications, particularly if you are implementing an interface, because a class cannot inherit two interface types that are different parameterizations of the same interface. For example, consider the Comparable interface. If you define a comparable class Value then it is natural to declare it as:

```
class Value implements Comparable<Value> {
    // ...
}
```

Suppose you now extend Value to add additional state. This ExtendedValue class should define objects that are comparable only to ExtendedValue objects, so you would expect to be able to define it so:

```
class ExtendedValue extends Value
    implements Comparable<ExtendedValue> { // INVALID!
    // ...
}
```

But this won't compile because ExtendedValue is attempting to implement both Comparable<Value> and Comparable<ExtendedValue> and that is not permitted. Once you extend or implement a parameterized type you fix that parameterization for the current class and all subclasses. So you need to think carefully about the implications of that. In the case of Comparable you have little choice but to accept the restriction, and although you can't change the type parameterization, you can override the implementation of compareTo to ensure that a subclass instance is accepted for comparison while a superclass instance is rejected. Recall from the SortedCollection example on page 258 that if you want to accept a Comparable object, the correct approach is to declare Comparable<? super T> rather than Comparable<T>. This is not only more general (as previously explained), it also allows for the fact that a comparable class T may not actually be able to implement Comparable<T>.

Generic types are a powerful tool for writing your programs more effectively, but they are a tool that is difficult to master and can easily be misused. A full treatment of generic types requires an understanding of type theory—in particular the characteristics of covariant and contravariant typing—that is beyond the scope of this book. If you are interested there is additional material on the subject listed in "Further Reading" on page 755.

> *Nearly all men can stand adversity,*
> *but if you want to test a man's character, give him power.*
> —Abraham Lincoln

CHAPTER 12

Exceptions and Assertions

A slipping gear could let your M203 grenade launcher fire when you least expect it.
That would make you quite unpopular in what's left of your unit.
—The U.S. Army's *PS* magazine, August 1993

DURING execution, applications can run into many kinds of errors of varying degrees of severity. When methods are invoked on an object, the object can discover internal state problems (inconsistent values of variables), detect errors with objects or data it manipulates (such as a file or network address), determine that it is violating its basic contract (such as reading data from an already closed stream), and so on.

Many programmers do not test for all possible error conditions, and for good reason: Code becomes unintelligible if each method invocation checks for all possible errors before the next statement is executed. This trade-off creates a tension between correctness (checking for all errors) and clarity (not cluttering the basic flow of code with many error checks).

Exceptions provide a clean way to check for errors without cluttering code. Exceptions also provide a mechanism to signal errors directly rather than indirectly with flags or side effects such as fields that must be checked. Exceptions make the error conditions that a method can signal an explicit part of the method's contract. The list of exceptions can be seen by the programmer, checked by the compiler, and preserved (if needed) by extended classes that override the method.

An exception is *thrown* when an unexpected error condition is encountered. The exception is then *caught* by an encompassing clause further up the method invocation stack. Uncaught exceptions result in the termination of the thread of execution, but before it terminates, the thread's `UncaughtExceptionHandler` is given the opportunity to handle the exception as best it can, usually printing useful information (such as a call stack) about where the exception was thrown—see "Threads and Exceptions" on page 379.

12.1 Creating Exception Types

Exceptions are objects. All exception types—that is, any class designed for throwable objects—must extend the class `Throwable` or one of its subclasses. The `Throwable` class contains a string that can be used to describe the exception—it is set via a constructor parameter and may be retrieved with the `getMessage` method. By convention, most new exception types extend `Exception`, a subclass of `Throwable`. Exception types are not allowed to be generic types.

Exceptions are primarily *checked exceptions,* meaning that the compiler checks that your methods throw only the exceptions they have declared themselves to throw. The standard runtime exceptions and errors extend one of the classes `RuntimeException` and `Error`, making them *unchecked exceptions.* Here is the top of the exception type hierarchy:

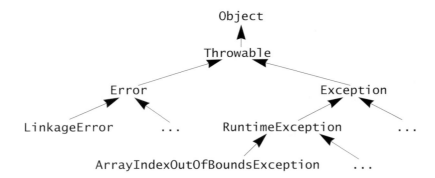

Checked exceptions represent conditions that, although exceptional, can reasonably be expected to occur, and if they do occur must be dealt with in some way. Making these exceptions checked documents the existence of the exception and ensures that the caller of a method deals with the exception in some way—or at least consciously chooses to ignore it.

Unchecked runtime exceptions represent conditions that, generally speaking, reflect errors in your program's logic and cannot be reasonably recovered from at run time. For example, the `ArrayIndexOutOfBoundsException` thrown when you access outside the bounds of an array tells you that your program calculated an index incorrectly, or failed to verify a value to be used as an index. These are errors that should be corrected in the program code. Given that you can make errors writing any statement it would be totally impractical to have to declare or catch all the exceptions that could arise from those errors—hence they are unchecked.

The `Error` class, through its subclasses, defines a range of errors that indicate something has failed in the virtual machine itself (`VirtualMachineError`), or in the virtual machine's attempt to execute your application (`LinkageError`). These are also unchecked because they are beyond the applications ability to control, or handle. Application code should rarely, if ever, throw these error exceptions directly.

Nearly all exceptions you create should extend `Exception`, making them checked exceptions. These new checked exceptions represent the exceptional conditions that can arise in your library or application. You can usually handle any runtime problems that arise in your code by throwing one of the existing runtime exception classes—there are sufficient of these that one of them is usually a good match to the kind of error that has occurred, or else the error is sufficiently general that throwing an instance of `RuntimeException` itself is sufficient. Occasionally, you may want to extend an existing runtime exception class to provide additional information about the error that occurred. Even more rarely, you might define a new class of runtime exception that is specific to your application domain. Just remember that when it comes to unchecked exceptions, proper usage relies on good documentation because the compiler will not be able to assist you.

Sometimes it is useful to have more data to describe the exceptional condition than what is in the `Exception` class. In such cases, you can extend `Exception` to create a class that contains the added data (usually set in the constructor).

For example, suppose a `replaceValue` method is added to the `Attributed` interface discussed in Chapter 4. This method replaces the current value of a named attribute with a new value. If the named attribute doesn't exist, an exception should be thrown, because it is reasonable to assume that one should replace only existing attributes. That exception should contain the name of the attribute. To represent the exception, we create the `NoSuchAttributeException` class:

```
public class NoSuchAttributeException extends Exception {
    public final String attrName;

    public NoSuchAttributeException(String name) {
        super("No attribute named \"" + name + "\" found");
        attrName = name;
    }
}
```

`NoSuchAttributeException` extends `Exception` to add a constructor that takes the name of the attribute; it also adds a public final field to store the data. The constructor invokes the superclass's constructor with a string description of what happened. This custom exception type helps when writing code that catches the exception because it holds both a human-usable description of the error and the data that created the error. Adding useful data is one reason to create a new exception type.

Another reason to create a new exception type is that the type of the exception is an important part of the exception data, because exceptions are caught according to their type. For this reason, you would invent `NoSuchAttributeException` even if you did not want to add data. In this way, a programmer who cared only about such an exception could catch it exclusive of other exceptions that might be generated either by the methods of the `Attributed` interface, or by other methods used on other objects in the same area of code.

In general, new exception types should be created when programmers will want to handle one kind of error differently from another kind. Programmers can then use the exception type to execute the correct code rather than examine the contents of the exception to determine whether they really care about the exception or they have caught an irrelevant exception by accident.

12.2 `throw`

You throw exceptions using the `throw` statement:

    throw *expression*;

where *expression* must evaluate to a value or variable that is assignable to `Throwable`—or in simple terms, a reference to a `Throwable` object. For example, here is an addition to `AttributedImpl` from Chapter 4 that implements `replaceValue`:

```
public void replaceValue(String name, Object newValue)
    throws NoSuchAttributeException
{
    Attr attr = find(name);            // look up the attr
    if (attr == null)                  // it isn't found
        throw new NoSuchAttributeException(name);
    attr.setValue(newValue);
}
```

The `replaceValue` method first looks up the current `Attr` object for the name. If there isn't one, it throws a new object of type `NoSuchAttributeException`, providing the constructor with the attribute name. Exceptions are objects, so they must be created before being thrown. If the attribute does exist, its value is replaced with the new value. You can also generate an exception by invoking a method that itself throws an exception.

12.2.1 Transfer of Control

When an exception is thrown, the statement or expression that caused the exception is said to *complete abruptly*. This abrupt completion of statements causes the call chain to gradually unwind as each block or method invocation completes abruptly until the exception is caught. If the exception is not caught, the thread of execution terminates, after giving the thread's `UncaughtExceptionHandler` a chance to handle the exception—see "Threads and Exceptions" on page 379.

Once an exception occurs, actions after the point at which the exception occurred do not take place. If evaluation of a left-operand causes an exception then no part of the right-operand is evaluated; if evaluation of a left argument expression results in an exception, then no argument to the right is evaluated. The next action to occur will be in either a `finally` block, or a `catch` block that catches the exception.

12.2.2 Asynchronous Exceptions

A `throw` statement results in a *synchronous* exception, as does, say, a divide-by-zero arithmetic exception—the exception occurs directly as a result of executing a particular instruction; either the `throw` or dividing by zero. In contrast an *asynchronous* exception is one that can occur at any time, regardless of the instructions being executed.

Asynchronous exceptions can occur in only two specific ways. The first is an internal error in the Java virtual machine—such exceptions are considered asynchronous because they are caused by the execution of instructions in the virtual machine, not the instructions of the program. Needless to say, there is little that you can do about an internal error.

The second mechanism is the use of the deprecated `Thread.stop` methods, or the related, and not deprecated, `stopThread` methods of the JVM™ Tool Interface (JVMTI)—a native code interface to the virtual machine that allows for the inspection, and control of, a running application. These methods allow an asynchronous exception of any kind (checked or unchecked) to be thrown at any point during the execution of the target thread. Such a mechanism is inherently dangerous, which is why it has been deprecated in the `Thread` class—we discuss this further in Chapter 14.

12.3 The `throws` Clause

The definition of the `replaceValue` method declares which checked exceptions it throws. The language requires such a declaration because programmers invoking a method need to know the exceptions it can throw just as much as they need to know its normal behavior. The checked exceptions that a method throws are as important as the type of value it returns. Both must be declared.

The checked exceptions a method can throw are declared with a `throws` clause, which declares a comma-separated list of exception types. Only those exceptions that are not caught within the method must be listed.

You can throw checked exceptions that are extensions of any type of exception in the `throws` clause because you can use a class polymorphically anywhere its superclass is expected. A method can throw many classes of checked exceptions—all of them extensions of a particular exception class—and declare only the superclass in the `throws` clause. By doing so, however, you hide potentially useful information from programmers invoking the method: They won't know which of the possible extended exception types could be thrown. For documentation purposes, the `throws` clause should be as complete and specific as possible.

The contract defined by the `throws` clause is strictly enforced—you can throw only a type of checked exception that has been declared in the `throws` clause. Throwing any other type of checked exception is invalid, whether you use `throw` directly or use it indirectly by invoking another method. If a method has no `throws` clause, that does not mean that *any* exceptions can be thrown: It means that *no* checked exceptions can be thrown.

All the standard runtime exceptions (such as `ClassCastException` and `ArithmeticException`) are extensions of the `RuntimeException` class. The more serious errors are signaled by exceptions that are extensions of `Error`, and these exceptions can occur at any time in any code. `RuntimeException` and `Error` are the only exceptions you do not need to list in your `throws` clauses. They are ubiquitous, and every method can potentially throw them. This is why they are unchecked by the compiler. Those runtime exceptions—such as `IllegalArgumentException`—thrown under specific conditions should always be documented, even though they do not appear in the `throws` clause; see Chapter 19 for details on how to document exceptions thrown by your methods.

Because checked exceptions must be declared in a `throws` clause, it follows that any code fragment outside a method, or constructor, with a `throws` clause cannot throw a checked exception. This means that static initializers and static initialization blocks cannot throw checked exceptions, either directly or by invoking a method that throws such an exception. Non-static initializers and non-static initialization blocks are considered to be part of the constructor for a class, and so they are allowed to throw checked exceptions only if all the constructors of the class declare those checked exceptions.

Checked exception handling is strictly enforced because doing so helps avoid bugs that come from not dealing with errors. Experience has shown that programmers forget to handle errors or defer writing code to handle them until some future time that never arrives. The `throws` clause states clearly which exceptions are being thrown by methods and makes sure they are dealt with in some way by the invoker.

If you invoke a method that lists a checked exception in its `throws` clause, you have three choices:

◆ Catch the exception and handle it.

◆ Catch the exception and map it into one of your exceptions by throwing an exception of a type declared in your own `throws` clause.

◆ Declare the exception in your `throws` clause and let the exception pass through your method (although you might have a `finally` clause that cleans up first; see "`finally`" on page 288 for details).

The first two choices require that you catch exceptions thrown by other methods—something you will learn about soon.

You should be explicit in your `throws` clause, listing all the exceptions you know that you throw, even when you could encompass several exceptions under some superclass they all share. This is good self-documentation. Deciding how explicit you should be requires some thought. If you are designing a general interface or superclass you have to think about how restrictive you want to be to the implementing classes. It may be quite reasonable to define a general exception you use in the interface's `throws` clause, and to expect that the implementing classes will be more specific where possible. This tactic is used by the `java.io` package, which defines a general `IOException` type for its methods to throw. This lets implementing classes throw exceptions specific to whatever kind of I/O is being done. For example, the classes that do I/O across network channels can throw various network-related subclasses of `IOException`, and those dealing with files throw file-related subclasses.

12.3.1 throws Clauses and Method Overriding

When you override an inherited method, or implement an inherited abstract method, the `throws` clause of the overriding method must be compatible with the `throws` clause of the inherited method (whether abstract or not).

The simple rule is that an overriding or implementing method is not allowed to declare more checked exceptions in the `throws` clause than the inherited method does. The reason for this rule is quite simple: Code written to deal with the original method declaration won't be prepared to catch any additional checked exceptions and so no such exceptions are allowed to be thrown. Subtypes of the declared exceptions can be thrown because they will be caught in a `catch` block for their supertype. If the overriding or implementing method does not throw a checked exception then it need not redeclare that exception. For example, as you saw in "Strategies for Cloning" on page 101, a class that implements `Cloneable` need not declare that `clone` may throw a `CloneNotSupportedException`. Whether to declare it or not is a matter of design—if you declare it in the overriding method then subclasses of your class will be allowed to throw the exception in that method, otherwise they will not.

If a method declaration is multiply inherited—that is, it exists in more than one inherited interface, or in both an inherited interface and a superclass—then the `throws` clause of that method must satisfy all the inherited `throws` clauses. As we discussed in "Inheriting, Overriding, and Overloading Methods" on page 125, the real issue in such multiple inheritance situations, is whether a single implementation of a method can honor all the inherited contracts.

12.3.2   `throws` Clauses and Native Methods

A native method declaration (see page 74) can provide a `throws` clause that forces all users of that method to catch or redeclare the specified checked exceptions. However, the implementation of native methods is beyond the control of the Java compiler and so they cannot be checked to ensure that only the declared exceptions are thrown. Well-written native methods, however, will throw only those checked exceptions that they declare.

Exercise 12.1: Create an `ObjectNotFoundException` class for the `LinkedList` class you built in previous exercises. Add a `find` method that looks for an object in the list and either returns the `LinkedList` object that contains the desired object or throws the exception if the object isn't found in the list. Why is this preferable to returning `null` if the object isn't found? What additional data if any should `ObjectNotFoundException` contain?

12.4   `try`, `catch`, and `finally`

You catch exceptions by enclosing code in `try` blocks. The basic syntax for a `try` block is:

```
try {
    statements
} catch (exception_type1 identifier1) {
    statements
} catch (exception_type2 identifier2) {
```

```
    statements
  . . .
} finally {
    statements
}
```

where either at least one `catch` clause, or the `finally` clause, must be present. The body of the `try` statement is executed until either an exception is thrown or the body finishes successfully. If an exception is thrown, each `catch` clause is examined in turn, from first to last, to see whether the type of the exception object is assignable to the type declared in the `catch`. When an assignable `catch` clause is found, its block is executed with its identifier set to reference the exception object. No other `catch` clause will be executed. Any number of `catch` clauses, including zero, can be associated with a particular `try` as long as each clause catches a different type of exception. If no appropriate `catch` is found, the exception percolates out of the `try` statement into any outer `try` that might have a `catch` clause to handle it.

If a `finally` clause is present with a `try`, its code is executed after all other processing in the `try` is complete. This happens no matter how completion was achieved, whether normally, through an exception, or through a control flow statement such as `return` or `break`.

This example code is prepared to handle one of the exceptions `replaceValue` throws:

```
Object value = new Integer(8);
try {
    attributedObj.replaceValue("Age", value);
} catch (NoSuchAttributeException e) {
    // shouldn't happen, but recover if it does
    Attr attr = new Attr(e.attrName, value);
    attributedObj.add(attr);
}
```

The `try` sets up a statement (which must be a block) that does something that is normally expected to succeed. If everything succeeds, the block is finished. If any exception is thrown during execution of the code in the `try` block, either directly via a `throw` or indirectly by a method invoked inside it, execution of the code inside the `try` stops, and the attached `catch` clause is examined to see whether it wants to catch the exception that was thrown.

A `catch` clause is somewhat like an embedded method that has one parameter—namely, the exception to be caught. As with method parameters, the exception "parameter" can be declared `final`, or can have annotations applied.

Inside a catch clause, you can attempt to recover from the exception, or you can clean up and rethrow the exception so that any code calling yours also has a chance to catch it. Or a catch can do what it needs to and then fall out the bottom, in which case control flows to the statement after the try statement (after executing the finally clause, if there is one).

A general catch clause—one that catches exceptions of type Exception, for example—is usually a poor implementation choice since it will catch *any* exception, not just the specific one you are interested in. Had we used such a clause in our code, it could have ended up handling, for example, a ClassCastException as if it were a missing attribute problem.

You cannot put a superclass catch clause before a catch of one of its subclasses. The catch clauses are examined in order, so a catch that picked up one exception type before a catch for an extended type of exception would be a mistake. The first clause would always catch the exception, and the second clause would never be reached. The compiler will not accept the following code:

```
class SuperException extends Exception { }
class SubException extends SuperException { }

class BadCatch {
    public void goodTry() {
        /* This is an INVALID catch ordering */
        try {
            throw new SubException();
        } catch (SuperException superRef) {
            // Catches both SuperException and SubException
        } catch (SubException subRef) {
            // This would never be reached
        }
    }
}
```

Only one exception is handled by any single encounter with a try clause. If a catch or finally clause throws another exception, the catch clauses of the try are not reexamined. The catch and finally clauses are outside the protection of the try clause itself. Such exceptions can, of course, be handled by any encompassing try block in which the inner catch or finally clauses were nested.

12.4.1 finally

The finally clause of a try statement provides a mechanism for executing a section of code whether or not an exception is thrown. Usually, the finally clause is used to clean up internal state or to release non-object resources, such as open files stored in local variables. Here is a method that closes a file when its work is done, even if an error occurs:

```
public boolean searchFor(String file, String word)
    throws StreamException
{
    Stream input = null;

    try {
        input = new Stream(file);
        while (!input.eof())
            if (input.next().equals(word))
                return true;
        return false;        // not found
    } finally {
        if (input != null)
            input.close();
    }
}
```

If the new fails, input will never be changed from its initial null value. If the new succeeds, input will reference the object that represents the open file. When the finally clause is executed, the input stream is closed only if it has been open. Whether or not the operations on the stream generate an exception, the contents of the finally clause ensure that the file is closed, thereby conserving the limited resource of simultaneous open files. The searchFor method declares that it throws StreamException so that any exceptions generated are passed through to the invoking code after cleanup, including any StreamException thrown by the invocation of close.

There are two main coding idioms for correctly using finally. The general situation is that we have two actions, call them pre and post, such that if pre occurs then post must occur—regardless of what other actions occur between pre and post and regardless of whether those actions complete successfully or throw exceptions. One idiom for ensuring this is:

```
pre();
try {
    // other actions
} finally {
    post();
}
```

If pre succeeds then we enter the try block and no matter what occurs we are guaranteed that post gets executed. Conversely, if pre itself fails for some reason and throws an exception, then post does not get executed—it is important that pre occur outside the try block in this situation because post must not execute if pre fails.

You saw the second form of the idiom in the stream searching example. In that case pre returns a value that can be used to determine whether or not it completed successfully. Only if pre completed successfully is post invoked in the finally clause:

```
Object val = null;
try {
    val = pre();
    // other actions
} finally {
    if (val != null)
        post();
}
```

In this case, we could still invoke pre outside the try block, and then we would not need the if statement in the finally clause. The advantage of placing pre inside the try block comes when we want to catch both the exceptions that may be thrown by pre and those that may be thrown by the other actions—with pre inside the try block we can have one set of catch blocks, but if pre were outside the try block we would need to use an outer try-catch block to catch the exceptions from pre. Having nested try blocks can be further complicated if both pre and the other actions can throw the same exceptions—quite common with I/O operations—and we wish to propagate the exception after using it in some way; an exception thrown by the other actions would get caught twice and we would have to code our catch blocks to watch for and deal with that situation.

A finally clause can also be used to clean up for break, continue, and return, which is one reason you will sometimes see a try clause with no catch clauses. When any control transfer statement is executed, all relevant finally clauses are executed. There is no way to leave a try block without executing its finally clause.

The preceding example relies on finally in this way to clean up even with a normal return. One of the most common reasons goto is used in other languages is to ensure that certain things are cleaned up when a block of code is complete, whether or not it was successful. In our example, the finally clause ensures that the file is closed when either the return statement is executed or the stream throws an exception.

A `finally` clause is always entered with a reason. That reason may be that the `try` code finished normally, that it executed a control flow statement such as `return`, or that an exception was thrown in code executed in the `try` block. The reason is remembered when the `finally` clause exits by falling out the bottom. However, if the `finally` block creates its own reason to leave by executing a control flow statement (such as `break` or `return`) or by throwing an exception, that reason supersedes the original one, and the original reason is forgotten. For example, consider the following code:

```
try {
    // ... do something ...
    return 1;
} finally {
    return 2;
}
```

When the `try` block executes its return, the `finally` block is entered with the "reason" of returning the value 1. However, inside the `finally` block the value 2 is returned, so the initial intention is forgotten. In fact, if any of the other code in the `try` block had thrown an exception, the result would still be to return 2. If the `finally` block did not return a value but simply fell out the bottom, the "return the value 1" reason would be remembered and carried out.

12.5 Exception Chaining

Exceptions sometimes are caused by other exceptions. In "A Quick Tour", Section 1.14 on page 32, you saw an example where this was true:

```
public double[] getDataSet(String setName)
    throws BadDataSetException
{
    String file = setName + ".dset";
    FileInputStream in = null;
    try {
        in = new FileInputStream(file);
        return readDataSet(in);
    } catch (IOException e) {
        throw new BadDataSetException();
    } finally {
        try {
            if (in != null)
```

```
                    in.close();
          } catch (IOException e) {
              ;       // ignore: we either read the data OK
                      // or we're throwing BadDataSetException
          }
      }
}
// ... definition of readDataSet ...
```

This method throws a BadDataSetException on any I/O exception or data format error. The problem is that any information about the original exception is lost,
and it might be a needed clue to fixing the problem.

   Replacing exceptions with other ones is an important way to raise the level of
abstraction. To any code invoking the above method, all failures can be recovered
from in the same way. The particulars of the failure probably don't much matter to
what the program will do, which is to handle the failure of the data file. But
humans fixing the problem can require knowledge of the exact failure, so they will
want to have that information available—see "Stack Traces" on page 294.

   Situations like this are common enough that the exception mechanism
includes the notion of one exception being *caused* by another exception. The
initCause method, defined in Throwable, sets one exception's cause to be the
exception object passed as a parameter. For example, the previous example can
have its IOException catch clause rewritten as:

```
} catch (IOException e) {
    BadDataSetException bdse = new BadDataSetException();
    bdse.initCause(e);
    throw bdse;
} finally {
    // ...
}
```

Here initCause is used to remember the exception that made the data bad. This
means that the invoking code can handle all bad data simply with one exception
handler but still know the kind of exception that caused the underlying problem.
The invoking code can use the getCause method to retrieve the exception.

   The example can be simplified further by writing BadDataSetException to
expect to have a cause, at least some of the time, and so provide a constructor to
accept that cause if it is known. The idiomatic way to define a new exception class

is to provide at least the following four constructor forms—or variants thereof that deal with exception specific data:

```
class BadDataSetException extends Exception {
    public BadDataSetException() {}

    public BadDataSetException(String details) {
        super(details);
    }

    public BadDataSetException(Throwable cause) {
        super(cause);
    }

    public BadDataSetException(String details,
                               Throwable cause) {
        super(details, cause);
    }
}
```

Now the catch clause in the example simply becomes:

```
} catch (IOException e) {
    throw new BadDataSetException(e);
} finally {
    // ...
}
```

Not all exception classes provide cause-taking constructors, but all support the `initCause` method. To make it easier to use `initCause` with such exception classes, it returns the exception instance that it is invoked on. The idea is that you can use it like this:

```
throw new BadDataSetException().initCause(e); // Error?
```

The only problem is that this will nearly always result in a compile-time error: `initCause` returns a `Throwable` instance, and you can only throw a `Throwable` if your method's `throws` clause lists `Throwable`—which it rarely, if ever, should! Consequently, you have to modify the above, to cast the `Throwable` back to the actual exception type you are creating:

```
throw (BadDataSetException)
    new BadDataSetException().initCause(e);
```

Note that an exception can only have it's cause set once—either via a constructor, or by a single call to `initCause`—any attempt to set it again will cause an `IllegalStateException` to be thrown.

12.6 Stack Traces

When an exception is created, a stack trace of the call is saved in the exception object. This is done by the `Throwable` constructor invoking its own `fillInStacktrace` method. You can print this stack trace by using `printStackTrace`, and you can replace it with the current stack information by invoking `fillInStackTrace` again. If an exception has a cause, then typically `printStackTrace` will print the current exceptions stack trace, followed by the stack trace of its cause—however, the details of stack trace printing depend on the virtual-machine implementation.

A stack trace is represented by an array of `StackTraceElement` objects that you can get from `getStackTrace`. You can use this array to examine the stack or to create your own display of the information. Each `StackTraceElement` object represents one method invocation on the call stack. You can query these with the methods `getFileName`, `getClassName`, `getMethodName`, `getLineNumber`, and `isNativeMethod`.

You can also set the stack trace with `setStackTrace`, but you would have to be writing a very unusual program for this to be a good idea. The real information contained in a stack trace is quite valuable. Do not discard it without compelling need. Proper reasons for changing a stack trace are vital, but very rare.

12.7 When to Use Exceptions

We used the phrase "unexpected error condition" at the beginning of this chapter when describing when to throw exceptions. Exceptions are not meant for simple, expected situations. For example, reaching the end of a stream of input is expected, so the method that returns the next input from the stream has "hitting the end" as part of its expected behavior. A return flag that signals the end of input is reasonable because it is easy for callers to check the return value, and such a convention is also easier to understand. Consider the following typical loop that uses a return flag:

```
while ((token = stream.next()) != Stream.END)
    process(token);
stream.close();
```

Compare that to this loop, which relies on an exception to signal the end of input:

```
try {
    for (;;) {
        process(stream.next());
    }
} catch (StreamEndException e) {
    stream.close();
}
```

In the first case, the flow of control is direct and clear. The code loops until it reaches the end of the stream, and then it closes the stream. In the second case, the code seems to loop forever. Unless you know that end of input is signaled with a `StreamEndException`, you don't know the loop's natural range. Even when you know about `StreamEndException`, this construction can be confusing since it moves the loop termination from inside the `for` loop into the surrounding `try` block.

In some situations no reasonable flag value exists. For example, a class for a stream of `double` values can contain any valid `double`, and there is no possible end-of-stream marker. The most reasonable design is to add an explicit `eof` test method that should be called before any read from the stream:

```
while (!stream.eof())
    process(stream.nextDouble());
stream.close();
```

On the other hand, continuing to read *past* the end of input is not expected. It means that the program didn't notice the end and is trying to do something it should never attempt. This is an excellent case for a `ReadPastEndException`. Such behavior is outside the expected use of your stream class, and throwing an exception is the right way to handle it.

Deciding which situations are expected and which are not is a fuzzy area. The point is not to abuse exceptions as a way to report expected situations.

Exercise 12.2: Decide which way the following conditions should be communicated to the programmer:

- Someone tries to set the capacity of a `PassengerVehicle` object to a negative value.
- A syntax error is found in a configuration file that an object uses to set its initial state.

◆ A method that searches for a programmer-specified word in a string array cannot find any occurrence of the word.

◆ A file provided to an "open" method does not exist.

◆ A file provided to an "open" method exists, but security prevents the user from using it.

◆ During an attempt to open a network connection to a remote server process, the remote machine cannot be contacted.

◆ In the middle of a conversation with a remote server process, the network connection stops operating.

12.8 Assertions

An *assertion* is used to check an *invariant,* a condition that should always be true. If the assertion is found to be false then an exception is thrown. If your code assumes that something is true, adding an assertion to test it gives you a way to catch mistakes before they cause odd effects. For example, in a linked list the last element in the list usually has a `null` reference to the next element:

```java
public void append(Object value) {
    ListNode node = new ListNode(value);
    if (tail != null)
        tail.next = node;
    tail = node;
    assert tail.next == null;
}
```

When the append method has done its work, the `assert` double-checks that the last node is properly formed. If it is not, then an `AssertionError` is thrown.

By default, assertions are not evaluated. It is possible to turn assertion evaluation on and off for packages, classes, and entire class loaders, as you will soon see. When assertions are turned off, the assertions are not evaluated at all. This means that you must be careful about side effects that affect non-assertion code. For example, the following code is very dangerous:

```java
assert ++i < max;
```

When assertions are being evaluated, the value of i will be incremented to the next value. But when someone turns off assertions the entire expression will logically vanish from the code leaving i perpetually unchanged. Don't ever do anything like this. Split it up:

```
    i++;
    assert i < max;
```

12.8.1 The `assert` Statement

The syntax for an assertion is:

```
    assert eval-expr [: detail-expr];
```

where *eval-expr* is either a `boolean` or `Boolean` expression and *detail-expr* is an optional expression that will be passed to the `AssertionError` constructor to help describe the problem. The detail expression is optional; if present, it provides information to a person who looks at the statement or thrown exception. If the detail is a `Throwable` it will become the cause of the `AssertionError`; that is, it will be the value returned by the error's `getCause` method. Otherwise, the detail will be converted to a string and become the detail message for the error.

When an `assert` is encountered in the code, the first expression is evaluated. If the resulting value is `true`, the assertion passes. If it is `false`, the assertion fails, and an `AssertionError` will be constructed and thrown.

12.9 When to Use Assertions

Assertions are typically used to make sure those things that "can't happen" are noticed if they do happen. This is why a failed assertion throws a kind of `Error` instead of an `Exception`. A failed assertion means that the current state is basically insane.

You should not use assertions to test for things that you know will actually happen sometimes (`IOException`) or for which other means are common (`IllegalArgumentException`, `NullPointerException`, ...). You want to deal with these problems whether or not assertions are being evaluated. Assertions are for testing for things that should never happen—in a properly functioning program no assertion should ever fail. The next few sections show some good examples of when to use assertions.

12.9.1 State Assertions

Some assertions are used to test that the current state is always as it should be.

```
    public void setEnds(Point p1, Point p2) {
        this.p1 = p1;
        this.p2 = p2;
```

```
        distance = calculateDistance(p1, p2);
        assert (distance >= 0) : "Negative distance";
    }
```

In the above code, setting the endpoints causes the distance field to be recalculated. The distance calculation should always result in a positive value. Any bug that gives distance a negative value would produce odd effects when the value is used in the future. The assertion shown will catch such a bug right at the source. Simple assertions of this form can be used in many places to ensure the sanity of your state and algorithms.

The terms *precondition* and *postcondition* refer to particular kinds of state assertion. A precondition is something that must be true before a particular chunk of code (usually a method) is executed; a postcondition must be true after. You can use assert to check pre- and postconditions, such as:

```
public boolean remove(Object value) {
    assert count >= 0;
    if (value == null)
        throw new NullPointerException("value");
    int orig = count;
    boolean foundIt = false;
    try {
        // remove element from list (if it's there)
        return foundIt;
    } finally {
        assert ((!foundIt && count == orig) ||
                count == orig - 1);
    }
}
```

Here the method enforces the precondition that the list size must be non-negative before the operation, and the postcondition that the list size should be reduced by one after removal of an element, unless the element was not in the list.

Note that the check for whether the element to remove is null is not an assert, but instead throws a NullPointerException. In general you should expect that users of your class will make mistakes, and so, where possible, you should always check for them and have defined what happens for when they make them, such as returning a flag value or throwing an exception. In effect an assertion is a way of checking that there are no bugs or unexpected usage in the code, not that the code that calls it is bug free—so do not use assertions to validate arguments passed to your non-private methods.

Assert statements may or may not be executed, so the compiler will not always consider them reachable. A variable that is initialized only in an assert statement will be considered potentially uninitialized because if asserts are disabled it will be uninitialized. This will be true even if all uses of the variable are in other assert statements.

12.9.2 Control Flow Assertions

You can also use assertions to verify that the control flow of some code is always what you want it to be:

```
// value must always be present
private void replace(int val, int nval) {
    for (int i = 0; i < values.length; i++) {
        if (values[i] == val) {
            values[i] = nval;
            return;
        }
    }
    assert false : "replace: can't find " + val;
}
```

This loop should never reach the end, because some index in the loop ought to cause a return. If this doesn't happen, the loop will unexpectedly fall out the bottom and the program will continue silently on its unexpected way. The `assert false` after the loop means that if the control flow ever gets there you will be told.

In this kind of case you can reasonably avoid the assertion mechanism entirely and go straight to throwing the error yourself, replacing the `assert` with a `throw`:

```
throw new AssertionError("replace: can't find " + val);
```

Using a `throw` is especially valuable for methods that return values. Without a `throw` the compiler would not know that the method cannot get to the bottom, so it insists that you return a value at the end. That code typically looks like this:

```
return -1;   // never happens
```

The comment "never happens" asserts something to be true but doesn't check or enforce it. Only a human reading the code knows the invariant. And an `assert false` could be turned off, so the compiler would still require the code to have a bogus `return`. The `throw` enforces what you already know.

The compiler will not let you have an `assert` statement it believes to be unreachable, just like it won't let you have any other unreachable statement. When

the compiler can determine that a line is unreachable, not only do you need no
`assert`, you may not put one there.

12.10 Turning Assertions On and Off

By default, assertion evaluation is turned off. You can turn on all assertion evaluation in a virtual machine, or on a package, class, or class loader basis. Because
they can be on or off, you must be careful to avoid side effects that affect non-
assertion code.

   You control assertion evaluation either by passing command-line options to
the virtual machine—described shortly—or by using methods provided by the
class loader—see "Controlling Assertions at Runtime" on page 444.

12.10.1 Why Turn Assertions On and Off?

The first question to answer is why you would want to be able to switch assertion
evaluation on and off. The usual example is to turn assertions on during development, but turn them off when your system is shipping. The argument is that you
will have caught any insanities during the development cycle so the overhead of
doing all the checks is not worth the effort.

   This is tempting logic, but you can open yourself up to serious problems. The
point of assertions is to catch bugs early before they corrupt things and cause
bizarre side effects. When someone else is running your code, tracking down
causes for problems is much more difficult, so catching them early and reporting
them clearly is much more important, even if it should happen a lot less often. You
should only turn off assertions in code where they have very noticeable performance effects. In those critical sections of code, though, you will want to turn
them off.

12.10.2 Controlling Assertions on the Command Line

Assertion evaluation is off by default. To change this, you can use standard command line options if you are using a command-line-driven virtual machine:

`-enableassertions/-ea[`*`descriptor`*`]`

> Enables (turns on) assertion evaluation as defined by the *descriptor*. If
> there is no descriptor, assertions are enabled for all classes except those
> loaded by the system class loader—see "Loading Classes" on page 435.

`-disableassertions/-da[`*`descriptor`*`]`

> Disables (turns off) assertion evaluation for all classes as defined by the *`descriptor`*. If there is no descriptor, assertions are disabled for all classes.

The *`descriptor`* allows you to specify particular packages or classes that will be affected by the option. An absent descriptor means the option applies to all non-system classes (that is, classes loaded by any class loader but the system class loader). Packages are defined by name, followed by ... which means to apply the option to all subpackages. For example, the option

```
-enableassertions:com.acme...
```

would turn on assertions in all classes in `com.acme` and all its subpackages. If the descriptor consists only of ... it represents the unnamed package in the current working directory. Without the ... the descriptor is assumed to be the full name of a class.

```
-enableassertions:com.acme.Plotter
```

turns on assertions for the class `com.acme.Plotter`. So if you want to turn on all assertions in `com.acme`, but the class `com.acme.Evalutor` is not relevant, you could say

```
-enableassertions:com.acme... -da:com.acme.Evaluator
```

This applies the option to the `Evaluator` class and any of its nested types.

If you are using assertions in your code, the obvious thing you should do is always use `-ea` with enough specificity to get all your relevant code.

Multiple options are evaluated in order from the command line. Class-specific options take precedence over package ones, and a more specific package option takes precedence over a less specific one. For example, given

```
-da:com.acme.Plotter -ea:com.acme... -da:com.acme.products
-ea:com.acme.products.Rocket
```

assertions will be enabled for all classes and subpackages of `com.acme`, except the class `com.acme.Plotter`, and disabled for all classes and subpackages of `com.acme.products`, except for the class `com.acme.products.Rocket`.

The system classes are controlled separately because you are more likely to be searching for bugs in your code than in the system code. To affect system classes, use the "system" variants of the options: `-enablesystemassertions/-esa` and `-disablesystemassertions/-dsa` (the latter option is primarily for symmetry).

The assertion status of a class is determined when that class is initialized—see "Preparing a Class for Use" on page 441—and never changes. This determination is made before any static initializers for the class are executed, but after the initialization of the superclass. If a superclass static initializer causes a static method of its own subclass to be executed, it is possible for that static method to execute before its own class is initialized, and before the assertion status of that class has been determined. In such circumstances, the execution of any assert statements must be dealt with as if assertions were enabled for the class.

12.10.3 Complete Removal

Even though assertions may never get executed at runtime, the code associated with them still exists, and they can still consume virtual machine resources and add overhead to the performance of an application. For most applications this isn't something you should worry about—and a good just-in-time compiler will take care of the overhead—but sometimes, in resource constrained environments, you do have to worry about it. The only way to guarantee the complete removal of assertion related code is to edit the code and remove the assertions. But there is a standard Java programming idiom that gives the source code compiler a hint that you don't want certain sections of code present under some circumstances:

```
private static final boolean doAssert = true;

    if (doAssert)
        assert (cleared || size == origSize);
```

In the above code fragment, asserts will be checked only if the doAssert variable is true. The doAssert variable is a compile-time constant—it is static, final, and initialized with a constant value—and references to compile-time constants are replaced, at compile time, with the value of that constant. If doAssert is false nothing will ever cause the assert to get executed, so the if statement can be completely removed by the compiler, if it chooses. You can also use this technique to elide debugging print statements, for example.

12.10.4 Making Assertions Required

Sometimes (rarely) you may need to ensure that some class never has its assertions turned off. You can do this with code like the following

```
static {
    boolean assertsEnabled = false;
    assert assertsEnabled = true;
```

```
        if (!assertsEnabled)
            throw new IllegalStateException("Asserts required");
    }
```

In this code we purposefully use a side effect of the `assert` statement so that the code can determine whether asserts have been turned off—if they have then the class will not load. This is a nearly unique case in which side effects are a good thing.

Requiring assertions to be on complicates the running environment of the code since it must always turn on assertions for this class even if they are off elsewhere. You should do this almost, if not actually, never.

> *The greatest of all faults is to be conscious of none.*
> —-Thomas Carlyle

CHAPTER 13

Strings and Regular Expressions

What's the use of a good quotation if you can't change it?
—Dr. Who, *The Two Doctors*

Sᴛʀɪɴɢs are standard objects with built-in language support. You have already seen many examples of using string literals to create string objects. You've also seen the + and += operators that concatenate strings to create new strings. The `String` class, however, has much more functionality to offer. `String` objects are immutable (read-only), so you also have a `StringBuilder` class for mutable strings. This chapter describes `String` and `StringBuilder` and some related classes, including utilities for regular expression matching.

13.1 Character Sequences

As described in "Character Set" on page 161, the Java programming language represents text consisting of Unicode characters as sequences of `char` values using the UTF-16 encoding format. The `String` class defines objects that represent such character sequences. More generally, the `java.lang.CharSequence` interface is implemented by any class that represents such a character sequence—this includes the `String`, `StringBuilder`, and `StringBuffer` classes described in this chapter, together with the `java.nio.CharBuffer` class that is used for performing I/O.

The `CharSequence` interface is simple, defining only four methods:

`public char charAt(int index)`

Returns the `char` in this sequence at the given `index`. Sequences are indexed from zero to `length()-1` (just as arrays are indexed). As this is a UTF-16 sequence of characters, the returned value may be an actual character or a value that is part of a surrogate pair. If the index is negative or not less than the length of the sequence, then an `IndexOutOfBoundsException` is thrown.

`public int length()`
Returns the length of this character sequence.

`public CharSequence subSequence(int start, int end)`
Returns a new `CharSequence` that contains the `char` values in this sequence consisting of `charAt(start)` through to `charAt(end-1)`. If end is less than `start` or if use of either value would try to index outside this sequence, then an `IndexOutOfBoundsException` is thrown. Be careful to ensure that the specified range doesn't split any surrogate pairs.

`public String toString()`
Overrides the contract of `Object.toString` to specify that it returns the character sequence represented by this `CharSequence`.

13.2 The `String` Class

Strings are immutable (read-only) character sequences: Their contents can never be changed after the string is constructed. The `String` class provides numerous methods for working with strings—searching, comparing, interacting with other character sequences—an overview of which is given in the following sections.

13.2.1 Basic `String` Operations

You can create strings implicitly either by using a string literal (such as "Größe") or by using + or += on two `String` objects to create a new one.

You can also construct `String` objects explicitly using new. The `String` class supports the following simple constructors (other constructors are shown in later sections):

`public String()`
Constructs a new `String` with the value ""—an empty string.

`public String(String value)`
Constructs a new `String` that is a copy of the specified `String` object `value`—this is a copy constructor. Because `String` objects are immutable, this is rarely used.

public **String(StringBuilder value)**
> Constructs a new String with the same contents as the given StringBuilder.

public **String(StringBuffer value)**
> Constructs a new String with the same contents as the given StringBuffer.

The most basic methods of String objects are length and charAt, as defined by the CharSequence interface. This loop counts the number of each kind of character in a string:

```
for (int i = 0; i < str.length(); i++)
    counts[str.charAt(i)]++;
```

Note that length is a method for String, while for array it is a field—it's common for beginners to confuse the two.

In most String methods, a string index position less than zero or greater than length()-1 throws an IndexOutOfBoundsException. Some implementations throw the more specific StringIndexOutOfBoundsException, which can take the illegal index as a constructor argument and then include it in a detailed message. Methods or constructors that copy values to or from an array will also throw IndexOutOfBoundsException if any attempt is made to access outside the bounds of that array.

There are also simple methods to find the first or last occurrence of a particular character or substring in a string. The following method returns the number of characters between the first and last occurrences of a given character in a string:

```
static int countBetween(String str, char ch) {
    int begPos = str.indexOf(ch);
    if (begPos < 0)          // not there
        return -1;
    int endPos = str.lastIndexOf(ch);
    return endPos - begPos - 1;
}
```

The countBetween method finds the first and last positions of the character ch in the string str. If the character does not occur twice in the string, the method returns -1. The difference between the two character positions is one more than the number of characters in between (if the two positions were 2 and 3, the number of characters in between is zero).

Several overloads of the method indexOf search forward in a string, and several overloads of lastIndexOf search backward. Each method returns the index of what it found, or –1 if the search was unsuccessful:

Method	Returns Index Of...
indexOf(int ch)	first position of ch
indexOf(int ch, int start)	first position of ch ≥ start
indexOf(String str)	first position of str
indexOf(String str, int start)	first position of str ≥ start
lastIndexOf(int ch)	last position of ch
lastIndexOf(int ch, int start)	last position of ch ≤ start
lastIndexOf(String str)	last position of str
lastIndexOf(String str, int start)	last position of str ≤ start

The indexing methods that take an int parameter for the character to look for will search for the given character if the value is less than 0xFFFF, or else the code point with the given value—see "Working with UTF-16" on page 336.

If you don't care about the actual index of the substring, you can use the contains method, which returns true if the current string contains a given CharSequence as a subsequence. If you want to find the index of an arbitrary CharSequence you must invoke toString on the CharSequence and pass that to indexOf instead.

Exercise 13.1: Write a method that counts the number of occurrences of a given character in a string.

Exercise 13.2: Write a method that counts the number of occurrences of a particular string in another string.

13.2.2 String Comparisons

The String class supports several methods to compare strings and parts of strings. Before we describe the methods, though, you should be aware that internationalization and localization issues of full Unicode strings are not addressed with these methods. For example, when you're comparing two strings to determine which is "greater," characters in strings are compared numerically by their Unicode values, not by their localized notion of order. To a French speaker, c and ç are the same letter, differing only by a small diacritical mark. Sorting a set of strings in French should ignore the difference between them, placing "açb" before "acz" because b comes before z. But the Unicode characters are different—c (\u0063) comes before ç (\u00e7) in the Unicode character set—so these strings will actually sort the other way around. Internationalization and localization are discussed in Chapter 24.

The first compare operation is `equals`, which returns `true` if it is passed a reference to a `String` object having the same contents—that is, the two strings have the same length and exactly the same Unicode characters. If the other object isn't a `String` or if the contents are different, `String.equals` returns `false`. As you learned on page 100, this overrides `Object.equals` to define equivalence instead of identity.

To compare strings while ignoring case, use the `equalsIgnoreCase` method. By "ignore case," we mean that Ë and ë are considered the same but are different from E and e. Characters with no case distinctions, such as punctuation, compare equal only to themselves. Unicode has many interesting case issues, including a notion of "titlecase." Case issues in `String` are handled in terms of the case-related methods of the `Character` class, as described in "`Character`" on page 192.

A `String` can be compared with an arbitrary `CharSequence` by using the `contentEquals` method, which returns `true` if both objects represent exactly the same sequence of characters.

To sort strings, you need a way to order them, so `String` implements the interface `Comparable<String>`—the `Comparable` interface was described on page 118. The `compareTo` method returns an `int` that is less than, equal to, or greater than zero when the string on which it is invoked is less than, equal to, or greater than the other string. The ordering used is Unicode character ordering. The `String` class also defines a `compareToIgnoreCase` method.

The `compareTo` method is useful for creating an internal canonical ordering of strings. A binary search, for example, requires a sorted list of elements, but it is unimportant that the sorted order be local language order. Here is a binary search lookup method for a class that has a sorted array of strings:

```java
private String[] table;

public int position(String key) {
    int lo = 0;
    int hi = table.length - 1;
    while (lo <= hi) {
        int mid = lo + (hi - lo) / 2;
        int cmp = key.compareTo(table[mid]);
        if (cmp == 0)          // found it!
            return mid;
        else if (cmp < 0)      // search the lower part
            hi = mid - 1;
```

```
        else                    // search the upper part
            lo = mid + 1;
    }
    return -1;                   // not found
}
```

This is the basic binary search algorithm. It first checks the midpoint of the search range to determine whether the key is greater than, equal to, or less than the element at that position. If they are the same, the element has been found and the search is over. If the key is less than the element at the position, the lower half of the range is searched; otherwise, the upper half is searched. Eventually, either the element is found or the lower end of the range becomes greater than the higher end, in which case the key is not in the list.

In addition to entire strings, regions of strings can also be compared for equality. The method for this is regionMatches, and it has two forms:

public boolean **regionMatches(int start, String other, int ostart, int count)**

> Returns true if the given region of this String has the same Unicode characters as the given region of the string other. Checking starts in this string at the position start, and in the other string at position ostart. Only the first count characters are compared.

public boolean **regionMatches(boolean ignoreCase, int start, String other, int ostart, int count)**

> This version of regionMatches behaves exactly like the previous one, but the boolean ignoreCase controls whether case is significant.

For example:

```
class RegionMatch {
    public static void main(String[] args) {
        String str = "Look, look!";
        boolean b1, b2, b3;

        b1 = str.regionMatches(6, "Look", 0, 4);
        b2 = str.regionMatches(true, 6, "Look", 0, 4);
        b3 = str.regionMatches(true, 6, "Look", 0, 5);

        System.out.println("b1 = " + b1);
        System.out.println("b2 = " + b2);
        System.out.println("b3 = " + b3);
    }
}
```

Here is its output:

```
b1 = false
b2 = true
b3 = false
```

The first comparison yields `false` because the character at position 6 of the main string is `'l'` and the character at position 0 of the other string is `'L'`. The second comparison yields `true` because case is not significant. The third comparison yields `false` because the comparison length is now 5 and the two strings are not the same over five characters, even ignoring case.

In querying methods, such as `regionMatches` and those we mention next, any invalid indexes simply cause `false` to be returned rather than throwing exceptions. Passing a `null` argument when an object is expected generates a `NullPointerException`.

You can do simple tests for the beginnings and ends of strings by using `startsWith` and `endsWith`:

public boolean **startsWith(String prefix, int start)**
> Returns `true` if this `String` starts (at `start`) with the given `prefix`.

public boolean **startsWith(String prefix)**
> Equivalent to `startsWith(prefix, 0)`.

public boolean **endsWith(String suffix)**
> Returns `true` if this `String` ends with the given `suffix`.

13.2.3 String Literals, Equivalence and Interning

In general, using `==` to compare strings will give you the wrong results. Consider the following code:

```
if (str == "¿Peña?")
    answer(str);
```

This does not compare the contents of the two strings. It compares one object reference (`str`) to another (the string object representing the literal `"¿Peña?"`). Even if `str` contains the string `"¿Peña?"` this `==` expression will almost always yield `false` because the two strings will be held in different objects. Using `==` on objects only tests whether the two references refer to the same object, not whether they are equivalent objects.

However, any two string *literals* with the same contents will refer to the same String object. For example, == works correctly in the following code:

```
String str = "¿Peña?";
// ...
if (str == "¿Peña?")
    answer(str);
```

Because str is initially set to a string literal, comparing with another string literal is equivalent to comparing the strings for equal contents. But be careful—this works only if you are sure that all string references involved are references to string literals. If str is changed to refer to a manufactured String object, such as the result of a user typing some input, the == operator will return false even if the user types ¿Peña? as the string.

To overcome this problem you can *intern* the strings that you don't know for certain refer to string literals. The intern method returns a String that has the same contents as the one it is invoked on. However, any two strings with the same contents return the same String object from intern, which enables you to compare string references to test equality, instead of the slower test of string contents. For example:

```
int putIn(String key) {
    String unique = key.intern();
    int i;
    // see if it's in the table already
    for (i = 0; i < tableSize; i++)
        if (table[i] == unique)
            return i;
    // it's not there--add it in
    table[i] = unique;
    tableSize++;
    return i;
}
```

All the strings stored in the table array are the result of an intern invocation. The table is searched for a string that was the result of an intern invocation on another string that had the same contents as the key. If this string is found, the search is finished. If not, we add the unique representative of the key at the end. Dealing with the results of intern makes comparing object references equivalent to comparing string contents, but much faster.

Any two strings with the same contents are guaranteed to have the same hash code—the String class overrides Object.hashCode—although two different strings might also have the same hash code. Hash codes are useful for hashtables, such as the HashMap class in java.util—see "HashMap" on page 590.

13.2.4 Making Related Strings

Several String methods return new strings that are like the old one but with a specified modification. New strings are returned because String objects are immutable. You could extract delimited substrings from another string by using a method like this one:

```
public static String delimitedString(
    String from, char start, char end)
{
    int startPos = from.indexOf(start);
    int endPos = from.lastIndexOf(end);
    if (startPos == -1)          // no start found
        return null;
    else if (endPos == -1)       // no end found
        return from.substring(startPos);
    else if (startPos > endPos) // start after end
        return null;
    else                         // both start and end found
        return from.substring(startPos, endPos + 1);
}
```

The method delimitedString returns a new String object containing the string inside from that is delimited by start and end—that is, it starts with the character start and ends with the character end. If start is found but not end, the method returns a new String object containing everything from the start position to the end of the string. The method delimitedString works by using the two overloaded forms of substring. The first form takes only an initial start position and returns a new string containing everything in the original string from that point on. The second form takes both a start and an end position and returns a new string that contains all the characters in the original string from the start to the endpoint, including the character at the start but *not* the one at the end. This "up to but not including the end" behavior is the reason that the method adds one to endPos to include the delimiter characters in the returned string. For example, the string returned by

```
delimitedString("Il a dit «Bonjour!»", '«', '»');
```

is

«Bonjour!»

Here are the rest of the "related string" methods:

public String **replace(char oldChar, char newChar)**
> Returns a `String` with all instances of `oldChar` replaced with the character `newChar`.

public String **replace(CharSequence oldSeq, CharSquence newSeq)**
> Returns a `String` with each occurrence of the subsequence `oldSeq` replaced by the subsequence `newSeq`.

public String **trim()**
> Returns a `String` with leading and trailing whitespace stripped. Whitespace characters are those identified as such by the `Character.isWhitespace` method and include space, tab, and newline.

A number of methods return related strings based on a match with a given regular expression—see "Regular Expression Matching" on page 321:

public String **replaceFirst(String regex, String repStr)**
> Returns a `String` with the first substring that matches the regular expression `regex` replaced by `repStr`. Invoked on `str`, this is equivalent to `Pattern.compile(regex).matcher(str).replaceFirst(repStr)`.

public String **replaceAll(String regex, String repStr)**
> Returns a `String` with all substrings that match the regular expression `regex` replaced by `repStr`. Invoked on `str`, this is equivalent to `Pattern.compile(regex).matcher(str).replaceAll(repStr)`.

public String[] **split(String regex)**
> Equivalent to `split(regex,0)` (see below).

public String[] **split(String regex, int limit)**
> Returns an array of strings resulting from splitting up this string according to the regular expression. Each match of the regular expression will cause a split in the string, with the matched part of the string removed. The `limit` affects the number of times the regular expression will be applied to the string to create the array. Any positive number n limits the number of applications to $n-1$, with the remainder of the string returned as the last element of the array (so the array will be no larger than n). Any negative limit means that there is no limit to the number of applications and the array can have any length. A limit of zero behaves like a negative limit, but trailing empty strings will be discarded. Invoked on `str`, this is equivalent to `Pattern.compile(regex).split(str, limit)`.

This is easier to understand with an example. The following table shows the array elements returned from `split("--", n)` invoked on the string `"w--x--y--"` for n equal to –1, 0, 1, 2, 3, and 4:

Limit:	-1	0	1	2	3	4
Results						
[0]:	w	w	w--x--y--	w	w	w
[1]:	x	x		x--y--	x	x
[2]:	y	y			y--	y
[3]:	""					""

With a negative or zero limit we remove all occurrences of `"--"`, with the difference between the two being the trailing empty string in the negative case. With a limit of one we don't actually apply the pattern and so the whole string is returned as the zeroth element. A limit of two applies the pattern once, breaking the string into two substrings. A limit of three gives us three substrings. A limit of four gives us four substrings, with the fourth being the empty string due to the original string ending with the pattern we were splitting on. Any limit greater than four will return the same results as a limit of four.

In all the above, if the regular expression syntax is incorrect a `PatternSyntaxException` is thrown.

These are all convenience methods that avoid the need to work with `Pattern` and `Matcher` objects directly, but they require that the regular expression be compiled each time. If you just want to know if a given string matches a given regular expression, the `matches` method returns a `boolean` to tell you.

Case issues are *locale sensitive*—that is, they vary from place to place and from culture to culture. The platform allows users to specify a locale, which includes language and character case issues. Locales are represented by `Locale` objects, which you'll learn about in more detail in Chapter 24. The methods `toLowerCase` and `toUpperCase` use the current default locale, or you can pass a specific locale as an argument:

public String **toLowerCase()**

> Returns a `String` with each character converted to its lowercase equivalent if it has one according to the default locale.

public String **toUpperCase()**

> Returns a `String` with each character converted to its uppercase equivalent if it has one according to the default locale.

public String **toLowerCase(Locale loc)**

> Returns a `String` with each character converted to its lowercase equivalent if it has one according to the specified locale.

```
public String toUpperCase(Locale loc)
```
> Returns a `String` with each character converted to its uppercase equivalent if it has one according to the specified locale.

The `concat` method returns a new string that is equivalent to the string returned when you use + on two strings. The following two statements are equivalent:

```
newStr = oldStr.concat(" not");
newStr = oldStr + " not";
```

Exercise 13.3: As shown, the `delimitedString` method assumes only one such string per input string. Write a version that will pull out all the delimited strings and return an array.

Exercise 13.4: Write a program to read an input string with lines of the form "*type value*", where `type` is one of the wrapper class names (`Boolean`, `Character`, and so on) and `value` is a string that the type's constructor can decode. For each such entry, create an object of that type with that value and add it to an `ArrayList`—see "`ArrayList`" on page 582. Display the final result when all the lines have been read. Assume a line is ended simply by the newline character `'\n'`.

13.2.5 String Conversions

You often need to convert strings to and from something else, such as integers or booleans. The convention is that the type being converted *to* has the method that does the conversion. For example, converting from a `String` to an `int` requires a static method in class `Integer`. This table shows all the types that you can convert, and how to convert each to and from a `String`:

Type	**To String**	**From String**
boolean	String.valueOf(boolean)	Boolean.parseBoolean(String)
byte	String.valueOf(int)	Byte.parseByte(String, int base)
char	String.valueOf(char)	*str*.charAt(0)
short	String.valueOf(int)	Short.parseShort(String, int base)
int	String.valueOf(int)	Integer.parseInt(String, int base)
long	String.valueOf(long)	Long.parseLong(String, int base)
float	String.valueOf(float)	Float.parseFloat(String)
double	String.valueOf(double)	Double.parseDouble(String)

To convert a primitive type to a `String` you invoke one of the static `valueOf` methods of `String`, which for numeric types produces a base 10 representation.

The `Integer` and `Long` wrapper classes—as described in Chapter 8—also provide methods `toBinaryString`, `toOctalString`, and `toHexString` for other representations.

To convert, or more accurately to parse a string into a primitive type you invoke the static `parseType` method of the primitives type's corresponding wrapper class. Each parsing method has its own rules about the allowed format of the string, for example `Float.parseFloat` will accept a floating-point literal of the form `"3.14f"`, whereas `Long.parseLong` will not accept the string `"25L"`. These numeric parsing methods have two overloaded forms: one that takes a numeric base between 2 and 32 in addition to the string to parse; and one that takes only the string and assumes base 10. These parsing methods will also reject the string if it has characters representing the base of the number, such as `"0x12FE"` for a hexadecimal value, or `"\033"` for an octal value. However, the `Integer` and `Long` wrapper classes also provide a static `decode` method that will parse a string that does include this base information. For the numeric types, if the string does not represent a valid value of that type, a `NumberFormatException` is thrown.

To convert a `String` to a `char` you simply extract the first `char` from the `String`.

Your classes can support string encoding and decoding by having an appropriate `toString` method and a constructor that creates a new object given the string description. The method `String.valueOf(Object obj)` is defined to return either `"null"` (if `obj` is `null`) or the result of `obj.toString`. The `String` class provides enough overloads of `valueOf` that you can convert any value of any type to a `String` by invoking `valueOf`.

13.2.6 Strings and char Arrays

A `String` maps to an array of `char` and vice versa. You often want to build a string in a `char` array and then create a `String` object from the contents. Assuming that the writable `StringBuilder` class (described later) isn't adequate, several `String` methods and constructors help you convert a `String` to an array of `char`, or convert an array of `char` to a `String`.

There are two constructors for creating a `String` from a `char` array:

`public String(char[] chars, int start, int count)`
> Constructs a new `String` whose contents are the same as the `chars` array, from index `start` up to a maximum of `count` characters.

`public String(char[] chars)`
> Equivalent to `String(chars, 0, chars.length)`.

Both of these constructors make copies of the array, so you can change the array contents after you have created a `String` from it without affecting the contents of the `String`.

For example, the following simple algorithm squeezes out all occurrences of a character from a string:

```
public static String squeezeOut(String from, char toss) {
    char[] chars = from.toCharArray();
    int len = chars.length;
    int put = 0;
    for (int i = 0; i < len; i++)
        if (chars[i] != toss)
            chars[put++] = chars[i];
    return new String(chars, 0, put);
}
```

The method `squeezeOut` first converts its input string `from` into a character array using the method `toCharArray`. It then sets up `put`, which will be the next position into which to put a character. After that it loops, copying into the array any character that isn't a `toss` character. When the method is finished looping over the array, it returns a new `String` object that contains the squeezed string.

You can use the two static `String.copyValueOf` methods instead of the constructors if you prefer. For instance, `squeezeOut` could have been ended with

```
return String.copyValueOf(chars, 0, put);
```

There is also a single-argument form of `copyValueOf` that copies the entire array. For completeness, two static `valueOf` methods are also equivalent to the two `String` constructors.

The `toCharArray` method is simple and sufficient for most needs. When you need more control over copying pieces of a string into a character array, you can use the `getChars` method:

public void getChars(int srcBegin, int srcEnd, char[] dst,
**   int dstBegin)**

> Copies characters from this `String` into the specified array. The characters of the specified substring are copied into the character array, starting at `dst[dstBegin]`. The specified substring is the part of the string starting at `srcBegin`, up to but *not* including `srcEnd`.

13.2.7 Strings and byte Arrays

Strings represent characters encoded as char values with the UTF-16 encoding format. To convert those char values into raw byte values requires that another encoding format be used. Similarly, to convert individual "characters" or arrays of raw 8-bit "characters" into char values requires that the encoding format of the raw bytes is known. For example, you would convert an array of ASCII or Latin-1 bytes to Unicode characters simply by setting the high bits to zero, but that would not work for other 8-bit character set encodings such as those for Hebrew. Different character sets are discussed shortly. In the following constructors and methods, you can name a character set encoding or use the user's or platform's default encoding:

public **String(byte[] bytes, int start, int count)**
> Constructs a new String by converting the bytes, from index start up to a maximum of count bytes, into characters using the default encoding for the default locale.

public **String(byte[] bytes)**
> Equivalent to String(bytes, 0, bytes.length).

public **String(byte[] bytes, int start, int count, String enc)**
> throws UnsupportedEncodingException
> Constructs a new String by converting the bytes, from index start up to a maximum of count bytes, into characters using the encoding named by enc.

public **String(byte[] bytes, String enc)**
> throws UnsupportedEncodingException
> Equivalent to String(bytes, 0, bytes.length, enc).

public byte[] **getBytes()**
> Returns a byte array that encodes the contents of the string using the default encoding for the default locale.

public byte[] **getBytes(String enc)**
> throws UnsupportedEncodingException
> Returns a byte array that encodes the contents of the string using the encoding named by enc.

The String constructors for building from byte arrays make copies of the data, so further modifications to the arrays will not affect the contents of the String.

13.2.8 Character Set Encoding

A character set encoding specifies how to convert between raw 8-bit "characters" and their 16-bit Unicode equivalents. Character sets are named using their standard and common names. The local platform defines which character set encodings are understood, but every implementation is required to support the following:

US-ASCII	7-bit ASCII, also known as ISO646-US, and as the Basic Latin block of the Unicode character set
ISO-8859-1	ISO Latin Alphabet No. 1, also known as ISO-LATIN-1
UTF-8	8-bit Unicode Transformation Format
UTF-16BE	16-bit Unicode Transformation Format, big-endian byte order
UTF-16LE	16-bit Unicode Transformation Format, little-endian byte order
UTF-16	16-bit Unicode Transformation Format, byte order specified by a mandatory initial byte-order mark (either order accepted on input, big-endian used on output)

Consult the release documentation for your implementation to see if any other character set encodings are supported.

Character sets and their encoding mechanisms are represented by specific classes within the java.nio.charset package:

Charset

A named mapping (such as US-ASCII or UTF-8) between sequences of 16-bit Unicode code units and sequences of bytes. This contains general information on the sequence encoding, simple mechanisms for encoding and decoding, and methods to create CharsetEncoder and CharsetDecoder objects for richer abilities.

CharsetEncoder

An object that can transform a sequence of 16-bit Unicode code units into a sequence of bytes in a specific character set. The encoder object also has methods to describe the encoding.

CharsetDecoder

An object that can transform a sequence of bytes in a specific character set into a sequence of 16-bit Unicode code units. The decoder object also has methods to describe the decoding.

You can obtain a Charset via its own static forName method, though usually you will just specify the character set name to some other method (such as the

String constructor or an I/O operation) rather than working with the Charset object directly. To test whether a given character set is supported use the forName method, and if you get an UnsuppportedCharsetException then it is not.

You can find a list of available character sets from the static availableCharsets method, which returns a SortedMap of names and Charset instances, of all known character sets. For example, to print out the names of all the known character sets you can use:

```java
for (String name : Charset.availableCharsets().keySet())
    System.out.println(name);
```

Every instance of the Java virtual machine has a default character set that is determined during virtual-machine startup and typically depends on the locale and encoding being used by the underlying operating system. You can obtain the default Charset using the static defaultCharset method.

13.3 Regular Expression Matching

The package java.util.regex provides you a way to find if a string matches a general description of a category of strings called a *regular expression*. A regular expression describes a class of strings by using wildcards that match or exclude groups of characters, markers to require matches in particular places, etc. The package uses a common kind of regular expression, quite similar to those used in the popular perl programming language, which itself evolved from those used in several Unix utilities.

You can use regular expressions to ask if strings match a pattern and pick out parts of strings using a rich expression language. First you will learn what regular expressions are. Then you will learn how to compile and use them.

13.3.1 Regular Expressions

A full description of regular expressions is complex and many other works describe them. So we will not attempt a complete tutorial, but instead will simply give some examples of the most commonly used features. (A full reference alone would take several pages.) A list of resources for understanding regular expressions is in "Further Reading" on page 758.

Regular expressions search in character sequences, as defined by java.lang.CharSequence, implemented by String and StringBuilder. You can implement it yourself if you want to provide new sources.

A regular expression defines a pattern that can be applied to a character sequence to search for matches. The simplest form is something that is matched exactly; the pattern xyz matches the string xyzzy but not the string plugh. Wildcards make the pattern more general. For example, . (dot) matches any single character, so the pattern .op matches both hop and pop, and * matches zero or more of the thing before it, so xyz* matches xy, xyz, and xyzzy.

Other useful wildcards include simple sets (p[aeiou]p matches pop and pup but not pgp, while [a-z] matches any single lowercase letter); negations ([^aeiou] matches anything that is not a single lowercase vowel); predefined sets (\d matches any digit; \s any whitespace character); and boundaries (^twisty matches the word "twisty" only at the beginning of a line; \balike matches "alike" only after a word boundary, that is, at the beginning of a word).

Special symbols for particular characters include \t for tab; \n for newline; \a for the alert (bell) character; \e for escape; and \\ for backslash itself. Any character that would otherwise have a special meaning can be preceded by a \ to remove that meaning; in other words \c always represents the character c. This is how, for example, you would match a * in an expression—by using *.

Special symbols start with the \ character, which is also the character used to introduce an escape character. This means, for example, that in the string expression "\balike", the actual pattern will consist of a backspace character followed by the word "alike", while "\s" would not be a pattern for whitespace but would cause a compile-time error because \s is not valid escape character. To use the special symbols within a string expression the leading \ must itself be escaped using \\, so the example strings become "\\balike" and "\\s", respectively. To include an actual backslash in a pattern it has to be escaped twice, using four backslash characters: "\\\\". Each backslash pair becomes a single backslash within the string, resulting in a single backslash pair being included in the pattern, which is then interpreted as a single backslash character.

Regular expressions can also *capture* parts of the string for later use, either inside the regular expression itself or as a means of picking out parts of the string. You capture parts of the expression inside parentheses. For example, the regular expression (.)-(.*)-\2-\1 matches x-yup-yup-x or ñ-å-å-ñ or any other similar string because \1 matches the group (.) and \2 matches the group (.*).[1] Groups are numbered from one, in order of the appearance of their opening parenthesis.

---

[1]   The .* means "zero or more characters," because . means "any character" and * means "zero or more of the thing I follow," so together they mean "zero or more of any character."

13.3.2 Compiling and Matching with Regular Expressions

Evaluating a regular expression can be compute intensive, and in many instances a single regular expression will be used repeatedly. This can be addressed by *compiling* the regular expression once and using the result. In addition, a single character sequence might be checked repeatedly against the same pattern to find multiple matches, which can be done fastest by remembering some information about previous matches. To address both these opportunities for optimization, the full model of using a regular expression is this:

1. First you turn your regular expression string into a `Pattern` object that is the compiled version of the pattern.
2. Next you ask the `Pattern` object for a `Matcher` object that applies that pattern to a particular `CharSequence` (such as a `String` or `StringBuilder`).
3. Finally you ask the `Matcher` to perform operations on the sequence using the compiled pattern.

Or, expressed in code:

```
Pattern pat = Pattern.compile(regularExpression);
Matcher matcher = pat.matcher(sequence);
boolean foundMatch = matcher.find();
```

If you are only using a pattern once, or are only matching each string against that pattern once, you need not actually deal with the intermediate objects. As you will see, there are convenience methods on `Pattern` for matching without a `Matcher`, and methods that create their own `Pattern` and `Matcher`. These are easy to use, but inefficient if you are using the same pattern multiple times, or matching against the same string with the same pattern repeatedly.

The `Pattern` class has the following methods:

public static Pattern **compile(String regex)**
throws PatternSyntaxException
> Compiles the given regular expression into a pattern.

public static Pattern **compile(String regex, int flags)**
throws PatternSyntaxException
> Compiles the given regular expression into a pattern with the given flags. The flags control how certain interesting cases are handled, as you will soon learn.

public String **pattern()**
> Returns the regular expression from which this pattern was compiled.

```
public int flags()
```
Returns this pattern's match flags.

```
public Matcher matcher(CharSequence input)
```
Creates a matcher that will match the given input against this pattern.

```
public String[] split(CharSequence input, int limit)
```
A convenience method that splits the given input sequence around matches of this pattern. Useful when you do not need to reuse the matcher. The `limit` affects the number of times the pattern will be applied to the input to create the array—see the `String` method `split(String regex, int limit)` on page 314 for a detailed example of how the limit applies.

```
public String[] split(CharSequence input)
```
A convenience method that splits the given input sequence around matches of this pattern. Equivalent to `split(input, 0)`.

```
public static boolean matches(String regex, CharSequence input)
```
A convenience method that compiles the given regular expression and attempts to match the given input against it. Useful when you do not need to reuse either parser or matcher. Returns `true` if a match is found.

```
public static String quote(String str)
```
Returns a string that can be used to create a pattern that would match with `str`.

The `toString` method of a `Pattern` also returns the regular expression from which the pattern was compiled.

The flags you can specify when creating the pattern object affect how the matching will be done. Some of these affect the performance of the matching, occasionally severely, but they may be functionality you need.

Flag	Meaning
CASE_INSENSITIVE	Case-insensitive matching. By default, only handle case for the ASCII characters.
UNICODE_CASE	Unicode-aware case folding when combined with CASE_INSENSITIVE
CANON_EQ	Canonical equivalence. If a character has multiple expressions, treat them as equivalent. For example, å is canonically equivalent to a\u030A.
DOTALL	Dot-all mode, where . matches line breaks, which it otherwise does not.
MULTILINE	Multiline mode, where ∧ and $ match at lines embedded in the sequence, not just at the start and end of the entire sequence

Flag	Meaning
UNIX_LINES	Unix lines mode, where only \n is considered a line terminator.
COMMENTS	Comments and whitespace in pattern. Whitespace will be ignored, and comments starting with # are ignored up to the next end of line.
LITERAL	Enable literal parsing of the pattern

The Matcher class has methods to match against the sequence. Each of these returns a boolean indicating success or failure. If successful, the position and other state associated with the match can then be retrieved from the Matcher object via the start, end, and group methods. The matching queries are

public boolean **matches()**

> Attempts to match the entire input sequence against the pattern.

public boolean **lookingAt()**

> Attempts to match the input sequence, starting at the beginning, against the pattern. Like the matches method, this method always starts at the beginning of the input sequence; unlike that method, it does not require that the entire input sequence be matched.

public boolean **find()**

> Attempts to find the next subsequence of the input sequence that matches the pattern. This method starts at the beginning of the input sequence or, if a previous invocation of find was successful and the matcher has not since been reset, at the first character not matched by the previous match.

public boolean **find(int start)**

> Resets this matcher and then attempts to find the next subsequence of the input sequence that matches the pattern, starting at the specified index. If a match is found, subsequent invocations of the find method will start at the first character not matched by this match.

Once matching has commenced, the following methods allow the state of the matcher to be modified:

public Matcher **reset()**

> Resets this matcher. This discards all state and resets the append position (see below) to zero. The returned Matcher is the one on which the method was invoked.

public Matcher **reset(CharSequence input)**

> Resets this matcher to use a new input sequence. The returned Matcher is the one on which the method was invoked.

```
public Matcher usePattern(Pattern pattern)
```
Changes the pattern used by this matcher to be `pattern`. Any group information is discarded, but the input and append positions remain the same.

Once a match has been found, the following methods return more information about the match:

```
public int start()
```
Returns the start index of the previous match.

```
public int end()
```
Returns the index of the last character matched, plus one.

```
public String group()
```
Returns the input subsequence matched by the previous match; in other words, the substring defined by `start` and `end`.

```
public int groupCount()
```
Returns the number of capturing groups in this matcher's pattern. Group numbers range from zero to one less than this count.

```
public String group(int group)
```
Returns the input subsequence matched by the given group in the previous match. Group zero is the entire matched pattern, so `group(0)` is equivalent to `group()`.

```
public int start(int group)
```
Returns the start index of the given group from the previous match.

```
public int end(int group)
```
Returns the index of the last character matched of the given group, plus one.

Together these methods form the `MatchResult` interface, which allows a match result to be queried but not modified. You can convert the current matcher state to a `MatchResult` instance by invoking its `toMatchResult` method. Any subsequent changes to the matcher state do not affect the existing `MatchResult` objects.

13.3.3 Replacing

You will often want to pair finding matches with replacing the matched characters with new ones. For example, if you want to replace all instances of sun with moon, your code might look like this:[2]

---

[2] The `StringBuffer` class (see page 335) is an appendable character sequence (you can modify its contents). The `Matcher` class should have been updated in the 5.0 release to work with any appendable character sequence, such as `StringBuilder`, but this was overlooked.

```
Pattern pat = Pattern.compile("sun");
Matcher matcher = pat.matcher(input);
StringBuffer result = new StringBuffer();
boolean found;
while ((found = matcher.find()))
    matcher.appendReplacement(result, "moon");
matcher.appendTail(result);
```

The loop continues as long as there are matches to sun. On each iteration through the loop, all the characters from the append position (the position after the last match; initially zero) to the start of the current match are copied into the string buffer. Then the replacement string moon is copied. When there are no more matches, appendTail copies any remaining characters into the buffer.

The replacement methods of Matcher are

public String **replaceFirst(String replacement)**

Replaces the first occurrence of this matcher's pattern with the replacement string, returning the result. The matcher is first reset and is not reset after the operation.

public String **replaceAll(String replacement)**

Replaces all occurrences of this matcher's pattern with the replacement string, returning the result. The matcher is first reset and is not reset after the operation.

public Matcher **appendReplacement(StringBuffer buf,**
   String replacement)

Adds to the string buffer the characters between the current append and match positions, followed by the replacement string, and then moves the append position to be after the match. As shown above, this can be used as part of a replacement loop. Returns this matcher.

public StringBuffer **appendTail(StringBuffer buf)**

Adds to the string buffer all characters from the current append position until the end of the sequence. Returns the buffer.

So the previous example can be written more simply with replaceAll:

```
Pattern pat = Pattern.compile("sun");
Matcher matcher = pat.matcher(input);
String result = matcher.replaceAll("moon");
```

As an example of a more complex usage of regular expressions, here is code that will replace every number with the next largest number:

```
Pattern pat = Pattern.compile("[-+]?[0-9]+");
Matcher matcher = pat.matcher(input);
StringBuffer result = new StringBuffer();
boolean found;
while ((found = matcher.find())) {
    String numStr = matcher.group();
    int num = Integer.parseInt(numStr);
    String plusOne = Integer.toString(num + 1);
    matcher.appendReplacement(result, plusOne);
}
matcher.appendTail(result);
```

Here we decode the number found by the match, add one to it, and replace the old value with the new one.

The replacement string can contain a g, which will be replaced with the value from the gth capturing group in the expression. The following method uses this feature to swap all instances of two adjacent words:

```
public static String
    swapWords(String w1, String w2, String input)
{
    String regex = "\\b(" + w1 + ")(\\W+)(" + w2 + ")\\b";
    Pattern pat = Pattern.compile(regex);
    Matcher matcher = pat.matcher(input);
    return matcher.replaceAll("$3$2$1");
}
```

First we build a pattern from the two words, using parenthesis to capture groups of characters. A \b in a pattern matches a word boundary (otherwise the word "crow" would match part of "crown"), and \W matches any character that would not be part of a word. The original pattern matches groups one (the first word), two (the separator characters), and three (the second word), which the "$3$2$1" replacement string inverts.

For example, the invocation

```
swapWords("up", "down",
            "The yo-yo goes up, down, up, down, ...");
```

would return the string

```
The yo-yo goes down, up, down, up, ...
```

If we only wanted to swap the first time the words were encountered we could use `replaceFirst`:

```
public static String
    swapFirstWords(String w1, String w2, String input) {

    String regex = "\\b(" + w1 + ")(\\W+)(" + w2 + ")\\b";
    Pattern pat = Pattern.compile(regex);
    Matcher matcher = pat.matcher(input);
    return matcher.replaceFirst("$3$2$1");
}
```

13.3.4 Regions

A `Matcher` looks for matches in the character sequence that it is given as input. By default, the entire character sequence is considered when looking for a match. You can control the *region* of the character sequence to be used, through the method `region` which takes a starting index and an ending index to define the subsequence in the input character sequence. The methods `regionStart` and `regionEnd` return, respectively, the current start index and the current end index.

You can control whether a region is considered to be the true start and end of the input, so that matching with the beginning or end of a line will work, by invoking `useAnchoringBounds` with an argument of `true` (the default). If you don't want the region to match with the line anchors then use `false`. The method `hasAnchoringBounds` will return the current setting.

Similarly, you can control whether the bounds of the region are transparent to matching methods that want to look-ahead, look-behind, or detect a boundary. By default bounds are opaque—that is, they will appear to be hard bounds on the input sequence—but you can change that with `useTransparentBounds`. The `hasTransparentBounds` method returns the current setting.

13.3.5 Efficiency

Suppose you want to parse a string into two parts that are separated by a comma. The pattern `(.*),(.*)` is clear and straightforward, but it is not necessarily the most efficient way to do this. The first `.*` will attempt to consume the entire input. The matcher will have to then back up to the last comma and then expand the rest into the second `.*`. You could help this along by being clear that a comma is not part of the group: `([^,]*),([^,]*)`. Now it is clear that the matcher should only go so far as the first comma and stop, which needs no backing up. On the other hand, the second expression is somewhat less clear to the casual user of regular expressions.

You should avoid trading clarity for efficiency unless you are writing a performance critical part of the code. Regular expressions are by nature already cryptic. Sophisticated techniques make them even more difficult to understand, and so should be used only when needed. And when you do need to be more efficient be sure that you are doing things that are more efficient—as with all optimizations, you should test carefully what is actually faster. In the example we give, a sufficiently smart pattern compiler and matcher might make both patterns comparably quick. Then you would have traded clarity for nothing. And even if today one is more efficient than the other, a better implementation tomorrow may make that vanish. With regular expressions, as with any other part of programming, choosing optimization over clarity is a choice to be made sparingly.

13.4 The `StringBuilder` Class

If immutable strings were the only kind available, you would have to create a new `String` object for each intermediate result in a sequence of `String` manipulations. Consider, for example, how the compiler would evaluate the following expression:

```
public static String guillemete(String quote) {
    return '«' + quote + '»';
}
```

If the compiler were restricted to `String` expressions, it would have to do the following:

```
quoted = String.valueOf('«').concat(quote)
            .concat(String.valueOf('»'));
```

Each `valueOf` and `concat` invocation creates another `String` object, so this operation would construct four `String` objects, of which only one would be used afterward. The others strings would have incurred overhead to create, to set to proper values, and to garbage collect.

The compiler is more efficient than this. It uses a `StringBuilder` object to build strings from expressions, creating the final `String` only when necessary. `StringBuilder` objects can be modified, so new objects are not needed to hold

intermediate results. With StringBuilder, the previous string expression would
be represented as

```
quoted = new StringBuilder().append('«')
            .append(quote).append('»').toString();
```

This code creates just one StringBuilder object to hold the construction,
appends stuff to it, and then uses toString to create a String from the result.

To build and modify a string, you probably want to use the StringBuilder
class. StringBuilder provides the following constructors:

public **StringBuilder()**

> Constructs a StringBuilder with an initial value of "" (an empty string)
> and a capacity of 16.

public **StringBuilder(int capacity)**

> Constructs a StringBuilder with an initial value of "" and the given capac-
> ity.

public **StringBuilder(String str)**

> Constructs a StringBuilder with an initial value copied from str.

public **StringBuilder(CharSequence seq)**

> Constructs a StringBuilder with an initial value copied from seq.

StringBuilder is similar to String, and it supports many methods that have
the same names and contracts as some String methods—indexOf,
lastIndexof, replace, substring. However, StringBuilder does not extend
String nor vice versa. They are independent implementations of CharSequence.

13.4.1 Modifying the Buffer

There are several ways to modify the buffer of a StringBuilder object, including appending to the end and inserting in the middle. The simplest method is
setCharAt, which changes the character at a specific position. The following
replace method does what String.replace does, except that it uses a
StringBuilder object. The replace method doesn't need to create a new object to
hold the results, so successive replace calls can operate on one buffer:

```
public static void
    replace(StringBuilder str, char oldChar, char newChar) {

    for (int i = 0; i < str.length(); i++)
        if (str.charAt(i) == oldChar)
            str.setCharAt(i, newChar);
}
```

The setLength method truncates or extends the string in the buffer. If you invoke setLength with a length smaller than the length of the current string, the string is truncated to the specified length. If the length is longer than the current string, the string is extended with null characters ('\u0000').

There are also append and insert methods to convert any data type to a String and then append the result to the end or insert the result at a specified position. The insert methods shift characters over to make room for inserted characters as needed. The following types are converted by these append and insert methods:

```
Object       String       CharSequence  char[]
boolean      char         int           long
float        double
```

There are also append and insert methods that take part of a CharSequence or char array as an argument. Here is some code that uses various append invocations to create a StringBuilder that describes the square root of an integer:

```
String sqrtInt(int i) {
    StringBuilder buf = new StringBuilder();

    buf.append("sqrt(").append(i).append(')');
    buf.append(" = ").append(Math.sqrt(i));
    return buf.toString();
}
```

The append and insert methods return the StringBuilder object itself, enabling you to append to the result of a previous append.

A few append methods together form the java.lang.Appendable interface. These methods are

public Appendable **append(char c)**

public Appendable **append(CharSequence seq)**

public Appendable **append(CharSequence seq, int start, int end)**

The Appendable interface is used to mark classes that can receive formatted output from a java.util.Formatter object—see "Formatter" on page 624.

The insert methods take two parameters. The first is the index at which to insert characters into the StringBuilder. The second is the value to insert, after conversion to a `String` if necessary. Here is a method to put the current date at the beginning of a buffer:

```
public static StringBuilder addDate(StringBuilder buf) {
    String now = new java.util.Date().toString();
    buf.insert(0, now).insert(now.length(), ": ");
    return buf;
}
```

The `addDate` method first creates a string with the current time using `java.util.Date`, whose default constructor creates an object that represents the time it was created. Then `addDate` inserts the string that represents the current date, followed by a simple separator string. Finally, it returns the buffer it was passed so that invoking code can use the same kind of method concatenation that proved useful in `StringBuilder`'s own methods.

The `reverse` method reverses the order of characters in the `StringBuilder`. For example, if the contents of the buffer are `"good"`, the contents after `reverse` are `"doog"`.

You can remove part of the buffer with `delete`, which takes a starting and ending index. The segment of the string up to but *not* including the ending index is removed from the buffer, and the buffer is shortened. You can remove a single character by using `deleteCharAt`.

You can also replace characters in the buffer:

public StringBuilder **replace(int start, int end, String str)**
> Replace the characters starting at `start` up to but *not* including end with the contents of `str`. The buffer is grown or shrunk as the length of `str` is greater than or less than the range of characters replaced.

13.4.2 Getting Data Out

To get a `String` object from a `StringBuilder` object, you simply invoke the `toString` method. If you need a substring of the buffer, the `substring` methods works analogously to those of `String`. If you want some or all of the contents as a character array, you can use `getChars`, which is analogous to `String.getChars`.

public void **getChars(int srcBegin, int srcEnd, char[] dst,**
   int dstBegin)
> Copies characters from this `StringBuilder` into the specified array. The characters of the specified substring are copied into the character array, starting at `dst[dstBegin]`. The specified substring is the part of the string buffer from `srcBegin` up to but *not* including `srcEnd`.

Here is a method that uses `getChars` to remove part of a buffer:

```
public static StringBuilder
    remove(StringBuilder buf, int pos, int cnt) {

    if (pos < 0 || cnt < 0 || pos + cnt > buf.length())
        throw new IndexOutOfBoundsException();

    int leftover = buf.length() - (pos + cnt);
    if (leftover == 0) {     // a simple truncation
        buf.setLength(pos);
        return buf;
    }

    char[] chrs = new char[leftover];
    buf.getChars(pos + cnt, buf.length(), chrs, 0);
    buf.setLength(pos);
    buf.append(chrs);
    return buf;
}
```

First `remove` ensures that the array references will stay in bounds. You could handle the actual exception later, but checking now gives you more control. Then `remove` calculates how many characters follow the removed portion. If there are none, it truncates and returns. Otherwise, `remove` retrieves them using `getChars` and then truncates the buffer and appends the leftover characters before returning.

13.4.3 Capacity Management

The buffer of a `StringBuilder` object has a capacity, which is the length of the string it can store before it must allocate more space. The buffer grows automatically as characters are added, but it is more efficient to specify the size of the buffer only once.

You set the initial size of a `StringBuilder` object by using the constructor that takes a single `int`:

public **StringBuilder(int capacity)**
> Constructs a `StringBuilder` with the given initial `capacity` and an initial value of `""`.

public void **ensureCapacity(int minimum)**
> Ensures that the capacity of the buffer is at least the specified `minimum`.

```
public int capacity()
```
> Returns the current capacity of the buffer.

```
public void trimToSize()
```
> Attempts to reduce the capacity of the buffer to accommodate the current sequence of characters. There is no guarantee that this will actually reduce the capacity of the buffer, but this gives a hint to the system that it may be a good time to try and reclaim some storage space.

You can use these methods to avoid repeatedly growing the buffer. Here, for example, is a rewrite of the `sqrtInt` method from page 332 that ensures that you allocate new space for the buffer at most once:

```
String sqrtIntFaster(int i) {
    StringBuilder buf = new StringBuilder(50);
    buf.append("sqrt(").append(i).append(')');
    buf.append(" = ").append(Math.sqrt(i));
    return buf.toString();
}
```

The only change is to use a constructor that creates a `StringBuilder` object large enough to contain the result string. The value 50 is somewhat larger than required; therefore, the buffer will never have to grow.

13.4.4 The `StringBuffer` Class

The `StringBuffer` class is essentially identical to the `StringBuilder` class except for one thing: It provides a *thread-safe* implementation of an appendable character sequence—see Chapter 14 for more on thread safety. This difference would normally relegate discussion of `StringBuffer` to a discussion on thread-safe data structures, were it not for one mitigating factor: The `StringBuffer` class is older, and previously filled the role that `StringBuilder` does now as the standard class for mutable character sequences. For this reason, you will often find methods that take or return `StringBuffer` rather than `StringBuilder`, `CharSequence`, or `Appendable`. These historical uses of `StringBuffer` are likely to be enshrined in the existing APIs for many years to come.

Exercise 13.5: Write a method to convert strings containing decimal numbers into comma-punctuated numbers, with a comma every third digit from the right. For example, given the string "1543729", the method should return the string "1,543,729".

Exercise 13.6: Modify the method to accept parameters specifying the separator character to use and the number of digits between separator characters.

13.5 Working with UTF-16

In "Working with UTF-16" on page 196, we described a number of utility methods provided by the `Character` class to ease working with the supplementary Unicode characters (those greater in value than 0xFFFF that require encoding as a pair of char values in a `CharSequence`). Each of the `String`, `StringBuilder`, and `StringBuffer` classes provides these methods:

public int **codePointAt(int index)**
> Returns the code point defined at the given index in `this`, taking into account that it may be a supplementary character represented by the pair `this.charAt(index)` and `this.charAt(index+1)`.

public int **codePointBefore(int index)**
> Returns the code point defined preceding the given index in `this`, taking into account that it may be a supplementary character represented by the pair `this.charAt(index-2)` and `this.charAt(index-1)`.

public int **codePointCount(int start, int end)**
> Returns the number of code points defined in `this.charAt(start)` to `this.charAt(end)`, taking into account surrogate pairs. Any unpaired surrogate values count as one code point each.

public int **offsetByCodePoints(int index, int numberOfCodePoints)**
> Returns the index into `this` that is `numberOfCodePoints` away from `index`, taking into account surrogate pairs.

In addition, the `StringBuilder` and `StringBuffer` classes define the `appendCodePoint` method that takes an `int` representing an arbitrary Unicode character, encodes it as a surrogate pair if needed, and appends it to the end of the buffer. Curiously, there is no corresponding `insertCodePoint` method.

Finally, the `String` class also provides the following constructor:

public **String(int[] codePoints, int start, int count)**
> Constructs a new `String` with the contents from `codePoints[start]` up to a maximum of `count` code points, with supplementary characters encoded as surrogate pairs as needed. If any value in the array is not a valid Unicode code point, then `IllegalArgumentException` is thrown.

When ideas fail, words come in very handy.
—Johann Wolfgang von Goethe

CHAPTER **14**

Threads

At some point, you have to jump out of the plane under the assumption
that you can *get the parachute sewn together in time to deploy it.*
—Jack Rickard

WE usually write programs that operate one step at a time, in a sequence. In the
following picture, the value of a bank balance is fetched, it is increased by the
value of the deposit, and then it is copied back into the account record:

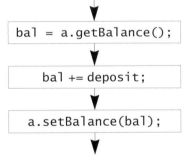

Real bank tellers and computer programs go through similar sequences. In a computer, a sequence of steps executed one at a time is called a *thread*. This *single-
threaded* programming model is the one most programmers use.

In a real bank, more than one thing happens at a time:

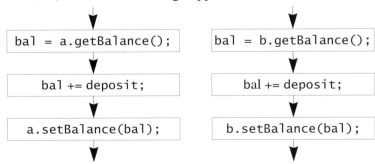

337

Inside a computer, the analogue to having multiple real-world bank tellers is called *multithreading*. A thread, like a bank teller, can perform a task independent of other threads. And just as two bank tellers can use the same filing cabinets, threads can share access to objects.

This shared access is simultaneously one of the most useful features of multithreading and one of its greatest pitfalls. This kind of get–modify–set sequence has what is known as a *race hazard* or *race condition*. A race hazard exists when two threads can potentially modify the same piece of data in an interleaved way that can corrupt data. In the bank example, imagine that someone walks up to a bank teller to deposit money into an account. At almost the same time, a second customer asks another teller to handle a deposit into the same account. Each teller

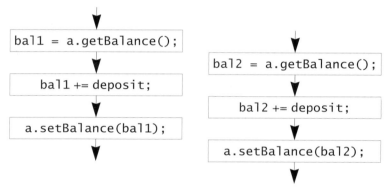

goes to the filing cabinet to get the current account balance (assuming this is an old-fashioned bank that still uses paper files) and gets the same information. Then the tellers go back to their stations, add in the deposit, and return to the filing cabinet to record their separately calculated results. With this procedure, only the last deposit recorded actually affects the balance. The first modification is lost.

A real bank can handle this problem by having the first teller put a note into the file that says, "I'm working on this one, wait until I'm finished." Essentially the same thing is done inside the computer: A *lock* is associated with an object to tell when the object is or is not being used.

Many real-world software problems can best be solved by using multiple threads of control. For example, an interactive program that graphically displays data often needs to let users change display parameters in real time. Interactive programs often obtain their best dynamic behavior by using threads. Single-threaded systems usually provide an illusion of multiple threads either by using interrupts or by *polling*. Polling mixes the display and user input parts of an application. In particular, the display code must be written so it will poll often enough to respond to user input in fractions of a second. Display code either must ensure that display operations take minimal time or must interrupt its own operations to poll. The resulting mixture of two unrelated functional aspects of a program leads to complex and often unmaintainable code.

These kinds of problems are more easily solved in a multithreaded system. One thread of control updates the display with current data, and another thread responds to user input. If user input is complex—for example, filling out a form—display code can run independently until it receives new data. In a polling model, either display updates must pause for complex input or complicated handshaking must be used so that display updates can continue while the user types data into the form. Such a model of shared control within a process can be directly supported in a multithreaded system instead of being handcrafted for each new polling case.

This chapter describes the basic constructs, classes, and methods that control multithreading in the Java programming language, but it cannot teach you effective multithreaded program design. The package `java.util.concurrent` and its subpackages provide higher-level concurrency utilities to ease the task of writing sophisticated multithreaded programs, but again the detailed use of such tools is beyond the scope of this book—an overview is given in Section 25.9.1 on page 733. You can read *Concurrent Programming in Java*™, *Second Edition,* a book in this series, to get advice on how to create well-designed multithreaded programs. "Further Reading" on page 755 has other useful references to give you a background in thread and synchronization design.

14.1 Creating Threads

To create a thread of control, you start by creating a `Thread` object:

```
Thread worker = new Thread();
```

After a `Thread` object is created, you can configure it and then run it. Configuring a thread involves setting its initial priority, name, and so on. When the thread is ready to run, you invoke its `start` method. The `start` method spawns a new thread of control based on the data in the `Thread` object, then returns. Now the virtual machine invokes the new thread's `run` method, making the thread active. You can invoke `start` only once for each thread—invoking it again results in an `IllegalThreadStateException`.

When a thread's `run` method returns, the thread has exited. You can request that a thread cease running by invoking its `interrupt` method—a request a well-written thread will always respond to. While a thread is running you can interact with it in other ways, as you shall soon see.

The standard implementation of `Thread.run` does nothing. To get a thread that does something you must either extend `Thread` to provide a new `run` method or create a `Runnable` object and pass it to the thread's constructor. We first discuss how to create new kinds of threads by extending `Thread`. We describe how to use `Runnable` in the next section.

Here is a simple two-threaded program that prints the words "ping" and "PONG" at different rates:

```
public class PingPong extends Thread {
    private String word;   // what word to print
    private int delay;     // how long to pause

    public PingPong(String whatToSay, int delayTime) {
        word = whatToSay;
        delay = delayTime;
    }

    public void run() {
        try {
            for (;;) {
                System.out.print(word + " ");
                Thread.sleep(delay); // wait until next time
            }
        } catch (InterruptedException e) {
            return;                 // end this thread
        }
    }
    public static void main(String[] args) {
        new PingPong("ping",  33).start(); // 1/30 second
        new PingPong("PONG", 100).start(); // 1/10 second
    }
}
```

We define a type of thread called `PingPong`. Its run method loops forever, printing its `word` field and sleeping for `delay` milliseconds. `PingPong.run` cannot throw exceptions because `Thread.run`, which it overrides, doesn't throw any exceptions. Accordingly, we must catch the `InterruptedException` that `sleep` can throw (more on `InterruptedException` later).

Now we can create some working threads, and `PingPong.main` does just that. It creates two `PingPong` objects, each with its own word and delay cycle, and invokes each thread object's `start` method. Now the threads are off and running. Here is some example output:

```
ping PONG ping ping PONG ping ping ping PONG ping
ping PONG ping ping ping PONG ping ping PONG ping
ping ping PONG ping ping PONG ping ping ping PONG
ping ping PONG ping ping ping PONG ping ping PONG
ping ping ping PONG ping ping PONG ping ping ping
PONG ping ping PONG ping ping ping PONG ping ping ...
```

You can give a thread a name, either as a `String` parameter to the constructor or as the parameter of a `setName` invocation. You can get the current name of a thread by invoking `getName`. Thread names are strictly for programmer convenience—they are not used by the runtime system—but a thread must have a name and so if none is specified, the runtime system will give it one, usually using a simple numbering scheme like `Thread-1`, `Thread-2`, and so on.

You can obtain the `Thread` object for the currently running thread by invoking the static method `Thread.currentThread`. There is always a currently running thread, even if you did not create one explicitly—`main` itself is executed by a thread created by the runtime system.

Exercise 14.1: Write a program that displays the name of the thread that executes `main`.

14.2 Using `Runnable`

Threads abstract the concept of a worker—an entity that gets something done. The work done by a thread is packaged up in its `run` method. When you need to get some work done, you need both a worker and the work—the `Runnable` interface abstracts the concept of work and allows that work to be associated with a worker—the thread. The `Runnable` interface declares a single method:

```
public void run();
```

The `Thread` class itself implements the `Runnable` interface because a thread can also define a unit of work.

You have seen that `Thread` can be extended to provide specific computation for a thread, but this approach is awkward in many cases. First, class extension is single inheritance—if you extend a class to make it runnable in a thread, you cannot extend any other class, even if you need to. Also, if your class needs only to be runnable, inheriting all the overhead of `Thread` is more than you need.

Implementing `Runnable` is easier in many cases. You can execute a `Runnable` object in its own thread by passing it to a `Thread` constructor. If a `Thread` object is constructed with a Runnable object, the implementation of Thread.run will invoke the runnable object's run method.

Here is a Runnable version of the PingPong class. If you compare the versions, you will see that they look almost identical. The major differences are in the supertype (implementing Runnable versus extending Thread) and in main.

```java
class RunPingPong implements Runnable {
    private String word;      // what word to print
    private int delay;        // how long to pause

    RunPingPong(String whatToSay, int delayTime) {
        word = whatToSay;
        delay = delayTime;
    }

    public void run() {
        try {
            for (;;) {
                System.out.print(word + " ");
                Thread.sleep(delay); // wait until next time
            }
        } catch (InterruptedException e) {
            return;               // end this thread
        }
    }

    public static void main(String[] args) {
        Runnable ping = new RunPingPong("ping",  33);
        Runnable pong = new RunPingPong("PONG", 100);
        new Thread(ping).start();
        new Thread(pong).start();
    }
}
```

First, a new class that implements Runnable is defined. Its implementation of the run method is the same as PingPong's. In main, two RunPingPong objects with different timings are created; a new Thread object is then created for each object and is started immediately.

Five Thread constructors enable you to specify a Runnable object:

public **Thread(Runnable target)**

Constructs a new Thread that uses the run method of the specified target.

public **Thread(Runnable target, String name)**

> Constructs a new Thread with the specified name and uses the run method of the specified target.

public **Thread(ThreadGroup group, Runnable target)**

> Constructs a new Thread in the specified ThreadGroup and uses the run method of the specified target. You will learn about ThreadGroup later.

public **Thread(ThreadGroup group, Runnable target, String name)**

> Constructs a new Thread in the specified ThreadGroup with the specified name and uses the run method of the specified target.

public **Thread(ThreadGroup group, Runnable target, String name, long stacksize)**

> Constructs a new Thread in the specified ThreadGroup with the specified name and uses the run method of the specified target. The stackSize parameter allows a stack size for the thread to be suggested. The values appropriate for a stack size are completely system dependent and the system does not have to honor the request. Such a facility is not needed by the vast majority of applications, but like most things of this nature, when you do need it, it is indispensable.

Classes that have only a run method are not very interesting. Real classes define complete state and behavior, where having something execute in a separate thread is only a part of their functionality. For example, consider a print server that spools print requests to a printer. Clients invoke the print method to submit print jobs. But all the print method actually does is place the job in a queue and a separate thread then pulls jobs from the queue and sends them to the printer. This allows clients to submit print jobs without waiting for the actual printing to take place.

```java
class PrintServer implements Runnable {
    private final PrintQueue requests = new PrintQueue();
    public PrintServer() {
        new Thread(this).start();
    }
    public void print(PrintJob job) {
        requests.add(job);
    }
    public void run() {
        for(;;)
            realPrint(requests.remove());
    }
    private void realPrint(PrintJob job) {
```

```
        // do the real work of printing
    }
}
```

When a `PrintServer` is created, it creates a new `Thread` to do the actual printing and passes itself as the `Runnable` instance. Starting a thread in a constructor in this way can be risky if a class can be extended. If it becomes extended, the thread could access fields of the object before the extended class constructor had been executed.

The `requests` queue takes care of synchronizing the different threads that access it—those calling `print` and our own internal thread—we look at such synchronization in later sections and define the `PrintQueue` class on page 356.

You may be wondering about the fact that we don't have a reference to the thread we created—doesn't that mean that the thread can be garbage collected? The answer is no. While we didn't keep a reference to the thread, when the thread itself was created, it stored a reference to itself in its `ThreadGroup`—we talk more about thread groups later.

The work that you define within a `run` method is normally of a fairly private nature—it should be performed only by the worker to whom the work was assigned. However, as part of an interface, `run` is public and so can be invoked indiscriminately by anyone with access to your object—something you usually don't desire. For example, we definitely don't want clients to invoke the `run` method of `PrintServer`. One solution is to use `Thread.currentThread` to establish the identity of the thread that invokes `run` and to compare it with the intended worker thread. But a simpler solution is not to implement `Runnable`, but to define an inner `Runnable` object. For example, we can rewrite `PrintServer` as follows:

```
class PrintServer2 {
    private final PrintQueue requests = new PrintQueue();
    public PrintServer2() {
        Runnable service = new Runnable() {
            public void run() {
                for(;;)
                    realPrint(requests.remove());
            }
        };
        new Thread(service).start();
    }
    public void print(PrintJob job) {
        requests.add(job);
    }
```

```
        private void realPrint(PrintJob job) {
            // do the real work of printing
        }
    }
```

The run method is exactly the same as before, but now it is part of an anonymous inner class that implements Runnable. When the thread is created we pass service as the Runnable to execute. Now the work to be performed by the thread is completely private and can't be misused.

Using Runnable objects you can create very flexible multithreaded designs. Each Runnable becomes a unit of work and each can be passed around from one part of the system to another. We can store Runnable objects in a queue and have a pool of worker threads servicing the work requests in the queue—a very common design used in multithreaded server applications.

Exercise 14.2: Modify the first version of PrintServer so that only the thread created in the constructor can successfully execute run, using the identity of the thread as suggested.

14.3 Synchronization

Recall the bank teller example from the beginning of this chapter. When two tellers (threads) need to use the same file (object), there is a possibility of interleaved operations that can corrupt the data. Such potentially interfering actions are termed *critical sections* or *critical regions,* and you prevent *interference* by *synchronizing* access to those critical regions. In the bank, tellers synchronize their actions by putting notes in the files and agreeing to the protocol that a note in the file means that the file can't be used. The equivalent action in multithreading is to acquire a *lock* on an object. Threads cooperate by agreeing to the protocol that before certain actions can occur on an object, the lock of the object must be acquired. Acquiring the lock on an object prevents any other thread from acquiring that lock until the holder of the lock releases it. If done correctly, multiple threads won't simultaneously perform actions that could interfere with each other.

Every object has a lock associated with it, and that lock can be acquired and released through the use of synchronized methods and statements. The term *synchronized code* describes any code that is inside a synchronized method or statement.

14.3.1 synchronized Methods

A class whose objects must be protected from interference in a multithreaded environment usually has appropriate methods declared synchronized ("appropriate" is defined later). If one thread invokes a synchronized method on an object, the lock of that object is first acquired, the method body executed, and then the lock released. Another thread invoking a synchronized method on that same object will block until the lock is released:

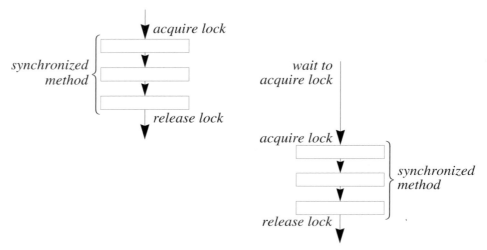

Synchronization forces execution of the two threads to be *mutually exclusive* in time. Unsynchronized access does not wait for any locks but proceeds regardless of locks that may be held on the object.

Locks are owned *per thread,* so invoking a synchronized method from within another method synchronized on the same object will proceed without blocking, releasing the lock only when the outermost synchronized method returns. This per-thread behavior prevents a thread from blocking on a lock it already has, and permits recursive method invocations and invocations of inherited methods, which themselves may be synchronized.

The lock is released as soon as the synchronized method terminates—whether normally, with a return statement or by reaching the end of the method body, or abnormally by throwing an exception. In contrast to systems in which locks must be explicitly acquired and released, this synchronization scheme makes it impossible to forget to release a lock.

Synchronization makes the interleaved execution example work: If the code is in a synchronized method, then when the second thread attempts to access the object while the first thread is using it, the second thread is blocked until the first one finishes.

For example, if the BankAccount class were written to live in a multithreaded environment it would look like this:

```
public class BankAccount {
    private long number;     // account number
    private long balance;    // current balance (in cents)
    public BankAccount(long initialDeposit) {
        balance = initialDeposit;
    }
    public synchronized long getBalance() {
        return balance;
    }
    public synchronized void deposit(long amount) {
        balance += amount;
    }
    // ... rest of methods ...
}
```

Now we can explain what is "appropriate" in synchronizing methods.

The constructor does not need to be synchronized because it is executed only when creating an object, and that can happen in only one thread for any given new object. Constructors, in fact, cannot be declared synchronized.

The balance field is defended from unsynchronized modification by the synchronized accessor methods. If the value of a field can change, its value should never be read at the same time another thread is writing it. If one thread were reading the value while another was setting it, the read might return an invalid value. Even if the value were valid, a get–modify–set sequence requires that the value not change between being read and being set, otherwise the set value will be wrong. Access to the field must be synchronized. This is yet another reason to prefer accessor methods to public or protected fields: Using methods, you can synchronize access to the data, but you have no way to do so if the fields can be accessed directly outside your class.

With the synchronized declaration, two or more running threads are guaranteed not to interfere with each other. Each of the methods will execute in mutual exclusion—once one invocation of a method starts execution, no other invocations of any of the methods can commence until the original has completed. However, there is no guarantee as to the order of operations. If the balance is queried about the same time that a deposit occurs, one of them will complete first but you can't tell which. If you want actions to happen in a guaranteed order, threads must coordinate their activities in some application-specific way.

You can ask whether the current thread holds the lock on a given object by passing that object to the Thread class's static holdsLock method, which returns true if the current thread does hold the lock on that object. This is typically used to assert that a lock is held when needed. For example, a private method that expects to be invoked only from synchronized public methods might assert that fact:

```
assert Thread.holdsLock(this);
```

You will also occasionally find it important that a certain lock not be held in a method. And in some rare circumstances you might want to choose whether or not to acquire a given lock depending on whether or not another lock is held.

When an extended class overrides a synchronized method, the new method can be synchronized or not. The superclass's method will still be synchronized when it is invoked. If the unsynchronized method uses super to invoke the superclass's method, the object's lock will be acquired at that time and will be released when the superclass's method returns. Synchronization requirements are a part of the implementation of a class. An extended class may be able to modify a data structure such that concurrent invocations of a method do not interfere and so the method need not be synchronized; conversely the extended class may enhance the behavior of the method in such a way that interference becomes possible and so it must be synchronized.

14.3.2 Static synchronized Methods

Static methods can also be declared synchronized. Associated with every class is a Class object—see "The Class Class" on page 399. A static synchronized method acquires the lock of the Class object for its class. Two threads cannot execute static synchronized methods of the same class at the same time, just as two threads cannot execute synchronized methods on the same object at the same time. If static data is shared between threads then access to it must be protected by static synchronized methods.

Acquiring the Class object lock in a static synchronized method has no effect on any objects of that class. You can still invoke synchronized methods on an object while another thread holds the Class object lock in a static synchronized method. Only other static synchronized methods are blocked.

14.3.3 synchronized Statements

The synchronized statement enables you to execute synchronized code that acquires the lock of any object, not just the current object, or for durations less than the entire invocation of a method. The synchronized statement has two parts: an object whose lock is to be acquired and a statement to execute when the lock is obtained. The general form of the synchronized statement is

```
synchronized (expr) {
    statements
}
```

The expression *expr* must evaluate to an object reference. After the lock is obtained, the `statements` in the block are executed. At the end of the block the lock is released—if an uncaught exception occurs within the block, the lock is still released. A `synchronized` method is simply a syntactic shorthand for a method whose body is wrapped in a `synchronized` statement with a reference to `this`.

Here is a method to replace each element in an array with its absolute value, relying on a `synchronized` statement to control access to the array:

```
/** make all elements in the array non-negative */
public static void abs(int[] values) {
    synchronized (values) {
        for (int i = 0; i < values.length; i++) {
            if (values[i] < 0)
                values[i] = -values[i];
        }
    }
}
```

The `values` array contains the elements to be modified. We synchronize `values` by naming it as the object of the `synchronized` statement. Now the loop can proceed, guaranteed that the array is not changed during execution by any other code that is similarly synchronized on the `values` array. This is an example of what is generally termed *client-side* synchronization—all the clients using the shared object (in this case the array) agree to synchronize on that object before manipulating it. For objects such as arrays, this is the only way to protect them when they can be shared directly, since they have no methods that can be synchronized.

The `synchronized` statement has a number of uses and advantages over a synchronized method. First, it can define a synchronized region of code that is smaller than a method. Synchronization affects performance—while one thread has a lock another thread can't get it—and a general rule of concurrent programming is to hold locks for as short a period as possible. Using a `synchronized` statement, you can choose to hold a lock only when it is absolutely needed—for example, a method that performs a complex calculation and then assigns the result to a field often needs to protect only the actual field assignment not the calculation process.

Second, `synchronized` statements allow you to synchronize on objects other than `this`, allowing a number of different synchronization designs to be implemented. Sometimes you want to increase the concurrency level of a class by using a finer granularity of locking. It may be that different groups of methods within a class act on different data within that class, and so while mutual exclusion is needed within a group, it is not needed between groups. Instead of making all the methods synchronized, you can define separate objects to be used as locks for each such group and have the methods use synchronized statements with the appropriate lock object. For example:

```
class SeparateGroups {
    private double aVal = 0.0;
    private double bVal = 1.1;
    protected final Object lockA = new Object();
    protected final Object lockB = new Object();

    public double getA() {
        synchronized (lockA) {
            return aVal;
        }
    }
    public void setA(double val) {
        synchronized (lockA) {
            aVal = val;
        }
    }
    public double getB() {
        synchronized (lockB) {
            return bVal;
        }
    }
    public void setB(double val) {
        synchronized (lockB) {
            bVal = val;
        }
    }
    public void reset() {
        synchronized (lockA) {
            synchronized (lockB) {
                aVal = bVal = 0.0;
            }
        }
    }
}
```

The two lock references are protected so that an extended class can correctly synchronize its own methods—such as a method to set aVal and bVal to the same
value. Also notice how reset acquires both locks before modifying both values.

Another common use of the synchronized statement is for an inner object to
synchronize on its enclosing object:

```
public class Outer {
    private int data;
    // ...

    private class Inner {
        void setOuterData() {
            synchronized (Outer.this) {
                data = 12;
            }
        }
    }
}
```

Like any other object, an inner object is independently synchronized—acquiring
the lock of an inner object has no effect on its enclosing object's lock, nor does
acquiring the lock of an enclosing object affect any enclosed inner objects. An
inner class that needs to synchronize with its enclosing object must do so explicitly and a synchronized statement is a perfect tool—the alternative is to declare a
synchronized method in the enclosing class just for the inner class to use.

If you need a synchronized statement to use the same lock used by static
synchronized methods, you can use the class literal for your class (see example
below). This also applies if you need to protect access to static data from within
non-static code. For example, consider the Body class. It maintains a static field,
nextID, to hold the next identifier for a new Body object. That field is accessed in
the Body class's no-arg constructor. If Body objects were created concurrently,
interference could occur when the nextID field is updated. To prevent that from
happening you can use a synchronized statement within the Body constructor
that uses the lock of the Body.class object:

```
Body() {
    synchronized (Body.class) {
        idNum = nextID++;
    }
}
```

The synchronized statement in the constructor acquires the lock of the Class
object for Body in the same way a synchronized static method of the class

would. Synchronizing on `this` would use a different object for each invocation and so would not prevent threads from accessing `nextID` concurrently. It would also be wrong to use the `Object` method `getClass` to retrieve the `Class` object for the current instance: In an extended class, such as `AttributedBody`, that would return the `Class` object for `AttributedBody` not `Body`, and so again, different locks would be used and interference would not be prevented. The simplest rule is to always protect access to static data using the lock of the `Class` object for the class in which the static data was declared.

In many cases, instead of using a `synchronized` statement you can factor the code to be protected into a `synchronized` method of its own. You'll need to use your own experience and judgment to decide when this is preferable. For example, in the `Body` class we could encapsulate access to `nextID` in a static synchronized method `getNextID`.

Finally, the ability to acquire locks of arbitrary objects with `synchronized` statements makes it possible to perform the client-side synchronization that you saw in the array example. This capability is important, not only for protecting access to objects that don't have synchronized methods, but also for synchronizing a series of accesses to an object. We look more at this in the next section.

14.3.4 Synchronization Designs

Designing the appropriate synchronization for a class can be a complex matter and it is beyond the scope of this book to delve too deeply into these design issues. We can take a brief look at some of the issues involved.

Client-side synchronization is done by having all the clients of a shared object use `synchronized` statements to lock the object before using it. Such a protocol is fragile—it relies on all of the clients doing the right thing. It is generally better to have shared objects protect access to themselves by making their methods `synchronized` (or using appropriate `synchronized` statements inside those methods). This makes it impossible for a client to use the object in a way that is not synchronized. This approach is sometimes termed *server-side* synchronization, but it is just an extension of the object-oriented perspective that objects encapsulate their own behavior, in this case synchronization.

Sometimes a designer hasn't considered a multithreaded environment when designing a class, and none of the class's methods are synchronized. To use such a class in a multithreaded environment, you have to decide whether to use client-side synchronization via `synchronized` statements or to create an extended class to override the appropriate methods, declare them `synchronized`, and forward method calls through the `super` reference.

If you are working with an interface instead of a class, you can provide an alternate implementation that wraps the methods of the interface in synchronized methods that forward the calls to another unsynchronized object that implements the same interface. This will work with any implementation of the interface, and is therefore a better solution than extending each class to use super in a synchronized method. This flexibility is another reason to use interfaces to design your system. You can see an example of this synchronized wrapper technique in the collections classes; see "The Synchronized Wrappers" on page 602.

The synchronization you have learned about so far is the simplest notion of "thread safety"—the idea that methods on objects can be invoked by multiple threads concurrently and each thread will have the method perform its expected job. Synchronization, however, has to extend to more complex situations involving multiple method invocations on an object, or even method invocations on multiple objects. If these series of invocations must appear as an atomic action you will need synchronization. In the case of multiple method invocations, you can encapsulate the series of invocations within another method and synchronize that method, but generally this is impractical—you can't define all combinations of the basic methods as methods themselves, nor are you likely to know at the time the class is designed which method combinations may be needed. In the case of operations on multiple objects, where could you put a synchronized method?

In these situations, the ability to use client-side synchronization through synchronized statements is often the only practical approach. An object can have its lock acquired, which prevents any of its synchronized methods from being invoked except by the lock holder performing the series of invocations. Similarly, you can acquire the locks of each of the objects involved and then invoke the series of methods on those objects—but watch out for deadlock (see Section 14.7 on page 362). As long as the object's methods are already synchronized on the current object's lock, then other clients of the object need not use client-side synchronization.

The way that synchronization is enforced in a class is an implementation detail. The fact that it is enforced is an important part of the contract of the class and must be clearly documented—the presence of the synchronized modifier on a method might only be an implementation detail of the class, not part of a binding contract. Additionally, the synchronization mechanism used within a class may need to be documented and made accessible to users of the class and/or to extended classes. An extended class needs to adhere to the synchronization policy enforced by its superclass and it can do that only if the programmer knows what that policy is and has access to the mechanisms that enforce it. For example, a class that uses a private field as a lock object prevents an extended class from using the same synchronization mechanism—the extended class would have to define its own lock object (perhaps this) and override every method of the superclass to use this new synchronization mechanism. Users of a class may need to know what synchronization mechanism is used so that they can safely apply client-side synchronization to invoke multiple methods on an object, without need-ing all users of that object to apply client-side synchronization.

Exercise 14.3: Write a class whose objects hold a current value and have a method that will add to that value, printing the new value. Write a program that creates such an object, creates multiple threads, and invokes the adding method repeatedly from each thread. Write the class so that no addition can be lost.

Exercise 14.4: Modify your code from Exercise 14.3 to use static data and methods.

Exercise 14.5: Modify your code from Exercise 14.4 so that threads can safely dec-rement the value without using a static synchronized method.

14.4 `wait`, `notifyAll`, and `notify`

The `synchronized` locking mechanism suffices for keeping threads from inter-fering with each other, but you also need a way to communicate between threads. For this purpose, the `wait` method lets one thread wait until some condition occurs, and the notification methods `notifyAll` and `notify` tell waiting threads that something has occurred that might satisfy that condition. The `wait` and notifi-cation methods are defined in class `Object` and are inherited by all classes. They apply to particular objects, just as locks do.

There is a standard pattern that is important to use with `wait` and notification. The thread waiting for a condition should always do something like this:

```
synchronized void doWhenCondition() {
    while (!condition)
        wait();
    … Do what must be done when the condition is true …
}
```

A number of things are going on here:

◆ Everything is executed within synchronized code. If it were not, the state of the object would not be stable. For example, if the method were not declared `synchronized`, then after the `while` statement, there would be no guarantee that the condition remained `true`: Another thread might have changed the situation that the condition tests.

◆ One of the important aspects of the definition of wait is that when it pauses the thread, it *atomically* releases the lock on the object. Saying that the thread suspension and lock release are atomic means that they happen together, indivisibly. Otherwise, there would be a race hazard: A notification could happen after the lock is released but before the thread is suspended. The notification would have no effect on the thread, effectively getting lost. When a thread is restarted after being notified, the lock is atomically reacquired.

◆ The condition test should *always* be in a loop. Never assume that being awakened means that the condition has been satisfied—it may have changed again since being satisfied. In other words, don't change the while to an if.

On the other side, the notification methods are invoked by synchronized code that changes one or more conditions on which some other thread may be waiting. Notification code typically looks something like this:

```
synchronized void changeCondition() {
    … change some value used in a condition test …
    notifyAll(); // or notify()
}
```

Using notifyAll wakes up all waiting threads, whereas notify picks only one thread to wake up.

Multiple threads may be waiting on the same object, possibly for different conditions. If they are waiting for different conditions, you should always use notifyAll to wake up all waiting threads instead of using notify. Otherwise, you may wake up a thread that is waiting for a different condition from the one you satisfied. That thread will discover that its condition has not been satisfied and go back to waiting, while some thread waiting on the condition you *did* satisfy will never get awakened. Using notify is an optimization that can be applied only when:

◆ All threads are waiting for the same condition

◆ At most one thread can benefit from the condition being met

◆ This is contractually true for *all* possible subclasses

Otherwise you must use notifyAll. If a subclass violates either of the first two conditions, code in the superclass that uses notify may well be broken. To that end it is important that waiting and notification strategies, which include identifying the reference used (this or some other field), are documented for use by extended classes.

The following example implements the `PrintQueue` class that we used with the `PrintServer` on page 343. We reuse the `SingleLinkQueue` class that we defined in Chapter 11 to actually store the print jobs, and add the necessary synchronization:

```
class PrintQueue {
    private SingleLinkQueue<PrintJob> queue =
        new SingleLinkQueue<PrintJob>();

    public synchronized void add(PrintJob j) {
        queue.add(j);
        notifyAll();        // Tell waiters: print job added
    }

    public synchronized PrintJob remove()
        throws InterruptedException
    {
        while (queue.size() == 0)
            wait();         // Wait for a print job

        return queue.remove();
    }
}
```

In contrast to `SingleLinkQueue` itself, the methods are synchronized to avoid interference. When an item is added to the queue, waiters are notified; and instead of returning `null` when the queue is empty, the `remove` method waits for some other thread to insert something so that `take` will block until an item is available. Many threads (not just one) may be adding items to the queue, and many threads (again, not just one) may be removing items from the queue. Because `wait` can throw `InterruptedException`, we declare that in the throws clause—you'll learn about `InterruptedException` a little later.

Looking back at the `PrintServer` example, you can now see that although the internal thread appears to sit in an infinite loop, continually trying to remove jobs from the queue, the use of `wait` means that the thread is suspended whenever there is no work for it to do. In contrast, if we used a queue that returned `null` when empty, the printing thread would continually invoke `remove`, using the CPU the whole time—a situation known as *busy-waiting*. In a multithreaded system you very rarely want to busy-wait. You should always suspend until told that what you are waiting for may have happened. This is the essence of thread communication with the `wait` and `notifyAll`/`notify` mechanism.

14.5   Details of Waiting and Notification

There are three forms of `wait` and two forms of notification. All of them are methods in the `Object` class, and all are `final` so that their behavior cannot be changed:

public final void **wait(long timeout)** throws InterruptedException
>   The current thread waits until one of four things happens: `notify` is invoked on this object and this thread is selected to be runnable; `notifyAll` is invoked on this object; the specified `timeout` expires; or the thread has its `interrupt` method invoked. `timeout` is in milliseconds. If `timeout` is zero, the wait will not time out but will wait indefinitely for notification. During the wait the lock of the object is released and is automatically reacquired before `wait` completes—regardless of how or why `wait` completes. An `InterruptedException` is thrown if the wait completes because the thread is interrupted.

public final void **wait(long timeout, int nanos)**
>   throws InterruptedException
>   A finer-grained `wait`, with the time-out interval as the sum of the two parameters: `timeout` in milliseconds and `nanos` in nanoseconds, in the range 0–999999).

public final void **wait()** throws InterruptedException
>   Equivalent to `wait(0)`.

public final void **notifyAll()**
>   Notifies *all* the threads waiting for a condition to change. Threads will return from the `wait` invocation once they can reacquire the object's lock.

public final void **notify()**
>   Notifies *at most one* thread waiting for a condition to change. You cannot choose which thread will be notified, so use this form of `notify` only when you are sure you know which threads are waiting for what at which times. If you are not sure of any of these factors, you should use `notifyAll`.

If no threads are waiting when either `notifyAll` or `notify` is invoked, the notification is not remembered. If a thread subsequently decides to `wait`, an earlier notification will have no effect on it. Only notifications that occur after the `wait` commences will affect a waiting thread.

You can invoke these methods only from within synchronized code, using the lock for the object on which they are invoked. The invocation can be directly made from the synchronized code, or can be made indirectly from a method invoked in such code. You will get an `IllegalMonitorStateException` if you attempt to invoke these methods on an object when you don't hold its lock.

When a `wait` completes because the time-out period expires, there is no indication that this occurred rather than the thread being notified. If a thread needs to know whether or not it timed out, it has to track elapsed time itself. The use of a time-out is a defensive programming measure that allows you to recover when some condition should have been met but for some reason (probably a failure in another thread) has not. Because the lock of the object must be reacquired, the use of a time-out cannot guarantee that `wait` will return in a finite amount of time.

It is also possible that some virtual machine implementations will allow so-called "spurious wakeups" to occur—when a thread returns from `wait` without being the recipient of a notification, interruption, or time-out. This is another reason that `wait` should always be performed in a loop that tests the condition being waited on.

Exercise 14.6: Write a program that prints the elapsed time each second from the start of execution, with another thread that prints a message every fifteen seconds. Have the message-printing thread be notified by the time-printing thread as each second passes by. Add another thread that prints a different message every seven seconds without modifying the time-printing thread.

14.6 Thread Scheduling

Threads perform different tasks within your programs and those tasks can have different importance levels attached to them. To reflect the importance of the tasks they are performing, each thread has a *priority* that is used by the runtime system to help determine which thread should be running at any given time. Programs can be run on both single- and multiprocessor machines and you can run with multiple threads or a single thread, so the thread scheduling guarantees are very general. On a system with *N* available processors, you will usually see *N* of the highest-priority runnable threads executing. Lower-priority threads generally run only when higher-priority threads are blocked (not runnable). But lower-priority threads might, in fact, run at other times to prevent starvation—a feature generally known as *priority aging*—though you cannot rely on it.

A running thread continues to run until it performs a blocking operation (such as `wait`, `sleep`, or some types of I/O) or it is preempted. A thread can be preempted by a higher-priority thread becoming runnable or because the thread scheduler decides it's another thread's turn to get some cycles—for example, *time slicing* limits the amount of time a single thread can run before being preempted.

Exactly when preemption can occur depends on the virtual machine you have. There are no guarantees, only a general expectation that preference is typically given to running higher-priority threads. Use priority only to affect scheduling policy for efficiency. Do not rely on thread priority for algorithm correctness. To write correct, cross-platform multithreaded code you must assume that a thread could be preempted at any time, and so you always protect access to shared resources. If you require that preemption occur at some specific time, you must use explicit thread communication mechanisms such as `wait` and `notify`. You also can make no assumptions about the order in which locks are granted to threads, nor the order in which waiting threads will receive notifications—these are all system dependent.

A thread's priority is initially the same as the priority of the thread that created it. You can change the priority using `setPriority` with a value between `Thread`'s constants `MIN_PRIORITY` and `MAX_PRIORITY`. The standard priority for the default thread is `NORM_PRIORITY`. The priority of a running thread can be changed at any time. If you assign a thread a priority lower than its current one, the system may let another thread run because the original thread may no longer be among those with the highest priority. The `getPriority` method returns the priority of a thread.

Generally, if you are to worry about priorities at all, the continuously running part of your application should run in a lower-priority thread than the thread dealing with rarer events such as user input. When users push a "Cancel" button, for example, they expect the application to cancel what it's doing. If display update and user input are at the same priority and the display is updating, considerable time may pass before the user input thread reacts to the button. If you put the display thread at a lower priority, it will still run most of the time because the user interface thread will be blocked waiting for user input. When user input is available, the user interface thread will typically preempt the display thread to act on the user's request. For this reason, a thread that does continual updates is often set to `NORM_PRIORITY-1` so that it doesn't hog all available cycles, while a user interface thread is often set to `NORM_PRIORITY+1`.

Using small "delta" values around the normal priority level is usually preferable to using `MIN_PRIORITY` or `MAX_PRIORITY` directly. Exactly what effect priorities have depends on the system you are running on. In some systems your thread priorities not only assign an importance relative to your program, they assign an importance relative to other applications running on the system.[1] Extreme priority settings may result in undesirable behavior and so should be avoided unless their effects are known and needed.

Some algorithms are sensitive to the number of processors available to the virtual machine to run threads on. For example, an algorithm might split work up

---

[1] Check the release notes for your virtual-machine implementation; some implementations treat ranges of priority values as the same, thus reducing the number of distinct scheduling classes.

into smaller chunks to take advantage of more parallel processing power. The availableProcessors method of the Runtime class (see Chapter 23) returns the number of processors currently available. Note that the number of processors can change at any time, so you want to check this number when it is important rather than remember the number from a previous check.

14.6.1 Voluntary Rescheduling

Several methods of the Thread class allow a thread to relinquish its use of the CPU. By convention, static methods of the Thread class always apply to the currently executing thread, and since you can never take the CPU from another thread, these voluntary rescheduling methods are all static:

public static void **sleep(long millis)** throws InterruptedException
> Puts the currently executing thread to sleep for at least the specified number of milliseconds. "At least" means there is no guarantee the thread will wake up in exactly the specified time. Other thread scheduling can interfere, as can the granularity and accuracy of the system clock, among other factors. If the thread is interrupted while it is sleeping, then an InterruptedException is thrown.

public static void **sleep(long millis, int nanos)**
throws InterruptedException
> Puts the currently executing thread to sleep for at least the specified number of milliseconds and nanoseconds. Nanoseconds are in the range 0–999999.

public static void **yield()**
> Provides a hint to the scheduler that the current thread need not run at the present time, so the scheduler may choose another thread to run. The scheduler may follow or ignore this suggestion as it sees fit—you can generally rely on the scheduler to "do the right thing" even though there is no specification of exactly what that is.

The following program illustrates how yield can affect thread scheduling. The application takes a list of words and creates a thread for each that is responsible for printing that word. The first parameter to the application says whether each thread will yield after each println; the second parameter is the number of times each thread should repeat its word. The remaining parameters are the words to be repeated:

```
class Babble extends Thread {
    static boolean doYield;  // yield to other threads?
    static int howOften;     // how many times to print
```

```
    private String word;     // my word

    Babble(String whatToSay) {
        word = whatToSay;
    }

    public void run() {
        for (int i = 0; i < howOften; i++) {
            System.out.println(word);
            if (doYield)
                Thread.yield(); // let other threads run
        }
    }

    public static void main(String[] args) {
        doYield = new Boolean(args[0]).booleanValue();
        howOften = Integer.parseInt(args[1]);

        // create a thread for each word
        for (int i = 2; i < args.length; i++)
            new Babble(args[i]).start();
    }
}
```

When the threads do not yield, each thread gets large chunks of time, usually enough to finish all the prints without any other thread getting any cycles. For example, suppose the program is run with doYield set to false in the following way:

```
Babble false 2 Did DidNot
```

The output may well look like this:

```
Did
Did
DidNot
DidNot
```

If each thread yields after each println, other printing threads will have a chance to run. Suppose we set doYield to true with an invocation such as this:

```
Babble true 2 Did DidNot
```

The yields give the other threads a chance to run, and the other threads will yield in turn, producing an output more like this:

```
Did
DidNot
DidNot
Did
```

The output shown is only approximate—perhaps you expected the words to alternate? A different thread implementation could give different results, or the same implementation might give different results on different runs of the application. But under all implementations, invoking `yield` can give other threads a more equitable chance at getting cycles.

Two other factors affect the behavior of this program (and many like it that try to demonstrate scheduling behavior). The first is that `println` uses synchronization, so the different threads must all contend for the same lock.

The second factor is that there are three threads in the program, not two. The main thread has to create and start the two `Babble` threads and that means that it contends with them for scheduling as well. It is entirely possible that the first `Babble` thread will run to completion before the main thread even gets the chance to create a second `Babble` thread.

Exercise 14.7: Run `Babble` multiple times and examine the output: Is it always the same? If possible, run it on different systems and compare.

14.7 Deadlocks

Whenever you have two threads and two objects with locks, you can have a *deadlock,* in which each thread has the lock on one of the objects and is waiting for the lock on the other object. If object *X* has a `synchronized` method that invokes a `synchronized` method on object *Y,* which in turn has a `synchronized` method invoking a `synchronized` method on object *X,* two threads may wait for each other to complete in order to get a lock, and neither thread will be able to run. This situation is also called a *deadly embrace.* Here's a `Friendly` class in which one friend, upon being hugged, insists on hugging back:

```
class Friendly {
    private Friendly partner;
    private String name;

    public Friendly(String name) {
```

```
            this.name = name;
        }

        public synchronized void hug() {
            System.out.println(Thread.currentThread().getName()+
                " in " + name + ".hug() trying to invoke " +
                partner.name + ".hugBack()");
            partner.hugBack();
        }

        private synchronized void hugBack() {
            System.out.println(Thread.currentThread().getName()+
                " in " + name + ".hugBack()");
        }

        public void becomeFriend(Friendly partner) {
            this.partner = partner;
        }
    }
```

Now consider this scenario, in which jareth and cory are two Friendly objects that have become friends:

1. Thread number 1 invokes synchronized method jareth.hug. Thread number 1 now has the lock on jareth.

2. Thread number 2 invokes synchronized method cory.hug. Thread number 2 now has the lock on cory.

3. Now jareth.hug invokes synchronized method cory.hugBack. Thread number 1 is now blocked waiting for the lock on cory (currently held by thread number 2) to become available.

4. Finally, cory.hug invokes synchronized method jareth.hugBack. Thread number 2 is now blocked waiting for the lock on jareth (currently held by thread number 1) to become available.

We have now achieved deadlock: cory won't proceed until the lock on jareth is released and vice versa, so the two threads are stuck in a permanent embrace.

We can try to set up this scenario:

```
public static void main(String[] args) {
    final Friendly jareth = new Friendly("jareth");
    final Friendly cory = new Friendly("cory");
```

```
        jareth.becomeFriend(cory);
        cory.becomeFriend(jareth);

        new Thread(new Runnable() {
            public void run() { jareth.hug(); }
        }, "Thread1").start();

        new Thread(new Runnable() {
            public void run() { cory.hug(); }
        }, "Thread2").start();
    }
```

And when you run the program, you might get the following output before the program "hangs":

```
Thread1 in jareth.hug() trying to invoke cory.hugBack()
Thread2 in cory.hug() trying to invoke jareth.hugBack()
```

You could get lucky, of course, and have one thread complete the entire hug without the other one starting. If steps 2 and 3 happened to occur in the opposite order, jareth would complete both hug and hugBack before cory needed the lock on jareth. But a future run of the same application might deadlock because of a different choice of the thread scheduler. Several design changes would fix this problem. The simplest would be to make hug and hugBack not synchronized but have both methods synchronize on a single object shared by all Friendly objects. This technique would mean that only one hug could happen at a time in all the threads of a single application, but it would eliminate the possibility of deadlock. Other, more complicated techniques would enable multiple simultaneous hugs without deadlock.

You are responsible for avoiding deadlock. The runtime system neither detects nor prevents deadlocks. It can be frustrating to debug deadlock problems, so you should solve them by avoiding the possibility in your design. One common technique is to use *resource ordering.* With resource ordering you assign an order on all objects whose locks must be acquired and make sure that you always acquire locks in that order. This makes it impossible for two threads to hold one lock each and be trying to acquire the lock held by the other—they must both request the locks in the same order, and so once one thread has the first lock, the second thread will block trying to acquire that lock, and then the first thread can safely acquire the second lock.

Exercise 14.8: Experiment with the Friendly program. How often does the deadlock actually happen on your system? If you add yield calls, can you change the likelihood of deadlock? If you can, try this exercise on more than one kind of system. Remove the deadlock potential without getting rid of the synchronization.

14.8 Ending Thread Execution

A thread that has been started becomes *alive* and the `isAlive` method will return `true` for that thread. A thread continues to be alive until it terminates, which can occur in one of three ways:

- The `run` method returns normally.
- The `run` method completes abruptly.
- The application terminates.

Having `run` return is the normal way for a thread to terminate. Every thread performs a task and when that task is over the thread should go away. If something goes wrong, however, and an exception occurs that is not caught, then that will also terminate the thread—we look at this further in Section 14.12 on page 379. By the time a thread terminates it will not hold any locks, because all synchronized code must have been exited by the time `run` has completed.

A thread can also be terminated when its application terminates, which you'll learn about in "Ending Application Execution" on page 369.

14.8.1 Cancelling a Thread

There are often occasions when you create a thread to perform some work and then need to cancel that work before it is complete—the most obvious example being a user clicking a cancel button in a user interface. To make a thread *cancellable* takes a bit of work on the programmer's part, but it is a clean and safe mechanism for getting a thread to terminate. You request cancellation by *interrupting* the thread and by writing the thread such that it watches for, and responds to, being interrupted. For example:

Thread 1

```
thread2.interrupt();
```

Thread 2

```
while (!interrupted()) {
    // do a little work
}
```

Interrupting the thread advises it that you want it to pay attention, usually to get it to halt execution. An interrupt does *not* force the thread to halt, although it will interrupt the slumber of a sleeping or waiting thread.

Interruption is also useful when you want to give the running thread some control over when it will handle an event. For example, a display update loop might need to access some database information using a transaction and would prefer to handle a user's "cancel" after waiting until that transaction completes normally. The user-interface thread might implement a "Cancel" button by interrupting the display thread to give the display thread that control. This approach will work well as long as the display thread is well behaved and checks at the end of every transaction to see whether it has been interrupted, halting if it has.

The following methods relate to interrupting a thread: `interrupt`, which sends an interrupt to a thread; `isInterrupted`, which tests whether a thread has been interrupted; and `interrupted`, a `static` method that tests whether the current thread has been interrupted and then clears the "interrupted" state of the thread. The interrupted state of a thread can be cleared only by that thread—there is no way to "uninterrupt" another thread. There is generally little point in querying the interrupted state of another thread, so these methods tend to be used by the current thread on itself. When a thread detects that it has been interrupted, it often needs to perform some cleanup before actually responding to the interrupt. That cleanup may involve actions that could be affected if the thread is left in the interrupted state, so the thread will test and clear its interrupted state using `interrupted`.

Interrupting a thread will normally not affect what it is doing, but a few methods, such as `sleep` and `wait`, throw `InterruptedException`. If your thread is executing one of these methods when it is interrupted, the method will throw the `InterruptedException`. Such a thrown interruption clears the interrupted state of the thread, so handling code for `InterruptedException` commonly looks like this:

```
void tick(int count, long pauseTime) {
    try {
        for (int i = 0; i < count; i++) {
            System.out.println('.');
            System.out.flush();
            Thread.sleep(pauseTime);
        }
    } catch (InterruptedException e) {
        Thread.currentThread().interrupt();
    }
}
```

The `tick` method prints a dot every `pauseTime` milliseconds up to a maximum of `count` times—see "Timer and TimerTask" on page 653 for a better way to do this. If something interrupts the thread in which `tick` is running, `sleep` will throw

`InterruptedException`. The ticking will then cease, and the `catch` clause will reinterrupt the thread. You could instead declare that `tick` itself throws `InterruptedException` and simply let the exception percolate upward, but then every invoker of `tick` would have to handle the same possibility. Reinterrupting the thread allows `tick` to clean up its own behavior and then let other code handle the interrupt as it normally would.

In general any method that performs a blocking operation (either directly or indirectly) should allow that blocking operation to be cancelled with `interrupt` and should throw an appropriate exception if that occurs. This is what `sleep` and `wait` do. In some systems, blocking I/O operations will respond to interruption by throwing `InterruptedIOException` (which is a subclass of the general `IOException` that most I/O methods can throw—see Chapter 20 for more details on I/O). Even if the interruption cannot be responded to during the I/O operation, systems may check for interruption at the start of the operation and throw the exception—hence the need for an interrupted thread to clear its interrupted state if it needs to perform I/O as part of its cleanup. In general, however, you cannot assume that `interrupt` will unblock a thread that is performing I/O.

Every method of every class executes in some thread, but the behavior defined by those methods generally concerns the state of the object involved, not the state of the thread executing the method. Given that, how do you write methods that will allow threads to respond to interrupts and be cancellable? If your method can block, then it should respond to interruption as just discussed. Otherwise, you must decide what interruption or cancellation would mean for your method and then make that behavior part of the methods contract—in the majority of cases methods need not concern themselves with interruption at all. The golden rule, however, is to never hide an interrupt by clearing it explicitly or by catching an `InterruptedException` and continuing normally—that prevents any thread from being cancellable when executing your code.

The interruption mechanism is a tool that cooperating code can use to make multithreading effective. Neither it, nor any other mechanism, can deal with hostile or malicious code.

14.8.2 Waiting for a Thread to Complete

One thread can wait for another thread to terminate by using one of the `join` methods. The simple form waits forever for a particular thread to complete:

```
class CalcThread extends Thread {
    private double result;

    public void run() {
```

```
                result = calculate();
        }

        public double getResult() {
            return result;
        }

        public double calculate() {
            // ... calculate a value for "result"
        }
    }

    class ShowJoin {
        public static void main(String[] args) {
            CalcThread calc = new CalcThread();
            calc.start();
            doSomethingElse();
            try {
                calc.join();
                System.out.println("result is "
                    + calc.getResult());
            } catch (InterruptedException e) {
                System.out.println("No answer: interrupted");
            }
        }
        // ... definition of doSomethingElse ...
    }
```

First, a new thread type, CalcThread, is defined to calculate a result. We start a CalcThread, do something else for a while, and then join that thread. When join returns, CalcThread.run is guaranteed to have finished, and result will be set. If CalcThread is already finished when doSomethingElse has completed, join returns immediately. When a thread dies, its Thread object doesn't go away, so you can still access its state. You are not required to join a thread before it can terminate.

Two other forms of join take time-out values analogous to wait. Here are the three forms of join:

public final void **join(long millis)**
   throws InterruptedException
        Waits for this thread to finish or for the specified number of milliseconds to
        elapse, whichever comes first. A time-out of zero milliseconds means to wait

forever. If the thread is interrupted while it is waiting you will get an `InterruptedException`.

public final void **join(long millis, int nanos)**
   throws InterruptedException
     Waits for this thread to finish, with more precise timing. Again, a total time-out of zero nanoseconds means to wait forever. Nanoseconds are in the range 0–999,999.

public final void **join()** throws InterruptedException
     Equivalent to `join(0)`.

Internally, `join` is defined in terms of `isAlive` and can be logically considered to act as if written as

```
while (isAlive())
    wait();
```

with the understanding that the runtime system will invoke `notifyAll` when the thread actually terminates.

14.9 Ending Application Execution

Each application starts with one thread—the one that executes `main`. If your application creates no other threads, the application will finish when `main` returns. But if you create other threads, what happens to them when `main` returns?

There are two kinds of threads: *user* and *daemon*. The presence of a user thread keeps the application running, whereas a daemon thread is expendable. When the last user thread is finished, any daemon threads are terminated and the application is finished. This termination is like that of invoking `destroy`—abrupt and with no chance for any cleanup—so daemon threads are limited in what they can do. You use the method `setDaemon(true)` to mark a thread as a daemon thread, and you use `isDaemon` to test that flag. By default, daemon status is inherited from the thread that creates the new thread and cannot be changed after a thread is started; an `IllegalThreadStateException` is thrown if you try.

If your `main` method spawns a thread, that thread inherits the user-thread status of the original thread. When `main` finishes, the application will continue to run until the other thread finishes, too. There is nothing special about the original thread—it just happened to be the first one to get started for a particular run of an application, and it is treated just like any other user thread. An application will run until all user threads have completed. For all the runtime system knows, the original thread was designed to spawn another thread and die, letting the spawned thread do the real work. If you want your application to exit when the original thread dies, you can mark all the threads you create as daemon threads.

You can force an application to end by invoking either the `System` or `Runtime` method `exit`. This method terminates the current execution of the Java virtual machine and again is like invoking `destroy` on each thread. However, an application can install special threads to be run before the application shuts down—the methods for doing this are described in "Shutdown" on page 672.

Many classes implicitly create threads within an application. For example, the Abstract Window Toolkit (AWT), described briefly in Chapter 25, provides an event-based graphical user-interface and creates a special thread for dealing with all associated events. Similarly, Remote Method Invocation, also mentioned in Chapter 25, creates threads for responding to remote method invocations. Some of these threads may be daemons and others may not, so use of these classes can keep your application running longer than you may intend. In these circumstances the use of the `exit` method becomes essential if there is no other way to terminate the threads.

14.10 The Memory Model: Synchronization and `volatile`

Any mutable (that is, changeable) value shared between different threads should always be accessed under synchronization to prevent interference from occurring. Synchronization comes at a cost, however, and may not always be necessary to prevent interference. The language guarantees that reading or writing any variables, other than those of type `long` or `double`, is atomic—the variable will only ever hold a value that was written by some thread, never a partial value intermixing two different writes. This means, for example, that an atomic variable that is only written by one thread and read by many threads need not have access to it synchronized to prevent corruption because there is no possibility of interference. This does not help with get–modify–set sequences (such as ++), which always require synchronization.

Atomic access does not ensure that a thread will always read the most recently written value of a variable. In fact, without synchronization, a value written by one thread may *never* become visible to another thread. A number of factors affect when a variable written by one thread becomes visible to another thread. Modern multiprocessing hardware can do very strange things when it comes to the way in which shared memory values get updated, as can dynamic compilation environments at runtime. Further, in the absence of synchronization the order in which variables are seen to be updated by different threads can be completely different. To the programmer these things are not only strange, they often seem completely unreasonable and invariably not what the programmer wanted. The rules that determine how memory accesses are ordered and when they are guaranteed to be visible are known as the *memory model* of the Java programming language.

The actions of a thread are determined by the semantics of the statements in the methods that it executes. Logically, these statements are executed in the order the statements are written—an order known as *program order.* However, the values of any variables read by the thread are determined by the memory model. The memory model defines the set of allowed values that can be returned when a variable is read. In this context variables consist only of fields (both static and non-static) and array elements. From a programmer's perspective this set of values should only consist of a single value: that value most recently written by some thread. However, as we shall see, in the absence of proper synchronization, the actual set of values available may consist of many different values.

For example, suppose you had a field, `currentValue`, that was continuously displayed by a graphics thread and that could be changed by other threads using a non-synchronized method:

```
public void updateCurrent() {
    currentValue = (int) Math.random();
}
```

The display code might look something like this:

```
currentValue = 5;
for (;;) {
    display.showValue(currentValue);
    Thread.sleep(1000); // wait 1 second
}
```

When the loop is first entered (assuming no calls to `updateCurrent` have occurred in other threads) the only possible value for `currentValue` is 5. However, because there is no synchronization, each time a thread invokes `updateCurrent` the new value is added to the set of possible values to be read. By the time `currentValue` is read in the loop, the possible values might consist of 5, 25, 42, and 326, any of which may be returned by the read. According to the rules of the memory model any value written by some thread (but not some "out of thin air" value) may be returned by the read. In practical terms, if there is no way for `showValue` to change the value of `currentValue`, the compiler can assume that it can treat `currentValue` as unchanged inside the loop and simply use the constant 5 each time it invokes `showValue`. This is consistent with the memory model because 5 is one of the available values and the memory model doesn't control which value gets returned. For the program to work as desired we have to do something such that when `currentValue` is written, that written value becomes the only value that the memory model will allow to be read. To do that we have to synchronize the writes and the reads of variables.

14.10.1 Synchronization Actions

Certain actions a thread performs are defined as *synchronization actions,* and the order in which these actions are executed is termed the *synchronization order* of the program—the synchronization order is always consistent with the program order. These synchronization actions synchronize reads and writes of variables.

The most familiar synchronization action is the use of synchronized methods and blocks to ensure exclusive access to shared variables. The release of a monitor lock is said to *synchronize with* all subsequent acquisitions and releases of that monitor lock. If all reads and writes to a variable occur only when a specific monitor is held, then each read of the variable is guaranteed by the memory model to return the value that was most recently written to it.

There is a second synchronization mechanism that doesn't provide the exclusive access of monitors, but that again ensures that each read of a variable returns the most recently written value—the use of *volatile* variables. Fields (but not array elements) can be declared with the `volatile` modifier. A write to a volatile variable synchronizes with all subsequent reads of that variable. If `currentValue` was declared as volatile then the example code we showed would be correctly synchronized and the latest value would always be displayed. The use of volatile variables is seldom a replacement for the use of synchronized methods or statements on its own, because they don't provide atomicity across different actions. Rather, volatile variables are most often used for simple flags to indicate something has occurred, or for writing lock-free algorithms that incorporate use of the atomic variables mentioned in Section 25.9.1 on page 733.

An additional effect of making a variable volatile is that reads and writes are guaranteed to be atomic. This extends the basic atomicity guarantee to cover `long` and `double` variables.

A few other synchronization actions help make multithreading work nicely:

- Starting a thread synchronizes with the first action performed by that thread when it executes. This ensures that a newly started thread sees any data that was initialized by the creating thread—including the thread's own fields.

- The final action of a thread synchronizes with any action that detects that the thread has terminated—such as calling `isAlive` or invoking `join` on that thread. This ensures, for example, that if you join a thread you can see all data written by that thread before it terminated—such as the results of its computation.

♦ Interrupting a thread synchronizes with any other action that determines that the thread has been interrupted, such as the thread throwing `InterruptedException` or another thread invoking `isInterrupted` on the thread.

♦ The write of the default value (zero, null, or false) to any field synchronizes with the first action in any thread. This ensures that even in incorrectly synchronized programs a thread will never see arbitrary values in fields—either a specific value written by some thread will be seen or the default value of the field will be seen.

14.10.2 Final Fields and Security

We described in Section 2.2.3 on page 46 how final fields are used to define immutable values; indeed you can use final fields to define immutable objects. There is a common misconception that shared access to immutable objects does not require any synchronization because the state of the object never changes. This is a misconception in general because it relies on the assumption that a thread will be guaranteed to see the initialized state of the immutable object, and that need not be the case. The problem is that, while the shared object is immutable, the reference used to access the shared object is itself shared and often mutable— consequently, a correctly synchronized program must synchronize access to that shared reference, but often programs do not do this, because programmers do not recognize the need to do it. For example, suppose one thread creates a `String` object and stores a reference to it in a static field. A second thread then uses that reference to access the string. There is no guarantee, based on what we've discussed so far, that the values written by the first thread when constructing the string will be seen by the second thread when it accesses the string.

The memory model defines the semantics for multithreaded programs and tells you what you need to do to correctly synchronize your programs. But additionally, you need safeguards that ensure that incorrectly synchronized programs cannot violate the integrity of the language, or the virtual machine implementation, or the security architecture that prevents sensitive APIs from being misused— see "Security" on page 677. These safeguards come in the form of additional rules in the memory model covering the use of final fields.

The first rule for final fields covers the situation we described with the shared string. Basically, the rule states that if a reference to an object is stored after the object has been constructed, then any thread that reads that reference is guaranteed to see initialized values for the object's final fields. Note that there is no guarantee concerning non-final fields of the object that are read without synchronization.

The second rule expands on the first to apply transitively to objects reachable via final fields. There is little point being guaranteed to see a reference stored in a final field, if the fields of that object are not guaranteed to be seen. What the second rule states, in general terms, is that if you read a reference from a final field, then any non-final fields in the referenced object will have a value at least as recent as the value they had when the reference was written. For example, this means that if one thread constructs an object and uses methods on that object to set its state, then a second thread will see the state set by the first thread if the reference used to access the object was written to a final field after the state changes were made. Any final fields in such objects are covered by the first rule.

To preserve the integrity of the system, classes must use final fields appropriately to protect sensitive data, if correct synchronization cannot be relied on. For this reason, the `String` class uses final fields internally so that `String` values are both immutable and guaranteed to be visible.

14.10.3 The Happens-Before Relationship

The description of synchronizations actions above is a simplification of the operation of the memory model. The use of synchronized blocks and methods and the use of volatile variables provide guarantees concerning the reading and writing of variables beyond the volatile variables themselves or the variables accessed within the synchronized block. These synchronization actions establish what is called a *happens-before* relationship and it is this relationship that determines what values can be returned by a read of a variable. The happens-before relationship is transitive, and a statement that occurs ahead of another in program order happens-before that second statement. This allows actions other than synchronization actions to become synchronized across threads. For example, if a non-volatile variable is written before a volatile variable, and in another thread the same volatile variable is read before reading the non-volatile variable, then the write of the non-volatile variable happens-before the read of that variable and so the read is guaranteed to return the value written. Consider the following:

```
static Data data;
static volatile boolean dataReady;
```

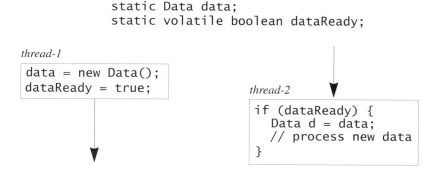

```
thread-1
data = new Data();
dataReady = true;
```

```
thread-2
if (dataReady) {
   Data d = data;
   // process new data
}
```

If the read of `dataReady` by thread-2 yields `true`, then the write of `dataReady` by thread-1 happened-before that read. Since the write to `data` by thread-1 happens-before the write to `dataReady` by thread-1, it follows that it also happens-before the read of `dataReady` by thread-2, hence the read of `data` by thread-2. In short, if thread-2 sees `dataReady` is `true` then it is guaranteed to see the new `Data` object created by thread-1. This is true because `dataReady` is a volatile variable,[2] even though `data` is not itself a volatile variable.

Finally, note that the actual execution order of instructions and memory accesses can be in any order as long as the actions of the thread appear to that thread as if program order were followed, and provided all values read are allowed for by the memory model. This allows the programmer to fully understand the semantics of the programs they write, and it allows compiler writers and virtual machine implementors to perform complex optimizations that a simpler memory model would not permit.

This discussion gives you an idea of how the memory model interacts with multithreading. The full details of the memory model are beyond the scope of this book. Fortunately, if you pursue a straightforward locking strategy using the tools in this book, the subtleties of the memory model will work for you and your code will be fine.

14.11 Thread Management, Security, and `ThreadGroup`

When you're programming multiple threads—some of them created by library classes—it can be useful to organize them into related groups, manage the threads in a group as a unit, and, if necessary, place limitations on what threads in different groups can do.

Threads are organized into *thread groups* for management and security reasons. A thread group can be contained within another thread group, providing a hierarchy—originating with the top-level or system thread group. Threads within a group can be managed as a unit, for example, by interrupting all threads in the group at once, or placing a limit on the maximum priority of threads in a group. The thread group can also be used to define a security domain. Threads within a thread group can generally modify other threads in that group, including any threads farther down the hierarchy. In this context "modifying" means invoking any method that could affect a thread's behavior—such as changing its priority, or interrupting it. However, an application can define a security policy that prevents a thread from modifying threads outside of its group. Threads within different

---

[2] The same would be true if `dataReady` were not volatile but instead had synchronized `get` and `set` methods.

thread groups can also be granted different permissions for performing actions within the application, such as performing I/O.

Generally speaking, security-sensitive methods always check with any installed security manager before proceeding. If the security policy in force forbids the action, the method throws a `SecurityException`. By default there is no security manager installed when an application starts. If your code is executed in the context of another application, however, such as an applet within a browser, you can be fairly certain that a security manager has been installed. Actions such as creating threads, controlling threads, performing I/O, or terminating an application, are all security sensitive. For further details, see "Security" on page 677.

Every thread belongs to a thread group. Each thread group is represented by a `ThreadGroup` object that describes the limits on threads in that group and allows the threads in the group to be interacted with as a group. You can specify the thread group for a new thread by passing it to the thread constructor. By default each new thread is placed in the same thread group as that of the thread that created it, unless a security manager specifies differently. For example, if some event-handling code in an applet creates a new thread, the security manager can make the new thread part of the applet thread group rather than the system thread group of the event-processing thread. When a thread terminates, the `Thread` object is removed from its group and so may be garbage collected if no other references to it remain.

There are four `Thread` constructors that allow you to specify the `ThreadGroup` of the thread. You saw three of them on page 343 when looking at `Runnable`. The fourth is:

`public` **`Thread(ThreadGroup group, String name)`**
      Constructs a new thread in the specified thread group with the given name.

To prevent threads from being created in arbitrary thread groups (which would defeat the security mechanism), these constructors can themselves throw `SecurityException` if the current thread is not permitted to place a thread in the specified thread group.

The `ThreadGroup` object associated with a thread cannot be changed after the thread is created. You can get a thread's group by invoking its `getThreadGroup` method. You can also check whether you are allowed to modify a `Thread` by invoking its `checkAccess` method, which throws `SecurityException` if you cannot modify the thread and simply returns if you can (it is a `void` method).

A thread group can be a *daemon group*—which is totally unrelated to the concept of daemon threads. A daemon `ThreadGroup` is automatically destroyed when it becomes empty. Setting a `ThreadGroup` to be a daemon group does not affect whether any thread or group contained in that group is a daemon. It affects only what happens when the group becomes empty.

Thread groups can also be used to set an upper limit on the priority of the threads they contain. After you invoke setMaxPriority with a maximum priority, any attempt to set a thread priority higher than the thread group's maximum is silently reduced to that maximum. Existing threads are not affected by this invocation. To ensure that no other thread in the group will ever have a higher priority than that of a particular thread, you can set that thread's priority and then set the group's maximum priority to be less than that. The limit also applies to the thread group itself. Any attempt to set a new maximum priority for the group that is higher than the current maximum will be silently reduced.

```
static synchronized void
    maxThread(Thread thr, int priority)
{
    ThreadGroup grp = thr.getThreadGroup();
    thr.setPriority(priority);
    grp.setMaxPriority(thr.getPriority() - 1);
}
```

This method works by setting the thread's priority to the desired value and then setting the group's maximum allowable priority to less than the thread's priority. The new group maximum is set to one less than the thread's actual priority—not to priority - 1 because an existing group maximum might limit your ability to set the thread to that priority. Of course, this method assumes that no thread in the group already has a higher priority.

ThreadGroup supports the following constructors and methods:

public **ThreadGroup(String name)**
> Creates a new ThreadGroup. Its parent will be the ThreadGroup of the current thread. Like Thread names, the name of a group is not used by the runtime system—but it can be null.

public **ThreadGroup(ThreadGroup parent, String name)**
> Creates a new ThreadGroup with a specified name in the ThreadGroup parent. A NullPointerException is thrown if parent is null.

public final String **getName()**
> Returns the name of this ThreadGroup.

public final ThreadGroup **getParent()**
> Returns the parent ThreadGroup, or null if it has none (which can only occur for the top-level thread group).

public final void **setDaemon(boolean daemon)**
> Sets the daemon status of this thread group.

`public final boolean` **`isDaemon()`**
  Returns the daemon status of this thread group.

`public final void` **`setMaxPriority(int maxPri)`**
  Sets the maximum priority of this thread group.

`public final int` **`getMaxPriority()`**
  Gets the current maximum priority of this thread group.

`public final boolean` **`parentOf(ThreadGroup g)`**
  Checks whether this thread group is a parent of the group g, or is the group
  g. This might be better thought of as "part of," since a group is part of itself.

`public final void` **`checkAccess()`**
  Throws `SecurityException` if the current thread is not allowed to modify
  this group. Otherwise, this method simply returns.

`public final void` **`destroy()`**
  Destroys this thread group. The thread group must contain no threads or this
  method throws `IllegalThreadStateException`. If the group contains
  other groups, they must also be empty of threads. This does *not* destroy the
  threads in the group.

  You can examine the contents of a thread group using two parallel sets of
methods: One gets the threads contained in the group, and the other gets the thread
groups contained in the group.

`public int` **`activeCount()`**
  Returns an estimate of the number of active threads in this group, including
  threads contained in all subgroups. This is an estimate because by the time
  you get the number it may be out of date. Threads may have died, or new
  ones may have been created, during or after the invocation of `activeCount`.
  An active thread is one for which `isAlive` returns true.

`public int` **`enumerate(Thread[] threadsInGroup, boolean recurse)`**
  Fills the `threadsInGroup` array with a reference to every active thread in
  the group, up to the size of the array, and returns the number of threads
  stored. If `recurse` is `false`, only threads directly in the group are included;
  If it is `true`, all threads in the group's hierarchy will be included.
  `ThreadGroup.enumerate` gives you control over whether you recurse, but
  `ThreadGroup.activeCount` does not. You can get a reasonable estimate of
  the size of an array needed to hold the results of a recursive enumeration, but
  you will overestimate the size needed for a non-recursive `enumerate`.

`public int` **`enumerate(Thread[] threadsInGroup)`**
  Equivalent to enumerate(threadsInGroup, true).

`public int` **`activeGroupCount()`**

> Like `activeCount`, but counts groups, instead of threads, in all subgroups. "Active" means "existing." There is no concept of an inactive group; the term "active" is used for consistency with `activeCount`.

`public int`
  `enumerate(ThreadGroup[] groupsInGroup, boolean recurse)`

> Like the similar `enumerate` method for threads, but fills an array of `ThreadGroup` references instead of `Thread` references.

`public int` **`enumerate(ThreadGroup[] groupsInGroup)`**

> Equivalent to `enumerate(groupsInGroup, true)`.

You can also use a `ThreadGroup` to manage threads in the group. Invoking `interrupt` on a group invokes the `interrupt` method on each thread in the group, including threads in all subgroups. This method is the only way to use a `ThreadGroup` to directly affect threads—there used to be others but they have been deprecated.

There are also two static methods in the `Thread` class to act on the current thread's group. They are shorthands for invoking `currentThread`, invoking `getThreadGroup` on that thread, and then invoking the method on that group.

`public static int` **`activeCount()`**

> Returns the number of active threads in the current thread's `ThreadGroup`.

`public static int` **`enumerate(Thread[] threadsInGroup)`**

> Equivalent to invoking the method `enumerate(threadsInGroup)` on the `ThreadGroup` of the current thread.

The `ThreadGroup` class also supports a method that is invoked when a thread dies because of an uncaught exception:

`public void` **`uncaughtException(Thread thr, Throwable exc)`**

We'll look at this in more detail in the next section.

Exercise 14.9: Write a method that takes a thread group and starts a thread that periodically prints the hierarchy of threads and thread groups within that group, using the methods just described. Test it with a program that creates several short-lived threads in various groups.

14.12 Threads and Exceptions

Exceptions always occur in a specific thread, due to the actions of that thread—for example, trying to perform division by zero, or explicitly throwing an exception.

Such exceptions are synchronous exceptions and always remain within the thread. If a "parent" thread wants to know why a "child" terminated, the child will have to store that information somewhere the "parent" can get it. Placing a thread start invocation in a try-catch block does *not* catch exceptions that may be thrown by the new thread—it simply catches any exception thrown by start.

When an exception is thrown it causes statements to complete abruptly and propagates up the call stack as each method invocation completes abruptly. If the exception is not caught by the time the run method completes abruptly then it is, by definition, an *uncaught exception.* At that point the thread that experienced the exception has terminated and the exception no longer exists. Because uncaught exceptions are usually a sign of a serious error, their occurrence needs to be tracked in some way. To enable this, every thread can have associated with it an instance of UncaughtExceptionHandler. The UncaughtExceptionHandler interface is a nested interface of class Thread and declares a single method:

public void **uncaughtException(Thread thr, Throwable exc)**
    Invoked when thr terminated due to exc being thrown.

A thread's uncaught exception handler can be set, if security permissions allow it, using its setUncaughtExceptionHandler method.

When a thread is about to terminate due to an uncaught exception, the runtime queries it for its handler by invoking the getUncaughtExceptionHandler method on it, and invokes the returned handler's uncaughtException method, passing the thread and the exception as parameters.

The getUncaughtExceptionHandler method will return the handler explicitly set by the thread's setUncaughtExceptionHandler method, or if no handler has been explicitly set, then the thread's ThreadGroup object is returned. Once a thread has terminated, and it has no group, getUncaughtExceptionHandler may return null.

The default implementation of the ThreadGroup uncaughtException method invokes uncaughtException on the group's parent group if there is one. If the thread group has no parent, then the system is queried for a default uncaught exception handler, using the static Thread class method getDefaultUncaughtExceptionHandler. If such a default handler exists, its uncaughtException method is called with the thread and exception. If there is no default handler, ThreadGroup's uncaughtException method simply invokes the exception's printStackTrace method to display information about the exception that occurred (unless it is an instance of ThreadDeath in which case nothing further happens).

An application can control the handling of uncaught exceptions, both for the threads it creates, and threads created by libraries it uses, at three levels:

♦ At the system level, by setting a default handler using the static `Thread` class method `setDefaultUncaughtExceptionHandler`. This operation is security checked to ensure the application has permission to control this.

♦ At the group level, by extending `ThreadGroup` and overriding it's definition of `uncaughtException`.

♦ At the thread level, by invoking `setUncaughtExceptionHandler` on that thread.

For example, if you were writing a graphical environment, you might want to display the stack trace in a window rather than simply print it to `System.err`, which is where the method `printStackTrace` puts its output. You could define your own `UncaughtExceptionHandler` that implement `uncaughtException` to create the window you need and redirect the stack trace into the window.

14.12.1 Don't `stop`

We mentioned in Chapter 12 that two forms of asynchronous exceptions are defined—internal errors in the Java virtual machine, and exceptions caused by the invocation of the deprecated `Thread.stop` method.

As a general rule we don't discuss deprecated methods in this book, but `stop` is special—partly because of what it does, but mostly because it is, as they say, "out there" and you may well come across code that uses it (or tries to).

The `stop` method causes an asynchronous `ThreadDeath` exception to be thrown in the thread on which it is invoked. There is nothing special about this exception—just like any other exception it can be caught, and if it is not caught it will propagate until eventually the thread terminates. The exception can occur at almost any point during the execution of a thread, but not while trying to acquire a lock.

The intent of `stop` was to force a thread to terminate in a controlled manner. By throwing an exception that was unlikely to be caught, it allowed the normal cleanup procedure of using `finally` clauses to tidy up as the thread's call stack unwound. But `stop` failed to achieve this in two ways. First, it couldn't *force* any thread to terminate because a thread could catch the exception that was thrown and ignore it—hence it was ineffective against malicious code. Second, rather than allowing a controlled cleanup, it actually allowed the corruption of objects. If `stop` was invoked while a thread was in a critical section, the synchronization lock would be released as the exception propagated, but the object could have been left in a corrupt state due to the partial completion of the critical section. Because of these serious flaws `stop` was deprecated. Instead, `interrupt` should be used for cooperative cancellation of a thread's actions.

A second form of stop took any Throwable object as an argument and caused that to be the exception thrown in the target thread—this is even more insidious because it allows "impossible" checked exceptions to be thrown from code that doesn't declare them.

14.12.2 Stack Traces

Any thread that is alive, can be queried for its current execution stack trace. The getStackTrace method returns an array of StackTraceElement objects—as described in "Stack Traces" on page 294—where the zeroth element represents the currently executing method of the thread. If the thread is not alive then a zero-length array is returned.

You can access the stack traces of all threads in the system using the static Thread class method getAllStackTraces, which returns a map from each thread to its corresponding StackTraceElement array.

Stack trace information is generally used for debugging and monitoring purposes—for example, if your application "hangs," a monitoring thread might display all the stack traces, showing you what each thread is doing. Of course, if your application hangs because of an error in your code, any such monitoring thread may itself not get a chance to execute. The virtual machine is not required to produce non-zero-length stack traces for any given thread, and it is also allowed to omit some methods from the stack trace information.

14.13 ThreadLocal Variables

The ThreadLocal class allows you to have a single logical variable that has independent values in each separate thread. Each ThreadLocal object has a set method that lets you set the value of the variable in the current thread, and a get method that returns the value for the current thread. It is as if you had defined a new field in each thread class, but without the need to actually change any thread class. This is a feature you may well never need, but if you do need it ThreadLocal may simplify your work.

For example, you might want to have a user object associated with all operations, set on a per-thread basis. You could create a ThreadLocal object to hold each thread's current user object:

```
public class Operations {
    private static ThreadLocal<User> users =
        new ThreadLocal<User>() {
            /** Initially start as the "unknown user". */
```

```
            protected User initialValue() {
                return User.UNKNOWN_USER;
            }
        };

    private static User currentUser() {
        return users.get();
    }

    public static void setUser(User newUser) {
        users.set(newUser);
    }

    public void setValue(int newValue) {
        User user = currentUser();
        if (!canChange(user))
            throw new SecurityException();
        // ... modify the value ...
    }

    // ...
}
```

The static field users holds a ThreadLocal variable whose initial value in each thread will be User.UNKNOWN_USER. This initial value is defined by overriding the method initialValue, whose default behavior is to return null. The programmer can set the user for a given thread by invoking setUser. Once set, the method currentUser will return that value when invoked in that thread. As shown in the method setValue, the current user might be used to determine privileges.

You can clear the value in a ThreadLocal by invoking its remove method. If get is invoked again, then initialValue will again be used to determine what to return.

When a thread dies, the values set in ThreadLocal variables for that thread are not reachable, and so can be collected as garbage if not otherwise referenced.

When you spawn a new thread, the values of ThreadLocal variables for that thread will be the value returned by its initialValue method. If you want the value in a new thread to be inherited from the spawning thread, you can use the class InheritableThreadLocal, a subclass of ThreadLocal. It has a protected method childValue that is invoked to get the child's (spawned thread's) initial value. The method is passed the parent's value for the variable and returns the value for the child. The default implementation of childValue returns the parent's value, but you can subclass to do something different, such as cloning the parent's value for the child.

Use of `ThreadLocal` objects is an inherently risky tool. You should use them only where you thoroughly understand the thread model that will be used. The problems arise with *thread pooling,* a technique that is sometimes used to reuse threads instead of creating new ones for each task. In a thread pooling system a thread might be used several times. Any `ThreadLocal` object used in such an environment would contain the state set by the last code that happened to use the same thread, instead of an uninitialized state expected at the beginning of a new thread of execution. If you write a general class that uses `ThreadLocal` objects and someone uses your class in a thread pool, the behavior might be dangerously wrong.

For example, the `users` variable in the `Operations` example above could have just this problem—if an `Operations` object was used in multiple threads, or different `Operations` objects were used in the same thread, the "current user" notion could easily be wrong. Programmers who use `Operations` objects must understand this and only use the objects in threading situations that match the assumptions of the class's code.

14.14 Debugging Threads

A few `Thread` methods are designed to help you debug a multithreaded application. These print-style debugging aids can be used to print the state of an application. You can invoke the following methods on a `Thread` object to help you debug your threads:

`public String` **`toString()`**
> Returns a string representation of the thread, including its name, its priority, and the name of its thread group.

`public long` **`getId()`**
> Returns a positive value that uniquely identifies this thread while it is alive.

`public Thread.State` **`getState()`**
> Returns the current state of this thread. `Thread.State` is a nested enum that defines the constants: NEW, RUNNABLE, BLOCKED, WAITING, TIMED_WAITING, and TERMINATED. A newly created thread has state NEW, until it is started, at which time it becomes RUNNABLE until it terminates and becomes TERMINATED. While a thread is runnable, but before it terminates it can switch between being RUNNABLE and being BLOCKED (such as acquiring a monitor lock), WAITING (having invoked `wait`), or TIMED_WAITING (having invoked a timed version of `wait`).

`public static void` **dumpStack()**
> Prints a stack trace for the current thread on `System.err`.

There are also debugging aids to track the state of a thread group. You can invoke the following methods on `ThreadGroup` objects to print their state:

`public String` **toString()**
> Returns a string representation of the `ThreadGroup`, including its name and priority.

`public void` **list()**
> Lists this `ThreadGroup` recursively to `System.out`. This prints the `toString` value for each of the threads and thread groups within this group.

> *I'll play it first and tell you what it is later.*
> —Miles Davis

CHAPTER 15

Annotations

I don't like spinach, and I'm glad I don't,
because if I liked it I'd eat it,
and I just hate it.
—Clarence Darrow

THE source code for our programs is usually accompanied by copious amounts of informal documentation that typically is contained within comments in the source code file. For example, many organizations have a standard preamble that they place at the top of class source files that contains things like copyright information, the programmers name, the date the class was created, the date the class was last modified, the current revision number, and so forth. Other comments may reflect intended usage of a class or a method, or usage limitations, such as documenting that the instances of a class are not thread-safe and so shouldn't be used concurrently. Other comments may be provided for processing by external tools that assist in the management and deployment of an application, such as version control in a source code management system, or deployment descriptors on how a class should be managed by an application server. These comment-based annotations serve a useful purpose, but they are informal and ad hoc. A better way to document these things is to annotate the program elements directly using *annotation types* to describe the form of the annotations. Annotation types present the information in a standard and structured way that is amenable to automated processing by tools.

While this chapter presents the syntax and semantics of using annotations and defining annotation types, it can't tell you what annotations to use when because very few such annotations exist within the language. The annotations you use will be those supported by the tools in your development or deployment environment. Annotation is centered on types in the package `java.lang.annotation`, and the standard types introduced in this chapter come from this package.

15.1 A Simple Annotation Example

Consider an informal, comment-based class preamble:

```
/*-------------------------------
   Created:          Jan 31 2005
   Created By:       James Gosling
   Last Modified:    Feb 9 2005
   Last Modified By: Ken Arnold
   Revision:         3
-------------------------------*/
public class Foo {
    // ...
}
```

You can define an annotation type that can hold all of the desired information:

```
@interface ClassInfo {
    String created();
    String createdBy();
    String lastModified();
    String lastModifiedBy();
    int revision();
}
```

An annotation type is a special kind of interface, designated by the @ character preceding the `interface` keyword.[1] Annotations are applied to *program elements,* such as a class or field declaration. What appear to be methods in the annotation type are actually special *annotation element* declarations. An annotation element is rather like a field, and has a value for each program element that has that type of annotation. So a `ClassInfo` annotation contains four string elements and one `int` element. When you *annotate* (apply an annotation to) a program element, you supply values for each of the annotation elements. Annotations are modifiers and can appear anywhere a modifier is allowed. Here's how you would use `ClassInfo` with class Foo:

```
@ClassInfo (
    created = "Jan 31 2005",
    createdBy = "James Gosling",
    lastModified = "Feb 9 2005",
    lastModifiedBy = "Ken Arnold",
```

---

[1]   The @ character was chosen because it is pronounced "at": A-T, short for Annotation Type.

```
      revision = 3
)
public class Foo {
    // ...
}
```

The annotation is introduced using the @ character again, followed by the name of the annotation type. Values for the annotation elements are provided by a comma-separated list of name=value statements within parentheses. As you can see, an annotation can contain a lot of textual information that can easily obscure the actual program, so it is strongly recommended that you follow a consistent practice of always specifying annotations first, ahead of any other modifiers, and always on a separate line.

To use the ClassInfo annotation, a programmer should update the value for each changed element whenever they edit the source for Foo. Such updates could be automated through development tools that understand annotations.

15.2 Annotation Types

Annotation types are a special kind of interface, declared, as you have seen, with the interface keyword preceded by the @ character. Annotation types can be declared anywhere an interface can be declared—that is, as a top-level annotation type or nested within another type—and can have the same modifiers applied as interfaces. Characterizing annotation types as interfaces is a little misleading, however, as aside from borrowing some syntax and some associated usage rules, annotation types bear little resemblance to interfaces in normal use.[2]

The methods declared in an annotation type are known as the *elements* of the annotation type. These elements are constrained by strict rules:

- ◆ The type of the element can only be a primitive type, String, an enum type, another annotation type, Class (or a specific generic invocation of Class), or an array of one of the preceding types.
- ◆ The element cannot declare any parameters.
- ◆ The element cannot have a throws clause.
- ◆ The element cannot define a type parameter (that is, it can't be a generic method).

---

[2] Except when accessed reflectively at runtime—see "Annotation Queries" on page 414.

In essence, the elements of an annotation type are like the fields of an object, that is instantiated for each program element the annotation type is applied to. The values of these fields are determined by the initializers given when the annotation is applied or by the default value of the element if it has one.

You can give an element a default value by following the empty parameter list with the keyword `default` and a suitable value. For example, suppose you want to represent a revision number as a pair of integers for the major and minor revision, you could define the following annotation type that has a default revision number of 1.0:

```
@interface Revision {
    int major() default 1;
    int minor() default 0;
}
```

The values themselves must be constant expressions or literals (such as a class literal), but not `null`.

The `Revision` annotation type could be used to annotate a class or interface—we show you how to enforce this a little later—or used by other annotation types. In particular we can redefine the `ClassInfo` annotation type to use it:

```
@interface ClassInfo {
    String created();
    String createdBy();
    String lastModified();
    String lastModifiedBy();
    Revision revision();
}
```

When we first created class Foo we might have used `ClassInfo`:

```
@ClassInfo (
    created = "Jan 31 2005",
    createdBy = "James Gosling",
    lastModified = "Jan 31 2005",
    lastModifiedBy = "James Gosling",
    revision = @Revision
)
public class Foo {
    // ...
}
```

Notice how the initialization expression for an element of an annotation type uses the annotation syntax. In this case `@Revision` initializes the revision element with the default values for `major` and `minor`. When `Foo` is later edited, the revision element would be changed accordingly, for example:

```
@ClassInfo (
    created = "Jan 31 2005",
    createdBy = "James Gosling",
    lastModified = "Feb 9 2005",
    lastModifiedBy = "Ken Arnold",
    revision = @Revision(major = 3)
)
public class Foo {
    // ...
}
```

This updates the revision to be 3.0, by specifying the major value and again allowing the minor value to default to 0.

An annotation type can have zero elements, in which case it is called a *marker annotation*—similar to a marker interface. For example, the annotation type `java.lang.Deprecated` is a marker annotation that identifies a program element that should no longer be used. The compiler can issue a warning when a program element annotated with `@Deprecated` is used, as could an annotation-aware development environment.

If an annotation type has but a single element, then that element should be named `value`. This permits some syntactic shorthand that is described in the next section.

There are further restrictions on the form of an annotation type. An annotation type may not explicitly declare that it extends another interface, but all annotation types implicitly extend the interface `Annotation`. An annotation type is not allowed to be a generic type. Finally, an annotation type is not allowed to directly, or indirectly, have an element of its own type.[3]

If an interface explicitly extends `Annotation` it is not an annotation type—and `Annotation` itself is not an annotation type. Similarly, if an interface declares that it extends an annotation type, that interface is not itself an annotation type. Extending or implementing an annotation type is pointless, but if you do it, the annotation type is just a plain interface with the declared set of methods (including those inherited from `Annotation`).

Finally, just like any other interface, an annotation type can declare constants and (implicitly static) nested types.

---

[3] This restriction is aimed at preventing the possibility of infinite recursion if an annotation type had an element of its own type with a default value. Curiously, there are no attempts to prevent a similar infinite recursion with class types.

15.3 Annotating Elements

The program elements that can be annotated are all those for which modifiers can be specified: type declarations (classes, interfaces, enums, and annotation types), field declarations, method and constructor declarations, local variable declarations, and even parameter declarations. There is also a special mechanism to annotate packages, described in Section 18.5 on page 476.

As you have seen, to annotate an element you provide the name of the annotation type being applied, preceded by @ and followed by a parenthesized list of initializers for each element of the annotation type. A given program element can only be annotated once per annotation type.

If the annotation type is a marker annotation or if all its elements have default values, then the list of initializers can be omitted. For example, you can mark a method as deprecated:

```
@Deprecated
public void badMethod() { /* ... */ }
```

Equivalently, you can just specify an empty list of initializers:

```
@Deprecated()
public void badMethod() { /* ... */ }
```

Otherwise, for each element that does not have a default value you must list an initializer, of the form *name=value,* as you have seen with ClassInfo. The order of initializers is not significant, but each element can only appear once. If an element has a default value then it need not appear, but you can include it if you want to override the default value with a specific one, as you saw in the Revision annotation type with ClassInfo.

If an element has an array type, then it is initialized with an array initializer expression. For example, an annotation to track the bug fixes applied to a class might look like this:

```
@interface BugsFixed {
    String[] bugIDs();
}
```

The intent is that as each bug is fixed, its identifier is appended to the initializer list for bugIDs. Here's how it might be used:

```
@BugsFixed(bugIDs = { "457605", "532456"})
class Foo { /* ... */ }
```

If an array has only a single element, then you can use a shorthand to initialize the array, dispensing with the braces around the array elements. For example, the first bug fixed in Foo could be annotated like this:

```
@BugsFixed(bugIDs = "457605")
```

If an annotation type, like BugsFixed, has only a single element, then naming that element value allows for some additional shorthand:

```
@interface BugsFixed {
    String[] value();
}
```

The first use of BugsFixed above can now be written simply as

```
@BugsFixed({ "457605", "532456"})
```

If there is a single initializer expression, then it is assumed to initialize an element called value. If there is no such element by that name, then you will get a compile-time error. Combining this shorthand with the shorthand for arrays with one element, you can rewrite the second use of BugsFixed to be

```
@BugsFixed("457605")
```

You can have more than one element in the annotation type and still call one of them value. If you do, and all other elements have default values, then you can still use the shorthand form to initialize the value element. However, once you have more than one initializer expression, you must explicitly name each element.

Finally, you can annotate an annotation type with itself. For example, the Documented marker annotation indicates that the program element that is annotated should have its documentation comments processed—see Chapter 19. Because Documented should itself be documented it is annotated with itself:

```
@Documented
@interface Documented { }
```

Self-annotation is quite different from having an element of the annotation type within the annotation type—which, as you know, is not permitted.

15.4 Restricting Annotation Applicability

Annotations can appear anywhere a modifier is allowed, but as you can imagine, not every annotation makes sense for every program element—consider applying ClassInfo to a method parameter! You can restrict the applicability of an annotation type by annotating it with the @Target annotation. An annotation on an annotation type is known as a *meta-annotation*.

The Target annotation type is one of a small number of annotation types defined in the java.lang.annotation package—all the types mentioned here are in that package unless otherwise stated. Target is applied to annotation types, and controls where those types are themselves applicable. It has a single element—an array of the enum type ElementType—which following convention is called value. ElementType represents the different kinds of program elements to which annotations can be applied, and defines the constants ANNOTATION_TYPE, CONSTRUCTOR, METHOD, FIELD, LOCAL_VARIABLE, PARAMETER, PACKAGE, and TYPE. The compiler will check that any annotation applied to a program element is allowed to be applied to that kind of program element.

The ClassInfo annotation type should only be applied to type declarations (classes, interfaces, enums, or annotation types), so it should be declared:

```
@Target(ElementType.TYPE)
@interface ClassInfo {
    String created();
    String createdBy();
    String lastModified();
    String lastModifiedBy();
    Revision revision();
}
```

Now if you tried to annotate a parameter declaration with ClassInfo, you'd get a compile-time error.

You can specify multiple element types when applying the Target annotation. For example, an annotation type that only applies to fields or local variables would be annotated with

```
@Target({ ElementType.FIELD, ElementType.LOCAL_VARIABLE })
```

Our Revision annotation type could also be annotated with:

```
@Target(ElementType.TYPE)
```

to restrict its applicability to type declarations. If an annotation type has no @Target meta-annotation then it is applicable anywhere.

Don't confuse the applicability of an annotation type with the accessibility of the annotation type. If an annotation is public then it can be used anywhere, but its applicability might restrict what elements it can be applied to. Conversely, you can't apply an annotation if it is inaccessible, even if you are trying to apply it to the right kind of element. Restricting the applicability of an annotation does not affect its use within other annotation types. For example, if Revision were restricted to use on local variables (not that it makes sense), that doesn't stop ClassInfo from having an element of type Revision.

15.5 Retention Policies

Annotations can serve many different purposes and may be intended for different readers. Most of the annotations you have seen are intended to be read by programmers, or perhaps a development tool. Others, such as @Deprecated, are intended for the compiler to read. In some cases a tool may need to extract the annotations from a binary representation of a class, such as to determine how an application should be deployed. And sometimes annotations will need to be inspected at runtime.

Associated with every annotation type is a retention policy that determines when the annotation can be accessed. This retention policy is defined by the RetentionPolicy enum, and is controlled by the use of the Retention meta-annotation. There are three retention policy values:

- ◆ SOURCE—Annotations exist only in the source file, and are discarded by the compiler when producing a binary representation.
- ◆ CLASS—Annotations are preserved in the binary representation of the class, but need not be available at runtime.
- ◆ RUNTIME—Annotations are preserved in the binary representation of the class and must be available at runtime via the reflection mechanism.

The default retention policy is CLASS. Regardless of the retention policy, annotations on local variables are never available in the binary representation or at runtime. There is no place to store the information in the binary representation.

The reflection methods for accessing annotations at runtime are discussed in Section 16.2 on page 414. In essence, for each annotated element, the runtime system creates an object that implements the interface defined by the annotation type. You get the values of the annotation elements for that program element by invoking the corresponding method on that object.

15.6 Working with Annotations

Annotations can be very powerful, but they can easily be misused. It is easy to achieve annotation-overload when the number and verbosity of the annotations totally obscure the code itself. Annotations should be used sparingly and wisely.

The second problem with annotations is that anyone can define their own. A key benefit of annotations is their suitability for automatic analysis, generally via annotation processing tools, or APTs. But automation is most helpful if there are common, standard annotations. While you have seen how annotation types can be defined, in practice very few programmers should need to define their own types. There are currently only a few defined annotation types:[4]

- The meta-annotations @Target and @Retention, which you have seen.

- The @Deprecated and @Documented annotations, which you have also seen.

- The @Inherited meta-annotation that indicates an annotation should be inherited. For example, if a class Foo is queried for a specific annotation type that is not present on Foo, but that annotation type has the @Inherited meta-annotation, then Foo's superclass will be queried, and so forth.

- The @Override annotation, which informs the compiler that a method is meant to override an inherited method from a superclass. This allows the compiler to warn you if you mistakenly overload the method instead of overriding it (a common mistake).

- The @SuppressWarnings annotation tells the compiler to ignore certain warnings, as defined by the strings used to initialize the annotation. Unfortunately, there is no predefined set of warning strings, meaning that interoperability between different compilers could be a problem.

Without standards in this area, the effective use of annotations could be stifled.

Finally, another potential problem with annotations is that they could be misused to change the semantics of the code they are applied to. According to the *Java Language Specification,* "annotations are not permitted to affect the semantics of programs in the Java programming language in any way." Indeed, any unrecognized annotations should just be ignored by the compiler, the virtual machine, and any other annotation processing tool. However, it is easy to see how, with a suitable processing tool, annotations could be used to achieve a style of metaprogramming, that allows people to create specialized dialects of the Java programming language to meet their own specific needs. If programs become dependent on specialized annotation support, then the portability benefits of the Java platform will be lost.

> *I don't care who does the electin' as long as I get to do the nominatin'.*
> —Boss Tweed

---

[4]   Under the Java Community Process, JSR 250 is defining common annotations for future use.

CHAPTER 16

Reflection

*A sense of humor keen enough to show a man his own absurdities
will keep him from the commission of all sins,
or nearly all, save those that are worth committing.*
—Samuel Butler

THE package `java.lang.reflect` contains the *reflection* package, the classes you can use to examine a type in detail. You can write a complete type browser using these classes, or you can write an application that interprets code that a user writes, turning that code into actual uses of classes, creation of objects, invocations of methods, and so on. Almost all the types mentioned in this discussion on reflection are contained in the package `java.lang.reflect`, except for the classes `Class` and `Package`, which are part of the package `java.lang`, and `Annotation`, which is part of the `java.lang.annotation` package.

Reflection starts with a `Class` object. From the `Class` object you can obtain a complete list of members of the class, find out all the types of the class (the interfaces it implements, the classes it extends), and find out information about the class itself, such as the modifiers applied to it (`public`, `abstract`, `final`, and so on) or the package it is contained in. Reflection is also sometimes called *introspection;* both terms use the metaphor of asking the type to look at itself and tell you something. These capabilities can be used by type browsers to show the structure of an application. They also form the first step for you to dynamically create and manipulate objects.

Here's a simple example of a "type browser." Given the name of a class this program shows the class's immediate superclass and lists all the public methods it declares:

```
import java.lang.reflect.*;
import static java.lang.System.out;
import static java.lang.System.err;
```

```
public class SimpleClassDesc {
    public static void main(String[] args) {
        Class type = null;
        try {
            type = Class.forName(args[0]);
        } catch (ClassNotFoundException e) {
            err.println(e);
            return;
        }

        out.print("class " + type.getSimpleName());
        Class superclass = type.getSuperclass();
        if (superclass != null)
            out.println(" extends " +
                        superclass.getCanonicalName());
        else
            out.println();

        Method[] methods = type.getDeclaredMethods();
        for (Method m : methods)
            if (Modifier.isPublic(m.getModifiers()))
                out.println("    " + m);
    }
}
```

Given the fully qualified name of a class (such java.lang.String) the program first tries to obtain a Class object for that class, using the static method Class.forName. If the class can't be found an exception is thrown which the program catches and reports. Otherwise, the simple name of the class—String, for example—is printed. Next the Class object is asked for its superclass's Class object. As long as the named class is not Object and is a class rather than an interface, getSuperclass will return a superclass's Class object. The name of the super class is printed in full using getCanonicalName (there are a number of ways to name a class as you'll see in Section 16.1.4 on page 411). Next, the Class object is asked for all the methods that it declares. The declared methods include all methods actually declared in the class but none that are inherited. Since we're only interested in public methods, we ask the Method object for the method's modifiers and ask the Modifier class if those modifiers include public. If so the method is printed, otherwise it is ignored. Here's the output when given the name of the Attr class from page 76:

```
class Attr extends java.lang.Object
  public java.lang.String Attr.getName()
  public java.lang.String Attr.toString()
  public java.lang.Object Attr.getValue()
  public java.lang.Object Attr.setValue(java.lang.Object)
```

Over the next few pages you'll see how to perform a much more detailed examination of a class's supertypes and its members.

Reflection also allows you to write code that performs actions that you can more simply execute directly in code if you know what you are doing. Given the name of a class (which may not have existed when the program was written) you can obtain a Class object and use that Class object to create new instances of that class. You can interact with those objects just as you would with an object created via new. You can, for example, invoke a method using reflection, as you will soon see, but it is much harder to understand than a direct method invocation. You should use reflection only when you have exhausted all other object-oriented design mechanisms. For example, you should not use a Method object as a "method pointer," because interfaces and abstract classes are better tools. There are times when reflection is necessary—usually when you're interpreting or displaying some other code—but use more direct means whenever possible.

Figure 16–1 (see next page) shows the classes and interfaces that support introspection. At the top, Type represents all types that can exist in a Java program—it is a marker interface containing no methods. All concrete types are represented by an instance of class Class. The other types pertain to generic types: parameterized types, type variables, wildcards, and generic arrays. The Constructor, Method, and Field classes represent constructors, methods and fields, respectively. These are all Member instances and are also subclasses of AccessibleObject (which pertains to access control). The classes Class, Constructor, and Method are all GenericDeclaration instances because they can be declared in a generic way. Finally, the class Class, the AccessibleObject subclasses, and the Package class are all instances of AnnotatedElement because they can have annotations applied to them.

16.1 The Class Class

There is a Class object for every type. This includes each class, enum, interface, annotation, array, and the primitive types. There is also a special Class object representing the keyword void. These objects can be used for basic queries about the type and, for the reference types, to create new objects of that type.

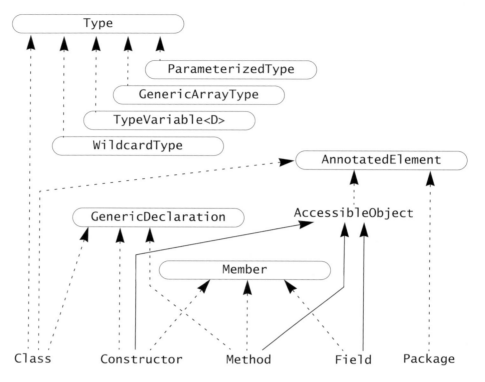

FIGURE 16–1: *The Introspection Hierarchy*

The Class class is the starting point for reflection. It also provides a tool to manipulate classes, primarily for creating objects of types whose names are specified by strings, and for loading classes using specialized techniques, such as across the network. We look in more detail at class loading in Section 16.13 on page 435.

You get a Class object in four ways: ask an object for its Class object using its getClass method; use a class literal (the name of the class followed by .class, as in String.class); look it up by its fully qualified name (all packages included) using the static method Class.forName; or get it from one of the reflection methods that return Class objects for nested classes and interfaces (such as Class.getClasses).

16.1.1 Type Tokens

Class is a generic class, declared as Class<T>. Each Class object for a reference type is of a parameterized type corresponding to the class it represents. For example, the type of String.class is Class<String>, the type of Integer.class is Class<Integer>, and so forth. The type of the Class object for a primitive type is the same type as that of its corresponding wrapper class. For example, the type of int.class is Class<Integer>, but note that int.class and Integer.class are two different instances of the same type of class. Parameterized types all share the Class object of their raw type—for example, the Class object for List<Integer> is the same as that for List<String> and the same as that for List.class, and its type is Class<List>.

A parameterized Class type is known as the *type token* for a given class. The easiest way to obtain a type token is to use a class literal, such as String.class, since this provides you with the exact type token. In contrast, Class.forName is declared to return a wildcard, Class<?>, that represents an unidentified type token—to use this type token effectively you need to establish its actual type, as you'll soon see. The Object method getClass returns the type token for the type of object it is invoked on, and its return type is also Class<?>, another wildcard. However, getClass receives special treatment by the compiler: If getClass is invoked on a reference with static type T, then the compiler treats the return type of getClass as being Class<? extends T>.[1] So this works:

```
String str = "Hello";
Class<String> c1 = String.class;  // exact type token
Class<? extends String> c2 =
    str.getClass();               // compiler magic
```

but this won't compile:

```
Class<? extends String> c3 =
    Class.forName("java.lang.String");  // INVALID
```

Taking an unknown type token Class<?> and turning it into a type token of a known type is a common action when working with reflection. What you need is something that acts like a cast, but as you already know, you can't perform casts involving parameterized types. The solution to this is another piece of "magic" in the shape of the asSubclass method of class Class:

public <T> Class<? extends T> **asSubclass(Class<T> subType)**

> Returns the Class object on which it is invoked, after casting it to represent a subclass of the given Class object. If the current Class object does not

---

[1]   It actually treats it as being Class<? extends S>, where S is the erasure of T. Parameterized types share the same Class object so the erasure is used to remove any parameterized types from the wildcard's bounds. For example, given List<String> l, then l.getClass() has the type Class<? extends List>.

represent a type that is a subtype of `subType`'s type (or `subType` itself), then `ClassCastException` is thrown.

The `asSubclass` method doesn't change the `Class` object at all; it simply changes the type of the expression it is invoked on, so we can use the additional type information—just as a cast does. For example, here's how you can use `asSubclass` with `forName` to fix the previous problem:

```
Class<? extends String> c3 =
    Class.forName("java.lang.String").
        asSubclass(String.class);          // OK
```

Note that you can't convert the unknown type token to be exactly `Class<String>`, but having `Class<? extends String>` should be sufficient. Of course, `String` is not a practical example for using reflection. A more typical example would be when you are loading an unknown class that implements a known interface and you want to create an instance of that class; you'll see an example of this in the Game class on page 436.

16.1.2 Class Inspection

The `Class` class provides a number of methods for obtaining information about a particular class. Some of these provide information on the type of the class—the interfaces it implements, the class it extends—and others return information on the members of the class, including nested classes and interfaces. You can ask if a class represents an interface or an array, or whether a particular object is an instance of that class. We look at these different methods over the next few pages.

The most basic `Class` methods are those that walk the type hierarchy, displaying information about the interfaces implemented and the classes extended. As an example, this program prints the complete type hierarchy of the type represented by a string passed as an argument:

```
import java.lang.reflect.*;

public class TypeDesc {
    public static void main(String[] args) {
        TypeDesc desc = new TypeDesc();
        for (String name : args) {
            try {
                Class<?> startClass = Class.forName(name);
                desc.printType(startClass, 0, basic);
            } catch (ClassNotFoundException e) {
                System.err.println(e);  // report the error
```

```
            }
        }
    }

    // by default print on standard output
    private java.io.PrintStream out = System.out;

    // used in printType() for labeling type names
    private static String[]
        basic   = { "class",   "interface",
                    "enum",    "annotation"  },
        supercl = { "extends", "implements" },
        iFace   = { null,      "extends"  };

    private void printType(
        Type type, int depth, String[] labels)
    {
        if (type == null) // stop recursion -- no supertype
            return;

        // turn the Type into a Class object
        Class<?> cls = null;
        if (type instanceof Class<?>)
            cls = (Class<?>) type;
        else if (type instanceof ParameterizedType)
            cls = (Class<?>)
                ((ParameterizedType)type).getRawType();
        else
            throw new Error("Unexpected non-class type");

        // print this type
        for (int i = 0; i < depth; i++)
            out.print("  ");
        int kind = cls.isAnnotation() ? 3 :
            cls.isEnum() ? 2 :
            cls.isInterface() ? 1 : 0;
        out.print(labels[kind] + " ");
        out.print(cls.getCanonicalName());

        // print generic type parameters if present
        TypeVariable<?>[] params = cls.getTypeParameters();
```

```
            if (params.length > 0) {
                out.print('<');
                for (TypeVariable<?> param : params) {
                    out.print(param.getName());
                    out.print(", ");
                }
                out.println("\b\b>");
            }
            else
                out.println();

            // print out all interfaces this class implements
            Type[] interfaces = cls.getGenericInterfaces();
            for (Type iface : interfaces) {
                printType(iface, depth + 1,
                        cls.isInterface() ? iFace : supercl);
            }
            // recurse on the superclass
            printType(cls.getGenericSuperclass(),
                    depth + 1, supercl);
        }
    }
```

This program loops through the names provided on the command line, obtains the
Class object for each named type and invokes printType on each of them. It
must do this inside a try block in case there is no class of the specified name.
Here is its output when invoked on the utility class java.util.HashMap:

```
class java.util.HashMap<K, V>
   implements java.util.Map<K, V>
   implements java.lang.Cloneable
   implements java.io.Serializable
   extends java.util.AbstractMap<K, V>
     implements java.util.Map<K, V>
     extends java.lang.Object
```

After the main method is the declaration of the output stream to use, by
default System.out. The String arrays are described shortly.

The printType method prints its own type parameter's description and then
invokes itself recursively to print the description of type's supertypes. Because
we initially have general Type objects, we first have to convert them to Class
objects. The depth parameter keeps track of how far up the type hierarchy it has

climbed, indenting each description line according to its depth. The depth is incremented at each recursion level. The `labels` array specifies how to label the class—`labels[0]` is the label if the type is a class; `labels[1]` is for interfaces; `labels[2]` for enums; and `labels[3]` for annotation types. Note the order in which we check what kind of type we have—an enum type is a class, and an annotation type is an interface, so we have to check for these more specific kinds of type first.

Three arrays are defined for these labels: `basic` is used at the top level, `supercl` is used for superclasses, and `iFace` is used for superinterfaces of interfaces, which extend, not implement, each other. After we print the right prefix, we use `getCanonicalName` to print the full name of the type. The `Class` class provides a `toString` method, but it already adds "class" or "interface" in front. We want to control the prefix, so we must create our own implementation. We look more at class names a little later.

Next, the type is examined to see if it is a generic type. All classes implement `GenericDeclaration`, which defines the single method `getTypeParameters` that returns an array of `TypeVariable` objects. If we have one or more type parameters then we print each of their names between angle brackets, just as they would appear in your source code.

After printing the type description, `printType` invokes itself recursively, first on all the interfaces that the original type implements and then on the superclass this type extends (if any), passing the appropriate label array to each. Eventually, it reaches the `Class` object for `Object`, which implements no interfaces and whose `getGenericSuperclass` method returns `null`, and the recursion ends.

Some simple query methods, a few of which you saw in the example, examine the kind of `Class` object that you are dealing with:

`public boolean` **`isEnum()`**
> Returns `true` if this `Class` object represents an enum.

`public boolean` **`isInterface()`**
> Returns `true` if this `Class` object represents an interface (which includes annotation types).

`public boolean` **`isAnnotation()`**
> Returns `true` if this `Class` object represents an annotation type.

`public boolean` **`isArray()`**
> Returns `true` if this `Class` object represents an array.

`public boolean` **`isPrimitive()`**
> Returns `true` if this `Class` object is one of the `Class` objects representing the eight primitive types or `void`.

`public boolean` **`isSynthetic()`**

Returns `true` if this `Class` object represents a synthetic type introduced by the compiler. A synthetic program element is anything for which there does not exist a corresponding construct in the source code.

`public int` **`getModifiers()`**

Returns the modifiers for the type, encoded as an integer. The value should be decoded using the constants and methods of class `Modifier`; see Section 16.3 on page 416. Type modifiers include the access modifiers (`public`, `protected`, `private`) as well as `abstract`, `final`, and `static`. For convenience, whether a type is an interface is also encoded as a modifier. Primitive types are always `public` and `final`. Array types are always `final` and have the same access modifier as their component type. In this context, an annotation is not considered a modifier because this encoding scheme predates the addition of annotations to the language.

You can also ask whether you have a top-level type or a nested type, and if nested, some information about which kind of nested type:

`public boolean` **`isMemberClass()`**

Returns `true` if this `Class` object represents a type that is a member of another type—that is, it is a nested type. If this method returns `false`, then you have a top-level type. Despite the name, this method applies to nested interfaces, as well as nested classes.

`public boolean` **`isLocalClass()`**

Returns `true` if this class represents a local inner class.

`public boolean` **`isAnonymousClass()`**

Returns `true` if this class represents an anonymous inner class.

Note that there is no way to determine if a member class is a static nested class or an inner class.

The example showed the two methods you can use to find out where a type fits in the type hierarchy:

`public Type[]` **`getGenericInterfaces()`**

Returns an array of `Type` objects for each of the interfaces implemented by this type. If no interfaces are implemented you will get a zero-length array. If an implemented interface is a parameterized type, then the `Type` object will be an instance of `ParameterizedType`; otherwise, the `Type` object will be a `Class` object.

`public Type` **`getGenericSuperclass()`**

Returns the `Type` object for the superclass of this type. This returns `null` if this `Class` object represents the `Object` class, an interface, `void`, or primitive type, since these have no superclass. If this Class object represents an array, the Class object for Object is returned. By invoking this recursively you can determine all superclasses of a class. If the superclass is a parameterized type, the Type object will be an instance of ParameterizedType; otherwise, the Type object will be a Class object.

The legacy methods getInterfaces and getSuperclass are similar to the above except they return Class objects instead of Type objects. Any parameterized type is returned as the Class object for the corresponding raw type.

Given all the different kinds of types there are, some methods only apply to a subset of those different kinds:

public Class<?> **getComponentType()**
Returns the Class object representing the component type of the array represented by this Class object. If this Class object doesn't represent an array, null is returned. For example, given an array of int, the getClass method will return a Class object for which isArray returns true and whose getComponentType method returns the same object as int.class.

public T[] **getEnumConstants()**
Returns the elements of this enum class, or null if this Class object does not represent an enum.

public Class<?> **getDeclaringClass()**
Returns the Class object for the type in which this nested type was declared as a *member.* If this type is not a nested member type, null is returned. For example, when invoked on a local inner class or an anonymous inner class, this method returns null.

public Class<?> **getEnclosingClass()**
Returns the Class object for the enclosing type in which this type was declared. If this type is a top-level type, null is returned.

public Constructor<?> **getEnclosingConstructor()**
Returns the Constructor object (discussed shortly) for the constructor in which this local or anonymous inner class was declared. If this isn't a local or anonymous inner class declared in a constructor, then null is returned.

public Method **getEnclosingMethod()**
Returns the Method object (discussed shortly) for the method in which this local or anonymous inner class was declared. If this isn't a local or anonymous inner class declared in a method, then null is returned.

Exercise 16.1: Modify TypeDesc to skip printing anything for the Object class. It is redundant because everything ultimately extends it. Use the reference for the Class object for the Object type.

Exercise 16.2: Modify `TypeDesc` to show whether the named type is a nested type, and if so, what other type it is nested within.

16.1.3 Examining Class Members

The `Class` class contains a set of methods you can use to examine the class's components: its fields, methods, constructors, and nested types. Special types are defined to represent each of these, which you will learn about in detail in later sections: `Field` objects for fields, `Method` objects for methods, `Constructor` objects for constructors, and for nested types, the `Class` objects you have already seen.

These methods come in four variants depending on whether you want all members or a particular member, only public members or any members, only members declared in the current class or inherited members as well.

You can request all the public members of a specific kind that are either declared in the class (interface) or inherited, by using one of the following:[2]

```
public Constructor[] getConstructors()
public Field[] getFields()
public Method[] getMethods()
public Class[] getClasses()
```

Because constructors are not inherited, `getConstructors` returns `Constructor` objects only for public constructors declared in the current class.

You can also ask for the members of a specific kind that are actually declared in the class (interface), as opposed to being inherited. Such members need not be public:

```
public Constructor[] getDeclaredConstructors()
public Field[] getDeclaredFields()
public Method[] getDeclaredMethods()
public Class[] getDeclaredClasses()
```

In each case, if there is no member of that kind, you will get an empty array. The `getClasses` and `getDeclaredClasses` methods return both nested classes and nested interfaces.

Requesting a particular member requires you to supply further information. For nested types this is simply the name of the nested type and, in fact, there are

---

[2] A number of methods return arrays of raw types, such as `Class[]` or `Constructor[]`. These methods should have been generified to return wildcard types: `Class<?>[]` or `Constructor<?>[]`.

no special methods to do this because `Class.forName` can be used for this purpose. Particular fields are requested using their name:

```
public Field getField(String name)
public Field getDeclaredField(String name)
```

The first form finds a public field that is either declared or inherited, while the second finds only a declared field that need not be public. If the named field does not exist, a `NoSuchFieldException` is thrown. Note that the implicit length field of an array is not returned when these methods are invoked on an array type.

Particular methods are identified by their signature—their name and a sequence of `Class` objects representing the number and type of their parameters. Remember that for a varargs method the last parameter will actually be an array.

```
public Method
    getMethod(String name, Class... parameterTypes)
public Method
    getDeclaredMethod(String name, Class... parameterTypes)
```

Similarly, constructors are identified by their parameter number and types:

```
public Constructor<T>
    getConstructor(Class... parameterTypes)
public Constructor<T>
    getDeclaredConstructor(Class... parameterTypes)
```

In both cases, if the specified method or constructor does not exist, you will get a `NoSuchMethodException`.

Note that when you ask for a single constructor you get a parameterized constructor type, `Constructor<T>`, that matches the type of the `Class` object, while the array returned for a group of constructors is not parameterized by T. This is because you can't create a generic array. Any constructor extracted from the array is essentially of an unknown kind, but this only affects use of the `invoke` method, which we discuss a little later.

All the above methods require a security check before they can proceed and so will interact with any installed security manager—see "Security" on page 677. If no security manager is installed then all these methods will be allowed. Typically, security managers will allow any code to invoke methods that request information on the public members of a type—this enforces the normal language level access rules. However, access to non-public member information will usually be restricted to privileged code within the system. Note that the only distinction made is between public and non-public members—security managers do not have enough information to enforce protected or package-level access. If access is not allowed, a `SecurityException` is thrown.

The following program lists the public fields, methods, and constructors of a given class:

```java
import java.lang.reflect.*;

public class ClassContents {
    public static void main(String[] args) {
        try {
            Class<?> c = Class.forName(args[0]);
            System.out.println(c);
            printMembers(c.getFields());
            printMembers(c.getConstructors());
            printMembers(c.getMethods());
        } catch (ClassNotFoundException e) {
            System.out.println("unknown class: " + args[0]);
        }
    }

    private static void printMembers(Member[] mems) {
        for (Member m : mems) {
            if (m.getDeclaringClass() == Object.class)
                continue;
            String decl = m.toString();
            System.out.print("    ");
            System.out.println(strip(decl, "java.lang."));
        }
    }

    // ... definition of strip ...
}
```

We first get the Class object for the named class. We then get and print the arrays of member objects that represent all the public fields, constructors, and methods of the class. The printMembers method uses the Member object's toString method to get a string that describes the member, skipping members that are inherited from Object (using getDeclaringClass to see which class the member belongs to) since these are present in all classes and so are not very useful to repeat each time (`strip` removes any leading `"java.lang."` from the name). Here is the output when the program is run on the `Attr` class from page 76:

```
class Attr
    public Attr(String)
    public Attr(String, Object)
    public String Attr.toString()
    public String Attr.getName()
    public Object Attr.getValue()
    public Object Attr.setValue(Object)
```

Exercise 16.3: Modify `ClassContents` to show information for all declared and all public inherited members. Make sure you don't list anything twice.

16.1.4 Naming Classes

The `Class` objects in the `TypeDesc` program are obtained using the static method `Class.forName`, which takes a string argument and returns a `Class` object for the type with that name. The name must be the *binary name* of a class or interface, or else be a specially named array type—these are defined below.

Every type is represented by a number of different names. The actual class or interface name is the *simple name* of the type. This is the shortest name you could write in your program to represent a given type. For example, the simple name of `java.lang.Object` is `Object`, the simple name of the nested `Entry` interface in the `java.util.Map` interface is `Entry`, the simple name of the type representing an array of `Object` instances is `Object[]`, and the simple name of an array of `int` is `int[]`. All types except for anonymous inner classes have simple names. You can get the simple name of a type from the `Class` method `getSimpleName`.

The *canonical name* of a type is its full name, as you would write it in your programs, including, if applicable, the package and enclosing type in which the type was *declared*. For example, the canonical name of `Object` is `java.lang.Object`; for the nested `Entry` interface it is `java.util.Map.Entry`; for an array of `Object` instances it is `java.lang.Object[]`; and for an array of `int` is `int[]`. In more specific terms, the canonical name of a top-level class or interface is its package name followed by dot, followed by its simple name. The canonical name of a nested type is the canonical name of the type in which it is declared, followed by dot, followed by its simple name. The canonical name of an array type is the canonical name of its element type followed by `[]`. Local inner classes and anonymous inner classes do not have canonical names. You can get the canonical name of a type from the `Class` method `getCanonicalName`.

The canonical name is an example of a *fully qualified name*—the simple name qualified by the package and enclosing type, if applicable. While simple names might be ambiguous in a given context, a fully qualified name uniquely determines a type. Each type has only one canonical name, but nested types (and so arrays of nested types) can have multiple fully qualified names. For example, the `java.util.SortedMap` interface extends `java.util.Map` and inherits the nested `Entry` interface. Consequently, you can identify the `Entry` type by the fully qualified name `java.util.SortedMap.Entry`.

The *binary name* of a class or interface (not array) is a name used to communicate with the virtual machine, such as by passing it to `Class.forName` to ask the virtual machine for a specific `Class` object. The binary name of a top-level class or interface is its canonical name. For nested types there is a special naming convention, as you learned in "Implementation of Nested Types" on page 149. Static nested types and inner classes (excluding local and anonymous inner classes) have a binary name that consists of the binary name of their immediately enclosing type, followed by $ and the simple name of the nested or inner type. For example, the binary name of the `Entry` interface is `java.util.Map$Entry`. For local inner classes, the binary name is the binary name of the enclosing class, followed by $, then a number, and then its simple name. For an anonymous inner class, the binary name is the binary name of the enclosing class, followed by $ and a number.[3] You get the binary name of a type from the `Class` method `getName`. This binary name is what `forName` expects as a class or interface name.

For their names, array types have a special notation, known as *internal format* because it is the format used inside the virtual machine. But for some reason this notation is *not* considered a binary name. This notation consists of a code representing the component type of the array, preceded by the character [. The component types are encoded as follows:

B	byte
C	char
D	double
F	float
I	int
J	long
L*classname*;	class or interface
S	short
Z	boolean

---

[3] Since the binary name is not uniquely specified for local and anonymous classes, you cannot use reflection to instantiate these classes in a portable way. Fortunately, it is exceedingly rare that you would want to.

For example, an array of `int` is named `[I`, while an array of `Object` is named `[Ljava.lang.Object;` (note the trailing semicolon). A multidimensional array is just an array whose component type is an array, so, for example, a type declared as `int[][]` is named `[[I`—an array whose component type is named `[I`. These internal format names can be passed to `forName` to obtain the class objects for array types, and it is this name that `getName` returns for array types.

For primitive types and void, the simple name, canonical name, and binary name are all the same—the keyword that presents that type, such as `int`, `float`, or `void`—and all the name methods return the same name. For these types, `Class` objects cannot be obtained from `forName`. You must use the class literals, such as `int.class`, or the `TYPE` field of the appropriate wrapper class, such as `Void.TYPE`. If a name representing one of these types is used with `forName`, it is assumed to be a user-defined class or interface and is unlikely to be found.

16.1.5 Obtaining Class Objects by Name

The `forName` method we have been using is a simpler form of the more general `forName` method:

`public static Class<?> `**`forName(String name, boolean initialize, ClassLoader loader)`**` throws ClassNotFoundException`
> Returns the `Class` object associated with the named class or interface, using the given class loader. Given the binary name for a class or interface (in the same format returned by `getName`) or an array name in internal format, this method attempts to locate, load, and link the class or interface. The specified class loader is used to load the class or interface. If `loader` is `null`, the class is loaded through the system class loader. The class is initialized only if `initialize` is `true` and it has not previously been initialized. For array types, the component type of the array is loaded, but not initialized.

As this method description indicates, obtaining the `Class` object for a class can involve loading, linking, and initializing the class—a fairly complex process that is described further in Section 16.13 on page 435. The simple `Class.forName` method uses the current class loader—the one that loaded the current class in which the `forName` invocation appears—and initializes the class if needed. If the class cannot be found then the checked exception `ClassNotFoundException` is thrown. The exception can contain a nested exception that describes the problem, which you can get from invoking `getCause` on the exception object. This will be either the nested exception or `null`. Because of the complexities of loading, linking, and initializing a class, these methods can also throw the unchecked exceptions `LinkageError` and `ExceptionInInitializerError`.

16.1.6 Runtime Type Queries

When writing your programs you can check the type of an object by using `instanceof` or change the type of an expression with a cast. In both cases you need to know the name of the type involved so you can write it in the code. When working with reflection, you have only `Class` objects to work with, so operators like `instanceof` and casts can't be used. The class `Class` provides several methods that provide functionality analogous to the language level operators:

`public boolean` **`isInstance(Object obj)`**
> Determines if `obj` is assignment compatible with this class. This is the dynamic equivalent of the `instanceof` operator. It returns `true` if `obj` could be assigned to a variable of the type represented by this `Class` object; and `false` otherwise.

`public T` **`cast(Object obj)`**
> Casts the object `obj` to the type represented by this `Class` object. If the cast fails then `ClassCastException` is thrown. This is needed in some rare circumstances when the type you want to cast to is represented by a type parameter and so you can't use an actual language-level cast.

`public boolean` **`isAssignableFrom(Class<?> type)`**
> Returns `true` if this `Class` object represents a supertype of `type` or `type` itself; otherwise returns `false`.

16.2 Annotation Queries

You can ask about the annotations applied to a class or interface using methods that are similar to those used for asking about members, but which differ slightly in the details. These methods are all part of the `AnnotatedElement` interface. `AnnotedElement` is implemented by all the reflection classes that represent program elements: `Class`, `Field`, `Method`, `Constructor`, and `Package`. The discussion here applies to all these `AnnotatedElement` instances.

The annotation queries can only provide information on those annotations that are available at runtime—that is, those annotations with a retention policy of `RetentionPolicy.RUNTIME` (see "Retention Policies" on page 395).

You can ask for all the annotations present on an element, whether declared directly or inherited, by using `getAnnotations`, which returns an array of `Annotation` instances. Or you can ask for only the directly applied annotations using `getDeclaredAnnotations`, which also returns an array of `Annotation` instances. You can ask for a specific annotation using `getAnnotation`, which takes the type of the annotation as an argument and returns the `Annotation` object or `null` if it is not present. You can ask whether a specific annotation type is present on an element using the `boolean isAnnotationPresent` method. In contrast to the similarly named methods for querying members, there is no notion of public versus non-public annotations, and also no security checks.

The annotation instances that are returned are proxy objects that implement the interface defined by a given annotation type. The methods of the annotation type can be invoked to obtain the annotation values for each annotation element. For example, assuming our `BugsFixed` annotation type (see page 392) had a runtime retention policy, then given

```
@BugsFixed( { "457605", "532456"} )
class Foo { /* ... */ }
```

the code

```
Class<Foo> cls = Foo.class;
BugsFixed bugsFixed =
    (BugsFixed) cls.getAnnotation(BugsFixed.class);
String[] bugIds = bugsFixed.value();
for (String id : bugIds)
    System.out.println(id);
```

would print

```
457605
532456
```

If an annotation method represents an annotation element with a `Class` type, and that class can not be found at runtime, then you will get a `TypeNotPresentException` (which is an unchecked exception that is analogous to `ClassNotFoundException`).

Since the annotation type that is available at runtime could be different from the annotation type used to annotate the class being inspected, it is possible that the two uses of the type are incompatible. If this occurs, then trying to access an element of the annotation may throw an `AnnotationTypeMismatchException` or `IncompleteAnnotationException`. If an element type is an enum and the enum constant in the annotation is no longer present in the enum, then an `EnumConstantNotPresentException` is thrown.

Exercise 16.4: Write a program that prints all the available annotations applied to a given type. (Only annotations with a retention policy of `RUNTIME` will be available.)

Exercise 16.5: Expand ClassContents to include the available annotation information for each member.

16.3   The Modifier Class

The Modifier class defines int constants for all non-annotation modifiers: ABSTRACT, FINAL, INTERFACE, NATIVE, PRIVATE, PROTECTED, PUBLIC, STATIC, STRICT, SYNCHRONIZED, TRANSIENT, and VOLATILE. For each constant there is a corresponding query method is*Mod*(int modifiers) that returns true if modifier *mod* is present in the specified value. For example, if a field is declared

```
public static final int OAK = 0;
```

the value returned by its Field object's getModifiers method would be

```
Modifier.PUBLIC | Modifier.STATIC | Modifier.FINAL
```

The strictfp modifier is reflected by the constant STRICT. If code or a class is to be evaluated in strict floating point (see "Strict and Non-Strict Floating-Point Arithmetic" on page 203), the modifiers for the method, class, or interface will include the STRICT flag.

The query methods can be used to ask questions in a more symbolic fashion. For example, the expression

```
Modifier.isPrivate(field.getModifiers())
```

is equivalent to the more opaque expression

```
(field.getModifiers() & Modifier.PRIVATE) != 0
```

16.4   The Member classes

The classes Field, Constructor, and Method all implement the interface Member, which has four methods for properties that all members share:

Class **getDeclaringClass()**
> Returns the Class object for the class in which this member is declared.

String **getName()**
> Returns the name of this member.

int **getModifiers()**
> Returns the language modifiers for the member encoded as an integer. This value should be decoded using the Modifier class.

boolean `isSynthetic()`
>   Returns `true` if this member is a synthetic member that was created by the compiler. For example, synthetic fields are often created in an inner class to hold a reference to the enclosing instance, and synthetic "bridge" methods are generated to support generic types—see Section A.3.1 on page 745.

Although a class or interface can be a member of another class, for historical reasons the class `Class` does not implement `Member`, although it supports methods of the same name and contract.

The `toString` method of all `Member` classes includes the complete declaration for the member, similar to how it would appear in your source code, including modifiers, type, and parameter types (where applicable). For historical reasons, `toString` does not include generic type information. The `toGenericString` method provides a more complete representation of the declaration of a member, including type parameters, and all use of parameterized types and type variables. For methods and constructors, the `throws` list is also included in the string.

16.5 Access Checking and `AccessibleObject`

The classes `Field`, `Constructor`, and `Method` are also all subclasses of the class `AccessibleObject`, which lets you enable or disable the checking of the language-level access modifiers, such as `public` and `private`. Normally, attempts to use reflection to access a member are subject to the same access checks that would be required for regular, explicit code—for example, if you cannot access a field directly in code, you cannot access it indirectly via reflection. You can disable this check by invoking `setAccessible` on the object with a value of `true`—the object is now accessible, regardless of language-level access control. This would be required, for example, if you were writing a debugger. The methods are:

public void `setAccessible(boolean flag)`
>   Sets the accessible flag for this object to the indicated boolean value. A value of `true` means that the object should suppress language-level access control (and so will always be accessible); `false` means the object should enforce language-level access control. If you are not allowed to change the accessibility of an object a `SecurityException` is thrown.

public static void
>   `setAccessible(AccessibleObject[] array, boolean flag)`
>   A convenience method that sets the accessible flag for an array of objects. If setting the flag of an object throws a `SecurityException` only objects earlier in the array will have their flags set to the given value, and all other objects are unchanged.

```
public boolean isAccessible()
```
    Returns the current value of the accessible flag for this object.

16.6 The Field Class

The Field class defines methods for asking the type of a field and for setting and getting the value of the field. Combined with the inherited Member methods, this allows you to find out everything about the field declaration and to manipulate the field of a specific object or class.

    The getGenericType method returns the instance of Type that represents the field's declared type. For a plain type, such as String or int, this returns the associated Class object—String.class and int.class, respectively. For a parameterized type like List<String>, it will return a ParameterizedType instance. For a type variable like T, it will return a TypeVariable instance.

    The getType legacy method returns the Class object for the type of the field. For plain types this acts the same as getGenericType. If the field's declared type is a parameterized type, then getType will return the class object for the erasure of the parameterized type—that is, the class object for the raw type. For example, for a field declared as List<String>, getType will return List.class. If the field's declared type is a type variable, then getType will return the class object for the erasure of the type variable. For example, given class Foo<T>, for a field declared with type T, getType would return Object.class. If Foo were declared as Foo<T extends Number>, then getType would return Number.class.

    You can ask whether a field is an enum constant using isEnumConstant. You can also get and set the value of a field using the get and set methods. There is a general-purpose form of these methods that take Object arguments and return Object values, and more specific forms that deal directly with primitive types. All of these methods take an argument specifying which object to operate on. For static fields the object is ignored and can be null. The following method prints the value of a short field of an object:

```
public static void printShortField(Object o, String name)
    throws NoSuchFieldException, IllegalAccessException
{
    Field field = o.getClass().getField(name);
    short value = (Short) field.get(o);
    System.out.println(value);
}
```

The return value of get is whatever object the field references or, if the field is a primitive type, a wrapper object of the appropriate type. For our short field, get returns a Short object that contains the value of the field—that value is automatically unboxed for storing in the local variable value.

The set method can be used in a similar way. A method to set a short field to a provided value might look like this:

```
public static void
    setShortField(Object o, String name, short nv)
    throws NoSuchFieldException, IllegalAccessException
{
    Field field = o.getClass().getField(name);
    field.set(o, nv);
}
```

Although set takes an Object parameter, we can pass a short directly and let a boxing conversion wrap it in a Short object.

If the field of the specified object is not accessible and access control is being enforced, an IllegalAccessException is thrown. If the passed object does not have a type that declares the underlying field, an IllegalArgumentException is thrown. If the field is non-static and the passed object reference is null, a NullPointerException is thrown. Accessing a static field can require initializing a class, so it is also possible for an ExceptionInInitializerError to be thrown.

The Field class also has specific methods for getting and setting primitive types. You can invoke get*PrimitiveType* and set*PrimitiveType* on a Field object, where *PrimitiveType* is the primitive type name (with an initial upper-case letter). The get example just shown could have used the statement

```
short value = field.getShort(o);
```

The set example could have used

```
field.setShort(o, nv);
```

and avoided the use of the wrapper object.

Field implements AnnotatedElement, and the annotations on a field can be queried as discussed in Section 16.2 on page 414.

With some work you can use a Field object as a way to manipulate an arbitrary value, but you should avoid this when possible. The language is designed to catch as many programming errors as possible when the program is compiled. The less you write using indirections such as the Field object, the more your errors will be prevented before they are compiled into code. Also, as you can see, it takes more reading to see what is happening in the preceding code compared with what it would take if the name of the field were simply used in the normal syntax.

16.6.1   Final Fields

Under normal circumstances attempting to set the value of a field declared as `final` will result in `IllegalAccessException` being thrown. This is what you would expect: Final fields should never have their value changed. There are special circumstances—such as during custom deserialization (see page 554)—where it makes sense to change the value of a final field. You can do this via reflection only on instance fields, and only if `setAccessible(true)` has been invoked on the `Field` object. Note that it is not enough that `setAccessible(true)` would succeed, it must actually be called.

This capability is provided for highly specialized contexts and is not intended for general use—we mention it only for completeness. Changing a final field can have unexpected, possibly tragic consequences unless performed in specific contexts, such as custom deserialization. Outside those contexts, changes to a final field are not guaranteed to be visible. Even in such contexts, code using this technique must be guaranteed that security will not thwart its work. Changing a final field that is a constant variable (see page 46) will never result in the change being seen, except through the use of reflection—don't do it!

Exercise 16.6: Create an `Interpret` program that creates an object of a requested type and allows the user to examine and modify fields of that object.

16.7   The Method Class

The `Method` class, together with its inherited `Member` methods allows you to obtain complete information about the declaration of a method:

public Type **getGenericReturnType()**
> Returns the `Type` object for the type returned by this method. If the method is declared `void` the returned object is `void.class`.

public Type[] **getGenericParameterTypes()**
> Returns an array of `Type` objects with the type of each parameter of this method, in the order in which the parameters are declared. If the method has no parameters an empty array is returned.

public Type[] **getGenericExceptionTypes()**
> Returns an array of `Type` objects for each of the exception types listed in the `throws` clause for this method, in the order they are declared. If there are no declared exceptions an empty array is returned.

There are also the legacy methods `getReturnType`, `getParameterTypes`, and `getExceptionTypes` that return `Class` objects instead of `Type` objects. As with

Field.getType, parameterized types and type variables are represented by the Class objects of their erasures.

Method implements AnnotatedElement, and the annotations on a method can be queried as discussed in Section 16.2 on page 414. Additionally, Method provides the getParameterAnnotations method to provide access to the annotations applied to the method's parameters. The getParameterAnnotations method return an array of Annotation arrays, with each element of the outermost array corresponding to the parameters of the method, in the order they are declared. If a parameter has no annotations then a zero-length Annotation array is provided for that parameter. If the Method object represents a method that is itself an element of an annotation, the getDefaultValue method returns an Object representing the default value of that element. If it is not an annotation element or if there is no default value, then null is returned.

The Method class also implements GenericDeclaration and so defines the method getTypeParameters which returns an array of TypeVariable objects. If a given Method object does not present a generic method, then an empty array is returned.

You can ask a Method object if it is a varargs (variable-argument) method using the isVarArgs method. The method isBridge asks if it is a bridge method (see Section A.3.1 on page 745).

The most interesting use of a Method object is to reflectively invoke it:

public Object **invoke(Object onThis, Object... args)**
  throws IllegalAccessException, IllegalArgumentException, InvocationTargetException

> Invokes the method defined by this Method object on the object onThis, setting the parameters of the method from the values in args. For non-static methods the actual type of onThis determines the method implementation that is invoked. For static methods onThis is ignored and is traditionally null. The number of args values must equal the number of parameters for the method, and the types of those values must all be assignable to those of the method. Otherwise you will get an IllegalArgumentException. Note that for a varargs method the last parameter is an array that you must fill with the actual "variable" arguments you want to pass. If you attempt to invoke a method to which you do not have access, an IllegalAccessException is thrown. If this method is not a method of the onThis object, an IllegalArgumentException is thrown. If onThis is null and the method is not static, a NullPointerException is thrown. If this Method object represents a static method and the class has yet to be initialized, you might get an ExceptionInInitializerError. If the method throws an exception, an InvocationTargetException is thrown whose cause is that exception.

When you use `invoke`, you can either pass primitive types directly, or use wrappers of suitable types. The type represented by a wrapper must be assignable to the declared parameter type. You can use a `Long`, `Float`, or `Double` to wrap a `double` argument, but you cannot use a `Double` to wrap a `long` or `float` argument because a `double` is not assignable to a `long` or a `float`. The `Object` returned by `invoke` is handled as with `Field.get`, returning primitive types as their wrapper classes. If the method is declared `void`, `invoke` returns `null`.

Simply put, you can use `invoke` only to invoke a method with the same types and values that would be legal in the language. The invocation

```
return str.indexOf(".", 8);
```

can be written using reflection in the following way:

```
Throwable failure;
try {
    Method indexM = String.class.
        getMethod("indexOf", String.class, int.class);
    return (Integer) indexM.invoke(str, ".", 8);
} catch (NoSuchMethodException e) {
    failure = e;
} catch (InvocationTargetException e) {
    failure = e.getCause();
} catch (IllegalAccessException e) {
    failure = e;
}
throw failure;
```

The reflection-based code has semantically equivalent safety checks, although the checks that are made by the compiler for direct invocation can be made only at run time when you use `invoke`. The access checking may be done in a somewhat different way—you might be denied access to a method in your package by the security manager, even if you could invoke that method directly.

These are good reasons to avoid using this kind of invocation when you can. It's reasonable to use `invoke`—or the `get`–`set` methods of `Field`—when you are writing a debugger or other generic applications that require interpreting user input as manipulations of objects. A `Method` object can be used somewhat like a method pointer in other languages, but there are better tools—notably interfaces, abstract classes, and nested classes—to address the problems typically solved by method pointers in those languages.

Exercise 16.7: Modify your `Interpret` program to invoke methods on the object. You should properly display any values returned or exceptions thrown.

16.8   Creating New Objects and the `Constructor` Class

You can use a `Class` object's `newInstance` method to create a new instance (object) of the type it represents. This method invokes the class's no-arg constructor and returns a reference to the newly created object. For a class object of type `Class<T>` the returned object is of type T.

Creating a new object in this way is useful when you want to write general code and let the user specify the class. For example, you could modify the general sorting algorithm tester from "Designing a Class to Be Extended" on page 108 so that the user could type the name of the class to be tested and use that as a parameter to the `forName` lookup method. Assuming that the given class name was valid, `newInstance` could then be invoked to create an object of that type. Here is a new `main` method for a general `TestSort` class:

```
static double[] testData = { 0.3, 1.3e-2, 7.9, 3.17 };

public static void main(String[] args) {
    try {
        for (String name : args) {
            Class<?> classFor = Class.forName(name);
            SortDouble sorter
                = (SortDouble) classFor.newInstance();
            SortMetrics metrics
                = sorter.sort(testData);
            System.out.println(name + ": " + metrics);
            for (double data : testData)
                System.out.println("\t" + data);
        }
    } catch (Exception e) {
        System.err.println(e);              // report the error
    }
}
```

This is almost exactly like `TestSort.main` (see page 112), but we have removed all type names. This `main` method can be used to test any subclass of `SortDouble` that provides a no-arg constructor. You don't have to write a `main` for each type of sorting algorithm—this generic `main` works for them all. All you need to do is execute

```
java TestSort TestClass ...
```

for any sorting class (such as `SimpleSortDouble`) and it will be loaded and run.

Note that whereas `newInstance` returns a `T`, `Class.forName` returns a `Class<?>`. This means that the actual kind of object returned by `newInstance` is unknown, so the cast is needed. You could instead get a class object of the exact type needed using `asSubclass`, and invoke `newInstance` without needing a cast:

```
Class<? extends SortDouble> classFor =
    Class.forName(name).asSubclass(SortDouble.class);
SortDouble sorter = classFor.newInstance();
```

In either case, if the named class is not a subtype of `SortDouble`, then a `ClassCastException` will be thrown.

The `newInstance` method can throw a number of different exceptions if used inappropriately. If the class doesn't have a no-arg constructor, is an abstract class, or interface, or if the creation fails for some other reason, you will get an `InstantiationException`. If the class or the no-arg constructor is not accessible an `IllegalAccessException` is thrown. If the current security policy disallows the creation of a new object a `SecurityException` is thrown. Finally, creating a new object may require the class to be initialized so it is also possible for an `ExceptionInInitializerError` to be thrown.

The `newInstance` method of `Class` invokes only a no-arg constructor. If you want to invoke any other constructor then you must use the `Class` object to get the relevant `Constructor` object and invoke `newInstance` on that `Constructor`, passing the appropriate parameters.

The `Constructor` class, together with its inherited `Member` methods allows you to obtain complete information about the declaration of a constructor and allows you to invoke the constructor to obtain a new instance of that class.

public Type[] **getGenericParameterTypes()**
> Returns an array of Type objects for each of the parameter types accepted by this constructor, in the order in which the parameters are declared. If the constructor has no parameters an empty array is returned.

public Type[] **getGenericExceptionTypes()**
> Returns an array of Type objects for each of the exception types listed in the throws clause for this constructor, in the order they are declared. If there are no declared exceptions an empty array is returned.

As with `Method` objects, the above are mirrored by the legacy versions `getParameterTypes` and `getExceptionTypes`, respectively.

The `Constructor` class is similar to `Method`, implementing the same interfaces (`AnnotatedElement` and `GenericDeclaration`) and defining similar methods (`getParameterAnnotations` and `isVarArgs`).

To create a new instance of a class from a `Constructor` object, you invoke its `newInstance` method.

```
public T newInstance(Object... args)
   throws InstantiationException, IllegalAccessException,
   IllegalArgumentException, InvocationTargetException
```
   Uses the constructor represented by this Constructor object to create and
   initialize a new instance of the constructor's declaring class, with the specified initialization arguments. A reference to the newly initialized object is
   returned. Constructor.newInstance is very similar to Method.invoke.
   The number of args values must equal the number of parameters for the
   constructor, and the types of those values must all be assignable to those of
   the constructor. Otherwise you will get an IllegalArgumentException.
   Again, note that for a varargs constructor the last parameter is an array that
   you must fill in with the actual "variable" arguments you want to pass. If the
   declaring class is abstract you will get an InstantiationException. If the
   constructor is one to which you do not have access, you will get an
   IllegalAccessException. If the constructor itself throws an exception,
   you will get an InvocationTargetException whose cause is that exception.

   If your constructor object is referenced through a wildcard reference, then you
must cast the object returned by newInstance to the right type.

Exercise 16.8: Modify your Interpret program further to let users invoke constructors of an arbitrary class, displaying any exceptions. If a construction is successful, let users invoke methods on the returned object.

16.8.1   Inner Class Constructors

An inner class (excluding local and anonymous inner classes) never has a no-arg
constructor, since the compiler transforms all inner class constructors to take a
first parameter that is a reference to the enclosing object. This means that you can
never use Class.newInstance to create an inner class object, so you must use
Constructor objects. The Constructor objects for an inner class reflect the
transformed code, not the code written by the programmer. For example, consider
the BankAccount class and its associated inner Action class from page 136. The
Action class had a single constructor that took a String parameter, representing
the action that had occurred (withdraw, deposit, and so on), and a long value, representing the amount involved. If you use getDeclaredConstructors to obtain
that Constructor object and print its signature using toString, you will get the
following:

```
BankAccount$Action(BankAccount,java.lang.String,long)
```

Here you can see both the use of the $ naming convention for inner classes and the implicitly added constructor argument that refers to the enclosing object. You can retrieve this constructor as follows:

```
Class<Action> actionClass = Action.class;
Constructor<Action> con =
    actionClass.getDeclaredConstructor(BankAccount.class,
            String.class, long.class);
```

If you want to construct an `Action` object you must supply an appropriate enclosing object reference as in

```
BankAccount acct = new BankAccount();
// ...
Action a = con.newInstance(acct, "Embezzle", 10000L);
```

16.9 Generic Type Inspection

As you saw in Figure 16–1 on page 400, there are a number of interfaces to represent the different kinds of types that can exist in your programs. So far we have focussed on `Class` objects and `Member` objects since they are the more commonly used reflection objects, and we have only mentioned the other kinds of `Type` objects in passing. This section looks at those other `Type` interfaces in more detail.

16.9.1 Type Variables

The `GenericDeclaration` interface, which is implemented by `Class`, `Method`, and `Constructor`, has the single method `getTypeParameters`, which returns an array of `TypeVariable` objects. The `TypeVariable` interface is itself a generic interface, declared as

```
interface TypeVariable<D extends GenericDeclaration>
```

So, for example, the `TypeVariable` objects `Method.getTypeParameters` returns would be of type `TypeVariable<Method>`.

Each type variable has a name returned by `getName`. It also has one or more upper bounds, obtained as a `Type[]` from `getBounds`. Recall that if there is no explicit upper bound then the upper bound is `Object`.

The `getGenericDeclaration` method returns the `Type` object for the `GenericDeclaration` in which the `TypeVariable` was declared. For example, the expression `TypeVariable.class.getTypeParameters()[0]` would yield a `TypeVariable` object that represents D in the declaration above. If you invoked getGenericDeclaration on this object, it would return the Class object for the TypeVariable interface. More generally, for any GenericDeclaration object g with at least one type parameter,

g.getTypeParameters()[i].getGenericDeclaration() == g

is always true (assuming i is a valid index of course).

Type variable objects are created on demand by the reflection methods that return them, and there is no requirement that you receive the same TypeVariable object each time you ask for the same type variable. However, the objects returned for a given type variable must be equivalent according to the equals method. The bounds for a type variable are not created until getBounds is invoked, so getBounds can throw TypeNotPresentException if a type used in the bounds cannot be found. It can also throw MalformedParameterizedTypeException if any of the bounds refers to a ParameterizedType instance that cannot be created for some reason.

16.9.2 Parameterized Types

Parameterized types, such as List<String>, are represented by objects that implement the ParameterizedType interface. You can obtain the actual type arguments for the parameterized type from getActualTypeArguments, which returns an array of Type objects. For example, getActualTypeArguments invoked on the parameterized type List<String> would yield an array of length one, containing String.class as its only element.

The getOwnerType method (which perhaps would have been better called getDeclaringType) returns the Type object for the type in which this ParameterizedType object is a member. If this is not a member of another type then null is returned. This is analogous to the Class.getDeclaringClass method except that a Type object is returned.

Like TypeVariable objects, ParameterizedType objects are created on demand and are not always the same object, so you should use equals not == to check for equivalent parameterized type objects. Also, when a parameterized type is created, all its type arguments are also created, and this applies recursively. Both of the above methods will sometimes throw either TypeNotFoundException or MalformedParameterizedTypeException.

Finally, ParameterizedType also has the method getRawType, which returns the Class object for the raw type of the parameterized type. For example, if getRawType were invoked on the parameterized type List<String> it would return List.class. Even though a raw type is by definition a non-generic class or interface, getRawType returns a Type instance rather than a Class<?>, so a cast must be applied, as you saw in the TypeDesc program.

16.9.3 Wildcards

A wildcard type parameter is represented by an instance that implements the
WildcardType interface. For example, given a parameterized type for
List<? extends Number>, getActualTypeArguments will give an array of
length one containing a WildcardType object representing "? extends Number".

WildcardType has two methods: getUpperBounds and getLowerBounds,
which return Type arrays representing the upper and lower bounds of the wildcard, respectively. If no upper bound was specified, the upper bound is Object. If
a wildcard has no lower bound, getLowerBounds returns an empty array.

As with TypeVariable, the type objects for bounds are created on demand,
so TypeNotPresentException or MalformedParameterizedTypeException
may be thrown.

16.9.4 Generic Arrays

The last of the type related interfaces is GenericArrayType. This represents
array types in which the component type is a parameterized type or a type variable.[4] GenericArrayType has a single method, getGenericComponentType,
which returns the Type for the component type of the array, which will be either a
ParameterizedType or a TypeVariable. For example, for a List<String>[]
field, getGenericType would return a GenericArrayType object whose
getComponentType would return a ParameterizedType for List<String>.

The component type object gets created when getGenericComponentType is
invoked, so as you might expect, you may get a TypeNotPresentException or
MalformedParameterizedTypeException.

16.9.5 String Representations of Type Objects

None of the interfaces described above define the toString method, or any other
general way to obtain a string representation of a type—with the exception of
TypeVariable, which has the getName method. However, all the type objects
will have a toString method defined. With no specification of what toString
should return for Type objects, you cannot rely on toString to give a reasonable

---

[4]   You may recall that you cannot create such an array, but you are permitted to declare vari-
      ables of that type. The actual array creation can use only an unbounded wildcard type, such
      as new List<?>[1]. When you first assign the new array to a more specific variable, such
      as a List<String>[], you will get an "unchecked" warning because the compiler cannot
      guarantee that the current or future contents of the array will actually be List<String>
      objects. Such arrays are inherently unsafe and should be used with extreme caution—you
      should generally not create methods that return such arrays or take them as parameters.

representation of the type. If you want a string representation of a type, you will need to assemble it yourself from the information available. For example, if a `WildcardType` object has no lower bound and an upper bound of X, then the wildcard is "`? extends X`". For a `ParameterizedType` you can construct the string representation using the raw type and the actual type parameter types.

Exercise 16.9: Use reflection to write a program that will print a full declaration of a named class, including everything except the import statements, comments, and code for initializers, constructors, and methods. The member declarations should appear just as you would write them. You will need to use all the reflection classes you have seen. Also note that the `toString` methods of many of the reflection objects will not provide the information you want in the correct format, so you will need to piece together the individual pieces of information.

16.10 Arrays

An array is an object but has no members—the implicit `length` "field" of an array is not an actual field. Asking the `Class` object of an array for fields, methods, or constructors will all yield empty arrays. To create arrays and to `get` and `set` the values of elements stored in an array, you can use the static methods of the `Array` class. You can create arrays with either of two `newInstance` methods.

`public static Object`
`newInstance(Class<?> componentType, int length)`
> Returns a reference to a new array of the specified length and with component type `componentType`.

`public static Object`
`newInstance(Class<?> componentType, int[] dimensions)`
> Returns a reference to a multidimensional array, with dimensions as specified by the elements of the `dimensions` array and with the component type `componentType`. If the `dimensions` array is empty or has a length greater than the number of dimensions allowed by the implementation (typically 255), an `IllegalArgumentException` is thrown.

For primitive types, use the class literal to obtain the `Class` object. For example, use `byte.class` to create a byte array. The statement

```
byte[] ba = (byte[]) Array.newInstance(byte.class, 13);
```

is equivalent to

```
byte[] ba = new byte[13];
```

The second `newInstance` method takes an array of dimensions. The statement

```
int[] dims = { 4, 4 };
double[][] matrix =
    (double[][]) Array.newInstance(double.class, dims);
```

is equivalent to

```
double[][] matrix = new double[4][4];
```

Because the component type could itself be an array type, the actual dimensions of the created array can be greater than that implied by the arguments to `newInstance`. For example, if `intArray` is a `Class` object for the type `int[]`, then the invocation `Array.newInstance(intArray, 13)` creates a two-dimensional array of type `int[][]`. When `componentType` is an array type, the component type of the created array is the component type of `componentType`. So, in the previous example, the resulting component type is `int`.

The static `getLength` method of `Array` returns the length of a given array.

The `Array` class also has static methods to `get` and `set` the individual elements of a specified array, similar to the `get` and `set` methods of class `Field`. The general `get` and `set` methods work with `Objects`. For example, given an `int` array, `xa`, the value `xa[i]` can be more laboriously and less clearly fetched as

```
Array.get(xa, i)
```

which returns an `Integer` object that must be unwrapped to extract the `int` value. You can `set` values in a similar way: `xa[i] = 23` is the same as the more awkward

```
Array.set(xa, i, 23);
```

If the object passed as the array is not actually an array, you will get an `IllegalArgumentException`. If the value to be set is not assignable to the component type of the array (after unwrapping, if necessary), you will get an `IllegalArgumentException`.

The `Array` class also supports a full set of get*Type* and set*Type* methods for all the primitive types, as in

```
Array.setInt(xa, i, 23);
```

These avoid the need for intermediate wrapper objects.

16.10.1 Genericity and Dynamic Arrays

Recall the `toArray` method of the `SingleLinkQueue` class from Chapter 11. We promised back then that we'd show you how to create the array directly (instead of having it passed in) by having the type token for the actual type argument of the queue passed in. Here's a first attempt:

```
public E[] toArray_v1(Class<E> type) {
    int size = size();
    E[] arr = (E[]) Array.newInstance(type, size);
    int i = 0;
    for (Cell<E> c = head;
         c != null && i < size;
         c = c.getNext())
        arr[i++] = c.getElement();
    return arr;
}
```

This code works, but is less desirable than the generic version that took in the array to fill. The main problem is that the above causes an "unchecked" warning from the compiler. As you may have already noticed, the cast to E[] is a cast involving a type parameter and such casts have a different meaning at runtime—the actual cast will be to Object, which is the erasure of E. Despite this, it is apparent that the code above is type-safe: We ask for an array that has a component type of E and we try to use the returned object as such an array. The existence of the "unchecked" warning is a consequence of a limitation in the Array API and can't be avoided.

The second problem with the above is that it suffers from the same limitation as the original non-generic version of toArray—it will only allow an array of the exact element type to be created, not an array of any supertype. We can address this latter problem by turning the current version into a generic method, as we did previously:

```
public <T> T[] toArray(Class<T> type) {
    int size = size();
    T[] arr = (T[]) Array.newInstance(type, size);
    int i = 0;
    Object[] tmp = arr;
    for (Cell<E> c = head;
         c != null && i < size;
         c = c.getNext())
        tmp[i++] = c.getElement();
    return arr;
}
```

This version still has the "unchecked" warning—that can't be avoided—but it allows any Class object to passed in and tries to return an array with that component type. As with the generic version that takes the array as an argument, this version relies on the runtime checking of array stores to ensure that the component type passed is actually compatible with the element type of the current queue.

So you're left with two approaches for dealing with the `toArray` requirement: have the caller pass in the array and avoid warnings, but be forced to deal with an array of the wrong size, or have the caller pass in the type token for the element type and create an array of the right size, but be subjected to the "unchecked" warning. Or you could do as the collection classes do and combine both: Take in an array, but if it is the wrong size dynamically create another one, and get the warning. While we normally advise that you avoid "unchecked" warnings at all costs, the case of `Array.newInstance` is an exception.[5]

Exercise 16.10: Modify `Interpret` further to allow users to specify a type and size of array to create; set and get the elements of that array; and access fields and invoke methods on specific elements of the array.

16.11 Packages

If you invoke the `getPackage` method on a `Class` object, you get a `Package` object that describes the package in which the class lives (the `Package` class is defined in `java.lang`). You can also get a `Package` object by invoking the static method `getPackage` with the name of the package, or you can use the static `getPackages` method which returns an array of all known packages in the system. The `getName` method returns the full name of the package.

Package objects are used differently than the other reflective types—you can't create or manipulate packages at run time. You use `Package` objects to obtain information about a package, such as its purpose, who created it, what version it is, and so on. We defer a discussion on this until we look at packages in detail in Chapter 18.

16.12 The Proxy Class

The `Proxy` class lets you create classes at runtime that implement one or more interfaces. This is an advanced, rarely needed feature, but when needed it is quite useful.

---

[5] For compilers that support "unchecked" as a warning type, this situation is an ideal candidate for use of the `@SuppressWarnings` annotation that was mentioned on page 396,

Suppose, for example, you want to log calls to an object so that when a failure happens you can print the last several methods invoked on the object. You could write such code by hand for a particular class, with a way to turn it on for a particular object. But that requires custom code for each type of object you want to monitor, as well as each object checking on each method invocation to see if calls should be logged.

You could instead write a general utility that used a `Proxy`-created class to log a call history. Objects created by that class would implement the relevant interfaces, interposing code that you provide between the caller's invocation of a method and the object's execution of it.

The `Proxy` model is that you invoke `Proxy.getProxyClass` with a class loader and an array of interfaces to get a `Class` object for the proxy. Proxy objects have one constructor, to which you pass an `InvocationHandler` object. You can get a `Constructor` object for this constructor from the `Class` object and use `newInstance` (passing in an invocation handler) to create a proxy object. The created object implements all the interfaces that were passed to `getProxyClass`, as well as the methods of `Object`. As a shortcut to get a proxy object, you can invoke `Proxy.newProxyInstance`, which takes a class loader, an array of interfaces, and an invocation handler. When methods are invoked on the proxy object, these method invocations are turned into calls to the invocation handler's `invoke` method.

Given all that, here is how a general debug logging class might look:

```java
public class DebugProxy implements InvocationHandler {
    private final Object obj;            // underlying object
    private final List<Method> methods;  // methods invoked
    private final List<Method> history;  // viewable history

    private DebugProxy(Object obj) {
        this.obj = obj;
        methods = new ArrayList<Method>();
        history = Collections.unmodifiableList(methods);
    }

    public static synchronized Object proxyFor(Object obj) {
        Class<?> objClass = obj.getClass();
        return Proxy.newProxyInstance(
            objClass.getClassLoader(),
            objClass.getInterfaces(),
            new DebugProxy(obj));
    }
```

```
    public Object
        invoke(Object proxy, Method method, Object[] args)
        throws Throwable
    {
        methods.add(method); // log the call
        try {
            // invoke the real method
            return method.invoke(obj, args);
        } catch (InvocationTargetException e) {
            throw e.getCause();
        }
    }

    public List<Method> getHistory() { return history; }
}
```

If you want a debug proxy for a given object, you invoke proxyFor, as in

```
Object proxyObj = DebugProxy.proxyFor(realObj);
```

The object proxyObj would implement all the interfaces that realObj implements, plus the methods of Object. The object proxyObj is also associated with the instance of DebugProxy that was created—this instance is the invocation handler for the proxy. When a method is invoked on proxyObj, this leads to an invocation of the invoke method on the associated DebugProxy instance, passing proxyObj as the proxy object, a Method object representing the method that was invoked, and all the arguments to the method call. In our example invoke logs the invocation by adding it to its list of invoked methods and then invokes the method on the underlying realObj object, which was stored in the obj field.

The (read-only) history of method invocations on the proxy object can be retrieved from its DebugProxy instance. This is obtained by passing the proxy to the static Proxy class method getInvocationHandler:

```
DebugProxy h =
    (DebugProxy) Proxy.getInvocationHandler(proxyObj);
List<Method> history = h.getHistory();
```

If we hadn't used the newProxyInstance shortcut we would have needed to write the following in ProxyFor:

```
Class<?> objClass = obj.getClass();
Class<?> proxyClass = Proxy.getProxyClass(
    objClass.getClassLoader(),
```

```
        objClass.getInterfaces());
    Constructor ctor = proxyClass.getConstructor(
        InvocationHandler.class);
    return ctor.newInstance(new DebugProxy(obj));
```

The invocation handler's `invoke` method can throw `Throwable`. However, if `invoke` throws any exception that the original method could not throw, the invoker will get an `UndeclaredThrowableException` that returns the offending exception from its `getCause` method.

If you invoke `getProxyClass` twice with the same parameters (the same class loader and the same interfaces in the same order) you will get back the same `Class` object. If the interfaces are in another order or the class loader is different, you will get back different `Class` objects. The interface order matters because two interfaces in the list can potentially have methods with the same name and signature. If this happens, the `Method` object passed to `invoke` will have a declaring class of the first interface listed that declares that method (defined by a depth-first search of interfaces and superinterfaces).

The declaring class for the public non-final methods of `Object`—`equals`, `hashCode`, and `toString`—is always `Object.class`. The other methods of `Object` are not "proxied"; their methods are handled directly by the proxy object itself, not via a call to `invoke`. Most importantly, this means that a lock on a proxy object is just that—a lock on the proxy. Whatever object or objects the proxy uses to do its work (for example, in our case the underlying object whose methods are being traced) is not involved in the lock, including any uses of `wait`, `notifyAll`, or `notify`.

You can ask if a `Class` object represents a dynamically generated proxy class using the static `Proxy.isProxyClass` method.

16.13 Loading Classes

The runtime system loads classes when they are needed. Details of loading classes vary between implementations, but most of them use a *class path* mechanism to search for a class referenced by your code but not yet loaded into the runtime system. The class path is a list of places in which the system looks for class files. This default mechanism works well in many cases, but much of the power of the Java virtual machine is its ability to load classes from places that make sense to your application. To write an application that loads classes in ways different from the default mechanism, you must provide a `ClassLoader` object that can get the bytecodes for class implementations and load them into the runtime system.

For example, you might set up a game so that any player could write a class to play the game using whatever strategy the player chooses. The design would look something like this:

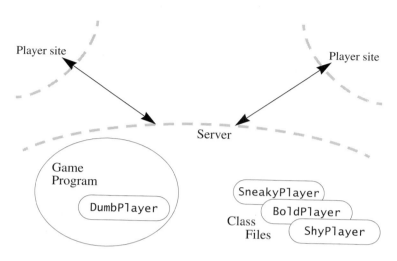

To make this work, you would provide a Player abstract class that players would extend to implement their strategy. When players were ready to try their strategy, they would send the compiled class's bytecodes to your system. The bytecodes would need to be loaded into the game and the strategy evaluated by playing it against others. The score would then be returned to the player.

At the server, the game program loads each waiting Player class, creates an object of the new type, and runs its strategy against the game algorithm. When the results are known, they are reported to the player who submitted the strategy.

The communication mechanism isn't specified here, but it could be as simple as electronic mail, with players mailing their classes and receiving the results by return mail.

The interesting part is how the game program loads the compiled class files into its runtime system. This is the province of a *class loader,* which must extend the abstract ClassLoader class and override its findClass method:

```
protected Class<?> findClass(String name)
    throws ClassNotFoundException
```
> Locates the bytecodes representing the class name and loads them into the virtual machine, returning the Class object created to represent that class.

In our example, we would provide a PlayerLoader class to read the bytecodes from the player classes and install each of them as a usable class. The basic loop would look like this:

```
public class Game {
    public static void main(String[] args) {
        String name;     // the class name
        while ((name = getNextPlayer()) != null) {
            try {
                PlayerLoader loader = new PlayerLoader();
                Class<? extends Player> classOf =
                    loader.loadClass(name).
                        asSubclass(Player.class);
                Player player = classOf.newInstance();
                Game game = new Game();
                player.play(game);
                game.reportScore(name);
            } catch (Exception e) {
                reportException(name, e);
            }
        }
    }

    // ... definition of other methods ...
}
```

Each new game creates a new `PlayerLoader` object to load the class for that run
of the game. The new loader loads the class, using `loadClass`, returning the
`Class` object that represents it. That `Class` object is used to create a new object of
the `Player` class. Then we create a new game and play it. When the game is finished, the score is reported. Without a new class loader for each run, attempting to
load a class with the same name as one that had already been loaded would return
the original class. This would prevent players from submitting updated versions of
their classes with the same name.

You can obtain the class loader for a given `Class` object from its
`getClassLoader` method. System classes need not have a class loader, so the
method may return `null`.

Class loaders define namespaces that separate the classes within an application. If two classes have different class loaders then they are distinct classes, even
if the binary data for the class was read from the same class file. Each distinct
class maintains its own set of static variables and modifications to the static variables of one class have no effect on the other class.

Each thread has an associated `ClassLoader` that will be used by default to
load classes. This *context class loader* can be specified at thread creation; if none
is specified the parent thread's context class loader will be used. The context class

loader of the first thread is typically the class loader used to load the application—the *system class loader.* The `Thread` methods `getContextClassLoader` and `setContextClassLoader` allow you to get and set the context class loader.

16.13.1 The `ClassLoader` Class

A class loader can delegate responsibility for loading a class to its *parent class loader.* The parent class loader can be specified as a constructor argument to `ClassLoader`:

protected **ClassLoader()**
> Creates a class loader with an implicit parent class loader of the system class loader, as returned by `getSystemClassLoader`.

protected **ClassLoader(ClassLoader parent)**
> Creates a class loader with the specified parent class loader.

A generic class loader, intended for use by others, should provide both forms of constructor to allow an explicit parent to be set.

The system class loader is typically the class loader used by the virtual machine to load the initial application class. You can get a reference to it from the static method `getSystemClassLoader`.

The *bootstrap* class loader is the class loader used to load those classes belonging to the virtual machine (classes like `Object`, `String`, `List`, and so forth). These classes are often referred to as *system classes,* a term which can lead to some confusion since the system classes are loaded by the bootstrap loader, whereas application classes are loaded by the system class loader. The bootstrap loader may or may not be represented by an actual `ClassLoader` object, so invoking `getClassLoader` on an instance of one of the system classes will typically return `null`, indicating it was loaded by the bootstrap loader.

You can get the parent class loader from the method `getParent`. If the class loader's parent is the bootstrap class loader, `getParent` may return `null`.

Class loaders are an integral part of the security architecture—see "Security" on page 677—so creating a class loader and asking for the parent class loader are checked operations that may throw a `SecurityException`.

The primary method of `ClassLoader` is `loadClass`:

public Class<?> **loadClass(String name)**
> throws ClassNotFoundException
> > Returns the `Class` object for the class with the specified binary name, loading the class if necessary. If the class cannot be loaded you will get a `ClassNotFoundException`.

The default implementation of loadClass, which is not usually overridden, attempts to load a class as follows:

1. It checks to see if the class has already been loaded by invoking findLoadedClass. ClassLoader maintains a table of Class objects for all the classes loaded by the current class loader. If a class has been previously loaded findLoadedClass will return the existing Class object.

2. If the class has not been loaded it invokes loadClass on the parent class loader. If the current class loader does not have a parent, the bootstrap class loader is used.

3. If the class still has not been loaded, findClass is invoked to locate and load the class.

Note that the parent class loader is always given the chance to load the class first; only if the bootstrap loader and the system class loader fail to load a given class will your custom class loader be given the opportunity to do so. The implication is that your custom class loader must search for classes in places that are different from those searched by the system or bootstrap class loaders.

The PlayerLoader class extends ClassLoader to override findClass:

```
class PlayerLoader extends ClassLoader {
    public Class<?> findClass(String name)
        throws ClassNotFoundException
    {
        try {
            byte[] buf = bytesForClass(name);
            return defineClass(name, buf, 0, buf.length);
        } catch (IOException e) {
            throw new ClassNotFoundException(e.toString());
        }
    }

    // ... bytesForClass, and any other methods ...
}
```

The findClass method generally has to perform two actions. First, it has to locate the bytecodes for the specified class and load them into a byte array—the job of bytesForClass in our example. Second, it uses the utility method defineClass to actually load the class defined by those bytes into the virtual machine and return a Class object for that class.

```
protected final Class<?> defineClass(String name, byte[] data,
    int offset, int length) throws ClassFormatError
```
Returns a Class object for the named class whose binary representation is held in data. Only the bytes in data from offset to offset+length-1 are used to define the class. If the bytes in the subarray do not conform to a valid class file format, a ClassFormatError is thrown. The defineClass method is responsible for storing the Class object into the table searched by findLoadedClass.

An overloaded form of defineClass takes an additional ProtectionDomain argument, while the above form uses a default protection domain. Protection domains define the security permissions for objects in that domain—again see "Security" on page 677 for further details. Both forms of defineClass may throw SecurityException.

Before you can define a class you have to read the bytes for the class, and that is the purpose of bytesForClass:

```
protected byte[] bytesForClass(String name)
    throws IOException, ClassNotFoundException
{
    FileInputStream in = null;
    try {
        in = streamFor(name + ".class");
        int length = in.available(); // get byte count
        if (length == 0)
            throw new ClassNotFoundException(name);
        byte[] buf = new byte[length];
        in.read(buf);                    // read the bytes
        return buf;
    } finally {
        if (in != null)
            in.close();
    }
}
```

This method uses streamFor (not shown) to get a FileInputStream to the class's bytecodes, assuming that the bytecodes are in a file named by the class name with a ".class" appended—streamFor knows where to search for the class files to be loaded. We then create a buffer for the bytes, read them all, and return the buffer.

When the class has been successfully loaded, findClass returns the new Class object returned by defineClass. There is no way to explicitly unload a class when it is no longer needed. You simply stop using it, allowing it to be gar-bage-collected when its `ClassLoader` is unreachable.

Exercise 16.11: Expand on `Game` and `Player` to implement a simple game, such as tic-tac-toe. Score some `Player` implementations over several runs each.

16.13.2 Preparing a Class for Use

The class loader assists in only the first stage of making a class available. There are three steps in all:

1. *Loading*—Getting the bytecodes that implement the class and creating a `Class` object.
2. *Linking*—Verifying that the class's bytecodes conform to the language rules, preparing the virtual machine by allocating space for static fields, and (optionally) resolving all references in the class by, if necessary, loading the classes referred to.
3. *Initialization*—Initializing the superclass (if necessary, including loading and linking it), then executing all the static initializers and static initialization blocks of the class.

The `Class` object returned by `defineClass` only represents a loaded class—it has not yet been linked. You can explicitly link by invoking the (misnamed) `resolveClass` method:

```
protected final void resolveClass(Class<?> c)
```
Links the specified class if it has not already been linked.

The `loadClass` method we described does not resolve the class that is loaded. A protected, overloaded form of `loadClass` takes an additional `boolean` flag indicating whether or not to resolve the class before returning. The virtual machine will ensure that a class is resolved (linked) before it is initialized.

A class must be initialized immediately before the first occurrence of: an instance of the class being created; a static method of the class being invoked; or a non-final static field of the class being accessed. This includes the use of reflec-tion methods to perform those actions. Additionally, before an `assert` statement is executed inside a nested type, the enclosing top-level class (if there is one) must be initialized. Using reflection to directly load a class may also trigger initializa-tion—such as use of `Class.forName(name)`—but note that simple use of a class literal does not trigger initialization.

16.13.3 Loading Related Resources

Classes are the primary resources a program needs, but some classes need other associated resources, such as text, images, or sounds. Class loaders have ways to find class resources, and they can use the same mechanisms to get arbitrary resources stored with the class. In our game example, a particular playing strategy might have an associated "book" that tells it how to respond to particular situations. The following code, in a BoldPlayer class, would get an InputStream for such a book:

```
String book = "BoldPlayer.book";
InputStream in;
ClassLoader loader = this.getClass().getClassLoader();
if (loader != null)
    in = loader.getResourceAsStream(book);
else
    in = ClassLoader.getSystemResourceAsStream(book);
```

System resources are associated with system classes (the classes that may have no associated class loader instance). The static ClassLoader method getSystemResourceAsStream returns an InputStream for a named resource. The preceding code checks to see whether it has a class loader. If it does not, the class has been loaded by the bootstrap class loader; otherwise, it uses the class loader's getResourceAsStream method to turn its resource name into a byte input stream. The resource methods return null if the resource is not found.

The Class class provides a getResourceAsStream method to simplify getting resources from a class's class loader. The preceding code could be written more simply as

```
String book = "BoldPlayer.book";
InputStream in = BoldPlayer.class.getResourceAsStream(book);
```

Resource names must be made up of one or more valid identifiers separated by / characters, specifying a path to the resource. Typically, a class loader will search for resources in the same places it will search for class files.

Two other resource methods—getResource and getSystemResource—return URL objects that name the resources. The class java.net.URL is covered briefly on page 725; it provides methods to use uniform resource locators to access resources. You can invoke the getContents method on the URL objects returned by the class loader methods to get an object that represents the contents of that URL.

The getResources method returns a java.util.Enumeration object (an older variant of the Iterator you've seen before) that can step through URL objects for all the resources stored under a given name. The static method getSystemResources does the same for system resources.

The resource-getting methods first ask the parent class loader for the resource, or they ask the bootstrap class loader if there is no parent. If the resource cannot be found, then findResource or findResources is invoked. Just as loadClass is built on top of a findClass that you provide when you subclass ClassLoader, so the resource methods are built on top of two methods that you can override to find resources:

public URL **findResource(String name)**
> Returns a URL object for the resource of the given name, or null if none was found. If there are multiple resources of the same name the implementation determines which should be returned. The default implementation in ClassLoader always returns null.

public Enumeration<URL> **findResources(String name)**
> Returns an Enumeration of URL objects for all the resources of the given name. The default implementation in ClassLoader returns an enumeration through zero resources.

Here is a findResource for PlayerLoader:

```
public java.net.URL findResource(String name) {
    File f = fileFor(name);
    if (!f.exists())
        return null;
    try {
        return f.toURL();
    } catch (java.net.MalformedURLException e) {
        return null;        // shouldn't happen
    }
}
```

The fileFor method is analogous to the streamFor method of PlayerLoader. It returns a java.io.File object that corresponds to the named resource in the file system. If the named file actually exists, then the URL for the resource is created from the path. (The File class represents a pathname in the file system—see "The File Class" on page 543.)

The BoldPlayer class might come with a BoldPlayer.book that can be found in the same place as the class file. You can replace this version with your own by simply placing yours in a location where it will be found first by the system class loader or the bootstrap loader.

Exercise 16.12: Modify your results for Exercise 16.11 to allow player strategies to use attached resources by implementing `findResource` and `findResources`.

16.14 Controlling Assertions at Runtime

In Chapter 12 you learned about assertions and how they can be turned on or off through command-line options that you pass to the virtual machine (see Section 12.10 on page 300). You can also affect assertion evaluation from running code, although this is rarely required. You will probably need to do this only if you are writing a harness for running other code and must provide your users with options to manage assertions. Such manipulation is done with methods on `ClassLoader`:

public void **setDefaultAssertionStatus(boolean enabled)**
> Sets the default assertion status for all classes loaded in this loader. Child loaders are not affected, whether they exist at the time this method is invoked or after. The initial default assertion status for a class loader is `false`.

public void **setPackageAssertionStatus(String packageName, boolean enabled)**
> Sets the default assertion status for all classes in the given package and it's subpackages that are loaded in this loader. A `null` package name means the unnamed package for this class loader—see Chapter 18, page 468.

public void **setClassAssertionStatus(String className, boolean enabled)**
> Sets the default assertion status for the given class and for all its nested classes when loaded in this loader. You can only name top-level classes; nested classes are turned off and on via their enclosing class.

public void **clearAssertionStatus()**
> Clears (turns off) all assertions for this class loader, wiping clear any previous settings, whether from method invocations or the command line.

In all cases the settings only apply to classes that are loaded and initialized in the future—you cannot change the assertion status of a class once it has been loaded. More specifically, the assertion status of a class is established during initialization: after initialization of the superclass, but before execution of any static initializers.

As with the command-line options, the class-specific declarations have precedence over the package-specific declarations, which in turn have precedence over the class loader's default status. In effect the command-line options simply request the virtual machine to invoke the appropriate method on the class loader. So the command-line options

```
-da:com.acme.Evaluator -ea:com.acme...
```

are equivalent to the calls

```
loader.setClassAssertionStatus("com.acme.Evaluator", false);
loader.setPackageAssertionStatus("com.acme", true);
```

where `loader` is the class loader that will be used. (Note that the methods do not use the ... syntax that the command line uses because it is apparent whether a name refers to a package or a class.)

> *Be and not seem.*
> —Ralph Waldo Emerson

CHAPTER **17**

Garbage Collection and Memory

Civilization is a limitless multiplication of unnecessary necessaries.
—Mark Twain

THE Java virtual machine uses a technique known as *garbage collection* to determine when an object is no longer referenced within a program, and so can be safely reclaimed to free up memory space. This chapter teaches the basic ideas behind garbage collection, how the programmer can be involved in the garbage collection process, and how special reference objects can be used to influence when an object may be considered garbage.

17.1 Garbage Collection

Objects are created with new, but there is no corresponding delete operation to reclaim the memory used by an object. When you are finished with an object, you simply stop referring to it—change your reference to refer to another object or to null, or return from a method so its local variables no longer exist and hence refer to nothing. Objects that are no longer referenced are termed *garbage,* and the process of finding and reclaiming these objects is known as *garbage collection.*

The Java virtual machine uses garbage collection both to ensure any referenced object will remain in memory, and to free up memory by deallocating objects that are no longer reachable from references in executing code. This is a strong guarantee—an object will not be collected if it can be reached by following a *chain* of references starting with a *root* reference, that is, a reference directly accessible from executing code.

In simple terms, when an object is no longer reachable from any executable code, the space it occupies can be reclaimed. We use the phrase "can be" because space is reclaimed at the garbage collector's discretion, usually only if more space is needed or if the collector wants to avoid running out of memory. A program may exit without running out of space or even coming close and so may never need to perform garbage collection. An object is "no longer reachable" when no reference to the object exists in any variable of any currently executing method, nor can a reference to the object be found by starting from such variables and then following each field or array element, and so on.

Garbage collection means never having to worry about *dangling references.* In systems in which you directly control when objects are deleted, you can delete an object to which some other object still has a reference. That other reference is now dangling, meaning it refers to space that the system considers free. Space that is thought to be free might be allocated to a new object, and the dangling reference would then reference something completely different from what the object thought it referenced. This situation could cause all manner of havoc when the program uses the values in that space as if they were part of something they are not. Garbage collection solves the dangling reference problem for you because an object that's still referenced somewhere will never be garbage-collected and so will never be considered free. Garbage collection also solves the problem of accidentally deleting an object multiple times—something that can also cause havoc.

Garbage is collected without your intervention, but collecting garbage still takes work. Creating and collecting large numbers of objects can interfere with time-critical applications. You should design such systems to be judicious in the number of objects they create and so reduce the amount of garbage to be collected.

Garbage collection is not a guarantee that memory will always be available for new objects. You could create objects indefinitely, place them in lists, and continue doing so until there is no more space and no unreferenced objects to reclaim. You could create a memory leak by, for example, allowing a list of objects to refer to objects you no longer need. Garbage collection solves many, but not all, memory allocation problems.

17.2 A Simple Model

Garbage collection is easier to understand with an explicit model so this section describes a simple one, but practical garbage collectors are far more sophisticated. Garbage collection is logically split into two phases: separating *live* objects from *dead* objects and then reclaiming the storage of the dead ones. Live objects are those that are *reachable* from running code—the objects that some action of your code can still potentially use. Dead objects are the garbage that can be reclaimed.

One obvious model of garbage collection is reference counting: When object X references object Y, the system increments a counter on Y, and when X drops its reference to Y, the system decrements the counter. When the counter reaches zero, Y is no longer live and can be collected, which will decrement the counts of any other objects to which Y refers.

Reference counting fails in the face of *cycles,* in which loops are created in the references. If X and Y reference each other, neither object's counter will ever become zero, and so neither X nor Y will ever be collected, nor will anything to which either object refers, directly or indirectly. Most garbage collectors do not use reference counting for this and other reasons.

The simplest model of garbage collection not subject to this problem is called *mark-and-sweep.* The name refers to the way the two phases of garbage collection are implemented. To find which objects are live, the garbage collector first determines a set of *roots* that contains the directly reachable objects: References in local variables on the stack, for example, are reachable because you can use those variables to manipulate the object. Objects referred to by local variables are therefore clearly live.

Once a set of roots is determined, the collector will mark the objects referenced by those roots as reachable. It will then examine references in each of those objects. If an object referred to by such a reference is already marked reachable from the first step, it is ignored. Otherwise. the object is marked reachable and *its* references are examined. This process continues until no more reachable objects remain unmarked. After this marking process is complete, the collector can reclaim the dead objects (those which are not marked) by sweeping them away.

Any change to the interconnection of objects during a run of mark-and-sweep will clearly interfere with the collection process. A marking run can miss an object that was unreachable at the beginning of the marking process, but which is assigned to a reachable reference in the middle. Running a basic mark-and-sweep pass requires freezing execution of the program, at least during the marking phase.

There are other problems with mark-and-sweep. Garbage collection is a complex area of research with no easy or universal answers. We present mark-and-sweep as a relatively simple mental model for you to use to understand garbage collection. Each virtual machine has its own collection strategy, and some let you choose among several. Use this mark-and-sweep model as a mental model only—do not assume that this is how any particular virtual machine actually works.

17.3 Finalization

You won't normally notice when an orphaned object's space is reclaimed—"it just works." But a class can implement a `finalize` method that is executed before an object's space is reclaimed—see "Strengths of Reference and Reachability" on page 455. Such a `finalize` method gives you a chance to use the state contained in the object to reclaim other non-memory resources. The `finalize` method is declared in the `Object` class:

protected void **finalize()** throws Throwable

> Is invoked by the garbage collector after it determines that this object is no longer reachable and its space is to be reclaimed. This method might clean up any non-memory resources used by this object. It is invoked at most once per object, even if execution of this method causes the object to become reachable again and later it becomes unreachable again. There is no guarantee, however, that `finalize` will be called in any specific time period; it may never be called at all. This method is declared to throw any exception but if an exception occurs it is ignored by the garbage collector. The virtual machine makes no guarantees about which thread will execute the `finalize` method of any given object, but it does guarantee that the thread will not hold any user-visible synchronization locks.

You should only rarely need to write a `finalize` method, and when you do, you should write it with great care. If your object has become garbage it is quite possible that other objects to which it refers are also garbage. As garbage, they may have been finalized before your `finalize` method is invoked and may therefore be in an unexpected state.

Garbage collection collects only memory. When you are dealing with non-memory resources that are not reclaimed by garbage collection, finalizers look like a neat solution. For example, open files are usually a limited resource, so closing them when you can is good behavior. But this usually cannot wait until the `finalize` phase of garbage collection. The code that asks you to perform an operation that opens a file should tell you when it's done—there is no guarantee that your object holding the open file will be collected before all the open file resources are used up.

Still, your objects that allocate external resources could provide a `finalize` method that cleans them up so that the class doesn't itself create a resource leak. For example, a class that opens a file to do its work should have some form of `close` method to close the file, enabling programmers using that class to explicitly manage the number-of-open-files resource. The `finalize` method can then invoke `close`. Just don't rely on this to prevent users of the class from having problems. They might get lucky and have the finalizer executed before they run out of open files, but that is risky—finalization is a safety-net to be used as a last resort, after the programmer has failed to release the resource manually. If you were to write such a method, it might look like this:

```java
public class ProcessFile {
    private FileReader file;

    public ProcessFile(String path) throws
        FileNotFoundException
    {
        file = new FileReader(path);
    }

    // ...

    public synchronized void close() throws IOException {
        if (file != null) {
            file.close();
            file = null;
        }
    }

    protected void finalize() throws Throwable {
        try {
            close();
        } finally {
            super.finalize();
        }
    }
}
```

Note that `close` is carefully written to be correct if it is invoked more than once. Otherwise, if someone invoked `close`, finalizing the object would cause another close on the file, which might not be allowed.

Note also that, in this example, `finalize` invokes `super.finalize` in a `finally` clause. Train yourself so that you always write that invocation in any `finalize` method you write. If you don't invoke `super.finalize`, you may correctly finalize your own part of the object, but the superclass's part will not get finalized. Invoking `super.finalize` is one of those good habits you should adopt even when your class doesn't extend any other class. In addition to being good training, invoking `super.finalize` in such a case means that you can always add a superclass to a class like `ProcessFile` without remembering to examine its `finalize` method for correctness. Invoking the superclass's `finalize` method in a `finally` clause ensures that the superclass's cleanup will happen even if your cleanup causes an exception.

The garbage collector may reclaim objects in any order or it may never reclaim them. Memory resources are reclaimed when the garbage collector thinks the time is appropriate. Not being bound to an ordering guarantee, the garbage collector can operate in whatever manner is most efficient, and that helps minimize the overhead of garbage collection. You can, if necessary, invoke the garbage collector to try to force earlier collection using `System.gc` or `Runtime.gc`, as you'll see in the next section, but there is no guarantee that garbage collection will actually occur.

When an application exits, no further garbage collection is performed, so any objects that have not yet been collected will not have their `finalize` methods invoked. In many cases this will not be a problem. For example, on most systems when the virtual machine exits, the underlying system automatically closes all open files and sockets. However, for non-system resources you will have to invent other solutions. (Temporary files can be marked as "delete on exit," which solves one of the more common issues—see "The `File` Class" on page 543.)

Reference queues—discussed on page 459—provide a better way of performing clean-up actions when an object is it about to be, or has been, reclaimed.

17.3.1 Resurrecting Objects during `finalize`

A `finalize` method can "resurrect" an object by making it referenced again—for example, by adding it to a static list of objects. Resurrection is discouraged, but there is nothing the system can do to stop you.

However, the virtual machine invokes `finalize` at most once on any object, even if that object becomes unreachable more than once because a previous `finalize` resurrected it. If resurrecting objects is important to your design, the object would be resurrected only once—probably not the behavior you wanted.

If you think you need to resurrect objects, you should review your design carefully—you may uncover a flaw. If your design review convinces you that you need something like resurrection, the best solution is to clone the object or create a new object, not to resurrect it. The `finalize` method can insert a reference to a new object that will continue the state of the dying object rather than a reference to the dying object itself. Being new, the cloned object's `finalize` method will be invoked in the future (if needed), enabling it to insert yet another copy of itself in yet another list, ensuring the survival, if not of itself, at least of its progeny.

17.4 Interacting with the Garbage Collector

Although the language has no explicit way to dispose of unwanted objects, you can directly invoke the garbage collector to look for unused objects. The `Runtime` class, together with some convenience methods in the System class, allows you to invoke the garbage collector, request that any pending finalizers be run, or query the current memory state:

public void **gc()**
>Asks the virtual machine to expend effort toward recycling unused objects so that their memory can be reused.

public void **runFinalization()**
>Asks the virtual machine to expend effort running the finalizers of objects that it has found to be unreachable but have not yet had their finalizers run.

public long **freeMemory()**
>Returns an estimate of free bytes in system memory.

public long **totalMemory()**
>Returns the total bytes in system memory.

public long **maxMemory()**
>Returns the maximum amount of memory, in bytes, that the virtual machine will ever attempt to use. If there is no limit, Long.MAX_VALUE is returned. There is no method to set the maximum; a virtual machine will typically have a command-line or other configuration option to set the maximum.

To invoke these methods you need to obtain a reference to the current Runtime object via the static method Runtime.getRuntime. The System class supports static gc and runFinalization methods that invoke the corresponding methods on the current Runtime; in other words, System.gc() is equivalent to Runtime.getRuntime().gc().

The garbage collector may not be able to free any additional memory when Runtime.gc is invoked. There may be no garbage to collect, and not all garbage collectors can find collectable objects on demand. So invoking the garbage collector may have no effect whatsoever. However, before creating a large number of objects—especially in a time-critical application that might be affected by garbage-collection overhead—invoking gc may be advisable. Doing so has two potential benefits: You start with as much free memory as possible, and you reduce the likelihood of the garbage collector running during the task. Here is a method that aggressively frees everything it can at the moment:

```
public static void fullGC() {
    Runtime rt = Runtime.getRuntime();
    long isFree = rt.freeMemory();
    long wasFree;
    do {
        wasFree = isFree;
```

```
            rt.runFinalization();
            rt.gc();
            isFree = rt.freeMemory();
        } while (isFree > wasFree);
    }
```

This method loops while the amount of freeMemory is being increased by successive calls to runFinalization and gc. When the amount of free memory doesn't increase, further calls will likely do nothing.

You will not usually need to invoke runFinalization, because finalize methods are called asynchronously by the garbage collector. Under some circumstances, such as running out of a resource that a finalize method reclaims, it is useful to force as much finalization as possible. But remember, there is no guarantee that any object actually awaiting finalization is using some of that resource, so runFinalization may be of no help.

The fullGC method is too aggressive for most purposes. In the unusual circumstance that you need to force garbage collection, a single invocation of the System.gc method will gather most if not all of the available garbage. Repeated invocations are progressively less productive—on many systems they will be completely unproductive.

Exercise 17.1: Write a program to examine the amount of memory available on start up and after allocation of a number of objects. Try invoking the garbage collector explicitly to see how the amount of free memory changes—make sure you don't hold references to the newly allocated objects of course.

17.5 Reachability States and Reference Objects

An object can be garbage collected only when there are no references to it, but sometimes you would like an object to be garbage collected even though you may have a specific reference to it. For example, suppose you are writing a web browser. There will be images that have been seen by the user but that are not currently visible. If memory becomes tight, you can theoretically free up some memory by writing those images to disk, or even by forgetting about them since you can presumably refetch them later if needed. But since the objects representing the images are referenced from running code (and hence *reachable*) they will not be released. You would like to be able to have a reference to an object that doesn't force the object to remain reachable if that is the only reference to the object. Such special references are provided by *reference objects*.

A reference object is an object whose sole purpose is to maintain a reference to another object, called the *referent*. Instead of maintaining direct references to objects, via fields or local variables, you maintain a direct reference to a reference object that wraps the actual object you are interested in. The garbage collector can determine that the only references to an object are through reference objects and so can decide whether to reclaim that object—if the object is reclaimed then, the reference object is usually cleared so that it no longer refers to that object. The strength of a reference object determines how the garbage collector will behave—normal references are the strongest references.

17.5.1 The Reference Class

The classes for the reference object types are contained in the package `java.lang.ref`. The primary class is the generic, abstract class `Reference<T>`, which is the superclass of all the specific reference classes. It has four methods:

`public T get()`
> Returns this reference object's referent object.

`public void clear()`
> Clears this reference object so it has no referent object.

`public boolean enqueue()`
> Adds this reference object to the reference queue with which it is registered, if any. Returns `true` if the reference object was enqueued and `false` if there is no registered queue or this reference object was already enqueued.

`public boolean isEnqueued()`
> Returns `true` if this reference object has been enqueued (either by the programmer or the garbage collector), and `false` otherwise.

We defer a discussion of reference queues until Section 17.5.3 on page 459.

Subclasses of `Reference` provide ways to bind the referent object to the reference object—the existing subclasses do this with a constructor argument. Once an object has been wrapped in a reference object you can retrieve the object via `get` (and thus have a normal strong reference to it) or you can clear the reference, perhaps making the referent unreachable. There is no means to change the object referred to by the reference object and you cannot subclass `Reference` directly.

17.5.2 Strengths of Reference and Reachability

In decreasing order of strength, the kinds of reference objects available to you are `SoftReference<T>`, `WeakReference<T>`, and `PhantomReference<T>`. These correspond to the reachability stages an object can pass through:

- ◆ An object is *strongly reachable* if it can be reached through at least one chain of strong references (the normal kind of references).

- ◆ An object is *softly reachable* if it is not strongly reachable, but is reachable through at least one chain containing a soft reference.

- ◆ An object is *weakly reachable* if it is not softly reachable, but is reachable through at least one chain containing a weak reference.

- ◆ An object is *phantom reachable* when it is not weakly reachable, has been finalized (if necessary), but is reachable through at least one chain containing a phantom reference.

- ◆ Finally, an object is *unreachable* if it is not reachable through any chain.

Once an object becomes weakly reachable (or less), it can be finalized. If after finalization the object is unreachable, it can be reclaimed.

Objects need not actually go through all these stages. For example, an object that is reachable only through strong references becomes unreachable when it is no longer strongly reachable.

The reachability stages of an object trigger behavior in the garbage collector appropriate to the corresponding reference object types:

- ◆ A softly reachable object may be reclaimed at the discretion of the garbage collector. If memory is low, the collector may clear a `SoftReference` object so that its referent can be reclaimed. There are no specific rules for the order in which this is done (but a good implementation will prefer keeping recently used or created references, where "used" is defined as "invoked `get`"). You can be sure that all `SoftReference`s to softly reachable objects will be cleared before an `OutOfMemoryError` is thrown.

- ◆ A weakly reachable object will be reclaimed by the garbage collector. When the garbage collector determines that an object is weakly reachable, all `WeakReference` objects that refer to that object will be cleared. The object then becomes finalizable and after finalization will be reclaimed (assuming it is not resurrected) unless it is phantom reachable.

- ◆ A phantom reachable object isn't really reachable in the normal sense because the referent object cannot be accessed via a `PhantomReference`— `get` always returns `null`. But the existence of the phantom reference prevents the object from being reclaimed until the phantom reference is explicitly cleared. Phantom references allow you to deal with objects whose `finalize` methods have been invoked and so can safely be considered "dead." Phantom references are used in conjunction with the reference queues we discuss in the next section.

Both SoftReference and WeakReference declare a constructor that takes a single referent object. All three classes declare a two-argument constructor that takes a referent object and a ReferenceQueue.

Soft references provide you with a kind of caching behavior, clearing older references while trying not to clear new or used ones. Consider our web browser scenario. If you maintain your images in soft references, they will be reclaimed as memory runs low. Images are probably relatively unimportant to keep in memory should memory run low, and clearing the oldest or least used images would be a reasonable approach. In contrast, if you used weak references then all images would be reclaimed as soon as memory got low—this would probably induce a lot of overhead as you reload images that it may not have been necessary to get rid of in the first place.

Weak references are a way of holding a reference to an object but saying "reclaim this object if this is the only type of reference to it."

Consider the following method that returns data read into memory from a file. The method has been optimized under the assumption that the same file is often named more than once in a row and that reading the data is expensive:

```java
import java.lang.ref.*;
import java.io.File;

class DataHandler {
    private File lastFile;              // last file read
    private WeakReference<byte[]>
                        lastData; // last data (maybe)

    byte[] readFile(File file) {
        byte[] data;

        // check to see if we remember the data
        if (file.equals(lastFile)) {
            data = lastData.get();
            if (data != null)
                return data;
        }

        // don't remember it, read it in
        data = readBytesFromFile(file);
        lastFile = file;
        lastData = new WeakReference<byte[]>(data);
```

```
            return data;
        }
    }
```

When readFile is called it first checks to see if the last file read was the same as the one being requested. If it is, readFile retrieves the reference stored in lastData, which is a weak reference to the last array of bytes returned. If the reference returned by get is null, the data has been garbage collected since it was last returned and so it must be re-read. The data is then wrapped in a new WeakReference. If get returns a non-null reference, the array has not been collected and can be returned.

If lastData were a direct, strong reference to the last data returned, that data would not be collected, even if the invoking program had long since dropped all references to the array. Such a strong reference would keep the object alive as long as the DataHandler object itself was reachable. This could be quite unfortunate. Using a WeakReference allows the space to be reclaimed, at the cost of occasionally re-reading the data from disk.

Notice that invoking get on lastData makes the byte array strongly reachable once again because its value is bound to an active local variable—a strong reference. If get returns a non-null reference there is no possibility of the byte array being reclaimed as long as readFile is executing, or the block of code to which readFile returns the reference is executing. That invoking code can store the reference in a reachable place or return it to another method, thereby ensuring the data's reachability. An object can only be less than strongly reachable when none of its references are strong. Storing a non-null reference fetched from a reference object's get method creates a strong reference that will be treated like any other strong reference.

Weak references typically store information about an object that might be time consuming to compute but that need not outlive the object itself. For example, if you had some complicated information built up from using reflection on an object, you might use the java.util.WeakHashMap class, which is a hashtable for mapping a weakly-held object to your information. If the object becomes unreachable the WeakHashMap will clean up the associated information, which presumably is no longer useful (since the object will not be used in any future computation because of its weak reachability). You will learn about WeakHashMap with the rest of the collection classes in Chapter 21, specifically in Section 21.9 on page 594.

Exercise 17.2: Modify DataHandler so that lastFile is also stored weakly.

17.5.3 Reference Queues

When an object changes reachability state, references to the object may be placed on a *reference queue*. These queues are used by the garbage collector to communicate with your code about reachability changes. They are usually the best way to detect such changes, although you can sometimes poll for changes as well, by seeing if get returns null.

Reference objects can be associated with a particular queue when they are constructed. Each of the Reference subclasses provide a constructor of the form

public *Strength*Reference(T referent, ReferenceQueue<? super T> q)
> Creates a new reference object with the given referent and registered with the given queue.

Both weak and soft references are enqueued at some point after the garbage collector determines that their referent has entered that particular reachability state, and in both cases they are cleared before being enqueued. Phantom references are also enqueued at some point after the garbage collector determines the referent is phantom reachable, but they are not cleared. Once a reference object has been queued by the garbage collector, it is guaranteed that get will return null, and so the object cannot be resurrected.

Registering a reference object with a reference queue does not create a reference between the queue and the reference object. If your reference object itself becomes unreachable, then it will never be enqueued. So your application needs to keep a strong reference to all reference objects.

The ReferenceQueue class provides three methods for removing references from the queue:

public Reference<? extends T> poll()
> Removes and returns the next reference object from this queue, or null if the queue is empty.

public Reference<? extends T> remove()
> throws InterruptedException
>> Removes and returns the next reference object from this queue. This method blocks indefinitely until a reference object is available from the queue.

public Reference<? extends T> remove(long timeout)
> throws InterruptedException
>> Removes and returns the next reference object from this queue. This method blocks until a reference object is available from the queue or the specified time-out period elapses. If the time-out expires, null is returned. A time-out of zero means wait indefinitely.

The `poll` method allows a thread to query the existence of a reference in a queue, taking action only if one is present, as in the example. The `remove` methods are intended for more complex (and rare) situations in which a dedicated thread is responsible for removing references from the queue and taking the appropriate action—the blocking behavior of these methods is the same as that defined by `Object.wait` (as discussed from page 354). You can ask whether a particular reference is in a queue via its `isEnqueued` method. You can force a reference into its queue by calling its `enqueue` method, but usually this is done by the garbage collector.

Reference queues are used with phantom references to determine when an object is about to be reclaimed. A phantom reference never lets you reach the object, even when it is otherwise reachable: Its `get` method always returns `null`. In effect it is the safest way to find out about a collected object—a weak or soft reference will be enqueued after an object is finalizable; a phantom reference is enqueued after the referent has been finalized and, therefore only after the last possible time that the object can do something. If you can, you should generally use a phantom reference because the other references still allow the possibility that a `finalize` method will use the object.

Consider a resource manager that controls access to some set of external resources. Objects can request access to a resource and use it until they are done, after which they should return the resource back to the resource manager. If the resource is shared, and use of it is passed from object to object, perhaps even across multiple threads, then it can be difficult to determine which use of the resource is the last use. That makes it difficult to determine which piece of code is responsible for returning the resource. To deal with this situation, the resource manager can automate the recovery of the resource by associating with it a special object called the *key*. As long as the key object is reachable, the resource is considered in use. As soon as the key object can be reclaimed, the resource is automatically released. Here's an abstract representation of such a resource:

```
interface Resource {
    void use(Object key, Object... args);
    void release();
}
```

When a resource is obtained, a key must be presented to the resource manager. The `Resource` instance that is given back will only allow use of the resource when presented with that key. This ensures that the resource cannot be used after the key has been reclaimed, even though the `Resource` object itself may still be reachable. Note that it is important that the `Resource` object not store a strong reference to the key object, since that would prevent the key from ever becoming unreachable, and so the resource could never be recovered. A Resource implementation class might be nested in the resource manager:

```
private static class ResourceImpl implements Resource {
    int keyHash;
    boolean needsRelease = false;

    ResourceImpl(Object key) {
        keyHash = System.identityHashCode(key);

        // .. set up the external resource

        needsRelease = true;
    }

    public void use(Object key, Object... args) {
        if (System.identityHashCode(key) != keyHash)
            throw new IllegalArgumentException("wrong key");

        // ... use the resource ...
    }

    public synchronized void release() {
        if (needsRelease) {
            needsRelease = false;

            // .. release the resource ...
        }
    }
}
```

When the resource is created it stores the identity hash code of the key, and whenever use is called, it checks that the same key was provided. Actually using the resource may require additional synchronization, but for simplicity this is elided. The release method is responsible for releasing the resource. It can either be called directly by the users of the resource when they have finished, or it will be called through the resource manager when the key object is no longer referenced. Because we will be using a separate thread to watch the reference queue, release has to be synchronized and it has to be tolerant to being called more than once.

The actual resource manager looks like this:

```
public final class ResourceManager {

    final ReferenceQueue<Object> queue;
    final Map<Reference<?>, Resource> refs;
    final Thread reaper;
    boolean shutdown = false;

    public ResourceManager() {
        queue = new ReferenceQueue<Object>();
        refs = new HashMap<Reference<?>, Resource>();
        reaper = new ReaperThread();
        reaper.start();

        // ... initialize resources ...
    }

    public synchronized void shutdown() {
        if (!shutdown) {
            shutdown = true;
            reaper.interrupt();
        }
    }

    public synchronized Resource getResource(Object key) {
        if (shutdown)
            throw new IllegalStateException();
        Resource res = new ResourceImpl(key);
        Reference<?> ref =
            new PhantomReference<Object>(key, queue);
        refs.put(ref, res);
        return res;
    }
}
```

The key object can be an arbitrary object—this gives great flexibility to the users of the resource, compared to having the resource manager assign a key. When getResource is invoked, a new ResourceImpl object is created, passing in the supplied key. A phantom reference is then created, with the key as the referent, and using the resource manager's reference queue. The phantom reference and the resource object are then stored into a map. This map serves two purposes:

First, it keeps all the phantom reference objects reachable; second it provides an easy way to find the actual resource object associated with each phantom reference. (The alternative would be to subclass `PhantomReference` and store the `Resource` object in a field.)

The resource manager uses a separate "reaper" thread to process resources when the key has become unreachable. The `shutdown` method "turns off" the resource manager by allowing the reaper to terminate (in response to the interruption) and causing `getResource` calls to throw `IllegalStateException`. In this simple design, any references enqueued after shutdown will not be processed. The actual reaper thread looks like this:

```
class ReaperThread extends Thread {
    public void run() {
        // run until interrupted
        while (true) {
            try {
                Reference<?> ref =  queue.remove();
                Resource res = null;
                synchronized(ResourceManager.this) {
                    res = refs.get(ref);
                    refs.remove(ref);
                }
                res.release();
                ref.clear();
            }
            catch (InterruptedException ex) {
                break; // all done
            }
        }
    }
}
```

`ReaperThread` is an inner class, and a given reaper thread runs until its associated resource manager is shut down. It blocks on `remove` until a phantom reference associated with a particular key has been enqueued. The phantom reference is used to get a reference to the `Resource` object from the map, and then that entry is removed from the map. The `Resource` object then has `release` invoked on it to release the resource. Finally, the phantom reference is cleared so that the key can actually be reclaimed.

As an alternative to using a separate thread, the `getResource` method could instead `poll` the queue whenever it is called and release any resources whose key has become unreachable. The `shutdown` method could then do a final poll, too.

The semantics for the resource manager necessarily depend on the actual kind of resource and its usage patterns.

A design that uses reference queues can be more reliable than direct use of finalization—particularly with phantom references—but remember that there are no guarantees as to exactly when or in what order a reference object will be enqueued. There are also no guarantees that by the time an application terminates, all enqueuable reference objects will have been enqueued. If you need to guarantee that all resources are released before the application terminates, you must install the necessary shutdown hooks (see "Shutdown" on page 672) or other application-defined protocols to ensure this happens.

Exercise 17.3: Rework the resource implementation class so that it uses a reference object to keep track of the key instead of using the hash code.

Exercise 17.4: Modify the reaper thread so that it stays alive after shutdown until all the allocated resources can be released.

Exercise 17.5: Redesign the resource manager to not use a reaper thread. Be clear on what semantics the resource manager has and on when resources will be released.

17.5.4 Finalization and Reachability

An object becomes finalizable when it becomes weakly reachable (or less). It would seem that to determine reachability you need simply examine the source code for your applications. Unfortunately, such an examination would often be wrong. Reachability is not determined by the statements in your source code, but by the actual state of the virtual machine at runtime. The virtual machine can perform certain optimizations that make an object unreachable much sooner than a simple examination of the source code would indicate.

For example, suppose a method creates an object that controls an external resource and that the only reference is through a local variable. The method then uses the external resource and finally nulls the local reference or simply returns, allowing the object to be finalized and release the external resource. The programmer might assume that the object is reachable until that reference is set to `null` or the method returns. But the virtual machine can detect that the object is not referenced within the method and may deem it unreachable and finalizable the instant after it was constructed, causing immediate finalization and release of the resource, which was not something the programmer intended. Even the reference queue designs that we have discussed depend on the referent remaining reachable as long as the programmer expects it to be reachable.

The optimizations under consideration only apply to references held on the stack—that is, references stored in local variables or parameters. If a reference is stored in a field, then the object remains reachable at least until the field no longer refers to it. This approach also covers the case of inner class objects—an inner class instance is reachable whenever its enclosing instance is reachable.

There are further subtle interactions between finalization, synchronization, and the memory model, but these are advanced topics unneeded by most programmers and are beyond the scope of this book.

> *Don't ever take a fence down until you know the reason why it was put up.*
> —G.K. Chesterton

CHAPTER 18

Packages

For some reason a glaze passes over people's faces when you say "Canada".
Maybe we should invade South Dakota or something.
—Sandra Gotlieb, wife of Canadian ambassador to U.S. (1981–1989)

PACKAGES define units of software that can be distributed independently and combined with other packages to form applications. Packages have members that are related classes, interfaces, and subpackages, and may contain additional resource files (such as images) used by the classes in the package. Packages are useful for several reasons:

- ◆ Packages create groupings for related interfaces and classes. For example, a set of library classes for performing statistical analysis could be grouped together in a `stats` package. The package can be placed in an archive file, together with a manifest describing the package, and shipped to customers for use in their applications.

- ◆ Packages create namespaces that help avoid naming conflicts between types. Interfaces and classes in a package can use popular public names (such as `List` and `Constants`) that make sense in one context but might conflict with the same name in another package.

- ◆ Packages provide a protection domain for developing application frameworks. Code within a package can cooperate using access to identifiers that are unavailable to external code.

Let us look at a package for the attribute classes you saw in previous chapters. We will name the package `attr`. Each source file whose classes and interfaces belong in the `attr` package states its membership with its `package` declaration:

```
package attr;
```

This statement declares that all classes and interfaces defined in this source file are part of the `attr` package. A `package` declaration must appear first in your source file, before any class or interface declarations. Only one package declaration can appear in a source file. The package name is implicitly prefixed to each type name contained within the package.

If a type is not declared as being part of an explicit package, it is placed in an unnamed package. Each system must support at least one unnamed package, but they can support more—typically one per class loader. The existence of the unnamed package makes it simple for you to write small programs without being encumbered by the organizational requirements imposed on the members of named packages. Any non-trivial program or set of library classes should always be part of a named package.

18.1 Package Naming

A package name should prevent collisions with other packages, so choosing a name that's both meaningful and unique is an important aspect of package design. But with programmers around the globe developing packages, there is no way to find out who is using what package names. So choosing unique package names is a problem. If you are certain a package will be used only inside your organization, you can use an internal arbiter to ensure that no projects pick clashing names.

But in the world at large, this approach is not practical. Package identifiers are simple names. A good way to ensure unique package names is to use an Internet domain name. If you worked at a company named Magic, Inc., that owned the domain name `magic.com`, the attribute package declaration should be

```
package com.magic.attr;
```

Notice that the components of the domain name are reversed from the normal domain name convention.

If you use this convention, your package names should not conflict with those of anyone else, except possibly within your organization. If such conflicts arise (likely in a large organization), you can further qualify using a more specific domain. Many large companies have internal subdomains with names such as `east` and `europe`. You could further qualify the package name with such a subdomain name:

```
package com.magic.japan.attr;
```

Package names can become quite long under this scheme, but it is relatively safe. No one else using this technique will choose the same package name, and programmers not using the technique are unlikely to pick your names.

18.2 Type Imports

Type imports are a generalization of the static imports that you learned about in Chapter 2 on page 71. They allow you to refer to types by their simple names instead of having to write their fully qualified name.

When you write code outside a package that needs types declared within that package you have two options. One is to use the fully qualified name of the type. This option is reasonable if you use only a few items from a package, but given the long names that packages tend to acquire (or even the shorter ones in the standard libraries) it can be quite tedious to use fully qualified names.

The other way to use types from a package is to *import* part or all of the package. A programmer who wants to use the `attr` package could put the following line near the top of a source file (after any `package` declaration but before anything else):

```
import attr.*;
```

Now the types in that package can be referred to simply by name, such as `Attributed`. An import that uses a * is called an *import on demand* declaration. You can also perform a *single type import:*

```
import attr.Attributed;
```

The name used with an import statement must be the canonical name of a package (for import on demand) or type (for single type import). As discussed in "Naming Classes" on page 411, the canonical name and fully qualified name can differ only for nested types. Note that generic types are imported using their raw type name—that name can then be used in a parameterized type without further qualification.

Code in a package imports the rest of its own package implicitly, so everything defined in a package is available to all types in the same package. The package `java.lang` is implicitly imported in all code.

The import mechanism is passive in that it does not cause information about the named packages and types to be read in at compile time—unless a type is used. The `import` statement simply tells the compiler how it can determine the fully qualified name for a type that is used in your program if it can't find that type defined locally. For example, as described on page 181, if your class declares a reference of type `Attributed` the compiler will search for the type in the following order:

1. The current type including inherited types.
2. A nested type of the current type.

3. Explicitly named imported types (single type import).

4. Other types declared in the same package.

5. Implicitly named imported types (import on demand).

If, after that, the type is still not found it is an error. It is also an error if any package named in an import statement cannot be located—even if there is no actual need to obtain a type from that package.

Resolving which type is being referred to requires some work by the compiler, and use of import on demand may involve more work than resolving a single type import. However, this is rarely significant in the compilation process. The choice between a single type import and import on demand is usually a matter of personal preference or local style rules. Naturally, to resolve conflicts or to ensure that a specific type is resolved correctly you may need to use a single type import.[1]

Type imports can also be used with nested class names. For example, in Chapter 5 we defined the `BankAcount` class and its nested `Permissions` class. If these classes were in the package `bank` and you imported `bank.BankAccount`, you would still need to use `BankAccount.Permissions` to name the `Permissions` class. However, you could instead import `bank.BankAccount.Permissions` and then use the simple name `Permissions`. You don't have to import `BankAccount` to import the class `BankAccount.Permissions`. Importing nested type names in this way should generally be avoided because it loses the important information that the type is actually a nested type.

Static nested types can be imported using either the type import mechanism or the static import mechanism. If you insist on importing nested types, then you should use the type import mechanism for consistency.

The `package` and `import` mechanisms give programmers control over potentially conflicting names. If a package used for another purpose, such as linguistics, has a class called `Attributed` for language attributes, programmers who want to use both types in the same source file have several options:

◆ Refer to all types by their fully qualified names, such as `attr.Attributed` and `lingua.Attributed`.

---

[1] For example, if you use import on demand for a given package and there is a type in that package with the same name as a type in the current package, then the current package type would be found ahead of the imported package. In this case you could use a single type import for that one type to make it clear that it is the type from the other package that is required. Alternatively, of course, you could just use the fully qualified name.

- Import only `attr.Attributed` or `attr.*`, use the simple name `Attributed` for `attr.Attributed`, and use the full name of `lingua.Attributed`.

- Do the converse: import `lingua.Attributed` or `lingua.*`, use the simple name `Attributed` for `lingua.Attributed`, and use the full name of `attr.Attributed`.

- Import all of both packages—`attr.*` and `lingua.*`—and use the fully qualified names `attr.Attributed` and `lingua.Attributed` in your code. (If a type with the same name exists in two packages imported on demand, you cannot use the simple name of either type.)

It is an error to import a specific type that exists as a top-level (that is non-nested) type within the current source file. For example, you can't declare your own `Vector` class and import `java.util.Vector`. Nor can you import the same type name from two different packages using two single type imports. As noted above, if two types of the same name are implicitly imported on demand, you cannot use the simple type name but must use the fully qualified name. Use of the simple name would be ambiguous and so result in a compile-time error.

18.3 Package Access

You have two options when declaring accessibility of top-level classes and interfaces within a package: package and public. A `public` class or interface is accessible to code outside that package. Types that are not `public` have package scope: They are available to all other code in the same package, but they are hidden outside the package and even from code in subpackages. Declare as `public` only those types needed by programmers using your package, hiding types that are package implementation details. This technique gives you flexibility when you want to change the implementation—programmers cannot rely on implementation types they cannot access, and that leaves you free to change them.

A class member that is not declared `public`, `protected`, or `private` can be used by any code within the package but is hidden outside the package. In other words, the default access for an identifier is "package" except for members of interfaces, which are implicitly public.

Fields or methods not declared `private` in a package are available to all other code in that package. Thus, classes within the same package are considered "friendly" or "trusted." This allows you to define application frameworks that are a combination of predefined code and placeholder code that is designed to be overridden by subclasses of the framework classes. The predefined code can use package access to invoke code intended for use by the cooperating package classes while making that code inaccessible to any external users of the package. However, subpackages are not trusted in enclosing packages or vice versa. For example, package identifiers in package dit are not available to code in package dit.dat, or vice versa.

Every type has therefore three different contracts that it defines:

◆ The public contract, defining the primary functionality of the type.

◆ The protected contract, defining the functionality available to subtypes for specialization purposes.

◆ The package contract, defining the functionality available within the package to effect cooperation between package types.

All of these contracts require careful consideration and design.

18.3.1 Accessibility and Overriding Methods

A method can be overridden in a subclass only if the method is accessible in the superclass. If the method is not accessible in the superclass then the method in the subclass does *not* override the method in the superclass even if it has the same signature. When a method is invoked at runtime the system has to consider the accessibility of the method when deciding which implementation of the method to run.

The following contrived example should make this clearer. Suppose we have a class AbstractBase declared in package P1:

```
package P1;

public abstract class AbstractBase {
    private   void pri() { print("AbstractBase.pri()"); }
              void pac() { print("AbstractBase.pac()"); }
    protected void pro() { print("AbstractBase.pro()"); }
    public    void pub() { print("AbstractBase.pub()"); }

    public final void show() {
        pri();
        pac();
        pro();
        pub();
    }
}
```

We have four methods, each with a different access modifier, each of which simply identifies itself. The method show invokes each of these methods on the current object. It will show which implementation of each method is invoked when applied to different subclass objects.

Now we define the class Concrete1, which extends AbstractBase but lives in the package P2:

```
package P2;

import P1.AbstractBase;

public class Concrete1 extends AbstractBase {
    public void pri() { print("Concrete1.pri()"); }
    public void pac() { print("Concrete1.pac()"); }
    public void pro() { print("Concrete1.pro()"); }
    public void pub() { print("Concrete1.pub()"); }
}
```

This class redeclares each of the methods from the superclass and changes their implementation to report that they are in class Concrete1. It also changes their access to public so that they are accessible to all other code. Executing the code

```
new Concrete1().show();
```

produces the following output:

```
AbstractBase.pri()
AbstractBase.pac()
Concrete1.pro()
Concrete1.pub()
```

Because the private method pri is inaccessible to subclasses (or to any other class) the implementation from AbstractBase is always the one invoked from show. The package accessible pac method of AbstractBase is not accessible in Concrete1, thus the implementation of pac in Concrete1 does not override that in AbstractBase, so it is AbstractBase.pac that show invokes. Both the pro and pub methods are accessible in Concrete1 and get overridden, so the implementation from Concrete1 is used in show.

Next we define the class `Concrete2`, which extends `Concrete1` but is in the same package P1 as `AbstractBase`:[2]

```
package P1;

import P2.Concrete1;

public class Concrete2 extends Concrete1 {
    public void pri() { print("Concrete2.pri()"); }
    public void pac() { print("Concrete2.pac()"); }
    public void pro() { print("Concrete2.pro()"); }
    public void pub() { print("Concrete2.pub()"); }
}
```

Each method of `Concrete2` overrides the version from `Concrete1` because they are all public and therefore accessible. Also, because `Concrete2` is in the same package as `AbstractBase`, the method `AbstractBase.pac` is accessible in `Concrete2` and so is overridden by `Concrete2.pac`. Invoking show on a `Concrete2` object prints

```
AbstractBase.pri()
Concrete2.pac()
Concrete2.pro()
Concrete2.pub()
```

Finally, we define the class `Concrete3`, which extends `Concrete2` but is in a different package P3:

```
package P3;

import P1.Concrete2;

public class Concrete3 extends Concrete2 {
    public void pri() { print("Concrete3.pri()"); }
    public void pac() { print("Concrete3.pac()"); }
    public void pro() { print("Concrete3.pro()"); }
    public void pub() { print("Concrete3.pub()"); }
}
```

---

[2] Having an inheritance hierarchy that weaves in and out of a package is generally a very bad idea. It is used here purely for illustration.

Invoking show on a Concrete3 object prints

```
AbstractBase.pri()
Concrete3.pac()
Concrete3.pro()
Concrete3.pub()
```

Here the method Concrete3.pac appears to have overridden the inaccessible AbstractBase.pac. In fact, Concrete3.pac overrides Concrete2.pac, and Concrete2.pac overrides AbstractBase.pac—therefore Concrete3.pac transitively overrides AbstractBase.pac. By redeclaring pac as public, Concrete2 made it accessible and overridable by any subclass.[3]

18.4 Package Contents

Packages should be designed carefully so that they contain only functionally related classes and interfaces. Classes in a package can freely access one another's non-private members. Protecting class members is intended to prevent misuse by classes that have access to internal details of other classes. Anything not declared private is available to all types in the package, so unrelated classes could end up working more intimately than expected with other classes.

Packages should also provide logical groupings for programmers who are looking for useful interfaces and classes. A package of unrelated classes makes the programmer work harder to figure out what is available. Logical grouping of classes helps programmers reuse your code because they can more easily find what they need. Including only related, coherent sets of types in a package also means that you can use obvious names for types, thereby avoiding name conflicts.

Packages can be nested inside other packages. For example, java.lang is a nested package in which lang is nested inside the larger java package. The java package contains only other packages. Nesting allows a hierarchical naming system for related packages.

For example, to create a set of packages for adaptive systems such as neural networks and genetic algorithms, you could create nested packages by naming the packages with dot-separated names:

```
package adaptive.neuralNet;
```

A source file with this declaration lives in the adaptive.neuralNet package, which is itself a subpackage of the adaptive package. The adaptive package

---

[3] This illustrates why weaving in and out of a package can be confusing and should be avoided.

might contain classes related to general adaptive algorithms, such as generic problem statement classes or benchmarking. Each package deeper in the hierarchy—such as `adaptive.neuralNet` or `adaptive.genetic`—would contain classes specific to the particular kind of adaptive algorithm.

Package nesting is an organizational tool for related packages, but it provides no special access between packages. Class code in `adaptive.genetic` cannot access package-accessible identifiers of the `adaptive` or `adaptive.neuralNet` packages. Package scope applies only to a particular package. Nesting can group related packages and help programmers find classes in a logical hierarchy, but it confers no other benefits.

18.5 Package Annotations

A package can have annotations applied to it. The problem is that there is no actual definition of a package to which you can apply such annotations—unlike a class or a method—because a package is an organizational structure, not a source code entity. So you annotate packages by applying the annotation to the package statement within a source file for that package. However, only one package declaration per package can have annotations applied to it.

So how do you actually annotate a package? There is no required way to deal with this "single annotated package statement" rule. The suggested approach is to create a file called `package-info.java` within the package directory, and to put in that file nothing but a package statement with any annotations for the package (plus any useful comments, of course). For example, a `package-info.java` file for the `attr` package might look like this:

```
@PackageSpec(name = "Attr Project", version = "1.0")
@DevelopmentSite("attr.project.org")
@DevelopmentModel("open-source")
package attr;
```

where `PackageSpec`, `DevelopmentSite`, and `DevelopmentModel` are made up annotation types—with a runtime retention policy, of course. The `package-info.java` file should be compiled along with the rest of the package source files.

The `package-info.java` file is recommended as the single place to put all package-related information. To that end, you can place a documentation comment at the start of the file, and that will be the package documentation for that package. Package documentation is covered in more detail in "Package and Overview Documentation" on page 496.

The java.lang.Package class implements AnnotatedElement, so you can ask about any applied annotations using the methods discussed in "Annotation Queries" on page 414.

18.6 Package Objects and Specifications

Packages typically implement a specification, and they are also typically from one organization. A Package object, unlike the other reflection types (see Chapter 16), is not used to create or manipulate packages, but acts only as a repository for information about the specification implemented by a package (its title, vendor, and version number) and for information about the implementation itself (its title, vendor, and version number). Although a package typically comes from a single organization, the specification for that package (such as a statistical analysis library) may have been defined by someone else. Programs using a package may need to be able to determine the version of the specification implemented by the package so that they use only functionality defined in that version. Similarly, programs may need to know which version of the implementation is provided, primarily to deal with bugs that may exist in different versions. The main methods of Package allow access to this information:

public String **getName()**
    Returns the name of this package.

public String **getSpecificationTitle()**
    Returns the title of the specification this package implements, or null if the title is unknown.

public String **getSpecificationVersion()**
    Returns a string describing the version of the specification that this package implements, or null if the version is unknown.

public String **getSpecificationVendor()**
    Returns the name of the vendor that owns and maintains the specification that this package implements, or null if the vendor is unknown.

public String **getImplementationTitle()**
    Returns the title of the implementation provided by this package, or null if the title is unknown.

public String **getImplementationVersion()**
    Returns a string describing the version of the implementation provided by this package, or null if the version is unknown.

`public String `**`getImplementationVendor()`**

> Returns the name of the organization (vendor) that provided this implementation, or `null` if the organization is unknown.

For example, extracting this information for the `java.lang` package on our system yielded the following:[4]

```
Specification Title:    Java Platform API Specification
Specification Version:  1.4
Specification Vendor:    Sun Microsystems, Inc.
Implementation Title:   Java Runtime Environment
Implementation Version: 1.5.0_02
Implementation Vendor:  Sun Microsystems, Inc.
```

Specification version numbers are non-negative numbers separated by periods, as in `"2.0"` or `"11.0.12"`. This pattern allows you to invoke the `isCompatibleWith` method to compare a version following this pattern with the version of the package. The method returns `true` if the package's specification version number is greater than or equal to the one passed in. Comparison is done one dot-separated number at a time. If any such value in the package's number is less than the one from the passed in version, the versions are not compatible. If one of the version numbers has more components than the other, the missing components in the shorter version number are considered to be zero. For example, if the package's specification version is `"1.4"` and you compare it to `"1.2"`, `"1.3.1"`, or `"1.1.8"`, you will get `true`, but if you compare it to `"1.4.2"` or `"1.5"`, you will get `false`. This comparison mechanism assumes backward compatibility between specification versions.

Implementation version numbers do not have a defined format because these will be defined by the different organizations providing the implementations. The only comparison you can perform between implementation versions is a test for equality—there is no assumption of backward compatibility.

Packages can be *sealed,* which means that no classes can be added to them. An unsealed package can have classes come from several different places in a class search path. A sealed package's contents must all come from one place—generally either a specific archive file or a location specified by a URL. Two methods ask if a package is sealed:

`public boolean `**`isSealed()`**

> Returns `true` if the package is sealed.

---

[4]   Yes the 1.4 specification version is a bug

```
public boolean isSealed(URL url)
```
Returns `true` if the package is sealed with respect to the given URL, that is, classes in the package can be loaded from the URL. Returns `false` if classes in the package cannot be loaded from the given URL or if the package is unsealed.

The specification and implementation information for a package is usually supplied as part of the manifest stored with the package—such as the manifest of a Java Archive (jar) file, as described in "Archive Files—`java.util.jar`" on page 735. This information is read when a class gets loaded from that package. A `ClassLoader` can dynamically define a `Package` object for the classes it loads:

```
protected Package definePackage(String name, String specTitle,
    String specVersion, String specVendor, String implTitle,
    String implVersion, String implVendor, URL sealBase)
```
Returns a `Package` object with the given name, and with specification and implementation values set to the corresponding arguments. If `sealBase` is `null` the package is unsealed, otherwise it is sealed with respect to that URL. The `Package` object for a class must be defined before the class is defined and package names must be unique within a class loader. If the package name duplicates an existing name, an `IllegalArgumentException` is thrown.

You can get the `Package` object for a given class from the `getPackage` method of the `Class` object for that class. You can also get a `Package` object by invoking either the static method `Package.getPackage` with the name of the package, or the static method `Package.getPackages`, which returns an array of all known packages. Both methods work with respect to the class loader of the code making the call by invoking the `getPackage` or `getPackages` method of that class loader. These class loader methods search the specific class loader and all of its parents. If there is no current class loader then the system class loader is used. Note that the class loader methods will return `null` if the package is unknown because no type from the package has been loaded.

> *When a shepherd goes to kill a wolf, and takes his dog along to see the sport,*
> *he should take care to avoid mistakes.*
> *The dog has certain relationships to the wolf the shepherd may have forgotten.*
> —Robert Prisig, *Zen and the Art of Motorcycle Maintenance*

CHAPTER 19

Documentation Comments

Any member introducing a dog into the Society's premises shall be liable to a fine of £10.
Any animal leading a blind person shall be deemed to be a cat.
—Rule 46, Oxford Union Society (circa 1997)

DOCUMENTATION comments, usually called *doc comments,* let you associate reference documentation for programmers directly with your code. The contents of the doc comment can be used to generate reference documentation, typically presented using HTML.

Doc comments are generally designed as fairly terse reference documentation. The reference documentation typically covers the contract of the documented interface, class, constructor, method, or field to the level of detail most programmers need. This approach is distinct from a full specification, which can be too long for reference documentation. A full specification might devote several pages of text to a single method, whereas reference documentation might be one or two paragraphs, possibly even short ones. Specifications should be produced separately, although they can be cross-referenced by the doc comment, as you will soon see.[1]

The procedure for generating documentation from the doc comments varies among development environments. One common procedure is to run the javadoc command on the packages or types; hence, the generated documentation is often called *javadoc.*

This chapter teaches what can go into documentation comments and how the contents are interpreted. You will also learn about features that are, strictly speaking, outside the language but are conventions for creating the generated documentation, such as overall package documentation and the location for images and other resources. Your development environment may not use these details in pre-

---

[1] This distinction is blurring and, for better or worse, documentation comments are being used to define full specifications.

cisely the same way as `javadoc` but it is likely to, and if not will usually have an analogous replacement. These features are covered in the section "External Conventions" on page 496.

19.1 The Anatomy of a Doc Comment

Doc comments start with the three characters /** and continue until the next */. Each doc comment describes the identifier whose declaration immediately follows. Leading * characters are ignored on doc comment lines, as are whitespace characters preceding a leading *. The first sentence of the comment is the summary for the identifier; "sentence" means all text up to the first period with following whitespace. Consider the doc comment:

```
/**
 * Do what the invoker intends.  "Intention" is defined by
 * an analysis of past behavior as described in ISO 4074-6.
 */
public void dwim() throws IntentUnknownException;
```

The summary for the method `dwim` will be "Do what the invoker intends." Your first sentence in a doc comment should be a good summary.

HTML tags are often embedded in doc comments as formatting directives or cross-reference links to other documentation. You can use almost any standard HTML tag. Be careful when using the header tags <h1>, <h2>, and so on, because they can disrupt the structure of the overall documentation—however, they are usually safe to use within class and package documentation. To insert the character <, >, or & you should use <, >, or &, respectively. If you must have an @ at the beginning of a line, use @—otherwise, an @ is assumed to start a doc comment tag.

Only doc comments that immediately precede a class, interface, method, or field are processed. If anything besides whitespace, comments, or annotations are between a doc comment and what it describes, the doc comment will be ignored. For example, if you put a doc comment at the top of a file with a `package` or `import` statement between the doc comment and the `class`, the doc comment will not be used. Doc comments apply to all fields declared in a single statement, so declaring multiple fields in a single statement is usually avoided where doc comments are used.

19.2 Tags

Doc comments can contain *tags* that hold particular kinds of information. Tags come in two forms:

◆ *Block tags* define stand-alone text elements. All these tags start with @, as in @see or @deprecated. These paragraphs are treated specially in the generated documentation, resulting in marked paragraphs, links to other documentation, and other special treatment. This section describes all tags except @serial, @serialData, and @serialField, which relate to object serialization and are described in "The Object Byte Streams" on page 549.

◆ *In-line tags* can occur anywhere within the text of a documentation comment and are used to apply special formatting, such as {@code} for use of code font, or to produce special text, such as creating a hypertext link using {@link}. In-line tags all have the form {@*tag-name args*} where the optional *args* value might provide text to be formatted or the target of the link, for example.

Except for tagged paragraphs and in-line tags, text in a doc comment is treated as input text for HTML. You can create paragraph breaks in the documentation with the standard <p> tag, blocks of example code using <pre>, and so on.

Not all tags need be processed by the javadoc tool by default; consult your tool documentation for details on what is needed to process which tags.

19.2.1 @see

The @see tag creates a cross-reference link to other javadoc documentation. You can name any identifier, although you must qualify it sufficiently. You can, for example, usually name a member of a class with its simple name. However, if the member is an overloaded method, you must specify which overload of the method you mean by listing the types of parameters. You can specify an interface or class that is in the current package by its unqualified name, but you must specify types from other packages with fully qualified names. You specify members of types by a # before the member name. The following are all potentially valid @see tags:

```
@see #getName
@see Attr
@see com.magic.attr.Attr
@see com.magic.attr.Deck#DECK_SIZE
@see com.magic.attr.Attr#getName
@see com.magic.attr.Attr#Attr(String)
```

```
@see com.magic.attr.Attr#Attr(String, Object)
@see com.magic.attr
@see <a href="spec.html#attr">Attribute Specification</a>
@see "The Java Developer's Almanac"
```

The first form refers to the method getName in the same class or interface as the doc comment itself, or in any enclosing class or interface; the same syntax can be used for constructors and fields. The second form refers to a class in the current package or an imported package. The third refers to a class by its fully qualified name.

The next four @see forms refer to members. The first two show forms for a field (DECK_SIZE) or method (getName). We can simply use the name of a method because exactly one getName method is defined in the Attr class. The next two forms refer to constructors of the Attr class, one that takes a String argument and another that takes a String and an Object. When a constructor or method is overloaded you must specify the arguments of the one you mean.

The next @see form directs readers to a specific package: com.magic.attr.

The final two forms allow you to reference other documentation. The first defines a link using <a...>. The second uses quotes to enclose the name of the document. You might use these to direct readers to other documentation, such as the full specification.

The @see forms that name a language entity (any of the above forms except the last two) can have a *label* following the entity. This label name will be the one used in the generated documentation instead of the entity's name. For example,

```
@see #getName Attribute Names
```

will create a link to the documentation of getName but will display the text "Attribute Names" not "getName". You should usually let the actual member name be used, but occasionally you may find this feature useful.

19.2.2 {@link} and {@linkplain}

The @see tag is useful for a "See also" section at the end of the documentation. You can embed an {@link} in-line tag in your text when the cross reference should belong in the text of your comment. The syntax for @link is

```
{@link package.class#member [label]}
```

The identifier specification is the same as for @see, as is the optional label. The following sentence embeds a link to the getValue method:

```
Changes the value returned by calls to {@link #getValue}.
```

The {@linkplain} tag acts just like {@link} except that the generated text uses a plain font rather code font. This is useful for replacing the link with a label that consists of plain text.

19.2.3 @param

The @param tag documents a single parameter to a method or constructor, or else a type parameter in a class, interface, or generic method. If you use @param tags you should have one for each parameter of the method. The first word of the paragraph is taken as the parameter name, and the rest is its description:

```
@param max    The maximum number of words to read.
```

When documenting type parameters you should use < and > around the type parameter name:

```
@param <E>  The element type of this List
```

Usually, though, type parameters don't require explicit documentation since their meaning is obvious.

19.2.4 @return

The @return tag documents the return value of a method:

```
@return       The number of words actually read.
```

19.2.5 @throws and @exception

The @throws tag documents an exception thrown by the method or constructor. If you use @throws tags you should have one for each type of exception the method throws. This list often includes more than just the checked exceptions that must be declared in the throws clause—it is a good idea to declare all exceptions in the throws clause whether or not they are required, and the same is true when you're using @throws tags. For example, suppose that your method checks its parameters to ensure that none is null, throwing NullPointerException if it finds a null argument. You should declare NullPointerException in your throws clause and your @throws tags.

```
@throws UnknownName    The name is unknown.
@throws java.io.IOException
                Reading the input stream failed; this exception
                is passed through from the input stream.
```

```
@throws NullPointerException
            The name is <code>null</code>.
```

The tag @exception is equivalent to @throws.

19.2.6 @deprecated

The @deprecated tag marks an identifier as being deprecated: unfit for continued use. Code using a deprecated type, constructor, method, or field *may* generate a warning when compiled. You should ensure that the deprecated entity continues working so that you don't break existing code that hasn't yet been updated. Deprecation helps you encourage users of your code to update to the latest version but preserves the integrity of existing code. Users can shift to newer mechanisms when they choose to instead of being forced to shift as soon as you release a new version of your types. You should direct users to a replacement for deprecated entities:

```
/**
 * Do what the invoker intends.  "Intention" is defined by
 * an analysis of past behavior as described in ISO 4074-6.
 *
 * @deprecated  You should use dwishm instead
 * @see         #dwishm
 */
@Deprecated
public void dwim() throws IntentUnknownException;
```

While the compiler *may* generate a warning if it sees the @deprecated tag, it is *guaranteed* to generate a warning if it sees the @Deprecated annotation. You should always use the two together: Use the @deprecated tag to document the reason for the deprecation, and use the @Deprecated annotation to inform the compiler.

19.2.7 @author

The @author tag specifies an author of a class or interface.

```
@author Aristophanes
@author Ursula K. LeGuin
@author Ibid
```

You can specify as many @author paragraphs as you desire. You should use only one author per @author paragraph to get consistent output in all circumstances.

19.2.8 @version

The @version tag lets you specify an arbitrary version specification for the class or interface.

```
@version 1.1
```

19.2.9 @since

The @since tag lets you specify an arbitrary version specification that denotes when the tagged entity was added to your system.

```
@since 2.1
```

Tagging the "birth version" can help you track which entities are newer and therefore may need intensified documentation or testing. By convention an @since tag on a class or interface applies to all members of the class or interface that don't have their own @since tag. For example, if the above @since tag preceded a class, then all constructors, fields, and methods of that class would be presumed to have been present in version 2.1 except any that had, for example, an @since 2.2 tag of its own.

19.2.10 {@literal} and {@code}

The {@literal *text*} in-line tag causes *text* to be printed exactly as is, without being interpreted as HTML source. This means that you can use &, <, and > rather than &, <, and >.

The {@code *text*} in-line tag behaves exactly like {@literal *text*} except that *text* is printed in code font. You'd get the same effect wrapping the {@literal *text*} tag in <code> and </code> HTML tags.

These in-line tags are exceedingly convenient for writing about generic types.

19.2.11 {@value}

The {@value *static-field-name*} tag is replaced by the actual value of the specified constant static field. This tag uses the same member syntax as the @see tag. For example, if a doc comment contained the text:

```
The valid range is 0 to {@value java.lang.Short#MAX_VALUE}.
```

Then the generated text would be

```
The valid range is 0 to 32767.
```

As a convenience, the value of the constant static field being documented can be referred to by {@value}, with no field name. For example, given

```
/** The default capacity of a new queue ({@value}). */
static final int DEFAULT_CAPACITY = 10;
```

the generated text would be

```
The default capacity of a new queue (10).
```

When specifying a particular field member, be careful not to leave any whitespace between the member name and the closing } because it will be treated as part of the name.

All constant fields are documented on the "Constant Field Values" page, generated by the javadoc tool.

19.2.12 {@docRoot}

The files generated by javadoc are put into a tree, with subdirectories that contain parts of the documentation. The exact placement of files in the tree is up to the javadoc implementation, and may change depending on your environment, user preferences, and the like. You may want to add things to the tree after it is built and then refer to those added pieces in your doc comments.

The in-line {@docRoot} tag lets you put into your doc comments a relative reference to other files in the documentation tree. The {@docRoot} tag will be replaced with a relative path to the top of the generated documentation tree. For example, the sentence

```
Check out <a href="{@docRoot}/license.html">our license</a>.
```

would result in a sentence with a link to the file license.html in the root of the documentation tree. After generating the documentation from the doc comments, you could copy license.html into the top of the generated documentation tree, and the above link would always go from the generated output to your license.html file. For some applications you may find the mechanism described in "The doc-files Directory" on page 497 more useful.

19.2.13 {@inheritDoc}

The {@inheritDoc} tag copies a documentation comment from the supertype. This is discussed in the next section.

19.3 Inheriting Method Documentation Comments

If no doc comment is given for an inherited method, the method "inherits" the doc comment from the supertype. This is often quite enough, especially when a class implements an interface—methods in the implementation often do nothing more than what the interface specifies, or at least nothing that belongs in a doc comment. It would be inconvenient, to say the least, if you had to duplicate all the doc comments from an interface or superclass to the class that defines the overriding method.

You should put in an explicit comment when you are inheriting doc comments so that someone reading your code doesn't think that you forgot to document the method, for example:

```
// inherit doc comment
public void dwim() throws IntentUnknownException {
    // ...
}
```

While overriding an interface method might not require any changes to the documentation, there is a good chance that overriding a superclass method involves changes to the method contract—such as weakening the precondition on a parameter, strengthening the postcondition on a return value, or reducing the types of exception that can be thrown. To make it easier to change only those parts of the documentation that need changing, the block tags define separate entities that can be inherited independently:

- ◆ The main doc comment for the method is known as the *body comment*. If you don't provide a body comment you will inherit the complete body comment from the supertype. If you provide any text as a body comment, then you won't inherit any part of the supertype's body comment.

- ◆ Each @param comment is inherited independently, based on the name of the parameter. If you don't provide an @param comment for a parameter, then you'll inherit the @param comment from the supertype.

- ◆ If no @return comment is specified then the @return comment from the supertype is inherited.

- ◆ There are special rules for @throws comments, as discussed below.

If a method inherits doc comments from both a superclass and superinterface the interface comment is used.

Often, the change to a doc comment only involves the addition of extra information. For example, an overriding method might guarantee that it never returns null, where the parent method could return null. To avoid manually copying the doc comment from the supertype, you can use the {@inheritDoc} tag to copy the doc comment from the supertype. The {@inheritDoc} tag can appear either in the body comment or within any of the block tags, and it copies the entire supertype's doc comment for that entity. For example, the method that no longer returns null could have a doc comment like this:

```
/**
 * @return   {@inheritDoc}
 * This implementation never returns null.
 */
```

The {@inheritDoc} tag allows you to easily add new documentation before or after the inherited documentation, but its effectiveness depends on how the original documentation was written. For example, if the previous method's original @return comment was

```
@return The value last set, or null if it has not been set.
```

then the additional documentation results in a less than clear description:

```
Returns: The value last set, or null if it has not been set.
         This implementation never returns null.
```

For the sake of clarity, it might be better to rewrite the entire doc comment rather than try to augment it.

19.3.1 Inheriting @throws Comments

There is a special rule for inheriting @throws comments: An overriding method only inherits the @throws comments for exceptions listed in its throws clause, and that are documented by the overridden method. For example, if the original method has an @throws comment for IOException and the overriding method declares that it throws IOException, then the comment is inherited. However, if the overriding method declares that it throws FileNotFoundException (a subclass of IOException) then the comment is not inherited because that exception type is not documented by the overridden method. This restriction on when inheritance of the @throws comment occurs is necessary because automatically inheriting @throws comments is often the wrong thing to do. Unfortunately, not inheriting them can also be the wrong thing to do.

An overriding method can throw fewer checked exceptions than the method it overrides, but not more. So automatically inheriting @throws comments for a checked exception that is not actually thrown would be the wrong thing to do. For checked exceptions it makes sense to inherit the documentation comments only for those exceptions listed in the throws clause. They are, after all, the only checked exceptions that can be thrown. So you inherit the comment if you still throw the exception and you don't inherit the comment if you don't.

Runtime exceptions, which are not typically declared in the throws clause, add a twist to the situation. You usually want to inherit @throws comments for exceptions like IllegalArgumentException because what is illegal for the method you override is typically illegal for your method—so if you don't automatically inherit the comment the exception won't be documented and that is wrong. But then consider, for example, an interface with optionally implemented methods that declare that they throw UnsupportedOperationException. This runtime exception is documented by an @throws comment. If the comment is automatically inherited then even if a particular class's implementation supports the operation and so never throws the exception, the exception will be documented as being thrown—which, again, is wrong.

By requiring that exceptions be listed in the throws clause before inheriting the associated @throws comment, the problem with inheriting inapplicable @throws comments is avoided. However, this promotes a style of programming where runtime exceptions are listed in a method's throws clause, which goes against standard practice. We recommend that you continue to list only checked exceptions in the throws clause of a method. Rather than trying to automatically inherit the doc comments for unchecked exceptions, we suggest that you manually rewrite the @throws comment, but use {@inheritDoc} to avoid the need to manually copy the exception description. For example, you can use the following to document that your method will still throw IllegalArgumentException when it's parent would:

```
@throws IllegalArgumentException {@inheritDoc}
```

The onus is still on you to remember that unchecked exceptions must be manually documented in this way.

19.4 A Simple Example

The following is a version of the Attr class from page 76 with an example of javadoc comments:

```
/**
 * An <code>Attr</code> object defines an attribute as a
 * name/value pair, where the name is a <code>String</code>
 * and the value an arbitrary <code>Object</code>.
```

```java
 *
 * @version 1.1
 * @author Plato
 * @since 1.0
 */
public class Attr {
    /** The attribute name. */
    private final String name;
    /** The attribute value. */
    private Object value = null;

    /**
     * Creates a new attribute with the given name and an
     * initial value of <code>null</code>.
     * @see Attr#Attr(String,Object)
     */
    public Attr(String name) {
        this.name = name;
    }

    /**
     * Creates a new attribute with the given name and
     * initial value.
     * @see Attr#Attr(String)
     */
    public Attr(String name, Object value) {
        this.name = name;
        this.value = value;
    }

    /** Returns this attribute's name. */
    public String getName() {
        return name;
    }

    /** Returns this attribute's value. */
    public Object getValue() {
        return value;
    }

    /**
```

```
 * Sets the value of this attribute.  Changes the
 * value returned by calls to {@link #getValue}.
 * @param newValue  The new value for the attribute.
 * @return  The original value.
 * @see #getValue()
 */
public Object setValue(Object newValue) {
    Object oldVal = value;
    value = newValue;
    return oldVal;
}


/**
 * Returns a string of the form <code>name=value</code>.
 */
public String toString() {
    return name + "='" + value + "'";
}
}
```

For simple methods like getName, whose whole description is what it returns, the @return tag is often omitted as overkill. Similarly, the constructors do not use @param tags because the description is sufficiently complete. Different organizations will make different choices of when to use each tag.

You should use doc comments to document all members, including private and package-accessible ones. Documentation generators such as javadoc let you specify whether you want to generate documentation from these comments. Having organized, readable documentation of your class's internals is quite useful when someone else needs to learn about them.

On the following two pages, you can see how the generated HTML javadoc output might look for this class.

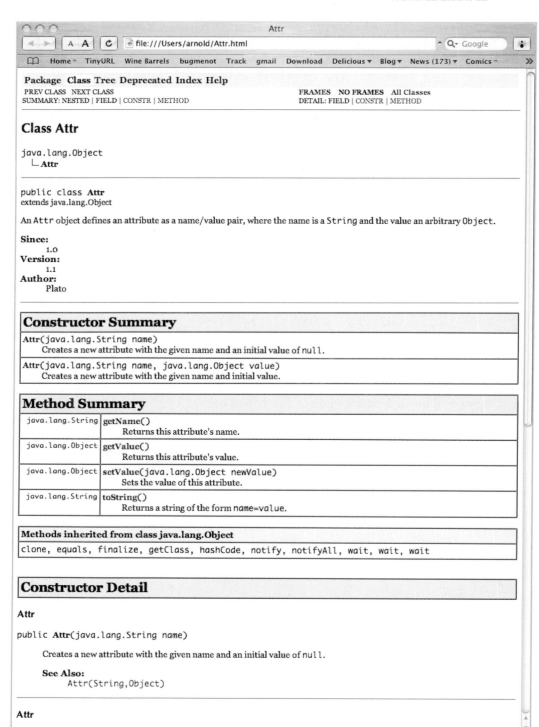

Attr

file:///Users/arnold/Attr.html

Package **Class** Tree Deprecated Index Help

PREV CLASS NEXT CLASS
SUMMARY: NESTED | FIELD | CONSTR | METHOD

FRAMES   NO FRAMES   All Classes
DETAIL: FIELD | CONSTR | METHOD

Class Attr

```
java.lang.Object
  └ Attr
```

public class **Attr**
extends java.lang.Object

An `Attr` object defines an attribute as a name/value pair, where the name is a `String` and the value an arbitrary `Object`.

Since:
  1.0
Version:
  1.1
Author:
  Plato

Constructor Summary

Attr(java.lang.String name)
  Creates a new attribute with the given name and an initial value of `null`.

Attr(java.lang.String name, java.lang.Object value)
  Creates a new attribute with the given name and initial value.

Method Summary

java.lang.String	**getName**() Returns this attribute's name.
java.lang.Object	**getValue**() Returns this attribute's value.
java.lang.Object	**setValue**(java.lang.Object newValue) Sets the value of this attribute.
java.lang.String	**toString**() Returns a string of the form `name=value`.

Methods inherited from class java.lang.Object

`clone, equals, finalize, getClass, hashCode, notify, notifyAll, wait, wait, wait`

Constructor Detail

Attr

public **Attr**(java.lang.String name)

   Creates a new attribute with the given name and an initial value of `null`.

   See Also:
     Attr(String,Object)

Attr

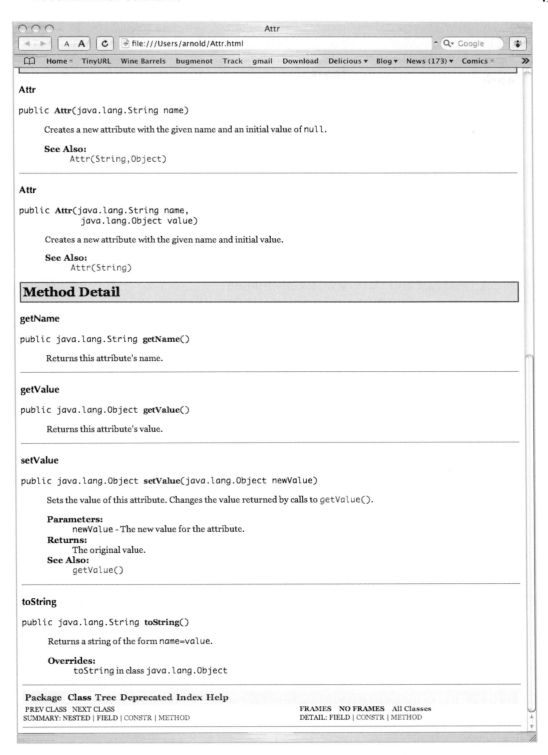

O O O   Attr

◄ ► | A A | C | file:///Users/arnold/Attr.html   ^ Q▾ Google   ☀

🕮 Home ▪ TinyURL Wine Barrels bugmenot Track gmail Download Delicious ▾ Blog ▾ News (173) ▾ Comics ▪   »

Attr

```
public Attr(java.lang.String name)
```

> Creates a new attribute with the given name and an initial value of null.
>
> **See Also:**
> > Attr(String,Object)

Attr

```
public Attr(java.lang.String name,
            java.lang.Object value)
```

> Creates a new attribute with the given name and initial value.
>
> **See Also:**
> > Attr(String)

Method Detail

getName

```
public java.lang.String getName()
```

> Returns this attribute's name.

---

getValue

```
public java.lang.Object getValue()
```

> Returns this attribute's value.

---

setValue

```
public java.lang.Object setValue(java.lang.Object newValue)
```

> Sets the value of this attribute. Changes the value returned by calls to getValue().
>
> **Parameters:**
> > newValue - The new value for the attribute.
>
> **Returns:**
> > The original value.
>
> **See Also:**
> > getValue()

---

toString

```
public java.lang.String toString()
```

> Returns a string of the form name=value.
>
> **Overrides:**
> > toString in class java.lang.Object

Package Class Tree Deprecated Index Help

PREV CLASS NEXT CLASS

FRAMES   NO FRAMES   All Classes

SUMMARY: NESTED | FIELD | CONSTR | METHOD

DETAIL: FIELD | CONSTR | METHOD

Exercise 19.1: Add doc comments to your `LinkedList` class from Exercise 2.16. Generate the javadoc and ask someone else to write a simple program using your class. Repeat, improving your doc comments if needed, until someone can do so.

Exercise 19.2: Expand on Exercise 19.1 by including the private members. Generate the full (private members included) javadoc and ask someone else to explain the class to you. Repeat, improving your comments if needed, until someone can do so.

19.5 External Conventions

Not all documentation needed for a package can be ascribed to a specific source file, nor are source files the only types of files that need to be referred to in documentation. You can incorporate such external elements in your documentation.

19.5.1 Package and Overview Documentation

Doc comments associate documentation with elements in source files, but packages are not defined in source files. The `javadoc` tool uses other conventions to allow packages to be documented.

The preferred mechanism, as mentioned in Section 18.5 on page 476, is to use the `package-info.java` file. This file should contain a single `package` statement identifying the package to which the file belongs, together with all annotations that apply to the package. In addition, if that package statement (with its applied annotations if any) is preceded by a doc comment, then that doc comment is treated as documentation for the overall package. This package documentation forms part of the package summary page that is produced by `javadoc`.

If there is no `package-info.java` file for a package, then `javadoc` will look for a file called `package.html`. If this file exists, then its contents between `<body>` and `</body>` will be read as if it were a doc comment for the package (although it should not have the `/**`, `*/`, or any leading `*`). Note that `package.html` will be ignored if `package-info.java` exists.

As with other doc comments, the first sentence of the package comment is used as a summary for the package. In the case of `package.html`, this is the first sentence after the `<body>` HTML tag. Any `@see` or `{@link}` tag that names a language element must use the fully qualified form of the entity's name, even for classes and interfaces within the package itself.

Finally, you can also provide an overview HTML file. An overview HTML file is read in the same way as a `package.html` file, and it can contain documentation for a set of packages or classes, giving an overview of what they do. You specify the HTML file to use as an overview when generating the documentation.

19.5.2 The doc-files Directory

The javadoc program will copy the contents of a doc-files directory in a given package into the generated documentation for that package. You can use this feature to include images, HTML, class files, or any other component you want to reference in your doc comment. For example, you could indirectly include a set of formal rules in a large number of doc comments:

```
@see <a href="doc-files/semantics.html">Formal Semantics</a>
```

Or you could use the directory to store useful images:

```
Made by Magic, Inc.<img src="doc-files/magiclogo.gif">
```

19.6 Notes on Usage

Tightly coupling the reference documentation to the source code has many advantages, but it does not turn all programmers into good documentation writers. Programmers will continue to vary in their ability and interest in writing good reference documentation. Many organizations have technical writers to produce the reference documentation. Doc comments require write access to the source, and technical writers often do not have permission to modify source code. The use of doc comments will require a change in such organizations.

Another issue is *comment skew,* in which comments become out of date as the source code changes over time. You can reduce this problem by putting only contractual information in your doc comments and not describing the implementation. When the implementation changes, the doc comment will still be correct as long as the contract remains unmodified. Changing the contract of an existing type, constructor, method, or field is a questionable practice in many cases, so such changes should be rare. Describing only the contract is generally a good practice in any case because it frees you to change details of the implementation in the future. Implementation details of methods need to be documented—use regular comments for this purpose.

You can further reduce the problem of comment skew by defining a standard marker for programmers to place in doc comments that need attention. For example, if you add a new method to a class, you could write the first draft of the doc comment, but flag the comment as one that might need review and rework by the documentation team:

```
/**
 * ...initial draft...
 * @docissue Review -- programmer's first draft
 */
```

A script run over the source could find @docissue markers and show them to the documentation team, alerting them to work that remains to be done. Some documentation generators allow you to add your own doc comment paragraph tags, so using an @ tag—such as @docissue shown above—allows you to flag these or other issues directly in the generated documentation as well as in the source itself.

> *The universe is made of stories,*
> *not atoms.*
> —Muriel Rukeyser

CHAPTER 20

The I/O Package

From a programmer's point of view,
the user is a peripheral that types when you issue a read *request.*
—Peter Williams

THE Java platform includes a number of packages that are concerned with the movement of data into and out of programs. These packages differ in the kinds of abstractions they provide for dealing with I/O (input/output).

The `java.io` package defines I/O in terms of *streams*. Streams are ordered sequences of data that have a *source* (input streams) or *destination* (output streams). The I/O classes isolate programmers from the specific details of the underlying operating system, while enabling access to system resources through files and other means. Most stream types (such as those dealing with files) support the methods of some basic interfaces and abstract classes, with few (if any) additions. The best way to understand the I/O package is to start with the basic interfaces and abstract classes.

The `java.nio` package and its subpackages define I/O in terms of *buffers* and *channels*. Buffers are data stores (similar to arrays) that can be read from or written to. Channels represent connections to entities capable of performing I/O operations, including buffers, files, and sockets. The "n" in `nio` is commonly understood as meaning "new" (the `nio` package predates the original stream-based `io` package), but it originally stood for "non-blocking" because one of the key differences between channel-based I/O and stream-based I/O is that channels allow for non-blocking I/O operations, as well as interruptible blocking operations. This is a powerful capability that is critical in the design of high throughput server-style applications.

The `java.net` package provides specific support for network I/O, based around the use of sockets, with an underlying stream or channel-based model.

This chapter is mainly concerned with the stream-based model of the `java.io` package. A short introduction to some of the capabilities of the `java.nio` package is given in "A Taste of New I/O" on page 565, but the use of non-blocking I/O and the `java.net` network I/O are advanced topics, beyond the scope of this book.

20.1 Streams Overview

The package `java.io` has two major parts: *character streams* and *byte streams.* Characters are 16-bit UTF-16 characters, whereas bytes are (as always) 8 bits. I/O is either text-based or data-based (binary). Text-based I/O works with streams of human-readable characters, such as the source code for a program. Data-based I/O works with streams of binary data, such as the bit pattern for an image. The character streams are used for text-based I/O, while byte streams are used for data-based I/O. Streams that work with bytes cannot properly carry characters, and some character-related issues are not meaningful with byte streams—though the byte streams can also be used for older text-based protocols that use 7- or 8-bit characters. The byte streams are called *input streams* and *output streams,* and the character streams are called *readers* and *writers.* For nearly every input stream there is a corresponding output stream, and for most input or output streams there is a corresponding reader or writer character stream of similar functionality, and vice versa.

Because of these overlaps, this chapter describes the streams in fairly general terms. When we talk simply about streams, we mean any of the streams. When we talk about input streams or output streams, we mean the byte variety. The character streams are referred to as readers and writers. For example, when we talk about the `Buffered` streams we mean the entire family of `BufferedInputStream`, `BufferedOutputStream`, `BufferedReader`, and `BufferedWriter`. When we talk about `Buffered` byte streams we mean both `BufferedInputStream` and `BufferedOutputStream`. When we talk about `Buffered` character streams, we mean `BufferedReader` and `BufferedWriter`.

The classes and interfaces in `java.io` can be broadly split into five groups:

- ◆ The general classes for building different types of byte and character streams—input and output streams, readers and writers, and classes for converting between them—are covered in Section 20.2 through to Section 20.4.

- ◆ A range of classes that define various types of streams—filtered streams, buffered streams, piped streams, and some specific instances of those streams, such as a line number reader and a stream tokenizer—are discussed in Section 20.5.

- ◆ The data stream classes and interfaces for reading and writing primitive values and strings are discussed in Section 20.6.

◆ Classes and interfaces for interacting with files in a system independent manner are discussed in Section 20.7.

◆ The classes and interfaces that form the *object serialization* mechanism, which transforms objects into byte streams and allows objects to be reconstituted from the data read from a byte stream, are discussed in Section 20.8.

Some of the output streams provide convenience methods for producing formatted output, using instances of the `java.util.Formatter` class. You get formatted input by binding an input stream to a `java.util.Scanner` object. Details of formatting and scanning are covered in Chapter 22.

The `IOException` class is used by many methods in `java.io` to signal exceptional conditions. Some extended classes of `IOException` signal specific problems, but most problems are signaled by an `IOException` object with a descriptive string. Details are provided in Section 20.9 on page 563. Any method that throws an `IOException` will do so when an error occurs that is directly related to the stream. In particular, invoking a method on a closed stream may result in an `IOException`. Unless there are particular circumstances under which the `IOException` will be thrown, this exception is not documented for each individual method of each class.

Similarly, `NullPointerException` and `IndexOutOfBoundsException` can be expected to be thrown whenever a `null` reference is passed to a method, or a supplied index accesses outside of an array. Only those situations where this does not occur are explicitly documented.

All code presented in this chapter uses the types in `java.io`, and every example has imported `java.io.*` even when there is no explicit `import` statement in the code.

20.2 Byte Streams

The `java.io` package defines abstract classes for basic byte input and output streams. These abstract classes are then extended to provide several useful stream types. Stream types are almost always paired: For example, where there is a `FileInputStream` to read from a file, there is usually a `FileOutputStream` to write to a file.

Before you can learn about specific kinds of input and output byte streams, it is important to understand the basic `InputStream` and `OutputStream` abstract classes. The type tree for the byte streams of `java.io` in Figure 20–1 shows the type hierarchy of the byte streams.

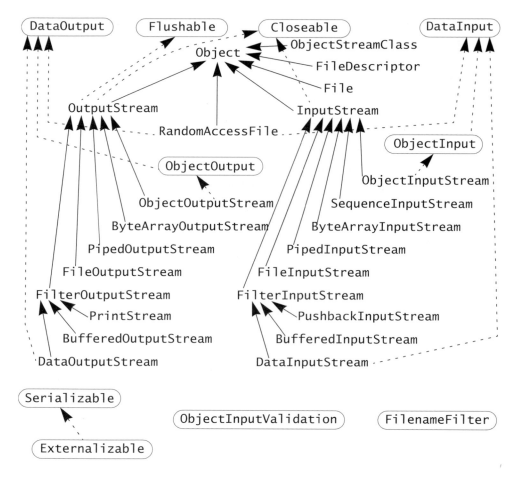

FIGURE 20–1: *Type Tree for Byte Streams in* **java.io**

All byte streams have some things in common. For example, all streams support the notion of being open or closed. You open a stream when you create it, and can read or write while it is open. You close a stream with its **close** method, defined in the **Closeable**[1] interface. Closing a stream releases resources (such as file descriptors) that the stream may have used and that should be reclaimed as soon as they are no longer needed. If a stream is not explicitly closed it will hold on to these resources. A stream class could define a **finalize** method to release these resources during garbage collection but, as you learned on page 449, that could be too late. You should usually close streams when you are done with them.

---

[1]   Yes, another misspelling.

All byte streams also share common synchronization policies and concurrent behavior. These are discussed in Section 20.5.1 on page 515.

20.2.1 `InputStream`

The abstract class `InputStream` declares methods to read bytes from a particular source. `InputStream` is the superclass of most byte input streams in `java.io`, and has the following methods:

`public abstract int` **`read()`** `throws IOException`

> Reads a single byte of data and returns the byte that was read, as an integer in the range 0 to 255, not –128 to 127; in other words, the byte value is treated as unsigned. If no byte is available because the end of the stream has been reached, the value –1 is returned. This method blocks until input is available, the end of stream is found, or an exception is thrown. The `read` method returns an `int` instead of an actual `byte` value because it needs to return all valid byte values plus a flag value to indicate the end of stream. This requires more values than can fit in a `byte` and so the larger `int` is used.

`public int` **`read(byte[] buf, int offset, int count)`**
  `throws IOException`

> Reads into a part of a `byte` array. The maximum number of bytes read is `count`. The bytes are stored from `buf[offset]` up to a maximum of `buf[offset+count-1]`—all other values in `buf` are left unchanged. The number of bytes actually read is returned. If no bytes are read because the end of the stream was found, the value –1 is returned. If `count` is zero then no bytes are read and zero is returned. This method blocks until input is available, the end of stream is found, or an exception is thrown. If the first byte cannot be read for any reason other than reaching the end of the stream—in particular, if the stream has already been closed—an `IOException` is thrown. Once a byte has been read, any failure that occurs while trying to read subsequent bytes is not reported with an exception but is treated as encountering the end of the stream—the method completes normally and returns the number of bytes read before the failure occurred.

`public int` **`read(byte[] buf)`** `throws IOException`

> Equivalent to `read(buf, 0, buf.length)`.

`public long` **`skip(long count)`** `throws IOException`

> Skips as many as `count` bytes of input or until the end of the stream is found. Returns the actual number of bytes skipped. If `count` is negative, no bytes are skipped.

public int **available()** throws IOException
> Returns the number of bytes that can be read (or skipped over) without blocking. The default implementation returns zero.

public void **close()** throws IOException
> Closes the input stream. This method should be invoked to release any resources (such as file descriptors) associated with the stream. Once a stream has been closed, further operations on the stream will throw an IOException. Closing a previously closed stream has no effect. The default implementation of close does nothing.

The implementation of InputStream requires only that a subclass provide the single-byte variant of read because the other read methods are defined in terms of this one. Most streams, however, can improve performance by overriding other methods as well. The default implementations of available and close will usually need to be overridden as appropriate for a particular stream.

The following program demonstrates the use of input streams to count the total number of bytes in a file, or from System.in if no file is specified:

```
import java.io.*;

class CountBytes {
    public static void main(String[] args)
        throws IOException
    {
        InputStream in;
        if (args.length == 0)
            in = System.in;
        else
            in = new FileInputStream(args[0]);

        int total = 0;
        while (in.read() != -1)
            total++;

        System.out.println(total + " bytes");
    }
}
```

This program takes a filename from the command line. The variable in represents the input stream. If a file name is not provided, it uses the standard input stream System.in; if one is provided, it creates an object of type FileInputStream, which is a subclass of InputStream.

The `while` loop counts the total number of bytes in the file. At the end, the results are printed. Here is the output of the program when used on itself:

```
318 bytes
```

You might be tempted to set `total` using `available`, but it won't work on many kinds of streams. The `available` method returns the number of bytes that can be read *without blocking*. For a file, the number of bytes available is usually its entire contents. If `System.in` is a stream associated with a keyboard, the answer can be as low as zero; when there is no pending input, the next `read` will block.

20.2.2 `OutputStream`

The abstract class `OutputStream` is analogous to `InputStream`; it provides an abstraction for writing bytes to a destination. Its methods are:

public abstract void **write(int b)** throws IOException
> Writes b as a byte. The byte is passed as an `int` because it is often the result of an arithmetic operation on a byte. Expressions involving bytes are type `int`, so making the parameter an `int` means that the result can be passed without a cast to `byte`. Note, however, that only the lowest 8 bits of the integer are written. This method blocks until the byte is written.

public void **write(byte[] buf, int offset, int count)**
  throws IOException
> Writes part of an array of bytes, starting at `buf[offset]` and writing count bytes. This method blocks until the bytes have been written.

public void **write(byte[] buf)** throws IOException
> Equivalent to `write(buf, 0, buf.length)`.

public void **flush()** throws IOException
> Flushes the stream. If the stream has buffered any bytes from the various `write` methods, `flush` writes them immediately to their destination. Then, if that destination is another stream, it is also flushed. One `flush` invocation will flush all the buffers in a chain of streams. If the stream is not buffered, `flush` may do nothing—the default implementation. This method is defined in the `Flushable` interface.

public void **close()** throws IOException
> Closes the output stream. This method should be invoked to release any resources (such as file descriptors) associated with the stream. Once a stream has been closed, further operations on the stream will throw an `IOException`. Closing a previously closed stream has no effect. The default implementation of `close` does nothing.

The implementation of OutputStream requires only that a subclass provide the single-byte variant of write because the other write methods are defined in terms of this one. Most streams, however, can improve performance by overriding other methods as well. The default implementations of flush and close will usually need to be overridden as appropriate for a particular stream—in particular, buffered streams may need to flush when closed.

Here is a program that copies its input to its output, translating one particular byte value to a different one along the way. The TranslateByte program takes two parameters: a from byte and a to byte. Bytes that match the value in the string from are translated into the value in the string to.

```java
import java.io.*;

class TranslateByte {
    public static void main(String[] args)
        throws IOException
    {
        byte from = (byte) args[0].charAt(0);
        byte to   = (byte) args[1].charAt(0);
        int b;
        while ((b = System.in.read()) != -1)
            System.out.write(b == from ? to : b);
    }
}
```

For example, if we invoked the program as

```java
java TranslateByte b B
```

and entered the text abracadabra!, we would get the output

```
aBracadaBra!
```

Manipulating data from a stream after it has been read, or before it is written, is often achieved by writing Filter streams, rather than hardcoding the manipulation in a program. You'll learn about filters in Section 20.5.2 on page 516.

Exercise 20.1: Rewrite the TranslateByte program as a method that translates the contents of an InputStream onto an OutputStream, in which the mapping and the streams are parameters. For each type of InputStream and OutputStream you read about in this chapter, write a new main method that uses the translation method to operate on a stream of that type. If you have paired input and output streams, you can cover both in one main method.

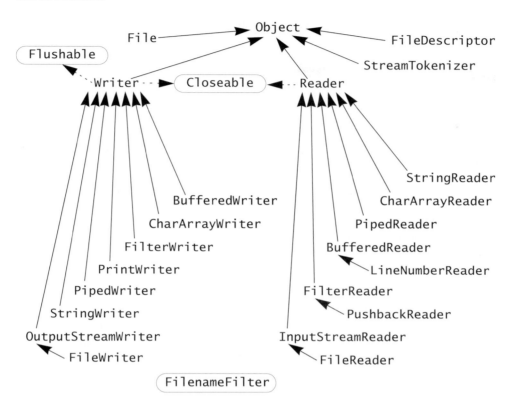

FIGURE 20–2: *Type Tree for Character Streams in* `java.io`

20.3 Character Streams

The abstract classes for reading and writing streams of characters are `Reader` and `Writer`. Each supports methods similar to those of its byte stream counterpart— `InputStream` and `OutputStream`, respectively. For example, `InputStream` has a `read` method that returns a `byte` as the lowest 8 bits of an `int`, and `Reader` has a `read` method that returns a `char` as the lowest 16 bits of an `int`. And where `OutputStream` has methods that write `byte` arrays, `Writer` has methods that write `char` arrays. The character streams were designed after the byte streams to provide full support for working with Unicode characters, and in the process the contracts of the classes were improved to make them easier to work with. The type tree for the character streams of `java.io` appears in Figure 20–2.

As with the byte streams, character streams should be explicitly closed to release resources associated with the stream. Character stream synchronization policies are discussed in Section 20.5.1 on page 515.

20.3.1 Reader

The abstract class `Reader` provides a character stream analogous to the byte stream `InputStream` and the methods of `Reader` essentially mirror those of `InputStream`:

`public int` **`read()`** `throws IOException`
> Reads a single character and returns it as an integer in the range 0 to 65535. If no character is available because the end of the stream has been reached, the value –1 is returned. This method blocks until input is available, the end of stream is found, or an exception is thrown.

`public abstract int` **`read(char[] buf, int offset, int count)`**
`throws IOException`
> Reads into a part of a char array. The maximum number of characters to read is `count`. The read characters are stored from `buf[offset]` up to a maximum of `buf[offset+count-1]`—all other values in `buf` are left unchanged. The number of characters actually read is returned. If no characters are read because the end of the stream was found, –1 is returned. If `count` is zero then no characters are read and zero is returned. This method blocks until input is available, the end of stream is found, or an exception is thrown. If the first character cannot be read for any reason other than finding the end of the stream—in particular, if the stream has already been closed—an `IOException` is thrown. Once a character has been read, any failure that occurs while trying to read characters does not cause an exception, but is treated just like finding the end of the stream—the method completes normally and returns the number of characters read before the failure occurred.

`public int` **`read(char[] buf)`** `throws IOException`
> Equivalent to `read(buf, 0, buf.length)`.

`public int` **`read(java.nio.CharBuffer buf)`** `throws IOException`
> Attempts to read as many characters as possible into the specified character buffer, without overflowing it. The number of characters actually read is returned. If no characters are read because the end of the stream was found, –1 is returned. This is equivalent to reading into an array that has the same length as the buffer has available capacity, and then copying the array into the buffer. This method is defined in the `java.lang.Readable` interface, and has no counterpart in `InputStream`.

```
public long skip(long count) throws IOException
```
Skips as many as count characters of input or until the end of the stream is found. Returns the actual number of characters skipped. The value of count must not be negative.

```
public boolean ready() throws IOException
```
Returns true if the stream is ready to read; that is, there is at least one character available to be read. Note that a return value of false does not guarantee that the next invocation of read will block because data could have become available by the time the invocation occurs.

```
public abstract void close() throws IOException
```
Closes the stream. This method should be invoked to release any resources (such as file descriptors) associated with the stream. Once a stream has been closed, further operations on the stream will throw an IOException. Closing a previously closed stream has no effect.

The implementation of Reader requires that a subclass provide an implementation of both the read method that reads into a char array, and the close method. Many subclasses will be able to improve performance if they also override some of the other methods.

There are a number of differences between Reader and InputStream. With Reader the fundamental reading method reads into a char array and the other read methods are defined in terms of this method. In contrast the InputStream class uses the single-byte read method as its fundamental reading method. In the Reader class subclasses must implement the abstract close method in contrast to inheriting an empty implementation—many stream classes will at least need to track whether or not they have been closed and so close will usually need to be overridden. Finally, where InputStream had an available method to tell you how much data was available to read, Reader simply has a ready method that tells you if there is any data.

As an example, the following program counts the number of whitespace characters in a character stream:

```
import java.io.*;

class CountSpace {
    public static void main(String[] args)
        throws IOException
    {
        Reader in;
        if (args.length == 0)
            in = new InputStreamReader(System.in);
```

```
        else
            in = new FileReader(args[0]);
        int ch;
        int total;
        int spaces = 0;
        for (total = 0; (ch = in.read()) != -1; total++) {
            if (Character.isWhitespace((char) ch))
                spaces++;
        }
        System.out.println(total + " chars, "
            + spaces + " spaces");
    }
}
```

This program takes a filename from the command line. The variable `in` represents the character stream. If a filename is not provided, the standard input stream, `System.in`, is used after wrapping it in an `InputStreamReader`, which converts an input byte stream into an input character stream; if a filename is provided, an object of type `FileReader` is created, which is a subclass of `Reader`.

The `for` loop counts the total number of characters in the file and the number of spaces, using the `Character` class's `isWhitespace` method to test whether a character is whitespace. At the end, the results are printed. Here is the output of the program when used on itself:

```
453 chars, 111 spaces
```

20.3.2 `Writer`

The abstract class `Writer` provides a stream analogous to `OutputStream` but designed for use with characters instead of bytes. The methods of `Writer` essentially mirror those of `OutputStream`, but add some other useful forms of `write`:

public void **write(int ch)** throws IOException
> Writes ch as a character. The character is passed as an `int` but only the lowest 16 bits of the integer are written. This method blocks until the character is written.

public abstract void **write(char[] buf, int offset, int count)**
    throws IOException
> Writes part of an array of characters, starting at `buf[offset]` and writing count characters. This method blocks until the characters have been written.

public void **write(char[] buf)** throws IOException
> Equivalent to `write(buf, 0, buf.length)`.

public void **write(String str, int offset, int count)**
   throws IOException
   Writes count characters from the string str onto the stream, starting with str.charAt(offset).

public void **write(String str)** throws IOException
   Equivalent to write(str, 0, str.length()).

public abstract void **flush()** throws IOException
   Flushes the stream. If the stream has buffered any characters from the various write methods, flush immediately writes them to their destination. Then, if that destination is another stream, it is also flushed. One flush invocation will flush all the buffers in a chain of streams. If a stream is not buffered flush will do nothing.

public abstract void **close()** throws IOException
   Closes the stream, flushing if necessary. This method should be invoked to release any resources (such as file descriptors) associated with the stream. Once a stream has been closed, further operations on the stream will throw an IOException. Closing a previously closed stream has no effect.

Subclasses of Writer must implement the array writing variant of write, the close method, and the flush method. All other Writer methods are implemented in terms of these three. This contrasts with OutputStream which uses the single-byte variant of write method as the fundamental writing method, and which provides default implementations of flush and close. As with Reader, many subclasses can improve performance if they also override other methods.

Writer also implements the java.lang.Appendable interface—see page 332. The append(char c) method is equivalent to write(c); the append methods that take a CharSequence are equivalent to passing the String representations of the CharSequence objects to the write(String str) method.

20.3.3 Character Streams and the Standard Streams

The standard streams System.in, System.out, and System.err existed before the character streams were invented, so these streams are byte streams even though logically they should be character streams. This situation creates some anomalies. It is impossible, for example, to replace System.in with a LineNumberReader to keep track of the standard input stream's current line number. By attaching an InputStreamReader—an object that converts a byte input stream to a character input stream—to System.in, you can create a LineNumberReader object to keep track of the current line number (see "LineNumberReader" on page 527). But System.in is an InputStream, so you cannot replace it with a `LineNumberReader`, which is a type of `Reader`, not an `InputStream`.

`System.out` and `System.err` are `PrintStream` objects. `PrintStream` has been replaced by its equivalent character-based version `PrintWriter`. Generally, you should avoid creating `PrintStream` objects directly. You'll learn about the `Print` stream classes in Section 20.5.8 on page 525.

20.4 `InputStreamReader` and `OutputStreamWriter`

The conversion streams `InputStreamReader` and `OutputStreamWriter` translate between character and byte streams using either a specified character set encoding or the default encoding for the local system. These classes are the "glue" that lets you use existing 8-bit character encodings for local character sets in a consistent, platform-independent fashion. An `InputStreamReader` object is given a byte input stream as its source and produces the corresponding UTF-16 characters. An `OutputStreamWriter` object is given a byte output stream as its destination and produces encoded byte forms of the UTF-16 characters written on it. For example, the following code would read bytes encoded under ISO 8859-6 for Arabic characters, translating them into the appropriate UTF-16 characters:

```
public Reader readArabic(String file) throws IOException {
    InputStream fileIn = new FileInputStream(file);
    return new InputStreamReader(fileIn, "iso-8859-6");
}
```

By default, these conversion streams will work in the platform's default character set encoding, but other encodings can be specified. Encoding values were discussed in "Character Set Encoding" on page 320; they can be represented by name or a `Charset`, or by a `CharsetDecoder` or `CharsetEncoder` object from the `java.nio.charset` package.

`public` **`InputStreamReader(InputStream in)`**
> Creates an `InputStreamReader` to read from the given `InputStream` using the default character set encoding.

`public` **`InputStreamReader(InputStream in, Charset c)`**
> Creates an `InputStreamReader` to read from the given `InputStream` using the given character set encoding.

`public` **`InputStreamReader(InputStream in, CharsetDecoder c)`**
> Creates an `InputStreamReader` to read from the given `InputStream` using the given character set decoder.

public **InputStreamReader(InputStream in, String enc)**
> throws UnsupportedEncodingException
>> Creates an InputStreamReader to read from the given InputStream using the named character set encoding. If the named encoding is not supported an UnsupportedEncodingException is thrown.

public **OutputStreamWriter(OutputStream out)**
>> Creates an OutputStreamWriter to write to the given OutputStream using the default character set encoding.

public **OutputStreamWriter(OutputStream out, Charset c)**
>> Creates an OutputStreamWriter to write to the given OutputStream using the given character set encoding.

public **OutputStreamWriter(OutputStream out, CharsetEncoder c)**
>> Creates an OutputStreamWriter to write to the given OutputStream using the given character set encoder.

public **OutputStreamWriter(OutputStream out, String enc)**
> throws UnsupportedEncodingException
>> Creates an OutputStreamWriter to write to the given OutputStream using the named character set encoding. If the named encoding is not supported an UnsupportedEncodingException is thrown.

The read methods of InputStreamReader simply read bytes from their associated InputStream and convert them to characters using the appropriate encoding for that stream. Similarly, the write methods of OutputStreamWriter take the supplied characters, convert them to bytes with the appropriate encoding, and write them to the associated OutputStream.

In both classes, closing the conversion stream also closes the associated byte stream. This may not always be desirable—such as when you are converting the standard streams—so consider carefully when closing conversion streams.

Both classes also support the method getEncoding, which returns a string representing either the historical or canonical name of the stream's character encoding, or null if the stream has been closed.

The FileReader and FileWriter classes are subclasses of these conversion streams. This helps you read and write local files correctly in a consistent, Unicode-savvy fashion using the local encoding. However, if the default local encoding isn't what you need, you must use an explicit InputStreamReader or OutputStreamWriter object. You will learn about the file related streams in more detail in Section 20.7 on page 540.

You can also use the data output stream you will learn about in Section 20.6.2 on page 539 to write characters as bytes using a specific Unicode encoding.

There is no `ReaderInputStream` class to translate characters to bytes, nor a `WriterOutputStream` class to translate bytes to characters.

20.5 A Quick Tour of the Stream Classes

The `java.io` package defines several types of streams. The stream types usually have input/output pairs, and most have both byte stream and character stream variants. Some of these streams define general behavioral properties. For example:

- `Filter` streams are abstract classes representing streams with some filtering operation applied as data is read or written by another stream. For example, a `FilterReader` object gets input from another `Reader` object, processes (filters) the characters in some manner, and returns the filtered result. You build sequences of filtered streams by chaining various filters into one large filter. Output can be filtered similarly (Section 20.5.2).
- `Buffered` streams add buffering so that `read` and `write` need not, for example, access the file system for every invocation. The character variants of these streams also add the notion of line-oriented text (Section 20.5.3).
- `Piped` streams are pairs such that, say, characters written to a `PipedWriter` can be read from a `PipedReader` (Section 20.5.4).

A group of streams, called *in-memory streams,* allow you to use in-memory data structures as the source or destination for a stream:

- `ByteArray` streams use a `byte` array (Section 20.5.5).
- `CharArray` streams use a `char` array (Section 20.5.6).
- `String` streams use string types (Section 20.5.7).

The I/O package also has input and output streams that have no output or input counterpart:

- The `Print` streams provide `print` and `println` methods for formatting printed data in human-readable text form (Section 20.5.8).
- `LineNumberReader` is a buffered reader that tracks the line numbers of the input (characters only) (Section 20.5.9).
- `SequenceInputStream` converts a sequence of `InputStream` objects into a single `InputStream` so that a list of concatenated input streams can be treated as a single input stream (bytes only) (Section 20.5.10).

There are also streams that are useful for building parsers:

- ◆ Pushback streams add a pushback buffer you can use to put back data when you have read too far (Section 20.5.11).

- ◆ The StreamTokenizer class breaks a Reader into a stream of tokens—recognizable "words"— that are often needed when parsing user input (characters only) (Section 20.5.12).

These classes can be extended to create new kinds of stream classes for specific applications.

Each of these stream types is described in the following sections. Before looking at these streams in detail, however, you need to learn something about the synchronization behavior of the different streams.

20.5.1 Synchronization and Concurrency

Both the byte streams and the characters streams define synchronization policies though they do this in different ways. The concurrent behavior of the stream classes is not fully specified but can be broadly described as follows.

Each byte stream class synchronizes on the current stream object when performing operations that must be free from interference. This allows multiple threads to use the same streams yet still get well-defined behavior when invoking individual stream methods. For example, if two threads each try to read data from a stream in chunks of n bytes, then the data returned by each read operation will contain up to n bytes that appeared consecutively in the stream. Similarly, if two threads are writing to the same stream then the bytes written in each write operation will be sent consecutively to the stream, not intermixed at random points.

The character streams use a different synchronization strategy from the byte streams. The character streams synchronize on a protected lock field which, by default, is a reference to the stream object itself. However, both Reader and Writer provide a protected constructor that takes an object for lock to refer to. Some subclasses set the lock field to refer to a different object. For example, the StringWriter class that writes its character into a StringBuffer object sets its lock object to be the StringBuffer object. If you are writing a reader or writer, you should set the lock field to an appropriate object if this is not appropriate. Conversely, if you are extending an existing reader or writer you should always synchronize on lock and not this.

In many cases, a particular stream object simply wraps another stream instance and delegates the main stream methods to that instance, forming a chain of connected streams, as is the case with Filter streams. In this case, the synchronization behavior of the method will depend on the ultimate stream object being wrapped. This will only become an issue if the wrapping class needs to perform some additional action that must occur atomically with respect to the main stream action. In most cases filter streams simply manipulate data before writing it to, or after reading it from, the wrapped stream, so synchronization is not an issue.

Most input operations will block until data is available, and it is also possible that output stream operations can block trying to write data—the ultimate source or destination could be a stream tied to a network socket. To make the threads performing this blocking I/O more responsive to cancellation requests an implementation may respond to `Thread` interrupt requests (see page 365) by unblocking the thread and throwing an `InterruptedIOException`. This exception can report the number of bytes transferred before the interruption occurred—if the code that throws it sets the value.

For single byte transfers, interrupting an I/O operation is quite straightforward. In general, however, the state of a stream after a thread using it is interrupted is problematic. For example, suppose you use a particular stream to read HTTP requests across the network. If a thread reading the next request is interrupted after reading two bytes of the header field in the request packet, the next thread reading from that stream will get invalid data unless the stream takes steps to prevent this. Given the effort involved in writing classes that can deal effectively with these sorts of situations, most implementations *do not* allow a thread to be interrupted until the main I/O operation has completed, so you cannot rely on blocking I/O being interruptible. The interruptible channels provided in the `java.nio` package support interruption by closing the stream when any thread using the stream is interrupted—this ensures that there are no issues about what would next be read.

Even when interruption cannot be responded to during an I/O operation many systems will check for interruption at the start and/or end of the operation and throw the `InterruptedIOException` then. Also, if a thread is blocked on a stream when the stream is closed by another thread, most implementations will unblock the blocked thread and throw an `IOException`.

20.5.2 `Filter` Streams

`Filter` streams—`FilterInputStream`, `FilterOutputStream`, `FilterReader`, and `FilterWriter`—help you chain streams to produce composite streams of greater utility. Each filter stream is bound to another stream to which it delegates the actual input or output actions. `Filter` streams get their power from the ability to filter—process—what they read or write, transforming the data in some way.

`Filter` byte streams add new constructors that accept a stream of the appropriate type (input or output) to which to connect. `Filter` character streams similarly add a new constructor that accepts a character stream of the appropriate type (reader or writer). However, many character streams already have constructors that take another character stream, so those Reader and Writer classes can act as filters even if they do not extend FilterReader or FilterWriter.

The following shows an input filter that converts characters to uppercase:

```java
public class UppercaseConvertor extends FilterReader {
    public UppercaseConvertor(Reader in) {
        super(in);
    }

    public int read() throws IOException {
        int c = super.read();
        return (c == -1 ? c : Character.toUpperCase((char)c));
    }

    public int read(char[] buf, int offset, int count)
        throws IOException
    {
        int nread = super.read(buf, offset, count);
        int last = offset + nread;
        for (int i = offset; i < last; i++)
            buf[i] = Character.toUpperCase(buf[i]);
        return nread;
    }
}
```

We override each of the read methods to perform the actual read and then convert the characters to upper case. The actual reading is done by invoking an appropriate superclass method. Note that we don't invoke read on the stream in itself—this would bypass any filtering performed by our superclass. Note also that we have to watch for the end of the stream. In the case of the no-arg read this means an explicit test, but in the array version of read, a return value of –1 will prevent the for loop from executing. In the array version of read we also have to be careful to convert to uppercase only those characters that we stored in the buffer.

We can use our uppercase convertor as follows:

```java
public static void main(String[] args)
    throws IOException
{
    StringReader src = new StringReader(args[0]);
    FilterReader f = new UppercaseConvertor(src);
```

```
    int c;
    while ((c = f.read()) != -1)
        System.out.print((char)c);
    System.out.println();
}
```

We use a string as our data source by using a `StringReader` (see Section 20.5.7 on page 523). The `StringReader` is then wrapped by our `UppercaseConvertor`. Reading from the filtered stream converts all the characters from the string stream into uppercase. For the input `"no lowercase"` we get the output:

```
NO LOWERCASE
```

You can chain any number of `Filter` byte or character streams. The original source of input can be a stream that is not a `Filter` stream. You can use an `InputStreamReader` to convert a byte input stream to a character input stream.

`Filter` output streams can be chained similarly so that data written to one stream will filter and write data to the next output stream. All the streams, from the first to the next-to-last, must be `Filter` output stream objects, but the last stream can be any kind of output stream. You can use an `OutputStreamWriter` to convert a character output stream to a byte output stream.

Not all classes that are `Filter` streams actually alter the data. Some classes are behavioral filters, such as the buffered streams you'll learn about next, while others provide a new interface for using the streams, such as the print streams. These classes are `Filter` streams because they can form part of a filter chain.

Exercise 20.2: Rewrite the `TranslateByte` class as a filter.

Exercise 20.3: Create a pair of `Filter` stream classes that encrypt bytes using any algorithm you choose—such as XORing the bytes with some value—with your `DecryptInputStream` able to decrypt the bytes that your `EncryptOutputStream` class creates.

Exercise 20.4: Create a subclass of `FilterReader` that will return one line of input at a time via a method that blocks until a full line of input is available.

20.5.3 Buffered Streams

The `Buffered` stream classes—`BufferedInputStream`, `BufferedOutputStream`, `BufferedReader`, and `BufferedWriter`—buffer their data to avoid every `read` or `write` going directly to the next stream. These classes are often used in conjunction with `File` streams—accessing a disk file is much slower than using a memory buffer, and buffering helps reduce file accesses.

Each of the `Buffered` streams supports two constructors: One takes a reference to the wrapped stream and the size of the buffer to use, while the other only takes a reference to the wrapped stream and uses a default buffer size.

When `read` is invoked on an empty `Buffered` input stream, it invokes `read` on its source stream, fills the buffer with as much data as is available—only blocking if it needs the data being waited for—and returns the requested data from that buffer. Future `read` invocations return data from that buffer until its contents are exhausted, and that causes another `read` on the source stream. This process continues until the source stream is exhausted.

`Buffered` output streams behave similarly. When a `write` fills the buffer, the destination stream's `write` is invoked to empty the buffer. This buffering can turn many small `write` requests on the `Buffered` stream into a single `write` request on the underlying destination.

Here is how to create a buffered output stream to write bytes to a file:

```
new BufferedOutputStream(new FileOutputStream(path));
```

You create a `FileOutputStream` with the path, put a `BufferedOutputStream` in front of it, and use the buffered stream object. This scheme enables you to buffer output destined for the file.

You must retain a reference to the `FileOutputStream` object if you want to invoke methods on it later because there is no way to obtain the downstream object from a `Filter` stream. However, you should rarely need to work with the downstream object. If you do keep a reference to a downstream object, you must ensure that the first upstream object is flushed before operating on the downstream object because data written to upper streams may not have yet been written all the way downstream. Closing an upstream object also closes all downstream objects, so a retained reference may cease to be usable.

The `Buffered` character streams also understand lines of text. The `newLine` method of `BufferedWriter` writes a line separator to the stream. Each system defines what constitutes a line separator in the system `String` property `line.separator`, which need not be a single character. You should use `newLine` to end lines in text files that may be read by humans on the local system (see "System Properties" on page 663).

The method `readLine` in `BufferedReader` returns a line of text as a `String`. The method `readLine` accepts any of the standard set of line separators: line feed (\n), carriage return (\r), or carriage return followed by line feed (\r\n). This implies that you should never set `line.separator` to use any other sequence. Otherwise, lines terminated by `newLine` would not be recognized by `readLine`. The string returned by `readLine` does not include the line separator. If the end of stream is encountered before a line separator, then the text read to that point is returned. If only the end of stream is encountered readLine returns null.

20.5.4 Piped Streams

Piped streams—PipedInputStream, PipedOutputStream, PipedReader, and PipedWriter—are used as input/output pairs; data written on the output stream of a pair is the data read on the input stream. The pipe maintains an internal buffer with an implementation-defined capacity that allows writing and reading to proceed at different rates—there is no way to control the size of the buffer.

Pipes provide an I/O-based mechanism for communicating data between different threads. The only safe way to use Piped streams is with two threads: one for reading and one for writing. Writing on one end of the pipe blocks the thread when the pipe fills up. If the writer and reader are the same thread, that thread will block permanently. Reading from a pipe blocks the thread if no input is available.

To avoid blocking a thread forever when its counterpart at the other end of the pipe terminates, each pipe keeps track of the identity of the most recent reader and writer threads. The pipe checks to see that the thread at the other end is alive before blocking the current thread. If the thread at the other end has terminated, the current thread will get an IOException.

The following example uses a pipe stream to connect a TextGenerator thread with a thread that wants to read the generated text. First, the text generator:

```
class TextGenerator extends Thread {
    private Writer out;

    public TextGenerator(Writer out) {
        this.out = out;
    }

    public void run() {
        try {
            try {
                for (char c = 'a'; c <= 'z'; c++)
                    out.write(c);
            } finally {
                out.close();
            }
        } catch (IOException e) {
            getUncaughtExceptionHandler().
                uncaughtException(this, e);
```

```
            }
        }
    }
```

The `TextGenerator` simply writes to the output stream passed to its constructor. In the example that stream will actually be a piped stream to be read by the main thread:

```
class Pipe {
    public static void main(String[] args)
        throws IOException
    {
        PipedWriter out = new PipedWriter();
        PipedReader in = new PipedReader(out);
        TextGenerator data = new TextGenerator(out);
        data.start();
        int ch;
        while ((ch = in.read()) != -1)
            System.out.print((char) ch);
        System.out.println();
    }
}
```

We create the `Piped` streams, making the `PipedWriter` a parameter to the constructor for the `PipedReader`. The order is unimportant: The input pipe could be a parameter to the output pipe. What is important is that an input/output pair be attached to each other. We create the new `TextGenerator` object, with the `PipedWriter` as the output stream for the generated characters. Then we loop, reading characters from the text generator and writing them to the system output stream. At the end, we make sure that the last line of output is terminated.

Piped streams need not be connected when they are constructed—there is a no-arg constructor—but can be connected at a later stage via the `connect` method. `PipedReader.connect` takes a `PipedWriter` parameter and vice versa. As with the constructor, it does not matter whether you connect x to y, or y to x, the result is the same. Trying to use a `Piped` stream before it is connected or trying to connect it when it is already connected results in an `IOException`.

20.5.5 ByteArray Byte Streams

You can use arrays of bytes as the source or destination of byte streams by using `ByteArray` streams. The `ByteArrayInputStream` class uses a `byte` array as its input source, and reading on it can never block. It has two constructors:

public **ByteArrayInputStream(byte[] buf, int offset, int count)**
>   Creates a ByteArrayInputStream from the specified array of bytes using only the part of buf from buf[offset] to buf[offset+count-1] or the end of the array, whichever is smaller. The input array is used directly, not copied, so you should take care not to modify it while it is being used as an input source.

public **ByteArrayInputStream(byte[] buf)**
>   Equivalent to ByteArrayInputStream(buf, 0, buf.length).

The ByteArrayOutputStream class provides a dynamically growing byte array to hold output. It adds constructors and methods:

public **ByteArrayOutputStream()**
>   Creates a new ByteArrayOutputStream with a default initial array size.

public **ByteArrayOutputStream(int size)**
>   Creates a new ByteArrayOutputStream with the given initial array size.

public int **size()**
>   Returns the number of bytes generated thus far by output to the stream.

public byte[] **toByteArray()**
>   Returns a copy of the bytes generated thus far by output to the stream. When you are finished writing into a ByteArrayOutputStream via upstream filter streams, you should flush the upstream objects before using toByteArray.

public void **reset()**
>   Resets the stream to reuse the current buffer, discarding its contents.

public String **toString()**
>   Returns the current contents of the buffer as a String, translating bytes into characters according to the default character encoding.

public String **toString(String enc)**
>   throws UnsupportedEncodingException
>   Returns the current contents of the buffer as a String, translating bytes into characters according to the specified character encoding. If the encoding is not supported an UnsupportedEncodingException is thrown.

public void **writeTo(OutputStream out)** throws IOException
>   Writes the current contents of the buffer to the stream out.

20.5.6 CharArray Character Streams

The CharArray character streams are analogous to the ByteArray byte streams—they let you use char arrays as a source or destination without ever blocking. You construct CharArrayReader objects with an array of char:

public **CharArrayReader(char[] buf, int offset, int count)**
> Creates a CharArrayReader from the specified array of characters using only the subarray of buf from buf[offset] to buf[offset+count-1] or the end of the array, whichever is smaller. The input array is used directly, not copied, so you should take care not to modify it while it is being used as an input source.

public **CharArrayReader(char[] buf)**
> Equivalent to CharArrayReader(buf, 0, buf.length).

The CharArrayWriter class provides a dynamically growing char array to hold output. It adds constructors and methods:

public **CharArrayWriter()**
> Creates a new CharArrayWriter with a default initial array size.

public **CharArrayWriter(int size)**
> Creates a new CharArrayWriter with the given initial array size.

public int **size()**
> Returns the number of characters generated thus far by output to the stream.

public char[] **toCharArray()**
> Returns a copy of the characters generated thus far by output to the stream. When you are finished writing into a CharArrayWriter via upstream filter streams, you should flush the upstream objects before using toCharArray.

public void **reset()**
> Resets the stream to reuse the current buffer, discarding its contents.

public String **toString()**
> Returns the current contents of the buffer as a String.

public void **writeTo(Writer out)** throws IOException
> Writes the current contents of the buffer to the stream out.

20.5.7 String Character Streams

The StringReader reads its characters from a String and will never block. It provides a single constructor that takes the string from which to read. For example, the following program factors numbers read either from the command line or System.in:

```
class Factor {
    public static void main(String[] args) {
        if (args.length == 0) {
            factorNumbers(new InputStreamReader(System.in));
```

```
        } else {
            for (String str : args) {
                StringReader in = new StringReader(str);
                factorNumbers(in);
            }
        }
    }
    // ... definition of factorNumbers ...
}
```

If the command is invoked without parameters, factorNumbers parses numbers
from the standard input stream. When the command line contains some arguments, a StringReader is created for each parameter, and factorNumbers is
invoked on each one. The parameter to factorNumbers is a stream of characters containing numbers to be parsed; it does not know whether they come from the command
line or from standard input.

StringWriter lets you write results into a buffer that can be retrieved as a
String or StringBuffer object. It adds the following constructors and methods:

public **StringWriter()**

Creates a new StringWriter with a default initial buffer size.

public **StringWriter(int size)**

Creates a new StringWriter with the specified initial buffer size. Providing a good initial size estimate for the buffer will improve performance in
many cases.

public StringBuffer **getBuffer()**

Returns the actual StringBuffer being used by this stream. Because the
actual StringBuffer is returned, you should take care not to modify it
while it is being used as an output destination.

public String **toString()**

Returns the current contents of the buffer as a String.

The following code uses a StringWriter to create a string that contains the
output of a series of println calls on the contents of an array:

```
public static String arrayToStr(Object[] objs) {
    StringWriter strOut = new StringWriter();
    PrintWriter out = new PrintWriter(strOut);
    for (int i = 0; i < objs.length; i++)
        out.println(i + ": " + objs[i]);
    return strOut.toString();
}
```

20.5.8 Print Streams

The `Print` streams—`PrintStream` and `PrintWriter`—provide methods that make it easy to write the values of primitive types and objects to a stream, in a human-readable text format—as you have seen in many examples. The `Print` streams provide `print` and `println` methods for the following types:

```
char     int     float     Object     boolean
char[]   long    double    String
```

These methods are much more convenient than the raw stream `write` methods. For example, given a `float` variable `f` and a `PrintStream` reference `out`, the call `out.print(f)` is equivalent to

```
out.write(String.valueOf(f).getBytes());
```

The `println` method appends a line separator after writing its argument to the stream—a simple `println` with no parameters ends the current line. The line separator string is defined by the system property `line.separator` and is not necessarily a single newline character (\n).

Each of the `Print` streams acts as a `Filter` stream, so you can filter data on its way downstream.

The `PrintStream` class acts on byte streams while the `PrintWriter` class acts on character streams. Because printing is clearly character-related output, the `PrintWriter` class is the class you should use. However, for historical reasons `System.out` and `System.err` are `PrintStreams` that use the default character set encoding—these are the only `PrintStream` objects you should use. We describe only the `PrintWriter` class, though `PrintStream` provides essentially the same interface.

`PrintWriter` has eight constructors.

public **PrintWriter(Writer out, boolean autoflush)**
> Creates a new `PrintWriter` that will write to the stream `out`. If `autoflush` is `true`, `println` invokes `flush`. Otherwise, `println` invocations are treated like any other method, and `flush` is not invoked. Autoflush behavior cannot be changed after the stream is constructed.

public **PrintWriter(Writer out)**
> Equivalent to `PrintWriter(out, false)`.

public **PrintWriter(OutputStream out, boolean autoflush)**
> Equivalent to
> `PrintWriter(new OutputStreamWriter(out), autoflush)`.

public **PrintWriter(OutputStream out)**
> Equivalent to PrintWriter(new OutputStreamWriter(out), false).

public **PrintWriter(File file)** throws FileNotFoundException
> Equivalent to PrintWriter(new OutputStreamWriter(fos)), where fos is a FileOutputStream created with the given file.

public **PrintWriter(File file, String enc)**

> throws FileNotFoundException, UnsupportedEncodingException
> Equivalent to PrintWriter(new OutputStreamWriter(fos, enc)), where fos is a FileOutputStream created with the given file.

public **PrintWriter(String filename)** throws FileNotFoundException
> Equivalent to PrintWriter(new OutputStreamWriter(fos)), where fos is a FileOutputStream created with the given file name.

public **PrintWriter(String filename, String enc)**

> throws FileNotFoundException, UnsupportedEncodingException
> Equivalent to PrintWriter(new OutputStreamWriter(fos, enc)), where fos is a FileOutputStream created with the given file name.

The Print streams implement the Appendable interface which allows them to be targets for a Formatter. Additionally, the following convenience methods are provided for formatted output—see "Formatter" on page 624 for details:

public PrintWriter **format(String format, Object... args)**
> Acts like new Formatter(this).format(format, args), but a new Formatter need not be created for each call. The current PrintWriter is returned.

public PrintWriter

> **format(Locale l, String format, Object... args)**
> Acts like new Formatter(this, l).format(format, args), but a new Formatter need not be created for each call. The current PrintWriter is returned. Locales are described in Chapter 24.

There are two printf methods that behave exactly the same as the format methods—printf stands for "print formatted" and is an old friend from the C programming language.

One important characteristic of the Print streams is that none of the output methods throw IOException. If an error occurs while writing to the underlying stream the methods simply return normally. You should check whether an error occurred by invoking the boolean method checkError—this flushes the stream and checks its error state. Once an error has occurred, there is no way to clear it. If any of the underlying stream operations result in an InterruptedIOException, the error state is not set, but instead the current thread is re-interrupted using `Thread.currentThread().interrupt()`.

20.5.9 LineNumberReader

The `LineNumberReader` stream keeps track of line numbers while reading text. As usual a line is considered to be terminated by any one of a line feed (\n), a carriage return (\r), or a carriage return followed immediately by a linefeed (\r\n).

The following program prints the line number where the first instance of a particular character is found in a file:

```java
import java.io.*;

class FindChar {
    public static void main(String[] args)
        throws IOException
    {
        if (args.length != 2)
            throw new IllegalArgumentException(
                                    "need char and file");

        int match = args[0].charAt(0);
        FileReader fileIn = new FileReader(args[1]);
        LineNumberReader in = new LineNumberReader(fileIn);
        int ch;
        while ((ch = in.read()) != -1) {
            if (ch == match) {
                System.out.println("'" + (char)ch +
                    "' at line " + in.getLineNumber());
                return;
            }
        }
        System.out.println((char)match + " not found");
    }
}
```

This program creates a `FileReader` named `fileIn` to read from the named file and then inserts a `LineNumberReader`, named `in`, before it. `LineNumberReader` objects get their characters from the reader they are attached to, keeping track of line numbers as they read. The `getLineNumber` method returns the current line number; by default, lines are counted starting from *zero*. When this program is run on itself looking for the letter `'I'`, its output is

```
'I' at line 4
```

You can set the current line number with `setLineNumber`. This could be useful, for example, if you have a file that contains several sections of information. You could use `setLineNumber` to reset the line number to 1 at the start of each section so that problems would be reported to the user based on the line numbers within the section instead of within the file.

`LineNumberReader` is a `BufferedReader` that has two constructors: One takes a reference to the wrapped stream and the size of the buffer to use, while the other only takes a reference to the wrapped stream and uses a default buffer size.

Exercise 20.5: Write a program that reads a specified file and searches for a specified word, printing each line number and line in which the word is found.

20.5.10 `SequenceInputStream`

The `SequenceInputStream` class creates a single input stream from reading one or more byte input streams, reading the first stream until its end of input and then reading the next one, and so on through the last one. `SequenceInputStream` has two constructors: one for the common case of two input streams that are provided as the two parameters to the constructor, and the other for an arbitrary number of input streams using the `Enumeration` abstraction (described in "Enumeration" on page 617). `Enumeration` is an interface that provides an ordered iteration through a list of objects. For `SequenceInputStream`, the enumeration should contain only `InputStream` objects. If it contains anything else, a `ClassCastException` will be thrown when the `SequenceInputStream` tries to get that object from the list.

The following example program concatenates all its input to create a single output. This program is similar to a simple version of the UNIX utility `cat`—if no files are named, the input is simply forwarded to the output. Otherwise, the program opens all the files and uses a `SequenceInputStream` to model them as a single stream. Then the program writes its input to its output:

```java
import java.io.*;
import java.util.*;

class Concat {
    public static void main(String[] args)
        throws IOException
    {
```

```
            InputStream in; // stream to read characters from
            if (args.length == 0) {
                in = System.in;
            } else {
                InputStream fileIn, bufIn;
                List<InputStream> inputs =
                    new ArrayList<InputStream>(args.length);
                for (String arg : args) {
                    fileIn = new FileInputStream(arg);
                    bufIn = new BufferedInputStream(fileIn);
                    inputs.add(bufIn);
                }
                Enumeration<InputStream> files =
                    Collections.enumeration(inputs);
                in = new SequenceInputStream(files);
            }
            int ch;
            while ((ch = in.read()) != -1)
                System.out.write(ch);
        }
        // ...
    }
```

If there are no parameters, we use System.in for input. If there are parameters, we create an ArrayList large enough to hold as many BufferedInputStream objects as there are command-line arguments (see "ArrayList" on page 582). Then we create a stream for each named file and add the stream to the inputs list. When the loop is finished, we use the Collections class's enumeration method to get an Enumeration object for the list elements. We use this Enumeration in the constructor for SequenceInputStream to create a single stream that concatenates all the streams for the files into a single InputStream object. A simple loop then reads all the bytes from that stream and writes them on System.out.

   You could instead write your own implementation of Enumeration whose nextElement method creates a FileInputStream for each argument on demand, closing the previous stream, if any.

20.5.11 Pushback Streams

A Pushback stream lets you push back, or "unread," characters or bytes when you have read too far. Pushback is typically useful for breaking input into tokens. Lexical scanners, for example, often know that a token (such as an identifier) has ended only when they have read the first character that follows it. Having seen that character, the scanner must push it back onto the input stream so that it is available as the start of the next token. The following example uses PushbackInputStream to report the longest consecutive sequence of any single byte in its input:

```java
import java.io.*;

class SequenceCount {
    public static void main(String[] args)
        throws IOException
    {
        PushbackInputStream
            in = new PushbackInputStream(System.in);
        int max = 0;      // longest sequence found
        int maxB = -1;    // the byte in that sequence
        int b;            // current byte in input

        do {
            int cnt;
            int b1 = in.read(); // 1st byte in sequence
            for (cnt = 1; (b = in.read()) == b1; cnt++)
                continue;
            if (cnt > max) {
                max = cnt;  // remember length
                maxB = b1;  // remember which byte value
            }
            in.unread(b);   // pushback start of next seq
        } while (b != -1); // until we hit end of input

        System.out.println(max + " bytes of " + maxB);
    }
}
```

We know that we have reached the end of one sequence only when we read the first byte of the next sequence. We push this byte back using unread so that it is read again when we repeat the do loop for the next sequence.

Both PushbackInputStream and PushbackReader support two constructors: One takes a reference to the wrapped stream and the size of the pushback buffer to create, while the other only takes a reference to the wrapped stream and uses a pushback buffer with space for one piece of data (byte or char as appropriate). Attempting to push back more than the specified amount of data will cause an IOException.

Each Pushback stream has three variants of unread, matching the variants of read. We illustrate the character version of PushbackReader, but the byte equivalents for PushbackInputStream have the same behavior:

public void **unread(int c)** throws IOException
> Pushes back the single character c. If there is insufficient room in the pushback buffer an IOException is thrown.

public void **unread(char[] buf, int offset, int count)**
> throws IOException
>> Pushes back the characters in the specified subarray. The first character pushed back is buf[offset] and the last is buf[offset+count-1]. The subarray is prepended to the front of the pushback buffer, such that the next character to be read will be that at buf[offset], then buf[offset+1], and so on. If the pushback buffer is full an IOException is thrown.

public void **unread(char[] buf)** throws IOException
> Equivalent to unread(buf, 0, buf.length).

For example, after two consecutive unread calls on a PushbackReader with the characters '1' and '2', the next two characters read will be '2' and '1' because '2' was pushed back second. Each unread call sets its own list of characters by prepending to the buffer, so the code

```
pbr.unread(new char[] {'1', '2'});
pbr.unread(new char[] {'3', '4'});
for (int i = 0; i < 4; i++)
    System.out.println(i + ": " + (char)pbr.read());
```

produces the following lines of output:

```
0: 3
1: 4
2: 1
3: 2
```

Data from the last unread (the one with '3' and '4') is read back first, and within that unread the data comes from the beginning of the array through to the end. When that data is exhausted, the data from the first unread is returned in the same order. The unread method copies data into the pushback buffer, so changes made to an array after it is used with unread do not affect future calls to read.

20.5.12 `StreamTokenizer`

Tokenizing input text is a common application, and the `java.io` package provides a `StreamTokenizer` class for simple tokenization. A more general facility for scanning and converting input text is provided by the `java.util.Scanner` class—see "Scanner" on page 641.

class—see "Scanner" on page 641.

You can tokenize a stream by creating a `StreamTokenizer` with a `Reader` object as its source and then setting parameters for the scan. A scanner loop invokes `nextToken`, which returns the token type of the next token in the stream. Some token types have associated values that are found in fields in the `StreamTokenizer` object.

This class is designed primarily to parse programming language-style input; it is not a general tokenizer. However, many configuration files look similar enough to programming languages that they can be parsed by this tokenizer. When designing a new configuration file or other data, you can save work if you make it look enough like a language to be parsed with `StreamTokenizer`.

When `nextToken` recognizes a token, it returns the token type as its value and also sets the `ttype` field to the same value. There are four token types:

- ◆ `TT_WORD`: A word was scanned. The `String` field `sval` contains the word that was found.

- ◆ `TT_NUMBER`: A number was scanned. The `double` field `nval` contains the value of the number. Only decimal floating-point numbers (with or without a decimal point) are recognized. The tokenizer does not understand `3.4e79` as a floating-point number, nor `0xffff` as a hexadecimal number.

- ◆ `TT_EOL`: An end-of-line was found.

- ◆ `TT_EOF`: The end-of-file was reached.

The input text is assumed to consist of bytes in the range `\u0000` to `\u00FF`—Unicode characters outside this range are not handled correctly. Input is composed of both *special* and *ordinary* characters. Special characters are those that the tokenizer treats specially—namely whitespace, characters that make up numbers, characters that make up words, and so on. Any other character is considered ordinary. When an ordinary character is the next in the input, its token type is itself. For example, if the character `'¿'` is encountered in the input and is not special, the token return type (and the `ttype` field) is the `int` value of the character `'¿'`.

As one example, let's look at a method that sums the numeric values in a character stream it is given:

```
static double sumStream(Reader source) throws IOException {
    StreamTokenizer in = new StreamTokenizer(source);
    double result = 0.0;
    while (in.nextToken() != StreamTokenizer.TT_EOF) {
        if (in.ttype == StreamTokenizer.TT_NUMBER)
            result += in.nval;
    }
    return result;
}
```

We create a `StreamTokenizer` object from the reader and then loop, reading tokens from the stream, adding all the numbers found into the burgeoning result. When we get to the end of the input, we return the final sum.

Here is another example that reads an input source, looking for attributes of the form `name=value`, and stores them as attributes in `AttributedImpl` objects, described in "Implementing Interfaces" on page 127:

```
public static Attributed readAttrs(Reader source)
    throws IOException
{
    StreamTokenizer in = new StreamTokenizer(source);
    AttributedImpl attrs = new AttributedImpl();
    Attr attr = null;
    in.commentChar('#');      // '#' is ignore-to-end comment
    in.ordinaryChar('/');     // was original comment char
    while (in.nextToken() != StreamTokenizer.TT_EOF) {
        if (in.ttype == StreamTokenizer.TT_WORD) {
            if (attr != null) {
                attr.setValue(in.sval);
                attr = null;           // used this one up
            } else {
                attr = new Attr(in.sval);
                attrs.add(attr);
            }
        } else if (in.ttype == '=') {
            if (attr == null)
                throw new IOException("misplaced '='");
        } else {
            if (attr == null)          // expected a word
```

```
                      throw new IOException("bad Attr name");
                  attr.setValue(new Double(in.nval));
                  attr = null;
              }
          }
          return attrs;
      }
```

The attribute file uses '#' to mark comments. Ignoring these comments, the stream is searched for a string token followed by an optional '=' followed by a word or number. Each such attribute is put into an Attr object, which is added to a set of attributes in an AttributedImpl object. When the file has been parsed, the set of attributes is returned.

Setting the comment character to '#' sets its character class. The tokenizer recognizes several character classes that are set by the following methods:

public void **wordChars(int low, int hi)**
> Characters in this range are word characters: They can be part of a TT_WORD token. You can invoke this several times with different ranges. A word consists of one or more characters inside any of the legal ranges.

public void **whitespaceChars(int low, int hi)**
> Characters in this range are whitespace. Whitespace is ignored, except to separate tokens such as two consecutive words. As with the wordChars range, you can make several invocations, and the union of the invocations is the set of whitespace characters.

public void **ordinaryChars(int low, int hi)**
> Characters in this range are ordinary. An ordinary character is returned as itself, not as a token. This removes any special significance the characters may have had as comment characters, delimiters, word components, whitespace, or number characters. In the above example, we used ordinaryChar to remove the special comment significance of the '/' character.

public void **ordinaryChar(int ch)**
> Equivalent to ordinaryChars(ch, ch).

public void **commentChar(int ch)**
> The character ch starts a single-line comment—characters after ch up to the next end-of-line are treated as one run of whitespace.

public void **quoteChar(int ch)**
> Matching pairs of the character ch delimit String constants. When a String constant is recognized, the character ch is returned as the token, and

the field `sval` contains the body of the string with surrounding `ch` characters removed. When string constants are read, some of the standard \ processing is applied (for example, `\t` can be in the string). The string processing in `StreamTokenizer` is a subset of the language's strings. In particular, you cannot use `\u`*xxxx*, `\'`, `\"`, or (unfortunately) `\Q`, where Q is the quote character `ch`. You can have more than one quote character at a time on a stream, but strings must start and end with the same quote character. In other words, a string that starts with one quote character ends when the next instance of that same quote character is found. If a different quote character is found in between, it is simply part of the string.

public void **parseNumbers()**

Specifies that numbers should be parsed as double-precision floating-point numbers. When a number is found, the stream returns a type of TT_NUMBER, leaving the value in `nval`. There is no way to turn off just this feature—to turn it off you must either invoke `ordinaryChars` for all the number-related characters (don't forget the decimal point and minus sign) or invoke `resetSyntax`.

public void **resetSyntax()**

Resets the syntax table so that all characters are ordinary. If you do this and then start reading the stream, `nextToken` always returns the next character in the stream, just as when you invoke `InputStream.read`.

There are no methods to ask the character class of a given character or to add new classes of characters. Here are the default settings for a newly created `StreamTokenizer` object:

```
wordChars('a', 'z');      // lower case ASCII letters
wordChars('A', 'Z');      // upper case ASCII letters
wordChars(128 + 32, 255); // "high" non-ASCII values
whitespaceChars(0, ' ');  // ASCII control codes
commentChar('/');
quoteChar('"');
quoteChar('\'');
parseNumbers();
```

This leaves the ordinary characters consisting of most of the punctuation and arithmetic characters (;, :, [, {, +, =, and so forth).

The changes made to the character classes are cumulative, so, for example, invoking `wordChars` with two different ranges of characters defines both ranges as word characters. To replace a range you must first mark the old range as ordinary and then add the new range. Resetting the syntax table clears all settings, so if you want to return to the default settings, for example, you must manually make the invocations listed above.

Other methods control the basic behavior of the tokenizer:

public void **eolIsSignificant(boolean flag)**

If `flag` is `true`, ends of lines are significant and TT_EOL may be returned by `nextToken`. If `false`, ends of lines are treated as whitespace and TT_EOL is never returned. The default is `false`.

public void **slashStarComments(boolean flag)**

If `flag` is `true`, the tokenizer recognizes /*...*/ comments. This occurs independently of settings for any comment characters. The default is `false`.

public void **slashSlashComments(boolean flag)**

If `flag` is `true`, the tokenizer recognizes // to end-of-line comments. This occurs independently of the settings for any comment characters. The default is `false`.

public void **lowerCaseMode(boolean flag)**

If `flag` is `true`, all characters in TT_WORD tokens are converted to their low-ercase equivalent if they have one (using `String.toLowerCase`). The default is `false`. Because of the case issues described in "Character" on page 192, you cannot reliably use this for Unicode string equivalence—two tokens might be equivalent but have different lowercase representations. Use `String.equalsIgnoreCase` for reliable case-insensitive comparison.

There are three miscellaneous methods:

public void **pushBack()**

Pushes the previously returned token back into the stream. The next invocation of `nextToken` returns the same token again instead of proceeding to the next token. There is only a one-token pushback; multiple consecutive invocations to `pushBack` are equivalent to one invocation.

public int **lineno()**

Returns the current line number. Usually used for reporting errors you detect.

public String **toString()**

Returns a `String` representation of the last returned stream token, including its line number.

Exercise 20.6: Write a program that takes input of the form *name op value*, where *name* is one of three words of your choosing, *op* is +, -, or =, and *value* is a number. Apply each operator to the named value. When input is exhausted, print the three values. For extra credit, use the HashMap class that was used for AttributedImpl so that you can use an arbitrary number of named values.

20.6 The Data Byte Streams

Reading and writing text characters is useful, but you also frequently need to transmit the binary data of specific types across a stream. The DataInput and DataOutput interfaces define methods that transmit primitive types across a stream. The classes DataInputStream and DataOutputStream provide a default implementation for each interface. We cover the interfaces first, followed by their implementations.

20.6.1 DataInput and DataOutput

The interfaces for data input and output streams are almost mirror images. The parallel read and write methods for each type are

Read	Write	Type
readBoolean	writeBoolean	boolean
readChar	writeChar	char
readByte	writeByte	byte
readShort	writeShort	short
readInt	writeInt	int
readLong	writeLong	long
readFloat	writeFloat	float
readDouble	writeDouble	double
readUTF	writeUTF	String (in UTF format)

String values are read and written using a modified form of the UTF-8 character encoding. This differs from standard UTF-8 in three ways: the null byte (\u0000) is encoded in a 2-byte format so that the encoded string does not have embedded null bytes; only 1-byte, 2-byte, or 3-byte formats are used; and supplementary characters are encoded using surrogate pairs. Encoding Unicode characters into bytes is necessary in many situations because of the continuing transition from 8-bit to 16-bit character sets.

In addition to these paired methods, DataInput has several methods of its own, some of which are similar to those of InputStream:

public abstract void **readFully(byte[] buf, int offset, int count)**
    throws IOException
> Reads into part of a byte array. The maximum number of bytes read is count. The bytes are stored from buf[offset] up to a maximum of buf[offset+count-1]. If count is zero then no bytes are read. This method blocks until input is available, the end of the file (that is, stream) is

found—in which case an EOFException is thrown—or an exception is thrown because of an I/O error.

public abstract void **readFully(byte[] buf)** throws IOException
Equivalent to readFully(buf, 0, buf.length).

public abstract int **skipBytes(int count)** throws IOException
Attempts to skip over count bytes, discarding any bytes skipped over. Returns the actual number of bytes skipped. This method never throws an EOFException.

public abstract int **readUnsignedByte()** throws IOException
Reads one input byte, zero-extends it to type int, and returns the result, which is therefore in the range 0 through 255. This method is suitable for reading a byte written by the writeByte method of DataOutput if the argument to writeByte was a value in the range 0 through 255.

public abstract int **readUnsignedShort()** throws IOException
Reads two input bytes and returns an int value in the range 0 through 65535. The first byte read is made the high byte. This method is suitable for reading bytes written by the writeShort method of DataOutput if the argument to writeShort was a value in the range 0 through 65535.

The DataInput interface methods usually handle end-of-file (stream) by throwing EOFException when it occurs. EOFException extends IOException.

The DataOutput interface supports signatures equivalent to the three forms of write in OutputStream and with the same specified behavior. Additionally, it provides the following unmirrored methods:

public abstract void **writeBytes(String s)** throws IOException
Writes a String as a sequence of bytes. The upper byte in each character is lost, so unless you are willing to lose data, use this method only for strings that contain characters between \u0000 and \u00ff.

public abstract void **writeChars(String s)** throws IOException
Writes a String as a sequence of char. Each character is written as two bytes with the high byte written first.

There are no readBytes or readChars methods to read the same number of characters written by a writeBytes or writeChars invocation, therefore you must use a loop on readByte or readChar to read strings written with these methods. To do that you need a way to determine the length of the string, perhaps by writing the length of the string first, or by using an end-of-sequence character to mark its end. You could use readFully to read a full array of bytes if you wrote the length first, but that won't work for writeChars because you want char values, not byte values.

20.6.2 The Data Stream Classes

For each `Data` interface there is a corresponding `Data` stream. In addition, the `RandomAccessFile` class implements both the input and output `Data` interfaces (see Section 20.7.2 on page 541). Each `Data` class is an extension of its corresponding `Filter` class, so you can use `Data` streams to filter other streams. Each `Data` class has constructors that take another appropriate input or output stream. For example, you can use the filtering to write data to a file by putting a `DataOutputStream` in front of a `FileOutputStream` object. You can then read the data by putting a `DataInputStream` in front of a `FileInputStream` object:

```
public static void writeData(double[] data, String file)
    throws IOException
{
    OutputStream fout = new FileOutputStream(file);
    DataOutputStream out = new DataOutputStream(fout);
    out.writeInt(data.length);
    for (double d : data)
        out.writeDouble(d);
    out.close();
}

public static double[] readData(String file)
    throws IOException
{
    InputStream fin = new FileInputStream(file);
    DataInputStream in = new DataInputStream(fin);
    double[] data = new double[in.readInt()];
    for (int i = 0; i < data.length; i++)
        data[i] = in.readDouble();
    in.close();
    return data;
}
```

The `writeData` method first opens the file and writes the array length. It then loops, writing the contents of the array. The file can be read into an array with `readData`. These methods can be rewritten more simply using the `Object` streams you will learn about in Section 20.8 on page 549.

Exercise 20.7: Add a method to the `Attr` class of Chapter 3 that writes the contents of an object to a `DataOutputStream` and add a constructor that will read the state from a `DataInputStream`.

20.7 Working with Files

The java.io package provides a number of classes that help you work with files in the underlying system. The File stream classes allow you to read from and write to files and the FileDescriptor class allows the system to represent underlying file system resources as objects. RandomAccessFile lets you deal with files as randomly accessed streams of bytes or characters. Actual interaction with the local file system is through the File class, which provides an abstraction of file pathnames, including path component separators, and useful methods to manipulate file names.

20.7.1 File Streams and FileDescriptor

The File streams—FileInputStream, FileOutputStream, FileReader, and FileWriter—allow you to treat a file as a stream for input or output. Each type is instantiated with one of three constructors:

- ◆ A constructor that takes a String that is the name of the file.
- ◆ A constructor that takes a File object that refers to the file (see Section 20.7.3 on page 543).
- ◆ A constructor that takes a FileDescriptor object (see below).

If a file does not exist, the input streams will throw a FileNotFoundException. Accessing a file requires a security check and a SecurityException is thrown if you do not have permission to access that file—see "Security" on page 677.

   With a byte or character output stream, the first two constructor types create the file if it does not exist, or truncate it if it does exist. You can control truncation by using the overloaded forms of these two constructors that take a second argument: a boolean that, if true, causes each individual write to append to the file. If this boolean is false, the file will be truncated and new data added. If the file does not exist, the file will be created and the boolean will be ignored.

   The byte File streams also provide a getChannel method for integration with the java.nio facilities. It returns a java.nio.channels.FileChannel object for accessing the file.

   A FileDescriptor object represents a system-dependent value that describes an open file. You can get a file descriptor object by invoking getFD on a File byte stream—you cannot obtain the file descriptor from File character streams. You can test the validity of a FileDescriptor by invoking its boolean valid method—file descriptors created directly with the no-arg constructor of FileDescriptor are not valid.

FileDescriptor objects create a new File stream to the same file as another stream without needing to know the file's pathname. You must be careful to avoid unexpected interactions between two streams doing different things with the same file. You cannot predict what happens, for example, when two threads write to the same file using two different FileOutputStream objects at the same time.

The flush method of FileOutputStream and FileWriter guarantees that the buffer is flushed to the underlying file. It does not guarantee that the data is committed to disk—the underlying file system may do its own buffering. You can guarantee that the data is committed to disk by invoking the sync method on the file's FileDescriptor object, which will either force the data to disk or throw a SyncFailedException if the underlying system cannot fulfill this contract.

20.7.2 RandomAccessFile

The RandomAccessFile class provides a more sophisticated file mechanism than the File streams do. A random access file behaves like a large array of bytes stored in the file system. There is a kind of cursor, or index into the implied array, called the *file pointer;* input operations read bytes starting at the file pointer and advance the file pointer past the bytes read. If the random access file is created in read/write mode, then output operations are also available; output operations write bytes starting at the file pointer and advance the file pointer past the bytes written.

RandomAccessFile is not a subclass of InputStream, OutputStream, Reader, or Writer because it can do both input and output and can work with both characters and bytes. The constructor has a parameter that declares whether the stream is for input or for both input and output.

RandomAccessFile supports read and write methods of the same names and signatures as the byte streams. For example, read returns a single byte. RandomAccessFile also implements the DataInput and DataOutput interfaces (see page 537) and so can be used to read and write data types supported in those interfaces. Although you don't have to learn a new set of method names and semantics for the same kinds of tasks you do with the other streams, you cannot use a RandomAccessFile where any of the other streams are required.

The constructors for RandomAccessFile are

public **RandomAccessFile(String name, String mode)**
   throws FileNotFoundException
      Creates a random access file stream to read from, and optionally write to, a file with the specified name. The basic mode can be either "r" or "rw" for read or read/write, respectively. Variants of "rw" mode provide additional semantics: "rws" mode specifies that on each write the file contents and metadata (file size, last modification time, etc.) are written synchronously

through to the disk; "rwd" mode specifies that only the file contents are written synchronously to the disk. Specifying any other mode will get you an IllegalArgumentException. If the mode contains "rw" and the file does not exist, it will be created or, if that fails, a FileNotFoundException is thrown.

public **RandomAccessFile(File file, String mode)**
  throws FileNotFoundException
  Creates a random access file stream to read from, and optionally write to, the file specified by the File argument. Modes are the same as for the String-based constructor.

Since accessing a file requires a security check, these constructors could throw a SecurityException if you do not have permission to access the file in that mode—see "Security" on page 677.

The "random access" in the name of the class refers to the ability to set the read/write file pointer to any position in the file and then perform operations. The additional methods in RandomAccessFile to support this functionality are:

public long **getFilePointer()** throws IOException
  Returns the current location of the file pointer (in bytes) from the beginning of the file.

public void **seek(long pos)** throws IOException
  Sets the file pointer to the specified number of bytes from the beginning of the file. The next byte written or read will be the pos^{th} byte in the file, where the initial byte is the 0th. If you position the file pointer beyond the end of the file and write to the file, the file will grow.

public int **skipBytes(int count)** throws IOException
  Attempts to advance the file pointer count bytes. Any bytes skipped over can be read later after seek is used to reposition the file pointer. Returns the actual number of bytes skipped. This method is guaranteed never to throw an EOFException. If count is negative, no bytes are skipped.

public long **length()** throws IOException
  Returns the file length.

public void **setLength(long newLength)** throws IOException
  Sets the length of the file to newLength. If the file is currently shorter, the file is grown to the given length, filled in with any byte values the implementation chooses. If the file is currently longer, the data beyond this position is discarded. If the current position (as returned by getFilePointer) is greater than newLength, the position is set to newLength.

You can access the `FileDescriptor` for a `RandomAccessFile` by invoking
its `getFD` method. You can obtain a `FileChannel` for a `RandomAccessFile` by
invoking its `getChannel` method.

Exercise 20.8: Write a program that reads a file with entries separated by lines
starting with %% and creates a table file with the starting position of each such entry.
Then write a program that uses that table to print a random entry (see the
`Math.random` method described in "`Math and StrictMath`" on page 657).

20.7.3   The `File` Class

The `File` class (not to be confused with the file streams) provides several common manipulations that are useful with file names. It provides methods to separate
pathnames into subcomponents and to ask the file system about the file a pathname refers to.

A `File` object actually represents a path, not necessarily an underlying file.
For example, to find out whether a pathname represents an existing file, you create
a `File` object with the pathname and then invoke `exists` on that object.

A path is separated into directory and file parts by a char stored in the static
field `separatorChar` and available as a `String` in the static field `separator`.
The last occurrence of this character in the path separates the pathname into directory and file components. (*Directory* is the term used on most systems; some systems call such an entity a "folder" instead.)

`File` objects are created with one of four constructors:

public **`File(String path)`**
> Creates a `File` object to manipulate the specified `path`.

public **`File(String dirName, String name)`**
> Creates a `File` object for the file `name` in the directory named `dirName`. If
> `dirName` is `null`, only `name` is used. If `dirName` is an empty string, `name` is
> resolved against a system dependent default directory. Otherwise, this is
> equivalent to using `File(dirName + File.separator + name)`.

public **`File(File fileDir, String name)`**
> Creates a `File` object for the file `name` in the directory named by the `File`
> object `fileDir`. Equivalent to using `File(fileDir.getPath(), name)`.

public **`File(java.net.URI uri)`**
> Creates a `File` object for the pathname represented by the given `file:` URI
> (Uniform Resource Identifier). If the given URI is not a suitable file URI then
> `IllegalArgumentException` is thrown.

Five "get" methods retrieve information about the components of a `File` object's pathname. The following code invokes each of them after creating a `File` object for the file `"FileInfo.java"` in the `"ok"` subdirectory of the parent of the current directory (specified by `".."`):

```
File src = new File(".." + File.separator + "ok",
                    "FileInfo.java");
System.out.println("getName() = " + src.getName());
System.out.println("getPath() = " + src.getPath());
System.out.println("getAbsolutePath() = "
    + src.getAbsolutePath());
System.out.println("getCanonicalPath() = "
    + src.getCanonicalPath());
System.out.println("getParent() = " + src.getParent());
```

And here is the output:

```
getName() = FileInfo.java
getPath() = ../ok/FileInfo.java
getAbsolutePath() = /vob/java_prog/src/../ok/FileInfo.java
getCanonicalPath() = /vob/java_prog/ok/FileInfo.java
getParent() = ../ok
```

The canonical path is defined by each system. Usually, it is a form of the absolute path with relative components (such as `".."` to refer to the parent directory) renamed and with references to the current directory removed. Unlike the other "get" methods, `getCanonicalPath` can throw `IOException` because resolving path components can require calls to the underlying file system, which may fail.

The methods `getParentFile`, `getAbsoluteFile`, and `getCanonicalFile` are analogous to `getParent`, `getAbsolutePath`, and `getCanonicalPath`, but they return `File` objects instead of strings.

You can convert a `File` to a `java.net.URL` or `java.net.URI` object by invoking `toURL` or `toURI`, respectively.

The overriding method `File.equals` deserves mention. Two `File` objects are considered equal if they have the same path, not if they refer to the same underlying file system object. You cannot use `File.equals` to test whether two `File` objects denote the same file. For example, two `File` objects may refer to the same file but use different relative paths to refer to it, in which case they do not compare equal. Relatedly, you can compare two files using the `compareTo` method, which returns a number less than, equal to, or greater than zero as the current file's pathname is lexicographically less than, equal to, or greater than the pathname of the argument `File`. The `compareTo` method has two overloaded forms: one takes a File argument and the other takes an Object argument and so implements the Comparable interface.

Several boolean tests return information about the underlying file:

- ◆ exists returns true if the file exists in the file system.
- ◆ canRead returns true if a file exists and can be read.
- ◆ canWrite returns true if the file exists and can be written.
- ◆ isFile returns true if the file is not a directory or other special type of file.
- ◆ isDirectory returns true if the file is a directory.
- ◆ isAbsolute returns true if the path is an absolute pathname.
- ◆ isHidden returns true if the path is one normally hidden from users on the underlying system.

All the methods that inspect or modify the actual file system are security checked and can throw SecurityException if you don't have permission to perform the operation. Methods that ask for the filename itself are not security checked.

File objects have many other methods for manipulating files and directories. There are methods to inspect and manipulate the current file:

public long **lastModified()**
> Returns a long value representing the time the file was last modified or zero if the file does not exist.

public long **length()**
> Returns the file length in bytes, or zero if the file does not exist.

public boolean **renameTo(File newName)**
> Renames the file, returning true if the rename succeeded.

public boolean **delete()**
> Deletes the file or directory named in this File object, returning true if the deletion succeeded. Directories must be empty before they are deleted.

There are methods to create an underlying file or directory named by the current File:

public boolean **createNewFile()**
> Creates a new empty file, named by this File. Returns false if the file already exists or if the file cannot be created. The check for the existence of the file and its subsequent creation is performed atomically with respect to other file system operations.

`public boolean` **`mkdir()`**

> Creates a directory named by this `File`, returning `true` on success.

`public boolean` **`mkdirs()`**

> Creates all directories in the path named by this `File`, returning `true` if all were created. This is a way to ensure that a particular directory is created, even if it means creating other directories that don't currently exist above it in the directory hierarchy. Note that some of the directories may have been created even if `false` is returned.

However, files are usually created by `FileOutputStream` or `FileWriter` objects or `RandomAccessFile` objects, not using `File` objects.

Two methods let you change the state of the underlying file, assuming that one exists:

`public boolean` **`setLastModified(long time)`**

> Sets the "last modified" time for the file or returns `false` if it cannot do so.

`public boolean` **`setReadOnly()`**

> Makes the underlying file unmodifiable in the file system or returns `false` if it cannot do so. The file remains unmodifiable until it is deleted or externally marked as modifiable again—there is no method for making it modifiable again.

There are methods for listing the contents of directories and finding out about root directories:

`public String[]` **`list()`**

> Lists the files in this directory. If used on something that isn't a directory, it returns `null`. Otherwise, it returns an array of file names. This list includes all files in the directory except the equivalent of `"."` and `".."` (the current and parent directory, respectively).

`public String[]` **`list(FilenameFilter filter)`**

> Uses `filter` to selectively list files in this directory (see `FilenameFilter` described in the next section).

`public static File[]` **`listRoots()`**

> Returns the available filesystem roots, that is, roots of local hierarchical file systems. Windows platforms, for example, have a root directory for each active drive; UNIX platforms have a single / root directory. If none are available, the array has zero elements.

The methods `listFiles()` and `listFiles(FilenameFilter)` are analogous to `list()` and `list(FilenameFilter)`, but return arrays of `File` objects instead of arrays of strings. The method `listFiles(FileFilter)` is analogous to the `list` that uses a `FilenameFilter`.

Three methods relate primarily to temporary files (sometimes called "scratch files")—those files you need to create during a run of your program for storing data, or to pass between passes of your computation, but which are not needed after your program is finished.

public static File **createTempFile(String prefix, String suffix, File directory)** throws IOException
> Creates a new empty file in the specified directory, using the given prefix and suffix strings to generate its name. If this method returns successfully then it is guaranteed that the file denoted by the returned abstract pathname did not exist before this method was invoked, and neither this method nor any of its variants will return the same abstract pathname again in the current invocation of the virtual machine. The prefix argument must be at least three characters long, otherwise an IllegalArgumentException is thrown. It is recommended that the prefix be a short, meaningful string such as "hjb" or "mail". The suffix argument may be null, in which case the suffix ".tmp" will be used. Note that since there is no predefined separator between the file name and the suffix, any separator, such as '.', must be part of the suffix. If the directory argument is null then the system-dependent default temporary-file directory will be used. The default temporary-file directory is specified by the system property java.io.tmpdir.

public static File **createTempFile(String prefix, String suffix)** throws IOException
> Equivalent to createTempFile(prefix, suffix, null).

public void **deleteOnExit()**
> Requests the system to remove the file when the virtual machine terminates—see "Shutdown" on page 672. This request only applies to a normal termination of the virtual machine and cannot be revoked once issued.

When a temporary file is created, the prefix and the suffix may first be adjusted to fit the limitations of the underlying platform. If the prefix is too long then it will be truncated, but its first three characters will always be preserved. If the suffix is too long then it too will be truncated, but if it begins with a period (.) then the period and the first three characters following it will always be preserved. Once these adjustments have been made the name of the new file will be generated by concatenating the prefix, five or more internally generated characters, and the suffix. Temporary files are not automatically deleted on exit, although you will often invoke deleteOnExit on File objects returned by createTempFile.

Finally, the character File.pathSeparatorChar and its companion string File.pathSeparator represent the character that separates file or directory names in a search path. For example, UNIX separates components in the program search path with a colon, as in ".:/bin:/usr/bin", so pathSeparatorChar is a colon on UNIX systems.

Exercise 20.9: Write a method that, given one or more pathnames, will print all the information available about the file it represents (if any).

Exercise 20.10: Write a program that uses a StreamTokenizer object to break an input file into words and counts the number of times each word occurs in the file, printing the result. Use a HashMap to keep track of the words and counts.

20.7.4 FilenameFilter and FileFilter

The FilenameFilter interface provides objects that filter unwanted files from a list. It supports a single method:

boolean **accept(File dir, String name)**
> Returns true if the file named name in the directory dir should be part of the filtered output.

Here is an example that uses a FilenameFilter object to list only directories:

```
import java.io.*;

class DirFilter implements FilenameFilter {
    public boolean accept(File dir, String name) {
        return new File(dir, name).isDirectory();
    }

    public static void main(String[] args) {
        File dir = new File(args[0]);
        String[] files = dir.list(new DirFilter());
        System.out.println(files.length + " dir(s):");
        for (String file : files)
            System.out.println("\t" + file);
    }
}
```

First we create a File object to represent a directory specified on the command line. Then we create a DirFilter object and pass it to list. For each name in the directory, list invokes the accept method on the filtering object and includes the name in the list if the filtering object returns true. For our accept method, true means that the named file is a directory.

The `FileFilter` interface is analogous to `FilenameFilter`, but works with a single `File` object:

boolean **accept(File pathname)**

> Returns `true` if the file represented by `pathname` should be part of the filtered output.

Exercise 20.11: Using `FilenameFilter` or `FileFilter`, write a program that takes a directory and a suffix as parameters and prints all files it can find that have that suffix.

20.8 Object Serialization

The ability to save objects in a byte stream that can be transferred across the network (perhaps for use in remote method invocations), saved to disk in a file or database, and later reconstituted to form a live object, is an essential aspect of many real-world applications.

The process of converting an object's representation into a stream of bytes is known as *serialization,* while reconstituting an object from a byte stream is *deserialization.* When talking about the classes, interfaces, and language features involved in this overall process, we generally just use the term *serialization* and understand that it includes deserialization as well.

A number of classes and interfaces are involved with serialization. You have already learned about the basic mechanisms for reading and writing primitive types and strings using the `Data` stream classes (see page 537). This section covers the object byte streams—`ObjectInputStream` and `ObjectOutputStream`—that allow you to serialize and deserialize complete objects. Various other classes and interfaces provide specific support for the serialization process. In addition, the field modifier `transient` provides a language-level means of marking data that should not be serialized.

20.8.1 The `Object` Byte Streams

The `Object` streams—`ObjectInputStream` and `ObjectOutputStream`—allow you to read and write object graphs in addition to the well-known types (primitives, strings, and arrays). By "object graph" we mean that when you use `writeObject` to write an object to an `ObjectOutputStream`, bytes representing the object—including all other objects that it references—are written to the stream. This process of transforming an object into a stream of bytes is called *seri-*

alization. Because the serialized form is expressed in bytes, not characters, the `Object` streams have no `Reader` or `Writer` forms.

When bytes encoding a serialized graph of objects are read by the method `readObject` of `ObjectInputStream`—that is, *deserialized*—the result is a graph of objects equivalent to the input graph.

Suppose, for example, that you have a `HashMap` object that you wish to store into a file for future use. You could write the graph of objects that starts with the hash map this way:

```
FileOutputStream fileOut = new FileOutputStream("tab");
ObjectOutputStream out = new ObjectOutputStream(fileOut);
HashMap<?,?> hash = getHashMap();
out.writeObject(hash);
```

As you can see, this approach is quite straightforward. The single `writeObject` on `hash` writes the entire contents of the hash map, including all entries, all the objects that the entries refer to, and so on, until the entire graph of interconnected objects has been visited. A new copy of the hash map could be reconstituted from the serialized bytes:

```
FileInputStream fileIn = new FileInputStream("tab");
ObjectInputStream in = new ObjectInputStream(fileIn);
HashMap<?,?> newHash = (HashMap<?,?>) in.readObject();
```

Serialization preserves the integrity of the graph itself. Suppose, for example, that in a serialized hash map, an object was stored under two different keys:

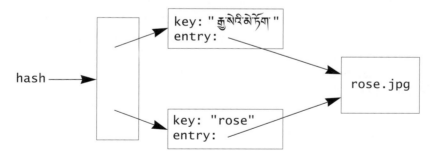

When the serialized hash map is deserialized, the two analogous entries in the new copy of the hash map will have references to a single copy of the `rose.jpg` object, not references to two separate copies of `rose.jpg`.[2]

---

[2] The first key field is the word "rose" in Tibetan.

Sometimes, however, sharing objects in this way is not what is desired. In that case you can use ObjectOutputStream's writeUnshared method to write the object as a new distinct object, rather than using a reference to an existing serialization of that object. Any object written into the graph by writeUnshared will only ever have one reference to it in the serialized data. The readUnshared method of ObjectInputStream reads an object that is expected to be unique. If the object is actually a reference to an existing deserialized object then an ObjectStreamException is thrown; similarly, if the deserialization process later tries to create a second reference to an object returned by readUnshared, an ObjectStreamException is thrown. These uniqueness checks only apply to the actual object passed to writeUnshared or read by readUnshared, not to any objects they refer to.

20.8.2 Making Your Classes Serializable

When an ObjectOutputStream writes a serialized object, the object must implement the Serializable marker interface. This marker interface declares that the class is designed to have its objects serialized.

Being serializable can be quite simple. The default serialization process is to serialize each field of the object that is neither transient nor static. Primitive types and strings are written in the same encoding used by DataOutputStream; objects are serialized by calling writeObject. With default serialization, all serialized fields that are object references must refer to serializable object types. Default serialization also requires either that your superclass have a no-arg constructor (so that deserialization can invoke it) or that it also be Serializable (in which case declaring your class to implement Serializable is redundant but harmless). For most classes this default serialization is sufficient, and the entire work necessary to make a class serializable is to mark it as such by declaring that it implements the Serializable interface:

```
public class Name implements java.io.Serializable {
    private String name;
    private long id;
    private transient boolean hashSet = false;
    private transient int hash;
    private static long nextID = 0;

    public Name(String name) {
        this.name = name;
        synchronized (Name.class) {
            id = nextID++;
```

```
            }
        }

        public int hashCode() {
            if (!hashSet) {
                hash = name.hashCode();
                hashSet = true;
            }
            return hash;
        }

        // ... override equals, provide other useful methods
    }
```

The class Name can be written to an ObjectOutputStream either directly
with writeObject, or indirectly if it is referenced by an object written to such a
stream. The name and id fields will be written to the stream; the fields nextID,
hashSet, and hash will not be written, nextID because it is static and the others because they are declared transient. Because hash is a cached value that can
easily be recalculated from name, there is no reason to consume the time and
space it takes to write it to the stream.

Default deserialization reads the values written during serialization. Static
fields in the class are left untouched—if the class needs to be loaded then the normal initialization of the class takes place, giving the static fields an initial value.
Each transient field in the reconstituted object is set to the default value for its
type. When a Name object is deserialized, the newly created object will have name
and id set to the same values as those of the original object, the static field
nextID will remain untouched, and the transient fields hashSet and hash will
have their default values (false and 0). These defaults work because when
hashSet is false the value of hash will be recalculated.

You will occasionally have a class that is generally serializable but has specific instances that are not serializable. For example, a container might itself be
serializable but contain references to objects that are not serializable. Any attempt
to serialize a non-serializable object will throw a NotSerializableException.

20.8.3 Serialization and Deserialization Order

Each class is responsible for properly serializing its own state—that is, its fields.
Objects are serialized and deserialized down the type tree—from the highest-level
class that is Serializable to the most specific class. This order is rarely impor-

tant when you're serializing, but it can be important when you're deserializing. Let us consider the following type tree for an HTTPInput class:

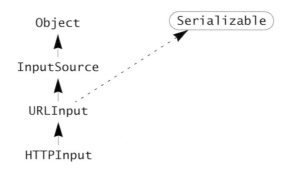

When deserializing an HTTPInput object, ObjectInputStream first allocates memory for the new object and then finds the first Serializable class in the object's type hierarchy—in this case URLInput. The stream invokes the no-arg constructor of that class's superclass (the object's last non-serializable class), which in this case is InputSource. If other state from the superclass must be preserved, URLInput is responsible for serializing that state and restoring it on deserialization. If your non-serializable superclass has state, you will almost certainly need to customize the first serializable class (see the next section). If the first serializable class directly extends Object (as the earlier Name class did), customizing is easy because Object has no state to preserve or restore.

Once the first serializable class has finished with its part of its superclass's state, it will set its own state from the stream. Then ObjectInputStream will walk down the type tree, deserializing the state for each class using readObject. When ObjectInputStream reaches the bottom of the type tree, the object has been completely deserialized.

As the stream is deserialized, other serialized objects will be found that were referenced from the object currently being deserialized. These other objects are deserialized as they are encountered. Thus, if URLInput had a reference to a HashMap, that hash map and its contents would be deserialized before the HTTPInput part of the object was deserialized.

Before any of this can happen, the relevant classes must first be loaded. This requires finding a class of the same name as the one written and checking to see that it is the same class. You'll learn about versioning issues shortly. Assuming it is the same class, the class must be loaded. If the class is not found or cannot be loaded for any reason, readObject will throw a ClassNotFoundException.

20.8.4 Customized Serialization

The default serialization methods work for many classes but not for all of them. For some classes default deserialization may be improper or inefficient. The HashMap class is an example of both problems. Default serialization would write all the data structures for the hash map, including the hash codes of the entries. This serialization is both wrong and inefficient.

It is wrong because hash codes may be different for deserialized entries. This will be true, for example, of entries using the default hashCode implementation.

It is inefficient because a hash map typically has a significant number of empty buckets. There is no point in serializing empty buckets. It would be more efficient to serialize the referenced keys and entries and rebuild a hash map from them than to serialize the entire data structure of the map.

For these reasons, java.util.HashMap provides private writeObject and readObject methods.[3] These methods are invoked by ObjectOutputStream and ObjectInputStream, respectively, when it is time to serialize or deserialize a HashMap object. These methods are invoked only on classes that provide them, and the methods are responsible only for the class's own state, including any state from non-serializable superclasses. A class's writeObject and readObject methods, if provided, should *not* invoke the superclass's readObject or writeObject method. Object serialization differs in this way from clone and finalize.

Let us suppose, for example, that you wanted to improve the Name class so that it didn't have to check whether the cached hash code was valid each time. You could do this by setting hash in the constructor, instead of lazily when it is asked for. But this causes a problem with serialization—since hash is transient it does not get written as part of serialization (nor should it), so when you are deserializing you need to explicitly set it. This means that you have to implement readObject to deserialize the main fields and then set hash, which implies that you have to implement writeObject so that you know how the main fields were serialized.

```
public class BetterName implements Serializable {
    private String name;
    private long id;
    private transient int hash;
```

---

[3] These methods are private because they should never be overridden and they should never be invoked by anyone using or subclassing your class. The serialization mechanism gains access to these private methods using reflection to disable the language level access control (see page 426). Of course this can only happen if the current security policy allows it—see "Security" on page 677.

```
    private static long nextID = 0;

    public BetterName(String name) {
        this.name = name;
        synchronized (BetterName.class) {
            id = nextID++;
        }
        hash = name.hashCode();
    }

    private void writeObject(ObjectOutputStream out)
        throws IOException
    {
        out.writeUTF(name);
        out.writeLong(id);
    }

    private void readObject(ObjectInputStream in)
        throws IOException, ClassNotFoundException
    {
        name = in.readUTF();
        id = in.readLong();
        hash = name.hashCode();
    }

    public int hashCode() {
        return hash;
    }

    // ... override equals, provide other useful methods
}
```

We use writeObject to write out each of the non-static, non-transient fields. It declares that it can throw IOException because the write methods it invokes can do so, and, if one does throw an exception, the serialization must be halted. When readObject gets the values from the stream, it can then set hash properly. It, too, must declare that it throws IOException because the read methods it invokes can do so, and this should stop deserialization. The readObject method must declare that it throws ClassNotFoundException because, in the general case, deserializing fields of the current object could require other classes to be loaded—though not in the example.

There is one restriction on customized serialization: You cannot directly set a `final` field within `readObject` because `final` fields can only be set in initializers or constructors. For example, if `name` was declared `final` the class `BetterName` would not compile. You will need to design your classes with this restriction in mind when considering custom serialization. The default serialization mechanism can bypass this restriction because it uses native code. This means that default serialization works fine with classes that have `final` fields. For custom serialization it is possible to use reflection to set a final field—see "Final Fields" on page 420—but the security restrictions for doing this means that it is seldom applicable. One circumstance in which it is applicable, for example, is if your classes are required to be installed as a standard extension and so have the necessary security privileges—see "Security Policies" on page 680.

The `readObject` and `writeObject` methods for `BetterName` show that you can use the methods of `DataInput` and `DataOutput` to transmit arbitrary data on the stream. However, the actual implementations replicate the default serialization and then add the necessary setup for `hash`. The read and write invocations of these methods could have been replaced with a simple invocation of methods that perform default serialization and deserialization:

```
private void writeObject(ObjectOutputStream out)
    throws IOException
{
    out.defaultWriteObject();
}


private void readObject(ObjectInputStream in)
    throws IOException, ClassNotFoundException
{
    in.defaultReadObject();
    hash = name.hashCode();
}
```

In fact, as you may have surmised, given that `writeObject` performs nothing but default serialization, we need not have implemented it at all.

A `writeObject` method can throw `NotSerializableException` if a particular object is not serializable. For example, in rare cases, objects of a class might be generally serializable, but a particular object might contain sensitive data.

You will occasionally find that an object cannot be initialized properly until the graph of which it is a part has been completely deserialized. You can have the `ObjectInputStream` invoke a method of your own devising by calling the stream's `registerValidation` method with a reference to an object that implements the interface `ObjectInputValidation`. When deserialization of the top-level object at the head of the graph is complete, your object's `validateObject` method will be invoked to make any needed validation operation or check.

Normally, an object is serialized as itself on the output stream, and a copy of the same type is reconstituted during deserialization. You will find a few classes for which this is not correct. For example, if you have a class that has objects that are supposed to be unique in each virtual machine for each unique value (so that `==` will return `true` if and only if `equals` also would return `true`), you would need to resolve an object being deserialized into an equivalent one in the local virtual machine. You can control these by providing `writeReplace` and `readResolve` methods of the following forms and at an appropriate access level:

<access> `Object` **`writeReplace()`** `throws ObjectStreamException`
> Returns an object that will replace the current object during serialization. Any object may be returned including the current one.

<access> `Object` **`readResolve()`** `throws ObjectStreamException`
> Returns an object that will replace the current object during deserialization. Any object may be returned including the current one.

In our example, `readResolve` would check to find the local object that was equivalent to the one just deserialized—if it exists it will be returned, otherwise we can register the current object (for use by `readResolve` in the future) and return `this`. These methods can be of any accessibility; they will be used if they are accessible to the object type being serialized. For example, if a class has a private `readResolve` method, it only affects deserialization of objects that are exactly of its type. A package-accessible `readResolve` affects only subclasses within the same package, while public and protected `readResolve` methods affect objects of all subclasses.

20.8.5 Object Versioning

Class implementations change over time. If a class's implementation changes between the time an object is serialized and the time it is deserialized, the `ObjectInputStream` can detect this change. When the object is written, the *serial version UID* (unique identifier), a 64-bit `long` value, is written with it. By default, this identifier is a secure hash of the full class name, superinterfaces, and members—the facts about the class that, if they change, signal a possible class incompatibility. Such a hash is essentially a fingerprint—it is nearly impossible for two different classes to have the same UID.

When an object is read from an `ObjectInputStream`, the serial version UID is also read. An attempt is then made to load the class. If no class with the same name is found or if the loaded class's UID does not match the UID in the stream, `readObject` throws an `InvalidClassException`. If the versions of all the classes in the object's type are found and all the UIDs match, the object can be deserialized.

This assumption is very conservative: Any change in the class creates an incompatible version. Many class changes are less drastic than this. Adding a cache to a class can be made compatible with earlier versions of the serialized form, as can adding optional behavior or values. Rather then relying on the default serial version UID, any serializable class should explicitly declare its own serial version UID value. Then when you make a change to a class that can be compatible with the serialized forms of earlier versions of the class, you can explicitly declare the serial version UID for the earlier class. A serial version UID is declared as follows:

```
private static final
    long serialVersionUID = -1307795172754062330L;
```

The `serialVersionUID` field must be a static, final field of type `long`. It should also be private since it is only applied to the declaring class. The value of `serialVersionUID` is provided by your development system. In many development systems, it is the output of a command called `serialver`. Other systems have different ways to provide you with this value, which is the serial version UID of the class before the first incompatible modification. (Nothing prevents you from using any number as this UID if you stamp it from the start, but it is usually a really bad idea. Your numbers will not be as carefully calculated to avoid conflict with other classes as the secure hash is.)

Now when the `ObjectInputStream` finds your class and compares the UID with that of the older version in the file, the UIDs will be the same even though the implementation has changed. If you invoke `defaultReadObject`, only those fields that were present in the original version will be set. Other fields will be left in their default state. If `writeObject` in the earlier version of the class wrote values on the field without using `defaultWriteObject`, you must read those values. If you try to read more values than were written, you will get an `EOFException`, which can inform you that you are deserializing an older form that wrote less information. If possible, you should design classes with a class version number instead of relying on an exception to signal the version of the original data.

When an object is written to an `ObjectOutputStream`, the `Class` object for that object is also written. Because `Class` objects are specific to each virtual machine, serializing the actual `Class` object would not be helpful. So `Class` objects on a stream are replaced by `ObjectStreamClass` objects that contain the information necessary to find an equivalent class when the object is deserialized.

This information includes the class's full name and its serial version UID. Unless you create one, you will never directly see an ObjectStreamClass object.

As a class evolves it is possible that a new superclass is introduced for that class. If an older serialized form of the class is deserialized it will not contain any serialized data for that superclass. Rather than making this an error, the system will set all fields declared by the superclass to their default initialized values. To override this default behavior, the new superclass (which must implement Serializable, of course) can declare the following method:

private void **readObjectNoData()** throws ObjectStreamException

If, as an object is deserialized, the serialized data lists the superclass as a known superclass then the superclass's readObject method will be invoked (if it exists), otherwise the superclass's readObjectNoData method will be invoked. The readObjectNoData method can then set appropriate values in the object's superclass fields.

20.8.6 Serialized Fields

The default serialization usually works well, but for more sophisticated classes and class evolution you may need to access the original fields. For example, suppose you were representing a rectangle in a geometric system by using two opposite corners. You would have four fields: x1, y1, x2, and y2. If you later want to use a corner, plus width and height, you would have four different fields: x, y, width, and height. Assuming default serialization of the four original fields you would also have a compatibility problem: the rectangles that were already serialized would have the old fields instead of the new ones. To solve this problem you could maintain the serialized format of the original class and convert between the old and new fields as you encounter them in readObject or writeObject. You do this using *serialized field* types to view the serialized form as an abstraction and to access individual fields:

```java
public class Rectangle implements Serializable {
    private static final
        long serialVersionUID = -1307795172754062330L;
    private static final
        ObjectStreamField[] serialPersistentFields = {
            new ObjectStreamField("x1", Double.TYPE),
            new ObjectStreamField("y1", Double.TYPE),
            new ObjectStreamField("x2", Double.TYPE),
            new ObjectStreamField("y2", Double.TYPE),
        };
```

```
private transient double x, y, width, height;

private void readObject(ObjectInputStream in)
    throws IOException, ClassNotFoundException
{
    ObjectInputStream.GetField fields;
    fields = in.readFields();
    x = fields.get("x1", 0.0);
    y = fields.get("y1", 0.0);
    double x2 = fields.get("x2", 0.0);
    double y2 = fields.get("y2", 0.0);
    width = (x2 - x);
    height = (y2 - y);
}

private void writeObject(ObjectOutputStream out)
    throws IOException
{
    ObjectOutputStream.PutField fields;
    fields = out.putFields();
    fields.put("x1", x);
    fields.put("y1", y);
    fields.put("x2", x + width);
    fields.put("y2", y + height);
    out.writeFields();
}
}
```

Rectangle keeps the serialVersionUID of the original version to declare that the versions are compatible. Changing fields that would be used by default serialization is otherwise considered to be an incompatible change.

To represent each of the old fields that will be found in the serialized data, you create an ObjectStreamField object. You construct each ObjectStreamField object by passing in the name of the field it represents, and the Class object for the type of the field it represents. An overloaded constructor also takes a boolean argument that specifies whether the field refers to an unshared object—that is, one written by writeUnshared or read by readUnshared. The serialization mechanism needs to know where to find these ObjectStreamField objects, so they must be defined in the static, final array called serialPersistentFields.

The fields x, y, width, and height are marked transient because they are not serialized—during serialization these new fields must be converted into appropriate values of the original fields so that we preserve the serialized form. So writeObject uses an ObjectOutputStream.PutField object to write out the old form, using x and y as the old x1 and y1, and calculating x2 and y2 from the rectangle's width and height. Each put method takes a field name as one argument and a value for that field as the other—the type of the value determines which overloaded form of put is invoked (one for each primitive type and Object). In this way the default serialization of the original class has been emulated and the serialized format preserved.

When a Rectangle object is deserialized, the reverse process occurs. Our readObject method gets an ObjectInputStream.GetField that allows access to fields by name from the serialized object. There is a get method for returning each primitive type, and one for returning an Object reference. Each get method takes two parameters: the name of the field and a value to return if it is not defined in the serialized object. The return value's type chooses which overload of get is used: A short return value will use the get that returns a short, for example. In our example, all values are double: We get the x1 and y1 fields to use for one corner of the rectangle, and the old x2 and y2 fields to calculate width and height.

Using the above technique the new Rectangle class can deserialize old rectangle objects and a new serialized rectangle can be deserialized by the original Rectangle class, provided that both virtual machines are using compatible versions of the serialization stream protocol. The stream protocol defines the actual layout of serialized objects in the stream regardless of whether they use default serialization or the serialized field objects. This means that the serialized form of an object is not dependent on, for example, the order in which you invoke put, nor do you have to know the order in which to invoke get—you can use get or put to access fields in any order any number of times.

20.8.7 The Externalizable Interface

The Externalizable interface extends Serializable. A class that implements Externalizable takes complete control over its serialized state, assuming responsibility for all the data of its superclasses, any versioning issues, and so on. You may need this, for example, when a repository for serialized objects mandates restrictions on the form of those objects that are incompatible with the provided serialization mechanism. The Externalizable interface has two methods:

```
public interface Externalizable extends Serializable {
    void writeExternal(ObjectOutput out)
        throws IOException;
```

```
    void readExternal(ObjectInput in)
        throws IOException, ClassNotFoundException;
}
```

These methods are invoked when the object is serialized and deserialized, respectively. They are normal public methods, so the exact type of the object determines which implementation will be used. Subclasses of an externalizable class will often need to invoke their superclass's implementation before serializing or deserializing their own state—in contrast to classes that use normal serialization.

You should note that the methods of the interface are public and so can be invoked by anyone at anytime. In particular, a malicious program might invoke readExternal to make an object overwrite its state from some serialized stream, possibly with invented content. If you are designing classes where such security counts you have to take this into account either by not using Externalizable or by writing your readExternal method to be only invoked once, and never at all if the object was created via one of your constructors.

20.8.8 Documentation Comment Tags

As you can see from the Rectangle code, the serialized form of an object can be an important thing, separate from its runtime form. This can happen over time due to evolution, or by initial design when the runtime form is not a good serialized form. When you write serializable classes that others will reimplement, you should document the persistent form so that other programmer's can properly reimplement the serialized form as well as the runtime behavior. You do this with the special javadoc tags @serial, @serialField, and @serialData.

Use @serial to document fields that use default serialization. For example, the original Rectangle class could have looked like this:

```
/** X-coordinate of one corner.
 *  @serial */
private double x1;
/** Y-coordinate of one corner.
 *  @serial */
private double y1;
/** X-coordinate of opposite corner.
 *  @serial */
private double x2;
/** Y-coordinate of opposite corner.
 *  @serial */
private double y2;
```

The @serial tag can include a description of the meaning of the field. If none is given (as above), then the description of the runtime field will be used. The javadoc tool will add all @serial information to a page, known as the *serialized form page*.

The @serial tag can also be applied to a class or package with the single argument include or exclude, to control whether serialization information is documented for that class or package. By default public and protected types are included, otherwise they are excluded. A class level @serial tag overrides a package level @serial tag.

The @serialField tag documents fields that are created by GetField and PutField invocations, such as those in our Rectangle example. The tag takes first the field name, then its type, and then a description. For example:

```
/** @serialField x1 double X-coordinate of one corner. */
/** @serialField y1 double Y-coordinate of one corner. */
/** @serialField x2 double X-coordinate of other corner. */
/** @serialField y2 double Y-coordinate of other corner. */
private transient double x, y, width, height;
```

You use the @serialData tag in the doc comment for a writeObject method to document any additional data written by the method. You can also use @serialData to document anything written by an Externalizable class's writeExternal method.

20.9 The IOException Classes

Every I/O-specific error detected by classes in java.io is signaled by an IOException or a subclass. Most I/O classes are designed to be general, so most of the exceptions cannot be listed specifically. For example, InputStream methods that throw IOException cannot detail which particular exceptions might be thrown, because any particular input stream class might throw a subclass of IOException for particular error conditions relevant to that stream. And the filter input and output streams pass through exceptions only from their downstream objects, which can also be of other stream types.

The specific subclasses of IOException used in the java.io package are

CharConversionException extends IOException
> Thrown when a character conversion problem occurs in a character stream operation that must convert local character codes to Unicode or vice versa.

EOFException extends IOException
> Thrown when the end of the file (stream) is detected while reading.

FileNotFoundException extends IOException
>   Thrown when the attempt to access the file specified by a given pathname fails—presumably because the file does not exist.

InterruptedIOException extends IOException
>   Thrown when a blocking I/O operation detects that the current thread has been interrupted before or during the operation. In principle, except for the Print stream methods, interrupting a thread should cause this exception if the thread is performing a blocking I/O operation. In practice most implementations only check for interruption before performing an operation and do not respond to interruption during the operation (see page 515) so you cannot rely on the ability to interrupt a blocked thread. This exception is also used to signify that a time-out occurred during network I/O.

InvalidClassException extends ObjectStreamException
>   Thrown when the serialization mechanism detects a problem with a class: The serial version of the class does not match that read from the stream, the class contains unknown data types, or the class does not have an accessible no-arg constructor when needed.

InvalidObjectException extends ObjectStreamException
>   Thrown when the validateObject method cannot make the object valid, thus aborting the deserialization.

NotActiveException extends ObjectStreamException
>   Thrown when a serialization method, such as defaultReadObject, is invoked when serialization is not under way on the stream.

NotSerializableException extends ObjectStreamException
>   Thrown either by the serialization mechanism or explicitly by a class when a class cannot be serialized.

ObjectStreamException extends IOException
>   The superclass for all the Object stream related exceptions.

OptionalDataException extends ObjectStreamException
>   Thrown when the optional data (that is, not part of default serialization) in the object input stream is corrupt or was not read by the reading method.

StreamCorruptedException extends ObjectStreamException
>   Thrown when internal object stream state is missing or invalid.

SyncFailedException extends IOException
>   Thrown by FileDescriptor.sync when the data cannot be guaranteed to have been written to the underlying media.

UnsupportedEncodingException extends IOException
>   Thrown when an unknown character encoding is specified.

UTFDataFormatException extends IOException
> Thrown by DataInputStream.readUTF when the string it is reading has malformed UTF syntax.

WriteAbortedException extends ObjectStreamException
> Thrown when an exception occurred during a serialization write operation.

In addition to these specific exceptions, other exceptional conditions in java.io are signaled with an IOException containing a string that describes the specific error encountered. For example, using a Piped stream object that has never been connected throws an exception object with a detail string such as "Pipe not connected", and trying to push more than the allowed number of characters onto a PushbackReader throws an exception with the string "Pushback buffer overflow". Such exceptions are difficult to catch explicitly, so this style of exception reporting is not in favor. Specific exception subtypes should be created for each category of exceptional circumstance.

20.10 A Taste of New I/O

The java.nio package ("New I/O") and its subpackages give you access to high performance I/O, albeit with more complexity. Instead of a simple stream model you have control over buffers, channels, and other abstractions to let you get maximum speed for your I/O needs. This is recommended only for those who have a demonstrated need.

The model for rapid I/O is to use buffers to walk through channels of primitive types. Buffers are containers for data and are associated with channels that connect to external data sources. There are buffer types for all primitive types: A FloatBuffer works with float values, for example. The ByteBuffer is more general; it can handle any primitive type with methods such as getFloat and putLong. MappedByteBuffer helps you map a large file into memory for quick access. You can use character set decoders and encoders to translate buffers of bytes to and from Unicode.

Channels come from objects that access external data, namely files and sockets. FileInputStream has a getChannel method that returns a channel for that stream, as do RandomAccessFile, java.net.Socket, and others.

Here is some code that will let you efficiently access a large text file in a specified encoding:

```
public static int count(File file, String charSet, char ch)
    throws IOException
{
    Charset charset = Charset.forName(charSet);
```

```
CharsetDecoder decoder = charset.newDecoder();
FileInputStream fis = new FileInputStream(file);
FileChannel fc = fis.getChannel();

// Get the file's size and then map it into memory
long size = fc.size();
MappedByteBuffer bb =
    fc.map(FileChannel.MapMode.READ_ONLY, 0, size);
CharBuffer cb = decoder.decode(bb);
int count = 0;
for (int i = 0; i < size && i < Integer.MAX_VALUE; i++)
    if (cb.charAt(i) == ch)
        count++;
fc.close();
return count;
}
```

We use a `FileInputStream` to get a channel for the file. Then we create a mapped buffer for the entire file. What a "mapped buffer" does may vary with the platform, but for large files (greater than a few tens of kilobytes) you can assume that it will be at least as efficient as streaming through the data, and nearly certainly much more efficient. We then get a decoder for the specified character set, which gives us a `CharBuffer` from which to read.[4]

The `CharBuffer` not only lets you read (decoded) characters from the file, it also acts as a `CharSequence` and, therefore, can be used with the regular expression mechanism.

In addition to high-performance I/O, the new I/O package also provides a different programming model that allows for non-blocking I/O operations to be performed. This is an advanced topic well beyond the scope of this book, but suffice it to say that this allows a small number of threads to efficiently manage a large number of simultaneous I/O connections.

There is also a reliable file locking mechanism: You can lock a `FileChannel` and receive a `java.nio.channels.FileLock` object that represents either a shared or exclusive lock on a file. You can release the `FileLock` when you are done with it.

> *Nothing has really happened until it has been recorded.*
> —Virginia Woolf

---

4. Note that there is an unfortunate discrepancy between the ability to map huge files and the fact that the returned buffer has a capacity that is limited to `Integer.MAX_VALUE`.

Collections

ANDREA: *Unhappy the land that has no heroes.*
GALILEO: *No, unhappy the land that* needs *heroes.*
—Bertolt Brecht, *Life of Galileo*

THE `java.util` package contains many useful interfaces, classes, and a range of subpackages. The classes and interfaces can be roughly divided into two categories: collections and everything else. This chapter describes the collection types. You will learn about the other general utilities in the next chapter.

21.1 Collections

Collections (sometimes called *containers*) are holders that let you store and organize objects in useful ways for efficient access. What will be efficient depends on how you need to use the collection, so collections come in many flavors. Most programming environments provide some collection types, ranging from impoverished up through gargantuan.

In the package `java.util` you will find interfaces and classes that provide a generic *collection* framework. This framework gives you a consistent and flexible set of collection interfaces and several useful implementations of these interfaces. You've already been briefly introduced to some of these, such as the interfaces `List`, `Set`, `Map`, and `Iterator`, and implementations `ArrayList` and `HashMap`.

The collection framework is designed to be concise. The principle is to have a core set of valuable collection abstractions and implementations that are broadly useful, rather than an exhaustive set that is complete but conceptually complex and unwieldy.

One way to keep the size down is to represent broad abstractions in the interfaces rather than fine-grained differences. Notions such as immutability and resizability are not represented by different interface types. The core collection

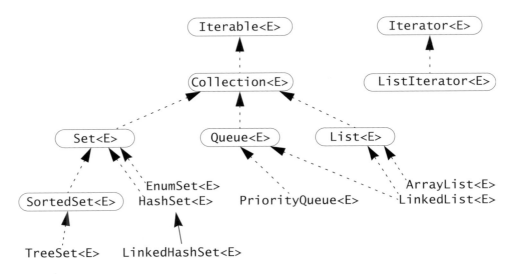

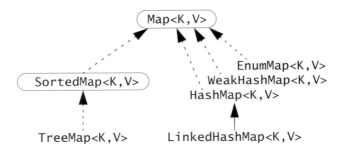

FIGURE 21–1: *Type Trees for Concrete Collections in* `java.util`

interfaces provide methods that allow all common operations, leaving it to specific implementations to refuse to execute particular improper operations by throwing the unchecked `java.lang.UnsupportedOperationException`.

Figure 21–1 shows the collections interfaces and the concrete implementations provided directly in `java.util`.[1] The collections interfaces are

◆ `Collection<E>`—The root interface for collections. Provides such methods as `add`, `remove`, `size`, and `toArray`.

---

[1]   The full list of collections includes abstract collections that help you write your own implementations. These are presented in Section 21.14 on page 611. Other specialized implementations are also elided for clarity, but are discussed later in the chapter.

- Set<E>—A collection in which no duplicate elements can be present, and whose elements are not necessarily stored in any particular order (extends Collection<E>).

- SortedSet<E>—A set whose elements are sorted (extends Set<E>).

- List<E>—A collection whose elements stay in a particular order unless the list is modified (extends Collection<E>). This is a general use of the word "list" and does not necessarily mean "linked list," although that is one possible implementation.

- Queue<E>—A collection with an implied ordering in its elements (extends Collection<E>). Every queue has a *head* element that is the target of specific operations like peek and poll.

- Map<K,V>—A mapping from keys to at most one value each. (Map does not extend Collection, although the concepts meaningful to both maps and collections are represented by methods of the same names, and maps can be viewed as collections.)

- SortedMap<K,V>—A map whose keys are sorted (extends Map<K,V>).

- Iterator<E>—An interface for objects that return elements from a collection one at a time. This is the type of object returned by the method Iterable.iterator.

- ListIterator<E>—An iterator for List objects that adds useful List-related methods. This is the type of object returned by List.listIterator.

- Iterable<E>—An object that provides an Iterator and so can be used in an enhanced for statement. Although defined in the java.lang package, this is considered part of the collection framework because the vast majority of standard iterable types are collections.

The interfaces SortedSet and SortedMap guarantee that iteration through the elements is done in sorted order. You will learn how to define an order for objects later in this chapter.

The java.util package also provides several useful concrete implementations of these interfaces that will suffice for most of your needs. For example:

- HashSet<E>—A Set implemented as a hashtable. A good, general-purpose implementation for which searching, adding, and removing are mostly insensitive to the size of the contents.

- TreeSet<E>—A SortedSet implemented as a balanced binary tree. Slower to search or modify than a HashSet, but keeps the elements sorted.

- ◆ ArrayList<E>—A List implemented using a resizable array. It is expensive to add or delete an element near the beginning if the list is large, but relatively cheap to create and fast for random access.

- ◆ LinkedList<E>—A doubly linked List and Queue implementation. Modification is cheap at any size, but random access is slow.

- ◆ HashMap<K,V>—A hashtable implementation of Map. A very generally useful collection with relatively cheap lookup and insertion times.

- ◆ TreeMap<K,V>—An implementation of SortedMap as a balanced binary tree to keep its elements ordered by key. Useful for ordered data sets that require moderately quick lookup by key.

- ◆ WeakHashMap<K,V>—An hashtable implementation of Map that references its keys with weak reference objects (see page 454). This is useful only in limited situations.

Nearly all the implementation classes in java.util are both Cloneable and Serializable. The exceptions are PriorityQueue which is not Cloneable, and WeakHashMap which is neither.

In this chapter you first learn about iteration because it is useful with all the collection classes. We then cover ordering since it is used by many of the collection types. We then present the details of the Collection-based types, followed by the Map-based types. After that we look at the various utilities available, and we show you how to make unmodifiable and type-safe versions of your collections. Next we show you the synchronized and concurrent collections. You will then learn how to write your own iteration and collection types in case you have a need that the provided classes do not fill. Finally, we cover the "legacy collections" in java.util that predate the overall collection system, but which you will find in some existing code. One of these legacy collection types—Properties—continues in common use.

For simplicity, we usually refer to the various interfaces without mentioning their type parameters—for example, Iterator or Collection—except where it is necessary to show that the same type parameter is being used—for example, that iterator has a return type Iterator<E> for a Collection<E>.

21.1.1 Exception Conventions

A few conventions related to exceptions are used throughout the collections classes and interfaces, and we do not wish to document them for every constructor and method where they may occur:

- Methods that are optional in an implementation of an interface throw `UnsupportedOperationException` when not implemented. We indicate which methods are optional as we go through—using "(Optional)" at the end of the method description.

- Methods or constructors that accept elements (either individually or as part of other collections) to be added to the current collection can throw `ClassCastException` if the element is not of an appropriate type for the collection, or for sorted collections, if the element cannot be compared with other elements. Methods that check for the existence of elements or try to remove them may also throw `ClassCastException`.

- Methods or constructors that accept elements (either individually or as part of other collections) to be added to the current collection throw `IllegalArgumentException` if the element's value is not appropriate for the collection—for example, some collections, such as subsets, define restricted ranges on the values of elements allowed in the collection.

- Methods that return individual elements of a collection will give you a `NoSuchElementException` if the collection is empty.

- Methods or constructors that take parameters of reference type usually throw `NullPointerException` if passed a `null` reference. The exceptions to this are collections that accept `null` elements, with which `null` can be used when adding, removing, or searching.

Any variations to the above, or other exceptions generated, are documented on a case-by-case basis.

21.2 Iteration

You've encountered iteration several times already during the course of this book—particularly in the discussion of the enhanced `for` loop in Chapter 10. This section reviews the basic operation of an iterator and covers its additional capabilities and the additional iterator types.

`Collection<E>` extends `Iterable<E>`, which defines an `iterator` method that returns an object that implements the `Iterator<E>` interface:

```
public boolean hasNext()
```
   Returns `true` if the iteration has more elements.

```
public E next()
```
   Returns the next element in the iteration. If there is no next element a `NoSuchElementException` is thrown.

```
public void remove()
```
> Removes the element returned most recently by the iteration from the under-
> lying collection. remove can be called only once per call of next. If next
> has not yet been called, or if remove has already been called since the last
> call to next, an IllegalStateException is thrown. (Optional)

The following code uses all three methods of Iterator to remove all long
strings from a collection:

```
public void removeLongStrings
    (Collection<? extends String> coll, int maxLen) {
    Iterator<? extends String> it = coll.iterator();
    while (it.hasNext()) {
        String str = it.next();
        if (str.length() > maxLen)
            it.remove();
    }
}
```

First we use iterator to get an Iterator object that steps through the contents
of the collection one element at a time (recall that the enhanced for loop can't be
used when you want to remove elements using the iterator). Then we loop as long
as hasNext returns true to indicate that there is at least one more element left in
the iteration. Each time through the loop we get the next element of the list using
next. If any string is longer than the maximum allowed length, we use the iterator's remove method to remove the most recent element returned by next. When
you use an iterator's remove method you modify the underlying collection safely
for that iterator—the iterator will properly move through the subsequent elements
of the collection. Removing elements from the collection any other way (using
operations on the collection or through a different iterator on the same collection)
is unsafe.

The ListIterator<E> interface extends Iterator<E>, adding methods you
can use to manipulate an ordered List object during iteration. You can iterate forward using hasNext and next, backward using hasPrevious and previous, or
back and forth by intermixing the calls as you please. The following code loops
backward through a list of strings:

```
ListIterator<String> it = list.listIterator(list.size());
while (it.hasPrevious()) {
    String obj = it.previous();
    System.out.println(obj);
    // ... use obj ...
}
```

This gets a `ListIterator` positioned one beyond the end of the list, and then backs up through the list one element at a time, printing each element. List elements are indexed by position, just like array elements, from 0 to `list.size()-`1. The methods `nextIndex` or `previousIndex` get the index of the element that a subsequent invocation of `next` or `previous` will return. The next index when the iterator is at the end of the list is returned as `list.size()`. The previous index when the iterator is at the first element in the list (index 0) is returned as −1.

The `remove` method on a `ListIterator` removes the last value returned by either `next` or `previous`. In addition to `remove`, you can use two additional methods to modify the list's contents:

`public void` **set(E elem)**

> Replaces the last element returned by `next` or `previous` with `elem`. If you have called `remove` or `add` on the iterator since the last call to `next` or `previous`, calling `set` throws `IllegalStateException`. (Optional)

`public void` **add(E elem)**

> Inserts `elem` into the list in front of the next element that would be returned, or at the end if `hasNext` returns `false`. The iterator is moved forward; if you invoke `previous` after an `add` you will get the added element. (Optional)

The contract of `remove` is extended such that an `IllegalStateException` is thrown if `remove` is invoked and either `set` or `add` has been invoked since the last call to `next` or `previous`.

The contracts for `Iterator` and `ListIterator` do not include a *snapshot* guarantee. In other words, changing the contents of the collection while the iterator is in use can affect the values returned by the methods. For example, if the implementation of `next` uses the contents of the original collection for its list, it is dangerous to remove elements from the list as you step through it except through the iterator's own methods. A snapshot would return the elements as they were when the `Iterator` or `ListIterator` object was created, immune from future changes. You can rely on having a snapshot of the contents only if the method that returns an iterator object explicitly makes a snapshot guarantee. If you need a snapshot but don't have such a guarantee, you can create a snapshot by making a simple copy of the collection, such as with an `ArrayList`:

```
public <T> Iterator<T>
    snapshotIterator(Collection<? extends T> coll) {
    return new ArrayList<T>(coll).iterator();
}
```

Any utility method that returns a collection will invariably be a generic method. We introduce the type variable T to represent the unknown type of the collection being passed in. The `snapshotIterator` method can accept any collection of T or a subtype of T, but only guarantees that it returns an `Iterator<T>`.[2]

Many of the iterators defined in the `java.util` package are what is known as *fail-fast* iterators. Such iterators detect when a collection has been modified other than through the iterator itself, and fail quickly and cleanly by throwing an exception—a `ConcurrentModificationException`—rather than risk performing an action whose behavior may be unsafe.

21.3   Ordering with `Comparable` and `Comparator`

The interface `java.lang.Comparable<T>` can be implemented by any class whose objects can be sorted. The interface has a single method:

`public int` **`compareTo(T other)`**

> Returns a value that is less than, equal to, or greater than zero as this object is less than, equal to, or greater than the `other` object. This method should return zero only if `equals` with the same object would return `true`. If the objects are not mutually comparable (such as an `Integer` with a `String`), a `ClassCastException` is thrown.

The ordering defined by `compareTo` is a class's *natural ordering,* that is, the ordering that is most natural to objects of the class. It is also a *total ordering,* meaning that any two objects of the same type must be mutually comparable— that is, you must be able to compare them in either order and always get the same result as to which is the larger. Similarly, the `equals` method defines a *natural equivalence.*

Many existing classes are `Comparable`, including `String`, `java.io.File`, `java.util.Date`, and all the primitive wrapper class types.

If a given class does not implement `Comparable` or if its natural ordering is wrong for some purpose, you can often provide a `java.util.Comparator` object instead. The `Comparator<T>` interface has the method

`public int` **`compare(T o1, T o2)`**

> Provides an ordering in the same manner as `Comparable.compareTo` for the two provided objects.

You can use `Comparable` and `Comparator` objects to sort and search `List` objects with the `Collections` class's static methods `sort` and `binarySearch`.

---

[2]   It is possible to return `Iterator<? super T>`, which is slightly more general than `Iterator<T>`, but to do so would mean you wouldn't be able to assign the result to a variable of type `Iterator<T>`. That would be a very annoying restriction.

The Collections class (see page 594) also provides static methods min and max to return the smallest and largest element in a Collection.

Comparing strings ignoring case is a common requirement, so the String class defines a Comparator object for this purpose, available from the field String.CASE_INSENSITIVE_ORDER.

21.4 The Collection Interface

As you have seen, most collection types are subtypes of the Collection interface. The only exceptions are those that are subtypes of Map. In this section we cover the Collection interface. The following sections describe the interfaces that extend Collection and the specific collection implementations provided in java.util. We leave Map and its related types for later. We also defer talking about implementing your own collection types.

The basis of much of the collection system is the Collection interface. As you saw in Figure 21–1, most of the actual collection types implement this interface, usually by implementing an extended interface such as Set or List. So Collection is a good place to start understanding collections. It has the following primary methods for working with an individual collection:

public int **size()**
>   Returns the size of this collection, that is, the number of elements it currently holds. The value returned is limited to Integer.MAX_VALUE even if the collection holds more elements.

public boolean **isEmpty()**
>   Returns true if this collection currently holds no elements.

public boolean **contains(Object elem)**
>   Returns true if the collection contains the object elem; that is, if this collection has an element on which invoking equals with elem returns true. If elem is null, returns true if there is a null element in the collection.

public Iterator<E> **iterator()**
>   Returns an iterator that steps through the elements of this collection.

public Object[] **toArray()**
>   Returns a new array that contains all the elements of this collection.

public <T> T[] **toArray(T[] dest)**
>   Returns an array that contains all the elements of this collection. If the elements will fit in dest, then they are placed in dest and it is dest that is returned. If dest has more elements than this collection, the first element in dest that follows the contents of the collection is set to null to mark the end

of the collection. If the elements do not fit in `dest`, a new, larger array is created of the same type as `dest`, filled in, and returned. If the type of `dest` is not compatible all the elements in the collection, an `ArrayStoreException` is thrown.

`public boolean` **`add(E elem)`**

Makes sure that this collection contains the object `elem`, returning `true` if this required changing the collection. If this collection allows duplicates, `add` will always return `true`. If duplicates are not allowed and an equivalent element is already in the collection, `add` will return `false`. (Optional)

`public boolean` **`remove(Object elem)`**

Removes a single instance of `elem` from the collection, returning `true` if this required changing the collection (that is, if the element existed in this collection). If `elem` is `null`, returns `true` if there was a `null` element in the collection. (Optional)

All methods that need the notion of equivalence (such as `contains` and `remove`) use the `equals` method on the relevant objects.

The `toArray` method that has no parameters returns an array of `Object`. You can use `toArray(T[])` to create arrays of other types. For example, if your collection contains `String` objects, you may want to create a `String` array. The following code will do that:

```
String[] strings = new String[collection.size()];
strings = collection.toArray(strings);
```

Notice that `strings` is assigned the return value of `toArray`. This is to be safe in case the size of the collection has increased since the array was allocated, in which case the returned array will not be the one originally allocated. You can also use an empty `String` array to pass in the desired type and let `toArray` allocate an array of exactly the right size:

```
String[] strings = collection.toArray(new String[0]);
```

Several methods of `Collection` operate in bulk from another collection. The methods are provided for convenience; also, a collection can often operate more efficiently in bulk.

`public boolean` **`containsAll(Collection<?> coll)`**

Returns `true` if this collection contains each of the elements in `coll`.

`public boolean` **`addAll(Collection<? extends E> coll)`**

Adds each element of `coll` to this collection, returning `true` if any addition required changing the collection. (Optional)

```
public boolean removeAll(Collection<?> coll)
```
Removes each element of coll from this collection, returning true if any removal required changing the collection. (Optional)

```
public boolean retainAll(Collection<?> coll)
```
Removes from this collection all elements that are not elements of coll, returning true if any removal required changing the collection. (Optional)

```
public void clear()
```
Removes all elements from this collection. (Optional)

This Collection interface is purposely very general. Each specific collection type can define restrictions on its parameters or other related behavior. A collection may or may not accept null elements, may be restricted to certain types of elements, may retain elements in a sorted order, and so on. Each collection that makes a restriction should state those restrictions in its documentation so that users can understand the contract for that collection.

21.5 Set and SortedSet

The Set<E> interface extends Collection<E>, providing a more specific contract for its methods, but adds no new methods of its own. A collection that is a Set contains no duplicate elements. If you add the same element twice to a set (in other words, if you add two objects that are equal), the first invocation will return true, while the second will return false. If after this, remove is similarly invoked twice, the first remove of the element will return true since the set was changed by removing the element, while the second will return false since the element was no longer present. A set may also contain at most one null element.

The SortedSet<E> interface extends Set<E> to specify an additional contract—iterators on such a set will always return the elements in a specified order. By default this will be the element's natural order. In the implementations of SortedSet provided in java.util you can also specify a Comparator object that will be used to order the elements instead of the natural order.

SortedSet adds some methods that make sense in an ordered set:

```
public Comparator<? super E> comparator()
```
Returns the Comparator being used by this sorted set, or null if the elements' natural order is being used. Note the use of the lower bounded wildcard in the return type; any implementation of this interface should accept a comparator that is typed the same way.

```
public E first()
```
Returns the first (lowest) object in this set.

public E **last()**

Returns the last (highest) object in this set.

public SortedSet<E> **subSet(E min, E max)**

Returns a view of the set that contains all the elements of this set whose values are greater than or equal to min and less than max. The view is *backed by* the collection; that is, changes to the collection that fall within the range will be visible through the returned subset and vice versa. If min is greater than max, or if this set is itself a view of another set and min or max fall outside the range of *that* view, an IllegalArgumentException is thrown. You will also get an IllegalArgumentException if you attempt to modify the returned set to contain an element that is outside the specified range.

public SortedSet<E> **headSet(E max)**

Returns a view of the set that contains all the elements of this set whose values are less than the value of max. This view is backed by the collection as with subSet. The exceptions thrown by this method or the returned set are the same as those of subSet.

public SortedSet<E> **tailSet(E min)**

Similar to headSet, but the returned set contains all the elements of this set whose values are greater than or equal to the value of min.

The notion of being *backed by* a collection is important in many methods. The sets returned by the subsetting methods are not snapshots of the matching contents. Rather, they are views onto the underlying collection that filter out certain elements, returning an empty collection if all elements are filtered out. Because the subsets are backed by the original collection, the views remain current no matter which set you use—the subset or the original set. You can create snapshots by making copies of the view, as in

```
public <T> SortedSet<T> copyHead(SortedSet<T> set, T max) {
    SortedSet<T> head = set.headSet(max);
    return new TreeSet<T>(head); // contents from head
}
```

This utilizes the copy constructor provided by most of the concrete collection implementations to create a new collection whose initial members are the same as the collection passed to the constructor.

The java.util package gives you two general-purpose Set implementations—HashSet and LinkedHashSet—and one SortedSet implementation, TreeSet.

21.5.1 HashSet

HashSet<E> is a Set<E> implemented with a hashtable. Modifying the contents of a HashSet or testing for containment are $O(1)$ constant-time operations[3]—that is, they do not get larger as the size of the set increases (assuming that the hashCode methods of the contents are well written to distribute the hash codes widely across the full range of int values). HashSet has four constructors:

public **HashSet(int initialCapacity, float loadFactor)**

    Creates a new HashSet with initialCapacity hash buckets and the given loadFactor, which must be a positive number. When the ratio of the number of elements in the set to the number of hash buckets is greater than or equal to the load factor, the number of buckets is increased.

public **HashSet(int initialCapacity)**

    Creates a new HashSet with initialCapacity and a default load factor.

public **HashSet()**

    Creates a new HashSet with a default initial capacity and load factor.

public **HashSet(Collection<? extends E> coll)**

    Creates a new HashSet whose initial contents are the elements in coll. The initial capacity is based on the size of coll, and the default load factor is used.

The initial capacity and load factor are used to construct the HashMap that underlies a HashSet. The meaning of these values is discussed in "HashMap" on page 590. Iteration of a HashSet requires a time proportional to the sum of the size and capacity.

---

[3] The notation $O(f)$ is used in computer science to mean that the order of time for the execution of an algorithm increases in the manner of f. In this notation, n is traditionally the magnitude of the data under consideration. An algorithm that is $O(\log n)$ takes longer as a function of the log of n—the number of elements—multiplied by some constant C. Generally speaking, the constant is irrelevant when algorithms are compared because as n gets large, the difference between an algorithm that is $O(\log n)$ compared to one that is, say, $O(n^2)$ is governed by n, not the constant—when n is 1000, for example, $\log n$ is 6.9, whereas n^2 is 1,000,000. The multiplying constant for the $O(\log n)$ algorithm would have to be extremely large to make it worse than the $O(n^2)$ algorithm. Of course, when two $O(\log n)$ algorithms are compared, the constant does matter, so in such a case it would be written. A similar argument means that for algorithms whose overhead has multiple terms, such as $O(C^2 + n)$, the smaller term is not relevant and so would be typically described as $O(n)$. An algorithm that is not sensitive to the size of n is written as $O(1)$ or sometimes $O(C)$. You will see "big O" notation in this chapter because it is an effective way of comparing different collection implementations.

21.5.2 LinkedHashSet

LinkedHashSet<E> extends HashSet<E> and refines the contract of HashSet by defining an order to the elements in the set. Iterating through the contents of a LinkedHashset will return the elements in *insertion order*—the order in which they were added. Aside from this, LinkedHashSet behaves the same as HashSet and defines constructors with the same form. The performance of a LinkedHashSet is likely to be a little slower than a HashSet because of the over-head of maintaining the linked list structure; however, iteration only requires a time proportional to the size, regardless of capacity.

21.5.3 TreeSet

If you need a SortedSet, you can use TreeSet, which stores its contents in a tree structure that is kept balanced. This means that the time required to modify or search the tree is $O(\log n)$. TreeSet has four constructors:

public **TreeSet()**
> Creates a new TreeSet that is sorted according to the natural order of the element types. All elements added to this set must implement the Comparable interface and be mutually comparable.

public **TreeSet(Collection<? extends E> coll)**
> Equivalent to using TreeSet() and then adding the elements of coll.

public **TreeSet(Comparator<? super E> comp)**
> Creates a new TreeSet that is sorted according to the order imposed by comp.

public **TreeSet(SortedSet<E> set)**
> Creates a new TreeSet whose initial contents will be the same as those in set and that is sorted in the same way as set.

21.6 List

The List<E> interface extends Collection<E> to define a collection whose elements have a defined order—each element exists in a particular position in the collection, indexed from 0 to list.size()-1. Or, in other words, a List defines a *sequence* of elements. This requires a refinement of the contracts of several methods inherited from Collection: when you add an element, it is placed at the end of the list; When you remove the nth element from the list, the element that was after it is shifted over, becoming the new n^{th} element; and the toArray methods fill in the array in the list's order.

List also adds several methods that make sense in an ordered collection:

public E **get(int index)**
> Returns the indexth entry in the list.

public E **set(int index, E elem)**
> Sets the indexth entry in the list to elem, replacing the previous element and returning it. (Optional)

public void **add(int index, E elem)**
> Adds the entry elem to the list at the indexth position, shifting every element farther in the list down one position. (Optional)

public E **remove(int index)**
> Removes and returns the indexth entry in the list, shifting every element farther in the list up one position. (Optional)

public int **indexOf(Object elem)**
> Returns the index of the first object in the list that is equal to elem, or that is null if elem is null. Returns –1 if no match is found.

public int **lastIndexOf(Object elem)**
> Returns the index of the last object in the list that is equal to elem, or that is null if elem is null. Returns –1 if no match is found.

public List<E> **subList(int min, int max)**
> Returns a List that is a view on this list over the range, starting with min up to, but not including, max. For example, subList(1, 5) would return a list containing elements number 1, 2, 3, and 4 from this list. The returned list is backed by this list, so changes made to the returned list are reflected in this list. Changes made directly to the backing list are not guaranteed to be visible to a sublist and can cause undefined results (so don't do it). Sublists allow you to do anything to part of a list that you could to do an entire list, so they can be a powerful tool. For example, you can remove part of a list using list.subList(min, max).clear().

public ListIterator<E> **listIterator(int index)**
> Returns a ListIterator object that will iterate through the elements of the list starting at the indexth entry.

public ListIterator<E> **listIterator()**
> Returns a ListIterator object that will iterate through the elements of the list starting at the beginning.

All the methods that take an index will throw IndexOutOfBoundsException if index is less than zero or greater than or equal to the list's size.

The java.util package provides two implementations of List—ArrayList and LinkedList.

21.6.1 ArrayList

ArrayList is a good basic list implementation that stores its elements in an underlying array. Adding and removing elements at the end is very simple—$O(1)$. Getting the element at a specific position is also $O(1)$. Adding and removing elements from the middle is more expensive—$O(n - i)$ where n is the size of the list and i is the position of the element being removed. Adding or removing the element requires copying the remainder of the array one position up or down.

An ArrayList has a *capacity*, which is the number of elements it can hold without allocating new memory for a larger array. As you add elements they are stored in the array, but when room runs out, a replacement array must be allocated. Setting your initial capacity correctly can improve performance. If the initial size of the data is significantly smaller than its final size, setting the initial capacity to a larger value reduces the number of times the underlying array must be replaced with a larger copy. Setting the size too large can waste space.

ArrayList has three constructors:

public **ArrayList()**
> Creates a new ArrayList with a default capacity.

public **ArrayList(int initialCapacity)**
> Creates a new ArrayList that initially can store initialCapacity elements without resizing.

public **ArrayList(Collection<? extends E> coll)**
> Creates a new ArrayList whose initial contents are the contents of coll. The capacity of the array is initially 110% of the size of coll to allow for some growth without resizing. The order is that returned by the collections iterator.

ArrayList also provides some methods to manage capacity:

public void **trimToSize()**
> Sets the capacity to be exactly the current size of the list. If the capacity is currently larger than the size, a new, smaller underlying array will be allocated and the current values copied in. You can thus reduce the amount of memory necessary to hold the list, although at some cost.

public void **ensureCapacity(int minCapacity)**
> Sets the capacity to minCapacity if the capacity is currently smaller. You can use this if you are about to add a large number of elements to the list, and so ensure the array will be reallocated at most once (when ensureCapacity is invoked) rather than possibly multiple times while the elements are added.

21.6.2 LinkedList

A LinkedList is a doubly linked list whose performance characteristics are virtually the reverse of ArrayList: Adding an element at the end is $O(1)$, but everything else is swapped. Adding or removing an element in the middle is $O(1)$ because it requires no copying, while getting the element at a specific position i is $O(i)$ since it requires starting at one end and walking through the list to the ith element.

LinkedList provides two constructors and adds methods that are useful and efficient for doubly linked lists:

public **LinkedList()**
> Creates a new empty LinkedList.

public **LinkedList(Collection<? extends E> coll)**
> Creates a new LinkedList whose initial contents are those of coll. The order is that returned by the collection's iterator.

public E **getFirst()**
> Returns the first object in this list.

public E **getLast()**
> Returns the last object in this list.

public E **removeFirst()**
> Removes the first object in this list.

public E **removeLast()**
> Removes the last object in this list.

public void **addFirst(E elem)**
> Adds elem into this list as the first element.

public void **addLast(E elem)**
> Adds elem into this list as the last element.

A LinkedList is a good base for a queue—and indeed it implements the Queue interface discussed next—or any other list in which most of the action is not at the end. For a stack, or for building up a list of elements as you find them, an ArrayList is more efficient because it requires fewer objects: the one array instead of one object for each element in the list. You can also efficiently scan an ArrayList without creating an Iterator object, by simply using an int as an index. This can be a good reason to use an ArrayList for a list that will be scanned frequently.

Here is a `Polygon` class that stores a list of `Point` objects that are the polygon's vertices:

```
import java.util.List;
import java.util.ArrayList;

public class Polygon {
    private List<Point> vertices =
        new ArrayList<Point>();

    public void add(Point p) {
        vertices.add(p);
    }

    public void remove(Point p) {
        vertices.remove(p);
    }

    public int numVertices() {
        return vertices.size();
    }

    // ... other methods ...
}
```

Notice that `vertices` is a `List` reference that is assigned an `ArrayList` object. You should declare a variable to be as abstract a type as possible, preferring the abstract `List` type to the implementation class `ArrayList`. As written, you could change `Polygon` to use a `LinkedList` if that would be more efficient by changing only one line of code—the line that creates the list. All the other code can remain unchanged.

Exercise 21.1: Write a program that opens a file and reads its lines one at a time, storing each line in a `List` sorted by `String.compareTo`. The line-reading class you created for Exercise 20.4 should prove helpful.

21.6.3 RandomAccess Lists

The marker interface `RandomAccess` marks list implementations that support fast random access. Random access means that any element of the list can be accessed directly. For example, `ArrayList` implements `RandomAccess` because any element can easily be accessed by its index. In contrast, a LinkedList does not implement RandomAccess because accessing an element by index requires traversing from one end of the list. Some algorithms for manipulating random access lists perform poorly when applied to sequential lists, so the purpose of the RandomAccess interface is to allow an algorithm to adapt depending on the kind of list it is given. As a rule of thumb, if code such as

```
for (int i = 0; i < list.size(); i++)
    process(list.get(i));
```

will typically be faster than using

```
Iterator it = list.iterator();
while (it.hasNext())
    process(it.next());
```

then your list should implement RandomAccess.

21.7 Queue

The Queue<E> interface extends Collection<E> to add some structure to the internal organization of the collection. A queue defines a *head* position, which is the next element that would be removed. Queues often operate on a *first-in-first-out* ordering, but it is also possible to have *last-in-first-out* ordering (commonly known as a *stack*) or to have a specific ordering defined by a comparator or by comparable elements. Each implementation must specify its ordering properties. The Queue interface adds several methods that work specifically with the head:

public E **element()**
> Returns, but does not remove, the head of the queue. If the queue is empty a NoSuchElementException is thrown.

public E **peek()**
> Returns, but does not remove, the head of the queue. If the queue is empty, null is returned. This differs from element only in its handling of an empty queue.

public E **remove()**
> Returns and removes the head of the queue. If the queue is empty a NoSuchElementException is thrown.

public E **poll()**
> Returns and removes the head of the queue. If the queue is empty, null is returned. This differs from remove only in its handling of an empty queue.

There is also a method for inserting into a queue:

public boolean **offer(E elem)**

> Attempts to insert the given element into this queue. If the attempt is successful, true is returned, otherwise false. For queues that have genuine reason to reject a request—such as a queue with finite capacity—this method is preferable to the Collection add method which can only indicate failure by throwing an exception.

Queues in general should not accept null elements because null is used as a sentinel value for poll and peek to indicate an empty queue.

The LinkedList class provides the simplest implementation of Queue. For historical reasons the LinkedList class accepts null elements, but you should avoid inserting null elements when using a LinkedList instance as a queue.

21.7.1 PriorityQueue

The other Queue implementation is PriorityQueue, an unbounded queue, based on a *priority heap*. The head of the queue is the *smallest* element in it, where smallest is determined either by the elements' natural order or by a supplied comparator. A PriorityQueue is *not* a sorted queue in the general sense—you can't pass it to a method expecting a sorted collection—because the iterator returned by iterator is *not* guaranteed to traverse the elements in priority order; rather it guarantees that removing elements from the queue occurs in a given order. The iterator can traverse the elements in any order. If you need ordered traversal you could extract the elements to an array and then sort the array (see "The Arrays Utility Class" on page 607).

Whether the smallest element represents the element with the highest or lowest "priority" depends on how the natural order or the comparator is defined. For example, if queuing Thread objects according to their execution priority, then the smallest element represents a Thread with the lowest execution priority.

The performance characteristics of a PriorityQueue are unspecified. A good implementation based on a priority heap would provide $O(1)$ operations on the head, with $O(\log n)$ for general insertion. Anything that requires traversing, such as removing a specific element or searching for one, would be $O(n)$.

There are six constructors:

public **PriorityQueue(int initialCapacity)**

> Creates a new PriorityQueue that can store initialCapacity elements without resizing and that orders the elements according to their natural order.

public **PriorityQueue()**

> Creates a new PriorityQueue with the default initial capacity, and that orders the elements according to their natural order.

public **PriorityQueue(int initialCapacity,**
  Comparator<? super E> comp)
> Creates a new PriorityQueue that can initially store initialCapacity elements without resizing, and that orders the elements according to the supplied comparator.

public **PriorityQueue(Collection<? extends E> coll)**
> Creates a new PriorityQueue whose initial contents are the contents of coll. The capacity of the queue is initially 110% of the size of coll to allow for some growth without resizing. If coll is a SortedSet or another PriorityQueue, then this queue will be ordered the same way; otherwise, the elements will be sorted according to their natural order. If any element in coll can't be compared, a ClassCastException is thrown.

public **PriorityQueue(SortedSet<? extends E> coll)**
> Creates a new PriorityQueue whose initial contents are the contents of coll. The capacity of the queue is initially 110% of the size of coll to allow for some growth without resizing. This queue will be ordered the same way as coll.

public **PriorityQueue(PriorityQueue<? extends E> coll)**
> Creates a new PriorityQueue whose initial contents are the contents of coll. The capacity of the queue is initially 110% of the size of coll to allow for some growth without resizing. This queue will be ordered the same way as coll.

Since PriorityQueue does not accept null elements, all constructors that take collections throw NullPointerException if a null element is encountered.

The comparator used to construct the priority queue can be retrieved with the comparator method. This has the same contract as the comparator method in SortedSet, returning null if the elements' natural ordering is being used.

21.8 Map and SortedMap

The interface Map<K,V> does not extend Collection because it has a contract that is different in important ways. The primary difference is that you do not add an element to a Map—you add a key/value pair. A Map allows you to look up the value stored under a key. A given key (as defined by the equals method of the key) maps to one value or no values. A value can be mapped to by as many keys as you like. For example, you might use a map to store a mapping of a person's name to their address. If you have an address listed under a name, there will be exactly one in the map. If you have no mapping, there will be no address value for that name. Multiple people might share a single address, so the map might return the same value for two or more names.

The basic methods of the Map interface are

`public int `**`size()`**
> Returns the size of this map, that is, the number of key/value mappings it currently holds. The return value is limited to `Integer.MAX_VALUE` even if the map contains more elements.

`public boolean `**`isEmpty()`**
> Returns `true` if this collection currently holds no mappings.

`public boolean `**`containsKey(Object key)`**
> Returns `true` if the collection contains a mapping for the given key.

`public boolean `**`containsValue(Object value)`**
> Returns `true` if the collection contains at least one mapping to the given value.

`public V `**`get(Object key)`**
> Returns the object to which `key` is mapped, or `null` if it is not mapped. Also returns `null` if `key` has been mapped to `null` in a map that allows `null` values. You can use `containsKey` to distinguish between the cases, although this adds overhead. It can be more efficient to put marker objects instead of `null` into the map to avoid the need for the second test.

`public V `**`put(K key, V value)`**
> Associates `key` with the given value in the map. If a map already exists for `key`, its value is changed and the original value is returned. If no mapping exists, `put` returns `null`, which may also mean that `key` was originally mapped to `null`. (Optional)

`public V `**`remove(Object key)`**
> Removes any mapping for the key. The return value has the same semantics as that of `put`. (Optional)

`public void `**`putAll(Map< ? extends K, ? extends V> otherMap)`**
> Puts all the mappings in `otherMap` into this map. (Optional)

`public void `**`clear()`**
> Removes all mappings. (Optional)

Methods that take keys as parameters may throw `ClassCastException` if the key is not of the appropriate type for this map, or `NullPointerException` if the key is `null` and this map does not accept `null` keys.

You can see that, though Map does not extend Collection, methods with the same meaning have the same names, and analogous methods have analogous names. This helps you remember the methods and what they do.

Generally, you can expect a Map to be optimized for finding values listed under keys. For example, the method containsKey will usually be much more efficient than containsValue on larger maps. In a HashMap, for example, containsKey is $O(1)$, whereas containsValue is $O(n)$—the key is found by hashing, but the value must be found by searching through each element until a match is found.

Map is not a collection, but there are methods that let you view the map using collections:

public Set<K> **keySet()**
>Returns a Set whose elements are the keys of this map.

public Collection<V> **values()**
>Returns a Collection whose elements are the values of this map.

public Set<Map.Entry<K,V>> **entrySet()**
>Returns a Set whose elements are Map.Entry objects that represent single
>mappings in the map. As you will see soon, Map.Entry is a nested interface
>with methods to manipulate the entry.

The collections returned by these methods are backed by the Map, so removing an element from one of these collections removes the corresponding key/value pair from the map. You cannot add elements to these collections—they do not support the optional methods for adding to a collection. If you iterate through the key and value sets in parallel you cannot rely on getting key/value pairs—they may return values from their respective sets in any order. If you need such pairing, you should use entrySet.

The interface Map.Entry<K,V> defines methods for manipulating the entries in the map, as returned from the Map interface's entrySet method:

public K **getKey()**
>Returns the key for this entry.

public V **getValue()**
>Returns the value for this entry.

public V **setValue(V value)**
>Sets the value for this entry and returns the old value.

Note that there is no setKey method—you change the key by removing the existing mapping for the original key and adding another mapping under the new key.

The SortedMap interface extends Map refining the contract to require that the keys be sorted. This ordering requirement affects the collections returned by keySet, values, and entrySet. SortedMap also adds methods that make sense in an ordered map:

```
public Comparator<? super K> comparator()
```
Returns the comparator being used for sorting this map. Returns null if none is being used, which means that the map is sorted using the keys' natural order.

```
public K firstKey()
```
Returns the first (lowest value) key in this map.

```
public K lastKey()
```
Returns the last (highest value) key in this map.

```
public SortedMap<K,V> subMap(K minKey, K maxKey)
```
Returns a view of the portion of the map whose keys are greater than or equal to minKey and less than maxKey.

```
public SortedMap<K,V> headMap(K maxKey)
```
Returns a view of the portion of the map whose keys are less than maxKey.

```
public SortedMap<K,V> tailMap(K minKey)
```
Returns a view of the portion of the map whose keys are greater than or equal to minKey.

Any returned map is backed by the original map so changes made to either are visible to the other.

A SortedMap is to Map what SortedSet is to Set and provides almost identical functionality except that SortedMap works with keys. The exceptions thrown by the SortedMap methods mirror those thrown by its SortedSet counterparts.

The java.util package gives you four general-purpose Map implementations—HashMap, LinkedHashMap, IdentityHashMap, and WeakHashMap—and one SortedMap implementation, TreeMap.

21.8.1 HashMap

HashMap implements Map with a hashtable, where each key's hashCode method is used to pick a place in the table. With a well-written hashCode method, adding, removing, or finding a key/value pair is $O(1)$. This makes a HashMap a very efficient way to associate a key with a value—HashMap is one of the most commonly used collections. You already have seen a HashMap in "Implementing Interfaces" on page 127. The constructors for HashMap are

```
public HashMap(int initialCapacity, float loadFactor)
```
Creates a new HashMap with initialCapacity hash buckets and the given loadFactor, which must be a positive number.

public **HashMap(int initialCapacity)**

> Creates a new HashMap with the given initialCapacity and a default load factor.

public **HashMap()**

> Creates a new HashMap with default initial capacity and load factor.

public **HashMap(Map<? extends K, ? extends V> map)**

> Creates a new HashMap whose initial mappings are copied from map. The initial capacity is based on the size of map; the default load factor is used.

The internal table used by a hash map consists of a number of buckets, initially determined by the initial capacity of the hash map. The hash code of an object (or a special hashing function used by the hash map implementation) determines which bucket an object should be stored in. The fewer the number of buckets, the more likely that different objects will get stored in the same bucket, so looking up the object will take longer because the bucket has to be examined in detail. The more buckets there are, the less likely it is that this will occur, and the lookup performance will improve—but the space occupied by the hash map will increase. Further, the more buckets there are, the longer iteration will take, so if iteration is important you may want to reduce the number of buckets—the cost of iteration is proportional to the sum of the hash map's size and capacity. The load factor determines when the hash map will automatically have its capacity increased. When the number of entries in the hash map exceeds the product of the load factor and the current capacity, the capacity will be doubled. Increasing the capacity requires that all the elements be rehashed and stored in the correct new bucket—a costly operation.

You need to consider the load factor and the initial capacity when creating the hash map, be aware of the expected number of elements the map will hold, and be aware of the expected usage patterns of the map. If the initial capacity is too small and the load factor too low, then numerous rehash operations will occur. In contrast, with a large enough initial capacity and load factor, a rehash might never be needed. You need to balance the cost of normal operations against the costs of iteration and rehashing. The default load factor of 0.75 provides a good general trade-off.

21.8.2 LinkedHashMap

LinkedHashMap<K,V> extends HashMap<K,V> and refines the contract of HashMap by defining an order to the entries in the map. Iterating through the contents of a LinkedHashMap (either the entry set or the key set) will, by default, return the entries in *insertion order*—the order in which they were added. Aside from this, LinkedHashMap behaves like HashMap and defines constructors of the same forms. The performance of a `LinkedHashMap` is likely to be a little slower than a `HashMap` due to the overhead of maintaining the linked list structure; however, iteration only requires a time proportional to the size, regardless of capacity.

Additionally, `LinkedHashMap` provides a constructor that takes the initial capacity, the load factor and a boolean flag `accessOrder`. If `accessOrder` is `false`, then the map behaves as previously described with respect to ordering. If `accessOrder` is `true`, then the map is sorted from the most recently accessed entry to the least recently accessed entry, making it suitable for implementing a Least Recently Used (LRU) cache. The only methods to count as an access of an entry are direct use of `put`, `get`, and `putAll`—however, if invoked on a different view of the map (see Section 21.10 on page 597), even these methods do not count as an access.

21.8.3 `IdentityHashMap`

The general contract of `Map` requires that equality for keys be based on equivalence (that is, using the `equals` method). But there are times when you really want a map that stores information about specific objects instead of treating all equivalent objects as a single key to information. Consider the serialization mechanism discussed in Chapter 20. When determining if an object in the serialization graph has already been seen, you need to check that it is the actual object, not just one that is equivalent. To support such requirements the `IdentityHashMap` class uses object identity (comparison using `==`) to determine if a given key is already present in the map. This is useful, but it does break the general contract of `Map`.

There are three constructors:

public **IdentityHashMap(int expectedSize)**
>   Creates a new `IdentityHashMap` with the given expected maximum size.

public **IdentityHashMap()**
>   Creates a new `IdentityHashMap` with the default expected maximum size.

public **IdentityHashMap(Map<? extends K, ? extends V> map)**
>   Creates a new `IdentityHashMap` containing the entries from the given map.

The expected maximum size is a hint for the initial capacity of the map, but its exact effects are not specified.

21.8.4 `WeakHashMap`

The collection implementations all use strong references for elements, values, and keys. As with strong references elsewhere, this is usually what you want. Just as you occasionally need reference objects to provide weaker references, you also occasionally need a collection that holds the objects it contains less strongly. You can use WeakHashMap in such cases.

WeakHashMap behaves like HashMap but with one difference—WeakHashMap refers to keys by using WeakReference objects instead of strong references. As you learned in Section 17.5 on page 454, weak references let the objects be collected as garbage, so you can put an object in a WeakHashMap without the map's reference forcing the object to stay in memory. When a key is only weakly reachable, its mapping may be removed from the map, which also drops the map's strong reference to the key's value object. If the value object is otherwise not strongly reachable, this could result in the value also being collected.

A WeakHashMap checks to find unreferenced keys when you invoke a method that can modify the contents (put, remove, or clear), but not before get. This makes the performance of such methods dependent on the number of keys that have become unreferenced since the last check. If you want to force removal you can invoke one of the modifying methods in a way that will have no effect, such as by removing a key for which there is no mapping (null, for example, if you do not use null as a key). Because entries in the map can disappear at any time, the behavior of some methods can be surprising—for example, successive calls to size can return smaller and smaller values; or an iterator for one of the set views can throw NoSuchElementException after hasNext returns true.

The WeakHashMap class exports the same constructors as HashMap: a no-arg constructor; a constructor that takes an initial capacity; a constructor that takes an initial capacity and a load factor; and a constructor that takes a Map whose contents will be the initial contents of the WeakHashMap.

Exercise 21.2: Rewrite the DataHandler class on page 457 to use a WeakHashMap to store the returned data instead of a single WeakReference.

Exercise 21.3: A WeakHashMap has weak keys and strong values. A WeakValueMap would have strong keys and weak values. Design a WeakValueMap. Be cautioned that this is not as simple as it might seem, in fact it is extremely complicated and requires a number of design choices to be made. For example, should iteration of values be allowed to yield null after hasNext has returned true, or should iteration keep the values alive while they are being iterated? Hint: Don't try to extend AbstractMap, delegate to a HashMap instead.

21.8.5 TreeMap

The TreeMap class implements SortedMap, keeping its keys sorted in the same way as TreeSet. This makes adding, removing, or finding a key/value pair

$O(\log n)$. So you generally use a TreeMap only if you need the sorting or if the hashCode method of your keys is poorly written, thereby destroying the $O(1)$ behavior of HashMap.

TreeMap has the following constructors:

public **TreeMap()**

> Creates a new TreeMap that is sorted according to the natural order of the keys. All elements added to this map must implement the Comparable interface and be mutually comparable.

public **TreeMap(Map<? extends K, ? extends V> map)**

> Equivalent to using TreeMap() and then adding all the key/value pairs of map to this map.

public **TreeMap(Comparator<? super K> comp)**

> Creates a new TreeMap that is sorted according to the order imposed by comp.

public **TreeMap(SortedMap<K, ? extends V> map)**

> Creates a new TreeMap whose initial contents will be the same as those in map and that is sorted the same way as map.

21.9   enum Collections

Two collections, EnumSet and EnumMap, are specifically designed for working efficiently with enum constants.

21.9.1   EnumSet

The abstract class EnumSet<E extends Enum<E>> represents a set of elements that are all enum constants from a specific enum type. Suppose you were writing a reflection related API, you could define an enum of the different field modifiers, and then have your Field class return the set of modifiers applicable to that field:

```
enum FieldModifiers { STATIC, FINAL, VOLATILE, TRANSIENT }

public class Field {
    public EnumSet<FieldModifiers> getModifiers() {
        // ...
    }
    // ... rest of Field methods ...
}
```

In general, whenever an enum represents a set of flags or "status bits," then you will probably want to group the set of flags applicable to a given element in an enum set.

EnumSet objects are not created directly but are obtained from a number of static factory methods in EnumSet.

```
public static <E extends Enum<E>> EnumSet<E>
```
allOf(Class<E> enumType)
> Creates an EnumSet containing all the elements of the given enum type.

```
public static <E extends Enum<E>> EnumSet<E>
```
noneOf(Class<E> enumType)
> Creates an empty EnumSet that can contain elements of the given enum type.

```
public static <E extends Enum<E>> EnumSet<E>
```
copyOf(EnumSet<E> set)
> Creates an EnumSet of the same enum type as set and containing all the elements of set.

```
public static <E extends Enum<E>> EnumSet<E>
```
complementOf(EnumSet<E> set)
> Creates an EnumSet of the same enum type as set and containing all the enum constants that are *not* contained in set.

```
public static <E extends Enum<E>> EnumSet<E>
```
copyOf(Collection<E> coll)
> Creates an EnumSet from the given collection. If the collection is an EnumSet, a copy is returned. Any other collection must contain one or more elements, all of which are constants from the same enum; this enum will be the enum type of the returned EnumSet. If coll is empty and is not an EnumSet then IllegalArgumentException is thrown because there is no specified enum type for this set.

The of method creates an enum set containing the given enum constant. It has five overloaded forms that take one through five elements as arguments. For example, here is the form that takes three elements:

```
public static <E extends Enum<E>> EnumSet<E>
```
of(E e1, E e2, E e3)
> Creates an EnumSet containing e1, e2, and e3.

A sixth overload takes an arbitrary number of elements:

```
public static <E extends Enum<E>> EnumSet<E>
```
of(E first, E... rest)
> Creates an EnumSet containing all the specified enum values.

Finally, the `range` method takes two enum constants that define the first and last elements that the enum set will contain. If first and last are in the wrong order then `IllegalArgumentException` is thrown.

Once you have obtained an enum set you can freely modify it in whatever way you need.

`EnumSet` uses a bit-vector internally so it is both compact and efficient. The iterator returned by `iterator` is not the usual fail-fast iterator of other collections. It is a *weakly consistent* iterator that returns the enum values in their natural order—the order in which the enum constants were declared. A weakly consistent iterator never throws `ConcurrentModificationException`, but it also may not reflect any changes that occur while the iteration is in progress.

21.9.2 EnumMap

The `EnumMap<K extends Enum<K>, V>` is a special map that uses enum values as keys. All values in the map must come from the same enum type. Just like `EnumSet` the enum values are ordered by their natural order, and the iterator is weakly consistent.

Suppose you were writing an application that dynamically builds and displays an on-line form, based on a description written in a structured format such as XML. Given the set of expected form elements as an enum

```
enum FormElements { NAME, STREET, CITY, ZIP }
```

you could create an enum map to represent a filled in form, where the keys are the form elements and the values are whatever the user entered.

`EnumMap` has three constructors:

`public EnumMap(Class<K> keyType)`
   Creates an empty `EnumMap` that can hold keys of the given enum type.

`public EnumMap(EnumMap<K, ? extends V> map)`
   Creates an `EnumMap` of the same enum type as `map` and containing all the elements of `map`.

`public EnumMap(Map<K, ? extends V> map)`
   Creates an `EnumMap` from the given map. If the map is an `EnumMap`, a copy is returned. Any other map must contain one or more keys, all of which are constants from the same enum; this enum will be the enum type of the returned `EnumMap`. If `map` is empty and is not an `EnumMap` then `IllegalArgumentException` is thrown because there is no specified enum type for this map.

`EnumMap` is implemented using arrays internally, so it is compact and efficient.

21.10 Wrapped Collections and the `Collections` Class

The `Collections` class defines a range of static utility methods that operate on collections. The utility methods can be broadly classified into two groups: those that provide wrapped collections and those that don't. The wrapped collections allow you to present a different view of an underlying collection. There are three different views: a read-only view, a type-safe view, and a synchronized view. The first two are discussed in this section, synchronized wrappers are discussed later with the concurrent collections. First we discuss the general utility methods.

21.10.1 The `Collections` Utilities

The `Collections` class defines many useful utility methods. You can find the minimum and maximum valued elements in a collection:

```
public static <T extends Object & Comparable<? super T>> T
  min(Collection<? extends T> coll)
```
    Returns the smallest valued element of the collection based on the elements' natural order.

```
public static <T> T
  min(Collection<? extends T> coll, Comparator<? super T> comp)
```
    Returns the smallest valued element of the collection according to `comp`.

```
public static <T extends Object & Comparable<? super T>> T
  max(Collection<? extends T> coll)
```
    Returns the largest valued element of the collection based on the elements' natural order.

```
public static <T> T
  max(Collection<? extends T> coll, Comparator<? super T> comp)
```
    Returns the largest valued element of the collection according to the comparator `comp`.

The declarations of the type variables for two of these methods seem rather complex. Basically, they just declare that `T` is a `Comparable` type. The inclusion of "extends `Object`" might seem redundant, but it changes the erasure of `T` to be `Object` rather than `Comparable`.

    You can obtain a `Comparator` that will reverse the natural ordering of the objects it compares, or that of a given comparator:

```
public static <T> Comparator<T> reverseOrder()
```
    Returns a `Comparator` that reverses the natural ordering of the objects it compares.

`public static <T> Comparator<T>` **`reverseOrder(Comparator<T> comp)`**
  Returns a `Comparator` the reverses the order of the given comparator.

Then there are some general convenience methods for collections:

`public static <T> boolean`
  `addAll(Collection<? super T> coll, T... elems)`
  Adds all of the specified elements to the given collection, returning `true` if
  the collection was changed. Naturally, if the collection does not support the
  add method then `UnsupportedOperationException` is thrown.

`public static boolean`
  `disjoint(Collection<?> coll1, Collection<?> coll2)`
  Returns `true` if the two given collections have no elements in common.

There are numerous methods for working with lists:

`public static <T> boolean`
  `replaceAll(List<T> list, T oldVal, T newVal)`
  Replaces all occurrences of `oldVal` in the list with `newVal`. Returns `true` if
  any replacements were made.

`public static void` **`reverse(List<?> list)`**
  Reverses the order of the elements of the list.

`public static void` **`rotate(List<?> list, int distance)`**
  Rotates all of the elements in the list by the specified distance. A positive distance moves elements toward the end of the list, wrapping around to the
  beginning. A negative distance moves elements toward the head of the list,
  wrapping around to the end. For example, given a list *v, w, x, y, z*, a rotate
  with distance 1 will change the list to be *z, v, w, x, y* (as will a rotation of 6,
  11, … or –4, –9, …).

`public static void` **`shuffle(List<?> list)`**
  Randomly shuffles the list.

`public static void` **`shuffle(List<?> list, Random randomSource)`**
  Randomly shuffles the list using `randomSource` as the source of random
  numbers (see "Random" on page 639).

`public static void` **`swap(List<?> list, int i, int j)`**
  Swaps the ith and j^{th} elements of the given list. This can be done efficiently
  inside the collection.

`public static <T> void` **`fill(List<? super T> list, T elem)`**
  Replaces each element of `list` with `elem`.

```
public static <T> void
```
   copy(List<? super T> dest, List<? extends T> src)
   Copies each element to dst from src. If dst is too small to contain all the elements, throws IndexOutOfBoundsException. You can use a sublist for either dst or src to copy only to or from parts of a list.

```
public static <T> List<T> nCopies(int n, T elem)
```
   Returns an immutable list that contains n elements, each of which is elem. This only requires storing one reference to elem, so n can be 100 and the returned list will take the same amount of space it would if n were one.

```
public static int indexOfSubList(List<?> source, List<?> target)
```
   Returns the index of the start of the first sublist of source that is equal to target.

```
public static int
```
   lastIndexOfSubList(List<?> source, List<?> target)
   Returns the index of the start of the last sublist of source that is equal to target.

There are also methods for sorting and searching lists:

```
public static <T extends Comparable<? super T>> void
```
   sort(List<T> list)
   Sorts list in ascending order, according to its elements' natural ordering.

```
public static <T> void
```
   sort(List<T> list, Comparator<? super T> comp)
   Sorts list according to comp.

```
public static <T> int
```
   binarySearch(List<? extends Comparable<? super T>> list,T key)
   Uses a binary search algorithm to find a key object in the list, returning its index. The list must be in its elements' natural order. If the object is not found, the index returned is a negative value encoding a safe insertion point.

```
public static <T> int binarySearch(List<? extends T> list, T key,
```
   Comparator<? super T> comp)
   Uses a binary search algorithm to find a key object in the list, returning its index. The list must be in the order defined by comp. If the object is not found, the index returned is a negative value encoding a safe insertion point.

The phrase "a negative value encoding a safe insertion point" requires some explanation. If you use a binarySearch method to search for a key that is not found, you will always get a negative value. Specifically, if i is the index at which the key could be inserted and maintain the order, the value returned will be $-(i + 1)$. (The return value algorithm ensures that the value will be negative when the key is not found, since zero is a valid index in a list.) So using the `binarySearch` methods you can maintain a list in sorted order: Search the list to see if the key is already present. If not, insert it according to the return value of `binarySearch`:

```
public static <T extends Comparable<? super T>>
    void ensureKnown(List<T> known, T value)
{
    int indexAt = Collections.binarySearch(known, value);
    if (indexAt < 0)           // not in the list -- insert it
        known.add(-(indexAt + 1), value);
}
```

If the list of `known` elements does not include the given `value`, this method will insert the value in its place in the list based on its natural ordering.

If you invoke one of the sorting or searching methods that relies on ordering on a list that contains objects that are not mutually comparable, or are not comparable by the relevant `Comparator`, you will get a `ClassCastException`.

You can ask how many times an element appears in a collection:

public static int **frequency(Collection<?> coll, Object elem)**
> Returns the number of times that the given element appears in the given collection.

There are also methods to create *singleton* collections—collections containing only a single element:

public static <T> Set<T> **singleton(T elem)**
> Returns an immutable set containing only `elem`.

public static <T> List<T> **singletonList(T elem)**
> Returns an immutable list containing only `elem`.

public static <K,V> Map<K,V> **singletonMap(K key, V value)**
> Returns an immutable map containing only one entry: a mapping from `key` to `value`.

And finally, there are methods that return empty collections:

public static <T> List<T> **emptyList()**
> Returns an empty, immutable list of the desired type.

public static <T> Set<T> **emptySet()**
> Returns an empty, immutable set of the desired type.

public static <K,V> Map<K,V> **emptyMap()**
> Returns an empty, immutable map of the desired type.

There are also legacy static final fields, EMPTY_LIST, EMPTY_SET, and EMPTY_MAP, of the raw types List, Set, and Map, initialized to refer to empty immutable collection objects. The use of these fields is not type-safe and is discouraged, as is all use of raw types.

21.10.2 The Unmodifiable Wrappers

The Collections class has static methods that return *unmodifiable wrappers* for all of the collection types: unmodifiableCollection, unmodifiableSet, unmodifiableSortedSet, unmodifiableList, unmodifiableMap, and unmodifiableSortedMap. The collections returned by these methods pass non-modifying methods through to the underlying collection. Modifying methods throw UnsupportedOperationException. The unmodifiable wrapper is backed by the original collection, so any changes you make to the collection will be visible through the wrapped collection. In other words, the contents of an unmodifiable wrapper can change, but not through the wrapper itself.

Unmodifiable wrappers are a reasonable way to expose information that may be changing but that shouldn't be changed by the observer. For example, consider the Attributed interface and the AttributedImpl class from Chapter 4. The attributes are exposed by having the attrs method return an Iterator—a reasonable design. An alternative, however, would be to return the attributes as an unmodifiable collection. Here's how AttributedImpl could implement this:

```
public Collection<Attr> attrs() {
    return Collections.
        unmodifiableCollection(attrTable.values());
}
```

Generally, iterators must be used immediately after they are obtained from the iterator method, with no intervening changes to the collection—otherwise, use of the iterator will encounter a ConcurrentModificationException. In contrast, you can ask for an unmodifiable collection, and then use it at some later time when the original collection has undergone arbitrary changes. Exposing information via a collection also allows the users of your class to utilize all the Collection utility methods. For example, if you expose your information as an unmodifiable list, it can be searched and sorted without your having to define search and sort methods.

21.10.3 The Checked Wrappers

A List<String> is guaranteed at compile time to only ever hold String objects—unless you have to pass it to legacy code as a raw type, in which case all guarantees are off (and you will get an "unchecked" warning). Dealing with legacy code that is unaware of generic types is a practical necessity. However, tracking down problems can be difficult. If you pass a List<String> to a legacy method that erroneously inserts a Number, you won't discover the problem until another part of your code tries to force the Number to be a String. The type-safe *checked wrappers* have been provided to help you with this problem. A checked wrapper will make a runtime check to enforce the type safety lost when the collection is used as a raw type. This allows errors to be detected as soon as they occur—when that erroneous Number is inserted.

public static <E> Collection<E>
    checkedCollection(Collection<E> coll, Class<E> type)
        Returns a dynamically typeset view of the given collection. Any attempt to insert an element that is not of the specified type will result in a ClassCastException.

The other type checked wrappers are obtained from checkedList, checkedSet, checkedSortedSet, checkedMap, and checkedSortedMap.

21.11 Synchronized Wrappers and Concurrent Collections

All the collection implementations provided in java.util are unsynchronized (except the legacy collections you will soon see). You must ensure any necessary synchronization for concurrent access from multiple threads. You can do this explicitly with synchronized methods or statements, or algorithmically by designing your code to use a given collection from only one thread. These techniques are how collections are often naturally used—as local variables in methods or as private fields of classes with synchronized code.

Thread-safety for collection classes themselves takes two main forms: lock-based synchronization to ensure that concurrent access is precluded, and the use of sophisticated data structures that allow (to varying degrees) truly concurrent use of a collection. The former is provided through the synchronized wrappers, while the latter are provided in the java.util.concurrent subpackage.

21.11.1 The Synchronized Wrappers

A *synchronized wrapper* passes through all method calls to the wrapped collection after adding any necessary synchronization. You can get a synchronized wrapper for a collection from one of the following static methods of Collections: synchronizedCollection, synchronizedSet, synchronizedSortedSet, synchronizedList, synchronizedMap, or synchronizedSortedMap. These factory methods return wrappers whose methods are fully synchronized and so are safe to use from multiple threads. For example, the following code creates a new HashMap that can be safely modified concurrently:

```
Map<String, String> unsyncMap =
    new HashMap<String, String>();
Map<String, String> syncMap =
    Collections.synchronizedMap(unsyncMap);
```

The map referred to by unsyncMap is a full, but unsynchronized, implementation of the Map interface. The Map returned by synchronizedMap has all relevant methods synchronized, passing all calls through to the wrapped map (that is, to unsyncMap). Modifications made through either map are visible to the other—there is really only one map with two different views: the unwrapped, unsynchronized view referenced by unsyncMap, and the wrapping, synchronized view referenced by syncMap:

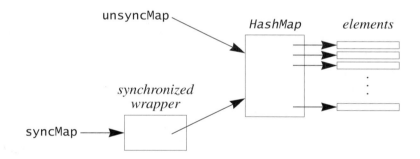

Because the underlying collection is unsynchronized, you must be very careful what you do with unsyncMap. The safest alternative is to drop the reference and do all work through syncMap. If you do not, you must be sure that you carefully control concurrency. The wrapper synchronizes on itself, so you could use syncMap to synchronize access on the collection and then use unsyncMap safely inside such code:

```
// add a lot of elements but grab the lock only once
synchronized (syncMap) {
    for (int i = 0; i < keys.length; i++)
        unsyncMap.put(keys[i], values[i]);
}
```

Iterators returned by synchronized wrappers are not synchronized but must be manually synchronized in a similar manner when needed:

```
synchronized (syncMap) {
    System.out.println("--- map contents:");
    for (String key : syncMap.keySet())
        System.out.println(key + ": " + syncMap.get(key));
}
```

If you use an unsynchronized collection concurrently the result is undefined—if you are lucky the error will be detected by the collection and you will get a ConcurrentModificationException. If you are unlucky the collection will quietly become corrupt.

21.11.2 The Concurrent Collections

The java.util.concurrent subpackage provides collection implementations that are not only safe for concurrent use but are specially designed to support such use.

When using a collection concurrently, you can't be sure when a collection might be empty, or, for a capacity constrained collection, when it might be full. In such circumstances it is useful to be able to wait until an element appears or until space for an element appears. The BlockingQueue<E> interface that extends Queue<E> defines such a capability:

public void **put(E elem)** throws InterruptedException
    Adds the specified element to this queue, waiting if necessary for space to become available.

public boolean **offer(E elem, long time, TimeUnit unit)**
   throws InterruptedException
    Adds the specified element to this queue, waiting if necessary up to the specified waiting time for space to become available. Returns true if the element was added, and false if the specified waiting time elapsed before space became available.

public E **take()** throws InterruptedException
    Returns and removes the head of this queue, waiting if necessary for the queue to be non-empty.

public E **poll(long time, TimeUnit unit)**
   throws InterruptedException
    Returns and removes the head of this queue, waiting if necessary up to the specified waiting time for the queue to be non-empty. Returns the head of

the queue, or `null` if the specified waiting time elapsed before an element became available.

As these are all potentially blocking operations. They support cancellation by throwing an `InterruptedException` in response to the current thread being interrupted.

You specify the waiting times with a `long` to indicate the time, and a value of the enum `java.util.concurrent.TimeUnit` to indicate the units. The enum `TimeUnit` has the constants NANOSECONDS, MICROSECONDS, MILLISECONDS, and SECONDS.

A `BlockingQueue` may be capacity constrained. The `remainingCapacity` method returns the number of elements that can be put in the queue without causing blocking—but note that if multiple threads are using the queue it doesn't guarantee how many elements an individual thread may be able to add without blocking. If there is no inherent limit `Integer.MAX_VALUE` is returned. If there is a capacity limit then `Collection.add` will throw `IllegalStateException` if the element cannot be added.

The `drainTo` method takes a collection and attempts to transfer all the elements of this queue into the given collection. The number of elements transferred is returned. An overloaded form of `drainTo` takes an additional `int` parameter that limits the maximum number of elements to transfer. This operation is provided as an alternative to repeated polling of the queue because some implementations will be able to implement it very efficiently—even atomically. However, the guarantees of this method are somewhat loose: It is possible that if an error occurs when an element is added to the target collection, the element may end up in one, neither, or both collections!

All `BlockingQueue` implementations must be thread-safe, but it is not required (unless explicitly documented by an implementation) that the bulk collection operations (`addAll`, `containsAll`, `retainAll`) are executed atomically.

The following blocking queue implementations are provided:

◆ `ArrayBlockingQueue`—A bounded blocking queue backed by an array. You construct one with a capacity and an optional fairness setting. If the queue is fair then blocked threads are processed in first-in-first-out order; otherwise, blocked threads can be unblocked in arbitrary order. The queue itself is ordered first-in-first-out. It provides a weakly consistent iterator.

◆ `LinkedBlockingQueue`—An optionally bounded queue based on a linked node implementation. The queue elements are ordered first-in-first-out. It provides a weakly consistent iterator.

A linked queue implementation will typically provide greater throughput than an array-based implementation when used concurrently. This is due to the use of algorithms that allow the head and tail to be locked independently. However, a linked queue implementation may require allocation for each insertion and produce garbage on each removal, which can add significant overhead. When the queue is used as a fixed size buffer that is constantly filled by one set of threads and then drained by another, this overhead is at its worst, and an array-based implementation may perform better than a bounded linked queue. Moreover, in the usage pattern described, the additional concurrency support of the linked queue isn't used because each thread within a set operates on the same end of the queue.

- `PriorityBlockingQueue`—An unbounded queue ordered the same way as a `PriorityQueue`. This implementation adds thread safety and the blocking retrieval operations. It provides an iterator that is thread-safe but fail-fast.

- `SynchronousQueue`—A specialized blocking queue where each `take` must wait for a `put`, and vice versa. A synchronous queue has no capacity, not even a capacity of one, so you cannot peek into a synchronous queue, nor can you iterate through it. From the perspective of most of the collection methods a synchronous queue acts like an empty collection.

- `DelayQueue`—A specialized unbounded blocking queue of `Delayed` elements. The `Delayed` interface has a single method, `getDelay`, which takes a `TimeUnit` constant and returns the delay in that time unit. A `Delayed` element cannot be removed from a `DelayQueue` until its delay has expired. The head of a delay queue is that element whose delay expired furthest in the past. If no elements have a delay that has passed then the head is `null`. It provides an iterator that is thread-safe but fail-fast.

In addition to the thread-safe blocking queues, `java.util.concurrent` provides a number of other concurrent collections.

`ConcurrentHashMap` provides a hash map implementation that allows for fully concurrent retrievals and up to a set number of concurrent insertions. Although all operations are thread-safe, they do not involve locking, and there is no way to externally synchronize the map to provide atomic sequences of operations. Because of this, some extra support is needed to do things like inserting a value in the map only if it is not present. The `ConcurrentMap<K,V>` interface, implemented by `ConcurrentHashMap`, defines a number of such methods:

public V **putIfAbsent(K key, V value)**

Atomically stores the given value in the map only if a mapping for `key` does not currently exist. The old value mapped to `key` is returned, or `null` if the key was not present—but be aware that `null` may be a legitimate value for some maps. (Optional if the map does not support `put`)

public boolean **remove(Object key, Object value)**
>Atomically remove the entry for key if it currently maps to value. Returns true if the entry was removed. (Optional if the map does not support remove)

public boolean **replace(K key, V oldValue, V newValue)**
>Atomically replaces the entry for key only if it currently maps to oldValue. Returns true if the entry was replaced. (Optional if the map does not support put)

public V **replace(K key, V value)**
>Atomically replaces the mapping for key if and only if a mapping currently exists. The old value mapped to key is returned, or null if the key was not present—but be aware that null may be a legitimate value for some maps. (Optional if the map does not support put)

The ConcurrentLinkedQueue<E> class provides an unbounded thread-safe queue based on a linked node representation. Operations on the queue are highly concurrent and do not utilize locks. Because of the concurrent nature an operation like size requires a complete traversal of the queue and so is quite expensive—however, knowing the size that a concurrently changing queue used to be is seldom, if ever, useful. The iterator provided by ConcurrentLinkedQueue is weakly consistent, it guarantees to traverse the elements that existed when the iterator was created, but may not reflect subsequent additions.

The CopyOnWriteArrayList<E> is a thread-safe variant of ArrayList. It allows iteration to be done over a snapshot of the contents without actually making a copy of the original list. Copies are made only when someone modifies the list—hence the name "copy on write." This makes a very efficient structure for lists that are read much more frequently than they are changed. Because the iterator sees a snapshot of the elements, it can never fail; but it does not support the remove operation.

The CopyOnWriteArraySet<E> class is an implementation of Set that uses a CopyOnWriteArrayList.

21.12 The Arrays Utility Class

The class Arrays provides useful static methods for dealing with arrays. Most of these methods have a full complement of overloads: one for arrays of each primitive type (except boolean for searching and sorting) and one for Object arrays. There are also two variants of some methods: one acting on the whole array and one acting on the subarray specified by two supplied indices. The methods are

◆ sort—Sorts an array into ascending order. The exact algorithm is not specified other than it must be stable for objects (that is, equal objects don't get reordered because of the sort). A good implementation would use a technique that is not worse than $O(n\log n)$.

◆ binarySearch—Searches a sorted array for a given key. Returns the key's index, or a negative value encoding a safe insertion point (as for the method Collections.binarySearch described previously). There are no subarray versions of these methods.

◆ fill—Fills in the array with a specified value.

◆ equals and deepEquals—Return true if the two arrays they are passed are the same object, are both null, or have the same size and equivalent contents. There are no subarray versions. The equals method for Object[] uses Object.equals on each non-null element of the array; null elements in the first array must be matched by null elements of the second. This does not treat nested arrays specially, so it cannot generally be used to compare arrays of arrays. The deepEquals method checks for equivalance of two Object[] recursively taking into account the equivalence of nested arrays.

◆ hashCode and deepHashCode—Return a hash code based on the contents of the given array. There are no subarray versions. The deepHashCode method computes a hash code for an Object[] recursively taking into account the contents of nested arrays.

◆ toString and deepToString—Return a string representation of the contents of the array. There are no subarray versions. The string consists of a comma seperated list of the array's contents, enclosed by '[' and ']'. The array contents are converted to strings with String.valueof. The toString method for Object[] converts any nested arrays to strings using Object.toString. The deepToString method returns a string representation of an Object[] recursively converting nested arrays to strings as defined by this method.

The methods sort and binarySearch have two overloads for Object arrays. One assumes that its elements are comparable (implement the Comparable interface). The second uses a provided Comparator object instead, so you can manipulate arrays of objects that are not comparable or for which you do not want to use the natural ordering.

You can view an array of objects as a List by using the object returned by the asList method.

```
public static <T> List<T> asList(T... elems)
```

This can take an actual array reference, or it can conveniently create an array from the given sequence of elements. The list is backed by the underlying array, so changes made to the array are visible to the list and vice versa. The returned list allows you to set elements, but not to add or remove them—it is a modifiable list, but not a resizable list. Using a List for access to an underlying array can give you useful features of List, such as using synchronized wrappers to synchronize access to the underlying array.

21.13 Writing Iterator Implementations

Iterators are generally useful, and you may want to write your own, even if you are not implementing a collection type. The following code demonstrates the basics of writing your own Iterator implementation, in this case for an iterator that will filter out strings longer than a given length:

```java
public class ShortStrings implements Iterator<String> {
    private Iterator<String> strings;  // source for strings
    private String nextShort;          // null if next not known
    private final int maxLen;          // only return strings <=

    public ShortStrings(Iterator<String> strings,
                        int maxLen) {
        this.strings = strings;
        this.maxLen = maxLen;
        nextShort = null;
    }

    public boolean hasNext() {
        if (nextShort != null)  // found it already
            return true;
        while (strings.hasNext()) {
            nextShort = strings.next();
            if (nextShort.length() <= maxLen)
                return true;
        }
        nextShort = null;        // didn't find one
        return false;
    }

    public String next() {
```

```
        if (nextShort == null && !hasNext())
            throw new NoSuchElementException();
        String n = nextShort;    // remember nextShort
        nextShort = null;        // consume nextShort
        return n;                // return nextShort
    }

    public void remove() {
        throw new UnsupportedOperationException();
    }
}
```

The class ShortStrings is a type of iterator that will read String objects from another iterator, returning only those that are no longer than a specified length. The constructor takes the iterator that will provide the strings and the maximum length, storing those in the object's fields. The field nextShort will hold the next short string, or null when there isn't one. If nextShort is null, the hasNext method searches for the next short string, remembering it in nextShort. If hasNext reaches the end of its source iteration without finding a short string it returns false.

The method next checks to see if there is a next short string, either returning it if there is one or throwing NoSuchElementException if there are none to return. Notice that hasNext does all the real work of finding the short strings, and next just returns the results, setting nextShort to null to indicate that the next short string, if any, is as yet undiscovered.

Finally, remove is not supported by this iterator implementation, so remove throws UnsupportedOperationException.

A few things to notice. First, hasNext is carefully written so that it will work if invoked multiple times before a next. This is required—the calling code may invoke hasNext as many times as it wants between invocations of next. Second, next is carefully written so that it works even if programmer using it has never invoked hasNext. Although generally a poor practice, you could never invoke hasNext and simply loop invoking next until an exception is generated.

Third, remove is not allowed because it cannot work correctly. Imagine, for example, if remove invoked remove on the underlying iterator. The following legal (although odd) code can cause incorrect behavior:

```
it.next();
it.hasNext();
it.remove();
```

Imagine that this were to happen when there was one more short string left in the iteration followed by some long ones. The invocation of next would return the last short string. Then hasNext would iterate through the list of strings, and finding no more short ones, return false. When remove was invoked, it would invoke remove on the underlying iterator, thereby removing the last (long) string that hasNext rejected. That would be incorrect. Since the above code is valid, you cannot fix the problem by forbidding the sequence of methods. You are effectively stuck. Because of this, you cannot build a filtering iterator on top of another Iterator object. You can build one on top of a ListIterator though, since it allows you to back up to the previously returned short string.

The methods of ListIterator have contracts similar to those of Iterator, as you have learned earlier in this chapter. You can provide ListIterator objects in some circumstances where you might otherwise write an Iterator. If you are writing a general utility class for others to use, you should implement ListIterator instead of Iterator if possible.

Exercise 21.4: Write a version of ShortStrings that implements ListIterator to filter a ListIterator object. Should your class extend ShortStrings?

21.14 Writing Collection Implementations

You will usually find that at least one of the collection implementations will satisfy your needs. If not, you can implement relevant collection interfaces yourself to provide collections that satisfy your particular needs. You will find skeletal implementations in the abstract classes AbstractCollection, AbstractSet, AbstractList, AbstractSequentialList, AbstractQueue, and AbstractMap. You can extend these classes to create your own collections, often with less work than starting from the interfaces directly. The concrete collections shown in Figure 21–1 on page 568 each extend the appropriate abstract collection type, as shown in the concrete type tree in Figure 21–1.

These abstract collection classes are designed to be helpful superclasses for your own collection implementations. They are not required—in some cases you will find it easier or more efficient to directly implement the interfaces.

Each abstract collection class declares a few abstract methods and uses them in default implementations of other methods of the collection type. For example, AbstractList has two abstract methods: size and get. All other querying methods of AbstractList, including its iterators, are implemented by using these methods. You need only write your own implementation of the other methods if you want to, typically to either increase efficiency or to allow something disallowed by default. For example, if your list is modifiable, your subclass of

AbstractList will have to provide an overriding implementation of the set method, which by default throws UnsupportedOperationException.

The root of the abstract collection types is AbstractCollection. If you need a collection that isn't a set, list, or map you can subclass this directly. Otherwise, you will probably find it more useful to subclass one of the more specific abstract collections classes.

If the Collection class you are creating is unmodifiable (if the modification methods of your collection should throw UnsupportedOperationException), your subclass of AbstractCollection need only provide an implementation of the size and iterator methods. This means you must at least write an implementation of Iterator for your collection. If your collection is modifiable, you must also override the default implementation of the add method (which throws UnsupportedOperationException) and your iterator must support remove.

AbstractSet extends AbstractCollection, and the methods you must implement and can override are the same, with the additional constraint that a subclass of AbstractSet must conform to the contract of the Set interface. It also overrides the implemention of equals and hashCode from Object.

AbstractQueue has the same requirements as AbstractCollection, with the additional requirements that you must implement offer, poll, and peek.

AbstractList requires you to implement only size and get(int) to define an unmodifiable list class. If you also override set(int,Object) you will get a modifiable list, but one whose size cannot change. Your list can change size if you also override the methods add(int,Object) and remove(int).

For example, suppose you need to view a bunch of arrays as a single list. You could use one of the existing List implementations, but at the cost of copying the information each time from the arrays into a new collection. You could instead subclass AbstractList to create an ArrayBunchList type that lets you do this without copying:

```java
public class ArrayBunchList<E> extends AbstractList<E> {
    private final E[][] arrays;
    private final int size;

    public ArrayBunchList(E[][] arrays) {
        this.arrays = arrays.clone();
        int s = 0;
        for (E[] array : arrays)
            s += array.length;
        size = s;
    }
```

```
    public int size() {
        return size;
    }

    public E get(int index) {
        int off = 0;      // offset from start of collection
        for (int i = 0; i < arrays.length; i++) {
            if (index < off + arrays[i].length)
                return arrays[i][index - off];
            off += arrays[i].length;
        }
        throw new ArrayIndexOutOfBoundsException(index);
    }

    public E set(int index, E value) {
        int off = 0;      // offset from start of collection
        for (int i = 0; i < arrays.length; i++) {
            if (index < off + arrays[i].length) {
                E ret = arrays[i][index - off];
                arrays[i][index - off] = value;
                return ret;
            }
            off += arrays[i].length;
        }
        throw new ArrayIndexOutOfBoundsException(index);
    }
}
```

When an ArrayBunchList is created, all the constituent arrays are remembered internally in the arrays field, and the total size of the collection in size. ArrayBunchList implements size, get, and set, but not add or remove. This means that the class provides a modifiable list, but one whose size cannot be changed. Any call that needs values from the underlying arrays will go through get. Any action that modifies the value of the ArrayBunchList will go through set, which modifies the appropriate underlying array.

AbstractList provides Iterator and ListIterator implementations on top of the other methods of the class. Because the iteration implementations use the methods of your underlying subclass of AbstractList, the modifying methods of the iteration will properly reflect the modifiability of your class.

The Iterator implementations of AbstractList use get to read values. As you will note, ArrayBunchList has a get that can do some significant work if the value is stored in one of the later arrays. We can make get smarter than shown here to help with this work, but we can be even more efficient for iteration because it accesses the data sequentially. Here is an optimized Iterator:

```
private class ABLIterator implements Iterator<E> {
    private int off;        // offset from start of list
    private int array;      // array we are currently in
    private int pos;        // position in current array

    ABLIterator() {
        off = 0;
        array = 0;
        pos = 0;
        // skip any initial empty arrays (or to end)
        for (array = 0; array < arrays.length; array++)
            if (arrays[array].length > 0)
                break;
    }

    public boolean hasNext() {
        return off + pos < size();
    }

    public E next() {
        if (!hasNext())
            throw new NoSuchElementException();
        E ret = arrays[array][pos++];

        // advance to the next element (or to end)
        while (pos >= arrays[array].length) {
            off += arrays[array++].length;
            pos = 0;
            if (array >= arrays.length)
                break;
        }
        return ret;
    }

    public void remove() {
```

```
            throw new UnsupportedOperationException();
    }
}
```

This implementation uses our knowledge of the underlying data structures to know exactly where the next element is coming from. This is more efficient than invoking `get` to implement the iterator's `next`. (It is also written to handle empty arrays and an empty `ArrayBunchList`.)

You can often substantially increase the performance of a resizable list by overriding the protected `removeRange` method, which takes two `int` parameters, `min` and `max`, and removes the elements starting at `min`, up to but not including `max`. The `clear` method uses `removeRange` to remove elements from lists and sublists. The default implementation is to invoke `remove` on each element one at a time. Many data structures can do bulk removes much more efficiently.

`AbstractSequentialList` extends `AbstractList` to make it easier to implement lists that are backed by a *sequential access* data store where moving from one element of the data to another requires examining each element of the data. In such a store, random access requires work since you must traverse each element to get to the next. A linked list is a sequential access data store. By contrast, an array can be randomly accessed directly. This is why `ArrayList` extends `AbstractList`, while `LinkedList` extends `AbstractSequentialList`.

Where `AbstractList` implements its iterators via the random access method `get`, `AbstractSequentialList` implements the random access methods via an iterator you provide by implementing the `listIterator` method. You must also implement `size`. Your class will be modifiable in whatever ways your list iterator's methods allow. For example, if your iterator allows `set` but not `add` or `remove`, you will have a modifiable but non-resizable list.

To use the `AbstractMap` class you must implement the `entrySet` method to return an unmodifiable set of entries that contains the mappings of the map. This will implement an unmodifiable map. To make a modifiable map, you must override `put`, and the iterator your `entrySet` object returns must allow `remove`.

The abstract implementations provided in these classes are designed to be easy to extend, but efficiency is not always a consequence. You can often make your subclass of an abstract collection type much faster by judicious overriding of other methods, as shown for the `ArrayBunchList` iterator. As another example, the implementation of `get` in `AbstractMap`, having only a set of entries, must search through that set one at a time until it finds an appropriate entry. This is an $O(n)$ implementation. To get its $O(1)$ performance, `HashMap` overrides `get` and all other key-based methods to use its own hash buckets. However, `HashMap` does not override the implementation of `equals` because that requires iteration anyway and the implementation in `AbstractMap` is reasonably efficient.

Exercise 21.5: Implement a more efficient `ListIterator` for `ArrayBunchList`. Be careful of the specific contracts of `ListIterator` methods, such as `set` not being valid until either `next` or `previous` is invoked.

21.15 The Legacy Collection Types

The collection framework—the interfaces and classes described in this chapter, and shown in Figure 21–1 on page 568—has not always been a part of the package `java.util`, but that package has always contained some other collections. Most are superseded by the new collection types. Even so, they are not deprecated because they are in widespread use in existing code and will continue to be used until programs shift over to the new types. You are therefore likely to encounter these *legacy collections* so you should learn about them, including their relationship to the newer collection types. The legacy collections consist of the following types:

- `Enumeration`—Analogous to `Iterator`.
- `Vector`—Analogous to `ArrayList`, maintains an ordered list of elements that are stored in an underlying array.
- `Stack`—A subclass of `Vector` that adds methods to push and pop elements so that you can treat the vector by using the terms normal to a stack.
- `Dictionary`—Analogous to the `Map` interface, although `Dictionary` is an abstract class, not an interface.[4]
- `Hashtable`—Analogous to `HashMap`.
- `Properties`—A subclass of `Hashtable`. Maintains a map of key/value pairs where the keys and values are strings. If a key is not found in a properties object a "default" properties object can be searched.

Of these types, only `Properties` is in active use—it is used to contain system properties, as described in "System Properties" on page 663 and by some applications to store configuration data. We describe the other legacy collections by contrasting them with their analogous types. We then describe `Properties` in more detail since you are more likely to actually need to write code that uses it.

---

[4] `Dictionary` is not an interface because it predates the addition of interfaces to the language, which gives you some idea of how old these legacy collections are.

21.15.1 Enumeration

Enumeration<E> is analogous to Iterator, but has just two methods: hasMoreElements which behaves like hasNext, and nextElement which behaves like next. You can get an Enumeration that iterates through a non-legacy collection from the static method Collections.enumeration.

You can convert an Enumeration to a List via the static Collections.list method, which returns an ArrayList containing all the elements accessible by the enumeration, in the order the enumeration returned them.

Exercise 21.6: Rewrite the example program Concat on page 528 so that it uses an implementation of Enumeration that has only one FileInputStream object open at a time.

21.15.2 Vector

The Vector<E> class is analogous to ArrayList<E>. Although Vector is a legacy class, it has been made to implement List, so it works as a Collection. All methods that access the contents of a Vector are synchronized. As a legacy collection, Vector contains many methods and constructors that are analogous to those of ArrayList, in addition to those it inherits from List. The legacy constructors and methods of Vector and their analogues in ArrayList are

public **Vector(int initialCapacity, int capacityIncrement)**
    No analogue. Creates a new Vector with the given initialCapacity that will grow by capacityIncrement elements at a time.

public **Vector(int initialCapacity)**
    Analogous to ArrayList(initialCapacity).

public **Vector()**
    Analogous to ArrayList().

public **Vector(Collection<? extends E> coll)**
    Analogous to ArrayList(coll).

public final void **addElement(E elem)**
    Analogous to add(elem).

public final void **insertElementAt(E elem, int index)**
    Analogous to add(index, elem).

public final void **setElementAt(E elem, int index)**
    Analogous to set(index, elem).

public final void **removeElementAt(int index)**
    Analogous to remove(index).

public final boolean **removeElement(Object elem)**
> Analogous to remove(elem).

public final void **removeAllElements()**
> Analogous to clear().

public final E **elementAt(int index)**
> Analogous to get(index).

public final void **copyInto(Object[] anArray)**
> No direct analogue; the closest is toArray(Object[]), although toArray allocates a new array if the array is too small, where copyInto will throw an IndexOutOfBoundsException.

public final int **indexOf(Object elem, int index)**
> Searches for the first occurrence of elem, beginning the search at index, and testing for equality using equals. The closest analogue would be to create a sublist covering the range and use indexOf on the sublist.

public final int **lastIndexOf(Object elem, int index)**
> Searches backward for the last occurrence of elem, beginning the search at index, and testing for equality using equals. The closest analogue would be to create a sublist covering the range and use lastIndexOf on the sublist.

public final Enumeration<E> **elements()**
> Analogous to iterator(). Equivalent to Collections.enumeration.

public final E **firstElement()**
> Analogous to get(0).

public final E **lastElement()**
> Analogous to get(size() - 1).

public final void **setSize(int newSize)**
> No analogue. If newSize is less than the current size, extra data is dropped. If newSize is larger than the current size, any added elements are null.

public final int **capacity()**
> No analogue. Returns the current capacity of the vector.

In addition to these public methods, protected fields are available to classes that subclass the Vector class. Be careful what you do (if anything) with these fields because, for example, methods in Vector rely on elementCount being less than or equal to the length of the elementData array.

protected Object[] **elementData**
> The buffer where elements are stored.

protected int **elementCount**
> The number of elements currently used in the buffer.

`protected int `**`capacityIncrement`**
> The number of elements to add to the capacity when `elementData` runs out of space. If zero, the size of the buffer is doubled every time it needs to grow.

21.15.3 Stack

The `Stack<E>` class extends `Vector<E>` to add methods for a simple last-in-first-out stack of objects. Use `push` to push an object onto the stack and use `pop` to remove the top element from the stack. The `peek` method returns the top item on the stack without removing it. The `empty` method returns `true` if the stack is empty. Trying to `pop` or `peek` in an empty `Stack` object will throw an `EmptyStackException`.

You can use `search` to find an object's distance from the top of the stack, with 1 being the top of the stack. If the object isn't found, –1 is returned. The `search` method uses `Object.equals` to test whether an object in the stack is the same as the one it is searching for.

These methods are trivial uses of the `Vector` methods, so using an `ArrayList` to implement a `Stack` would be simple: using `add` to implement push, and so on. There is no analogue to `Stack` in the collections.

Exercise 21.7: Implement a stack using `ArrayList`. Should your stack class be a subclass of `ArrayList` or use an `ArrayList` internally, providing different stack-specific methods?

21.15.4 `Dictionary`

The `Dictionary<K,V>` abstract class is essentially an interface. It is analogous to the `Map` interface but uses the terms *key* and *element* instead of *key* and *value*. With two exceptions, each method in `Dictionary` has the same name as its analogous method in `Map`: `get`, `put`, `remove`, `size`, and `isEmpty`. The two exceptions are `keys` and `elements`. In `Map`, you get a `Set` of keys or values that you can iterate over or otherwise manipulate. In `Dictionary`, you can only get an `Enumeration` (iterator) for the keys and elements, using the `keys` and `elements` methods, respectively. The legacy collections did not contain a `Set` type, and so `Dictionary` could not be expressed in those terms.

21.15.5 `Hashtable`

The `Hashtable<K,V>` class is similar to the `HashMap` class, but implements the methods of `Dictionary` as well as (more recently) implementing the `Map` interface. All methods of `Hashtable` are synchronized, unlike `HashMap`. Beyond the methods inherited from `Dictionary` and `Map`, `Hashtable` adds the following methods and constructors:

public **Hashtable()**
>   Analogous to HashMap().

public **Hashtable(int initialCapacity)**
>   Analogous to HashMap(initalCapacity).

public **Hashtable(int initialCapacity, float loadFactor)**
>   Analogous to HashMap(initialCapacity, loadFactor).

public **Hashtable(Map<? extends K,? extends V> t)**
>   Analogous to HashMap(map).

public boolean **contains(Object elem)**
>   Analogous to containsValue(elem).

21.16 Properties

A `Properties` object is used to store string keys and associated string elements. This kind of hashtable often has a default `Properties` object in which to look for properties that are not specified in the table itself. The `Properties` class extends `Hashtable<Object,Object>`. Standard `Hashtable` methods are used for almost all manipulation of a `Properties` object, but to get and set properties, you can use string-based methods. In addition to inherited methods, the following methods and constructors are provided:

public **Properties()**
>   Creates an empty property map.

public **Properties(Properties defaults)**
>   Creates an empty property map with the specified default `Properties` object. If a property lookup fails, the default `Properties` object is queried. The default `Properties` object can have its own default `Properties` object, and so on. The chain of default objects can be arbitrarily deep.

public String **getProperty(String key)**
>   Gets the property element for key. If the key is not found in this object, the default `Properties` object (if any) is searched. Returns null if the property is not found.

public String **getProperty(String key, String defaultElement)**
>   Gets the property element for key. If the key is not found in this object, the default `Properties` object (if any) is searched. Returns defaultElement if the property is not found.

`public Object` **`setProperty(String key, String value)`**
> Adds the property key to the map with the given `value`. This only affects the `Properties` object on which it is invoked—the default `Properties` object (if any) is unaffected. Returns the previous value that was mapped to this key, or `null` if there was none.

`public void` **`store(OutputStream out, String header)`**
   `throws IOException`
> Saves properties to an `OutputStream`. This only works if this `Properties` object contains only string keys and values (as the specification says it must); otherwise you get a `ClassCastException`. If not `null`, the `header` string is written to the output stream as a single-line comment. Do not use a multiline header string, or else the saved properties will not be loadable. Only properties in this object are saved to the file; the default `Properties` object (if any) is not saved.

`public void` **`load(InputStream in)`** `throws IOException`
> Loads properties from an `InputStream`. The property list is presumed to have been created previously by `store`. This method puts values into this `Properties` object; it does not set values in the default `Properties` object.

`public Enumeration<?>` **`propertyNames()`**
> Enumerates the keys, including those of any default `Properties` object. This method provides a snapshot, and hence can be expensive. The inherited keys method, by contrast, returns only those properties defined in this object itself.

`public void` **`list(PrintWriter out)`**
> Lists (prints) properties on the given `PrintWriter`. Useful for debugging.

`public void` **`list(PrintStream out)`**
> Lists (prints) properties on the given `PrintStream`. Also useful for debugging.

The default `Properties` object cannot be changed after the object is created. To change the default `Properties` object, you can subclass the `Properties` class and modify the protected field named `defaults` that contains the default `Properties` object.

> *Science is facts;*
> *just as houses are made of stones, so is science made of facts;*
> *but a pile of stones is not a house and a collection of facts is not necessarily science.*
> —Henri Poincaré

CHAPTER 22

Miscellaneous Utilities

The best way to make a fire with two sticks is to make sure one of them is a match.

—Will Rogers

Y OU will find several standard utility interfaces and classes in the `java.util` package. You have seen the collection classes already in Chapter 21. This chapter covers the remainder of the classes except those used for localization, which are in Chapter 24. The `java.util` classes covered in this chapter are

- ◆ `Formatter`—A class for producing formatted text.
- ◆ `BitSet`—A dynamically sized bit vector.
- ◆ `Observer/Observable`—An interface/class pair that enables an object to be `Observable` by having one or more `Observer` objects that are notified when something interesting happens in the `Observable` object.
- ◆ `Random`—A class to generate sequences of pseudorandom numbers.
- ◆ `Scanner`—A class for scanning text and parsing it into values of primitive types or strings, based on regular expression patterns.
- ◆ `StringTokenizer`—A class that splits a string into tokens based on delimiters (by default, whitespace).
- ◆ `Timer/TimerTask`—A way to schedule tasks to be run in the future.
- ◆ `UUID`—A class that represents a universally unique identifier (UUID).

Finally, we look at two other useful classes, housed in the `java.lang` package:

- ◆ `Math`—A class for performing basic mathematical operations, such as trigonometric functions, exponentiation, logarithms, and so on.
- ◆ `StrictMath`—Defines the same methods as `Math` but guarantees the use of specific algorithms that ensure the same results on every virtual machine.

22.1 Formatter

The Formatter class allows you to control the way in which primitive values and objects are represented as text. The common way to represent objects or values as text is to convert the object or value to a string, using either the toString method of the object or the toString method of the appropriate wrapper class. This is often done implicitly, either through use of string concatenation or by invoking a particular overload of the PrintStream or PrintWriter print methods. This is easy and convenient, but it doesn't give you any control over the exact form of the string. For example, if you invoke

```
System.out.println("The value of Math.PI is " + Math.PI);
```

the output is

```
The value of Math.PI is 3.141592653589793
```

This is correct and informative, but it might provide more detail than the reader really needs to see, or more than you have room to show. Using a formatter you can control the format of the converted text, such as restricting the value to only three decimal places, or padding the converted string with spaces so that it occupies a minimum width regardless of the actual value being converted. All of these operations are possible starting from the result of toString, but it is much easier to have a formatter do it for you.

The primary method of a Formatter object is the format method. In its simplest form it takes a *format string* followed by a sequence of arguments, which are the objects and values you want to format. For convenience the PrintStream and PrintWriter classes provide a printf method (for "print formatted") that takes the same arguments as format and passes them through to an associated Formatter instance. We use the System.out.printf method to demonstrate how format strings are used.

The format string contains normal text together with *format specifiers* that tell the formatter how you want the following values to be formatted. For example, you can print the value of Math.PI to three decimal places using

```
System.out.printf("The value of Math.PI is %.3f %n", Math.PI);
```

which prints

```
The value of Math.PI is 3.142
```

A format specifier starts with a % character and ends with a character that indicates the type of conversion to perform. In the example above, the f conversion means that the argument is expected to be a floating-point value and that it should be formatted in the normal decimal format. In contrast, an e conversion is a floating-point conversion that produces output in scientific notation (such as 3.142e+00). Other conversions include 'd for integers in decimal format, x for integers in hexadecimal, and s for strings or general object conversions. Conversion indicators that can produce non-digit text are defined in both a lowercase and uppercase form, such as e and E, where the uppercase form indicates that all text in the output will be converted to uppercase (as if the resulting String had toUpperCase invoked on it).

In addition to the conversion indicator, a format specifier can contain other values that control the layout of the converted value. In the example above the ".3" is a *precision* indicator, which for a floating-point decimal conversion indicates how many decimal places should appear in the result, with the value rounded up or down as appropriate. You can also control the *width* of the output text, ensuring that different formatted elements line up correctly (such as for printing data in a tabular form) regardless of the actual value being formatted. There are also *flags* that can be specified to control things like the justification (left or right) and the padding character to use to maintain the minimum width. The exact meaning of precision, width, and flags depends on the conversion being applied.

There are two special conversions that we quickly mention. The first is the % conversion used to output the % character. Because the % character marks the start of a format specifier, you need a way to include a % character that should actually appear in the output. The format specifier %% will do just that (just as the escape character \\ is used to produce the single character \). You can specify a width with this conversion to pad the output with spaces: on the left if no flags are given, and on the right if the – flag is given to request left-justification.

The second special conversion is the line separator conversion n. A format specifier of %n (as used in the example) outputs the platform specific line separator. The line separator string is defined by the system property line.separator and is not necessarily a single newline character (\n)—see "System Properties" on page 663. Unlike println that outputs the line separator for you, printf and format require that you remember to do this yourself. No width, precision, or flag values can be used with the line separator conversion.

The following sections look at the format specifiers for numeric, character, and general conversions. The formatting conversions for dates and times are discussed in "Using Formatter with Dates and Times" on page 706. The Formatter class also supports formatting for instances of the java.math.BigInteger and java.math.BigDecimal classes, but those are not discussed here—consult the Formatter class documentation for information concerning those classes.

22.1.1 Format Specifiers

The general form of a format specifier for general, character, or numeric conversions is

```
%[argument_index][flags][width][.precision]conversion
```

where everything except the % and the conversion indicator are optional.

If there is an error in the format string, a mismatch between the conversion and the other formatting requests, or a mismatch between the conversion and the argument type supplied, then an `IllegalFormatException` of some form will be thrown. These exceptions are described later.

The argument index is an optional indicator of which argument this format specifier should be applied to. This is very useful for referring to the same argument multiple times within the same format string. The argument index can take two forms: a number indicating which argument it applies to, followed by a $ character; or the < character meaning "the same argument as the previous format specifier." If the argument index is not present, then each unmarked format specifier is numbered sequentially, and it is that argument to which the format specifier is applied. This numbering ignores the presence of any indexed format specifiers. For example, given

```
System.out.printf("%3$d %d %2$d %<d %d %n", 1, 2, 3);
```

the output is

```
3 1 2 2 2
```

The first specifier explicitly applies to argument three; the second is the first non-indexed specifier so it applies to argument one; the third specifier explicitly applies to argument two; the fourth specifier applies to whatever the third did, so that is again two; the fifth specifier is the second non-indexed specifier so it also applies to argument two.

If any format specifier indicates an argument that does not exist, then you get a `MissingFormatArgumentException`. Examples of this kind of error are using %3$ when there are only two arguments, or using %< as the first format specifier.

The meaning of flags, width, and precision is similar for the different conversions but the details differ depending on the exact kind of conversion, as discussed in the following sections.

When you consider which argument types are expected for each conversion, remember that anything that applies to a primitive type also applies to its wrapper. For brevity we don't mention the wrapper classes explicitly.

22.1.2 Integer Conversions

The integer conversions apply to arguments of type `byte`, `short`, `int`, and `long`. The different conversions are

- d—decimal format
- o—octal format
- x, X—hexadecimal format

The width value specifies the minimum number of characters to output—including additional characters that the flags may cause to be included. No precision value may be given. The flags applicable to each conversion are shown in the following table. An entry with a × means the flag is not allowed.

Flag	d	o	x/X	Meaning
'−'				Left justify (otherwise right justify)
'#'	×			Include radix: 0 for octal and 0x or 0X for hexadecimal
'+'		×	×	Always include the sign
' '		×	×	(space) Include a leading space for positive values
'0'				Use zero-padding (else spaces)
','		×	×	Include grouping separators
'('		×	×	Enclose negative values in parentheses

For example, to print a zero-padded, hexadecimal value with a radix indicator and a minimum width of 10, you could use

```
System.out.printf("%0#10x %n", val);
```

which for `val` equal to 32 prints

```
0x00000020
```

You cannot use + and space together, nor can you use − and 0 together. If either of 0 or − is given then a width must be given.

22.1.3 Floating-Point Conversions

The floating-point conversions apply to arguments of type `float` and `double`. The different conversions are

- e, E—computerized scientific notation (such as 3.142e+00)
- f, F—decimal format (such as 3.142)

♦ g, G—general scientific notation (see below)

♦ a, A—hexadecimal exponential format (as used for hexadecimal floating-point literals—see page 168)

In each case a value of NaN or infinity produces the strings "NaN" or "Infinity".

The width value specifies the minimum number of characters to output, with the result being padded if necessary to fit the requested width. For everything except general scientific conversion, the precision value specifies the number of digits to output after the decimal point (or hexadecimal point), with the value rounded as necessary to match that precision. If no precision is given then it defaults to 6, except for the hexadecimal exponential form where no precision means to use as many places as needed.

A conversion to general scientific notation chooses the output format based on the magnitude of the value and the precision that is given. In this case precision indicates the number of significant digits (not the number of fractional digits). If after rounding to the specified precision, the value is smaller than 10^{-4}, or it is greater than or equal to $10^{precision}$, then computerized scientific notation is used; otherwise, decimal format is used. For example, given

```
System.out.
    printf("%1$.5g %1$.4g %1$.3g %1$.2g %n", Math.PI * 100);
```

The output is:

```
314.16 314.2 314 3.1e+02
```

You can see the value being rounded according to the number of significant digits requested, and see the switch to scientific notation when the value exceeds 10^2.

For the general scientific notation conversion, if the precision is not given it defaults to 6, but a precision of zero is treated as a precision of 1.

The flags applicable to each conversion are shown in the following table. An entry with × means the flag is not allowed.

Flag	e/E	f/F	g/G	a/A	Meaning
'-'					Left justify (otherwise right justify)
'#'			×		Always include the (hexa)decimal point
'+'					Always include the sign
' '					(space) Leading space for positive values
'0'					Use zero-padding (else spaces)
','	×			×	Include grouping separators
'('				×	Enclose negative values in parentheses

As with the integer conversions, you cannot use + and space together, nor can you use – and 0 together. If either of 0 or – is given then a width must be given.

22.1.4 Character Conversions

The character conversions apply to argument types of `byte`, `short`, and `char`, together with `int` provided that the `int` value represents a valid Unicode code point (otherwise `IllegalFormatCodePointException` is thrown).

The conversion indicator for characters is `c` or `C` and formats the argument as a Unicode character.

A width value specifies the minimum number of characters to output, with spaces used to pad the output as necessary. No precision value may be supplied. The only applicable flag is – to left-justify the output. If the – flag is given then a width must be given.

22.1.5 General Conversions

There are three general conversions that are unrelated but that are not numeric or character conversions, so we describe them together. They apply to an argument of any type.

The `b` and `B` conversions are boolean conversions. If the argument is `null` then the output is the string `"false"`. If the argument is a `boolean` then the output is either the string `"true"` or the string `"false"` depending on the argument's value, otherwise the output is the string `"true"`.

The `h` and `H` conversions are hash code conversions. If the argument is `null` then the output is the string `"null"`. Otherwise, the output is the string obtained by passing the object's `hashCode` result to `Integer.toHexString`.

The `s` and `S` conversions are string conversions. If the argument is `null` then the output is the string `"null"`. Otherwise, if the argument implements the `Formattable` interface (see next section) then its `formatTo` method is invoked to produce a customized output; otherwise, the output is the result of invoking `toString` on the argument. The `#` flag can be passed only to a `Formattable` argument, and its effect is determined by the object.

For all the general conversions, the width specifies the minimum number of characters, while the precision indicates the maximum. Spaces will be used to pad the output to the minimum width if necessary. The precision is applied first so if it is smaller than the width, the output will be truncated to that maximum size. The only flag applicable is the – flag to left-justify the output. If the – flag is given then a width must be given.

22.1.6   Custom Formatting

A class can support custom formatting by implementing the `Formattable` inter-face, which defines the single method `formatTo`. If an instance of that class is passed as an argument for a string conversion (s or S) then its `formatTo` method will be invoked, passing the current formatter as an argument.

public void **formatTo(Formatter formatter, int flags, int width,**
  int precision)

> Outputs the representation of the current object by appending the desired text to the destination of the given formatter, obtained from its `out` method (see Section 22.1.8 on page 631). The `flags`, `width`, and `precision` argu-ments contain the flags, width, and precision values that were used in the string conversion format specifier. If no width or precision was given, then −1 is passed. The flags are encoded as a bit mask from the constants of the `FormattableFlags` class. Only two flags are supported: LEFT_JUSTIFY, which indicates the − flag for left-justification, and ALTERNATE, which indi-cates the # flag. Each `Formattable` class is free to define what ALTERNATE means.

Additionally, the flag value encodes whether the conversion indicator was lowercase or uppercase using the `FormattableFlags.UPPERCASE` constant. You can test whether a flag is set by ANDing the `flags` value with the desired constant and seeing if the result is non-zero.

By implementing `Formattable` a class can provide greater flexibility in how it represents itself textually, compared to the fixed output of the `toString` method. For example, it can use a long or short form, depending on the width and precision that were supplied; or it can adapt itself to the locale used by the format-ter—see page 632.

22.1.7   Format Exceptions

If any errors occur while processing a format string with a given set of arguments, an exception that is a subclass of `IllegalFormatException` will be thrown. The types of exception you can encounter are

- `DuplicateFormatFlagsException`—A flag was used more than once.
- `FormatFlagsConversionMismatchException`—A flag was incompatible with the conversion.
- `IllegalFormatCodePointException`—An integer value was passed that was not a valid Unicode codepoint.

- `IllegalFormatConversionException`—The argument was the wrong type for the conversion.

- `IllegalFormatFlagsException`—The combination of flags was invalid.

- `IllegalFormatPrecisionException`—The precision value was invalid, or the conversion does not support a precision value.

- `IllegalFormatWidthException`—The width value was invalid, or the conversion does not support a width value.

- `MissingFormatArgumentException`—No argument was supplied in the position expected by a conversion modifier.

- `MissingFormatWidthException`—No width was specified when it was required.

- `UnknownFormatConversionException`—A format's conversion indicator was not known.

- `UnknownFormatFlagsExceptions`—An unknown flag was given.

22.1.8 The `Formatter` Class

A `Formatter` object is always associated with some object that is the destination for the formatted text produced by the formatter. By default the destination is a `StringBuilder`. The other destination objects that can be passed to the various constructors are

- An arbitrary `Appendable` object. This is any object to which characters or `CharSequence` objects can be appended—see page 332 for the methods defined by `Appendable`.

- A file, specified either as a `File` object or a string representing the file name

- An `OutputStream`

The constructors for the byte-oriented destinations (files and output streams) either work with the platform's default encoding or take an additional string parameter that represents the character set encoding name to use. An additional constructor takes a `PrintStream` as a destination, but only the default platform encoding is used.

`Formatter` supports localization (see Chapter 24) and for each type of destination there is an additional constructor that takes a `Locale` object with which the formatter should work. If you do not specify a locale to the constructor, the default locale is used. The locale being used is returned by the `locale` method.

The destination of a `Formatter` object can be obtained from the `out` method, which returns an `Appendable` object.

If writing to the destination object could throw an `IOException`, then the last `IOException` to occur (if any) can be obtained from the `ioException` method.

`Formatter` implements `Closeable` and `Flushable`. If `close` or `flush` are invoked, then the destination is also closed or flushed if it too implements `Closeable` or `Flushable`. Once a formatter has been closed the only method that can be invoked is `ioException`; all others throw `FormatterClosedException`.

The primary method of `Formatter` is, of course, `format`:

`public Formatter` **`format(String format, Object... args)`**
> Formats the given arguments according to the given format string and writes them through to the destination object. The current `Formatter` object is returned, allowing `format` invocations to be chained together.

`public Formatter` **`format(Locale loc, String format, Object... args)`**
> Like the above `format` method, but uses the specified locale instead of the one from the current `Formatter`.

The `Formatter` class's support of localized output is restricted to a subset of the numeric conversions (and the date/time conversions discussed in Chapter 24). The localized numeric conversions are the integer decimal conversion (d) and the three main floating-point conversions (e, f, g and their uppercase counterparts). For these conversions, digit characters are taken from the active locale, and the correct sign characters, decimal point character, and grouping character (for the , flag) are also taken from the locale. Similarly, if zero-padding is requested the zero character is that defined by the locale. The `NumberFormat` class described in Chapter 24, on page 710, provides more extensive formatting capabilities for localized numbers.

Exercise 22.1: Write a method that takes an array of floating-point values and a number indicating how many columns to use, and prints the array contents. Try to ensure that the entries in each column line up neatly. Assume a line is 80 characters wide.

22.2 `BitSet`

The `BitSet` class provides a way to create a bit vector that grows dynamically. In effect, a bit set is a vector of `true` or `false` bits indexed from 0 to `Integer.MAX_VALUE`, all of them initially `false`. These bits can be individually set, cleared, or retrieved. `BitSet` uses only sufficient storage to hold the highest index bit that has been set—any bits beyond that are deemed to be `false`.

Methods that take indices into the set throw `IndexOutOfBoundsException` if a supplied index is negative or, where relevant, if the `from` index is greater than the `to` index.

There are two constructors for `BitSet`:

`public` **`BitSet(int size)`**

> Creates a new bit set with enough initial storage to explicitly represent bits indexed from 0 to `size-1`. All bits are initially `false`.

`public` **`BitSet()`**

> Creates a new bit set with a default amount of initial storage. All bits are initially `false`.

There are four methods for dealing with individual bits.

`public void` **`set(int index)`**

> Sets the bit specified by `index` to `true`.

`public void` **`clear(int index)`**

> Sets the bit specified by `index` to `false`.

`public void` **`flip(int index)`**

> Sets the bit specified by `index` to the complement of its current value—`true` becomes `false`, and `false` becomes `true`.

`public boolean` **`get(int index)`**

> Returns the value of the bit specified by `index`.

A second overloaded form of each of the above methods works on a range of bits. These overloads take a `from` index and a `to` index and either sets, clears, flips, or returns all bits in the range, starting with `from` and up to but not including `to`. For `get`, the values are returned as a new `BitSet`. A third overload of `clear` takes no arguments and clears the entire set to `false`. A second variant of the `set` method takes both the index (or range) and a boolean value to apply to the bits. This makes it easier for you to change bits arbitrarily without having to work out whether you need to invoke `set` or `clear`.

You can find the index of the next clear or set bit, that is at or after a given index, using the `nextClearBit` and `nextSetBit` methods. If there is no next set bit from that index then −1 is returned.[1]

Other methods modify the current bit set by applying bitwise logical operations using the bits from another bit set:

---

[1]   The only time there can be no next clear bit is if the bit at index `Integer.MAX_VALUE` has been set—something that is extremely unlikely in practice because the bit set could use a huge amount of memory.

```
public void and(BitSet other)
```
Logically ANDs this bit set with other and changes the value of this set to the result. The resulting value of a bit in this bit set is true only if it was originally true and the corresponding bit in other is also true.

```
public void andNot(BitSet other)
```
Clears all bits in this bit set that are set in other. The resulting value of a bit in this bit set is true only if it was originally true and the corresponding bit in other is false.

```
public void or(BitSet other)
```
Logically ORs this bit set with other and changes the value of this set to the result. The resulting value of a bit in this bit set is true only if it was originally true or the corresponding bit in other is true.

```
public void xor(BitSet other)
```
Logically XORs this bit set with other and changes the value of this set to the result. The resulting value of a bit in this bit set is true only if it has a value different from the corresponding bit in other.

You can also ask whether the current bit set has any true bits in common with a second bit set by using the intersects method.

The remaining methods are

```
public int cardinality()
```
Returns the number of bits in this bit set that are true.

```
public int size()
```
Returns the number of bits actually stored in this BitSet. Setting a bit index greater than or equal to this value may increase the storage used by the set.

```
public int length()
```
Returns the index of the highest set bit in this BitSet plus one.

```
public boolean isEmpty()
```
Returns true if this bit set has no true bits.

```
public int hashCode()
```
Returns a hash code for this set based on the values of its bits. Do not change values of bits while a BitSet is in a hash map, or the set will be misplaced.

```
public boolean equals(Object other)
```
Returns true if all the bits in other are the same as those in this set.

Here is a class that uses a BitSet to mark which characters occur in a string. Each position in the bit set represents the numerical value of a character: The 0th position represents the null character (\u0000), the 97th bit represents the character a, and so on. The bit set can be printed to show the characters that it found:

```
public class WhichChars {
    private BitSet used = new BitSet();

    public WhichChars(String str) {
        for (int i = 0; i < str.length(); i++)
            used.set(str.charAt(i));    // set bit for char
    }

    public String toString() {
        String desc = "[";
        for (int i = used.nextSetBit(0);
             i >= 0;
             i = used.nextSetBit(i+1) ) {
            desc += (char) i;
        }
        return desc + "]";
    }
}
```

If we pass `WhichChars` the string "Testing 1 2 3" we get back

```
[ 123Teginst]
```

which shows each of the characters (including the spaces) that were used in the input string, and which, incidentally, have now been sorted into numerical order. Notice how easy it is to iterate through all the set bits in a bit set.

Exercise 22.2: The `WhichChars` class has a problem marking characters near the top of the Unicode range because the high character values will leave many unused bits in the lower ranges. Use a `HashSet` to solve this problem by storing `Character` objects for each character seen.

Exercise 22.3: Now use a `HashMap` to store a `BitSet` object for each different top byte (high 8 bits) encountered in the input string, with each `BitSet` storing the low bytes that have been seen with the particular high byte.

22.3 Observer/Observable

The `Observer/Observable` types provide a protocol for an arbitrary number of `Observer` objects to watch for changes and events in any number of `Observable` objects. An `Observable` object subclasses the `Observable` class, which provides methods to maintain a list of `Observer` objects that want to know about changes in the `Observable` object. All objects in the "interested" list must implement the `Observer` interface. When an `Observable` object experiences a noteworthy change or an event that `Observer` objects may care about, the `Observable` object invokes its `notifyObservers` method, which invokes each `Observer` object's `update` method.

The `Observer` interface consists of a single method:

public void **update(Observable obj, Object arg)**

> This method is invoked when the `Observable` object `obj` has a change or an event to report. The `arg` parameter is a way to pass an arbitrary object to describe the change or event to the observer.

The `Observer`/`Observable` mechanism is designed to be general. Each `Observable` class is left to define the circumstances under which an `Observer` object's `update` method will be invoked. The `Observable` object maintains a "changed" flag which subclass methods use to indicate when something of interest has occurred.

protected void **setChanged()**

> Marks this object as having been changed—`hasChanged` will now return `true`—but does not notify observers.

protected void **clearChanged()**

> Indicates that this object is no longer changed or has notified all observers of the last change—`hasChanged` will now return `false`.

public boolean **hasChanged()**

> Returns the current value of the "changed" flag.

When a change occurs, the `Observable` object should invoke its `setChanged` method and then notify its observers with one of the following methods:

public void **notifyObservers(Object arg)**

> Notifies all `Observer` objects in the list that something has happened, and then clears the "changed" flag. For each observer in the list, its `update` method is invoked with this `Observable` object as the first argument and `arg` as the second.

public void **notifyObservers()**

> Equivalent to `notifyObservers(null)`.

The following `Observable` methods maintain the list of `Observer` objects:

public void **addObserver(Observer o)**

> Adds the observer `o` to the observer list if it's not already there.

public void **deleteObserver(Observer o)**

> Deletes the observer `o` from the observer list.

```
public void deleteObservers()
```
Deletes all Observer objects from the observer list.

```
public int countObservers()
```
Returns the number of observers in the observer list.

The methods of Observable use synchronization to ensure consistency when concurrent access to the object occurs. For example, one thread can be trying to add an observer while another is trying to remove one and a third is effecting a change on the Observable object. While synchronization is necessary for maintaining the observer list and making changes to the "changed" flag, no synchronization lock should be held when the update method of the observers is invoked. Otherwise it would be very easy to create deadlocks. The default implementation of notifyObservers takes a synchronized snapshot of the current observer list before invoking update. This means that an observer that is removed while notifyObservers is still in progress will still be notified of the last change. Conversely, an observer that is added while notifyObservers is still in progress will not be notified of the current change. If the Observable object allows concurrent invocations of methods that generate notifications, it is possible for update to be called concurrently on each Observer object. Consequently, Observer objects must use appropriate synchronization within update to ensure proper operation.

The default implementation of notifyObservers uses the invoking thread to invoke update on each observer. The order in which observers are notified is not specified. A subclass could specialize notifyObservers to use a different threading model, and/or to provide ordering guarantees.

The following example illustrates how Observer/Observable might be used to monitor users of a system. First, we define a Users class that is Observable:

```
import java.util.*;

public class Users extends Observable {
    private Map<String, UserState> loggedIn =
        new HashMap<String, UserState>();

    public void login(String name, String password)
        throws BadUserException
    {
        if (!passwordValid(name, password))
            throw new BadUserException(name);

        UserState state = new UserState(name);
        loggedIn.put(name, state);
        setChanged();
```

```
            notifyObservers(state);
    }

    public void logout(UserState state) {
        loggedIn.remove(state.name());
        setChanged();
        notifyObservers(state);
    }

    // ...
}
```

A `Users` object stores a map of users who are logged in and maintains `UserState` objects for each login. When someone logs in or out, all `Observer` objects will be passed that user's `UserState` object. The `notifyObservers` method sends messages only if the state changes, so you must invoke `setChanged` on `Users`; otherwise, `notifyObservers` would do nothing.

Here is how an `Observer` that maintains a constant display of logged-in users might implement `update` to watch a `Users` object:

```
import java.util.*;

public class Eye implements Observer {
    Users watching;

    public Eye(Users users) {
        watching = users;
        watching.addObserver(this);
    }
    public void update(Observable users, Object whichState)
    {
        if (users != watching)
            throw new IllegalArgumentException();

        UserState state = (UserState) whichState;
        if (watching.loggedIn(state))    // user logged in
            addUser(state);              // add to my list
        else
            removeUser(state);           // remove from list
    }
    // ...
}
```

Each Eye object watches a particular Users object. When a user logs in or out, Eye is notified because it invoked the Users object's addObserver method with itself as the interested object. When update is invoked, it checks the correctness of its parameters and then modifies its display depending on whether the user in question has logged in or out.

The check for what happened with the UserState object is simple here. You could avoid it by passing an object describing what happened and to whom instead of passing the UserState object itself. Such a design makes it easier to add new actions without breaking existing code.

The Observer/Observable mechanism is a looser, more flexible analogue to the wait/notify mechanism for threads described in "wait, notifyAll, and notify" on page 354. The thread mechanism ensures that synchronized access protects you from undesired concurrency. The observation mechanism enables any relationship to be built between two participants, whatever the threading model. Both patterns have producers of information (Observable and the invoker of notify) and consumers of that information (Observer and the invoker of wait), but each one fills a different need. Use wait/notify when you design a thread-based mechanism, and use Observer/Observable when you need something more general.

Exercise 22.4: Provide an implementation of the Attributed interface that uses Observer/Observable to notify observers of changes.

22.4 Random

The Random class creates objects that manage independent sequences of pseudo-random numbers. If you don't care what the sequence is and want it as a sequence of double values, use the method java.lang.Math.random, which creates a single Random object the first time it is invoked and returns pseudorandom numbers from that object—see Section 22.9 on page 657. You can gain more control over the sequence (for example, the ability to set the seed) by creating a Random object and getting values from it.

public **Random()**

Creates a new random number generator. Its seed will be initialized to a value based on the current time.

public **Random(long seed)**

Creates a new random number generator using the specified seed. Two Random objects created with the same initial seed will return the same sequence of pseudorandom numbers.

`public void` **`setSeed(long seed)`**
> Sets the seed of the random number generator to `seed`. This method can be invoked at any time and resets the sequence to start with the given seed.

`public boolean` **`nextBoolean()`**
> Returns a pseudorandom uniformly distributed `boolean` value.

`public int` **`nextInt()`**
> Returns a pseudorandom uniformly distributed `int` value between the two values `Integer.MIN_VALUE` and `Integer.MAX_VALUE`, inclusive.

`public int` **`nextInt(int ceiling)`**
> Like `nextInt()`, but returns a value that is at least zero and is less than the value `ceiling`. Use this instead of using `nextInt()` and `%` to get a range. If `ceiling` is negative, an `IllegalArgumentException` is thrown.

`public long` **`nextLong()`**
> Returns a pseudorandom uniformly distributed `long` value between `Long.MIN_VALUE` and `Long.MAX_VALUE`, inclusive.

`public void` **`nextBytes(byte[] buf)`**
> Fills the array `buf` with random bytes.

`public float` **`nextFloat()`**
> Returns a pseudorandom uniformly distributed `float` value between `0.0f` (inclusive) and `1.0f` (exclusive).

`public double` **`nextDouble()`**
> Returns a pseudorandom uniformly distributed `double` value between `0.0` (inclusive) and `1.0` (exclusive).

`public double` **`nextGaussian()`**
> Returns a pseudorandom Gaussian-distributed `double` value with mean of 0.0 and standard deviation of 1.0.

All the next*Type* methods use the protected method `next`. The `next` method takes an `int` that represents the number of random bits to produce (between 1 and 32) and returns an `int` with that many bits. These random bits are then converted to the requested type. For example, `nextInt` simply returns `next(32)`, while `nextBoolean` returns `true` if `next(1)` is not zero, else it returns `false`.

You can safely use `Random` from multiple threads.

The `Random` class specifies the algorithms to be used to generate the pseudo-random numbers but permits different algorithms to be used provided the general contract of each method is adhered to. The basic algorithm (a linear congruential generator) is defined in the `next` method and is used for all other methods except `nextGaussian`. You can create your own random number generator by overriding the `next` method to provide a different generating algorithm.

Exercise 22.5: Given a certain number of six-sided dice, you can calculate the theoretical probability of each possible total. For example, with two six-sided dice, the probability of a total of seven is one in six. Write a program that compares the theoretical distribution of sums for a given number of six-sided dice with the actual results over a large number of "rolls" using Random to generate numbers between one and six. Does it matter which of the number-generating methods you use?

Exercise 22.6: Write a program that tests nextGaussian, displaying the results of a large number of runs as a graph (a bar chart of * characters will do).

22.5 Scanner

The Scanner class will help you read files of formatted data, such as those you might generate from a method that used printf. It uses regular expressions to locate the desired data, and parsers to convert them into known types. For example, it knows how to use localized number parsing to read in values that humans might type (such as "20,352").

Many of the methods of Scanner can take a pattern to indicate how the scanner should match input. These methods all have two overloaded forms: One takes the pattern as a String and the other takes it as a java.util.regex.Pattern. When we say that a method takes a pattern, you should infer from this that there are two variants of the method as just described. Supplying a pattern as a string may require that it be compiled each time (using Pattern.compile), so if a pattern is to be reused it may be more efficient to use a Pattern object directly. See Section 13.3 on page 321 for a refresher on regular expression patterns.

There are two primary approaches to using Scanner, although they can be reasonably intermixed as desired, with care. The first is to use it to read a stream of values. The second is line-oriented.

22.5.1 Stream of Values

When reading input as a stream of values, you simply ask Scanner to return the next value in the stream. The scanner determines the next value by first skipping over any delimiter characters in the input (which by default matches whitespace) and examining the input up to the next delimiter. For example, the following code is a rewrite of the sumStream example from page 533:

```
static double sumStream(Readable source) throws IOException {
    Scanner in = new Scanner(source);
    double result = 0.0;
```

```
while (in.hasNext()) {
    if (in.hasNextDouble())
        result += in.nextDouble();
    else
        in.next();
}
IOException ex = in.ioException();
if (ex != null)
    throw ex;

return result;
}
```

You can iterate through the input one token at a time, asking if the next token is a string, int, or double value, and so forth, and storing it into a variable of the appropriate type.[2] In contrast to StreamTokenizer, Scanner can produce primitive values other than just double, and it recognizes numbers in a range of formats, not just the common decimal format. (Essentially, how ever Formatter— see page 624—might write out a number as a string, Scanner can read it back as a number.)

A scanner needs a source of characters to read from, which in the most general case is represented by an object that implements the java.lang.Readable interface—this interface defines a single method, read, that takes a java.nio.CharBuffer object into which the characters read from the Readable should be stored. The sumStream method accepts a Readable parameter and passes it to the constructor for Scanner to indicate it should be used as the input source for that scanner. The java.io.Reader class implements Readable, so any of the input character streams can be used as a source for a Scanner object.

The loop continues as long as hasNext indicates that the scanner has another token available. Knowing that there is a token doesn't tell you what kind of token it may be, so we use the hasNextDouble method to ask if the token is a double value. If so, the value is read with nextDouble and added to the sum. Otherwise, the value is read (as a String) with next and ignored. The hasNext and next methods should be familiar to you—they are two of the methods of Iterator. And indeed Scanner implements Iterator<String> so you can easily iterate through the tokens in an input source.[3] The remove method of Scanner throws UnSupportedOperationException.

---

[2] The Scanner class also supports scanning of values into java.math.BigInteger and java.math.BigDecimal objects.

[3] Note that Scanner is an Iterator not an Iterable, so it can not be used with the enhanced for loop. This limitation may be removed in the future.

The `hasNext` method returns `true` if the scanner has another token to return from `next`. For each primitive type except `char`, `hasNextType` asks if the next token is of that type, and if so, `nextType` will return it. For the integer types there are overloads of `hasNextType` and `nextType` that take an `int` radix for the number. For example, `hasNextInt(8)` will return `true` if the next token is a valid octal representation of an `int` value. The default radix of the scanner (initially 10) can be changed with the `useRadix` method, and retrieved from the `radix` method.

The `hasNext` method also has two additional overloads that take a pattern and will return `true` only if the next token matches the given pattern. Similarly, `next` also has two overloads that take a pattern describing the token to return.

All the methods that get the next token operate as follows: Delimiters from the current position to the first non-delimiter are ignored; then the next delimiter is found; if the input between the delimiters matches the pattern then a token has been found and the current position is advanced to the first character after the token. If there is no next token then `NoSuchElementException` is thrown. If the method requires a specific type of token or a token that matches a given radix or pattern, and the next token does not meet those criteria, then `InputMismatchException` is thrown. If an exception is thrown then the position of the scanner is unchanged.

Input sources for scanners can come from several places. There is a constructor that takes a `Readable` character source, one that takes a `String`, and several that take byte sources: `File`, `InputStream` or `java.nio.ReadableByteBuffer`. By default these byte sources will be converted to characters using the platform's default encoding, or you can use a form of the constructor that takes the character set name to use as the encoding.

When the source for a scanner is a file or other input stream, it is possible that when the scanner tries to read the source it will encounter an `IOException`. The scanner methods themselves do not declare or throw the `IOException`. The responsibility for dealing with these potential exceptions falls to you. If the scanner encounters an `IOException` it considers the end of the input source to have been reached—so `hasNext` will return false, and any attempt to take the next token will cause `NoSuchElementException` to be thrown. To determine whether tokenizing of the source ended because of a true end of input or an exception, you can use the `ioException` method. It returns the last `IOException` that was thrown by the underlying source, or `null` if there have been no exceptions. So, as in the example, when the iteration is complete you should check to see that it didn't complete prematurely due to an exception.

A scanner identifies tokens by looking for a delimiter pattern in the input stream of characters. By default the delimiter pattern matches any whitespace, as determined by the `Character.isWhitespace` method. You can set the delimiter to a different pattern with the `useDelimiter` method. The current delimiter pattern is returned as a `Pattern` object from the `delimiter` method. For example, here is a simple method that reads values from a source that is in *comma-separated-values* (CSV) format and returns them in a `List`:

```
public static List<String> readCSV(Readable source)
    throws IOException {
    Scanner in = new Scanner(source);
    in.useDelimiter(",|" +LINE_SEPARATOR_PATTERN);
    List<String> vals = new ArrayList<String>();

    while (in.hasNext())
        vals.add(in.next());

    IOException ex = in.ioException();
    if (ex!= null)
        throw ex;

    return vals;
}
```

Here the delimiter pattern is either a single comma or a line separator, since the values themselves can contain any other characters, including whitespace. The definition of a line separator is documented in the `Pattern` class. To make it easier to read the example, we defined a constant to represent that pattern:

```
static final String LINE_SEPARATOR_PATTERN =
    "\r\n|[\n\r\u2028\u2029\u0085]";
```

The `Scanner` class also provides a `close` method. When you invoke `close` on a scanner, the input source will be closed if it is `Closeable`. Once a scanner has been closed, attempts to invoke any of the scanning operations will result in an `IllegalStateException`. Take care when closing a scanner: The input source may not be yours to close, such as an `InputStreamReader` for `System.in`. As a general rule, don't close a scanner unless you opened its input source.

22.5.2 Scanning Lines

In line mode, the scanner can process a line at a time using the regular expression pattern that you supply. If the line matches the pattern then a `java.util.regex.MatchResult` object can be obtained from the `match` method, from which you can extract the groups the pattern defined. Line matching is done with the `findInLine` method.

```
public String findInLine(Pattern pattern)
```
Attempts to find the given pattern before the next line separator is encountered. The delimiters of the scanner are ignored during this search. If the pattern is found then the scanner advances to the next position after the matching input, and the matching input is returned. If the pattern is not found then `null` is returned and the position of the scanner is unchanged.

Note that if the pattern does not match the entire line then the scanner will be positioned to continue reading the remainder of the current line; and if the pattern starts in the middle of the line, then all preceding input is skipped. As usual a second form of this method takes a `String` representing the pattern.

You can use a scanner's `hasNextLine` and `nextLine` methods to tokenize input a complete line at a time. The `hasNextLine` method returns `true` if there is another line of input in this scanner. This means that between the current position of the scanner and the end of the input there is either a line separator or one or more other characters. The `nextLine` method advances the scanner to the start of the next line and returns all the input that was skipped, excluding the line separator itself.

Consider the example of input that is in comma-separated-value format. This format is often used to export values from a table, where each line in the output represents a row of the table and each value before a comma (or a newline) represents the contents of a cell. With a fixed number of cells per row we can process each line of input as a single entity:

```
static final int CELLS = 4;

public static List<String[]> readCSVTable(Readable source)
        throws IOException {
    Scanner in = new Scanner(source);
    List<String[]> vals = new ArrayList<String[]>();
    String exp = "^(.*),(.*),(.*),(.*)";
    Pattern pat = Pattern.compile(exp, Pattern.MULTILINE);
    while (in.hasNextLine()) {
        String line = in.findInLine(pat);
        if (line != null) {
            String[] cells = new String[CELLS];
            MatchResult match = in.match();
            for (int i = 0; i < CELLS; i++)
                cells[i] = match.group(i+1);
            vals.add(cells);
            in.nextLine();  // skip newline
        }
```

```
        else {
            throw new IOException("input format error");
        }
    }

    IOException ex = in.ioException();
    if (ex!= null)
        throw ex;

    return vals;
}
```

Each line of the input is expected to have four values separated by commas (naturally you'd want to adapt the pattern to account for different numbers of cells in different calls to the method). If the line matches what is expected then each value is extracted from the match group. When a match is found, the newline is left in the input so we use nextLine to skip over it. As we don't know how many lines there will be, we use a List to accumulate the rows.

The use of a pattern in multiline mode is common when scanning line-oriented input. The pattern we used has to match from the start of a line, so we need to include the start-of-line (∧) boundary marker, and that only matches actual lines when the pattern is in multiline mode.

The findWithinHorizon methods operate similarly to findInLine except that they take an additional int parameter that specifies the maximum number of characters to look-ahead through. This "horizon" value is treated as a transparent, non-anchoring bound (see the Matcher class for details—Section 13.3.4 on page 329). A horizon of zero means there is no look-ahead limit.

The skip method can be used to skip over the input that matches a given pattern. As with findInLine and findWithinHorizon, it ignores the scanner's delimiters when looking for the pattern. The skipped input is not returned, rather skip returns the scanner itself so that invocations can be chained together.

Exercise 22.7: Rewrite readCSVTable so that the number of cells of data expected is passed as an argument.

Exercise 22.8: As it stands, readCSVTable is both too strict and too lenient on the input format it expects. It is too strict because an empty line at the end of the input will cause the IOException to be thrown. It is too lenient because a line of input with more than three commas will not cause an exception. Rectify both of these problems.

Exercise 22.9: Referring back to the discussion of efficiency of regular expressions on page 329, devise at least four patterns that will parse a line of comma-separated-values. (Hint: In addition to the suggestion on page 329 also consider the use of greedy versus non-greedy quantifiers.) Write a benchmark program that compares the efficiency of each pattern, and be sure that you test with both short strings between commas and very long strings.

22.5.3 Using Scanner

`Scanner` and `StreamTokenizer` have some overlap in functionality, but they have quite different operational models. `Scanner` is based on regular expressions and so can match tokens based on whatever regular expressions you devise. However, some seemingly simple tasks can be difficult to express in terms of regular expression patterns. On the other hand, `StreamTokenizer` basically processes input a character at a time and uses the defined character classes to identify words, numbers, whitespace, and ordinary characters. You can control the character classes to some extent, but you don't have as much flexibility as with regular expressions. So some things easily expressed with one class are difficult, or at best awkward, to express with the other. For example, the built-in ability to handle comment lines is a boon for `StringTokenizer`, while using a scanner on commented text requires explicit, unobvious handling. For example:

```
Scanner in = new Scanner(source);
Pattern COMMENT = Pattern.compile("#.*");
String comment;
// ...
while (in.hasNext()) {
    if (in.hasNext(COMMENT)) {
        comment = in.nextLine();
    }
    else {
        // process other tokens
    }
}
```

This *mostly* works. The intent is that if we find that the next token matches a comment, then we skip the rest of the line by using `nextLine`. Note that you can't, for example, use a pattern of `"#.*$"` to try to match from the comment character to the end of the line, unless you are guaranteed there are no delimiters in the comment itself.

The above fails to work because it can act like there were two comments when there was only one. Consider a non-comment line followed by a comment line. The input stream might look something like this:

```
token\n# This is a comment line\ntoken2
```

After the last token on the non-comment line is processed, the current input position is just before the line separator that delimited the end of that token. When hasNext is invoked it looks past the line separator and sees that there is something there, so it returns true, leaving the current input position where it was. When hasNext(COMMENT) is invoked, it too ignores the line separator delimiter and sees a pattern on the next line that matches the comment, so it also returns true, leaving the current input position where it was. When nextLine is invoked its job is to advance the current position to the beginning of the next line and return the input that was skipped. The current position is immediately before the line separator, so moving it after the line separator is a very short move and, other than the line separator, no input is skipped. Consequently, nextLine returns an empty string. In our example this is not a problem because we loop around again and match the comment a second time, and this time we remove it properly. However, if your code assumed that the comment itself was gone after nextLine was invoked, then that assumption would be incorrect. We can fix this problem like so:

```
Scanner in = new Scanner(source);
Pattern COMMENT = Pattern.compile("#.*");
String comment;
// ...
while (in.hasNext()) {
    if (in.hasNext(COMMENT)) {
        comment = in.findWithinHorizon(COMMENT, 0);
        in.nextLine();
    }
    else {
        // process other tokens
    }
}
```

Now when hasNext(COMMENT) tells us that there is a comment ahead, we use findWithinHorizon(COMMENT, 0) to skip the line separator, find the actual comment, and return it. We don't need to set any horizon because we know from hasNext that the comment is there. After findWithinHorizon returns the comment, the current position is just before the line separator at the end of the comment line, so we use nextLine to skip over that to the next line.

Another way to get the scanner to skip comments would be to make the comment pattern part of the delimiter pattern. But that is not quite as straightforward as it might sound. We leave that approach as an exercise for the reader.

So skipping comments was trivial with `StreamTokenizer` and quite involved with `Scanner`. In contrast, it is quite simple to change the scanner's delimiter to parse a comma-separated-variable file, but to do the same with `StringTokenizer` requires careful manipulation of the character classes to make the comma a whitespace character and to stop space from being considered a whitespace character. Although relatively simple to state, the API makes it awkward to do and it is conceptually bizarre.

`StreamTokenizer` is very good for working with free-format files such as that used in the attribute reading example on page 533. It read input that consisted of names and values, seperated by whitespace, with an optional = character in between, and stored them into an `Attr` object. The names were simply words, and values could be words or numbers, while the = character was an ordinary character. Pairing of names and values was trivially done, as was detecting a misplaced = character. In contrast, `Scanner` has a lot of trouble dealing with such a flexible format. If you add the = character to the delimiter it isn't too hard to simply treat every two words as a name and value pair. However, because delimiters are ignored, you can't detect misplaced = characters. If you don't make the = character a delimiter, then you have problems when there is no whitespace between the = and the name or value.

If you wanted to store `Attr` objects and read them back with a `Scanner`, you could have more flexibility with the values than if you used `StreamTokenizer`, but the file would be more restricted in format. For example, here is a pair of methods to print and scan attributes:

```
public static void printAttrs(Writer dest, Attr[] attrs) {
    PrintWriter out = new PrintWriter(dest);
    out.printf("%d attrs%n", attrs.length);
    for (int i = 0; i < attrs.length; i++) {
        Attr attr = attrs[i];
        out.printf("%s=%s%n",
                attr.getName(), attr.getValue());
    }
    out.flush();
}

public static Attr[] scanAttrs(Reader source) {
    Scanner in = new Scanner(source);
    int count = in.nextInt();
    in.nextLine();    // skip rest of line
```

```
Attr[] attrs = new Attr[count];
Pattern attrPat =
    Pattern.compile("(.*?)=(.*)$", Pattern.MULTILINE);
for (int i = 0; i < count; i++) {
    in.findInLine(attrPat);
    MatchResult m = in.match();
    attrs[i] = new Attr(m.group(1), m.group(2));
}
return attrs;
}
```

The printAttrs method uses printf to print an attribute in one line, using a = character to separate name from value. The scanAttrs method will read such a file back in. It uses a combination of stream-based and line-based Scanner calls. It first reads back the count as an int and then consumes the rest of the line (the "attrs" from the printf is just for human readability). It then loops getting name/value lines. The pattern used has two capture groups, the first to get the attribute name (using a non-greedy qualifier to get the fewest possible characters before the =) and the second to get the value. These groups are pulled out to create the actual Attr object.

It is no accident that these two methods are paired. Although a Scanner can read many formats of data, it is best used for data formatted in relatively straight-forward ways. Stream mode is useful for reading user input as well, but when you use Scanner for data you should be able to visualize (if not actually write) the printf usage that would generate that data. Scanner is extremely powerful, but that power can be difficult to harness.

Exercise 22.10: Write a method to tokenize input that ignores comments, using the comment pattern as part of the scanner's delimiter.

Exercise 22.11: Write a version of readCSV that uses a StreamTokenizer rather than a Scanner.

Exercise 22.12: Write a version of the attribute reading method from page 533 that uses a Scanner. For this exercise it is only necessary that both versions accept the same correctly formatted input.

Exercise 22.13: Extend your solution to Exercise 22.12 so that misplaced = characters are detected, as in the StreamTokenizer version. (Hint: You might want to try to dynamically change the delimiter pattern between certain tokens.)

22.5.4 Localization

Localization is covered in detail in Chapter 24, but since the `Scanner` class has some support for localization, we cover that briefly here.

By default a scanner works in the current locale, but you can change it with the `useLocale` method, which takes a `Locale` instance. The locale being used by the scanner can be retrieved from the `locale` method.

The type-specific numeric scanning methods, like `hasNextDouble` and `nextInt`, are fully localized. They recognize numerical values that are formed from the numeric digit characters of the locale being used, including the locale-specific decimal separator and grouping separator. In contrast, to use a regular expression to match a local number, you would need to know what the separator characters were so that you could account for them in your pattern. Further, any potentially numeric value that is obtained as a string from a `MatchResult` must be separately converted into a numeric value. To localize such numeric values you must use the parsing methods of the `java.text.NumberFormat` class described in Chapter 24.

22.6 `StringTokenizer`

The `StringTokenizer` class is an older and much simpler cousin of the `Scanner` class, and its use is discouraged in new code—the `String` `split` method (page 314) can be used as an alternative in many cases. A `StringTokenizer` breaks a string into parts, using delimiter characters. A sequence of tokens broken out of a string is, in effect, an ordered enumeration of those tokens, so `StringTokenizer` implements the `Enumeration` interface[4] (see page 617). `StringTokenizer` provides methods that are more specifically typed than `Enumeration`, which you can use if you know you are working on a `StringTokenizer` object. The `StringTokenizer` enumeration is effectively a snapshot because `String` objects are read-only. For example, the following loop breaks a string into tokens separated by spaces or commas:

```
String str = "Gone, and forgotten";
StringTokenizer tokens = new StringTokenizer(str, " ,");
while (tokens.hasMoreTokens())
    System.out.println(tokens.nextToken());
```

By including the comma in the list of delimiter characters in the `StringTokenizer` constructor, the tokenizer consumes commas along with

---

[4] For historical reasons it implements `Enumeration<Object>`, not `Enumeration<String>`.

spaces, leaving only the words of the string to be returned one at a time. The output of this example is

```
Gone
and
forgotten
```

The StringTokenizer class has several methods to control what is considered a word, whether it should understand numbers or strings specially, and so on:

public **StringTokenizer(String str, String delim,**
   boolean returnTokens)
   Constructs a StringTokenizer on the string str, using the characters in delim as the delimiter set. The returnTokens boolean determines whether delimiters are returned as tokens or skipped. If they are returned as tokens, each delimiter character is returned separately.

public **StringTokenizer(String str, String delim)**
   Equivalent to StringTokenizer(str, delim, false), meaning that delimiters are skipped, not returned.

public **StringTokenizer(String str)**
   Equivalent to StringTokenizer(str, " \t\n\r\f"), meaning that the delimiters are the whitespace characters and are skipped.

public boolean **hasMoreTokens()**
   Returns true if more tokens exist.

public String **nextToken()**
   Returns the next token of the string. If there are no more tokens, a NoSuchElementException is thrown.

public String **nextToken(String delim)**
   Switches the delimiter set to the characters in delim and returns the next token. There is no way to set a new delimiter set without getting the next token. If there are no more tokens, a NoSuchElementException is thrown.

public int **countTokens()**
   Returns the number of tokens remaining in the string using the current delimiter set. This is the number of times nextToken can return before it will generate an exception. When you need the number of tokens, this method is faster than repeatedly invoking nextToken because the token strings are merely counted, not constructed and returned.

The methods StringTokenizer implements for the Enumeration interface (hasMoreElements and nextElement) are equivalent to hasMoreTokens and nextToken, respectively.

The delimiter characters are processed individually when `StringTokenizer` looks for the next token, so it cannot identify tokens separated by a multicharacter delimiter. If you need a multicharacter delimiter, use either the `String` class's `split` method or a `Scanner`.

Exercise 22.14: Write a method that will take a string containing floating-point numbers, break it up using whitespace as the delimiter, and return the sum of the numbers.

22.7 Timer and TimerTask

The `Timer` class helps you set up tasks that will happen at some future point, including repeating events. Each `Timer` object has an associated thread that wakes up when one of its `TimerTask` objects is destined to run. For example, the following code will set up a task that prints the virtual machine's memory usage approximately once a second:

```
Timer timer = new Timer(true);
timer.scheduleAtFixedRate(new MemoryWatchTask(), 0, 1000);
```

This code creates a new `Timer` object that will be responsible for scheduling and executing a `MemoryWatchTask` (which you will see shortly). The `true` passed to the `Timer` constructor tells `Timer` to use a daemon thread (see page 369) so that the memory tracing activity will not keep the virtual machine alive when other threads are complete.

The `scheduleAtFixedRate` invocation shown tells `timer` to schedule the task starting with no delay (the 0 that is the second argument) and repeat it every thousand milliseconds (the 1000 that is the third argument). So starting immediately, `timer` will invoke the run method of a `MemoryWatchTask`:

```
import java.util.TimerTask;
import java.util.Date;

public class MemoryWatchTask extends TimerTask {
    public void run() {
        System.out.print(new Date() + ": " );
        Runtime rt = Runtime.getRuntime();
        System.out.print(rt.freeMemory() + " free, ");
        System.out.print(rt.totalMemory() + " total");
```

```
                     System.out.println();
              }
       }
```

MemoryWatchTask extends the abstract TimerTask to define a task that prints the current free and total memory, prefixed by the current time. TimerTask implements the Runnable interface, and its run method is what is invoked by a Timer object when a task is to be run. Because the setup code told timer to execute once a second, the thread used by timer will wait one second between task executions.

TimerTask has three methods:

public abstract void **run()**
> Defines the action to be performed by this TimerTask.

public boolean **cancel()**
> Cancels this TimerTask so that it will never run again (or at all if it hasn't run yet). Returns true if the task was scheduled for repeated execution or was a once-only task that had not yet been run. Returns false if the task was a once-only task that has already run, the task was never scheduled, or the task has previously been cancelled. Essentially, this method returns true if it prevented the task from having a scheduled execution.

public long **scheduledExecutionTime()**
> Returns the scheduled execution time of the most recent actual execution (possibly the in-progress execution) of this TimerTask. The returned value represents the time in milliseconds. This method is most often used inside run to see if the current execution of the task occurred soon enough to warrant execution; if the task was delayed too long run may decide not to do anything.

You can cancel either a single task or an entire timer by invoking the cancel method of TimerTask or Timer. Cancelling a task means that it will not be scheduled in the future. Cancelling a Timer object prevents any future execution of any of its tasks. If you purge a timer then all references to cancelled tasks are removed from its internal queue of tasks to schedule.

Each Timer object uses a single thread to schedule its task executions. You can control whether this thread is a daemon thread by the boolean you specify to the Timer constructor.

public **Timer(boolean isDaemon)**
> Creates a new Timer whose underlying thread has its daemon state set according to isDaemon.

public **Timer()**
> Equivalent to Timer(false).

public **Timer(String name)**
>   Equivalent to Timer(false) but gives the associated thread the given name. This is useful for debugging and monitoring purposes.

public **Timer(String name, boolean isdaemon)**
>   Equivalent to Timer(isDaemon) but gives the associated thread the given name. This is useful for debugging and monitoring purposes.

If the thread is not specified to be a daemon, it will be a user thread. When the timer is garbage collected—which can only happen when all references to it are dropped and no tasks remain to be executed—the user thread will terminate. You should not rely on this behavior since it depends on the garbage collector discovering the unreachability of the timer object, which can happen anytime or never.

There are three kinds of task scheduling. A *once-only* scheduling means that the task will be executed once. A *fixed-delay* scheduling lets you define the amount of time between the start of one execution and the next. The task essentially executes periodically, but any delay in the start of one execution (due to general thread scheduling considerations, garbage collection, or other background activity) causes the next execution to be similarly delayed, so that an execution starts relative to the start of the previous execution. In contrast, a *fixed-rate* scheduling starts each execution relative to the start of the initial execution. If one execution is delayed, there will be a shorter gap before the next execution—possibly no gap, depending on the extent of the delay. You use fixed-delay scheduling when the frequency of tasks is what matters, such as time delays between animation frames in some circumstances. You use fixed-rate scheduling when the absolute time matters, such as alarms or timers.

public void **schedule(TimerTask task, Date time)**
>   Schedules the given task for a once-only execution at the specified time.

public void **schedule(TimerTask task, long delay)**
>   Schedules the given task for a once-only execution after the specified delay (in milliseconds),

public void **schedule(TimerTask task, Date firstTime, long period)**
>   Schedules the given task to execute on a fixed-delay schedule until cancelled, starting at firstTime, executing every period milliseconds.

public void **schedule(TimerTask task, long delay, long period)**
>   Schedules the given task to execute on a fixed-delay schedule until cancelled, starting after the given delay, executing every period milliseconds.

public void **scheduleAtFixedRate(TimerTask task, Date firstTime, long period)**
>   Schedules the given task to execute on a fixed-rate schedule until cancelled, starting at firstTime, executing every period milliseconds.

```
public void scheduleAtFixedRate(TimerTask task, long delay, long
    period)
```
    Schedules the given `task` to execute on a fixed-rate schedule until cancelled, starting after the given `delay`, executing every `period` milliseconds.

Any time you specify that is in the past schedules an immediate execution. All times are in milliseconds—the `Date` class's `getTime` method converts a `Date` to milliseconds (see "Time, Dates, and Calendars" on page 695)—and are approximate because the timer uses `Thread.wait(long)` to schedule future executions, and `wait`, like `sleep`, does not guarantee precision. If a delay is so large that adding it to the current time would cause an overflow, you will get an `IllegalArgumentException`.

A `TimerTask` object can only be scheduled with one `Timer`, and a cancelled `Timer` cannot have any new tasks scheduled. If you attempt to schedule a task that violates either of these restrictions or if you schedule an already cancelled `TimerTask`, you will get an `IllegalStateException`.

A `Timer`'s thread is subject to the usual thread scheduling of a system and takes no steps to influence its priority in any way—it is created with the priority of the thread that created the `Timer`. If you need to boost the priority of a given task when it is executing, set the thread priority within the `run` method. If you want to boost the priority of the `Timer` thread itself, you must create the `Timer` from a thread that already has the desired priority level.

There is no way to ask which tasks are being governed by a particular `Timer`.

22.8 UUID

The `UUID` class provides immutable objects that represent universally unique identifiers. These are 128-bit values that are generated in such a way that they are guaranteed to be unique. There are four different versions of UUID values, generally known as types 1, 2, 3, and 4. You can ask a `UUID` object for its version by using the `version` method.

The usual way to create a type 4 (random) UUID is to use the static factory method `randomUUID`. A type 3 (name-based) UUID can be obtained from the static factory method `nameUUIDFromBytes`, which takes an array of bytes representing the name.

You can directly construct an arbitrary form UUID by supplying two `long` values that represent the upper and lower halves. Of course, there are no guarantees about uniqueness for such a constructed UUID—it is up to you to supply appropriate values. The two halves of a UUID object can be retrieved as `long` values from the `getMostSignificantBits` and `getLeastSignificantBits` methods.

The layout of a UUID is determined by which *variant* is used to implement it. There are four variants: 0, 2, 6, and 7. The UUID class always generates variant 2 UUID values—known as the *Leach-Salz* variant. The details of these variants are not important for this discussion. You can ask a UUID object for its variant by using the `variant` method. Two UUID objects are `equal` only if they have the same variant and 128-bit value.

The `toString` method returns a string representation of a UUID that can be passed into the static `fromString` factory method to get a UUID object.

The remaining methods are applicable only to type 1 (time-based) UUID values, and throw `UnsupportedOperationException` if invoked on other types:

`public long `**`timestamp()`**
> Returns the 60-bit timestamp associated with this UUID.

`public int `**`clockSequence()`**
> Returns the 14-bit clock sequence value associated with this UUID.

`public long `**`node()`**
> Returns the 48-bit node value associated with this UUID. This value relates to the host address of the machine on which this UUID was generated.

22.9 Math and StrictMath

The `Math` class consists of static constants and methods for common mathematical manipulations that use normal floating-point semantics. The `StrictMath` class defines the same constants and methods but always uses specific algorithms. This means that `StrictMath` methods always return the same values across different virtual machines, while `Math` methods are allowed to vary within specified limits. Both classes have two useful `double` constants: `E` approximates *e* (2.7182818284590452354), and `PI` approximates π (3.14159265358979323846). In the following table of the main `Math` and `StrictMath` methods, angles are in radians and all parameters and return values are `double` unless stated otherwise:

Function	Value
`sin(a)`	sine(a)
`cos(a)`	cosine(a)
`tan(a)`	tangent(a)
`asin(v)`	arcsine(v), with v in the range $[-1.0, 1.0]$
`acos(v)`	arccosine(v), with v in the range $[-1.0, 1.0]$
`atan(v)`	arctangent(v), returned in the range $[-\pi/2, \pi/2]$
`atan2(x,y)`	arctangent(x/y), returned in the range $[-\pi, \pi]$
`toRadians(d)`	given d in degrees, returns equivalent angle in radians

Function	Value
`toDegrees(r)`	given *r* in radians, returns equivalent angle in degrees
`exp(x)`	e^x
`sinh(x)`	hyperbolic sine of *x*
`cosh(x)`	hyperbolic cosine of *x*
`tanh(x)`	hyperbolic tangent of *x*
`pow(y,x)`	y^x
`log(x)`	ln *x* (natural log of *x*)
`log10(x)`	base 10 logarithm of *x*
`sqrt(x)`	Square root of *x*
`cbrt(x)`	Cubic root of *x*
`signum(x)`	signum function: 1 if x is positive; −1 if x is negative; 0 if x is zero. There are `double` and `float` versions
`ceil(x)`	Smallest whole number $\geq x$
`floor(x)`	Largest whole number $\leq x$
`rint(x)`	*x* rounded to the nearest integer; if neither integer is nearer, rounds to the even integer
`round(x)`	`(int) floor(x + 0.5)` for `float` *x* `(long) floor(x + 0.5)` for `double` *x*
`abs(x)`	$\lvert x \rvert$ for any numeric type. (the absolute value of the most negative value of an `int` or `long` is itself and therefore negative; that's how two's complement integers work)
`max(x,y)`	Larger of *x* and *y* for any numeric type
`min(x,y)`	Smaller of *x* and *y* for any numeric type
`hypot(x,y)`	Calculates the length of the hypotenuse of a right-angled triangle with sides of length *x* and *y*; that is, it calculates $\sqrt{x^2 + y^2}$ with no intermediate overflow or underflow

The static method `IEEEremainder` calculates remainder as defined by the IEEE 754 standard. The remainder operator %, as described in "Floating-Point Arithmetic" on page 202, behaves in an analogous manner to the remainder operator for integers. This preserves one kind of symmetry: Symmetry around zero. That is, if x%y is z, then changing the sign of either x or y will change only the sign of z, never its absolute value. For example, 7%2.5 is 2.0, and -7%2.5 is -2.0. The IEEE standard defines remainder for x and y differently, preserving symmetry of spacing along the number line—the result of `IEEEremainder(-7, 2.5)` is 0.5. The IEEE remainder mechanism keeps resulting values y units apart, as contrasted with the remainder operator's symmetry around zero. The method is provided because both kinds of remainder are useful.

The static method `random` generates a pseudorandom number r in the range $0.0 \le r < 1.0$. More control over pseudorandom number generation is provided by the `Random` class, as you learned on page 639.

The algorithms used in `StrictMath` are those defined in the FDLIBM "C" math library; if you need a complete understanding of these issues, consult *The Java*™ *Language Specification, Third Edition.*

See "`java.math`—Mathematics" on page 722 for brief coverage of some other math-related classes.

Exercise 22.15: Write a calculator that has all `Math` or `StrictMath` functions, as well as (at least) the basic operators +, -, *, /, and %. (The simplest form is probably a reverse Polish stack calculator because operator precedence is not an issue.)

> *Computers are useless—they can only give you answers.*
> —Pablo Picasso

CHAPTER 23

System Programming

> GLENDOWER: *I can call spirits from the vasty deep.*
> HOTSPUR: *Why, so can I, or so can any man;*
> *But will they come when you do call for them?*
> —William Shakespeare, *King Henry IV, Part 1*

Sometimes your application must interact with the runtime system of the Java virtual machine or the underlying operating system. Such interactions include executing other programs, shutting down the runtime system, and reading and writing the system properties that allow communication between the operating system and the runtime system. Three main classes in `java.lang` provide this access:

- The `System` class provides static methods to manipulate system state. It provides for the reading and writing of system properties, provides the standard input and output streams, and provides a number of miscellaneous utility functions. For convenience, several methods in `System` operate on the current `Runtime` object.

- The `Runtime` class provides an interface to the runtime system of the executing virtual machine. The current `Runtime` object provides access to functionality that is per-runtime, such as interacting with the garbage collector, executing other programs and shutting down the runtime system.

- The `Process` class represents a running process that was created by calling `Runtime.exec` to execute another program, or through direct use of a `ProcessBuilder` object.

These interactions and others can require security to protect your computer's integrity. So we also look at security and how different security policies are enforced in the runtime system. We start, though, by looking at the `System` class.

661

23.1   The System Class

The System class provides static methods to manipulate system state and acts as a repository for system-wide resources. System provides functionality in four general areas:

◆ The standard I/O streams

◆ Manipulating system properties

◆ Utilities and convenience methods for accessing the current Runtime

◆ Security

You'll learn about security in more detail in Section 23.5 on page 677.

23.1.1   Standard I/O Streams

The standard input, output, and error streams are available as static fields of the System class.

public static final InputStream **in**
    Standard input stream for reading data.

public static final PrintStream **out**
    Standard output stream for printing messages.

public static final PrintStream **err**
    Standard error stream for printing error messages. The user can often redirect standard output to a file. But applications also need to print error messages that the user will see even if standard output is redirected. The err stream is specifically devoted to error messages that are not rerouted with the regular output.

For historical reasons, both out and err are PrintStream objects, not PrintWriter objects. See "Print Streams" on page 525 for a discussion about PrintStream and PrintWriter types.

Although each of the standard stream references is declared final, the static methods setIn, setOut, and setErr allow you to redefine the actual streams to which these references are bound (by using native code to bypass the language level restriction of not assigning final variables). These methods are security checked and throw SecurityException if you do not have permission to change the standard streams.

23.1.2 System Properties

System properties define the system environment. They are stored by the System class in a Properties object (see page 620). Property names consist of multiple parts separated by periods. For example, here is a dump of the standard properties on one system:

```
# Standard System Properties
java.version=1.5.0_02
java.vendor=Sun Microsystems Inc.
java.vendor.url=http://java.sun.com/
java.vm.specification.version=1.0
java.vm.specification.vendor=Sun Microsystems Inc.
java.vm.specification.name=Java Virtual Machine Specification
java.vm.version=1.5.0_02-b09
java.vm.vendor=Sun Microsystems Inc.
java.vm.name=Java HotSpot(TM) Client VM
java.specification.version=1.5
java.specification.vendor=Sun Microsystems Inc.
java.specification.name=Java Platform API Specification
java.home=/opt/jdk1.5.0_02/jre
java.class.version=49.0
java.class.path=classes
java.library.path=/opt/jdk1.5.0_02/jre/lib/i386/client:/opt/
jdk1.5.0_02/jre/lib/i386:/opt/jdk1.5.0_02/jre/../lib/i386
java.io.tmpdir=/tmp
java.compiler=
java.ext.dirs=/opt/jdk1.5.0_02/jre/lib/ext
os.name=Linux
os.arch=i386
os.version=2.4.20-31.9smp
file.separator=/
path.separator=:
line.separator=\n
user.name=dholmes
user.home=/home/dholmes
user.dir=/home/dholmes/JPL-4e/src
```

These properties are defined on all systems, although the values will certainly vary. On any given system many more properties may be defined. Some of the standard properties are used by classes in the standard packages. The File class, for example, uses the file.separator property to build up and break down pathnames. You are also free to use properties. The following method looks for a personal configuration file in the user's home directory:

```
public static File personalConfig(String fileName) {
    String home = System.getProperty("user.home");
    if (home == null)
        return null;
    else
        return new File(home, fileName);
}
```

The methods of the System class that deal with the system properties are

public static Properties getProperties()
  Gets the Properties object that defines all system properties.

public static String getProperty(String key)
  Returns the value of the system property named in key.

public static String getProperty(String key, String defaultValue)
  Returns the value of the system property named in key. If it has no definition, it returns defaultValue.

public static String setProperty(String key, String value)
  Sets the value of the system property named in key to the given value, returning the previous value or null if the property was not previously set.

public static String clearProperty(String key)
  Removes the system property named in key, returning the previous value, or null if the property was not previously set.

public static void setProperties(Properties props)
  Sets the Properties object that defines all system properties to be props.

All these methods are security checked and may throw SecurityException. However, being denied access to the entire set of properties does not necessarily mean you will be denied access to individual properties.

Property values are stored as strings, but the strings can represent other types, such as integers or booleans. Methods are available to read properties and decode them into some of the primitive types. These decoding methods are static methods of the primitive type's class. Each method has a String parameter that names the property to retrieve. Some forms have a second parameter (shown as def later) that is the default value to return if no property is found with that name. Methods that lack a default value parameter return an object that contains the default value for the type. All these methods decode values in the standard formats for constants of the primitive type:

```
public static boolean Boolean.getBoolean(String name)
public static Integer Integer.getInteger(String name)
public static Integer
    Integer.getInteger(String name, Integer def)
public static Integer Integer.getInteger(String name, int def)
public static Long Long.getLong(String name)
public static Long Long.getLong(String name, Long def)
public static Long Long.getLong(String name, long def)
```

The getBoolean method is different from the others—it returns a boolean value instead of an object of class Boolean. If the property isn't present, getBoolean returns false; the other methods return null.

The classes Character, Byte, Short, Float, and Double do not have property fetching methods. You can get the value as a string and use the mechanisms described in "String Conversions" on page 316 to convert to the appropriate primitive type.

23.1.3 Utility Methods

The System class also contains a number of utility methods:

```
public static long currentTimeMillis()
```
> Returns the current time in milliseconds since the epoch (00:00:00 GMT, January 1, 1970). The time is returned in a long. Sophisticated applications may require more functionality (see "Time, Dates, and Calendars" on page 695).

```
public static long nanoTime()
```
> Returns the current value, in nanoseconds, of the most precise available system timer. This method can only be used to measure elapsed time and is not related to any notion of calendar time or wall-clock time, and is not relative to the epoch. Although the precision is in nanoseconds, there are no guarantees as to the accuracy.

```
public static void arraycopy(Object src, int srcPos, Object dst,
    int dstPos, int count)
```
> Copies the contents of the source array, starting at src[srcPos], to the destination array, starting at dst[dstPos]. Exactly count elements will be copied. If an attempt is made to access outside either array an IndexOutOfBoundsException is thrown. If the values in the source array are not compatible with the destination array an ArrayStoreException is thrown. "Compatible" means that each object in the source array must be

assignable to the component type of the destination array. For arrays of primitive types, the types must be the same, not just assignable; `arraycopy` cannot be used to copy an array of `short` to an array of `int`. The `arraycopy` method works correctly on overlapping arrays, so it can be used to copy one part of an array over another part. You can, for example, shift everything in an array one slot toward the beginning, as shown in the method `squeezeOut` on page 318.

`public static int` **`identityHashCode(Object obj)`**
Returns a hashcode for `obj` using the algorithm that `Object.hashCode` defines. This allows algorithms that rely on identity hashing to work even if the class of `obj` overrides `hashCode`.

A number of other methods in `System` are convenience methods that operate on the current `Runtime` object—which can be obtained via the static method `Runtime.getRuntime`. For each method an invocation `System.`*`method`* is equivalent to the invocation `Runtime.getRuntime().`*`method;`* consequently, these methods are described as we discuss the `Runtime` class. The methods are

`public static void` **`exit(int status)`**

`public static void` **`gc()`**

`public static void` **`runFinalization()`**

`public static void` **`loadLibrary(String libname)`**

`public static void` **`load(String filename)`**

23.2 Creating Processes

As you have learned, a running system can have many threads of execution. Most systems that host a Java virtual machine can also run multiple programs. You can execute new programs by using one of the `Runtime.exec` convenience methods. Each successful invocation of `exec` creates a new `Process` object that represents the program running in its own *process*. You can use a `Process` object to query the process's state and invoke methods to control its progress. `Process` is an abstract class whose subclasses are defined on each system to work with that system's processes. The two basic forms of `exec` are

`public Process` **`exec(String[] cmdArray)`** `throws IOException`
Runs the command in `cmdArray` on the current system. Returns a `Process` object (described below) to represent it. The string in `cmdArray[0]` is the name of the command, and any subsequent strings in the array are passed to the command as arguments.

public Process **exec(String command)** throws IOException
> Equivalent to the array form of exec with the string command split into an array wherever whitespace occurs, using a default StringTokenizer (see page 651).

The newly created process is called a *child* process. By analogy, the creating process is a *parent* process.

Creating processes is a privileged operation and a SecurityException is thrown if you are not permitted to do it. If anything goes wrong when the system tries to create the process, an IOException is thrown.

23.2.1 Process

The exec methods return a Process object for each child process created. This object represents the child process in two ways. First, it provides methods to get input, output, and error streams for the child process:[1]

public abstract OutputStream **getOutputStream()**
> Returns an OutputStream connected to the standard input of the child process. Data written on this stream is read by the child process as its input.

public abstract InputStream **getInputStream()**
> Returns an InputStream connected to the standard output of the child process. When the child writes data on its output, it can be read from this stream.

public abstract InputStream **getErrorStream()**
> Returns an InputStream connected to the error output stream of the child process. When the child writes data on its error output, it can be read from this stream.

Here, for example, is a method that connects the standard streams of the parent process to the standard streams of the child process so that whatever the user types will go to the specified program and whatever the program produces will be seen by the user:

```
public static Process userProg(String cmd)
    throws IOException
{
    Process proc = Runtime.getRuntime().exec(cmd);
    plugTogether(System.in,  proc.getOutputStream());
    plugTogether(System.out, proc.getInputStream());
```

---

[1] For historical reasons these are byte stream objects instead of character streams. You can use InputStreamReader and OutputStreamWriter to convert the bytes to characters under the system default encoding or another of your choosing.

```
        plugTogether(System.err, proc.getErrorStream());
        return proc;
    }
    // ... definition of plugTogether ...
```

This code assumes that a method plugTogether exists to connect two streams by reading the bytes from one stream and writing them onto the other.

The second way a Process object represents the child process is by providing methods to control the process and discover its termination status:

public abstract int waitFor() throws InterruptedException
Waits indefinitely for the process to complete, returning the value it passed to either System.exit or its equivalent (zero means success, nonzero means failure). If the process has already completed, the value is simply returned.

public abstract int exitValue()
Returns the exit value for the process. If the process has not completed, exitValue throws IllegalThreadStateException.

public abstract void destroy()
Kills the process. Does nothing if the process has already completed. Garbage collection of a Process object does not mean that the process is destroyed; it will merely be unavailable for manipulation.

For example, the following method returns a String array that contains the output of the ls command with the specified command-line arguments. It throws an LSFailedException if the command completed unsuccessfully:

```
    // We have imported java.io.* and java.util.*
    public String[] ls(String dir, String opts)
        throws LSFailedException
    {
        try {
            // start up the command
            String[] cmdArray = { "/bin/ls", opts, dir };
            Process child = Runtime.getRuntime().exec(cmdArray);
            InputStream lsOut = child.getInputStream();
            InputStreamReader r = new InputStreamReader(lsOut);
            BufferedReader in = new BufferedReader(r);

            // read the command's output
            List<String> lines = new ArrayList<String>();
            String line;
            while ((line = in.readLine()) != null)
                lines.add(line);
```

```
        if (child.waitFor() != 0)   // if the ls failed
            throw new LSFailedException(child.exitValue());
        return lines.toArray(new String[lines.size()]);
    } catch (LSFailedException e) {
        throw e;
    } catch (Exception e) {
        throw new LSFailedException(e.toString());
    }
}
```

In the `ls` method we want to treat the output as character data, so we wrap the input stream that lets us read the child's output through an `InputStreamReader`. If we wanted to treat the child's output as a stream of bytes, we could easily do that instead. If the example were written to use the second form of `exec`, the code would look like this:

```
String cmd = "/bin/ls " + opts + " " + dir;
Process child = Runtime.getRuntime().exec(cmd);
```

`Process` is an abstract class. Each implementation of a Java virtual machine may provide one or more appropriate extended classes of `Process` that can interact with processes on the underlying system. Such classes might have extended functionality that would be useful for programming on the underlying system. The local documentation should contain information about this extended functionality.

Note that there is no requirement that the child process execute asynchronously or concurrently with respect to the parent process—in a particular system `exec` could appear to block until the child process terminates.

Exercise 23.1: Write the `plugTogether` method. You will need threads.

23.2.2 Process Environments

Two other forms of `Runtime.exec` enable you to specify a set of *environment variables,* which are system-dependent values that can be queried as desired by the new process. Environment variables are passed to `exec` as a `String` array; each element of the array specifies the name and value of an environment variable in the form *name=value.* The name cannot contain any spaces, although the value can be any string. The environment variables are passed as the second parameter:

```
public Process exec(String[] cmdArray, String[] env)
    throws IOException
public Process exec(String command, String[] env)
    throws IOException
```

The single argument forms of exec are equivalent to passing null for env, which means that the created process inherits the environment variables of its parent.

Environment variables are interpreted in a system-dependent way by the child process's program. They can hold information such as the current user name, the current working directory, search paths, or other useful information that may be needed by a running program. The environment variables mechanism is supported because existing programs on many different kinds of platforms understand them. You can get the environment variables of the current runtime process from the System.getenv method, which returns an unmodifiable map of all the name/ value pairs. Individual values can be retrieved using the System.getenv method which takes a string argument representing the name of the environment variable. The preferred way to communicate between different virtual machine runtimes is with system properties (see page 663). However, this remains the only means of querying and subsequently modifying the environment when executing a non-Java program.

There remain two further forms of exec that allow the initial working directory of the child process to be specified:

```
public Process exec(String[] cmdArray, String[] env, File dir)
    throws IOException

public Process exec(String command, String[] env, File dir)
    throws IOException
```

The child process is given an initial working directory as specified by the path of dir. If dir is null, the child process inherits the current working directory of the parent—as specified by the system property user.dir. The one- and two-argument forms of exec are equivalent to passing null for dir.

23.2.3 ProcessBuilder

The exec methods of Runtime are convenience methods that use the more general ProcessBuilder class. ProcessBuilder encapsulates the three key attributes of an external process: the command, the environment, and the current working directory. You can then start an external process with those attributes by using the ProcessBuilder object's start method—which returns a Process object, just as exec does.

ProcessBuilder has two constructors: One takes a sequence of String objects that represent the command; the other a List<String> that represents the command.

A fourth attribute you can control with ProcessBuilder, but not with exec, is whether the standard error stream of the process is redirected to match the standard output stream of the process. Redirecting the error stream merges all output into one stream, which makes it much easier to correlate when errors occur relative to normal processing.

ProcessBuilder provides methods to query and set each of the four attributes. Each query method simply names the attribute and returns its value—for example, command returns the current command as a List<String>. The other query methods are

public File **directory()**

> Returns the working directory.

public Map<String, String> **environment()**

> Returns a map containing all the environment variable settings

public boolean **redirectErrorStream()**

> Returns true if the standard error stream should be redirected to the standard output stream.

The setting methods have the same names as the query methods, but they take suitable arguments for the attribute and return the ProcessBuilder object. However, there is no method to set the environment. Instead, the map returned by environment can be modified directly and that will affect the environment of any process subsequently started. Once a process has been started, any subsequent changes to the attributes of the ProcessBuilder that started it have no effect on that process.

By returning the ProcessBuilder object different calls to set attributes can be chained together and ultimately start invoked. For example, here is how we could rewrite the ls example, but with the error stream redirected:

```
public String[] ls(String dir, String opts)
    throws LSFailedException
{
    try {
        // start up the command
        Process child =
            new ProcessBuilder("/bin/ls", opts, dir).
                redirectErrorStream(true).start();

        // ... as before ...

}
```

23.2.4 Portability

Any program that uses `exec` or `ProcessBuilder` is not portable across all systems. Not all environments have processes, and those that have them can have widely varying commands and syntax for invoking those commands. Also, because running arbitrary commands raises serious security issues, the system may not allow all programs to start processes. Be very cautious about choosing to do this because it has a strong negative impact on your ability to run your program everywhere.

Exercise 23.2: Write a program that runs `exec` on its command-line arguments and prints the output from the command, preceding each line of output by its line number.

Exercise 23.3: Write a program that runs `exec` on command-line arguments and prints the output from the command, killing the command when a particular string appears in the output.

23.3 Shutdown

Normally, an execution of a virtual machine terminates when the last user thread terminates. A `Runtime` can also be shut down explicitly with its `exit` method, passing an integer status code that can be communicated to the environment executing the virtual machine—zero to indicate successful completion of a task and non-zero to indicate failure. This method abruptly terminates all threads in the runtime system no matter what their state. They are not interrupted or even stopped. They simply cease to exist as the virtual machine itself stops running—no `finally` clauses are executed.

In either case, when `exit` is invoked or the last user thread terminates, the shutdown sequence is initiated. The virtual machine can also be shut down externally, such as by a user interrupting the virtual machine from a keyboard (on many systems by typing control-C) or when the user logs out or the computer is shut down.

All the methods related to shutting down the runtime system are security checked and throw `SecurityException` if you don't have required permissions.

23.3.1 Shutdown Hooks

An application can register a *shutdown hook* with the runtime system. Shutdown hooks are threads that represent actions that should be taken before the virtual machine exits. Hooks typically clean up external resources such as files and network connections.

public void **addShutdownHook(Thread hook)**

Registers a new virtual-machine shutdown hook. If hook has already been registered or has already been started an IllegalArgumentException is thrown.

public boolean **removeShutdownHook(Thread hook)**

Unregisters a previously registered virtual machine shutdown hook. Returns true if hook was registered and has been unregistered. Returns false if hook was not previously registered.

You cannot add or remove shutdown hooks after shutdown has commenced; you will get IllegalStateException if you try.

When shutdown is initiated, the virtual machine will invoke the start method on all shutdown hook Thread objects. You cannot rely on any ordering— shutdown hook threads may be executed before, after, or at the same time as any other shutdown hook thread depending on thread scheduling.

You must be careful about this lack of ordering. Suppose, for example, you were writing a class that stored state in a database. You might register a shutdown hook that closed the database. However, a program using your class might want to register its own shutdown hook that writes some final state information through your class to the database. If your shutdown hook is run first (closing the database), the program's shutdown hook would fail in writing its final state. You can improve this situation by writing your class to reopen the database when needed, although this might add complexity to your class and possibly even some bad race conditions. Or you might design your class so that it doesn't need any shutdown hooks.

It is also important to realize that the shutdown hook threads will execute concurrently with other threads in the system. If shutdown was initiated because the last user thread terminated, then the shutdown hook threads will execute concurrently with any daemon threads in the system. If shutdown was initiated by a call to exit, then the shutdown hook threads will execute concurrently with both daemon and user threads. Your shutdown hook threads must be carefully written to ensure correct synchronization while avoiding potential deadlocks.

Your shutdown hooks should execute quickly. When users interrupt a program, for example, they expect the program to terminate quickly. And when a virtual machine is terminated because a user logs out or the computer is shut down, the virtual machine may be allowed only a small amount of time before it is killed forcibly. Interacting with a user should be done before shutdown, not during it.

23.3.2 The Shutdown Sequence

The shutdown sequence is initiated when the last user thread terminates, the `Runtime.exit` method is invoked, or the external environment signals the virtual machine to shutdown. When shutdown is initiated all the shutdown hook threads are started and allowed to run to completion. If any of these threads fails to terminate the shutdown sequence will not complete. If shutdown was initiated internally the virtual machine will not terminate. If shutdown was signaled from the external environment then failure to shutdown may result in a forced termination of the virtual machine.

If a shutdown hook thread incurs an uncaught exception, no special action is taken; it is handled like any other uncaught exception in a thread. In particular, it does not cause the shutdown process to abort.

When the last shutdown hook thread has terminated, the `halt` method will be invoked. It is `halt` that actually causes the virtual machine to cease running. The `halt` method also takes an integer status as an argument whose meaning is the same as that of `exit`: Zero indicates successful execution of the entire virtual machine. A shutdown hook can invoke `halt` to end the shutdown phase. Invoking `halt` directly—either before or during the shutdown phase—is dangerous since it prevents uncompleted hooks from doing their cleanup. You will probably never be in a situation where invoking `halt` is correct.

If `exit` is called while shutdown is in progress the call to `exit` will block indefinitely. The effect of this on the shutdown sequence is not specified, so don't do this.

In rare circumstances, the virtual machine will abort rather than perform an orderly shutdown. This can happen, for example, if an internal error is detected in the virtual machine that prevents an orderly shutdown—such as errant native code overwriting system data structures. However, the environment hosting the virtual machine can also force the virtual machine to abort—for example, under UNIX systems a SIGKILL signal will force the virtual machine to abort. When the virtual machine is forced to terminate in this way, no guarantees can be made about whether or not shutdown hooks will run.

23.3.3 Shutdown Strategies

Generally, you should let a program finish normally rather than forcibly shut it down with `exit`. This is particularly so with multithreaded programs, where the thread that decides it is time for the program to exit may have no idea what the other threads are doing.

Designing a multithreaded application in a way that makes it safe to exit at arbitrary points in the program is either trivial or extremely complex. It is trivial when none of the threads are performing actions that must be completed—for example, having a thousand threads all trying to solve a numerical problem. It is complex whenever any of the threads perform actions that must be completed.

You can communicate the fact that shutdown is required by writing your threads to respond to the `interrupt` method—as you learned on page 365. You can broadcast the shutdown request to all your threads by invoking the `interrupt` method of the parent `ThreadGroup` of your application. This is no guarantee that a program will terminate, however, because libraries that you have used may have created user threads that do not respond to interrupt requests—the AWT graphics library is one well-known example.

There are two circumstances when you must invoke `exit`: when it is the only way to terminate some of the threads and hence your application, and when your application must return a status code. In both cases you need to delay the call to `exit` until all your application threads have had a chance to terminate cleanly. One way is for the thread initiating the termination to `join` the other threads and so know when those threads have terminated. However, an application may have to maintain its own list of the threads it creates because simply inspecting the `ThreadGroup` may return library threads that do not terminate and for which `join` will not return.

The decision to shutdown a program should be made at a high-level within the application—often within `main` or the `run` method of a thread in the top-level application `ThreadGroup` or in the code that responds to events in a graphical user interface. Methods that encounter errors should simply report those errors via exceptions that allow the high-level code to take appropriate action. Utility code should never terminate an application because it encounters an error—this code lacks knowledge of the application that allows an informed decision to be made; hence, exceptions are used to communicate with higher-level code.

23.4 The Rest of `Runtime`

The `Runtime` class provides functionality in six different areas:

- ◆ Interacting with the garbage collector and querying memory usage
- ◆ Asking for the number of processors available
- ◆ Executing external programs
- ◆ Terminating the current `Runtime`
- ◆ Loading native code libraries
- ◆ Debugging

You have already learned about the first four of these areas (you learned about interacting with the garbage collector via the `gc` and `runFinalization` methods in Chapter 17, on page 452, and about `availableProcessors` in Chapter 14 on page 359). Now is the time to cover the final two.

23.4.1 Loading Native Code

In Chapter 2, you learned about the `native` modifier (see page 74) that can be applied to methods and which signifies that the method's implementation is being provided by native code. At runtime the native code for such methods must be loaded into the virtual machine so that the methods can be executed. The details of this process are system-dependent, but two methods in `Runtime` allow this activity to occur:

public void **loadLibrary(String libname)**
> Loads the dynamic library with the specified library name. The library corresponds to a file in the local file system that is located in some place where the system knows to look for library files. The actual mapping from the library name to a file name is system-dependent.

public void **load(String filename)**
> Loads the file specified by `filename` as a dynamic library. In contrast with `loadLibrary`, `load` allows the library file to be located anywhere in the file system.

Typically, classes that have native methods load the corresponding library as part of the initialization of the class by placing the `load` invocation in a static initialization block. However, the library could be lazily loaded when an actual invocation of the method occurs.

Loading native code libraries is, naturally, a privileged operation, and you will get a `SecurityException` if you do not have the required permissions. If the library cannot be found or if an error occurs while the system tries to load the library, an `UnsatisfiedLinkError` is thrown.

A related method in class `System`—`mapLibraryName`—maps a library name into a system-dependent library name. For example, the library name `"awt"` might map to `"awt.dll"` under Windows, while under UNIX it might map to `"libawt.so"`.

23.4.2 Debugging

Two methods in `Runtime` support the debugging of applications:

public void **traceInstructions(boolean on)**

> Enables or disables the tracing of instructions depending on the value of on. If on is true, this method suggests that the virtual machine emit debugging information for each instruction as it is executed.

public void **traceMethodCalls(boolean on)**

> Enables or disables the tracing of method calls depending on the value of on. If on is true, this method suggests that the virtual machine emit debugging information for each method when it is called.

The format of this debugging information and the file or other output stream to which it is emitted depend on the host environment. Each virtual machine is free to do what it wants with these calls, including ignoring them if the local runtime system has nowhere to put the trace output, although they are likely to work in a development environment.

These methods are fairly low-level debugging tools. Typically, a virtual machine will also support high-level debuggers and profilers through the JVM[TM] Tool Interface (JVMTI); interested readers should consult that specification for more information.

23.5 Security

Security is a very complex issue and a full discussion of it is well beyond the scope of this book—you can read *Inside Java*[TM] *2 Platform Security, Second Edition,* a companion book in this series, for all the details. What we can do, however, is provide an overview of the security architecture and some of its key components. Information on other aspects of security is given in "java.security and Related Packages—Security Tools" on page 732.

To perform a security-checked operation you must have *permission* to perform that operation. Together, all permissions in a system and the way in which they are assigned define the *security policy* for that system. A *protection domain* encloses a set of classes whose instances are granted the same set of permissions and that all come from the same *code source*. Protection domains are established via the class loading mechanism. To enable the security policy of a system and activate the protection domains, you need to install a *security manager.*[2]

---

[2] Some virtual machines allow a startup argument that causes a default security manager to be created and installed. For example, using the JDK[TM] 5.0 you define the system property java.security.manager by passing the argument -Djava.security.manager to the java command.

The classes and interfaces used for security are spread across a number of packages so we use the fully qualified name the first time we introduce a specific class or interface.

23.5.1 The SecurityManager Class

The `java.lang.SecurityManager` class allows applications to implement a security policy by determining, before performing a possibly unsafe or sensitive operation, whether it is being attempted in a security context that allows the operation to be performed. The application can then allow or disallow the operation.

The `SecurityManager` class contains many methods with names that begin with the word "check." These methods are called by various methods in the standard libraries before those methods perform certain potentially sensitive operations, such as accessing files, creating and controlling threads, creating class loaders, performing some forms of reflection, and controlling security itself. The invocation of such a check method typically looks like this:

```
SecurityManager security = System.getSecurityManager();
if (security != null) {
    security.checkXXX(...);
}
```

The security manager is given an opportunity to prevent completion of the operation by throwing an exception. A security manager routine simply returns if the operation is permitted but throws a `SecurityException` if the operation is not permitted.

You can get and set the security manager with methods of the `System` class:

public static void **setSecurityManager(SecurityManager s)**
> Sets the system security manager object. If a security manager already exists this new manager will replace it, provided the existing manager supports replacement and you have permission to replace it; otherwise, a `SecurityException` is thrown.

public static SecurityManager **getSecurityManager()**
> Gets the system security manager. If none has been set `null` is returned and you are assumed to have all permissions.

The security manager delegates the actual security check to an access control object. Each check method just invokes the security manager's `checkPermission` method, passing the appropriate `java.security.Permission` object for the requested action. The default implementation of `checkPermission` then calls

```
java.security.AccessController.checkPermission(perm);
```

If a requested access is allowed, checkPermission returns quietly. If denied, a java.security.AccessControlException (a type of SecurityException) is thrown.

This form of checkPermission always performs security checks within the context of the current thread—which is basically the set of protection domains of which it is a member. Given that a protection domain is a set of classes with the same permissions, a thread can be a member of multiple protection domains when the call stack contains active methods on objects of different classes.

The security manager's getSecurityContext method returns the security context for a thread as a java.security.AccessControlContext object. This class also defines a checkPermission method, but it evaluates that method in the context that it encapsulates, not in the context of the calling thread. This feature is used when one context (such as a thread) must perform a security check for another context. For example, consider a worker thread that executes work requests from different sources. The worker thread has permission to perform a range of actions, but the submitters of work requests may not have those same permissions. When a work request is submitted, the security context for the submitter is stored along with the work request. When the worker thread performs the work, it uses the stored context to ensure that any security checks are performed with respect to the submitter of the request, not the worker thread itself. In simple cases, this might involve invoking the security manager's two-argument checkPermission method, which takes both a Permission object and an AccessControlContext object as arguments. In more general situations, the worker thread may use the doPrivileged methods of AccessController, which you will learn about shortly.

23.5.2 Permissions

Permissions fall into a number of categories, each managed by a particular class, for example:

- File—java.io.FilePermission
- Network—java.net.NetPermission
- Properties—java.util.PropertyPermission
- Reflection—java.lang.reflect.ReflectPermission
- Runtime—java.lang.RuntimePermission
- Security—java.security.SecurityPermission
- Serialization—java.io.SerializablePermission
- Sockets—java.net.SocketPermission

All but `FilePermission` and `SocketPermission` are subclasses of `java.security.BasicPermission`, which itself is an abstract subclass of the top-level class for permissions, which is `java.security.Permission`. `BasicPermission` defines a simple permission based on the name. For example, the `RuntimePermission` with name `"exitVM"` represents the permission to invoke `Runtime.exit` to shutdown the virtual machine. Here are some other basic `RuntimePermission` names and what they represent:

- `"createClassLoader"`—Invoke the `ClassLoader` constructors.

- `"setSecurityManager"`—Invoke `System.setSecurityManager`.

- `"modifyThread"`—Invoke `Thread` methods `interrupt`, `setPriority`, `setDaemon`, or `setName`.

Basic permissions are something you either have or you don't. The names for basic permissions follow the hierarchical naming scheme used for system properties (see page 663). An asterisk may appear at the end of the name, following a `"."` or by itself, to signify a wildcard match. For example: `"java.*"` or `"*"` are valid; `"*java"` or `"x*y"` are not valid.

`FilePermission` and `SocketPermission` are subclasses of `Permission`. These classes can have a more complicated name syntax than that used for basic permissions. For example, for a `FilePermission` object, the permission name is the pathname of a file (or directory) and can cover multiple files by using `"*"` to mean all files in the specified directory and using `"-"` to mean all files in the specified directory as well as all files in all subdirectories.

All permissions can also have an *action list* associated with them that defines the different actions permitted by that object. For example, the action list for a `FilePermission` object can contain any combination of `"read"`, `"write"`, `"execute"`, or `"delete"`, specifying actions that can be performed on the named file (or directory). Many basic permissions do not use the action list, but some, such as `PropertyPermission` do. The name of a `PropertyPermission` is the name of the property it represents and the actions can be `"read"` or `"write"`, which let you invoke `System.getProperty` and `System.setProperty`, respectively, with that property name. For example, a `PropertyPermission` with the name `"java.*"` and action `"read"` allows you to retrieve the values of all system properties that start with `"java."`.

23.5.3 Security Policies

The security policy for a given execution of the runtime system is represented by a `java.security.Policy` object or, more specifically, by a concrete subclass of the abstract `Policy` class. The `Policy` object maintains the sets of permissions that have been assigned to the different protection domains, according to their code source. How the security policy is communicated to the Policy object is a function of the actual implementation of that policy. The default implementation is to use policy files to list the different permissions that are granted to each code source.

For example, a sample policy file entry granting code from the /home/ sysadmin directory read access to the file /tmp/abc is

```
grant codeBase "file:/home/sysadmin/" {
    permission java.io.FilePermission "/tmp/abc", "read";
};
```

To find out how security policies are defined in your local system, consult your local documentation.

Classes loaded by the bootstrap loader are considered to be trusted and do not need explicit permissions set in the security policy. Some virtual machine implementations also support the *standard extensions* mechanism, which allows classes to be identified as trusted by placing them in special locations accessed by the *extensions class loader.* These classes do not need explicit permissions set either.

23.5.4 Access Controllers and Privileged Execution

The AccessController class is used for three purposes:

◆ It provides the basic checkPermission method used by security managers to perform a security check.

◆ It provides a way to create a "snapshot" of the current calling context by using getContext, which returns an AccessControlContext.

◆ It provides a means to run code as *privileged,* thus changing the set of permissions that might otherwise be associated with the code.

We have discussed (to the extent we intend to) the first two of these. In this section we look at what it means to have privileged execution.

A *protection domain* (represented by java.security.ProtectionDomain) encompasses a *code source* (represented by java.security.CodeSource) and the permissions granted to code from that code source, as determined by the security policy currently in effect. A code source extends the notion of a code base (the location classes were loaded from) to include information about the digital certificates associated with those classes. Digital certificates can be used to verify the authenticity of a file and ensure that the file has not been tampered with in any way. Classes with the same certificates and from the same location are placed in the same domain, and a class belongs to one and only one protection domain. Classes that have the same permissions but are from different code sources belong to different domains.

Each applet or application runs in its appropriate domain, determined by its code source. For an applet (or an application running under a security manager) to be allowed to perform a secured action, the applet or application must be granted permission for that particular action. More specifically, whenever a secure action is attempted, all code traversed by the execution thread up to that point must have permission for that action unless some code on the thread has been marked as *privileged*. For example, suppose that access control checking occurs in a thread of execution that has a chain of multiple callers—think of this as multiple method calls that potentially cross the protection domain boundaries. When the `AccessController checkPermission` method is invoked by the most recent caller, the basic algorithm for deciding whether to allow or deny the requested action is as follows:

> If the code for any caller in the call chain does not have the requested permission, an `AccessControlException` is thrown, unless a caller whose code is granted the said permission has been marked as *privileged* and all parties subsequently called by this caller (directly or indirectly) have the said permission.

Marking code as *privileged* enables a piece of trusted code to temporarily enable access to more actions than are directly available to the code that called it. This is necessary in some situations. For example, an application may not be allowed direct access to files that contain fonts, but the system utility to display a document must obtain those fonts on behalf of the user. This requires that the system utility code becomes privileged while obtaining the fonts.

The `doPrivileged` method of `AccessController` take as an argument a `java.security.PrivilegedAction<T>` object whose `run` method defines the code to be marked as privileged. For example, your call to `doPrivileged` can look like the following:

```
void someMethod() {
    // ...normal code here...
    AccessController.doPrivileged(
        new PrivilegedAction<Object>() {
            public Object run() {
                // privileged code goes here, for example:
                System.loadLibrary("awt");
                return null; // nothing to return
```

```
            }
        }
    );
    // ...normal code here...
}
```

The `doPrivileged` method executes the `run` method in privileged mode. Privileged execution is a way for a class with a given permission to temporarily grant that permission to the thread that executes the privileged code. It will not let you gain permissions that you do not already have. The class defining `someMethod` must have the permission `RuntimePermission("loadLibrary.awt")`; otherwise, any thread that invokes `someMethod` will get a `SecurityException`. It is guaranteed that privileges will be revoked after the `PrivilegedAction` object's `run` method returns.

The `PrivilegedAction<T>` interface's single method `run` returns a T object. Another form of `doPrivileged` takes a `PrivilegedExceptionAction<T>` object, whose `run` method also returns T, but which can throw any checked exception. For both of these methods there is a second overloaded form of `doPrivileged` that takes an `AccessControlContext` as an argument and uses that context to establish the permissions that the privileged code should run with.

You should use `doPrivileged` with extreme care and ensure that your privileged sections of code are no longer than necessary and that they perform only actions you fully control. For example, it would be an extreme security risk for a method with, say, all I/O permissions, to accept a `Runnable` argument and invoke its `run` method within a privileged section of code, unless you wouldn't mind if that method removed all the files on your disk.

> *Power corrupts.*
> *Absolute power is kind of neat.*
> —John Lehman, U.S. Secretary of the Navy, 1981–1987

CHAPTER 24

Internationalization and Localization

Nobody can be exactly like me.
Sometimes even I have trouble doing it.
—Tallulah Bankhead

THE credo of "Write once, run anywhere™," means that your code will run in many places where languages and customs are different from yours. With a little care you can write programs that can adapt to these variations gracefully. Keeping your programs supple in this fashion is called *internationalization*. You have several tools for internationalizing your code. Using internationalization tools to adapt your program to a specific locale—such as by translating messages into the local language—is called *localization*.

The first tool is inherent in the language: Strings are in Unicode, which can express almost any written language on our planet. Someone must still translate the strings, and displaying the translated text to users requires fonts for those characters. Still, having Unicode is a big boost for localizing your code.

The nexus of internationalization and localization is the *locale*, which defines a "place." A place can be a language, culture, or country—anything with an associated set of customs that requires changes in program behavior. Each running program has a default locale that is the user's preferred place. It is up to each program to adapt to a locale's customs as best it can. The locale concept is represented by the `Locale` class, which is part of the `java.util` package.

Given a locale, several tools can help your program behave in a locally comprehensible fashion. A common pattern is for a class to define the methods for performing *locale-sensitive* operations. A generic "get instance" static method of this class returns an object (possibly of a subclass) suitable for the default locale. The class will also provide an overload of each "get instance" method that takes a locale argument and returns a suitable object for a particular locale. For example, by invoking the class's `getInstance` methods, you can get an appropriate `java.util.Calendar` object that works with the user's preferred dates and times. The returned `Calendar` object will understand how to translate system time into dates using the customs of the default locale. If the user were Mexican, an object that was a `Calendar` adapted to Mexican customs could be returned. A Chinese user might get an object of a different subclass that worked under the Chinese calendar customs.

If your program displays information to the user, you will likely want to localize the output: Saying "That's not right" to someone who doesn't understand English is probably pointless, so you would like to translate (localize) the message for speakers in other locales. The resource bundle mechanisms help you make this possible by mapping string keys to arbitrary resources. You use the values returned by a resource bundle to make your program speak in other tongues—instead of writing the literal message strings in your code, you look up the strings from a resource bundle by string keys. When the program is moved to another locale, someone can translate the messages in the resource bundle and your program will work for that new locale without your changing a line of code.

The classes described in this chapter come mostly from the package `java.util`. There are occasional brief discussions of classes in the text internationalization and localization package `java.text`, with an overview of some of its capabilities in Section 24.6 on page 708, but a full discussion on this subject is outside the scope of this book.

24.1 Locale

A `java.util.Locale` object describes a specific place—cultural, political, or geographical. Using a locale, objects can *localize* their behavior to a user's expectations. An object that does so is called *locale-sensitive*. For example, date formatting can be localized by using the locale-sensitive `DateFormat` class (described later in this chapter), so the date written in the United Kingdom as `26/11/72` would be written `26.11.72` in Iceland, `11/26/72` in the United States, or `72.26.11` in Latvia.

A single locale represents issues of language, country, and other traditions. There can be separate locales for U.S. English, U.K. English, Australian English, Pakistani English, and so forth. Although the language is arguably in common for these locales, the customs of date, currency, and numeric representation vary.

Your code will rarely get or create `Locale` objects directly but instead will use the default locale that reflects the user's preference. You typically use this locale implicitly by getting resources or resource bundles as shown with other locale-sensitive classes. For example, you get the default calendar object like this:

```
Calendar now = Calendar.getInstance();
```

The `Calendar` class's `getInstance` method looks up the default locale to configure the calendar object it returns. When you write your own locale-sensitive classes, you get the default locale from the static `getDefault` method of the `Locale` class.

If you write code that lets a user select a locale, you may need to create `Locale` objects. There are three constructors:

public **Locale(String language, String country, String variant)**
>   Creates a `Locale` object that represents the given language and country, where `language` is the two-letter ISO 639 code for the language (such as `"et"` for Estonian) and `country` is the two-letter ISO 3166 code for the country (such as `"KY"` for Cayman Islands). "Further Reading" on page 755 lists references for these codes. The `variant` can specify anything, such as an operating environment (such as `"POSIX"` or `"MAC"`) or company or era. If you specify more than one variant, separate the two with an underscore. To leave any part of the locale unspecified, use `""`, an empty string—not `null`.

public **Locale(String language, String country)**
>   Equivalent to `Locale(language, country, "")`.

public **Locale(String language)**
>   Equivalent to `Locale(language, "", "")`.

The language and country can be in any case, but they will always be translated to lowercase for the language and uppercase for the country to conform to the governing standards. The variant is translated into uppercase.

The `Locale` class defines static `Locale` objects for several well-known locales, such as `CANADA_FRENCH` and `KOREA` for countries, and `KOREAN` and `TRADITIONAL_CHINESE` for languages. These objects are simply conveniences and have no special privileges compared to any `Locale` object you may create.

The static method `setDefault` changes the default locale. The default locale is shared state and should always reflect the user's preference. If you have code that must operate in a different locale, you can specify that locale to locale-sensitive classes either as an argument when you get resources or on specific operations. You should rarely need to change the default locale.

`Locale` provides methods for getting the parts of the locale description. The methods `getCountry`, `getLanguage`, and `getVariant` return the values defined during construction. These are terse codes that most users will not know. These methods have "display" variants—`getDisplayCountry`, `getDisplayLanguage`, and `getDisplayVariant`—that return human-readable versions of the values.

The method `getDisplayName` returns a human-readable summary of the entire locale description, and `toString` returns the terse equivalent, using underscores to separate the parts. These "display" methods return values that are localized according to the default locale.

You can optionally provide a `Locale` argument to any of the "display" methods to get a description of the given locale under the provided locale. For example, if we print the value of

```
Locale.ITALY.getDisplayCountry(Locale.FRANCE)
```

we get

```
Italie
```

the French name for Italy.

The methods `getISO3Country` and `getISO3Language` return three-character ISO codes for the country and language of the locale, respectively.

24.2 Resource Bundles

When you internationalize code, you commonly have units of meaning—such as text or sounds—that must be translated or otherwise made appropriate for each locale. If you put English text directly into your program, localizing that code is difficult—it requires finding all the strings in your program, identifying which ones are shown to users, and translating them in the code, thereby creating a second version of your program for, say, Swahili users. When you repeat this process for a large number of locales the task becomes a nightmare.

The resource bundle classes in `java.util` help you address this problem in a cleaner and more flexible fashion. The abstract class `ResourceBundle` defines methods to look up resources in a bundle by string key and to provide a parent bundle that will be searched if a bundle doesn't have a key. This inheritance feature allows one bundle to be just like another bundle except that a few resource values are modified or added. For example, a U.S. English bundle might use a U.K. English bundle for a parent, providing replacements for resources that have different spelling. `ResourceBundle` provides the following public methods:

```
public final String getString(String key)
    throws MissingResourceException
```
  Returns the string stored in the bundle under the given key.

```
public final String[] getStringArray(String key)
    throws MissingResourceException
```
  Returns the string array stored in the bundle under the given key.

```
public final Object getObject(String key)
    throws MissingResourceException
```
Returns the object stored in the bundle under the given key.

```
public abstract Enumeration getKeys()
```
Returns an `Enumeration` of the keys understood by this bundle, including all those of the parent.

Each resource bundle defines a set of string keys that map to locale-sensitive resources. These strings can be anything you like, although it is best to make them mnemonic. When you want to use the resource you look it up by name. If the resource is not found a `MissingResourceException` is thrown. The resources themselves can be of any type but are commonly strings, so the *getString* methods are provided for convenience.

The following example shows an internationalized way to rewrite the "Hello, world" example. This internationalized version requires a program called `GlobalHello` and a resource bundle for the program's strings called `GlobalRes`, which will define a set of constants for the localizable strings. First, the program:

```
import java.util.*;

public class GlobalHello {
    public static void main(String[] args) {
        ResourceBundle res =
            ResourceBundle.getBundle("GlobalRes");
        String msg;
        if (args.length > 0)
            msg = res.getString(GlobalRes.GOODBYE);
        else
            msg = res.getString(GlobalRes.HELLO);
        System.out.println(msg);
    }
}
```

The program first gets its resource bundle. Then it checks whether any arguments are provided on the command line. If some are, it says good-bye; otherwise it says hello. The program logic determines which message to display, but the actual string to print is looked up by key (`GlobalRes.HELLO` or `GlobalRes.GOODBYE`).

Each resource bundle is a set of associated classes and property files. In our example, `GlobalRes` is the name of a class that extends `ResourceBundle`, implementing the methods necessary to map a message key to a localized translation of that message. You define classes for the various locales for which you want to localize the messages, naming the classes to reflect the locale. For example, the bundle class that manages GlobalRes messages for the Lingala language would be GlobalRes_ln because "ln" is the two-letter code for Lingala. French would be mapped in GlobalRes_fr, and Canadian French would be GlobalRes_fr_CA, which might have a parent bundle of GlobalRes_fr.

We have chosen to make the key strings constants in the GlobalRes class. Using constants prevents errors of misspelling. If you pass literal strings such as "hello" to getString, a misspelling will show up only when the erroneous getString is executed, and that might not happen during testing. If you use constants, a misspelling will be caught by the compiler (unless you are unlucky enough to accidentally spell the name of another constant).

You find resources by calling one of two static getBundle methods in ResourceBundle: the one we used, which searches the current locale for the best available version of the bundle you name; and the other method, which lets you specify both bundle name and desired locale. A fully qualified bundle name has the form *package.Bundle_la_CO_va,* where *package.Bundle* is the general fully qualified name for the bundle class (such as GlobalRes), *la* is the two-letter language code (lowercase), *CO* is the two-letter country code (uppercase), and *va* is the list of variants separated by underscores. If a bundle with the full name cannot be found, the last component is dropped and the search is repeated with this shorter name. This process is repeated until only the last locale modifier is left. If even this search fails and if you invoked getBundle with a specified locale, the search is restarted with the full name of the bundle for the default locale. If this second search ends with no bundle found or if you were searching in the default locale, getBundle checks using just the bundle name. If even that bundle does not exist, getBundle throws a MissingBundleException.

For example, suppose you ask for the bundle GlobalRes, specifying a locale for an Esperanto speaker living in Kiribati who is left-handed, and the default locale of the user is for a Nepali speaker in Bhutan who works for Acme, Inc. The longest possible search would be:

```
GlobalRes_eo_KI_left
GlobalRes_eo_KI
GlobalRes_eo
GlobalRes_ne_BT_Acme
GlobalRes_ne_BT
GlobalRes_ne
GlobalRes
```

The first resource bundle that is found ends the search, being considered the best available match.

The examples you have seen use resource bundles to fetch strings, but remember that you can use getObject to get any type of object. Bundles are used to store images, URLs, audio sources, graphics components, and any other kind of locale-sensitive resource that can be represented by an object.

Mapping string keys to localized resource objects is usually straightforward—simply use one of the provided subclasses of ResourceBundle that implement the lookup for you: ListResourceBundle and PropertyResourceBundle.

24.2.1 ListResourceBundle

ListResourceBundle maps a simple list of keys to their localized objects. It is an abstract subclass of ResourceBundle for which you provide a getContents method that returns an array of key/resource pairs as an array of arrays of Object. The keys must be strings, but the resources can be any kind of object. The ListResourceBundle takes this array and builds the maps for the various "get" methods. The following classes use ListResourceBundle to define a few locales for GlobalRes. First, the base bundle:

```
public class GlobalRes extends ListResourceBundle {
    public static final String HELLO = "hello";
    public static final String GOODBYE = "goodbye";

    public Object[][] getContents() {
        return contents;
    }

    private static final Object[][] contents = {
        { GlobalRes.HELLO,     "Ciao" },
        { GlobalRes.GOODBYE,   "Ciao" },
    };
}
```

This is the top-level bundle—when no other bundle is found, this will be used. We have chosen Italian for the default. Before any "get" method is executed, GlobalRes.getContents will be invoked and the contents array's values will seed the data structures used by the "get" methods. ListResourceBundle uses an internal lookup table for efficient access; it does not search through your array of keys. The GlobalRes class also defines the constants that name known resources in the bundle. Here is another bundle for a more specific locale:

```
public class GlobalRes_en extends ListResourceBundle {
    public Object[][] getContents() {
        return contents;
    }
```

```
        private static final Object[][] contents = {
            { GlobalRes.HELLO,       "Hello" },
            { GlobalRes.GOODBYE,     "Goodbye" },
        };
    }
```

This bundle covers the English-language locale en. It provides specific values for each localizable string. The next bundle uses the inheritance feature:

```
    public class GlobalRes_en_AU extends ListResourceBundle {
        // mostly like basic English  - our parent bundle

        public Object[][] getContents() { return contents; }

        private static final Object[][] contents = {
            { GlobalRes.HELLO,       "G'day" },
        };
    }
```

This bundle is for English speakers from Australia (AU). It provides a more colloquial version of the HELLO string and inherits all other strings from the general English locale GlobalRes_en. Whenever a resource bundle is instantiated, its parent chain is established. This proceeds by successively dropping the variant, country, and language components from the base bundle name and instantiating those bundles if they exist. If they do exist then setParent is called on the preceding bundle passing the new bundle as the parent. So in our example, when GlobalRes_en_AU is created, the system will create GlobalRes_en and set it as the parent of GlobalRes_en_AU. In turn, the parent of GlobalRes_en will be the base bundle GlobalRes.

Given these classes, someone with an English-language locale (en) would get the values returned by GlobalRes_en unless the locale also specified the country Australia (AU), in which case values from GlobalRes_en_AU would be used. Everyone else would see those in GlobalRes.

24.2.2 PropertyResourceBundle

PropertyResourceBundle is a subclass of ResourceBundle that reads its list of resources from a text property description. Instead of using an array of key/resource pairs, the text contains key/resource pairs as lines of the form

key=value

Both keys and values must be strings. A `PropertyResourceBundle` object reads the text from an `InputStream` passed to the `PropertyResourceBundle` constructor and uses the information it reads to build a lookup table for efficient access.

The bundle search process that we described earlier actually has an additional step that looks for a file *ResName*.`properties` after it looks for a class *ResName*. For example, if the search process doesn't find the class `GlobalRes_eo_KI_left` it will then look for the file `GlobalRes_eo_KI_left.properties` before looking for the next resources class. If that file exists, an input stream is created for it and used to construct a `PropertyResourceBundle` that will read the properties from the file.

It is easier to use property files than to create subclasses of `ListResourceBundle` but the files have two limitations. First, they can only define string resources whereas `ListResourceBundle` can define arbitrary objects. Second, the only legal character encoding for property files is the byte format of ISO 8859-1. This means that other Unicode characters must be encoded with \u*xxxx* escape sequences.

24.2.3 Subclassing `ResourceBundle`

`ListResourceBundle`, `PropertyResourceBundle`, and `.properties` files will be sufficient for most of your bundles, but you can create your own subclass of `ResourceBundle` if they are not. You must implement two methods:

`protected abstract Object `**`handleGetObject(String key)`**
> `throws MissingResourceException`
>> Returns the object associated with the given key. If the key is not defined in this bundle, it returns `null`, and that causes the `ResourceBundle` to check in the parent (if any). Do not throw `MissingResourceException` unless you check the parent instead of letting the bundle do it. All the "get" methods are written in terms of this one method.

`public abstract Enumeration `**`getKeys()`**
> Returns an `Enumeration` of the keys understood by this bundle, including all those of the parent.

Exercise 24.1: Get `GlobalHello` to work with the example locales. Add some more locales, using `ListResourceBundle`, `.properties` files, and your own specific subclass of `ResourceBundle`.

24.3 Currency

Currency encoding is highly sensitive to locale, and the `java.util.Currency` class helps you properly format currency values. You obtain a `Currency` object from one of its static `getInstance` methods, one of which takes a `Locale` object while the other takes a currency code as a `String` (codes are from the ISO 4217 standard).

The `Currency` class does not directly map currency values into localized strings but gives you information you need to do so. The information at your disposal is

`public String getSymbol()`
   Returns the symbol of this currency for the default locale.

`public String getSymbol(Locale locale)`
   Returns the symbol of this currency for the specified locale. If there is no locale specific symbol then the ISO 4217 currency code is returned. Many currencies share the same symbol in their own locale. For example, the $ symbol represents U.S. dollars in the United States, Canadian dollars in Canada, and Australian dollars in Australia—to name but a few. The local currency symbol is usually reserved for the local currency, so each locale can change the representation used for other currencies. For example, if this currency object represents the U.S. dollar, then invoking `getSymbol` with a U.S locale will return "$" because it is the local currency. However, invoking `getSymbol` with a Canadian locale will return "USD" (the currency code for the U.S. dollar) because the $ symbol is reserved for the Canadian dollar in the Canadian locale.

`public int getDefaultFractionDigits()`
   Returns the default number of fraction digits used with this currency. For example, the British pound would have a value of 2 because two digits usually follow the decimal point for pence (such as in £18.29), whereas the Japanese yen would have zero because yen values typically have no fractional part (such as ¥1200). Some "currencies" are not really currencies at all (IMF Special Drawing Rights, for example), and they return –1.

`public String getCurrencyCode()`
   Returns the ISO 4217 currency code of this currency.

Exercise 24.2: Select six different locales and six different currencies, and print a table showing the currency symbol for each currency in each locale.

24.4 Time, Dates, and Calendars

Time is represented as a `long` integer measured in milliseconds since midnight Greenwich Mean Time (GMT) January 1, 1970. This starting point for time measurement is known as the *epoch*. This value is signed, so negative values signify time before the beginning of the epoch. The `System.currentTimeMillis` method returns the current time. This value will express dates into the year A.D. 292,280,995, which should suffice for most purposes.

You can use `java.util.Date` to hold a time and perform some simple time-related operations. When a new `Date` object is created, you can specify a `long` value for its time. If you use the no-arg constructor, the `Date` object will mark the time of its creation. A `Date` object can be used for simple operations. For example, the simplest program to print the current time (repeated from page 37) is

```
import java.util.Date;

class Date2 {
    public static void main(String[] args) {
        Date now = new Date();
        System.out.println(now);
    }
}
```

This program will produce output such as the following:

```
Sun Mar 20 08:48:38 GMT+10:00 2005
```

Note that this is not localized output. No matter what the default locale, the date will be in this format, adjusted for the current time zone.

You can compare two dates with the `before` and `after` methods, which return `true` if the object on which they are invoked is before or after the other date. Or you can compare the `long` values you get from invoking `getTime` on the two objects. The method `setTime` lets you change the time to a different `long`.

The `Date` class provides no support for localization and has effectively been replaced by the more sophisticated and locale-sensitive `Calendar` and `DateFormat` classes.

24.4.1 Calendars

Calendars mark the passage of time. Most of the world uses the same calendar, commonly called the Gregorian calendar after Pope Gregory XIII, under whose auspices it was first instituted. Many other calendars exist in the world, and the calendar abstractions are designed to express such variations. A given moment in time is expressed as a date according to a particular calendar, and the same moment can be expressed as different dates by different calendars. The calendar abstraction is couched in the following form:

- ◆ An abstract `Calendar` class that represents various ways of marking time
- ◆ An abstract `TimeZone` class that represents time zone offsets and other adjustments, such as daylight saving time
- ◆ An abstract `java.text.DateFormat` class that defines how one can format and parse date and time strings

Because the Gregorian calendar is commonly used, you also have the following concrete implementations of the abstractions:

- ◆ A `GregorianCalendar` class
- ◆ A `SimpleTimeZone` class for use with `GregorianCalendar`
- ◆ A `java.text.SimpleDateFormat` class that formats and parses Gregorian dates and times

For example, the following code creates a `GregorianCalendar` object representing midnight (00:00:00), October 26, 1972, in the local time zone, then prints its value:

```
Calendar cal =
    new GregorianCalendar(1972, Calendar.OCTOBER, 26);
System.out.println(cal.getTime());
```

The method `getTime` returns a `Date` object for the calendar object's time, which was set by converting a year, month, and date into a millisecond-measured `long`. The output would be something like this (depending on your local time zone of course):

```
Thu Oct 26 00:00:00 GMT+10:00 1972
```

You can also work directly with the millisecond time value by using `getTimeInMillis` and `setTimeInMillis`. These are equivalent to working with a `Date` object; for example, `getTimeInMillis` is equivalent to invoking `getTime().getTime()`.

The abstract `Calendar` class provides a large set of constants that are useful in many calendars, such as `Calendar.AM` and `Calendar.PM` for calendars that use 12-hour clocks. Some constants are useful only for certain calendars, but no calendar class is required to use such constants. In particular, the month names in `Calendar` (such as `Calendar.JUNE`) are names for the various month numbers (such as 5—month numbers start at 0), with a special month UNDECIMBER for the thirteenth month that many calendars have. But no calendar is required to use these constants.

Each Calendar object represents a particular moment in time on that calendar. The Calendar class provides only constructors that create an object for the current time, either in the default locale and time zone or in specified ones.

Calendar objects represent a moment in time, but they are not responsible for displaying the date. That locale-sensitive procedure is the job of the DateFormat class, which will soon be described.

You can obtain a calendar object for a locale by invoking one of the static Calendar.getInstance methods. With no arguments, getInstance returns an object of the best available calendar type (currently only GregorianCalendar) for the default locale and time zone, set to the current time. The other overloads allow you to specify the locale, the time zone, or both. The static getAvailableLocales method returns an array of Locale objects for which calendars are installed on the system.

With a calendar object in hand, you can manipulate the date. The following example prints the next week of days for a given calendar object:

```
public static void oneWeek(PrintStream out, Calendar cal) {
    Calendar cur = (Calendar) cal.clone(); //modifiable copy
    int dow = cal.get(Calendar.DAY_OF_WEEK);
    do {
        out.println(cur.getTime());
        cur.add(Calendar.DAY_OF_WEEK, 1);
    } while (cur.get(Calendar.DAY_OF_WEEK) != dow);
}
```

First we make a copy of the calendar argument so that we can make changes without affecting the calendar we were passed.[1] Instead of assuming that there are seven days in a week (who knows what kind of calendar we were given?), we loop, printing the time and adding one day to that time, until we have printed a week's worth of days. We detect whether a week has passed by looking for the next day whose "day of the week" is the same as that of the original object.

The Calendar class defines many kinds of *calendar fields* for calendar objects, such as DAY_OF_WEEK in the preceding code. These calendar fields are

---

[1] For historical reasons Calendar.clone returns Object not Calendar, so a cast is required.

constants used in the methods that manipulate parts of the time:

MILLISECOND	DAY_OF_WEEK_IN_MONTH	YEAR
SECOND	DAY_OF_MONTH	ERA
MINUTE	DATE	ZONE_OFFSET
HOUR	DAY_OF_YEAR	DST_OFFSET
HOUR_OF_DAY	WEEK_OF_MONTH	FIELD_COUNT
AM_PM	WEEK_OF_YEAR	
DAY_OF_WEEK	MONTH	

An `int` is used to store values for all these calendar field types. You use these constants—or any others defined by a particular calendar class—to specify a calendar field to the following methods (always as the first argument):

get	Returns the value of the field
set	Sets the value of the field to the provided `int`
clear	Clears the value of the field to "unspecified"
isSet	Returns `true` if the field has been set
add	Adds an `int` amount to the specified field
roll	Rolls the field up to the next value if the second `boolean` argument is `true`, or down if it is `false`
getMinimum	Gets the minimum valid value for the field
getMaximum	Gets the maximum valid value for the field
getGreatestMinimum	Gets the highest minimum value for the field; if it varies, this can be different from `getMinimum`
getLeastMaximum	Gets the smallest maximum value for the field; if it varies, this can be different from `getMaximum`

The greatest minimum and least maximum describe cases in which a value can vary within the overall boundaries. For example, the least maximum value for DAY_OF_MONTH on the Gregorian calendar is 28 because February, the shortest month, can have as few as 28 days. The maximum value is 31 because no month has more than 31 days.

The `set` method allows you to specify a date by certain calendar fields and then calculate the time associated with that date. For example, you can calculate on which day of the week a particular date falls:

```
public static int dotw(int year, int month, int date) {
    Calendar cal = new GregorianCalendar();
    cal.set(Calendar.YEAR, year);
    cal.set(Calendar.MONTH, month);
```

```
        cal.set(Calendar.DATE, date);
        return cal.get(Calendar.DAY_OF_WEEK);
}
```

The method dotw calculates the day of the week on the Gregorian calendar for the given date. It creates a Gregorian calendar object, sets the date fields for year, month, and day, and returns the resulting day of the week.

The clear method can be used to reset a field's value to be unspecified. You can use clear with no parameters to clear all calendar fields. The isSet method returns true if a field currently has a value set.

Three variants of set change particular fields you commonly need to manipulate, leaving unspecified fields alone:

public void **set(int year, int month, int date)**

public void **set(int year, int month, int date, int hrs, int min)**

public void **set(int year, int month, int date, int hrs, int min, int sec)**

You can also use setTime to set the calendar's time from a Date object.

A calendar field that is out of range can be interpreted correctly. For example, January 32 can be equivalent to February 1. Whether it is treated as such or as an error depends on whether the calendar is considered to be *lenient*. A lenient calendar will do its best to interpret values as valid. A strict (non-lenient) calendar will not accept any values out of range, throwing IllegalArgumentException. The setLenient method takes a boolean that specifies whether parsing should be lenient; isLenient returns the current setting.

A week can start on any day, depending on the calendar. You can discover the first day of the week with the method getFirstDayOfWeek. In a Gregorian calendar for the United States this method would return SUNDAY, whereas Ireland uses MONDAY. You can change this by invoking setFirstDayOfWeek with a valid weekday index.

Some calendars require a minimum number of days in the first week of the year. The method getMinimalDaysInFirstWeek returns that number; the method setMinimalDaysInFirstWeek lets you change it. The minimum number of days in a week is important when you are trying to determine in which week a particular date falls—for example, in some calendars, if January 1 is a Friday it may be considered part of the last week of the preceding year.

You can compare two Calendar objects by using compareTo since Calendar implements Comparable. If you prefer, you can use the before and after methods to compare the objects.

24.4.2   Time Zones

TimeZone is an abstract class that encapsulates not only offset from GMT but also other offset issues, such as daylight saving time. As with other locale-sensitive classes, you can get the default TimeZone by invoking the static method getDefault. You can change the default time zone by passing setDefault a new TimeZone object to use—or null to reset to the original default time zone. Time zones are understood by particular calendar types, so you should ensure that the default calendar and time zone are compatible.

Each time zone has a string identifier that is interpreted by the time zone object and can be displayed to the user. These identifiers use a long form consisting of a major and minor regional name, separated by '/'. For example, the following are all valid time zone identifiers: America/New_York, Australia/Brisbane, Africa/Timbuktu. Many time zones have a short form identifier—often just a three letter acronym—some of which are recognized by TimeZone for backward compatibility. You should endeavor to always use the long form—after all, while many people know that EST stands for "Eastern Standard Time," that doesn't tell you for which country. TimeZone also recognizes generic identifiers expressed as the difference in time from GMT. For example, GMT+10:00 and GMT-4:00 are both valid generic time zone identifiers. You can get an array of all the identifiers available on your system from the static method getAvailableIDs. If you want only those for a given offset from GMT, you can invoke getAvailableIDs with that offset. An offset might, for example, have identifiers for both daylight saving and standard time zones.

You can find the identifier of a given TimeZone object from getID, and you can set it with setID. Setting the identifier changes only the identifier on the time zone—it does not change the offset or other values. You can get the time zone for a given identifier by passing it to the static method getTimeZone.

A time zone can be converted into a displayable form by using one of the getDisplayName methods, similar to those of Locale. These methods allow you to specify whether to use the default locale or a specified one, and whether to use a short or long format. The string returned by the display methods is controlled by a DateFormat object (which you'll see a little later). These objects maintain their own tables of information on how to format different time zones. On a given system they may not maintain information for all the supported time zones, in which case the generic identifier form is used, such as in the example on page 696.

Each time zone has a *raw offset* from GMT, which can be either positive or negative. You can get or set the raw offset by using getRawOffset or setRawOffset, but you should rarely need to do this.

Daylight saving time supplements the raw offset with a seasonal time shift. The value of this shift can be obtained from getDSTSavings—the default implementation returns 3,600,000 (the number of milliseconds in an hour). You can ask whether a time zone ever uses daylight saving time during the year by invoking the method `useDaylightTime`, which returns a `boolean`. The method `inDaylightTime` returns `true` if the `Date` argument you pass would fall inside daylight saving time in the zone.

You can obtain the exact offset for a time zone on a given date by specifying that date in milliseconds or by using calendar fields to specify the year and month and so on.

public int **getOffset(long date)**
> Returns the offset from GMT for the given time in this time zone, taking any daylight saving time offset into account

public abstract int **getOffset(int era, int year, int month, int day, int dayOfWeek, int milliseconds)**
> Returns the offset from GMT for the given time in this time zone, taking any daylight saving time offset into account. All parameters are interpreted relative to the calendar for which the particular time zone implementation is designed. The `era` parameter represents calendar-specific eras, such as B.C. and A.D. in the Gregorian calendar.

24.4.3 GregorianCalendar and SimpleTimeZone

The `GregorianCalendar` class is a concrete subclass of `Calendar` that reflects UTC (Coordinated Universal Time), although it cannot always do so exactly. Imprecise behavior is inherited from the time mechanisms of the underlying system.[2] Parts of a date are specified in UTC standard units and ranges. Here are the ranges for `GregorianCalendar`:

```
YEAR         1–292278994
MONTH        0–11
DATE         Day of the month, 1–31
HOUR_OF_DAY  0–23
```

---

[2] Almost all modern systems assume that one day is 24*60*60 seconds. In UTC, about once a year an extra second, called a *leap second,* is added to a day to account for the wobble of the Earth. Most computer clocks are not accurate enough to reflect this distinction, so neither is the `Date` class. Some computer standards are defined in GMT, which is the "civil" name for the standard; UT is the scientific name for the same standard. The distinction between UTC and UT is that UT is based on an atomic clock and UTC is based on astronomical observations. For almost all practical purposes, this is an invisibly fine hair to split. See "Further Reading" on page 755 for references.

```
MINUTE       0–59
SECOND       0–59
MILLISECOND  0–999
```

The GregorianCalendar class supports several constructors:

public **GregorianCalendar()**
> Creates a GregorianCalendar object that represents the current time in the default time zone with the default locale.

public **GregorianCalendar(int year, int month, int date, int hrs, int min, int sec)**
> Creates a GregorianCalendar object that represents the given date in the default time zone with the default locale.

public **GregorianCalendar(int year, int month, int date, int hrs, int min)**
> Equivalent to GregorianCalendar(year, month, date, hrs, min, 0)—that is, the beginning of the specified minute.

public **GregorianCalendar(int year, int month, int date)**
> Equivalent to GregorianCalendar(year, month, date, 0, 0, 0)—that is, midnight on the given date (which is considered to be the start of the day).

public **GregorianCalendar(Locale locale)**
> Creates a GregorianCalendar object that represents the current time in the default time zone with the given locale.

public **GregorianCalendar(TimeZone timeZone)**
> Creates a GregorianCalendar object that represents the current time in the given timeZone with the default locale.

public **GregorianCalendar(TimeZone zone, Locale locale)**
> Creates a GregorianCalendar object that represents the current time in the given timeZone with the given locale.

In addition to the methods it inherits from Calendar, GregorianCalendar provides an isLeapYear method that returns true if the passed in year is a leap year in that calendar.

The Gregorian calendar was preceded by the Julian calendar in many places. In a GregorianCalendar object, the default date at which this change happened is midnight local time on October 15, 1582. This is when the first countries switched, but others changed later. The getGregorianChange method returns the time the calendar is currently using for the change as a Date. You can set a calendar's change-over time by using setGregorianChange with a Date object.

The `SimpleTimeZone` class is a concrete subclass of `TimeZone` that expresses values for Gregorian calendars. It does not handle historical complexities, but instead projects current practices onto all times. For historical dates that precede the use of daylight saving time, for example, you will want to use a calendar with a time zone you have selected that ignores daylight saving time. For future dates, `SimpleTimeZone` is probably as good a guess as any.

24.5 Formatting and Parsing Dates and Times

Date and time formatting is a separate issue from calendars, although they are closely related. Formatting is localized in a different way. Not only are the names of days and months different in different locales that share the same calendar, but also the order in which a dates' components are expressed changes. In the United States it is customary in short dates to put the month before the date, so that July 5 is written as 7/5. In many European countries the date comes first, so 5 July becomes 5/7 or 5.7 or …

In the previous sections the word "date" meant a number of milliseconds since the epoch, which could be interpreted as year, month, day-of-month, hours, minutes, and seconds information. When dealing with the formatting classes you must distinguish between *dates,* which deal with year, month, and day-of-month information, and *times,* which deal with hours, minutes, and seconds.

Date and time formatting issues are text issues, so the classes for formatting are in the `java.text` package—though the `java.util.Formatter` class (see page 624) also supports some localized date formatting as you shall see. The `Date2` program on page 695 is simple because it does not localize its output. If you want localization, you need a `DateFormat` object.

`DateFormat` provides several ways to format and parse dates and times. It is a subclass of the general `Format` class, discussed in Section 24.6.2 on page 710. There are three kinds of formatters, each returned by different static methods: date formatters from `getDateInstance`, time formatters from `getTimeInstance`, and date/time formatters from `getDateTimeInstance`. Each of these formatters understands four formatting styles: SHORT, MEDIUM, LONG, and FULL, which are constants defined in `DateFormat`. And for each of them you can either use the default locale or specify one. For example, to get a medium date formatter in the default locale, you would use

```
Format fmt = DateFormat.getDateInstance(DateFormat.MEDIUM);
```

To get a date and time formatter that uses dates in short form and times in full form in a Japanese locale, you would use

```
Locale japan = new Locale("ja", "JP");
Format fmt = DateFormat.getDateTimeInstance(
            DateFormat.SHORT, DateFormat.FULL, japan
        );
```

For all the various "get instance" methods, if both formatting style and locale are specified the locale is the last parameter. The date/time methods require two formatting styles: the first for the date part, the second for the time. The simplest `getInstance` method takes no arguments and returns a date/time formatter for short formats in the default locale. The `getAvailableLocales` method returns an array of `Locale` objects for which date and time formatting is configured.

The following list shows how each formatting style is expressed for the same date. The output is from a date/time formatter for U.S. locales, with the same formatting mode used for both dates and times:

```
FULL:    Friday, August 29, 1986 5:00:00 PM EDT
LONG:    August 29, 1986 5:00:00 PM EDT
MEDIUM:  Aug 29, 1986 5:00:00 PM
SHORT:   8/29/86 5:00 PM
```

Each `DateFormat` object has an associated calendar and time zone set by the "get instance" method that created it. They are returned by `getCalendar` and `getTimeZone`, respectively. You can set these values by using `setCalendar` and `setTimeZone`. Each `DateFormat` object has a reference to a `NumberFormat` object for formatting numbers. You can use the methods `getNumberFormat` and `setNumberFormat`. (Number formatting is covered briefly in Section 24.6.2 on page 710.)

You format dates with one of several `format` methods based on the formatting parameters described earlier:

public final String **format(Date date)**
> Returns a formatted string for `date`.

public abstract StringBuffer **format(Date date,**
  StringBuffer appendTo, FieldPosition pos)
> Adds the formatted string for `date` to the end of `appendTo`.

public abstract StringBuffer **format(Object obj,**
  StringBuffer appendTo, FieldPosition pos)
> Adds the formatted string for `obj` to the end of `appendTo`. The object can be either a `Date` or a `Number` whose `longValue` is a time in milliseconds.

The `pos` argument is a `FieldPosition` object that tracks the starting and ending index for a specific field within the formatted output. You create a `FieldPosition` object by passing an integer code that represents the field that the object should track. These codes are static fields in `DateFormat`, such as `MINUTE_FIELD` or `MONTH_FIELD`. Suppose you construct a `FieldPosition` object `pos` with `MINUTE_FIELD` and then pass it as an argument to a `format` method. When `format` returns, the `getBeginIndex` and `getEndIndex` methods of `pos` will return the start and end indices of the characters representing minutes within the formatted string. A specific formatter could also use the `FieldPosition` object to align the represented field within the formatted string. To make that happen, you would first invoke the `setBeginIndex` and `setEndIndex` methods of `pos`, passing the indices where you would like that field to start and end in the formatted string. Exactly how the formatter aligns the formatted text depends on the formatter implementation.

A `DateFormat` object can also be used to parse dates. Date parsing can be lenient or not, depending on your preference. Lenient date parsing is as forgiving as it can be, whereas strict parsing requires the format and information to be proper and complete. The default is to be lenient. You can use `setLenient` to set leniency to be `true` or `false`. You can test leniency via `isLenient`.

The parsing methods are

`public Date `**`parse(String text)`**` throws ParseException`
> Tries to parse `text` into a date and/or time. If successful, a `Date` object is returned; otherwise, a `ParseException` is thrown.

`public abstract Date `**`parse(String text, ParsePosition pos)`**
> Tries to parse `text` into a date and/or time. If successful, a `Date` object is returned; otherwise, returns a `null` reference. When the method is called, `pos` is the position at which to start parsing; at the end it will either be positioned after the parsed text or will remain unchanged if an error occurred.

`public Object `**`parseObject(String text, ParsePosition pos)`**
> Returns the result of `parse(text, pos)`. This method is provided to fulfill the generic contract of `Format`.

The class `java.text.SimpleDateFormat` is a concrete implementation of `DateFormat` that is used in many locales. If you are writing a `DateFormat` class, you may find it useful to extend `SimpleDateFormat`. `SimpleDateFormat` uses methods in the `DateFormatSymbols` class to get localized strings and symbols for date representation. When formatting or parsing dates, you should usually not create `SimpleDateFormat` objects; instead, you should use one of the "get instance" methods to return an appropriate formatter.

`DateFormat` has protected fields `calendar` and `numberFormat` that give direct access to the values publicly manipulated with the set and get methods.

Exercise 24.3: Write a program that takes a string argument that is parsed into the date to print, and print that date in all possible styles. How lenient will the date parsing be?

24.5.1 Using `Formatter` with Dates and Times

The `java.util.Formatter` class, described in Chapter 22, also supports the formatting of date and time information using a supplied `Date` or `Calendar` object, or a date represented as a `long` (or `Long`). Using the available format conversions you can extract information about that date/time, including things like the day of the month, the day of the week, the year, the hour of the day, and so forth.

The output of the formatter is localized according to the locale associated with that formatter, so things like the name of the day and month will be in the correct language—however, digits themselves are not localized. Unlike `DateFormat`, a formatter cannot help you with localization issues such as knowing whether the month or the day should come first in a date—it simply provides access to each individual component and your program must combine them in the right way.

A date/time conversion is indicated by a format conversion of `t` (or `T` for uppercase output), followed by various suffixes that indicate what is to be output and in what form. The following table lists the conversion suffixes related to times:

H	Hour of the day for 24-hour clock format. Two digits: 00–23
I	Hour of the day for 12-hour clock format. Two digits: 01–12
k	Hour of the day for 24-hour clock format: 0–23
l	Hour of the day for 12-hour clock format: 1–12
M	Minute within the hour. Two digits: 00–59
S	Seconds within the minute. Two digits: 00–60 (60 is a leap second)
L	Milliseconds within the second. Three digits: 000–999
N	Nanoseconds within the second. Nine digits: 000000000–999999999
p	Locale specific AM or PM marker.
z	Numeric offset from GMT (as per RFC 822). E.g. +1000
Z	String representing the abbreviation for the time zone
s	Seconds since the epoch.
Q	Milliseconds since the epoch.

So, for example, the following code will print out the current time in the familiar *hh:mm:ss* format:

```
System.out.printf("%1$tH:%1$tM:%1$tS %n", new Date());
```

The conversion suffixes that deal with dates are

B   Full month name
b   Abbreviated month name
h   Same as 'b'
A   Full name of the day of the week
a   Short name of the day of the week
C   The four digit year divided by 100. Two digits: 00–99
Y   Year. Four digits: 0000–9999
y   Year: Two digits: 00–99
j   Day of the year. Three digits: 001–999
m   Month in year. Two digits: 01–99
d   Day of month. Two digits: 01–99
e   Day of month: 1–99

Naturally, the valid range for day of month, month of year, and so forth, depends on the calendar that is being used. To continue the example, the following code will print the current date in the common *mm/dd/yy* format:

```
System.out.printf("%1$tm/%1$td/%1$ty %n", new Date());
```

As you can see, all the information about a date or time can be extracted and you can combine the pieces in whatever way you need. Doing so, however, is rather tedious both for the writer and any subsequent readers of the code. To ease the tedium a third set of conversion suffixes provides convenient shorthands for common combinations of the other conversions:

R   Time in 24-hour clock *hh:mm* format ("%tH:%tM")
T   Time in 24-hour clock *hh:mm:ss* format ("%tH:%tM:%tS")
r   Time in 12-hour clock *h:mm:ss am/pm* format ("%tI:%tM:%tS %Tp")
D   Date in *mm/dd/yy* format ("%tm/%td/%ty")
F   Complete date in ISO 8601 format ("%tY-%tm-%td")
c   Long date and time format ("%ta %tb %td %tT %tZ %tY")

So the previous examples could be combined in the more compact and somewhat more readable

```
System.out.printf("%1$tT %1$tD %n", new Date());
```

As with all format conversions a width can be specified before the conversion indicator, to specify the minimum number of characters to output. If the converted value is smaller than the width then the output is padded with spaces. The only format flag that can be specified with the date/time conversions is the '–' flag for left-justification—if this flag is given then a width must be supplied as well.

24.6 Internationalization and Localization for Text

The package `java.text` provides several types for localizing text behavior, such as collation (comparing strings), and formatting and parsing text, numbers, and dates. You have already learned about dates in detail so in this section we look at general formatting and parsing, and collation.

24.6.1 Collation

Comparing strings in a locale-sensitive fashion is called *collation*. The central class for collation is `Collator`, which provides a `compare` method that takes two strings and returns an `int` less than, equal to, or greater than zero as the first string is less than, equal to, or greater than the second.

As with most locale-sensitive classes, you get the best available `Collator` object for a locale from a `getInstance` method, either passing a specific `Locale` object or specifying no locale and so using the default locale. For example, you get the best available collator to sort a set of Russian-language strings like this:

```
Locale russian = new Locale("ru", "");
Collator coll = Collator.getInstance(russian);
```

You then can use `coll.compare` to determine the order of strings. A `Collator` object takes locality—not Unicode equivalence—into account when comparing. For example, in a French-speaking locale, the characters ç and c are considered equivalent for sorting purposes. A naïve sort that used `String.compare` would put all strings starting with ç after all those starting with c (indeed, it would put them after z), but in a French locale this would be wrong. They should be sorted according to the characters that follow the initial c or ç characters in the strings.

Determining collation factors for a string can be expensive. A `CollationKey` object examines a string once, so you can compare precomputed keys instead of comparing strings with a `Collator`. The method `Collator.getCollationKey` returns a key for a string. For example, because `Collator` implements the interface `Comparator`, you could use a `Collator` to maintain a sorted set of strings:

```
class CollatorSorting {
    private TreeSet<String> sortedStrings;

    CollatorSorting(Collator collator) {
```

```
        sortedStrings = new TreeSet<String>(collator);
    }

    void add(String str) {
        sortedStrings.add(str);
    }

    Iterator<String> strings() {
        return sortedStrings.iterator();
    }
}
```

Each time a new string is inserted in `sortedStrings`, the `Collator` is used as a `Comparator`, with its `compare` method invoked on various elements of the set until the `TreeSet` finds the proper place to insert the string. This results in several comparisons. You can make this quicker at the cost of space by creating a `TreeMap` that uses a `CollationKey` to map to the original string. `CollationKey` implements the interface `Comparable` with a `compareTo` method that can be much more efficient than using `Collator.compare`.

```
class CollationKeySorting {
    private TreeMap<CollationKey, String> sortedStrings;
    private Collator collator;

    CollationKeySorting(Collator collator) {
        this.collator = collator;
        sortedStrings = new TreeMap<CollationKey, String>();
    }

    void add(String str) {
        sortedStrings.put(
            collator.getCollationKey(str), str);
    }

    Iterator<String> strings() {
        return sortedStrings.values().iterator();
    }
}
```

24.6.2 Formatting and Parsing

The abstract `Format` class provides methods to format and parse objects according to a locale. `Format` declares a `format` method that takes an object and returns a formatted `String`, throwing `IllegalArgumentException` if the object is not of a type known to the formatting object. `Format` also declares a `parseObject` method that takes a `String` and returns an object initialized from the parsed data, throwing `ParseException` if the string is not understood. Each of these methods is implemented as appropriate for the particular kind of formatting. The package `java.text` provides three `Format` subclasses:

- `DateFormat` was discussed in the previous section.

- `MessageFormat` helps you localize output when printing messages that contain values from your program. Because word order varies among languages, you cannot simply use a localized string concatenated with your program's values. For example, the English phrase "a fantastic menu" would in French have the word order "un menu fantastique." A message that took adjectives and nouns from lists and displayed them in such a phrase could use a `MessageFormat` object to localize the order.

- `NumberFormat` is an abstract class that defines a general way to format and parse various kinds of numbers for different locales. It has two subclasses: `ChoiceFormat` to choose among alternatives based on number (such as picking between a singular or plural variant of a word); and `DecimalFormat` to format and parse decimal numbers. (The formatting capabilities of `NumberFormat` are more powerful than those provided by `java.util.Formatter`.)

`NumberFormat` in turn has four different kinds of "get instance" methods. Each method uses either a provided `Locale` object or the default locale.

- `getNumberInstance` returns a general number formatter/parser. This is the kind of object returned by the generic `getInstance` method.

- `getIntegerInstance` returns a number formatter/parser that rounds floating-point values to the nearest integer.

- `getCurrencyInstance` returns a formatter/parser for currency values. The `Currency` object used by a `NumberFormatter` can also be retrieved with the `getCurrency` method.

- `getPercentInstance` returns a formatter/parser for percentages.

Here is a method you can use to print a number using the format for several different locales:

```
public void reformat(double num, String[] locales) {
    for (String loc : locales) {
        Locale pl = parseLocale(loc);
        NumberFormat fmt = NumberFormat.getInstance(pl);
        System.out.print(fmt.format(num));
        System.out.println("\t" + pl.getDisplayName());
    }
}

public static Locale parseLocale(String desc) {
    StringTokenizer st = new StringTokenizer(desc, "_");
    String lang = "", ctry = "", var = "";
    try {
        lang = st.nextToken();
        ctry = st.nextToken();
        var = st.nextToken();
    } catch (java.util.NoSuchElementException e) {
        ; // fine, let the others default
    }
    return new Locale(lang, ctry, var);
}
```

The first argument to `reformat` is the number to format; the other arguments specify locales. We use a `StringTokenizer` to break locale argument strings into constituent components. For example, `cy_GB` will be broken into the language `cy` (Welsh), the country `GB` (United Kingdom), and the empty variant `""`. We create a `Locale` object from each result, get a number formatter for that locale, and then print the formatted number and the locale. When run with the number `5372.97` and the locale arguments `en_US`, `lv`, `it_CH`, and `lt`, `reformat` prints:

```
5,372.97        English (United States)
5 372,97        Latvian
5'372.97        Italian (Switzerland)
5.372,97        Lithuanian
```

A similar method can be written that takes a locale and a number formatted in that locale, uses the `parse` method to get a `Number` object, and prints the resulting value formatted according to a list of other locales:

```
public void parseAndReformat(String locale, String number,
                            String[] locales)
    throws ParseException
{
    Locale loc = LocalNumber.parseLocale(locale);
    NumberFormat parser = NumberFormat.getInstance(loc);
    Number num = parser.parse(number);
    for (String str : locales) {
        Locale pl = LocalNumber.parseLocale(str);
        NumberFormat fmt = NumberFormat.getInstance(pl);
        System.out.println(fmt.format(num));
    }
}
```

When run with the original locale it_CH, the number string "5'372.97" and the locale arguments en_US, lv, and lt, parseAndReformat prints:

```
5,372.97
5 372,97
5.372,97
```

24.6.3 Text Boundaries

Parsing requires finding boundaries in text. The class BreakIterator provides a locale-sensitive tool for locating such break points. It has four kinds of "get instance" methods that return specific types of BreakIterator objects:

- ◆ getCharacterInstance returns an iterator that shows valid breaks in a string for individual characters (not necessarily a char).

- ◆ getWordInstance returns an iterator that shows word breaks in a string.

- ◆ getLineInstance returns an iterator that shows where it is proper to break a line in a string, for purposes such as wrapping text.

- ◆ getSentenceInstance returns an iterator that shows where sentence breaks occur in a string.

The following code prints each break shown by a given BreakIterator:

```
static void showBreaks(BreakIterator breaks, String str) {
    breaks.setText(str);
    int start = breaks.first();
```

```
    int end = breaks.next();
    while (end != BreakIterator.DONE) {
        System.out.println(str.substring(start, end));
        start = end;
        end = breaks.next();
    }
    System.out.println(str.substring(start)); // the last
}
```

A `BreakIterator` is a different style of iterator from the usual `java.util.Iterator` objects you have seen. It provides several methods for iterating forward and backward within a string, looking for different break positions.

You should always use these boundary classes when breaking up text because the issues involved are subtle and widely varying. For example, the logical characters used in these classes are not necessarily equivalent to a single `char`. Unicode characters can be combined, so it can take more than one 16-bit Unicode value to constitute a logical character. And word breaks are not necessarily spaces—some languages do not even use spaces.

Never speak more clearly than you think
—Jeremey Bernstein

CHAPTER 25

Standard Packages

> *No unmet needs exist,*
> *and current unmet needs that are being met will continue to be met.*
> —Transportation Commission on Unmet Needs, California

THE Java™ 2 Platform Standard Edition comes with many standard packages. These packages, all subpackages of the root `java` package, define the main classes and interfaces for the platform. Throughout this book we have taught you about many of these classes, particularly those relating to the core language and those most commonly used in general programs. The main packages that we have covered are

- `java.lang`—The main language classes, such as `Object`, `String`, `Thread`, `Class`, and so on. The subpackage `java.lang.annotation` defines some annotation types and was covered in Chapter 15. The subpackage `java.lang.reflect` provides a way to examine types in detail and was covered in Chapter 16. The subpackage `java.lang.ref` defines the weak reference types that allow you to influence garbage collection and was covered in Chapter 17.

- `java.io`—Input and output and some file system manipulation. This package was covered extensively in Chapter 20.

- `java.util`—Classes of general utility. Defines the collection classes both new and legacy that were covered in Chapter 21 and the localization classes covered in Chapter 24. Miscellaneous utilities were covered in Chapter 22.

- `java.util.regex`—Classes for regular expressions. These were covered in Chapter 13.

- `java.security`—The platform security classes, which were briefly described in Chapter 23. It contains a number of other classes for encryption, authentication, digital signatures, and other useful security-related code.

◆ java.text—Internationalization and localization for formatting and parsing numbers and dates, sorting strings, and message lookup by key. These were touched on briefly in Chapter 24.

We mentioned these main packages briefly, without covering them in detail:

◆ java.nio—The "New I/O" classes that we briefly introduced at the end of Chapter 20. The CharBuffer class from this package also pops up in a couple of other places.

◆ java.nio.charset—Classes for defining character sets and their encodings. This package was briefly covered in Chapter 13.

◆ java.util.concurrent—Contains (amongst other things) the concurrent collections that were briefly discussed in Chapter 21.

In addition, there are main packages we haven't covered at all:

◆ java.awt—The Abstract Window Toolkit abstraction layer for writing platform-independent graphical user interfaces.

◆ java.applet—The Applet class and related types for writing subprograms that can be hosted inside other applications, such as HTML browsers.

◆ java.beans—The JavaBeans components for user-composable code.

◆ java.lang.instrument—Services for defining agents that can instrument applications running on a virtual machine.

◆ java.lang.management—Services for monitoring and managing both the virtual machine and the operating system on which it runs.

◆ java.math—Mathematical manipulations. Currently, this package has only three classes, which handle some kinds of arbitrary-precision arithmetic.

◆ java.net—Networking classes for sockets, URLs, and so on.

◆ java.rmi—Remote Method Invocation, with which you can invoke methods on objects running in other virtual machines, typically across a network.

◆ java.sql—The JDBC package for using relational databases.

◆ java.util.jar—Classes for reading and writing JAR (Java ARchive) files. These archive files can be used to distribute packages of related classes and resources, as covered in "Package Objects and Specifications" on page 477.

◆ java.util.logging—A framework for logging from within your code.

◆ java.util.prefs—Provides a mechanism for managing user and system preferences, as well as application configuration.

◆ `java.util.zip`—Classes for reading and writing ZIP files.

Further packages exist outside the `java` package of the platform, in what are known as the standard extensions, for example:

◆ `javax.accessibility`—A framework for developing GUIs that are more accessible to people with disabilities.

◆ `javax.naming`—Classes and subpackages for working with directory and naming services.

◆ `javax.sound`—Has subpackages for creating and manipulating sounds.

◆ `javax.swing`—The Swing package of GUI components.

And there are packages that provide interaction between the platform and other environments:

◆ `org.omg.CORBA`—Classes for the Common Object Request Broker Architecture (CORBA), object request brokers (ORB's).

◆ `org.omg.CosNaming`—The Common Object Service's naming classes.

Other versions of the platform, such as the Java[TM] 2 Platform Enterprise Edition, contain even more packages.

This book cannot be large enough to contain full coverage of every one of these packages—some of them require complete books of their own. This chapter discusses some of the `java` subpackages not otherwise covered in this book, giving an overview of the purpose and contents, as well as some of the other packages we have listed. All these packages are covered in detail in your local documentation and the `java` packages are covered in the volumes of *The Java[TM] Class Libraries, Second Edition*. Most of the `java` packages, including the AWT and applet packages and some extensions such as Swing, are taught in the different versions of *The Java[TM] Tutorial*. These books and all others cited in this chapter are part of this official series of documentation from the source—the people who invented the Java programming language, its virtual machine, and many of its packages.

25.1 `java.awt`—The Abstract Window Toolkit

The Abstract Window Toolkit allows you to write graphical user interfaces (GUIs) that will run on every system in a reasonable way. The AWT displays GUI components (such as buttons, labels, and text fields) using (by default) the local platform's look and feel, showing Macintosh buttons on a Mac, Motif buttons on X platforms, Windows buttons on Windows systems, and so on.

For this to work, you may need to change how you think about laying out your GUI. You may be accustomed to interactive tools that let you place the various GUI components on the screen exactly where you want them to be. Such *absolute placement* will not work for a portable interface because, for example, the size of a button is different on different systems. When your interface is used on a system other than the one on which you designed it, some buttons will overlap and others will have ugly gaps between them.

Although you can use absolute placement in AWT, it is not recommended. When you place a component into an AWT display frame, the frame's *layout manager* decides where to put it. Almost all the layout managers provided with the AWT use *relative placement:* Components are placed and sized relative to other components. All the provided layout managers implement either the interface `LayoutManager` or its extended interface `LayoutManager2`. Layout managers range from the simple (`FlowLayout` adds components to a line until they don't fit and then starts a new line) to the sophisticated (`GridBagLayout` has a great deal of flexibility). You can also write your own layout manager.

Instead of thinking about where a check box should go on the screen, you should think about how it should be placed relative to other components. Then choose a layout manager for the frame in which the check box will be placed and add the components so that they have the expected relationships. If you do this right, your interface will look clean on all platforms.

AWT has a set of standard GUI components: labels, buttons, check boxes, choice lists, scroll bars, text fields, text regions, and so on. Several top-level containers, such as dialog boxes and windows, let you place other components inside them (preferably using a relative-placement layout manager).

When you need to draw your own graphics on the screen, the simplest technique is to subclass `Component` or `Container`, overriding the `paint` method to draw what you need using the `Graphics` object passed to `paint`. `Component` is the basis for many customized user-interface components when no standard component does what is needed. You would subclass `Container` if your drawn component contained other components.

The AWT is an event-based system. When the user performs an action, such as moving a mouse, clicking a mouse button, or typing a key, an event is generated that identifies the underlying component as the source of that event and that encapsulates the nature of that event. The event is then placed in a central *event queue,* and will be serviced by a single *event thread.* The event thread takes events from the queue one at a time and dispatches them to their source components. You can also generate events programmatically—for example, invoking `repaint` on a component puts an UPDATE event into the event queue—or can create event objects and insert them directly into the event queue.

Components are notified of events (mouse up, mouse down, mouse drag, keyboard events, and the like) by having methods invoked on them by the event thread. You can also register *listener* objects that are notified when an event occurs within a component. For example, a button that lets the user exit the program might be set up like this:

```
Button b = new Button("Exit");
b.addActionListener(
    new ActionListener() {
        public void actionPerformed(ActionEvent e) {
            System.exit(0);
        }
    }
);
gui.add(b);
```

Action events come from the basic action on the component, such as pressing a button or selecting a check box. The ActionEvent class has details of an action event, such as the keyboard modifiers (such as the Alt or Control key) that were being pressed when the action occurred. To receive this event you must register interest in action events, either by adding an ActionListener to the component as shown here or by invoking enableEvents with an appropriate mask.

The ActionListener interface in the previous example is a *listener interface*. Listener interfaces extend java.util.EventListener and exist for many kinds of events: mouse, keyboard, window, item, text, container, and general component events. You use objects that implement listener interfaces to trigger method execution when events occur—all of which get executed by the event thread. When an event occurs, the component's processEvent method is called, which in turn calls *processXXXEvent* for the specific event, and that in turn will call the *XXXOccurred* method of all registered listeners for that event.

Other classes in java.awt allow you to set colors, fonts, and so on. All these properties are inherited by default from outer components—the default colors of a button are those of the frame in which it has been placed. You can override this setting at any level by explicitly specifying a color for a component. That component and all its contained components will change to the specified color unless a subcomponent has its color specified.

Various subpackages of java.awt allow you to manipulate images, sounds, and other media:

◆ java.awt.color—color manipulation tools

- ◆ `java.awt.datatransfer`—moving data between applications, such as with cut, copy, and paste

- ◆ `java.awt.dnd`—drag-and-drop functionality

- ◆ `java.awt.event`—various event listener and adapter classes for connecting events to your code

- ◆ `java.awt.font`—font manipulation APIs

- ◆ `java.awt.geom`—2D geometry

- ◆ `java.awt.im`—input method interfaces for localized input devices

- ◆ `java.awt.image`—several interfaces and classes for reading and manipulating images

- ◆ `java.awt.print`—printing APIs

25.2 `java.applet`—Applets

Applets are a way to run code inside another application—commonly a web browser. Applets are the first exposure many people have to the Java virtual machine and its uses. An applet is defined primarily by the protocol that governs its lifetime and the methods by which it can query and manipulate its runtime environment. The types in `java.applet`—primarily the `Applet` superclass itself—define this environment.

When an `<applet>` or `<object>` tag is found in a web page's HTML, the browser downloads the code for the named class from a URL, creates an object of that class, creates a region on the web page for that object to control, and then invokes the object's `init` method—often creating a `ThreadGroup` and `Thread` just for this applet. As the applet runs, it can download other classes from the server as needed. Applets are usually run in a tightly secured "sandbox" in which potentially dangerous operations (such as file access, network access, and running local programs) are restricted by the security policy.

The method `init` is one of four lifecycle methods defined for the applet in the `Applet` class. After `init` is called, `start` is called, which tells the applet that it is active and should perform its function. If the browser decides that the applet is no longer of interest to the user, for example, the user leaves the page the applet was on, the applet's `stop` method is invoked to tell it to stop what it was doing. If the user returns to the applet's page the browser may invoke `start` again to tell the applet to recommence—so the applet can cycle through a stop–start sequence as the user presses the "Back" and "Forward" buttons (or their equivalents) to visit and leave the page. When the browser decides that the applet is no longer of interest (perhaps because the user has moved a number of pages away) the applet's destroy method is invoked to free up any resources used by the applet. If the applet's page is now revisited the lifecycle will recommence with init being called again. The browser ultimately defines the lifecycle of an applet and may choose to invoke destroy immediately after stop when the user leaves the page. Whether or not an applet class is unloaded and reloaded between visits to the applet is again a feature of the browser.

These lifecycle methods are typically overridden by applet classes. For example, if an applet uses a thread to do its work, init would typically create the thread; start would invoke the thread's start method the first time and ask it to continue execution on subsequent invocations; stop could ask the thread to pause to prevent it from consuming resources while the page is not visible; and destroy could interrupt the thread because the thread would no longer be needed.

An applet can get parameters from a <param> tag to customize its behavior. It might get colors, fonts, or the URL of an image to display.

Applets usually run in a highly constrained security environment to protect your computer and network from unwelcome inspection or invasion by a hostile applet. This means that certain conveniences, such as a local scratch disk, may not be available by default. You can grant permission to perform particular actions to individual applets by specifying an appropriate security policy.

The applet model is a good example of how the Java platform provides power. The fact that the same code runs on all systems in the same way allows a single piece of code (an applet) to run in a variety of browsers on a variety of windowing systems running on a larger variety of operating systems. The portability of Java bytecodes allows you to execute part of your application on the server and another part on the client system via downloaded code, whichever is appropriate. It is the same platform on both sides: the Java virtual machine. The ability to move code from one place to another and execute it in a secure environment enables new ways of thinking about where to execute what part of your design.

25.3 java.beans—Components

The JavaBeans[TM] component architecture helps independent vendors write classes that can be treated as components of larger systems assembled by users. The java.beans package provides necessary and useful classes for writing such *beans*. A bean exports properties, generates events, and implements methods. By following certain design patterns or by implementing methods that provide a description of these facets of behavior, you can compose beans by using interactive tools to build a system the user needs.

Much of a bean's behavior is simplified if you follow expected design patterns. For example, if your bean class is called Ernest and you provide a class named `ErnestBeanInfo` that implements the `BeanInfo` interface, the JavaBeans tools will use `ErnestBeanInfo` as a source of information about the behavior of the bean: the events it supports, the icons it uses, and so on.

Providing a `BeanInfo` object is itself optional—the JavaBeans system will use reflection to infer events and properties. For example, if a class `Ernest` has methods named `getImportance` and `setImportance`, the JavaBeans system will assume that you have an `importance` property that can be set, either directly or via another bean. Builder tools are expected to present the properties and events to users, who can use them to connect beans as components to build custom applications.

AWT components are beans, and the event model described earlier for AWT components is also the JavaBeans event model.

The JavaBeans component architecture is designed to interoperate with existing component architectures, extending the "Write Once, Run Anywhere" capability to create a homogeneous component platform.

The subpackage `java.beans.beancontext` defines interfaces and classes that are used to talk about the context in which a bean or set of beans is executing. Bean contexts can be nested.

25.4 `java.math`—Mathematics

The package `java.math` is destined for classes that help with mathematical calculations. Currently, it has three classes—`BigInteger`, `BigDecimal` and `MathContext`—and an enum, `RoundingMode`, that defines different rounding modes.

The class `BigInteger` provides arbitrary-precision integer arithmetic, providing analogous operations for all integer operations except >>>, which is equivalent to >> because there is no sign bit to copy in an arbitrary-precision integer. Neither will the provided single-bit operations (`clearBit` and `setBit`) change the sign of the number on which they operate. `BigInteger` behaves as if it were defined in two's-complement notation—the same notation used by the primitive integer types. Binary bitwise operations start by extending the sign of the smaller number and then executing the operation, just as operations on primitive values do. `BigInteger` objects are immutable, so all operations on them produce new `BigInteger` objects. The following simple method returns an iterator over the prime factors of a number:

```
static final BigInteger ONE = BigInteger.valueOf(1);
static final BigInteger TWO = BigInteger.valueOf(2);
static final BigInteger THREE = BigInteger.valueOf(3);
```

```
public static Iterator<BigInteger> factors(BigInteger num) {
    ArrayList<BigInteger> factors =
        new ArrayList<BigInteger>();

    if (num.compareTo(ONE) <= 0) { // num<=ONE means skip it
        factors.add(num);
        return factors.iterator();
    }

    BigInteger div = TWO;                           // divisor
    BigInteger divsq = BigInteger.valueOf(4); // div squared

    while (num.compareTo(divsq) >= 0) {
        BigInteger[] res = num.divideAndRemainder(div);
        if (res[1].signum() == 0) { // if remainder is zero
            factors.add(div);
            num = res[0];
        } else {                           // try next divisor
            if (div == TWO)
                div = THREE;
            else
                div = div.add(TWO);
            divsq = div.multiply(div);
        }
    }
    if (!num.equals(ONE))    // leftover must be a factor
        factors.add(num);
    return factors.iterator();
}
```

The constants ONE, TWO, and THREE are used often, so we create objects for them once. If the number we are factoring is less than or equal to one, we treat it as its own factor (BigInteger and BigDecimal implement the Comparable interface described on page 574). After this validity test we perform the real work of the method: testing potential divisors. If a divisor divides into the number evenly, it is a prime factor, and we proceed with the result of the division to find more factors. We first try two, and then all odd numbers, until we reach a divisor whose square is larger than the current number. You could optimize this method in any number of ways, but it shows how to use some BigInteger functionality.

BigDecimal provides an arbitrary-precision signed decimal number consisting of an arbitrary-precision integer and an int scale that says how many decimal places are to the right of the decimal point. The actual precision required can be set through a MathContext object that is either associated with the BigDecimal at construction time or passed as an argument to the actual operation being performed.

Decimal division and changing a number's scale require rounding, which you can specify on each operation or through an associated MathContext object. You can require that rounding be up, down, toward zero, away from zero, or toward the nearest value. You can also assert that no rounding will be necessary, in which case ArithmeticException will be thrown if you are found to be wrong. The eight different rounding modes are defined by the RoundingMode enum.

25.5 java.net—The Network

The java.net package provides classes for working with network infrastructure, such as sockets, network addresses, Uniform Resource Identifiers (URIs), and Uniform Resource Locators (URLs).

The java.net package is centered around the Socket class, which represents a connection to another socket—possibly on another machine—across which bytes can flow. You typically create a socket with a host name or InetAddress and a port number. You can also specify a local InetAddress and port to which the socket will be bound. A ServerSocket class lets you listen on a port for incoming connection requests, creating a socket for each request. For example, the following program accepts input on a socket:

```java
import java.net.*;
import java.io.*;

public class AcceptInput {
    public static final int PORT = 0xCAFE;

    public static void main(String[] args)
        throws IOException
    {
        ServerSocket server = new ServerSocket(PORT);
        byte[] bytes = new byte[1024];
        for (;;) {
            try {
                System.out.println("--------------------");
```

```
                        Socket sock = server.accept();
                        InputStream in = sock.getInputStream();
                        int len;
                        while ((len = in.read(bytes)) > 0)
                            System.out.write(bytes, 0, len);
                        in.close();
                    } catch (IOException e) {
                        e.printStackTrace();
                    }
                }
            }
        }
```

This program creates a ServerSocket and repeatedly accepts connections to it. The Socket obtained for each connection is queried for an input stream and the data from that socket is read from the stream and written to the standard output stream, printing whatever bytes it receives. A client that shipped its standard input to the server might look like this:

```
import java.net.*;
import java.io.*;

public class WriteOutput {
    public static void main(String[] args)
        throws IOException
    {
        String host = args[0];
        Socket sock = new Socket(host, AcceptInput.PORT);
        OutputStream out = sock.getOutputStream();
        int ch;
        while ((ch = System.in.read()) != -1)
            out.write(ch);
        out.close();
    }
}
```

Once we have the actual Socket connection, I/O is performed, like all other I/O, using an appropriate input or output stream.

A URL object stores a URL, providing methods to examine and set its various parts (protocol, host, port number, and file). A URL object simply names a resource—you invoke openConnection to connect to the named resource. The openConnection method returns a URLConnection object that lets you get the header fields and content of the resource as input and output streams. The following program reads the contents of a URL:

```
import java.net.*;
import java.io.*;

public class ReadURL {
    public static void main(String[] args) {
        for (String url : args) {
            try {
                readURL(url);
            } catch (Exception e) {
                System.err.println(url + ":");
                e.printStackTrace();
            }
        }
    }

    private static void readURL(String name)
        throws MalformedURLException, IOException
    {
        URL url = new URL(name);
        URLConnection connect = url.openConnection();
        InputStream in = connect.getInputStream();
        byte[] bytes = new byte[1024];

        int len;          // number of bytes actually read
        while ((len = in.read(bytes)) >= 0)
            System.out.write(bytes, 0, len);
    }
}
```

The URLEncoder class lets you turn an ISO Latin-1 string (such as a user-typed query) into a form that can be included as part of a URL. ASCII letters and digits remain unchanged, the space character is converted to a +, and all other characters are represented by their lower 8 bits in hex preceded by a %.

The File.toURL method creates a file URL for the path specified by that File object.

You can create DatagramSocket objects for sockets that send and receive DatagramPacket objects, which contain an array of bytes. Datagrams are a connectionless packet delivery service, in which packets are individually addressed and routed and could be received in any order. With the MulticastSocket subclass of `DatagramSocket`, you can set up a socket that can send and receive packets to and from multiple addresses.

25.6 `java.rmi`—Remote Method Invocation

When you can download and run code on other systems, the face of distributed computing changes. The Java platform's Remote Method Invocation (RMI) gives you a way to create objects whose methods can be invoked from other virtual machines, including those running on completely different hosts. Because RMI is designed for communicating between Java virtual machines it can take advantage of the architecture's features and can operate in a natural fashion for programmers. RMI is contained in the package `java.rmi` and its subpackages, most notably the package `java.rmi.server` for RMI server implementations.

To use RMI you must first design one or more *remote interfaces*—interfaces whose methods can be invoked remotely. A remote interface extends the `Remote` interface, and its methods throw `RemoteException` in addition to any other exceptions. Here, for example, is a simple definition of a compute server interface that will accept `Task` objects for execution, returning the resulting `Object`:

```
import java.rmi.*;

public interface ComputeServer extends Remote {
    Object compute(Task task) throws RemoteException;
}
```

The `Task` interface is generic, allowing a `ComputeServer` to do any computation requested of it:

```
public interface Task extends java.io.Serializable {
    Object run();
}
```

`Task` itself is not a remote interface. Each `ComputeServer` object will run on a host and will be asked to execute tasks locally on its own host and return any results. (Traditionally, the application invoking a remote method is called the *client* of the invocation, and the application executing the method is called the *server,* although a client of one invocation may be the server of another.) `Task` extends `Serializable` because all local types passed to or returned from a remote method must be serializable.

Each method of a remote interface is required to throw `RemoteException` because any invocation of a remote method can have failures that must be signaled. Recovery from these failures is unlike recovery in local computation, where methods always arrive at their intended objects and either results are always returned or you clearly know that they were not returned.

When you invoke a remote method, network failures create new uncertainties—if the network fails after the request is transmitted from the client, the client doesn't know whether the request was received. The failure may have happened before the invocation reached the server, or it may have happened after it reached the server but before results could be returned. There is no way for the client to know which of these two cases actually happened. If the request is to withdraw money from your bank account, you would not want to simply retransmit the request—it might get there twice. Remote interfaces must be designed to allow clients to recover from such *partial failures*. Methods may be *idempotent*—meaning the method can safely be reinvoked—or some other recovery method may be provided for the interface, such as transactions that can be aborted when non-idempotent methods fail. The users of a remote object must recover from such failures, and the declared `RemoteException` helps them do so.

Here is a simple implementation of the `ComputeServer` interface:

```java
import java.rmi.*;
import java.rmi.server.*;

public class ComputeServerImpl
    extends UnicastRemoteObject
    implements ComputeServer
{
    public ComputeServerImpl() throws RemoteException { }

    public Object compute(Task task) {
        return task.run();
    }

    public static void main(String[] args)
        throws java.io.IOException
    {
        // use the default, restrictive security manager
        System.setSecurityManager(new RMISecurityManager());

        ComputeServer server = new ComputeServerImpl();
        Naming.rebind("ComputeServer", server);
        System.out.println("Ready to receive tasks");
    }
}
```

This code is also straightforward. When a `compute` invocation arrives from a client, `ComputeServerImpl` implements the `ComputeServer` interface by taking the `Task` object it is given and invoking its `run` method, returning the resulting `Object`. Each incoming request typically gets its own thread, so this compute server implementation could have many concurrently executing tasks for different clients. `ComputeServerImpl` extends `UnicastRemoteObject`, which provides references for single-server remote method invocation. `UnicastRemoteObject`, like most types needed only by servers, is defined in `java.rmi.server`. The `ComputeServerImpl` constructor declares that it throws `RemoteException` because it can be thrown by the (implicitly invoked) `UnicastRemoteObject` constructor when it registers the object with the RMI system.

Now comes the fun part. Clients can ask the server to perform any computation at all. Suppose, for example, that you want to compute π to some number of decimal places. You can have the compute server do this for you:

```java
import java.math.BigDecimal;

public class Pi implements Task {
    private int decimals;

    /** Calculate Pi to a given number of decimal places */
    public Pi(int decimals) {
        this.decimals = decimals;
    }

    public Object run() {
        BigDecimal res = computePi();
        return res;
    }

    BigDecimal computePi() {
        // ...
    }
}
```

The `Pi` class implements the `Task` interface with a `run` method that returns a `java.math.BigDecimal` object containing the computed result. You then put the compiled `Pi` class someplace where it can be downloaded from a URL, just as an applet class would be. The URL from which to download the code will be set as a property for your client.

When you invoke the compute server's `compute` method, passing a `Pi` object, the server will need the `Pi` class. It will look at the URL that has been implicitly passed with the request, download the class, and run it in a secure sandbox. It will then invoke the Pi object's run method and return the result.

This ComputeServer example leverages the Java virtual machine's homogeneous computing model, in which all code means the same thing on all platforms, and its security model, in which downloaded code can be run securely.

Many environments can use the basic infrastructure just described. A compute farm that uses a large number of computers to render animation can use such a system to feed those computers images to be rendered, sound computations, and other tasks. This simple example needs some hardening to be used in other situations, especially when Task objects could not be trusted to be friendly. All you need is a Java virtual machine at both ends of the network.

UnicastRemoteObject references are for remote services that are started by the user or system. You can use java.rmi.activation.Activatable for references to remote objects that you want to be started automatically when they are first needed.

Because of the dangers inherent in running downloaded code, RMI requires that a security manager be installed. The RMISecurityManager class is a very conservative security manager that you can install to prevent unauthorized access to your system, or you can provide your own security manager.

Your server class may not be able to extend an RMI server class because your class must extend a different class. For example, an applet class must extend Applet and so cannot extend UnicastRemoteObject. You can create servers that do not extend UnicastRemoteObject by having your class's constructor invoke a static method:

```
public class SnazzyApplet extends Applet
    implements SnazzyRemote
{
    public SnazzyApplet() throws RemoteException {
        UnicastRemoteObject.exportObject(this);
    }
    // ... implement SnazzyRemote and Applet methods ...
}
```

Classes are downloaded from client to server (or server to client) only if they are needed. Classes will often be known on both sides. For example, BigDecimal is part of the core, so both the client and the server already know about it and it will not be downloaded. User-defined classes are treated in the same way—if both the client and server have a class installed, it will not be downloaded across the network.

Arguments and return values of remote methods are handled somewhat differently from those of local methods. RMI passes arguments and return values by using object serialization (see page 549). When a remote reference is passed as an argument or return value, the receiver will get a reference to the same remote object that was passed. This is how local references act in local methods—an object reference refers to the same object in both the invoking code and the invoked method. Primitive types, too, are passed in the same way locally and remotely; the receiver gets a copy of the value.

References to local objects must be passed differently. Local objects are not designed to deal with partial failures, so it is not possible to pass across the network a remote reference to a local object. Local objects are instead passed by a deep copy made by serialization. Any remote references contained within the object or in any part of the graph of objects it denotes will be passed as described earlier. All other parts of the graph will be serialized on the sender's system and deserialized on the receiver's. Changes made on one side will not be visible to the other side, because each side has its own local copy of the object.

The RMI registry provides a simple naming system to store remote references for bootstrapping your clients. This is not a full naming system, but it will let you store objects that register or find top-level services. The registry is accessed via the Naming class.

Server objects are governed by a "best effort" distributed garbage collector. When no outstanding references to a remote object exist, that object can be collected. This is similar in principle to garbage collection for local objects, but the failures of distributed computing make surety impossible. If a client hasn't been in contact for a long time, it is presumed to have gone away without notifying the server (possibly the system crashed). If a long-lived network failure is actually at fault, the client may find that the server has been garbage-collected when the network reconnects. Every reasonable effort is made to preclude this possibility. A server can ensure that it will never be garbage-collected by simply holding on to a remote reference to itself, thus ensuring that at least one remote reference will keep it alive. This reference can be dropped when the server decides that it no longer must be forced to be alive.

RMI is explicitly designed to take advantage of having both client and server in the Java programming language. This gives it a form that is simple and direct for people who know the language. You can, of course, implement any server methods you like as native methods. Native methods can help you use RMI as a bridge to existing native code, such as in two- and three-tier systems.

The subpackage java.rmi.activation provides for activatable servers, which will be started when they receive messages if they are not already running. Multiple servers can be put in the same activation group, and will then be run in the same virtual machine.

25.7 `java.security` and Related Packages—Security Tools

The security architecture that was introduced in Chapter 23 is quite extensive and incorporates a range of mechanisms for encryption, authorization, authentication, and so forth. These mechanisms are spread across a number of packages.

The package `java.security` contains several useful tools for security-related functions: digital signatures, message digests, key management, and cryptographic keys. Subpackages define abstractions for certificates (`java.security.cert`), RSA and DSA keys (`java.security.interfaces`), and key and algorithm parameter specifications (`java.security.spec`).

The `javax.security` subpackages complement these tools with a full authentication and authorization framework (`javax.security.auth` and its subpackages), including support for the Simple Authentication and Security Layer (SASL) as defined by RFC 2222 (the `javax.security.sasl` package). The authorization component allows specification of access controls based on code location, code signers, and code executors (subjects), using common protocols such as Kerberos and X500.

The `javax.crypto` package and subpackages (`interfaces` and `spec`) provide rich mechanisms for cryptography, including encryption with various kinds of ciphers, MAC generation, and key creation and agreement.

The `org.ietf.jgss` package provides a framework that helps you use security services such as authentication, data integrity, and data confidentiality from a variety of underlying security mechanisms. The security mechanisms an application can choose are identified with unique object identifiers. For example, the Kerberos v5 GSS-API mechanism has the object identifier 1.2.840.113554.1.2.2. This mechanism is available through the default instance of the `GSSManager` class.

Because there are many ways to approach things like cryptography and authentication, and there will be many more in the future, the security architecture provides abstractions of security interactions. Implementations of the abstractions are supplied by *providers.* Each platform has one or more providers. The `java.security.Security` utility class provides methods to find out which providers are available. Providers can interoperate through the provided abstractions.

Much more information on these packages, and on security in general in the virtual machine, is in *Inside Java™ 2 Platform Security, Second Edition.*

25.8 `java.sql`—Relational Database Access

The package `java.sql` provides the Java Database Connectivity™ (JDBC) package for using relational databases. These classes and methods can be implemented directly by your database vendor or through the industry-standard Open Database

Connectivity (ODBC) interface. JDBC is, in effect, a mapping of ODBC. The JDBC package and other issues about relational databases are covered in *JDBC*[TM] *API Tutorial and Reference, Third Edition.*

25.9 Utility Subpackages

Some of the utility classes in `java.util` are not independent classes but groups of related classes that together provide a particular functionality. These classes are themselves grouped into subpackages within `java.util`.[1]

25.9.1 Concurrency Utilities—`java.util.concurrent`

The package `java.util.concurrent`, together with its subpackages provides a range of utilities for writing efficient multithreaded applications. These utilities expand the in-built synchronization facilities of the Java programming language to allow building concurrent applications that would not otherwise be possible with synchronized code, and to simplify common synchronization tasks that would otherwise be tedious and error-prone to write using the language facilities. The utilities provided can be divided into five categories:

◆ Concurrent collections—These were described in Chapter 21.

◆ Synchronizers—A group of utility classes that simplify common synchronization tasks (discussed below).

◆ Executor framework—A framework for asynchronous task execution, including a flexible, high-performance thread pool implementation.

◆ Locks and Conditions—Classes that provide locking and waiting capabilities that go beyond those of the built-in monitor capabilities.

◆ Atomic variables—A set of classes that allow safe expression of lock-free and wait-free algorithms within an application.

There are four synchronizer classes:

◆ `Semaphore`—A counting semaphore. Useful for many situations in which access to a resource must be controlled. To use the resource a thread must acquire a (conceptual) permit, or token, from the semaphore. If none is available then the thread blocks until one is. When finished with the resource the

---

[1] For pragmatic reasons the collections classes had to be defined at the top level of `java.util`, rather than in a subpackage, because of the existing legacy collections.

thread releases the permit back to the semaphore to allow other threads to proceed. A counting semaphore can hold an arbitrary number of permits; a binary semaphore is a semaphore with only one permit.

◆ CountDownLatch—A utility for blocking until a given number of events have occurred or until certain conditions hold. The latch is created with a given number of events to expect. Each thread that triggers an event or sets a condition calls the countDown method which decrements the initial count. A thread that calls the await method will block until the latch has counted down to zero.

◆ CyclicBarrier—A utility that forces all threads using the barrier to wait until all those threads are ready to pass the barrier. This is useful for multi-phase algorithms in which all threads must complete a given phase before any threads commence the next phase.

◆ Exchanger—A simple utility that allows two threads to exchange data. The first thread to arrive at the exchanger waits until the other arrives, they then exchange data and proceed.

An Executor knows how to execute a task—which is represented by a Runnable object—and replaces the direct creation of new threads within an application. Depending on the implementation used, the Executor may execute the task in the current thread, submit the task to a thread pool for later execution, or perhaps create a new thread to execute the task. The Executor abstracts all the details of thread creation and management and allows the problem of executing tasks to be separated from the problem of generating tasks. An ExecutorService expands on the basic executor to provide lifecycle management—such as shutting down an executor. Particular implementations of ExecutorService provide thread pools (ThreadPoolExecutor) and permit the scheduling of tasks in the future (ScheduledThreadPoolExecutor).

The Callable interface defines a task that can return a result (unlike a Runnable). A Future represents a computation—such as that in a Callable—that may not yet have completed or even begun. You can submit a Future to an Executor (using the concrete FutureTask class) knowing that at some time in the future the result of the computation will be available. You can use the Future to ask whether the task has completed or to block until the task completes and the result is available.

The java.util.concurrent.locks subpackage defines the Lock and Condition interfaces and the ReentrantLock implementation. Lock abstracts the functionality of locking, as implied in the use of synchronized blocks and methods, to allow more flexible locking. A Lock can be locked in one method and unlocked in a different one—something that is needed in some concurrent traversal algorithms, and which is impossible to do with `synchronized` blocks or methods. In addition, the methods of `Lock` allow you to acquire the lock only if it is available—that is, you don't block trying to acquire the lock—or to stop trying to acquire the lock if interrupted or if a certain time has elapsed.

A `Condition` abstracts the functionality of the `Object` monitor methods `wait`, `notify`, and `notifyAll` into a distinct interface with methods `await`, `signal`, and `signalAll`. `Condition` objects are used with `Lock` objects the same way that `wait`/`notify` are used with monitors. The advantage is that while there is only a single wait-set per object, a `Lock` can have as many associated `Condition` objects as you need. The `ReentrantLock` class is one useful implementation of `Lock` that gives you `Condition` objects that are functionally equivalent to `synchronized` methods and blocks, plus the use of the monitor methods.

The package also contains the `ReadWriteLock` interface—and an implementation—for a lock that allows for both exclusive use and shared use—informally, only one writer may hold the lock (exclusive) but arbitrarily many readers can hold the lock (shared).

The `java.util.concurrent.atomic` package provides classes that represents values (`int`, `long`, references, and arrays of these values) that can be manipulated atomically. These classes provide operations that without the use of locks or in-built synchronization can, for example, get, set, increment, or decrement an integer. Atomic variables are used in the implementation of high-performance concurrent algorithms. For each basic atomic variable class, such as `AtomicInteger`, there is a corresponding atomic field updater class, such as `AtomicIntegerFieldUpdater`, that allows you to access a given field of an object atomically. These classes also provide the `compareAndSet` operation that is the fundamental operation in most lock-free and wait-free concurrent algorithms. It will atomically set a variable to a new value only if the variable currently holds an expected value.

25.9.2 Archive Files—`java.util.jar`

The `java.util.jar` package provides classes for reading and writing the JAR (Java ARchive) file format, which is based on the standard ZIP file format with an optional manifest file. JAR files can be used to distribute the classes and resources of a `Package` as a single unit. The manifest stores information about the JAR file contents and provides the specification information for the `Package` contained therein—as we discussed on page 477.

Archive files define a format for storing multiple files within a single file, and allow for the compression of those original file contents. A full description of archive files, particularly the JAR format, is beyond the scope of this book. For illustration we briefly describe each of the classes within the `java.util.jar` package:

- `Attributes`—maps `Manifest` attribute names to associated string values.
- `Attributes.Name`—represents an attribute's name. The main function of this class is to define static `Attributes.Name` objects for each attribute that a manifest may have. For example, the object corresponding to the "Manifest-Version" attribute of a manifest is stored in the static field `Attributes.Name.MANIFEST_VERSION`.
- `JarEntry`—represents a JAR file entry.
- `JarFile`—represents an actual JAR file and allows that JAR file to be read or written.
- `JarInputStream`—reads a JAR file. Methods exist that read each entry of the JAR file into a new `JarEntry` object.
- `JarOutputStream`—writes a JAR file. Methods exist that take a `JarEntry` object that is written to the JAR file.
- `Manifest`—maintains manifest entry names and their associated attributes.

A `JarFile` represents an actual JAR file and allows its contents to be read or written with the appropriate streams. A JAR file consists of a manifest and a number of JAR entries that can be read or written individually. The manifest contains all the attributes of the JAR file and all the attributes of the entries in the JAR file. The manifest is decoded with the `Manifest` and `Attributes` classes. Each `JarEntry` contains the per-entry attributes extracted from the manifest.

Most users never need to use the classes within `java.util.jar`. JAR files can be created via tools supplied as part of your development environment and are read automatically by the class loader within the virtual machine when needed.

25.9.3 ZIP Files — `java.util.zip`

The `java.util.zip` package provides classes for reading and writing standard ZIP and GZIP file formats. We mention it only for completeness, as it predates the newer JAR file format and forms its basis.

- `ZipFile`—represents a ZIP or GZIP format file.
- `ZipEntry`—represents an entry in a ZIP or GZIP format file.
- `ZipInputStream`—reads ZIP file format.
- `ZipOutputStream`—writes ZIP file format.

- ◆ `GZIPInputStream`—reads GZIP file format.
- ◆ `GZIPOutputStream`—writes GZIP file format.
- ◆ `Deflater`—provides general support for using ZLIB compression.
- ◆ `DeflaterOutputStream`—writes using ZLIB compression
- ◆ `Inflater`—provides general support for using ZLIB decompression.
- ◆ `InflaterInputStream`—reads ZLIB compressed data.
- ◆ `CheckedInputStream`—reads a stream, creating a checksum of the data.
- ◆ `CheckedOutputStream`—writes a stream, creating a checksum of the data.
- ◆ `CRC32`—computes a checksum using the CRC-32 algorithm.
- ◆ `Adler32`—computes a checksum using the Adler-32 algorithm.

25.10 `javax.*`—Standard Extensions

Standard extensions are packages or collections of packages that can be downloaded to extend the capabilities of a particular virtual machine. They will usually have names starting with `javax`, although future exceptions may be made. Conversely, packages with `javax` in the name may become part of the main set of packages over time. For example, the `javax.swing` and `javax.accessibility` packages are part of the main set. The name indicates that they were at first not part of the main set, but integrated later.

Standard extensions are a mechanism that allows growth in the capabilities of the platform without further extensions to the core packages required of all virtual machines. New standard extensions can be defined and made available, but only installed where they are needed. Several standard extensions are defined, and more are on the way. Listing them all is far outside the scope of this book—you can find more information on the Web, especially at `http://java.sun.com`.

25.11 `javax.accessibility`—Accessibility for GUIs

Graphical user interfaces traditionally assume certain kinds of abilities on the part of the user, such as the ability to use a mouse or keyboard. These assumptions are a problem for some people. The `javax.accessiblity` interfaces and classes provide a way to write interfaces that can use assistive technologies for input and output, allowing people with different abilities to use the same interfaces. If an application fully supports the accessibility API, then it should be compatible with, and friendly toward, assistive technologies such as screen readers and magnifiers.

25.12 `javax.naming`—Directory and Naming Services

This package defines the naming operations of the Java Naming and Directory Interface™ (JNDI), with the subpackage `javax.naming.directory`, defining the directory operations. These are designed to be independent of any specific naming or directory service implementation. Thus a variety of services—new, emerging, and already deployed ones—can be accessed in a common way.

A context, represented by the `Context` interface, consists of a set of name-to-object bindings. `Context` is the core interface for looking up, binding, unbinding, and renaming objects, and for creating and destroying subcontexts. `lookup` is the most commonly used operation. You supply `lookup` the name of the object you want to look up, and it returns the object bound to that name. For example, the following code fragment looks up a printer and sends a document to the printer object to be printed:

```
Printer printer = (Printer) ctx.lookup("Duplex");
printer.print(report);
```

Every naming method in the `Context` interface has two overloads: one that accepts a `Name` argument and one that accepts a string name. `Name` is an interface that represents a generic name—an ordered sequence of zero or more components. For these methods, you can use `Name` to represent a composite name (`CompositeName`) so that you can use a name that spans multiple namespaces.

The overloads that accept `Name` arguments are useful for applications that need to manipulate names: composing them, comparing components, and so on. The overloads that accept string names are likely to be more useful for simple applications, such as those that simply read in a name and look up the corresponding object.

The `Binding` class represents a name-to-object binding. It is a tuple containing the name of the bound object, the name of the object's class, and the object itself. The `Binding` class is actually a subclass of `NameClassPair`, which consists simply of the object's name and the object's class name. The `NameClassPair` is useful when you only want information about the object's class and do not want to pay the extra cost of getting the object.

Objects are stored in naming and directory services in different ways. If an object store supports storing objects it might store that object in its serialized form. However, some naming and directory services do not support the storing of such objects. Furthermore, for some objects in the directory, Java programs are just one group of applications that access them. In this case, a serialized object might not be the most appropriate representation. JNDI defines a `Reference` that contains information on how to construct a copy of the object. JNDI will attempt to turn references looked up from the directory into the objects they represent so that JNDI clients have the illusion that what is stored in the directory are objects.

In JNDI, all naming and directory operations are performed relative to a context—there are no absolute roots. Therefore, JNDI defines an `InitialContext` class that provides a starting point for naming and directory operations. Once you have an initial context, you can use it to look up other contexts and objects.

The `DirContext` interface represents a directory context. It defines methods for examining and updating attributes associated with a directory object, or directory entry as it is sometimes called. You use `getAttributes` to retrieve the attributes associated with a directory object (for which you supply the name). You can add, replace, or remove attributes and/or attribute values with the `modifyAttributes` method.

`DirContext` also behaves as a naming context by extending the `Context` interface. This means that any directory object can also provide a naming context. For example, the directory object for a person might contain the attributes of that person, and also provide a context for naming objects relative to that person such as printers and home directory.

`DirContext` contains methods for performing content-based searching of the directory. In the simplest and most common form of usage, the application specifies a set of attributes—possibly with specific values—to match, and submits this attribute set to the `search` method. Other overloads of `search` support more sophisticated search filters.

The subpackage `javax.naming.event` supports event notification for directory and naming services. Events include adding or removing objects, as well as events signifying changes in the stored objects themselves.

The subpackage `javax.naming.spi` defines the Service Provider Interface (SPI) which allows for dynamically plugging in support for using JNDI.

25.13 `javax.sound`—Sound Manipulation

The `javax.sound` package consists only of subpackages. `javax.sound.midi` provides interfaces for reading, writing, sequencing, and synthesizing data that conforms to the Musical Instrument Digital Interface (MIDI) format. `javax.sound.sampled` provides classes and interfaces for capturing, processing, and playing back digital (sampled) audio data. Each of these has a SPI subpackage to support the dynamic addition of sound services.

25.14 `javax.swing`—Swing GUI Components

The Swing components are a rich set of graphical user-interface controls. They are written to look and behave for the user identically on all systems as far as possible. This is in contrast to the AWT components which rely on the native GUI components. An AWT button will look like a Windows button on a Windows machine, a Macintosh button on a Macintosh computer, and so forth—its interaction with the program is the same on all platforms, but the user will see the native look and feel. A Swing component can have the same look on all platforms—its code is written in the Java programming language. The look and feel is "pluggable"—you or the user can use one of the standard look-and-feels or invent one. Swing components are also give you more control over the look and behavior of the system. You only occasionally need such control, but it is nice to have it when you do need it.

The Swing components use the same event model as AWT and JavaBeans components, although the components do define some new events.

Several subpackages define interface objects, tools for defining a custom pluggable look-and-feel, support HTML and text editing, and support some of the more complex components, such as tree displays and tables.

25.15 `org.omg.CORBA`—CORBA APIs

The package `org.omg.CORBA`, its various subpackages and other `org.omg` subpackages (such as `CosNaming`) provide the mapping of the OMG CORBA APIs and services to the Java programming language. (The package names are different from the standard core package names because they are defined by the Object Management Group and incorporated into the core package set.) CORBA is a way to send messages between processes that are not necessarily written in the same programming language. This is distinct from RMI, which communicates between programs written, at least in part, in the Java programming language (we use the phrase "at least in part" because RMI programs can include native code).

Programming today is a race
between software engineers striving to build bigger and better idiot-proof programs,
and the universe trying to produce bigger and better idiots.
So far the universe is winning.
—Rich Cook

Application Evolution

With every passing hour our solar system
comes 43,000 miles closer to globular cluster M13 in the constellation Hercules,
and still there are some misfits who continue to insist that there is no such thing as progress.
—Ransom K. Ferm

THE Java platform has undergone a number of changes since it was first introduced, but none more significant than those that occurred with the 5.0 release. While in general we try to avoid issues concerning the evolution of the platform, it is impossible to ignore those issues now. For some time to come, there will be applications and libraries that still comply with the older 1.3 version of the platform (as documented in the third edition of this book), those that support the additional features introduced in the 1.4 release, and finally those moving forward to take full advantage of the new features of the 5.0 release. The technical issues involved in application evolution and migration can be complex, and many of the changes to the language and libraries for the 5.0 release were designed with backward compatibility and migration in mind. A full coverage of the technical issues, let alone the management and logistics issues involved, is beyond the scope of this book, but we do want to highlight a couple of areas for your consideration.

The first section gives a brief overview of how the compiler and virtual machine can deal with different versions of the language and runtime. Next, we look at some ways of dealing with the different dialects that language changes produce, using assertions as an example. Finally, we look at some of the issues involving the integration of generic and non-generic code.

A.1 Language, Library, and Virtual Machine Versions

Each new release of the Java platform potentially changes three things:

- ◆ The language itself, through the addition of new keywords or extensions to the use of existing keywords
- ◆ The libraries: new types and/or new methods on existing types
- ◆ The virtual machine, and in particular the format of the compiled classes that the virtual machine expects

Not every new platform release changes all three—in particular, changes to the class format occur rarely because of the major impact such changes can have.

The compiler that comes with the Java Development Kit (JDK) tracks changes to the language and virtual machine through the use of "source" and "target" options that can be passed to it. By supplying an appropriate source and target pair you can compile code that will run on current or older versions of the virtual machine—assuming the code is compatible with the source version of the language chosen.

The different source versions and their approximate meaning are as follows:

- ◆ 1.1—The oldest recognized definition of the language, which included the original language definition together with nested types and blank final variables. This source version is no longer supported by the compiler in the 5.0 release.
- ◆ 1.2—Introduced the `strictfp` modifier.
- ◆ 1.3—Same as 1.2; this version number was added for consistency.
- ◆ 1.4—Introduced `assert`.
- ◆ 1.5—Introduced generics, enums, annotations, and extended `for` loop. Also uses `StringBuilder` rather than `StringBuffer` for string concatenation.

Similarly, the target versions are

- ◆ 1.1—Compliant with the first edition of the Java Virtual Machine Specification (JVMS)
- ◆ 1.2—Compliant with the second edition of the JVMS. The main change involved the way static member accesses were encoded in the compiled class and resolved at runtime.
- ◆ 1.3—No known change
- ◆ 1.4—No known change
- ◆ 1.5—Compliant with the third edition of the JVMS. This enables support for enums, annotations, and some aspects of generics. It also modifies the way class literals are implemented.

Because some language changes require new library classes, a change in the source version may imply a minimum target value. For example, a source of 1.4 requires a target of 1.4 because an earlier version of the virtual machine won't have the classes or methods that support assertions. Not surprisingly, a source of 1.5 requires a target of 1.5 as well. Naturally, source and target versions that came into existence after a given compiler was released are not supported.

Each target version causes a change in the class file version number that is encoded in the compiled classes. Each virtual machine knows what class versions it supports and will generally refuse to load any class files that have a higher version number. This means, for example, that you can prevent a class from being loaded on an older virtual machine even if there is no missing functionality in the version.

The default settings for the compiler in the 5.0 release are source 1.5 and target 1.5 to enable all the latest features of the language. If you compile code to run on previous versions (which doesn't use the new features of course) you'll need to explicitly set the target to a suitable earlier version.

A.2 Dealing with Multiple Dialects

Adding new keywords to the language runs the risk of breaking existing code, especially if the word is an identifier as common as "assert" or "enum."[1] The choice to add a new keyword creates some interesting and important compatibility issues. Taking assertions as an example, you can choose whether or not `assert` is recognized in your code by selecting a source version of 1.4 or higher. This allows you to keep your old use of "assert" in one class, while using the language assertions in another—provided the different uses are independent. When asserts were introduced in the 1.4 release, the default source version was left at 1.3 so by default nothing changed and you had to explicitly tell the compiler when you were ready to use the new language feature. In the 5.0 release the presumption is that everyone will want to use at least some of the new features, so they are enabled by default—if you don't want them you must either specify the appropriate source version or use an older version of the compiler.

These side-by-side dialects can create problems. With only one dialect you could use the same compiler, and the same compiler options, on all your source code. With two or more dialects you might have some source files that require `assert` or `enum` and others that reject it. You will have to compile your source carefully to handle such a situation. At this point, there are three dialects: with

---

[1]   The keyword `strictfp` was added to the language in the 1.2 release but caused almost no problems because nearly nobody had ever used it as an identifier.

assert and enum (5.0), with assert but not enum (1.4), and without either (1.3 and earlier).

The obvious solution is to use a single dialect for all your source. But you will not always have that kind of control. If you are using source produced by another group they may have moved on while you cannot, or vice versa.

This is deeper than you might hope. Suppose you have two source files, Newer.java which uses the assert keyword and Older.java which uses "assert" as a method name. If the newer class depends on the older and neither has yet been compiled, compiling Newer.java will attempt to compile Older.java as well. With only one dialect this is a feature. But with the incompatible dialects you will be unable to compile Newer.java until you have already compiled Older.java under the non-assert dialect. This complicates your build process because the order in which you compile things has now become significant.

Of course, the ultimate problem is if Newer.java and Older.java depend on each other. Now you have a loop you cannot solve without modifying one source file. Presumably you would upgrade Older.java to use the new dialect, but if you cannot do so you will have to regress Newer.java to the older dialect.

Woe betide if you can modify neither.

A.3   Generics: Reification, Erasure, and Raw Types

The generic type system was added to the Java programming language for the 5.0 release. The design was strongly constrained by the need to maintain compatibility between independently developed code modules that may or may not include the use of generics. The key design decision was that generic types could not be reified at runtime. Rather, for each generic type declaration there would be a single type that was defined in terms of the erasure of its type variables. As we discussed in Chapter 11, in simple terms the type is defined such that each type variable is replaced by its bound—commonly Object. The reasoning behind this decision is beyond the scope of this book, but to quote JLS 4.7 (*The Java*™ *Language Specification, Third Edition*, Section 4.7):

> …the design of the generic type system seeks to support migration compatibility. Migration compatibility allows the evolution of existing code to take advantage of generics without imposing dependencies between independently developed software modules. The price of migration compatibility is that full reification of the generic type system is not possible, at least while the migration is taking place.

Note that in the future, this design decision might be changed.

A.3.1   Raw Types, "Unchecked" Warnings, and Bridge Methods

A consequence of the reification design decision is the existence and use of raw types. Raw types represent the erasure of a specific generic type. They exist so that code that was written to use a non-generic version of a class or interface can execute in a virtual machine that uses a generic version of that class or interface. Some of these uses may cause *"unchecked" warnings* to be issued by the compiler, but the uses are still permitted. "Unchecked" warnings are emitted in the following circumstances:

- Assignment from a raw type variable to a parameterized type variable—the raw type variable might not refer to an instance of the expected parameterized type.

- Casts involving type variables—the cast cannot be checked at runtime because the erasure of the type variable is used.

- Invocation of a method or constructor of a raw type if erasure changes the type of a parameter.

- Access to a field of a raw type if erasure changes the type of the field.

The conversion between a raw type and a parameterized type adds an additional conversion to those defined in Section 9.4 on page 216: the *unchecked conversion*. These unchecked conversions can be applied as the final step in most of the conversion contexts—for example, as part of an assignment. An unchecked conversion is always accompanied by an "unchecked" warning, unless it has been suppressed by using the annotation SuppressWarnings("unchecked")—if your compiler supports this.

Use of raw types can also lead to other complications. Consider a variation of the passThrough example from Chapter 11 repackaged as a generic interface:

```
interface PassThrough<T> {
    T passThrough(T t);
}
```

Now consider an implementation of that interface:

```
class PassThroughString implements PassThrough<String> {
    public String passThrough(String t) {
        return t;
    }
}
```

and the following incorrect use:

```
public static void main(String[] args) {
    PassThrough s = new PassThroughString();
    s.passThrough(args);
}
```

This results in an "unchecked" warning at compile time because the use of the raw type means that we don't know what type passThrough should take or return. But we can see that s.passThrough should only be accepting a String argument, and args is a String[] not a String. If the compiler rejected the above, we could appease the compiler by casting args to String, and then we should expect, and would get, a ClassCastException at runtime. However, the compiler doesn't reject this code, but in fact if we execute this method a ClassCastException is still thrown. This behavior is specified as a special rule of method invocation that deals with this situation in JLS 15.12.4.5:

> If the erasure of the type of the method being invoked differs in its signature from the erasure of the type of the compile-time declaration for the method invocation, then if any of the argument values is an object which is not an instance of a subclass or subinterface of the erasure of the corresponding formal parameter type in the compile-time declaration for the method invocation, then a ClassCastException is thrown.

In simple terms, the compiler has to accept incorrect invocations like the above at compile time, but it has to ensure that at runtime the bad argument is not actually passed to the method. The ClassCastException must be thrown before invoking the method (as if we had put in the bad cast ourselves). One way a compiler can ensure this is to introduce what is known as a *bridge method*. A suitable bridge method in this case would be the following:

```
public Object passThrough(Object o) {
    return passThrough((String)o);
}
```

The compiler would insert calls to this bridge method, rather than calls to the actual method. Thus, the cast will fail when it should and succeed otherwise. Because bridge methods are introduced by the compiler, they will be marked as synthetic.

Bridge methods also fill another role in maintaining backward compatibility. For example, prior to generics the Comparable interface's compareTo method took an Object argument, but now it takes a T, whatever that may be. However, code compiled against non-generified Comparable implementations have bytecodes to invoke a version of the method that takes an `Object`. No such version is defined in the source code, but the compiler generates a `compareTo(Object)` bridge method that casts the argument to the expected type and invokes the new `compareTo` method.

The use of raw types in code written after generics was added is strongly discouraged, as they exist only for backward compatibility and may be removed in a future version of the language.

A.3.2 API Issues

A second compatibility issue concerns the changes to the APIs themselves, within the class libraries. Many, if not all, the generic types in the class libraries would have been written slightly differently had they been written from scratch to be generic types. For example, a number of methods in the collections classes that define a collection of T still take parameters of type `Object`. That was what the old signature specified, and changing it would break compatibility.

As another example, the reflection method in `java.lang.reflect.Array` to create a new array is still defined as

```
public static Object newInstance(Class<?> type, int length)
```

which has the unfortunate consequence that use of this method always results in an "unchecked" warning by the compiler. A generic version might be specified as

```
public static <T> T[] newInstance(Class<T> type, int length)
```

but not only is that not backward compatible, it precludes creating arrays where the component type is a primitive type. So even with a type-safe generic method, you'd still need a second method to allow primitive array creation.

There is a similar problem with implementing the `clone` method: You cannot define a `clone` method for a parameterized type without getting an "unchecked" warning when you cast the `Object` result of `Object.clone` to the correct type. This is one of those rare occasions in which a cast using the expected parameterized type is the right thing to do. For example, given a generic class `Cell<E>`, the `clone` method should be declared to return an instance of `Cell<E>` because that will permit the caller of `clone` to use the returned object without the need for any casts. To declare `clone` in that way requires that the result of `super.clone` be cast to `Cell<E>`, which incurs the "unchecked" warning. But be warned, an erroneous or malicious clone implementation could still return an object of the wrong type.

As you generify you own applications and libraries you must be aware of these issues in order to maintain the right level of compatibility with users of your code.

> *Things will get better despite our efforts to improve them.*
> —Will Rogers

Useful Tables

How many seconds are there in a year?
If I tell you there are 3.155×10^7 you won't even try to remember it.
On the other hand, who could forget that, to within half a percent, π seconds is a nanocentury?
—Tom Duff, Bell Labs

TABLE 1: **Keywords**

abstract	continue	for	new	switch
assert	default	goto[†]	package	synchronized
boolean	do	if	private	this
break	double	implements	protected	throw
byte	else	import	public	throws
case	enum	instanceof	return	transient
catch	extends	int	short	try
char	final	interface	static	void
class	finally	long	strictfp	volatile
const[†]	float	native	super	while

NOTE: Keywords marked with [†] are unused

TABLE 2: **Operator Precedence**

Operator Type	Operator
Postfix operators	`[] . (params) expr++ expr--`
Unary operators	`++expr --expr +expr -expr ~ !`
Creation or cast	`new (type)expr`
Multiplicative	`* / %`
Additive	`+ -`
Shift	`<< >> >>>`
Relational	`< > >= <= instanceof`
Equality	`== !=`
AND	`&`
Exclusive OR	`^`
Inclusive OR	`|`
Conditional AND	`&&`
Conditional OR	`||`
Conditional	`?:`
Assignment	`= += -= *= /= %= >>= <<= >>>= &= ^= |=`

TABLE 3: **Special Characters Using **

Sequence	Meaning
`\n`	Newline (\u000A)
`\t`	Tab (\u0009)
`\b`	Backspace (\u0008)
`\r`	Return (\u000D)
`\f`	Form feed (\u000C)
`\\`	Backslash itself (\u005C)
`\'`	Single quote (\u0027)
`\"`	Double quote (\u0022)
`\ddd`	An octal char, with each *d* being an octal digit (0–7)
`\uxxxx`	A Unicode char, with each x being a hex digit (0–9, a–f, A–F)

TABLE 4: **Regular Expression Special Characters**

Construct	Matches
CHARACTERS	
x	The character *x*
\\	backslash
\0*n*	character with octal value 0*n*
\0*nn*	character with octal value 0*nn*
\0*nnn*	character with octal value 0*nnn* (*nnn* $\leq$ 377)
\x*hh*	character with hexadecimal 0x*hh*
\u*hhhh*	character with hexadecimal value 0x*hhhh*
\t	tab character ('\u0009')
\n	newline character ('\u000A')
\r	carriage-return character ('\u000D')
\f	form-feed character ('\u000C')
\a	alert (bell) character ('\u0007')
\e	escape character ('\u001B')
\c*x*	control character corresponding to *x*
CHARACTER CLASSES	
[abc]	a, b, or c (simple class)
[^abc]	any character except a, b, or c (negation)
[a-zA-Z]	a through z or A through Z, inclusive (range)
[a-d[m-p]]	a through d or m through p; [a-dm-p] (union)
[a-z&[def]]	d, e, or f; [def] (intersection)
[a-z&[^bc]]	a through z, except b or c; [ad-z] (subtraction)
[a-z&[^m-p]]	a through z, except m through p; [a-lq-z]
PREDEFINED CHARACTER CLASSES	
.	any character (might match line terminators)
\d	digit; [0-9]
\D	non-digit; [^0-9]
\s	whitespace character; [\t\n\x0B\f\r]
\S	non-whitespace character; [^\s]
\w	word character; [a-zA-Z_0-9]
\W	non-word character; [^\w]
JAVA CHARACTER CLASSES	
\p{javaLowerCase}	as defined by Character.isLowerCase
\p{javaUpperCase}	as defined by Character.isUpperCase
\p{javaWhitespace}	as defined by Character.isWhitespace
\p{javaMirrored}	as defined by Character.isMirrored

TABLE 4: **Regular Expression Special Characters**

Construct	Matches
POSIX CHARACTER CLASSES (US-ASCII ONLY)	
\p{Lower}	lowercase alphabetic character; [a-z]
\p{Upper}	uppercase alphabetic character; [A-Z]
\p{ASCII}	ASCII character; [\x00-\x7F]
\p{Alpha}	alphabetic character; [\p{Lower}\p{Upper}]
\p{Digit}	decimal digit; [0-9]
\p{Alnum}	alphanumeric character; [\p{Alpha}\p{Digit}]
\p{Punct}	punctuation; one of
	!"#$%&'()*+,-./:;<=>?@[\]^_'{|}~
\p{Graph}	visible character; [\p{Alnum}\p{Punct}]
\p{Print}	printable character; [\p{Graph}]
\p{Blank}	space or a tab; [\t]
\p{Cntrl}	control character; [\x00-\x1F\x7F]
\p{XDigit}	hexadecimal digit; [0-9a-fA-F]
\p{Space}	whitespace character; [\t\n\x0B\f\r]
CLASSES FOR UNICODE BLOCKS AND CATEGORIES	
\p{InGreek}	character in the Greek block (simple block)
\p{Lu}	uppercase letter (simple category)
\p{Sc}	currency symbol ($, ¥, £, etc.)
\P{InGreek}	character except one in the Greek block (negation)
[\p{L}&[^\p{Lu}]]	any letter except an uppercase letter (subtraction)
BOUNDARY MATCHERS	
^	beginning of a line (if in multiline mode)
$	end of a line (if in multiline mode)
\b	word boundary
\B	non-word boundary
\A	beginning of input
\G	end of previous match
\Z	end of input except any final terminator
\z	end of input
GREEDY QUANTIFIERS	
$X?$	X once or not at all
$X*$	X zero or more times
$X+$	X one or more times
$X\{n\}$	X exactly n times
$X(n,\}$	X at least n times
$X\{n,m\}$	X at least n but not more than m times

TABLE 4: **Regular Expression Special Characters**

Construct	Matches
RELUCTANT QUANTIFIERS	
$X??$	X once or not at all
$X*?$	X zero or more times
$X+?$	X one or more times
$X\{n\}?$	X exactly n times
$X(n,\}?$	X at least n times
$X\{n,m\}?$	X at least n but not more than m times
POSSESSIVE QUANTIFIERS	
$X?+$	X once or not at all
$X*+$	X zero or more times
$X++$	X one or more times
$X\{n\}+$	X exactly n times
$X(n,\}+$	X at least n times
$X\{n,m\}+$	X at least n but not more than m times
LOGICAL OPERATORS	
XY	X followed by Y
$X\vert Y$	either X or Y
(X)	X as a capturing group
BACK REFERENCES	
$\backslash n$	what the nth capturing group matched
QUOTATION	
$\backslash$	nothing, but quotes the following character
$\backslash Q$	nothing, but quotes all characters until \E
$\backslash E$	nothing, but ends quoting started by \Q
SPECIAL CONSTRUCTS (NON-CAPTURING)	
$(?:X)$	X as a non-capturing group
$(?idmsux-idmsux)$	nothing, but turns match flags on/off
$(?idmsux-idmsux:X)$	X as a non-capturing group with the given flags on/off
$(?=X)$	X via zero-width positive lookahead
$(?!X)$	X via zero-width negative lookahead
$(?<;=X)$	X via zero-width positive lookbehind
$(?<;!X)$	X via zero-width negative lookbehind
$(?>;X)$	X as an independent, non-capturing group

TABLE 5: **Documentation Comment Tags**

Tag	Description
@see	Cross reference to another doc comment or URL
{@link}	In-line cross reference to another doc comment or URL
{@linkPlain}	Similar to {@link} but uses regular font not code font
@param *p*	Description of the single parameter *p*
@return	Description of the return value of a method
@throws *E*	Description of an exception *E* that the method may throw
@exception *E*	Older form of @throws *E*
@deprecated	Deprecate, describing any replacement; the compiler generates warnings on use of deprecated entities
@author	An author of the code
@version	A version string for the entity
@since	The version string for when this entity first appeared
{@literal *text*}	Includes the given *text* as-is without treating it as HTML
{@code *text*}	Similar to {@literal} but uses code font
{@value *field*}	The value of the named static constant field
@serial	Identifies a field serialized using default serialization
@serialField	A field created by GetField or PutField objects
@serialData	Documents additional data written during serialization
{@inheritDoc}	Copies document comments from the supertype
{@docRoot}	Expands to a relative path to the root of the documentation tree; for use within links

TABLE 6: **Required Character Sets**

Charset	Description
US-ASCII	7-bit ASCII, also known as ISO-646-US and as the Basic Latin block of the Unicode character set
ISO-8859-1	ISO Latin Alphabet No. 1, also known as ISO-LATIN-1
UTF-8	8-bit Unicode Transformation Format
UTF-16BE	16-bit Unicode Transformation Format, big-endian order
UTF-16LE	16-bit Unicode Transformation Format, little-endian order
UTF-16	16-bit Unicode Transformation Format, byte order specified by a mandatory initial byte-order mark (either order accepted on input, big-endian used on output)

Comparing information and knowledge
is like asking whether the fatness of a pig
is more or less green than the designated hitter rule.
—David Guaspari

Further Reading

The best book on programming for the layman is Alice in Wonderland,
but that's because it's the best book on anything for the layman.
—Alan J. Perlis

WE offer this list of works for further reading on related topics. The list is necessarily duosyncratic—other excellent works exist on many of these topics. Of course, all the books in this series are recommended for their respective topics.

JAVA PLATFORM TOPICS

- `http://java.sun.com/`, Sun Microsystems, Inc.
  Current information on the Java programming language and related topics, including releases, security issues, and online documentation.

- `http://java.sun.com/Series/`, Sun Microsystems, Inc.
  Current information about books in this series, including errata and updates. Of special interest will be those errata and updates for this book.

- *The Unicode Standard 4.0,* Addison-Wesley, 2003, ISBN 0321185781.
  More data on Unicode is available at `http://www.unicode.org`.

- *IEEE/ANSI Standard for Binary Floating-Point Arithmetic.* Institute of Electrical and Electronics Engineers, 1985, IEEE Std 754-1985.

- `http://www.unicode.org/unicode/onlinedat/languages.html`
  One site where you can find two-letter ISO 639 codes for languages.

- `http://www.unicode.org/unicode/onlinedat/countries.html`
  One site where you can find two-letter ISO 3166 codes for countries.

- ◆ "Uniprocessor Garbage Collection Techniques," by Paul R. Wilson, University of Texas, in revision for *ACM Computing Surveys*—also available from `http://www.cs.utexas.edu/users/oops/`
  Although dated, this is a good survey of uniprocessor garbage collection techniques that may or may not be used by your particular virtual-machine implementations.

- ◆ *Garbage Collection: Algorithms for Automatic Dynamic Memory Management,* by Richard Jones, John Wiley, and Sons, 1999, ISBN 0-471-94148-4
  An extensive coverage of many different forms of garbage collection and their respective trade-offs. Information about the book is available from `http://www.cs.kent.ac.uk/people/staff/rej/gc.html`, including an extensive online bibliography of over 1800 papers.

- ◆ `http://www.w3.org/`
  Main site for the World Wide Web Consortium, where you can find documentation for HTML tags, which are usable in doc comments.

- ◆ `http://tycho.usno.navy.mil/systime.html`
  U.S. Naval Observatory data on the time paradigms used in the `Date` class.

OBJECT-ORIENTED DESIGN

- ◆ *An Introduction to Object-Oriented Programming, 3rd Edition,* by Timothy Budd. Addison-Wesley, 2001, ISBN 0201760312
  An introduction to object-oriented programming as well as a comparison of Java, C++, Objective C, Smalltalk, and Delphi.

- ◆ *Pitfalls of Object-Oriented Development,* by Bruce F. Webster. M&T Books, 1995, ISBN 1-55851-397-3.
  A collection of traps to avoid in object technology. Alerts you to problems you're likely to encounter and presents some solutions for them.

- ◆ *Design Patterns,* by Erich Gamma, Richard Helm, Ralph Johnson, and John Vlissides. Addison-Wesley, 1995, ISBN 0-201-63361-2.

- ◆ *Object-Oriented Analysis and Design with Applications, 2nd Edition,* by Grady Booch. Benjamin/Cummings, 1994, ISBN 0-805-35340-2.

- ◆ *Structured Programming,* by Ole-Johan Dahl, Edsger Wybe Dijkstra, and C. A. R. Hoare. Academic Press, 1972, ISBN 0-12-200550-3.

◆ *Object-Oriented Programming: An Evolutionary Approach, 2nd Edition,* by Brad J. Cox and Andrew Novobilski. Addison-Wesley, 1991, ISBN 0-201-54834-8.

MULTITHREADED PROGRAMMING

◆ *Concurrent Programming in Java™: Design Principles and Patterns, 2nd Edition,* by Doug Lea. Addison-Wesley, 1999, ISBN 0-201-31009-0.

◆ *Programming with Threads,* by Steve Kleiman, Devang Shah, and Bart Smaalders. Prentice Hall, 1996, ISBN 0-13-172389-8.

◆ *Programming with POSIX Threads,* by David R. Butenhof. Addison-Wesley, 1997, ISBN 0-201-63392-2.

◆ *The Architecture of Concurrent Programs,* by Per Brinch Hansen. Prentice Hall, 1977, ISBN 0-13-044628-9.

◆ "Monitors: An Operating System Structuring Concept," by C. A. R. Hoare. *Communications of the ACM,* Volume 17, number 10, 1974, pp. 549–557.
   The seminal paper on using monitors to synchronize concurrent tasks.

GENERICS

◆ "Making the Future Safe for the Past: Adding Genericity to the Java™ Programming Language," by Gilad Bracha, Martin Odersky, David Stoutamire, and Philip Wadler. In *Proceedings of the ACM Conf. on Object-Oriented Programming, Systems, Languages and Applications,* October 1998
   The original proposal for adding generic types to the Java programming language. The ideas expressed here underwent significant revision before generic types actually appeared in the language.

◆ "Adding Wildcards to the Java™ Programming Language," by Mads Torgersen, Erik Ernst, Christian Plesner Hansen, Peter von der Ahé, Gilad Bracha, and Neal Gafter. *Journal of Object Technology,* Volume 3, number 11, December 2004, Special issue: OOPS track at SAC 2004, Nicosia/Cyprus, pp. 97–116; `http://www.jot.fm/issues/issue_2004_12/article5`
   A good overview of how wildcards came about and their implications in the type system.

REGULAR EXPRESSIONS

◆ *Mastering Regular Expressions; Powerful Techniques for Perl and Other Tools,* Jeffrey E. F. Friedl, O'Reilly, 1997, ISBN 1-56592-257-3
An entire book devoted to regular expressions and their use. (You can easily know what is specific to the Perl programming language and what is more general.)

◆ "Unicode Technical Report #18: Unicode Regular Expression Guidelines," http://www.unicode.org/unicode/reports/tr18
Covers how Unicode characters fit into a regular expression language. The simple answer is "about the same as you'd guess," but this has the formal details.

GENERAL PROGRAMMING TECHNIQUES

◆ *Hacker's Delight,* by Henry S. Warren, Jr. Addison-Wesley, 2002, ISBN 0-201-91465-4.

RELATED LANGUAGES

◆ *The C Programming Language, 2nd Edition,* by Brian W. Kernighan and Dennis M. Ritchie. Prentice Hall, 1988, ISBN 0-13-110362-8 and ISBN 0-13-110370-9 (hardcover).

◆ *The C++ Programming Language, 3rd Edition,* by Bjarne Stroustrup. Addison-Wesley, 1997, ISBN 0-201-88954-4.

◆ *The Evolution of C++,* edited by Jim Waldo. A USENIX Association book from MIT Press, ISBN 0-262-73107-X.
A history of C++ as told by many of the people who contributed.

◆ *Eiffel: The Language,* by Bertrand Meyer. Prentice Hall, 1992, ISBN 0-13-247925-7.

◆ "A Structural View of the Cedar Programming Environment," by Daniel Swinehart, Polle Zellweger, Richard Beach, and Robert Hagmann. *ACM Transactions on Programming Languages and Systems,* Volume 8, number 4, Oct. 1986.

◆ *Mesa Language Manual,* version 5.0, by James G. Mitchell, William Maybury, and Richard Sweet. Xerox Palo Alto Research Center Report CSL-79-3, April 1979.

- *Systems Programming with Modula-3,* edited by Greg Nelson. Prentice Hall, 1991, ISBN-0-13-590464-1.

  Introduces Modula-3. Chapter 4 is an excellent discussion of thread programming. Chapter 8 is a fascinating case history of language design.

- *Programming in Oberon—Steps Beyond Pascal and Modula,* by Martin Reiser and Niklaus Wirth. Addison-Wesley, 1992, ISBN 0-201-56543-9.

- *Objective C: Object-Oriented Programming Techniques,* by Lewis J. Pinson and Richard S. Wiener. Addison-Wesley, 1991, ISBN 0-201-50828-1.

- "Self: The Power of Simplicity," by David Ungar and Randall B. Smith. Sun Microsystems Laboratories Technical Report SMLI-TR-94-30, 1994.

- *Data Processing—Programming Languages—SIMULA.* Swedish standard SS 636114, SIS, 1987, ISBN 91-7162-234-9.

- *Smalltalk-80: The Language,* by Adele Goldberg and Dave Robson. Addison-Wesley, 1989, ISBN 0-201-13688-0.

SOFTWARE ENGINEERING

- *The Decline and Fall of the American Programmer,* by Ed Yourdon. Yourdon Press, 1993, ISBN 0-13-203670-3.

  Analysis of the revolution taking place in programming. Several chapters discuss object-oriented design. Two chapters of particular interest are "The Lure of the Silver Bullet" and "Programming Methodologies."

- *The Mythical Man-Month, Anniversary Edition,* by Frederick P. Brooks, Jr. Addison-Wesley, 1995, ISBN 0-201-83595-9.

  Essays describing how software projects are really managed and how they should be managed. Especially read Chapter 16, "No Silver Bullet: Essence and Accidents of Software Engineering." You cannot design good classes without understanding how they will be used and changed over time.

- *Peopleware,* by Tom DeMarco and Timothy Lister. Dorset House, 1987, ISBN 0-932633-05-6.

VISUAL DESIGN & GUI DESIGN

- *Designing Visual Interfaces,* by Kevin Mullet and Darrel Sano. Prentice Hall, 1995, ISBN 0-13-303389-9.

  This book describes fundamental techniques that can be used to enhance the visual quality of graphical user interfaces.

- *About Face,* by Alan Cooper. Hungry Minds Inc., 1995, ISBN 1568843224.
  Basics of good GUI design in a straightforward presentation.

- *Usability Engineering,* by Jakob Nielsen. Academic Press, 1993,
  ISBN 0-12-518405-0.
  A direct how-to guide on testing your interfaces to make sure they are usable by actual human beings.

- *The Visual Display of Quantitative Information,* by Edward R. Tufte.
  Graphics Press, 1983.
  You shouldn't communicate using graphical media without reading this.

- *The Non-Designer's Design Book,* by Robin Williams. Peachpit Press, 1994,
  ISBN 1-56609-159-4.
  How to use type, space, alignment, and other basic techniques to make your designs visually appealing and user-friendly. Applicable to paper documents, HTML documents, displaying data, and user interfaces.

- *The Design of Everyday Things,* by Donald A. Norman. Doubleday/Currency, 1988, ISBN 0-385-26774-6.
  Discusses usability design for everyday items (doors, typewriters, and so on) with lessons applicable to any design that humans are meant to use.

The cure for boredom is curiosity.
There is no cure for curiosity.
—Dorothy Parker

Index

It's a d–mn poor mind that can only think of one way to spell a word!
—Andrew Jackson

Numbers

0 (zero)
floating-point conversion use (table); 628
integer conversion use (table); 627
0X/0x (zero x) prefix
hexadecimal literal indicator; 167
hexadecimal floating-point literal indicator;
168
2D geometry
`java.awt.geom` package; 720

Symbols

(space)
floating-point conversion use (table); 628
integer conversion use (table); 627
! (bang)
logical negation operator; 207
!= (bang equals)
inequality operator; 99, 206
term definition; 5
" (double quote)
string literals use of; 3, 168
 # (pound sign)
floating-point conversion use (table); 628
integer conversion use (table); 627
specifying member names with, doc
comments; 483
string conversion use; 628
$ (dollar sign)
format specifier use; 626
multiline mode, dot-all mode pattern
matching; 324
nested type internal name use; 149

% (percent)
format specifier prefix, examples of; 23
format specifier use; 624
remainder operator; 201
preserving symmetry around zero; 658
term definition; 11
%% (percent percent)
outputting percent sign; 625
& (ampersand)
AND operator; 20
bitwise AND operator; 208
doc comment use; 482
generic type declaration use; 253
logical AND operator; 207
Unicode sequence for; 482
@ HTML tag,
doc comment use; 482
&& (ampersand ampersand)
conditional AND operator; 20, 207
evaluation order differences; 215
& HTML tag,
doc comment use; 482
> HTML tag,
doc comment use; 482
< HTML tag,
doc comment use; 482
' (single quote)
character literals use of; 167
((left parenthesis)
floating-point conversion use (table); 628
integer conversion use (table); 627
() (parentheses)
method invocation operator; 224
parameter list use; 2
precedence control in expressions; 222
type casting operator; 27, 91, 219

761

Then the bowsprit got mixed with the rudder sometimes...
—Lewis Carroll, *The Hunting of the Snark (an Agony in Eight Fits)*

Colophon

A vacuum is a hell of a lot better than some of the stuff that nature replaces it with.
—Tennessee Williams

THIS book is primarily 11-point Times. Code text is Lucida Sans Typewriter at 85% of the size of the surrounding text. A few decorations are Zapf Dingbats.

The text was written in FrameMaker on several Sun Solaris systems, Macintosh computers, and PC's running various versions of Windows, including, for a mercifully brief while, a 486i laptop running Windows 3.1.

The non-ISO Latin-1 text on pages 162, 165, and 550 were created on Macintosh computers using Adobe Illustrator to make PostScript drawings of the letters included as pictures in the text. The fonts used are Kourier for Cyrillic, ParsZiba for Persian, Palladam for Tamil, Ryumin for Kanji, and Sambhota for Tibetan.

Code examples were written, compiled, and tested, then broken into fragments by a Perl script looking for specially formatted comments. Source fragments and generated output were inserted in the book by another Perl script.

NOTE TO TRANSLATORS

These fonts have been chosen carefully. The code font, when mixed with body text, has the same "x" height and roughly the same weight and "color." Code in text looks even—if you read quickly it can seem like body text, yet it is easy to tell that code text *is* different. Please use the fonts we have used (we would be happy to help you locate any) or choose other fonts that are balanced together.

Someday, Weederman, we'll look back on all this and laugh...
It will probably be one of those deep, eerie ones
that slowly builds to a blood-curdling maniacal scream, but still it will be a laugh.
—Joe Martin, *Mister Boffo*

A child can go only so far in life without potty training.
It is not mere coincidence that six of the last seven presidents were potty trained,
not to mention nearly half of the nation's state legislators.
—Dave Barry

The Java™ Series

ISBN 0-201-63456-2   ISBN 0-201-70433-1   ISBN 0-201-31005-8   ISBN 0-321-24575-X   ISBN 0-201-70393-9   ISBN 0-201-48558-3

ISBN 0-201-74622-0   ISBN 0-201-75280-8   ISBN 0-201-76810-0   ISBN 0-201-31002-3   ISBN 0-201-31003-1   ISBN 0-201-48552-4

ISBN 0-201-71102-8   ISBN 0-201-70329-7   ISBN 0-201-30955-6   ISBN 0-201-31008-2   ISBN 0-201-78472-6   ISBN 0-201-78791-1

ISBN 0-201-31009-0   ISBN 0-201-70502-8   ISBN 0-201-32577-2   ISBN 0-201-43294-3   ISBN 0-201-91466-2

ISBN 0-321-19801-8   ISBN 0-201-74627-1   ISBN 0-201-70456-0   ISBN 0-201-77580-8   ISBN 0-201-78790-3

ISBN 0-201-77582-4   ISBN 0-201-91467-0   ISBN 0-201-70969-4   ISBN 0-321-17384-8

Visit www.awprofessional.com/javaseries for more information on these titles.

inform**IT**

www.informit.com

YOUR GUIDE TO IT REFERENCE

Articles

Keep your edge with thousands of free articles, in-depth features, interviews, and IT reference recommendations – all written by experts you know and trust.

Online Books

Answers in an instant from **InformIT Online Book's** 600+ fully searchable on line books. For a limited time, you can get your first 14 days **free**.

POWERED BY

Safari®

TECH BOOKS ONLINE®

Catalog

Review online sample chapters, author biographies and customer rankings and choose exactly the right book from a selection of over 5,000 titles.